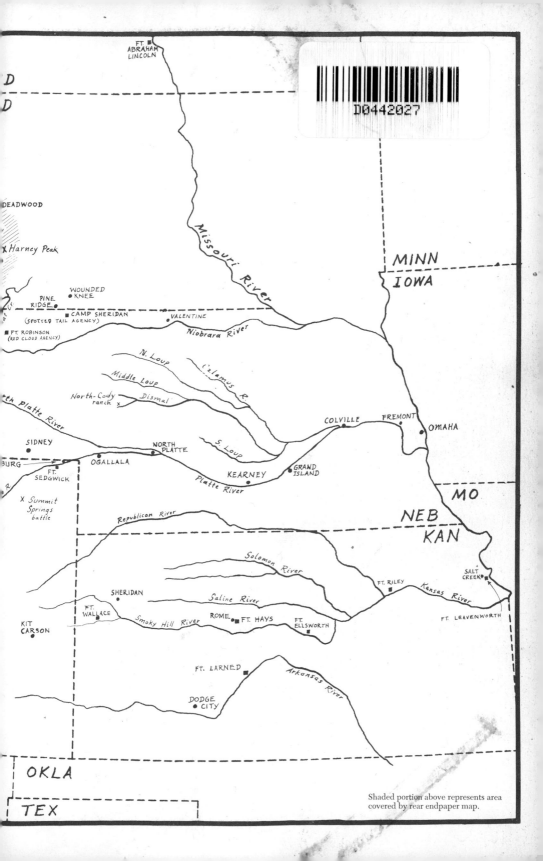

FT. ABRAHAM LINCOLN

D
D

DEADWOOD

X Harney Peak

MINN

IOWA

Missouri River

WOUNDED KNEE

PINE RIDGE

CAMP SHERIDAN
(SPOTTED TAIL AGENCY)

VALENTINE

FT. ROBINSON
(RED CLOUD AGENCY)

Niobrara River

N. Loup

Calamus R.

Middle Loup

North-Cody ranch X

Dismal

th Platte River

S. Loup

COLVILLE

FREMONT

OMAHA

SIDNEY

NORTH PLATTE

URG

FT. SEDGWICK

OGALLALA

KEARNEY

GRAND ISLAND

Platte River

MO

X Summit Springs battle

Republican River

NEB

KAN

Solomon River

SHERIDAN

FT. WALLACE

Saline River

FT. RILEY

SALT CREEK

Kansas River

KIT CARSON

Smoky Hill River

ROME

FT. HAYS

FT. ELLSWORTH

FT. LEAVENWORTH

FT. LARNED

Arkansas River

DODGE CITY

OKLA

TEX

Shaded portion above represents area
covered by rear endpaper map.

BUFFALO
BILL

Nellie Snyder Yost

BUFFALO BILL

His Family, Friends, Fame, Failures, and Fortunes

SAGE BOOKS

THE SWALLOW PRESS INC.
CHICAGO

ß

First Edition
  First Printing

Sage Books are published by
The Swallow Press Incorporated
811 West Junior Terrace
Chicago, Illinois 60613

Frontispiece courtesy David R. Phillips Collection

ISBN 0-8040-0766-7
Library of Congress Catalog Card Number 78-60434

*This book
is dedicated
to all those good people,
living or dead,
who knew and liked Buffalo Bill.*

Contents

Illustrations

Maps

Introduction

William Frederick (Buffalo Bill) Cody occupies a secure place in the foremost ranks of controversial historical characters. Misinformation and exaggeration concerning almost every facet of his adventuresome life have been rife, not only since his death more than half a century ago but even while he lived. Probably not a season passes but something more is published about him, much of it merely a rehash of inaccurate accounts of former years; some of it new tales told by someone who remembers that somebody's uncle, who was there, had told someone, who told him, that Buffalo Bill either did or did not ride for the Pony Express, handle a stagecoach run, kill Yellow Hand or Tall Bull, shoot glass balls with a rifle, and on and on.

Since reliable records *are* available for most of these events, it is strange that so few have bothered to go back to army files, or even to the newspapers of the time, to see how it really was. Don Russell, author of *The Lives and Legends of Buffalo Bill,* is one who did, and consequently has written the most factual account of Cody's life now in existence. His well-documented book carefully covers most of the many lives of Buffalo Bill, as scout, hunter, showman, author, and citizen.

Cody himself was somewhat at fault in perpetuating some of the exaggerated and untrue stories about himself. The explanation, however, is logical. By the time he got around to writing the first of his autobiographies, many others had already written of his deeds in lurid prose, often distorting them out of all semblance to the truth, and his enthusiastic public had believed every word. By then Cody was a color-

1

ful showman, portraying many of the alleged feats on the nation's
stages. So the showman-turned-author, hurriedly composing his books,
lifted whole passages from such works and incorporated them in his
own, or in stories written over his signature. It was good for show business.

Still later, his sister, Helen Cody Wetmore, writing and publishing
her *Last of the Great Scouts* (1899), not only repeated many of the distorted tales, such as the "duel with Yellow Hand," but even added to
the exaggeration. She seemed determined to portray her brother all of
ten feet tall, not only for the sake of his show business but for the
successful sale of her own book as well. But why she should be so
careless with other matters, the correct sequence of the births of the
Cody children, for instance, or the data on his Nebraska ranches
(doubling the size of the North Platte ranch and placing the Dismal
River outfit on the Dakota border), is harder to understand.

Most disturbing of all is the handling of the Cody story as told by
Mrs. W. F. Cody (Louisa) to Courtney Ryley Cooper in *Memories of
Buffalo Bill*, published in 1920. Buffalo Bill was dead by then and
Louisa was in her late seventies, but she surely did not make the mistake of locating North Platte, her home for thirty-five years, "near the
Wyoming line," or disregarding the existence of the Union Pacific railroad for years while she and her family traveled a parallel route by
stagecoach. Even Cooper must have known better. If not, only a curs-
ory glance at a map or a history book would have set him right. Furthermore, since Cooper knew Mrs. Cody personally, there is only one
answer to why he consistently pictured her as frail and fragile, given
to swooning in a crisis, when she was in reality a large, sensible,
solidly built woman. Cooper, too, was romanticizing his tale for the
benefit of eastern readers who demanded that heroines confronting
Indians and the rigors of frontier life and stagecoach travel be frail,
fragile, and given to swooning.

But even more important than my desire to help set straight the
many versions of the life of Mr. Cody is my wish to fill in a wide gap
in the life of this complex and colorful man and that of his family. None
of his previous biographers have bothered to write much about North
Platte, which for thirty-five years the Colonel made his home and headquarters; it is this part of his life that I especially wish to furnish with
the rich portraits of Buffalo Bill Cody as husband, father, neighbor, and
citizen in the town he adopted and loved. He made his money in far
places, but he spent much of it generously in the little town at the forks

of the Platte. There he developed a ranch second to none in western Nebraska, with the finest buildings, the most elaborate landscaping, the most productive of irrigated lands, and the best blooded livestock within hundreds of miles.

There he provided his wife and daughters with the handsomest house in town. There he gave lavishly to aid the town's churches, to outfit its band and its fire department, and to promote the county fairs. There, because of Colonel Cody, some of the finest shows then touring the United States, including opera, stopped to perform, and he saw to it that every kid in town, the ragged and barefoot as well as the others, saw those shows at his expense. There he performed countless little acts of kindness for his town's poor and unfortunate, kindnesses long unknown to any but the recipients. There, in later years, after the famous scout had gone to his eternal rest on Lookout Mountain, many of his fellow townsmen were to remember him as generous, honest, and friendly, a perfect gentleman and a loyal friend.

In his *Lives and Legends* bibliography, Russell lists more than 225 books and articles written by or about Buffalo Bill. Some are so laudatory as to be patently unbelievable, for the man did have his share of faults. One or two are vicious attempts to debunk and defame him. Another, though written in the first person and claimed to be fact, is almost entirely fictional.

And so the Cody story, with all its distortions and embellishments, has grown and continues to grow. Strangely enough, the true story of W. F. Cody and his family is more exciting, glamorous, and interesting than any fictitious tale that has been or could be written. Just reading the newspapers printed during the years when the Cody name appeared therein regularly, or listening to the reminiscences of those who knew the Codys—merchants, bankers, hired girls, neighbors, stable boys, members of the Wild West show—has been an adventure in itself. It has been my privilege during these years of research to come to feel as though I had personally known Will and Louisa, Arta and Orra, Kit and Irma; and it is now my pleasure to write their story as it must have really happened.

1

Fort McPherson 1869

LeClaire, Iowa, claims Buffalo Bill was born there; North Platte, Nebraska, claims he lived there; and Lookout Mountain, Colorado, claims he is buried there.

History verifies the fact that William Frederick Cody was born near LeClaire, Scott County, Iowa, on February 26, 1846. It is also true that he is buried on Lookout Mountain, near Golden, Colorado, where thousands visit his grave each year.

W. F. Cody's part in the history of North Platte and Lincoln County began on May 20, 1869, the day he came to Fort McPherson, a cavalry post, with Brevet Major General Eugene A. Carr and the Fifth U.S. Cavalry. Accompanied by a large wagon train of supplies, these troops, with Cody as guide, had been sent up from Fort Lyon, Kansas, to reinforce the post on the Platte. Cody was twenty-three years old, already well known as a dead shot and a top scout. He was to make his home, or at least his headquarters, in that section of Nebraska for most of the next forty-four years.

All of Cody's biographers agree that the young scout was tall and handsome, but few concur on further details of his appearance. As measured by a friend, Major M. C. Harrington, at Scout's Rest Ranch in 1888, he was 6'3/4" tall,[1] although he has been recorded by others as from 5'10" to 6'3". His hair has been described as both black and blonde but was, according to the most reliable informants, dark brown and wavy. When Cody came to Fort McPherson, he did not wear his hair long, nor did he yet wear the mustache and goatee that later became famous. He probably weighed about 200 pounds, although he

4

later became a little heavier; but his carriage, then and all his life, was arrow-straight. His complexion has often been described as exceptionally fine and smooth, and his hands, too, were well-shaped and soft.

Fort McPherson, as Cody saw it that soft spring day in 1869, was still a raw frontier post. Although it had been less than six years since the parade ground had been laid out and the first log buildings put up, it was a bustling, busy place, its thirty-nine buildings, together with extensive horse corrals and stables, spread out over a thirty-eight-acre tract or "reservation." Some of the buildings were log, the rest frame, all uniformly painted with "fire proof" brown paint. The parade quadrangle, 844x560 feet, centered the reservation, and the lofty, jointed cedar flagpole centered the quadrangle. From it flew the thirty-seven-star United States flag, Nebraska's star the thirty-seventh.

Beginning with the commodious houses of Officers Row on the north side of the parade ground, the accommodations grew progressively poorer as they ranged southward, ending in the stables and corrals on the far south side. The commanding officer's dwelling, heading the Row on the northwest corner, was a spacious frame structure, 68x20 feet, with a 24x20-foot wing. Seven more officers' homes, all roomy and comfortable for that period in frontier history, completed the Row.

The enlisted mens' quarters on the quadrangle's south side, rough log barracks 120x20 feet, housed sixteen men in each twenty-feet-square partitioned room. Back of the barracks the laudresses' quarters made up "Soap Suds Row." Roofed with sod and floored with straw, they were only a degree or so better than the stables. The army furnished laundresses in the proportion of one to each nineteen enlisted men and fed, housed, and paid these ladies of the washboard. The food and pay corresponded to the housing, but all equipment—wooden washtubs, washboards, and strong lye soap—was furnished.

On the south, within arrow range of the corrals and nearer buildings, rose a range of high, convoluted hills and deep, rugged canyons. West of the parade ground stood a scatterment of post workshops, blacksmith and carpenter shops, and the bakery. On the east were the barbership, sutler's store, post office, and two billiard rooms, one for officers, one for enlisted men. The adjutant's office, guardhouse, powder magazine, warehouses, hospital, and a few other structures made up the full complement of the post's buildings.

A short distance to the west, Cottonwood Canyon, a twisted, twenty-mile-long gash in the steep-sided hills, debouched onto the river valley. It was this canyon, long a pathway for migrating Indians, that ac-

counted for the fort's location at this point. The only major post between Fort Kearny and Fort Laramie, its troops patrolled east toward
Kearny, west to Julesburg, Colorado, and south to the Republican
River—a vast territory. Because of hostile Indians, this sector of the
Overland Trail—south of the Platte River and the Union Pacific railroad and between the rivers from North Platte on westward—was considered the most dangerous between the Missouri River and the Pacific
coast; hence the need for additional troops that spring of 1869.

A decade earlier, one Isaac Boyer had built a trading post about a
half mile east of the canyon's mouth, near a huge cottonwood tree that
stood at the end of a short gulch from which bubbled a large spring. At
that time (1858) the far-ranging canyons to the south were heavily
wooded with tall red cedars, while the wide, grassy valley stretching
east and west along the Platte River was almost completely treeless,
making a notable landmark of the great lone cottonwood tree.

Boyer, a small man of French extraction, who with an uncle, Joseph
Robideaux, had come from Illinois by way of St. Joseph, Missouri, was
the first white man to settle within the boundaries of what is now Lincoln County.[2] Traffic was extremely heavy on the trail, trading posts
west of Fort Kearny were almost nonexistent, and the pair had seen the
excellent possibilities for such an establishment near the spring, already
a favored camp site for freighters and travelers.

With cedar logs from the adjacent canyons, the Frenchmen built a
good-sized trading post and a large stable, enclosing the whole in a
solid log stockade that was both a corral and protection from Indians.
The big spring supplied good water, and a long island in the river, un-
grazed by emigrants' stock, afforded grazing and hay for their own.
The men were soon doing a thriving business, both with Indians and
white travelers.

The Indians were peaceful at the time the Frenchmen first came to
the valley, and Boyer soon brought his wife there to live. Within a year
a daughter was born to them, and later a son, Felix. The Boyers (Robideaux had gone back to St. Joseph), however, did not long enjoy their
monopoly at Cottonwood Springs, for William Bishop (history unknown) had built a little trading post of his own there the following
year, and the next, 1860, saw the arrival of Charles McDonald, a native
of Tennessee. McDonald built a larger and more impressive layout
some 200 yards south of Boyer's place. His trading post was a two-
story structure, 40x20 feet in size, with a 50-feet-long, one-story, sod-
roofed wing extending to the west. The main building housed his store

and saloon, with living quarters in the back. His huge stockade corral enclosed the trading post, blacksmith shop, warehouse, and stable and still afforded room for 200 head of oxen and horses. In front of his store and between his place and Boyer's store, where ran the Overland Trail, he dug a huge square well, forty feet deep and always filled with cold, clean water.[3]

Although Fort McPherson's first log buildings had been laid up in the fall of 1863, by 1869 two or three other log cabins had been built in the open space between the east line of the military reservation and the two trading posts. A little way to the north the broad, shining, shallow Platte River rippled east over its gravelly bed. Beyond it rose low ranges of lightly grassed, uninhabited sandhills, and to the east and west, as far as the eye could see, stretched the treeless valley of the Platte.

This then was the fort, the village, and the river valley as the young scout saw them, and he was to find the place both busy and exciting in the days ahead. The last spike in the Union Pacific railroad had been driven at Promontory, Utah, ten days before his arrival on the Platte, but wagon traffic was still heavy on the trail during the grass season, and would be for years to come. Troops were continually coming and going. Eastern government officials and military brass, riding the cars to McPherson Station, about four miles north across the river, almost daily visited the fort, some anticipating a bit of hunting, others making "tours of inspection" or performing other official duties.

From reville and the morning gun salute at daylight until taps sounded at 9:00 in the evening, there was always something doing. Mounted patrols were arriving and departing as troops were dispatched north to the Dismal, the Niobrara, and the Loups; south to the Republican; or east and west along some 200 miles of the Overland Trail and the Union Pacific tracks. Mounted couriers pounded into the fort on tired horses and dashed away on fresh ones. Mail from the east and west arrived every morning from McPherson Station, brought across the river on the narrow, railless wagon bridge that had been laid across the wide, quicksandy stream bed only that winter.

For entertainment there were the two company libraries, one for the officers, furnished with 362 volumes, the other for enlisted men, with twenty-six books; and the post theater, built by a detachment of Battery E, Third U.S. Artillery, in the fall of 1867. The theater, the pride of the post, constructed of "logs and boards," was 54 feet long by 30 wide. It had a stage and dressing rooms, and performances were given by the troops every Saturday night. Both "dramas and comedies were rendered exceedingly well for amateurs,"[4] and all were well attended by the officers and their ladies, as well as by the enlisted men. One wonders, though, how often vacancies were created in the cast by orders that suddenly took some of the actors away on scout or patrol duty.

Dances, too, were popular at the fort. Neighbors and settlers from outside were invited, as were cowboys from ranches far and wide: John Bratt's Double 0, John Burke's Flatiron, Nichols' 96, Walker's LW, and others. Probably every man at the post not incarcerated in the guardhouse or detailed to guard duty showed up for the revelries. But disciplinary measures no doubt cut attendance considerably at the enlisted men's hops, for it was not unusual for two dozen or more men to be detained in the solid log guardhouse at one time.

Young Cody fraternized freely with the officers and was on full friendship terms with those of humbler status, so he likely attended all the dances. That he had a good time goes almost without saying, and that he helped others have a good time is unquestionable, for his friends often said there was always something doing where Bill Cody was.

Nebraska,
Marriage, Buffalo Hunter
1857-1868

That May day in 1869 was not the first time W. F. Cody had seen this valley where the fort now stood, for he had first traveled the overland route up the Platte in 1857. As a lad of eleven, in the employ of Russell, Majors & Waddell, he had that year accompanied a wagon train under the command of wagon master Lewis Simpson to Wyoming.[1] Not even Boyer's trading post near the big cottonwood broke the emptiness of the valley that year.

On October 5, Simpson's train was captured by Lot Smith's Mormons on Big Sandy Creek, a tributary to the Green River in western Wyoming. Allowed to keep one wagon and a few supplies, Simpson and his crew made their way to Fort Bridger, where they spent the winter. When the party returned to Leavenworth, Kansas, the following summer, the valley at Cottonwood Springs was probably still empty, for Boyer and Robideaux did not build their trading post until the fall of 1858.

When Billy went west again in the late spring of the next year, headed for the gold fields of Colorado, he doubtless saw the Boyer buildings, and perhaps the Bishop trading store, too, giving the place the appearance of a thriving settlement. Fifteen miles east of Cottonwood Springs, his party must have passed the Gilman brothers' road ranch and perhaps stopped for awhile. The New Hampshire-born Gilmans, John and Jeremiah, had also earlier been headed for the gold fields, but their heavily loaded wagon broke down at the mouth of a gulch; while laid up for repairs, they took note of the endless stream of wagons passing all day on the trail and decided to stay where they were and open a store.

The brothers were both tall, but Jeremiah was thin as a lath while John was broad and well built. When the Pony Express went into operation the next year, their ranch was a "home station," and also an Overland Stage stop until the railroad built through in 1867. The ranch was most widely known, however, for the iron pitcher pump the brothers had set on the pipe above their dug well; the pump set it apart from other ranch wells, which still used buckets. The Indians for some reason associated the pump only with John and named him Wechoxcha, The Old Man With The Pump. Jeremiah, because of his red hair and beard, was Poteshasha, Red Whiskers.[2]

After Billy returned to Kansas in the summer of 1859, an unsuccessful miner, he probably did not see the Platte Valley below the forks of the river until he came there with Carr, ten years later. Cody's Pony Express riding did take him fairly close by, but his leg of the route lay about eighty miles farther west, on the Slade Division in Colorado, and he probably reached it by traveling northwest from Kansas and bypassing the trail up the Platte.

During the Civil War, Billy's activities were all south of Nebraska Territory. After various misadventures in the state of Kansas, where his widowed mother and his sisters lived, he enlisted in the Seventh Kansas Volunteer Cavalry on February 19, 1864. A year and seven months later, September 29, 1865, he was mustered out of the army. During the next few months, he did some scouting between Leavenworth, Kansas, and Fort Kearny, Nebraska, for General William Tecumseh Sherman, commanding general of the Military Division of the Mississippi. Then, for a short time, he drove stage under the famous Bill Trotter, veteran agent of the Overland Stage line, between Fort Kearny and Plum Creek, twenty-five miles on west. He quit the stage line in February 1866, to go to St. Louis to marry his Louisa.

The pretty young lady who had won the scout's heart was the daughter of John Frederici, an immigrant from Alsace-Lorraine. Educated in a St. Louis convent, she was living at home when she met William Cody. There are many versions of their first meeting, their courtship, and their marriage. In one account, Cody is quoted as saying:

The spring of 1865 found us again in Springfield, where we remained about two months, recuperating and replenishing our stock. I now got a furlough of 30 days and went to St. Louis, where I invested part of the $1000 I had saved in fashionable clothes and in rooms at one of the best hotels. It was while there that I met a young lady of a southern family to whom I paid a great deal of attention and from whom I finally extracted a promise that if I would come back to St. Louis at the end of the war she would marry me.[3]

He does not say where he earned the money from which he saved the $1,000, but it is characteristic of him to spend it for clothes and expensive hotel accommodations.

Another St. Louis tale has Cody riding down the street one morning when he spied a group of drunken soldiers annoying some young women. He sailed into the band, of course, knocked out two or three of the ruffians, and rescued the girls. Later he married one of them. Still another tale has him riding in a St. Louis park, where he sees a beautiful young lady, also taking her "morning constitutional" on horseback. For several mornings he returns to the park where the lady rides every day. He was still trying to figure out a proper way to meet her when, most conveniently, her bridle rein breaks and her horse runs away with her. Cody, of course, dashes to the rescue, catches the horse just before it dashes its frightened rider to destruction, and so makes her acquaintance.

Cody himself writes: "In the winter of 1864-65 I was permitted to spend a time at military headquarters in St. Louis on detached service. . . . I became acquainted with a young lady named Louisa Frederici, whom I greatly admired and in whose charming society I spent many a pleasant hour." Following his discharge in 1865, Cody returned to St. Louis where, "having made up my mind to capture the heart of Miss Frederici, whom I now adored above any other young lady I had ever seen," he ardently pressed his suit. He continues: "Her lovely face, her gentle disposition and her graceful manner, won my admiration and love; and I was not slow in declaring my sentiments to her. The result was that I obtained her consent to marry me in the near future."[4]

In her own story of her life, as told to Courtney Ryley Cooper in *Memories of Buffalo Bill*, the meeting is described as follows: On May 1, 1865, Louisa Frederici sat curled up in a big chair in front of a grate fire in her home in old French town, St. Louis. She was reading a book when the chair was violently pulled from under her. She scrambled to her feet, whirled, and slapped a man. Her cousin, Will McDonald, was the jokester, but the man she slapped in the face was his companion, Will Cody, whom she had never seen before. Embarrassed and apologetic, she stammered and blushed when they were introduced. Their courtship began that evening. This account has Cody writing poetry to her and holding her spellbound with tales of his many western adventures and Indian fights. He takes her picture with him when he leaves.[5]

Regardless of how they actually met, we do know that the next spring, March 6, 1866, they were married in her house, in the room with the grate fireplace. Will, as Louisa always called him, was twenty; she was twenty-three. They left immediately on their honeymoon, a boat trip up the Missouri to Leavenworth. Cooper's description of the journey is very tender, colorful, and romantic. The bride is frightened by a fight on the river bank at a landing and faints in her gallant bridegroom's arms. Cooper has Will so sorry about it all that he offers to give up the life in his beloved West, to which he was taking her, and try to make a place for himself "back east" where she belongs. But she would not allow him to make such a sacrifice for her, and so they go on.

They were met at the Leavenworth landing by Will's sister, Eliza, and her husband, George Myers. About sixty of Will's friends, including officers from Fort Leavenworth and a brass band arranged for in advance by the groom, were also waiting at the dock to greet the newlyweds with a high-style charivari. As Cooper has it, "they were waiting, with carriages and flowers and greetings and happiness." Since the bride had expected only savage Indians at this far western outpost, she was almost hysterical with happiness. Indeed, the "cultured men and cultured women" she met at the fort, and the dances and carriage rides by which she was entertained, made her first weeks in Kansas most delightful.[6]

Will rented the big house in nearby Salt Creek Valley that had belonged to his mother until her death in 1863, and where he had lived until the age of eleven. He named it the Golden Rule House and, with his wife's help, attempted to run a hotel. Due to his generous habit of treating his many friends to free rooms and meals, he had to abandon the hotel business six months later.

W. F. Cody then headed further west to keep his date with destiny and become the fabulous Buffalo Bill of dime novel fame and of history. Lulu, as he affectionately called his wife, stayed on for awhile in Leavenworth where, on December 16, 1866, their daughter was born. Will came home to see the baby and help select her name, Arta. Shortly afterward he returned to Fort Ellsworth, near the present town of the same name, and Lulu and the baby went home to St. Louis for a visit.

As Cooper has Louisa tell it, Will wrote her long letters that winter and spring of 1867, telling her of his scouting with Custer and other officers, of savage Indian battles, and of other derring-do. Next he writes of the splendid new town he and his partner, William Rose, had established out on the Kansas prairie on the Union Pacific Railway, Eastern Division, then building west toward Sheridan.[7] He would soon be coming to take her and the baby "home" to Rome, he told her.

Before long, Cody makes his promise good, more or less; he journeys to St. Louis and takes his family back to Kansas, only to find on their arrival that the whole town had moved to a new location—all, that is, but a lone saloon. Rome had been a flourishing reality when Cody left it for St. Louis, but while he was gone another promoter had established a new town site a mile away and offered superior inducements to settlers. Within three days Rome was deserted.

It was dark when Will and Lulu arrived at the deserted town site, according to Cooper. Furthermore, no sooner do they set foot on the ground than Cody is urgently summoned to Fort Hays on official business. Quickly establishing his wife and baby in a room at the rear of the saloon, the scout gallops away into the night. Louisa, alone and frightened, all but swoons when a noisy brawl breaks out on the other side of the partition that separates her from the saloon. When the shooting and yelling waken the baby, who begins to wail, she is convinced that all is lost. But the men on the other side of the wall hear the infant's cries, even above the noise of the fighting, and want to come in and see the baby. Too terror stricken to deny them, Louisa admits "ten dirty, unkempt, bearded men." Their hats in their hands, they come quietly in to stare in wonder at the baby. The tender tale ends with the gallant bartender sending the men away and closing the saloon for the rest of the night, so our heroine could get some sleep.

Cooper goes on to relate how Will moved his family to the fort but could find no suitable shelter or accommodations for them, so housed them in a tent and went off hunting and scouting. The next adventure to befall the allegedly delicate young mother was a terrific fight between some drunken soldiers which took place right over her tent, knocking it down and putting Louisa and the baby in imminent danger of being trampled to death. In the nick of time she finds the pistol her husband had given her, fights her way out of the smothering folds of the tent, and, with her baby on her other arm, points the gun at a ruffian and orders him out of her way. But another of the drunken men strikes her, knocking the gun from her hand. Almost fainting, she can only scream for help, which miraculously arrives from somewhere and she is saved.

After the feminine fashion of the time, she is then ill for a long while, even though Will came as soon as he heard of the trouble, found a place for her and Arta in the already overcrowded hotel, and savagely and manfully threatened to kill every ruffian involved in the fight. She eventually recovered and stayed on at the fort, where assorted thrilling experiences quickly came her way. Will teaches her to shoot her pistol with sure-fire accuracy and tells her next time to "shoot to kill." He next teaches her to shoot while riding a galloping horse, after which he takes her buffalo hunting.

Louisa, of course, rode sidesaddle, as all ladies did in those days. But Cooper's readers expected more than a mere description of their heroine riding sideways at full gallop, bringing down a thundering buffalo with every shot, and all this in spite of the very real danger of the running horse stepping in a prairie dog hole or a buffalo charging the horse and rider. So Cooper has Louisa doing it with little Arta *strapped on her lap* while she shoots three buffalo on her first hunt, and does it with her pistol.

Louisa soon begs her husband to buy her a buggy of her own. He protests, fearing she will drive too far from the post and have Indian trouble. She begs so hard that he finally gives in and orders her a rig from Kansas City. When it came he hitched his buffalo hunting horse, Brigham, in the shafts and took her for a drive. When he started to turn back, Lulu insisted they go on a little farther. His warning that Indians might be about could not dissuade her, so they went too far and were chased by yelling savages. While Will urged Brigham on ever faster and faster, he held a loaded gun to Lulu's head, ready to shoot if they lost the race. Again, just in the nick of time, some of the boys from the post, providentially alerted by Cody before they started on the drive, came riding to the rescue and chased the Indians away. Louisa's frail health broken by their hairbreadth escape, Will again had to take her back to St. Louis to recover.

In the spring of 1867, while Louisa and the baby were still in St. Louis, Cody *did* guide General Custer from Fort Hays to Fort Larned, a distance of sixty-five miles. A little later he accompanied Brevet Major General Armes and some troops as scout while pursuing Indians, during which action the major and several soldiers were wounded in a skirmish.

Late that spring, Cody *did* meet Rose in Ellsworth and they *did* form a partnership to promote their new town, Rome. Will *did* establish a store and saloon, with living quarters in the back, to which he brought his wife and daughter. Rome prospered mightily for a few months, before it lost out to the newer town of Hays, and Cody's dream of wealth through the sale of town lots faded fast, after which Lulu and Arta went back to St. Louis.[8] Alas for the exciting tales of the saloon brawl and the drunken soldiers fighting above the tent. These events just did not happen.

At this time Cody already owned Brigham, the first of his many celebrated horses.[9] Rose, who had secured a contract for grading five miles of the Union Pacific roadbed, needed help. So Cody and Brigham went to work, Brigham in work harness pulling a scraper.

One day a small herd of buffalo came by, heading toward a creek. Bill at once unhitched Brigham, threw off the harness, except for the bridle with its "workhorse blinders," leaped on, and started after the buffalo, armed with his needle gun which he had named Lucretia Borgia. Before he came up with the buffalo, he met five officers from Fort Hays. They found it amusing that a workman on a rawboned workhorse wearing a blind-bridle should be attempting to run down a herd of buffalo. They told him kindly that it required a fast horse to overtake these animals, but they would be glad to shoot the buffalo and let him have the meat.

They dashed off toward the herd of eleven buffalo, and Cody trailed along on his sorry-looking mount. As he had already noted, the herd was angling toward the creek for water, so while the officers chased after the herd, he cut across toward the creek and was in a good position when the buffalo, with their pursuers in their rear, came thundering down to the creek. "The buffaloes," said Cody, "came rushing past me not a hundred yards distant, with the officers about three hundred yards in the rear. . . . I pulled the blind-bridle from my horse . . . [and] the moment [it] was off, he started at the top of his speed, . . . and with a few jumps he brought me alongside of the rear buffalo. Raising old 'Lucretia Borgia' to my shoulder, I fired, and killed the animal at the first shot. My horse then carried me alongside the next one, not ten feet away, and I dropped him at the next fire."[10] In this manner Bill and his well-trained buffalo horse killed the eleven buffalo. He then presented the officers with the tongues and tenderloins and took a wagon load of hindquartrs back to camp for the workmen.

In October, Cody entered into an agreement with Goddard Brothers, who had contracted with the Union Pacific to board the workmen, to provide at least twelve buffalo a day until the contract expired. For this he was paid $500 a month. The job lasted until May 1868, a period of eight months. Shortly after he began supplying the daily ration of meat for the railroad workers, the Leavenworth *Daily Conservative* carried an item mentioning "Captain Graham . . . Buffalo Bill and other scouts."[11] Captain George Graham was one of the officers who had watched Cody down the eleven buffalo some weeks earlier, so he may have been the first to apply the nickname of Buffalo Bill to the scout and hunter.[12] From this it would appear that he acquired his famous cognomen *before* he killed those 4,280 buffalo. This famous figure was first given in his own story of his life,[13] and thereafter quoted without question by scores of writers. As Don Russell notes, at the minimum of twelve buffalo a day for an eight-month period, Cody would have killed almost 3,000 animals.[14] And he likely, with many good shooting days, averaged seventeen or eighteen per day.

His success with the buffalo contract was no doubt responsible for the notoriety and glamour that began to surround the name of "Buffalo Bill"—and the fact he made $500 a month for the life of the contract, extremely high wages for those times, helped. The money made it possible for him to have his family with him again (whenever he could spare the time to find a home for them), and the fame presumably led to the contest for the title of "Champion Buffalo Hunter of the Plains."[15]

William Comstock, a post guide and interpreter and also a well-known buffalo hunter, had many backers among the officers and men at Fort Wallace. The men at Fort Hays were just as certain that Bill Cody was the better man when it came to shooting buffalo. The result was the famous shooting match, with the officers of both posts backing the two hunters with cash bets.

According to Cooper, the hunt was advertised as far away as St. Louis, where Louisa came upon "a glaring poster, flaunting forth from a [downtown] wall." The poster announced a "Grand Excursion to Fort Sheridan, Kansas Pacific Railroad. Buffalo Shooting Match for $500 a side and the Championship of the World between Billy Comstock (The famous scout) and W. F. Cody (Buffalo Bill) famous buffalo killer for the Kansas Pacific Railroad."[16]

Cody in his autobiography relates that the contest "had been pretty well advertised and noised abroad, [and] a large crowd witnessed the interesting and exciting scene. An excursion party, mostly from St. Louis, consisting of about a hundred gentlemen and ladies, came out on a special train to view the sport, and among the number was my wife, with little baby Arta, who had come to remain with me for a while."[17] Until the train arrived at its destination, Louisa and Will had not seen each other since her return to St. Louis after the fall of Rome the previous autumn.

The hunt, as Buffalo Bill tells it, was to last from eight o'clock in the morning until four in the afternoon. The hunters were to ride into the herd at the same time, each to kill as many buffalo as he could. An official referee, or scorekeeper, was to follow each hunter.

Cody rode Brigham and carried his favorite gun, Lucretia Borgia. Out of their first herd, he killed thirty-eight buffalo, Comstock twenty-three; from the second herd, Cody killed eighteen, Comstock fourteen; of the third herd, Cody dropped thirteen, "the last one of which I had driven down close to the wagons, where the ladies were." The final score was sixty-nine for Cody, forty-six for Comstock, thus securing the championship *and* the title "Buffalo Bill" for Cody for all time.[18]

If in fact the Cody-Comstock hunt contest took place at all! It seems to be the most dateless, placeless, undocumented occasion in Cody's life. No eyewitness account (other than Cody's and his wife's) has ever turned up, and no newspaper record of the event has ever been found. Cody biographers in telling the Cody-Comstock story have to rely upon Cody's autobiography itself, and biographical pieces on Comstock can do no better.[19] The poster referred to and used as an illustration in Cooper's book is no help; though one may not want to agree with John Gray that the poster is an "obvious forgery," it does generate skepticism "by withholding the date and giving a location unknown to the railroad!"[20] In addition, a hundred-spectator Grand Excursion from St. Louis would not have been an obscure event from an obscure place; surely some newspaper somewhere or some memoir would have mentioned it. The answer probably lies in the fact that if indeed the Shooting Match took place, it has been exaggerated in the telling. We likely do better to think of it not as a widely publicized contest (certainly not for the Championship of the World, as Cooper has it) but instead somewhat analogous to a pick-up game of sand-lot baseball gotten up more or less on the spur of the moment by the neighborhood fellows.

Following the Cody-Comstock contest, Louisa went to Leavenworth to live, and Will was taken on again as a scout, this time by Brevet Major General George Armes of the Tenth Cavalry at Fort Hays. By September he was scouting out of Fort Larned. In October he joined the Fifth Cavalry, the regiment with which he was to win enduring fame; at $75 per month, he received the top pay authorized for a scout. He was gone so much that winter on long scouting expeditions that Louisa and Arta once more went back to St. Louis.

That fall General Philip H. Sheridan had moved his headquarters to Fort Hays and laid plans for an extensive winter campaign against the Indians. To further his plans, seven companies of the Fifth Cavalry,

brought together from various southern states, were gathered at Fort
Hays, where they picked up their assigned scout, W. F. Cody, and
their orders from General Sheridan, after which they rode out in search
of Indians.

Late in October Brevet Major General Eugene A. Carr, senior major
of the Fifth, had met the troops at Buffalo Tank on the Union Pacific
and taken command. In February (1869), after a busy winter of scouting across vast areas of the great plains, during which he covered himself with considerable glory and earned high praise from his general,
Will again went to visit Lulu in St. Louis. (No doubt that was the
occasion when he took her the news that he was to be transferred to
Fort McPherson in the spring. Certainly it was not *after* returning
from the battle of Summit Springs, as Cooper has it, for by then he
was already stationed in Nebraska.) Cody's wife heard her husband's
"booming" voice as he burst into her parents' home. "I could only stare
at him," she recorded. "Where the close cropped hair had been were
long, flowing curls now. A mustache weaved its way outward from his
upper lip, while a small goatee showed black and spot-like on his
chin."21

3

Scout
1869-1870

Cody and the Fifth had little time to get acquainted with their new quarters, for serious trouble broke out on the Republican the day after they reached Fort McPherson. During the week of May 21-28, 1869, Indians killed thirteen whites in raids along that river, and on May 29 derailed a Kansas Pacific train and killed most of the crew. The next day a band under Tall Bull raided a German settlement on the Solomon, over in Kansas, killed several people, and took prisoner two white women, Mrs. Thomas Alderdice and Mrs. G. Weichel. On June 7 Carr and his troops received orders to leave Fort McPherson on June 9 and clear the Republican country of Indians.[1]

On June 8 the "Dandy Fifth," at Carr's command, put on a full dress review; Eugene A. Carr, West Point graduate, class of 1850, a tall, handsome "bearded Cossack"[2] and an experienced Indian fighter, loved such military displays and provided them at the slightest excuse. Brevet Major General C. C. Augur, commander of the Department of the Platte, came out from Omaha on the train for this one. Brevet Brigadier General Thomas Duncan, commandant at the fort and lieutenant colonel of the Fifth, welcomed him with proper pomp and ceremony. Of course the entire McPherson garrison and their families, as well as all the villagers of Cottonwood Springs, turned out to watch. The day was warm and bright with sun. Drums rolled, the regimental band struck up a military march, and sabers glittered in salute as the Fifth passed in review. Following the blue and yellow ranks of cavalry came the Pawnee Battalion. The Pawnee Scouts, under Major Frank North,

19

had been serving with army troops in the West since 1864. Hereditary enemies of the Sioux, these colorful Indians were of great help to the military during the years of warfare in western Nebraska.[3]

W. F. Cody, who enjoyed pomp and flourish every bit as much as Carr, was no doubt very noticeable that day, tall and straight on some splendid horse. That evening the troops began to break camp in preparation for leaving. Next morning the drums rolled again, the band blared martial music, and, flags flying, the column marched out of the fort toward the south.

Marching for 300 miles under a broiling sun and over swollen streams and through heavy sandhills, the eight companies of the command finally on July 11 came up with the Dog Cheyennes, "notoriously the worst band of Indians on the plains."[4] The Indians, seemingly believing themselves safe from pursuit, as over a month had now passed since the Kansas attacks, had set up a loosely guarded camp at Summit Springs, just over the line into Colorado Territory.

Cody and a half dozen of the Pawnee scouts located the camp, a large one made up of men, women, and children and some 600 horses. Leaving the scouts to keep watch, Cody hurried to report the location of the camp to Carr and to suggest a plan by which he believed the village could be surrounded and taken by surprise. About two o'clock that afternoon, his plan was put into operation: 244 officers and soldiers and 50 Pawnee scouts crept up, undetected, to encircle the village. The surprise was complete, and the Cheyennes fled in all directions. Carr's command captured 85 lodges, 418 horses and mules, many weapons, and much ammunition. He reported 52 Indians killed on the field and 17 women and children taken prisoner. Tall Bull was dead, Mrs. Alderdice had been tomahawked to death as the soldiers dashed into the camp, and Mrs. Weichel, though wounded, was rescued.

As with nearly everything else that had anything to do with Buffalo Bill, many conflicting stories are told of the battle of Summit Springs, building up a controversy that goes on to this day.[5] There are various accounts as to who discovered the whereabouts of the Cheyenne village. Army records and accounts left by men who were there agree that it was Cody who located the Indian camp and brought the word to Carr, together with a plan for surrounding the horse herd and lodges.

Captain Luther North claimed otherwise and told his versions to George Bird Grinnell and others who included the tales in popular and well-read books.[6] In his own book, *Man of the Plains*, North relates that Tall Bull's band had separated into three parties on July 10 and that upon coming onto these trails on July 11, General Carr also divided his command three ways. Royall and some of his men, with Cody as scout, were sent on "the right hand trail toward the northeast." North goes on to state that Royall's party had not yet returned when General Carr, after waiting for the absent men, ordered the attack on the village. This was why Cody and his party, he concludes, did not come into camp until the battle was over.[7] Another North version explaining why Cody was not in the fight at all has Cody off driving a pair of condemned government plugs "hooked up to a wagon with stuff such as soldiers would buy—tobacco, groceries . . . — a sort of mobile canteen, a moving grocery."[8]

There is also the matter of who killed Tall Bull. Luther states flatly that his brother, Major Frank North, killed the chief and that he saw him do it.[9] Cody wrote that after the battle and while the Indian camp and supplies were being burned, some mounted Indians came charging back to try to rescue some of their possessions. One went dashing about on a fine big bay horse, exhorting the others to follow him and fight until they died. The bay horse attracted Cody's eye, and he determined to have the animal. Hiding in the head of a ravine, he waited until the Indian came by at close range and shot him off the horse. Lieutenant George F. Mason jumped from his own horse and secured the fallen Indian's fine warbonnet while Sergeant McGrath, who had seen Cody kill the rider, caught the horse and handed it over to him.

Buffalo Bill rode the horse down to the place where the soldiers were holding their Indian prisoners. There one of the women "began crying in a pitiful and hysterical manner at sight of the horse, and upon inquiry I found that she was Tall Bull's wife, the same squaw that had killed one of the white women and wounded the other. She stated that this was her husband's favorite war horse and that only a short time ago she had seen Tall Bull riding him." Cody then told her that henceforth he would call the gallant steed Tall Bull in honor of her husband.[10]

In later years various members of the Fifth Cavalry, including General Carr, wrote or stated that Cody killed Tall Bull at the battle of Summit Springs. Captain Leicester Walker, who took part in the fight but does not say who killed the chief, also tells an interesting story. He relates how the Indian trail was followed "until we reached the Platte River between old Fort Sedgwick and Denver."

Here the trail was lost. No sign of any trail could be seen. General Carr ordered Cody to try to find the trail. He also ordered Major North to send some of his best Scouts to locate the trail if possible.

Six Pawnee Scouts left the command, going down the river. Cody went alone over the hills to the west. In about an hour Cody returned to the command with the report that he had found the village, that it was about one-half mile long, located at some springs. He reported that there was a large band with their families and several hundred mules and ponies. While Cody was reporting to the General the Pawnee Scouts returned, informing the General that they had found a trail. General Carr ordered me to take a squadron of cavalry and Captain North's company of Indians, but left it to me to return if I found the trail to be of no service.

General Carr started with the balance of the command with Cody as guide. I soon found the trail to be of no service and returned to the point where I had left the main command and followed General Carr. After marching about five miles I overtook the command. We were now near the point where Cody said we would find the camp. The command was halted in a valley and General Carr, Cody and Captain North and myself traveled up to the top of the hill over-looking the valley where the Indians were located. We estimated the distance from the top of the hill to the camp to be one mile. This ground had to be covered before we could strike a blow, and this would give the Indians time to mount and give us battle.[11]

Walker describes how the troops were divided and sent right and left to stations surrounding the camp. "I had five companies to charge center," he wrote. "In going from the hills to the point where the charge was ordered we went at a fast gallop. . . . At this time we did not know of swampy ground between us and the Indian village . . . a marsh formed by the springs, and quite a number of my troops foundered in the mire . . . my horse went down and I mounted a horse of one of my men."

Because of the unforeseen delay in crossing the marsh, which looked quite like the surrounding grassy terrain, some of the Indians broke through at this point, the only opening in the encirclement, and Walker explains, "I followed the Indians about three miles beyond the village and captured quite a large number of mules and ponies."

Walker concludes his account: "When Tall Bull was killed his horse, a fine race horse, was given to Cody by General Carr. The credit for locating the Indians is to Cody. He made it possible for the troops to clear the country of these bands of Indians."

Captain George Price, regimental historian of the Fifth, as well as the official records of the expedition and attack, substantiate all of the foregoing accounts except North's.[12] And finally, seventy years after Cody's triumphant return to Fort McPherson with the fleet horse, Tall Bull, William McDonald, son of the post trader, Charles McDonald, said:

> I well remember the first time I saw Cody. It was in 1869. He was twenty-three and I had just turned seven. I had just returned from an errand to a neighbor's when I saw Cody, a tall man of six feet, standing in front of I. P. Boyer's bowling alley. The Fifth Cavalry and the Pawnee Scouts had just returned to Fort McPherson from the battle of Summit Springs. Cody was the chief of scouts and Walker was captain, with General Carr in command. I remember my father and the scout talking in the barn. Cody had the horse that had belonged to Chief Tall Bull, who had been killed in the battle, and I know it was generally understood at the fort that Cody killed Tall Bull.[13]

Luther North, Leicester Walker, and William McDonald were all old men when they told their stories of Cody and the battle of Summit Springs, and all could have been mistaken on some of the details, but North had a special reason for remembering his version. It is not difficult to understand why the old man so tenaciously stuck to his claim that his brother Frank killed Tall Bull or that Cody was not even present at the battle. After long years of neglect and obscurity, Luther was discovered and made much of by writers and historians. As one of the few living men who had had a part in the stirring events of Nebraka frontier history, he was considered a valuable source of firsthand information, most of which seems to have been accepted without question. In the meantime, his brother, Frank, whom he admired and revered, had died in 1885, after an injury suffered while performing in Cody's Wild West show. During the following thirty years, Cody had risen to world-wide fame, acclaimed on every hand.

As Luther grew old (he died in 1935 at the age of eighty-nine), it pained him to see how Cody's fame increased and endured while his own and his brother's not inconsiderable parts in the drama of the West were all but forgotten. Consequently, when historians began beating a path to his door, seeking information on those long-gone days, he saw his opportunity, and with each successive telling of the tales he and Frank did better. Perhaps the old man really remembered most of it as he told it. Anyway, Cody and most of the others were dead, and seemingly no one bothered to consult the dusty files and records that were available to any who cared to ask for them. As a result, numerous books and feature stories detailing Luther's version were published from the 1930s on through the 1950s and accepted as historical truth by most of their readers.

According to Luther and his chroniclers, it was shortly after the fight at Summit Springs that Ned Buntline came to Fort Sedgwick, where the troops had gone to report the engagement and deliver their prisoners. E. Z. C. Judson (pen name: Ned Buntline) was allegedly looking for Frank North, the killer of Tall Bull, for the purpose of making him the hero of some forthcoming dime novels. But Frank, according to Luther, refuses bruskly, points to Cody, napping under his "grocery wagon," and tells Buntline, "There is your hero." The writer is then supposed to have wakened the scout, interviewed him, and put him into numerous wild west Buffalo Bill novels, setting him on the road to enduring fame. Later writers copied the tale intact, except that they somehow changed the meeting place to Fort McPherson.

There are several things wrong with the story. As Don Russell after careful research points out, Frank North could not have met Buntline at either Fort Sedgwick or Fort McPherson at the time Luther says, for Frank had taken the train from Fort Sedgwick to his home at Columbus, Nebraska, on July 17, *before* the dime novel writer reached either Colorado or Nebraska. Also, Buntline, a New Yorker, rather than being on his way west in search of a hero, was actually on his way east from California, following a temperance lecture tour. He did stop at Fort Sedgwick, but saw neither North nor Cody, for the former had gone home the week before and Cody was then on his way to Fort McPherson, where he arrived on July 23. Within hours two occurrences would stabilize Cody's immediate future and would radically change any long-range future he might then have imagined.

On July 10, while Cody and the troops were absent on the Summit Springs expedition, Brevet Major General William H. Emory had arrived at Fort McPherson to establish regimental headquarters for the Fifth Cavalry. When the expedition returned, the general assured Cody his employment as scout would be permanent and that a log house would be built for him and his family. Happy over his good news, he went at once to the post office[14] to send Lulu a letter telling her to prepare to come west again soon.

Almost immediately Cody was assigned to another scout, with troops from Company F under Brevet Major William H. Brown. On July 24, shortly before the expedition left, Major Brown introduced Cody to

Ned Buntline, who had come to Cottonwood Springs to give a temperance lecture. On that day Frank North was in Omaha, serving as interpreter at a Pawnee Indian murder trial. Buntline, deciding to skip his lecture, accompanied the expedition up the Platte as far as O'Fallon's Station, where he resumed his trip east on the train. The scouting party, on the trail of a marauding Indian band, finally abandoned the chase and went on to Fort Sedgwick. While there the troops had a payday, and Bill proceeded to fill his pockets with winnings earned by the racing prowess of his new horse, Tall Bull.

It was of course Cody's introduction to Buntline that changed Buffalo Bill's future—not because Buntline made Cody famous through his dime novels, as the popular version goes, but because through Buntline's influence Cody went on the stage; and from there (without Buntline) one thing led to another. However, in late July of 1869 Cody, naturally, knew none of this; all he knew then was that between Fort McPherson and O'Fallon's Station, Buntline "asked me a great many questions."[15]

Presumably inspired by this brief encounter in the West, Buntline wrote an adventure tale, "Buffalo Bill, the King of Border Men," which was serialized in the *New York Weekly* beginning December 1869. Interestingly, this further undermines Luther North's story, for North claimed that Cody "was given by Ned Buntline the credit for having killed Tall Bull";[16] however, Buntline's tale does not even mention Summit Springs or Tall Bull. Nor do any of his subsequent stories. Three years later Buntline wrote two more Buffalo Bill tales, and a third in 1885, but in none of them did he mention Summit Springs or Tall Bull.

The July 1869 expedition was closely followed by another that led south toward the Frenchman Fork of the Republican, then north again across the South Platte, across the North Platte, and on across the Niobrara in the far northwestern section of the state; there the pursuit was abandoned and the troops turned back on August 11, arriving at the post on August 22. Cody found that his new house was not finished, but according to letters from Lulu, she and little Arta were already on their way to Nebraska. When they reached the fort a few days later, he found lodging for them with William Reed at the trading post until the house was ready.

The Cody's two-room cabin and small log barn were located a little way east of the post reservation, between the last post buildings and the McDonald trading post. Like the officers' houses, the Cody cabin

had a rain barrel at one corner to catch run-off water from the roof
for laundry purposes; when it did not rain, a big tank wagon manned
by enlisted men brought water from the river to fill the barrels. In
either case, before it could be used the water had to be carefully poured
off the mud that settled to the bottoms of the barrels.[17]

Mrs. Cody and Mrs. Charles McDonald were soon good friends.
"Together," Lulu says, "we would do our sewing or laundry, [for]
servants were an unknown quantity at Fort McPherson." Servants, of
course, were not an unknown quantity at the fort but were, in fact,
fairly plentiful and could be hired for fifty cents to a dollar a week, with
room and board thrown in. All of the officers' wives had servant girls,
many of whom married enlisted men or settlers and stayed to make
their homes in the valley.

Louisa also tells of the time when some apparently hostile Indians
came prowling about, and she and Mrs. McDonald hurriedly drank
from a bottle of tea which the trader's wife always carried with her for
protection. They then pretended to be very drunk, and the Indians,
mortally afraid of a drunken woman, fled in terror. On another occasion, Lulu had prepared a very special dinner for some friends her husband had invited to their cabin home. Mrs. McDonald helped her cook
the meal, which was the finest that could be gotten together on the
frontier. Cooper lists the guests as "Lord and Lady Dunraven from
England and Lord Finn from Australia." When they arrived, the Codys
welcomed them at the front door. Soon Lulu excused herself to go to
the kitchen to take up the dinner, politely declining Dunraven's wife's
offer to help. When she stepped into the kitchen, she found six Indians
finishing off her dinner.

Frances Fulton, who visited Mrs. Cody in North Platte in 1883 and
heard the tale, related it as follows: Mrs. Cody told me of a dinner
she had prepared "at great expense for six officers at Fort McPherson";
while she and her husband were receiving the guests at the front door,
six Indians entered by the kitchen door, "surrounded the table and
without ceremony or carving knife," ate her roasted chickens and other
delicacies. Concluded Mrs. Cody, "the dinner was completely spoiled,
but while I cried with mortification the officers laughed and enjoyed
the joke."[18]

There is little doubt that both the "tea" incident and the Indian dinner incident are true, for the McDonald family related both of them
in later years, but it is doubtful the guests were British nobility. Certainly Lord Adair (Earl of Dunraven) and his wife did not visit Fort

McPherson in 1869. For Cooper's purposes, however, lords and ladies at the Codys' table in the log cabin on the plains was much more impressive than mere American officers, however high their rank.[19]

Of even more questionable authenticity is the Louisa-Cooper tale involving some Sioux and Pawnee Indians. One afternoon Louisa and little Arta were sunning themselves in a big chair in the parlor when they heard the door slam in the other room and the "hurried swish of moccasined feet." Slipping to the door and peeking in, Louisa saw a small band of frightened Pawnees, taking refuge in her kitchen from a larger band of Sioux, just then coming out of a nearby ravine. Buffalo Bill and his friend, Texas Jack, had left for the fort a short while before, so Louisa pushed Arta, then three or four years old, out the front door and told her to run to the fort and tell her father the Sioux were coming to their cabin. She watched the little girl dash bravely away, then went into the kitchen to confront the Sioux and order them out. When they paid no attention to her, she tried to reach her gun, but the Sioux leader got to it first. She knew the Sioux were after the Pawnees and not her, but it was still a "desperate" situation.

Then, "far away, up at the fort, I heard the faint call of the bugle. I knew the call . . . Boots and Saddles! But the Sioux did not seem to hear, and it would mean a good ten minutes before the soldiers could mount and reach the house." Since it was no more than two city blocks from the cabin to either the fort or the McDonald trading post, the soldiers who were saddling and mounting could have run the distance on foot as quickly as Arta had just done—but that would have been a tame rescue compared to Cooper's colorful charge of mounted troops.

Meanwhile, the Pawnees and Sioux were fighting savagely in the cabin. But in the nick of time Buffalo Bill and Texas Jack came riding to succor brave but terror-stricken Lulu, and the Indians began "piling out of the house into the little yard, where they faced the revolvers of Texas Jack and my husband. Will came into the house, paused just long enough to kiss me, then opened the door to the kitchen," which was still full of Pawnees. What a thrilling scene: the gallant scout lovingly kissing his frightened little wife before dashing into the kitchen to complete her rescue.

"When the scouting ended in October 1869, Cody found himself stranded at Fort McPherson, with no occupation and no income."[20] He was then reduced to making a living for himself and his family by racing his horse, as long as he could find anyone to match a race against him, for Tall Bull was a consistent winner. This means of making a living was so precarious that his wife had to take in washing to keep groceries on their table.

"Facts" such as the above are as groundless as the rescue just described, yet they have been printed over and over. Army records show that from the day Cody joined the Fifth Cavalry as scout on October 5, 1868, until he resigned in December 1872, he was never off the government payroll. During the first part of this period, October 5, 1868 to October 28, 1869, as chief of scouts he took part in seven expeditions against Indians and in nine Indian fights, and had been acclaimed for his able and efficient service by Generals Carr, Sheridan, Emory, and Augur.[21]

Fort McPherson, however, *did* have a properly laid-out one-mile race track, and the men of the post *did* enjoy the sport of kings whenever their duties permitted. Men and officers from other cavalry posts were frequent visitors at the fort; and settlers, travelers on the Oregon Trail, and horsemen from North Platte were always stopping in. It was easy to get a crowd together, and horse racing at Fort McPherson probably reached its peak the fall and winter after Buffalo Bill brought the long-legged bay horse home with him from Summit Springs. Before the winter was over, he had beaten every horse that had any claim whatever to speed and could match no more races with men who knew Tall Bull's reputation.

At this point he and Lieutenant Edward Spaulding matched a race in which Cody wagered he could jump off of and onto Tall Bull eight times in the race and still win. Describing the race, Cody wrote: "I rode the horse bareback, seized his mane with my left hand, rested my right on his withers, and while he was going at full speed, I jumped to the ground, and sprang again upon his back, eight times in succession. Such feats I had seen performed in the circus and I had practiced considerably at it with Tall Bull, so that I was certain of winning the race in the manner agreed upon."[22]

During the two weeks that elapsed between the arrival of the Fifth at Fort McPherson and its departure on the trail of Chief Tall Bull, Cody had seen the circus that gave him the inspiration for the race. On May 29, Dan Costello's Great Show, Circus, Menagerie, and Abyssinian Caravan, on its first coast-to-coast tour over the newly completed Union Pacific railroad, had played in North Platte. A few weeks later Buffalo Bill had captured the Tall Bull horse, tried the stunt, and found that it worked.

By the fall of 1870 the Codys had saved enough money to buy some much-needed new furniture for their cabin home. When Will was called to Fort D. A. Russell in Wyoming to testify in a court martial, it seemed a good time to buy the furniture in Cheyenne and have it shipped home. Cody arrived at the fort, found the case had been postponed for a week, and had to lay over there. Of course he met many old friends and had a good time, with the result: "I woke up one morning and found that I was dead broke, . . . and to raise necessary funds I sold my race-horse Tall Bull."[23]

Before the fine race horse passes from the scene, it can be told that he was beaten once. This happened, according to Bill McDonald, when a ten-year-old-boy, riding a pony owned by Lieutenant Hayes, told Cody the pony could beat Tall Bull on a four-mile run. Cody raced with him and lost.[24] Tall Bull, unbeatable in short-distance dashes, was not a long-distance runner.

4

The Platte Valley
1860s

The Platte Valley, east of the forks of the river, must have seemed to Buffalo Bill to be fairly swarming with ranchers, settlers, and tradesmen that summer of 1869.

Although the Gilman brothers were gone, having grown wealthy, sold out, and moved to Nebraska City, the purchaser, Ben Gallagher, occupied the ranch. Gallagher, the first sutler or post trader at Fort McPherson in 1863, was already well on his way to wealth by 1868 when he bought the ranch and made it his headquarters. An Iowa youth, he had branched out rapidly after coming to the post, establishing a chain of trading posts to the west, following the tide of settlement. By 1869 he was also well launched in the cattle business, and Cody often stopped in at his ranch.

Nearer Fort McPherson were the ranches of John Burke and Washington Hinman. Both dealt in cattle—oxen at first, beef animals later. Big John Burke was the first man to build a bridge across the wide and treacherous Platte within the present borders of the state. This first bridge, located north and a little west of the post, connected it with McPherson Station, the depot and little village on the Union Pacific. It was only a very narrow roadway constructed of logs atop the running gears of scores of government wagons lined up in the river bed, the tongues pointing downstream, and did not prove very substantial or successful. His second bridge, built in the winter and spring of 1869, was a pile-driven, railless affair, floored with split cedar logs. Although not a structure to inspire confidence in the user, many tons of government freight and hundreds of passengers were transported across it

from the Station to the fort within the next few years. When the annual spring flooding of the Platte washed out one of its spans in 1872,
its builder was drowned while ferrying some government freight across
the gap, after which one of his eight sons took over the ranch and
freighting business.

Hinman, born in Pennsylvania, first passed up the Overland Trail on
his way to California in 1849. By 1860 he was back at Cottonwood
Springs, setting up his ranch, a blacksmith shop, and a steam sawmill.
He had long fraternized with the Indians, spoke the Sioux language
fluently, and had a Sioux wife. When the area was first organized into
Shorter County in 1860, he became treasurer. Jeremiah Gilman was its
first sheriff and Jack Morrow one of its commissioners.

Jack Morrow was without doubt the county's most notorious resident. He has been described as "a tall, raw-boned, dangerous-looking
man, wearing a mustache, and a goatee."[1] He also "wore a diamond
(said to be valued at $1000.00) in his yellow and badly soiled shirt
bosom."[2] Morrow's infamous road ranch was located against the hills
about a mile south of the junction of the Platte rivers. His log ranch
house, sixty feet long and two-and-one-half stories high, housed a store,
a saloon, a public dining room, and space on the upper floors for travelers who stayed overnight. The ranch early acquired a dreaded reputation, due to his alleged practice of robbing travelers on the Trail. A
thorough rascal, he and his renegade followers not only "rolled" his
overnight customers but ran off the oxen and other livestock belonging
to wagon trains camped in the vicinity. "Bad" Indians and unscrupulous
whites, including sundry squawmen who hung out at his Junction
Ranch, did the raiding, driving the animals well back into the rugged
hills to the south. The next morning Morrow, all sympathy, called on
the stranded trains and offered to sell them stock to replace their losses
and enable them to continue on their way.

In time, of course, wagon bosses camped their trains as far from the
ranch as possible, down near the river, until Morrow spiked this move
by digging a deep and narrow ditch from his ranch to the Platte. A
wagon bridge spanned the ditch near his house, forcing all wagons and
livestock to cross in his very dooryard. In an 1860 diary, a writer noted
that "no charge [is] made for crossing it."[3] How generous of the ranchman not to charge his intended victims for crossing his bridge.

Morrow also traded with the Indians, many of them relatives of his
various wives, accumulating vast stores of furs, hides, buffalo robes,
dried meat, and tongues. Once a year he headed a long caravan of such

goods to Omaha, where he sold his produce at good prices and went on drunken spees so stupendous they were talked about all the way back to Denver. A man who enjoyed the best in food and wine, he kept champagne at the ranch and served it in tin cups to guests invited to his big parties. He was still owner of the ranch in 1869, and Buffalo Bill was no doubt a visitor there a few times before Morrow, at the request of the commander at Fort McPherson, sold out and left the community.

Bill Paxton was another of the daring fraternity who pioneered in the ranching business in Nebraska. A former ox-team freighter, in 1868 he first bought cattle in Texas for resale in the north. The next year, in partnership with Ben Gallagher and Jack Morrow, he signed a five-year contract with the U.S. government to furnish up to 75,000 head of cattle annually to the Indian reservations in the northern part of the state. In 1875 he established his huge Keystone spread in western Nebraska, with headquarters at Alkali (now Paxton), thirty miles upriver from North Platte. Paxton and Cody early became close friends, and in 1895 the two of them witnessed the will of millionaire Ben Gallagher. By that time both Gallagher and Paxton had fine homes in Omaha, where Buffalo Bill was always a welcome guest.

John Bratt, another long-time friend of Bill Cody's, established a large beef cattle ranch east of Morrow's place about the time that notorious fellow pulled out. Bratt, an Englishman, came to America in 1864 at the age of twenty-one and made several wagon-freighting trips from Omaha to Fort Laramie before he came to Fort McPherson to fill a government hay contract in July 1869. That fall, in partnership with Isaac Coe and Levi Carter, he went into the cattle business. The following year he established his ranch headquarters in the edge of the hills about four miles southeast of North Platte and there built a set of sod barns with cedar pole corrals and a sturdy sod house with portholes for fighting off Indian attacks. Bratt had first met Buffalo Bill while putting up hay at Fort McPherson.

M. C. Keith, Guy Barton, Isaac Dillon, and Major Leicester Walker also became ranchmen in the North Platte area: Walker and Dillon northeast of town and Barton and Keith directly east. These men all directed the operations of their ranches from their homes in town, as did Russell Watts, a New Yorker, who had a vast range to the south and west.

Keith, a former freighter and stage line operator from Iowa, not only ran cattle on his Pawnee Springs ranch but with the help of his wife operated the Pacific House, a huge hotel and dining room housed in the main section of the Union Pacific depot. Guy Barton, Keith's partner in that early cattle business, came to North Platte about the time Cody did, invested his savings in cattle, became wealthy, built one of the finest houses in town, and served in the state legislature, 1872-1876, all within less than a decade.

Dillon, a nephew of Sidney Dillon, president of the Union Pacific railroad, built a big house a little way north of the depot and laid out a fine half-mile race track, enclosed by a solid board fence. A trotting horse fancier, he trained some good horses on his private track and held innumerable racing meets there. Keith, another trotting horse enthusiast, trained his speedy trotters on any straight, hard stretch of road in the valley.

A year or so after the battle of Summit Springs, Major Walker had been assigned command of the North Platte barracks. At the close of 1870 he resigned his command to go into the cattle business and built a comfortable home for his family near the Dillon house, north of the tracks. A short time later he founded the first bank in the town, later selling it to Charles McDonald. With the possible exception of Dillon, Watts, and Walker, all of these men began as very poor boys and became wealthy; all were good friends of W. F. Cody.

Another couple whose friendship was to mean a great deal to Buffalo Bill was Mr. and Mrs. Lew Baker. At the time of Cody's arrival in Nebraska, Baker was operating a saloon in North Platte, but until the coming of the railroad he and his wife had run a road ranch and stage station at O'Fallon's, said to have been one of the most dangerous on the whole length of the Oregon Trail because of the frequency of Indian attacks upon it. They were good, homelike people, according to John Bratt, and the best was never too good for anyone who stopped at their place.

It was that summer of 1869 that the first big herd of "commercial" cattle came to North Platte. Texas Jack Omohundro had trailed the 3,000 head of Longhorns up from Texas. Keith and Barton bought 1,000 two- to six-year-old cows from the herd. Mahlon Brown bought 500, and the rest were sold out in smaller bunches, after which all the trail men except Texas Jack went back to Texas. The tall cowboy, John Omohundro, stayed on in North Platte to tend bar for Lew Baker in one of the many saloons ranged along Front Street in the three-year-old village.

Charles Stamp, a teen-age newcomer from Illinois, heated the branding irons for the crew that branded out the Texas cattle. The branding done, Stamp took a job tending bar in another saloon, "not over twenty feet from where he [Texas Jack] worked. There wasn't much to do in the daytime, so I got pretty well acquainted with Texas Jack. I didn't work nights, as I was just a kid then, and an older man tended bar at night." Stamp goes on to say, "Buffalo Bill's first entry to North Platte was to [see] the Dan Costello circus."[4] This was on May 29.[5] Cody and the Fifth had arrived at Fort McPherson nine days earlier. Since they did not leave the post on Tall Bull's trail until June 9, it is reasonable to conclude that most of them rode up to North Platte to see the circus.

The foregoing pinpoints Buffalo Bill's first known visit to North Platte, the town that was to play such an intimate part in his life for the next forty-four years, and indeed to the very end of his days. It was only a straggling village then, sprawled crookedly between the forks of the river, some eighteen miles west of Fort McPherson.

The town had its beginning in the spring of 1866 when Mahlon H. Brown, formerly a stage station operator at O'Fallon's Bluff, hauled cedar logs from Cottonwood Canyon and built three cabins on what was soon to become the corner of Locust (now Jeffers) and Front Streets. When Brown moved his wife, Hester, into one of the cabins on March 6, she became the first white woman to live on the site.[6] Before the year was done, the place was the lively town of North Platte. In December of that year, "this station on the world's great highway" was described as follows:

> some twenty buildings, including a brick engine roundhouse, calcu-lated for forty engines, founded on a stone foundation, at present nearly completed for ten engines; a water tank of beautiful propor-tions, as they all are along the road, kept from freezing by being warmed by a stove, also a fixture in every tank house; a frame depot of the usual beautiful design; a large frame hotel [in the same build-ing with the depot], nearly finished, to cost about $18,000; a long, spacious movable building, belonging to General Casement, and his brother, Daniel Casement, the great tracklayers of the continent, cal-culated for a store, eating-house, and for storage purposes; together with sundry other buildings.[7]

Other buildings known to be there before 1869 included the Cedar Hotel, a log building across from the new depot-hotel, and the frame store put up by Miller and Peniston across from the Brown cabin.

William Star Peniston, one of the partners in the town's first permanent store, had been born in Kingston, Jamaica, in 1834. He was a nephew of Lord Peniston of England, and his father, at one time the largest ship owner in North America, lived in Quebec, where William had obtained his education. In 1858 he drove stage from St. Joseph to Salt Lake City and the following year came to Nebraska, and finally to North Platte in 1866, where he died forty years later. A. J. Miller was his brother-in-law, business partner, and friend.

By year's end, with the Union Pacific rails laid to the east bank of the North Platte River, just above its junction with the South Platte, and the long, new trestle bridge across the river completed, the town had become a brawling, sleepless, end-of-track conglomeration. With a shipment of goods brought in on one of the first trains to pull up to the new depot, Miller and Peniston had opened their doors on November 9, 1866.

North Platte City claimed a population of more than 3,000 by the following May when the *Missouri Democrat* of St. Louis sent a reporter out to get a story on Indian depredations, the killing of settlers, and the burning of ranches. The reporter, one Henry M. Stanley, who was to become famous a few years later seeking Dr. Livingston on the bleak shores of Tanganyika, made the trip out from Omaha on a fast passenger train in fifteen hours, traveling at a speed of nineteen miles an hour. A part of Stanley's published report read:

North Platte is a gay frontier hamlet, with the days of Pike's Peak and the California Gold Rush revived. Its citizens are a motley crowd of construction camp denizens, roughs, toughs, and gamblers, emigrants but a few months from the countries of the Old World. Women from the dance halls, bullwhackers and teamsters would line the tracks to see the train come in. Timid passengers, fearing to face so desperate appearing a multitude, were glad to follow hotel runners to a hastily constructed hostelry that charged a lot but gave little in the way of comfort. A gambling establishment was conducted in a large tent where games of chance seemed never to stop.[8]

Stanley estimated there were 15,000 tons of government freight awaiting transportation by ox team to military posts beyond the end of the railroad, and "camped in the vicinity were 1,236 wagons of Mormons, Utah bound. A newspaper, the Pioneer on Wheels, is being published in a boxcar near the engine shed . . . ready to move on as soon as the rails are laid farther west—as would the whole population excepting a few railroad men—the location seemingly being wholly unsuited for a townsite, being intersected by numerous sloughs populated by swarms of mosquitoes."9

The fine hotel mentioned by Simpson as nearly finished in December 1866, must not have been in operation yet in May 1867, for Stanley is apparently referring to the Cedar Hotel, as does Bishop D. S. Tuttle, a New York City churchman, a few days later. Traveling with two other ministers and two ladies to engage in missionary work in Montana, Idaho, and Utah, they came by train to North Platte to take stage for the west but were stranded five days in the town because of Indian raids that stopped all travel in that direction. "The one little frontier hotel," the bishop wrote over fifty years later, "was crowded full"; and though Tuttle managed to get a room for the ladies, the men, wrapped in blankets, had to sleep on a floor.

Before leaving, the bishop and his party held, in the little log hotel, what may have been the first Sunday church service in the town, noting: "At North Platte no religious services of any kind are held on Sunday. Men work and trade and buy and sell just as usual, and gamble and quarrel more than usual."10

The town as yet had neither a municipal government nor a peace officer, and the county sheriff, O. O. Austin, had an almost boundless territory to police. Consequently, every man was his own law and there were no restraints except such as a man could enforce against his neighbors.

In July 1867, the end-of-track population moved on to Julesburg, and overnight the brawling town became a village of some 150 souls, mostly Union Pacific employees and their families. Mahlon Brown stayed, as did Miller and Peniston, and M. C. Keith who, with the aid of his wife, was running the now finished Union Pacific hotel, the Pacific House. A blacksmith shop, livery stable, and, of course, the numerous saloons completed the business section of North Platte City.

By the time Buffalo Bill first saw the town, that day of the circus, the Cedar Hotel was no more, having burned down the previous winter, and the big Union Pacific hotel was a still smoldering heap of blackened embers. Sparks from the smokestack of a passing engine had set the vast two-story structure afire a few days earlier, but already huge piles of pine-scented lumber waited at the site, and a new depot-hotel would rise on the ashes of the old before the summer was done.

The prairie around the little business section was dotted with small houses, built so haphazardly that a few years later when the town fathers wanted to lay out streets they had to ask the owners to move their buildings this way or that to line them up in some sort of order. Wagon roads and paths wound from house to house, detouring around the sloughs and swales where ducks swam and mosquitoes buzzed. The houses, some log, some frame, but "mostly unplastered, were secured against the penetrating winds of winter by robes, skins and suchlike, tacked to the walls. With these, and a hot cook stove going day and night while cold spells and blizzards lasted, the inmates managed to get along."[11]

On the day of the circus, Cody and his army friends no doubt visited the North Platte barracks, strung out on the south side of the tracks beyond the west end of Front and (what is now) Sixth Streets. To protect the town, the track layers, the telegraph line, and west-bound traffic on the Trail, the government had established a military post there early in 1867 and garrisoned it with two companies of cavalry. When hostile Indians were known, or believed, to be in the area, the men at the new brick roundhouse were alerted and a special long blast blown on its whistle, warning everybody within hearing to head for the roundhouse and fort up there.

In the gap between the last business building on the west end of Front Street and the east end of the barracks stood two small houses. One was the W. J. Patterson home; the other belonged to Robert Rowland, a Front Street saloon keeper. Mrs. Patterson and everybody within hearing distance of the whistle always ran for the roundhouse, but Mrs. Rowland never did. Refusing to leave her home for any old Indians whatever, she calmly went on about her work. Although the citizens were happy to have the protection of the cavalry, the best families would not allow their daughters to associate or dance with the enlisted men. Officers, of course, were a different matter.

In the summer of 1868, word went out to all Indians of the Platte country to come in for a treaty conference to be held in the new machine shops on September 24. Toward the end of July, small bands of Sioux began to arrive, followed later by Pawnees and Cheyennes, all filing slowly along west of the roundhouse toward camp grounds on the north side of the river. Many had ponies pulling drags or travois. With their families, Chiefs Spotted Tail, Standing Elk, Swift Bear, Pawnee Killer, Big Mouth, and others went into camp a little west of the Union Pacific shops.[12]

With the chiefs were the squawmen John Y. Nelson and Hank and Monte Clifford and their Indian wives and mixed-blood children. The men were well known at Fort McPherson as well as in North Platte. Nelson, a native Virginian and an adopted member of Spotted Tail's tribe, had worked for the Gilmans, buying furs and hides from the Indians in 1862-1863. He spoke Sioux fluently and was in demand as an interpreter at such affairs as the upcoming treaty meeting. One of his various Indian wives was a relative of Chief Red Cloud.

The Clifford brothers, whose lodges, along with Nelson's, stood in a bend of the Medicine Creek, eighteen miles south of Fort McPherson, were white men who liked the Indian way of life better than that of their own race. As squawmen, however, they ran into some peculiar problems, chief of which was the likelihood of their wives' numerous relatives moving in with them every now and then. Since they were usually better off than Indian household heads and could get credit at the trading posts when the Indians could not, they often had visitors. And if a squawman wanted to maintain his standing in the tribe, it behooved him to provide for all the guests who came to dinner and stayed for the winter. Consequently, both Nelson and the Clifford brothers were constantly in debt to Miller and Peniston and other area traders because of this custom. During the winter of 1870, when they had killed enough buffalo to provide 10,000 pounds of meat, 1,000 dried tongues, and a goodly supply of tanned robes, all intended for shipment east for cash, sixty Indian relatives moved in and stayed until the merchandise was all used up in their entertainment.[13] Of necessity, both Nelson and the Cliffords made a business of buffalo hunting until the great herds were gone.

At the time of the 1868 treaty in North Platte, trade was unusually brisk at Miller and Peniston's and at Otto Uhlig's new store for a few days, while the Indians and squawmen exchanged their robes, hides, and pelts for store goods. Then General Sherman, Brigadier General John B. Sanborn, General William S. Harney, Brevet Major General Alfred Terry, and Brevet Major General C. C. Augur arrived to get the conference under way. During their stay in town, the officers were lavishly entertained by the most prominent citizens, and numerous dinners and parties were given in their honor. At a wedding held in the dining room of the Union Pacific hotel, General Sherman was accorded the honor of being first to kiss the bride.[14]

Pleasures
1869-1870

When Cody returned to winter quarters at Fort McPherson after the active summer and fall of 1869, military matters were quiet, and Will and Louisa had time to enjoy the social life at the post and its environs. In addition to the weekly stage plays, dinners and dances were frequent, and the Codys were popular at such affairs.

Charles McDonald, the trader, every now and then cleared out his store enough to make dancing space and held open house for the countryside. People came from twenty-five miles around and danced until breakfast time. Settlers, soldiers, cowboys from Bratt's Double O, Burke's Flatiron, Walker's LW, and anybody else who happened to be around or traveling by on the trail, all were welcome. Since men always outnumbered women at such frontier outposts, every lady present was sure to be danced off her feet by morning.

One night Louisa danced with a heavy-set young German, introduced to her as Magnus Cohen but popularly known as "Maggie." He told her he had arrived at the fort with his company in time to help raise the flag over the post on July 4, 1866, but was now about to be mustered out of the army, after which he planned to contract to furnish butchered beef to the fort, as he had been a butcher back in Pennsylvania. Before they finished their dance, the soldier told her she danced exactly like a girl he had once danced with in St. Louis. A bit more backtracking and they discovered they had danced together there, before Louisa had met her Will or Maggie Cohen had known he would be coming to the Platte Valley to make his home for the rest of his life.

Fiddlers, seemingly always in good supply at these frontier gatherings, furnished the dance music outside the post, while dances held on the reservation usually depended on the military band. Whenever Company L of the Fifth Cavalry entertained, the men cleared out a large sleeping room for the dance. The wife of Company L's first sergeant, Henry Clark, said one of these dances stood out above the others because of a trick played on the dancers by some of the officers. Sergeant Clark's office was a small room adjoining the one cleared for dancing, and the men set up a bed in it for the accommodation of sleeping babies belonging to the invited families. While the dance was in full swing, two or three officers slipped in and rewrapped the sleeping small fry, shifting blankets and coats. At dawn the tired and sleepy parents sorted out their offspring by identifying the wrappings and left, each with the wrong baby. When everyone had had time to go home and come back again, a more careful job of sorting was executed, along with some earburning comments on the tricksters.[1]

Social life for the feminine contingent at Fort McPherson was rounded out by formal dinners and teas, to which Mrs. McDonald, Louisa Cody, and others outside the post were invited. Mrs. Helen Randall, widow of a former postmaster general of the United States, Alexander Randall, was often among the guests. The government provided transportation for Mrs. Randall, Nebraska's first cattle queen, and to bring her to the post in fitting style four-horse ambulances, complete with uniformed cavalry outriders, were dispatched to her ranch home northwest of North Platte.[2]

The fraternal orders, too, soon caught up with the far frontier, and on Monday evening, November 15, 1869, Platte Valley Lodge No. 32 A. F. and A.M. was born in the quarters of Captain W. H. Brown, the officer who had introduced Buffalo Bill to Buntline the previous July. The new Masonic lodge was the first to be chartered west of Fremont in Nebraska, and the first regular meeting was held in the big room above McDonald's store in December of that year; the trader had become a Mason in Rogersville, Tennessee, in 1857. Buffalo Bill was among those who made up the charter membership of the new lodge; a little over a year later, on January 10, 1871, Cody received the degree of Master Mason while still a scout at the fort.[3]

The only account of Christmas at Fort McPherson is the one left by Cooper. He has Louisa enthusiastically relating how Will rode off to Cheyenne (which Cooper still believes is just a little jaunt to the west), with a wagon following him, to bring back gifts and all the other necessities of the season. While he was gone, Louisa and the other women at the post decorated the "big hall," passed out parts for the program, set up the Christmas tree, and cooked and baked great quantities of food for the holiday board.

Will comes back, "loaded down with packages, to say nothing of the wagon which followed him." The account lists only three children. "In that great camp, where lived the men who guarded the West, were only . . . three girls, the band-leader's child, Mrs. McDonald's little daughter, and Arta. And for them the soldiers had saved their money that they might have a real Christmas." There must have been other children included in that Christmas celebration, for young Will McDonald would have been nine or ten years old then, and several of the officers had their families with them on the post. At any rate, the program, as planned by Mrs. Cody and the other ladies, came off in high style, except that little Arta presumably embarrassed her mother no end by standing up in her turn and reciting a bit of silly doggerel her father had taught her, instead of the appropriate recitation her mother had selected for her.[4]

Texas Jack Omohundro, at the urging of Cody, quit his bartender's job sometime in the winter of '69 and moved down to the fort, where he taught school for awhile. Though the tall, well-mannered cowboy has been remembered as a popular square dance caller at the post, he was best known as a U.S. Army scout and a friend of Buffalo Bill. John Burwell Omohundro, a Virginian only five months younger than Cody, had served in the Fifth Virginia Cavalry during the war. Afterward he drifted to Florida, taught school for awhile there, and moved on to Texas where he did a little Indian fighting before coming up the trail with the longhorns that were sold off in North Platte.

Another close friendship that began that winter and was to last through the years was that of Cody and Dr. Frank Powell, contract surgeon at the post. Powell, a Kentuckian a year younger than Cody, obtained his medical education at the University of Louisville. As a thirty-second degree Mason and as Deputy Grand Master for Nebraska and for Colorado and Wyoming Territories when the Masons organized at Cottonwood Springs, he conferred the various degrees of the lodge on Buffalo Bill, Magnus Cohen, and others during the next year or so.[5] Powell was also a newspaper man and supplied the Omaha papers with accounts of any worthwhile news from the post.[6]

The spring of 1870 started out quietly enough and continued so until June 7, when, early in the morning, a band of Indians made off with twenty-one horses belonging to the Fort McPherson herd and some belonging to John Burke and Ben Gallagher. With Cody as guide, Fifth Cavalry troops took up the trail. Buffalo Bill had a very personal interest in the pursuit, for one of his favorite mounts, Powder Face, was among the stolen horses. By dark they were near Red Willow Creek, sixty miles south of the fort. Cody scouted on ahead and found the Indians in camp on the creek, about four miles from where the troops had halted. At dawn Cody guided the attack on the Indians, but they fled, abandoning everything but the horses they rode. It was on this occasion that Bill, with a single shot, killed two Indians mounted on one horse; but the Indian riding the fleet Powder Face got away, and the scout never saw the horse again.

As far back as the beginning of recorded history, the great Platte Valley and the vast ranges of hills on either side had been the accustomed grazing grounds of immense herds of buffalo, elk, deer, and other wild game. During the spring and fall migrating seasons, it was said the many canyons debouching onto the valley were like moving black rivers with endless miles of marching buffalo.

Since supplying his post with game was a part of a scout's duties, Buffalo Bill had good reason to do all the hunting he liked, and plenty of company when he wanted it, for hunting was probably predominant over all other entertainment offered at the post. And in addition to his friends, who seldom missed an opportunity to go hunting with him, there were nearly always some visiting dignitaries on hand eager to try their skills at bringing down big game.

Completion of the first transcontinental railroad the year before now made it possible for sportsmen to journey in comfort to the grazing grounds of the big herds, and once on the scene all they needed were experienced guides and horses and wagons to haul their gear. All of this was readily available at government expense to prominent persons, since the bulk of the meat brought in went to feed the troops at the post providing the equipment.

In the summer of 1870, the army outfitted and escorted an engaging visitor, but it was a different kind of hunt. Yale University's Othniel Charles Marsh, first professor of paleontology in the U.S., and a party of students came to the Great Plains to hunt fossils and old bones. Cody and Major Frank North were the army scouts for this expedition, but after only one day Cody was recalled for other duties; however, it was the beginning of a long friendship. Cody wrote of that initial acquaintance: Professor Marsh "gave me a geological history of the country . . . and otherwise entertained me with several scientific yarns."[7] In later years Buffalo Bill was often a guest in the eminent scientist's New Haven home.

Cody almost missed another outing that summer—a hunt arranged, during his absence, for four special guests: his sisters, May (Mary Hannah) and Helen (Laura Ella), and General Augur's two daughters. Twenty-nine years later Helen wrote a book about her famous brother, *The Last of the Great Scouts*, in which she tells the story. "A gay party it was," she wrote. "For men, there were a number of officers, and . . . Dr. Frank Powell . . . ; for women, the wives of two of the officers, the daughters of General Augur, May, and myself."[8]

After twenty miles on horseback, the party sighted a herd of buffalo. Dr. Powell proposed that the ladies do the shooting and a gun was put into May's hands. After being given "explicit directions as to its handling," she fired, wounding the buffalo, which dropped its shaggy head and charged. The officers then fired into "the mountain of flesh," but only enraged the buffalo the more. The writer leaves her young sister at this point, with the infuriated animal bearing down upon her and the rest of the party apparently helpless to aid her, while she explains that Buffalo Bill had been away on a scouting trip and not only had been unable to go on the hunt but had known nothing about it until his return to the post. As soon as he learned of the expedition he set out in pursuit of the party.

Thus it was that barely in time he galloped onto the scene, shot the charging buffalo, and saved his young sister's life. After he scolded them all roundly for going so far from the fort and running the danger of encountering hostile Indians, they hurriedly set out for home. The ladies, especially Helen, were exhausted by the time they reached the Jester ranch, five miles east of the post. Alexander Jester, described by Helen as a "wealthy bachelor," gives them supper and sends the weary women on to the fort in a carriage. "The next day's Omaha paper contained an account of the hunt from Dr. Powell's graphic pen, and in it May Cody received all the glory of the shot that laid the buffalo low."[9]

Helen returned to Kansas in the fall, but May stayed on and was still at her brother's home when the Cody's only son, little Kit Carson, was born on November 26, 1870. Helen lists the boy as the third of the Cody children, stating that the second daughter, Orra, had arrived two years earlier. The post records show that she was born on August 15, 1872, at 3:00 P.M., nearly two years *after* her brother's birth.

Cooper also makes a mistake when he has Kit born following Will's trip to New York in the spring of 1872, still more than a year in the future. It is easy to see why Cooper put it so far out of line, for it added much to the sentimental excitement of his tale and also provided a convenient reason why Louisa did not go to New York with him. But why Helen should shift the children about as she did is anybody's guess. Also, from this account of the sisters' visit to their brother's home, it would seem that the jealousy between the women in Cody's family, later so apparent, had not yet developed. Perhaps it was his later fame and riches that made each of the women want to claim his affection and attention for herself.

In the spring of the next year, 1871, Helen married Alexander Jester at the home of a family friend in Leavenworth and returned with him to his ranch to make her home.[10]

Justice of the Peace, Cody's Favorite Hunt 1870-1871

The year 1871 was also peaceful on the Platte, with only one brief encounter with Indians when Cody led thirty men under Lieutenant Edward Hayes on the trail of six Sioux who had made off with sixty horses and mules. On May 24 the troops surprised the Indians on Birdwood Creek, a tributary of the North Platte, northwest of North Platte, captured them, and took back the horses. The scout was mentioned for "conspicuous and gallant conduct" in the skirmish.[1]

Buffalo Bill, however, had other affairs to keep him busy that year, for he had been appointed justice of the peace at Cottonwood Springs. Since the army had little jurisdiction beyond the limits of its own military grounds, outlaws and sharpers of various sorts hung about the fringes of the reservation, preying upon soldiers, settlers, and travelers. Crooked gambling and stealing of government property had become so prevalent that General Emory, deciding something had to be done, recommended the appointment of W. F. Cody to the office,[2] figuring that someone also sympathetic to the army's side of controversies would be most helpful. Cody insisted that he didn't "know any more about law than a government mule does about book-keeping."[3] Helen phrased it slightly differently, writing that the appointment was much to her brother's dismay, for he "knew no more of law than a mule knows of singing."[4] Louisa, however, had Cody accepting the appointment of "judge" with glee and assuring her that "I know as much law as I need to know around here."[5]

Few details of this period survive except some humorous tales left by Buffalo Bill himself and some comments by his wife and sister. In his own story he says his most frightening experience was the occasion on which a couple came to him to be married. He couldn't remember how the ritual went nor could he find any help in the *Statutes of Nebraska,* so he made up a ceremony and went ahead. It ended with "whomsoever God and Buffalo Bill have joined together let no man put asunder,"[6] words that have become famous in western tales told and retold a thousand times since then.

As Cooper tells it, it was Will's wife who engineered the wedding at which her husband officiated. After describing the ceremony and the famous last words, she goes on to tell of another couple who sought him out and asked him to divorce them. He couldn't find anything in the *Statutes* on that either, and having not the slightest notion how to proceed, he solved the whole thing by talking the pair into traveling awhile longer in "double harness."[7]

While Buffalo Bill had no peer at finding his way over the trackless prairies and was even able to scout out workable trails through the mazes of the law while justice of the peace, he presumably needed help in the city. The Omaha *Daily Herald* of November 13, 1870 describes what was probably Cody's first visit to that place:

> Buffalo Bill is in town. Our readers are, no doubt, familiar with some of the exploits of this famous scout and guide. One of our reporters interviewed the gentleman yesterday and found him a modest, quiet man. His real name is William Cody. He was born in Davenport, Ia., and is 34. [He was 24.] He has been on the plains 27 years and for the last seven has been an army scout. He is a strongly built man, 6 feet 1 inch, and rather good looking. . . . Although Buffalo Bill is able to "hoe his own row" on the plains, he feels rather strange in a city, and consequently has engaged a guide to "take him around" while he remains in Omaha.

Without doubt Omaha *Herald* readers, as well as those of the big eastern papers, became much more familiar with Buffalo Bill the following September when he guided General Sheridan's buffalo hunting party to resounding success on the plains. Sheridan's guests included, from New York, James Gordon Bennett, editor of the New York *Herald*; Carroll Livingston; Lawrence R. Jerome, and his older brother Leonard W. Jerome, financier and three years later grandfather of Winston Churchill; General Anson Stager of the Western Union Telegraph Co. Also General H. E. Davies, who wrote a booklet, *Ten Days on the Plains*, describing the hunt; Charles L. Wilson, editor of the Chicago Evening *Journal*; Major General John C. Hecksher; General Charles Fitzhugh of Pittsburgh; Colonel John Schuyler Crosby and Captain M. Edward Rogers of Philadelphia; Brevet Major Morris J. Asch, assistant surgeon of General Sheridan's staff; Colonel M. C. Sheridan, the general's brother; and Colonel Daniel H. Rucker, acting quartermaster general and soon to be Philip Sheridan's father-in-law.

The august party was met at the North Platte depot by General Emory and Major Brown, with a full company of cavalry as escort and a sufficient number of wagons to carry the guests and their baggage. A brisk drive of less than two hours over a hard, smooth road took them to the fort, where they found the entire garrison, five companies of the Fifth under command of General Carr, on parade awaiting their arrival. While the band played, "the cavalry passed very handsomely in review before General Sheridan,"[8] after which the general introduced Buffalo Bill to the guests and assigned them to their quarters in large, comfortable tents just outside the post. The remainder of the day was spent entertaining the visitors at "dinner and supper parties, and music and dancing; at a late hour they retired to rest in their tents."[9] Naturally the officers of the post and their ladies drained the great occasion of the last ounce of its entertainment value. The finest linens, glassware, and china were brought out to grace the tables for the dinner and supper parties, and the ballroom glittered that night with gold braid, silks, velvets, and jewels.

That the hunt was important in Buffalo Bill's eyes is indicated by the fact that he dressed up for it as he had not done before. He writes that in spite of the lateness of the retirement hour, "At five o'clock next morning . . . I rose fresh and eager for the trip, and as it was a nobby and high-toned outfit which I was to accompany, I determined to put on a little style myself. So I dressed in a new suit of light buckskin, trimmed along the seams with fringes of the same material; and I put on a crimson shirt handsomely ornamented on the bosom, while on my head I wore a broad *sombrero*. Then mounting a snowy white horse—a gallant stepper—I rode down from the fort to the camp, rifle in hand. I felt first-rate that morning, and looked well."[10]

Quite likely Louisa was responsible for the handsome ornamentation on the bosom of the red shirt, for she was an expert with a needle, and in her own story she describes some of the elaborate outfits she made for her Will. And that Buffalo Bill was not mistaken in his own estimate of the fine figure he cut that morning is borne out by General Davies' description of him as Cody rode into camp: "The most striking feature of the whole was . . . our friend Buffalo Bill . . . . [H]e realized to perfection the bold hunter and gallant sportsman of the plains."[11]

Davies goes on to write eloquently of "the far-famed Buffalo Bill, whose name has been lately used to 'point a moral and adorn a tale,' in the New York Ledger, and whose life and adventures have furnished the material for the brilliant drama that under his name has drawn crowded and delighted audiences at one of our metropolitan theatres." He also refers to their guide as "William Cody, Esquire—which title he holds of right, being, in the county in which his home is, a justice of the peace." He describes him as "a mild, agreeable, well-mannered man, quiet and retiring in disposition, though well informed and always ready to talk well and earnestly upon any subject of interest. . . . Tall and somewhat slight in figure, though possessed of great strength and iron endurance; straight and erect as an arrow, and with strikingly handsome features, he at once attracted to him all with whom he became acquainted, and the better knowledge we gained of him during the days he spent with our party increased the good impression he made upon his introduction."[12]

The expedition was soon under way, heading up Cottonwood Canyon toward the divide that separated the valleys of the Platte and the Republican. One hundred troopers under command of Major Brown and a train of sixteen wagons carrying baggage, supplies (including a load of ice), and forage for the trip accompanied the celebrities on the excursion. There were three four-horse ambulances in which to carry the guns, and to which saddle-weary members of the party might repair to rest. Five greyhounds, brought along to course rabbits and antelope, were also hauled in the ambulances when they tired of the chase. A load of linen, china, and glassware was looked after by French chefs, and the meals of many courses were served by waiters in evening dress.[13]

The cavalcade made seventeen miles the first day and went into camp on Fox Creek, a tributary of the Republican River. The next day, in addition to finding and shooting several buffalo, the easterners and their escort visited the camp of the squawmen, the Clifford brothers and John Y. Nelson, who, with their Indian families, were engaged in hunting and making buffalo robes.

The much publicized hunt lasted ten days, progressing on down the ladder of rivers by way of Medicine Creek and the Republican River in Nebraska, across Beaver and Prairie Dog Creeks to the Solomon and

Saline Rivers in Kansas, arriving at Fort Hays on October 2, nearly two hundred miles from their starting point. On the way they had bagged hundreds of buffalo, elk, antelope, and wild turkeys, so much game in fact that the Salt Lake *Tribune*, looking ahead to rumors of a still more grandiose hunt soon to take place, observed on the conclusion of this one: "Enough game will be left, we hope, for the Grand Duke Alexis when he takes a scurry over the hunting grounds."

The New Yorkers, with splendid cooks and plenty of wine, had a wonderful time, and with each day out their admiration for Buffalo Bill increased. They marveled at the sureness with which he led them through the limitless network of hills and canyons, always bringing them out on a pretty tree-bordered stream at camping time. They were amazed at his skill in building a bridge across a stream that could not be forded with the wagons. They admired his knowledge of horse flesh when they found that Buckskin Joe, "a dismal looking dun colored brute," was the finest buffalo hunting horse in the cavvy. At Fort Hays, as General Sheridan and his guests prepared to board the train that would take them home, Bennett and the New Yorkers urged Buffalo Bill to visit them in their own bailiwick the first chance he might have to go east. Sheridan gave his permission for such a leave but indicated it would have to wait until after Grand Duke Alexis' visit, for he was appointing Cody guide for that royal extravaganza, the most famous buffalo hunt of all time.[14]

With admiring editors of two of the nation's biggest newspapers in Sheridan's hunting party, our popular guide stood to gain a good share of the publicity surrounding stories told of the hunt upon the party members' return home. Bennett's New York paper had already carried some items about the hunt and Buffalo Bill, but Wilson, Stager, Sheridan, and the general's staff officers were to be denied a festive re-living in Chicago of their Plains excursion, for only days after their return the great fire devastated the city. Wilson's newspaper carried only fire news, and Sheridan became embroiled in the responsibilities and controversy of administering a city under martial law.

Nonetheless, with the plum assignment to the royal hunt party under his belt and with the publication only a few months away of Davies' book describing the New York party ramble, Buffalo Bill's reputation as guide and hunter was solidly and nationally made.

Back at the post it was more of the same. As Cody recalled, "we returned to Fort McPherson and found General Carr about to start out on a twenty days' scout, not so much for the purpose of finding

Indians, but more for the object of taking some friends on a hunt"—
two visiting Englishmen and a Mr. McCarthy of Syracuse, New York, a
relative of Colonel William H. Emory. "Of course I was called on to
accompany the expedition."[15]

It was not all play and no work. Toward the end of October, after
weeks of fun and a round of practical jokes, General Carr's expedition
returned to Fort McPherson to find that Indians had killed the Buck
party on Beaver Creek. "Two companies of cavalry were sent," Cody
wrote, "and I accompanied them as a guide." The troops had little
success, finding no hostiles, but they did discover "some of the remains,
which we buried; but nothing further. It was now getting late in the
fall and we accordingly returned to Fort McPherson."[16]

The Fifth Cavalry was soon ordered to Arizona. Cody was inclined
to accompany his friends, but General Sheridan instructed him to stay
in Nebraska and await the January 1872 preparations for the Grand
Duke hunt. "During the next few weeks I had but little to do," Cody
remembered.[17]

7

Grand Duke Alexis
1872

There are countless versions of the Duke Alexis buffalo hunt of January 1872. The briefest and probably the most accurate account is the following: In 1871 Alexander I, czar of all the Russians, was desirous of getting his handsome twenty-one-year-old son out of his homeland for awhile in order to break up an undesirable or unsuitable romance. America seemed far enough away, and the royal parent made his wish known to President U. S. Grant, who turned the matter over to his top general, Phil Sheridan, since it was known that the Grand Duke had expressed a desire to visit the Great Plains of America and was also very fond of hunting.

Sheridan first made sure of the services of Buffalo Bill, now the country's best-known hunting guide, then laid plans for the most famous hunt ever to take place on American soil. As a result, Alexis sailed from England in September 1871, escorted by a Russian battle fleet. He arrived in New York more than a month later and was royally entertained there and in Washington for several weeks before proceeding west to see the vast prairies of which he had heard so much.

About January 1, 1872, General George A. Forsyth and Dr. Morris J. Asch went out to Fort McPherson to make the necessary preparations and have everything in readiness for the royal guest's arrival. There Buffalo Bill assured them there were plenty of buffalo in the country, especially over on the Red Willow, sixty miles to the south. The day following the officers' arrival, guided by Cody and accompanied by Lieutenant Hayes, Fifth Cavalry quartermaster, and a small escort of men and wagons, they proceeded to the Red Willow, where they chose a pleasant campsite on a grassy knoll above the timbered creek. Leaving the rest of the party to stake out the boundaries of the big camp, Bill set out early the following morning to hunt the winter camp of Spotted Tail and his band, somewhere on the Frenchman's Fork of the Republican, about 150 miles from the fort. This he did at the special request of General Sheridan, who thought it a good idea to invite Spotted Tail and "about one hundred of his leading warriors and chiefs" to the hunt, so the Duke could see how Indians killed buffalo, and also observe a grand war dance of the Sioux.

Cody found the Indian camp and invited the chief and his men to come to the old Government Crossing on the Red Willow in about ten sleeps to meet a great chief from across the water who was coming as the guest of the Great White Father in Washington. Spotted Tail promised that he and his men would be there, and Bill returned to the chosen campsite, where he found a company of the Second Cavalry leveling ground, preparatory to setting up tents and establishing a camp fit for a king.[1]

One newspaper report (Lincoln *Daily State Journal*, January 6, 1872) suggests that such elaborate preparations were superfluous: "General Sheridan has completed plans for a buffalo hunt, and the parties will leave the railroad at Ft. McPherson and expect to be on the hunt for six or eight days. No servants, carriages or luxuries will be indulged in, the design being to rough it." However, as is evident from all accounts, the design was not very closely followed.

Lieutenant Hayes had already selected seventy-five head of the best horses from the post herd of 500-600 head and sent them to the Red Willow camp for the use of the royal party. A huge supply of provisions, liquors, bedding, and furniture arrived from Chicago to be loaded onto wagons and sent across the hills to the camp, where two hospital tents, ten wall tents, and scores of "A" tents (these last for the servants and soldiers) had been set up. Three of the wall tents were floored, and one, the Duke's, was carpeted. Box and Sibley stoves were installed in the hospital tents, which served as dining halls for the expedition, and in the Duke's and officers' tents. "Roughing it," Russian style, was not too bad.

At seven o'clock on the morning of January 13 the Grand Duke and his party, in charge of Francis Thompson of the Union Pacific, pulled into North Platte aboard a special train provided by the U.S. government. A splendid array of brass and gold braid from the fort was there to greet the visitors. This welcoming party included Brevet

Major General George A. Custer, Brevet Major General E. O. C. Ord, Brevet Major General Innis N. Palmer, Brevet Brigadier General George A. Forsyth, and his brother, Lieutenant Colonel James W. Forsyth. With them were Buffalo Bill, Captain James Egan, quartermaster, five or six ambulances, fifteen or twenty extra saddle horses, two companies of cavalry, two of infantry, and the regimental band of the Second Cavalry. Cody conservatively estimated the entire party at 500 persons.[2]

Most of North Platte turned out, too, to see the train come in and the illustrious party alight from the cars. An Omaha *Weekly Herald* reporter, who was to accompany the hunting party, was there, and Bill McDonald says his parents, Charles and Orra, had driven up from Cottonwood Springs to see the royal visitor.

According to an unidentified newspaper dispatch from North Platte, as the party left the train General Sheridan singled out the tall figure of Buffalo Bill and presented him to the Duke as follows: "Your highness, this is Mr. Cody, otherwise and universally known as Buffalo Bill. Bill, this is the Grand Duke." "I am glad to know you," said Buffalo Bill.,

The Duke's party was fairly large. Besides his staff and servants, he was accompanied by several military officers, friends, and lesser royalty, including Dr. Vladimir Kadrin, Count Okenfieff, Consul Bodisco, and Admiral Possier.[3]

Cody described Alexis as "a large, fine-looking young man." Bill McDonald recalls his parents saying he was "tall, good looking, and wore grey trousers and jacket, trimmed in green. The buttons bore the imperial coat of arms and his pants were tucked into shining black boots. His headgear was a close-fitting cloth turbin. In his belt he carried a Russian hunting knife and a S&W revolver bearing the Russian and U.S. seals, a gift from the manufacturer."[4] Others have described the Russian prince as 6'2" tall, straight, broad, and handsome.

Inside half an hour, according to Cody, the visitors and their luggage were off-loaded, the luggage reloaded into wagons, the guests either mounted on horses or seated in ambulances, and the whole party "dashing away towards the south, across the South Platte and towards the Medicine."

Although the Grand Duke himself was quietly dressed, "some of his party were apparelled in gold and lace and all the trappings of royalty. These gorgeous Russian uniforms greatly impressed the colored troopers who were along to assist in the camp work. As the cavalcade moved south . . . at a rapid pace a colored sergeant ran his horse up to the head of the column, saluted Buffalo Bill and said, 'Ah begs leave to report, sah, another one of dem kings has fell off his hoss.' "[5]

According to the *Herald* reporter, at Medicine Creek, where the horses were changed from relays waiting there, a sumptuous lunch was served before the journey was resumed. And from there the "magnificent Second Cavalry band went on ahead, and when the remainder of the party reached the Red Willow camp at 4:30 that afternoon, the Duke and his escort was welcomed by the enthusiastic rendition of Hail to the Chief."[6]

Spotted Tail and *265 lodges, or nearly 1,000 of his people*, were also awaiting the arrival of the Great Chief from across the water. The noted Sioux, in order to do proper honor to the occasion, had brought along his own family; Chiefs Two Strike, Cut Leg, White Bear, and Little Eagle, with their families; and many other warriors and families. General Custer, Cody wrote, carried on a mild flirtation with Spotted Tail's daughter, and the Duke paid considerable attention to another pretty Indian maiden.

That evening the Sioux put on their grand war dance, and the next day, January 14, Alexis' twenty-first birthday, Buffalo Bill put the guests onto a good herd of buffalo and "twenty to thirty head were killed in the first two hours."[7] That night, according to Bill McDonald, the guests and their hosts dined magnificently. The dinner began with buffalo tail soup, followed by broiled fish, salami of prairie dog, stewed rabbit, and fillet of buffalo with mushrooms. Then came roast elk, antelope chops, buffalo calf steaks, blacktail deer and wild turkey, and broiled teal and mallard. With all this the diners had sweet and white mashed potatoes and green peas. Tapioca pudding was the dessert, if anybody wanted it, and throughout the meal there was an abundance of champagne frappé, claret, whisky, brandy, and ale.[8]

The hunt lasted five days and many buffalo were killed, the hunters celebrating the fall of each in champagne. The evenings were spent around big campfires, with story telling and Indian dances for entertainment. Before breaking camp, Spotted Tail and his people were presented one thousand pounds of tobacco and other gifts. Last of all, the choicest buffalo heads and skins were selected for mounting and tanning.

On the return trip, as Bill tells it, the Grand Duke and Sheridan rode in "a heavy double-seated open carriage . . . drawn by six spirited cavalry horses which were not much used to the harness. The driver was Bill Reed, an old overland stage driver. . . .[T]he Grand Duke frequently expressed his admiration of the skillful manner in which Reed handled the reins. General Sheridan informed the Duke that I also had been a stage driver in the Rocky Mountains, and thereupon His Royal Highness expressed a desire to see me drive. I was in advance at the time, and General Sheridan sang out to me, 'Cody, get in here and show the Duke how you can drive.' "

Cody and Reed changed places and "in a few moments I had the reins and we were rattling away over the prairie. When we were approaching Medicine creek, General Sheridan said, 'Shake 'em up a little Bill, and give us some old-time stage driving.' "

Cody shook 'em up and soon they were flying over the ground. "[A]t last we reached a steep hill, or divide, which led down into the valley of the Medicine. There was no brake on the wagon, and the horses were not much on the hold back. I saw that it would be impossible to stop them. All I could do was to keep them straight in the track and let them go it down the hill, for three miles, which . . . . I believe, was made in about six minutes. Every once in a while the hind wheels would strike a rut and take a bound, and not touch the ground again for fifteen or twenty feet. The Duke and the General were kept rather busy in holding their positions on the seats, and when they saw that I was keeping the horses straight in the road, they seemed to enjoy the dash. . . . I was unable to stop the team until they ran into the camp where we were to obtain a fresh relay."

Cody concludes his version of the hunt with the statement: "On arriving at the railroad, the Duke invited me into his car, and made me some valuable presents, at the same time giving me a cordial invitation to visit him, if ever I should come to his country. At the same time General Sheridan took occasion to remind me of [the] invitation to visit New York which I had received . . . in September. . . . Said he, 'You will never have a better opportunity to accept that invitation than now. I have had a talk with General Ord concerning you, and he will give you leave of absence whenever you are ready to start.'"[9]

In describing the ride her brother gave the Duke and the General in the "closed carriage," Helen, in her account written a quarter century later, gives them ten minutes to cover the three miles and has moved those three miles from the Medicine to the Platte, where she has them making the dash across the valley to the railroad station. And Helen is probably the inventor of the Duke's widely quoted expression of thanks for the ride: "I would not have missed it for a large sum of money; but rather than repeat it, I would return to Russia via

Alaska, swim Bering Strait, and finish my journey on one of your government mules."[10]

Elsewhere Buffalo Bill tells how, upon arriving at North Platte, "the Grand Duke invited me into his car, and there, over a few bottles of champagne, we went over all the details of the hunt. . . . As I was leaving the car one of his suite approached me, and, extending a big roll of greenbacks, begged me to accept it." Cody refuses the money but does accept the magnificent overcoat, made of many fine Russian furs, which the Duke had worn on the hunt. This story also has Alexis telegraphing "the most famous of New York jewelers" to order a set of cuff links and a scarf pin, studded with diamonds and rubies, each piece in the form of a buffalo head as large as a silver half-dollar, as a gift for Buffalo Bill.[11]

Cooper, of course, tops all other accounts with the one Louisa is supposed to have told him. All that winter Will had been growing famous, she said, due to the Buntline tales. "Every week, some new thrilling story, in which Buffalo Bill rescued maidens in distress, killed off Indians by the score and hunted buffalo in his sleep, appeared in the romantic magazines."[12]

This leads up to the visit of Duke Alexis and the account of how Louisa and Will entertained the royal party in their cabin prior to the hunt. Recalling her former experience when dining nobility, Louisa "determined that there would be no more visits from Indians, and that, this time, [her] kitchen would have some protection." A picket fence, she figured, would take care of the problem, so she went over to the post and asked "the Major" for some wood to build her fence. The major said there was none, that all he could supply in the way of wood was whiskey barrel staves.

"So thus it was that our little log cabin came to have a picket fence in honor of the visit of Grand Duke Alexis. And every picket in that enclosure was a barrel stave! What was more, every one had been firmly put into place by Buffalo Bill's wife—I wanted to be sure that no Indians were coming in to eat up my cakes and pies and game meats this time!" (One wonders what effect a mere picket fence, especially one made of barrel staves, would have on Indians, who seldom paid any attention even to closed doors.)

The tall tale goes on: "It was a wonderful day at the fort when the Grand Duke and his retinue arrived. By cramping every foot of space, we managed some way to get them all about the table in our little log house, but when it came to the reception that followed, that was a different matter. We had to hold it in the yard, in the confines of the picket fence—although such a thing as boundaries made little difference. The day was balmy, and every one at the fort was there at one time or another."[13]

A couple of other side accounts of the famous hunt, as told locally, are interesting—and presumably "truer." One is told by Mayme Watts Langford, daughter of the North Platte ranchman, Russell Watts, as she heard it many times from her parents. The army wasn't able to provide enough wagons to haul the royal equipment over the hills to camp Alexis, she said, and area ranchers were asked to bring their roundup mess wagons and come along. Watts was one who accepted, and when the party returned, late in the afternoon of a cold January day almost a week later, he brought the top army brass, Buffalo Bill, the Duke, and his friends home with him for supper, "the coldest, tiredest and most elated bunch of men you ever saw."

The hunters brought plenty of venison with them, of course, but it was frozen, and Mary Watts, a bride of a little over a year, fried up huge platters of it, "the quickest way to get a meal ready for hungry men, and after dinner the Duke asked her how she prepared the venison. He wanted to know so he could have more cooked in the same way."

Before Alexis left town, Mrs. Langford said, Buffalo Bill and Russell Watts held a banquet in his honor in M. C. Keith's Union Pacific dining room and invited all the leading citizens. The Union Pacific chef baked the venison, but the guests who had eaten at the Watts' home the evening before agreed it was *not* as good as that fried by Mrs. Watts.

When Alexis got back to Russia, he had one of his buffalo hides made into a splendid floor robe, decorated on the skin side with a solid pattern of brightly colored beads in a "Russian art design," which he sent to Mrs. Watts. The Watts' son was born shortly after the Duke's visit, and four years later Mayme completed the family circle. "With a stove for heat and wood for fuel, the robe on the floor made a fine place for us to play in winter," Mayme concluded.[14]

An oft-quoted story is that Ena Raymonde, a well-born, young, and attractive white woman took part in the royal hunt. A crack rifle shot and a first-rate horsewoman, she would have added much to the glamour of the affair, but she was not there for the simple reason that she did not come to Nebraska, to visit her brother on the Medicine, until July, nearly six months after Alexis had gone home, and so she missed her chance to go down in history as the only white woman on the celebrated hunt.

However, Ena's brother, William Herbert Palmer, did join the hunt a few days after it had begun. He later told of his meeting with the Duke on the Red Willow. "None but those high in office could approach or speak to him. I thought while in Frontier County I could and had a right to speak genteely to any person, and that no man stood above me: so I went up to Duke Alexis and said: 'How do you do, Duke?' He said, 'I have not been introduced to you.' I said, 'It don't make any difference to me. How do you do, Duke?' He said to General Sheridan: 'General, you are very familiar with your men.' General Sheridan said: 'Sir, we are Americans.' "[15]

The Duke has generally been described as a very friendly fellow, and if the incident actually took place his reluctance to shake hands with Paddy may have been generated by the man's unsavory appearance. His home on the Medicine was a dugout, a mere hole in the ground, and like a few other scions of well-to-do families on the frontier, he had degenerated in dress and cleanliness to an almost savage condition.

After the royal hunt, Alexis left North Platte and went by rail to Denver, accompanied by Generals Sheridan and Custer and other staff members. In Colorado he was met and escorted by the governor, the ex-governor, and other territorial officials; and on the evening of January 18 the Pioneer Club of Colorado hosted a grand ball for the distinguished visitor.

Elegant entertainment, however, was not the only thing on the minds of the Duke's hosts. Word of the grand buffalo hunt in neighboring Nebraska had, of course, preceded Alexis' visit to Colorado, and local pride prompted a replay of the recent extravaganza. At the town of Kit Carson, Colorado, the Duke's train pulled to a stop and discharged its passengers for Colorado's version of buffalo hunting. Chauvinism likely distorted the newspaper treatment of the day-long hunt as overly enthusiastic reporters announced that the "exciting hunt on the Nebraska Plains in the early part of the week dwindles into insignificance compared with the chases, uncertainties, and final triumphs of this last campaign." Even the buffalo in Colorado were better: "Unlike the sluggard animals of the Nebraska Plains, these were disposed to make a desperate effort for escape." But their efforts, whether greater or lesser than the Nebraska beasts, were not entirely successful, for the Duke "brought down five buffaloes altogether, and retained the tail of each as trophies of the day's sport."[16]

Buffalo Bill, though absent, was present in terms of his reputation that was already national. The newspaper reported an exciting confrontation during the Kit Carson hunt when a buffalo turned upon Alexis and charged with great fierceness. The account concluded: "The Grand Duke and his experienced horse were equal to the emergency, and although they dodged the infuriated animal every time, the escapes were sufficiently narrow for even a Buffalo Bill to boast of."[17]

The Colorado hunt, though shorter and less sumptuous than the Nebraska one, must have nevertheless seemed to Alexis a fine and successful outing. He had killed eight buffalo in Nebraska, now five in Colorado. And the following day, as the train "jogged along . . . leisurely" across Kansas, he, General Sheridan, General Custer, and other passengers fired from the car windows at buffalo herds along the track; "the Duke probably brought down no less than half a dozen of the animals."[18]

General Sheridan left the train at St. Louis. General Custer continued with the Duke to New Orleans, meeting Mrs. Custer en route in Kentucky. From New Orleans, Alexis and his party left by train for Pensacola, Florida, and sailed from there with the Russian fleet on February 22, 1872.

8

Celebrity
1872

At the conclusion of the Red Willow buffalo hunt, Cooper, with his usual disregard of facts, had Louisa telling of the goodbye aboard the Grand Duke's special train: Alexis offered Will "anything—anything in the world" to show his gratitude for the superlative entertainment provided him the past few days. So Will named the one thing he wanted most. The Duke promised him he should have it, and "six weeks later, came a letter. . . . A long strip ticket was in the envelope . . . —a ticket back East, all the way to New York and a pass from General Sheridan."[1] Actually, it was General Stager who sent the railroad passes, after Cody had been granted thirty days' leave of absence, with pay; and James Gordon Bennett sent $500 for expenses.[2]

Louisa, being pregnant ("a beautiful little reason why I could not accompany him," as she delicately expresses it), stayed at home, but she saw to it that her Will was appropriately dressed for his excursion into eastern society. "We procured some blue cloth at the commissary and, sewing day and night, I made Will his first real soldier suit, with a Colonel's gold braid on it, with stripes and cords and all the other gingerbread of an old-fashioned suit of 'blues.'" Although she couldn't go to New York with him, she did accompany him to the stage landing;[3] Cooper is still determined not to patronize the Union Pacific railroad in any part of his story of Louisa's life on the frontier.

Cody's wealthy eastern friends went all out to wine and dine their renowned guest, who was very much the lion of the day while scouting the canyons of New York. He also looked up Edward Judson (Ned Buntline) who, delighted to see him, hastened to revive the melodrama written from Ned's tale, "Buffalo Bill, the King of Border Men," and produced the previous year. The revival took place at the Bowery Theatre, and Ned had Buffalo Bill there in a box seat on opening night, watching himself played by actor J. B. Studley. Ned also saw to it that the audience learned the real Buffalo Bill was present. Of course he was invited to come forward and take a bow. Out on the stage he was very frightened, he said, and when he was offered $500 a week to stay on and play himself in the show, he firmly refused. You "might as well try to make an actor out of a government mule," he told Freligh, the manager.[4]

All in all, Cody had such a good time meeting important people and going to "swell" dinners given in his honor that when General Sheridan dropped in to see how he was doing, he told him he had struck the best camp he'd ever seen and he'd like to have his leave extended another ten days. Sheridan agreed to the extension but told Bill he would be needed at the post at the end of the ten days.

Cody had no sooner left New York than Buntline began his second Buffalo Bill dime novel, for by now the colorful scout's name was on every tongue, and the time was ripe to take advantage of his popularity. Bill was scarcely back on the plains before "Buffalo Bill's Best Shot; or, The Heart of Spotted Tail" was appearing as a serial in the *New York Weekly*.

Of his return to Fort McPherson, Cody says in one account that he was simply ordered out with a company of troopers to pursue and punish some Indians who had made a raid on McPherson Station, "killing two or three men and running off quite a large number of horses." Cody was the guide for the expedition, Texas Jack Omohundro his assistant.[5] In Cody's *Autobiography*, however, there is a much more exciting tale. His extra leave had not quite expired, according to this version, and he was attending a dinner given in his honor by Mr. Bennett, when he was handed a telegram from General Sheridan ordering him to leave at once for Fort McPherson, as serious Indian trouble had broken loose on the Platte. Although he left New York the next morning, he stopped over a day in Westchester to visit some of his relatives and participate in a fox hunt they had arranged for him.

In Chicago he was met with orders from Sheridan to hurry on to Fort McPherson as quickly as possible, because the expedition was waiting for him. But at Omaha a party of his friends took him off the train and entertained him until time for the next train. The friends had heard that Buffalo Bill had worn full dress while in New York, so now they insisted he dress up and let them see how he looked. "My trunk was taken to the Paxton Hotel and I put on the clawhammer and all that went with it. About fifty of my Omaha friends accompanied me to the train; in my silk hat and evening dress I was an imposing spectacle."[6]   The five-story Paxton, a truly plush establishment, partly owned by Cody's friend, Bill Paxton, was the finest hostelry in Omaha at that time, and Buffalo Bill in his split-tailed suit with his host of friends must, indeed, have been something to see. But in the excitement of the parade to the depot they forgot Bill's trunk and everyday clothes. So the scout was soon on his way west to chase Indians in clothes fit only for a banquet. His friends had, however, filled his stateroom with champagne, and the abundance of liquor helped temper the reception by his army friends when they saw his outlandish get-up. "They laughed a good deal at my stovepipe hat and evening dress, but because of the champagne they let me off without as much guying as I would otherwise have received."[7]

It is more than likely that Cody did stop in Omaha on his way home from New York in the spring of 1872, that he was luxuriously enter-tained by his friends, that they celebrated to the extent they forgot his trunk when they put him on the train for McPherson Station, that he did get off there in a full-dress suit, and that he afterward told the ridiculous story on himself; but the rest of the "facts" are somewhat different.

At that time there was no Indian trouble on the Platte that required his services, so there was no telegram from General Sheridan delivered at the banquet, and his slow dash west was actually only his routine return trip home. The rest of the tale, then, was likely only a buildup to explain his arrival at the station in the clawhammer outfit, and he really did not mount Buckskin Joe and dash away after Indians in a full-dress suit and silk hat.

Of his return, Louisa says that Will came home declaring, "Why Mamma, I'm such a tenderfoot right now from being away, that I'd run if I even saw an Injun!" She goes on to say that Will was soon away on another expedition, and while he was gone their son was born.[8] This was only partially correct: their only son was already nearly two years old, and the baby born following Cody's return from New York was their second daughter, Orra Maude,[9] named for their friend Orra McDonald.

Following his eastern trip, Buffalo Bill accompanied the troops on various expeditions in Nebraska and Dakota. One, with Company I of the Third Cavalry, involved a march of 496 miles, ending at Fort McPherson on July 21; another, into the Loup country with Company B, Third Cavalry, under Captain Charles Meinhold, resulted in his being awarded the Medal of Honor on May 22, 1872, for his excellent services to the military.[10]

In September Cody took another civilian hunting party southwest of the post. The story of this hunt, under the title "The Last Romantic Buffalo Hunt on the Plains of Nebraska," was written by James L. Webster of Omaha, and is remarkable for more than its flowery prose style. With attorney Webster on the Pullman coach from Omaha to North Platte were Colonel Smith, Judge Neville, and Judge Dundy. Watson B. Smith was clerk of the U.S. District and Circuit Courts of Nebraska and James Neville was U.S. district attorney. Elmer S. Dundy came to Nebraska in 1857 and was appointed a territorial judge in 1863; when the territory became a state in 1867, he was its first U.S. district judge.[11]

The distinguished party was met at the station by Buffalo Bill and Lieutenant Frederick Schwatka, an officer from the military post at North Platte, which furnished the necessary army horses and equipment for the hunt. Lieutenant Schwatka, at that time an officer in the regular army, later became famous as an arctic explorer and writer of three well-known books about his adventures in the far north.

Accompanied by a squad of cavalry to protect the judicial party from stray bands of roving and possibly hostile Indians, and guided by Cody, the hunters, all frankly amateurs, rode down to Fort McPherson to make their first camp, where they slept on the ground with only army blankets and small army tents for warmth and shelter. The next morning, "without the luxury of a bath or a change of wearing apparel," the cavalcade resumed its journey over what, to the city men, "seemed almost a barren waste of undulating private [—] no habitations, no fields, no farms." As the afternoon wore on the saddle-weary pilgrims took turns riding in the army wagon with the supplies.

The hunters camped in the wilderness that night, with sentries posted to guard the horses. Webster wrote that it was a somewhat sleepless night, with the city dwellers worrying about how they would ever get back to civilization if Indians got away with their horses. On the afternoon of the third day they saw their first buffalo, a very small band. Under the guidance of Buffalo Bill they were able to approach quite near to the game, "and then the chase began."

Webster admits that none of the "amateurs" came anywhere near shooting a buffalo, but describes some "unusual and soul-stirring amusement" furnished by Buffalo Bill when he roped the biggest bull buffalo in the herd and tied him to a tree. Bill writes that this was a feat he had often performed and that the gentlemen, who had heard of his skill with a lariat, had requested him to do it for them—and that is all he says about it.[12]

But Webster goes on to tell what happened after that. They left the lassoed buffalo out on the plain, solitary and alone, and when they went back to get him the next morning they found he had broken his leg in his struggle to get free. Rather than shooting the crippled animal or turning him loose on the prairie as he was, Cody solved(?) the problem in a strange way: the buffalo was led to a nearby ranch house where Cody borrowed a butcher knife, handsaw, bar of iron, and proceeded to amputate the leg above the break, after which he seared the wound with the hot iron to stop the bleeding. "The buffalo was then left in the ranchman's corral with the understanding that the animal would be well cared for."[13]

Webster says nothing about how many men it must have taken to lead the wild, powerful, and understandably angry buffalo bull anywhere; or to put on more ropes, throw him, and hold him while Cody performed his surgery; and it is certain the indignant, suffering animal would not have remained for any time at all in any kind of corral to be found on the plains. One wonders if Webster wasn't simply trying to top some of Buffalo Bill's tall stories with one of his own.

Webster tells another corker—shades of Buffalo Bill's return-home-from-Omaha (tall) tale. Cody verifies it, but perhaps we will be forgiven our skepticism in questioning the credibility of the witness! Webster tells us that Judge Neville boarded the train in Omaha in his habitual outfit—formal wear and high silk hat—and without any other change of clothing. Thus he participated in the hunt, "riding pell-mell over the prairies after the buffalo . . . astride his running war-horse, . . . his spike-tailed coat floating out behind him on the breeze, . . . a picture against the horizon that does not have its parallel in all pioneer history!"[14] Cody found the judge's attire a "very comical rig for a hunter, . . . enough to make a horse laugh, and I actually believe old Buckskin Joe did laugh."[15]

The Earl of Dunraven came west in 1872.[16] Of the various Plains settlements, especially the small and isolated ones, the British sportsman wrote: "They look as if Providence had been carrying a box of toy houses, and had dropped the lid and spilt out the contents on the earth. The houses have all come down right end uppermost, it is true, but otherwise they show no evidence of design."[17] The earl had visited General Philip Sheridan in Chicago, and upon seeing a magnificent mounted elk head in the general's headquarters, had at once determined to have one like it. Sheridan communicated with the commander at Fort McPherson, authorized a hunt and a military escort, and asked that Cody be designated guide for Dunraven and his friends. About his arrival at North Platte, the earl reflected:

> At one of these lonely little stations I was deposited [from the train] one fine evening in the early fall just before sundown. For a few moments only the place was all alive with bustle and confusion. The train represented everything that was civilised, all the luxuries that could be carried in a train were to be found on board of it, the people were all clothed in fashionable dresses, it was like a slice cut out of one of the Eastern cities set down bodily in the midst of a perfect wilderness. In a few seconds it was gone, civilisation vanished with it, the station relapsed into its normal condition of desolation, and I found myself almost alone in the heart of the desert.[18]

Buffalo Bill and Texas Jack met the Britishers at the station. Cody wore "a pair of corduroys tucked into his high boots, and a blue flannel shirt," a broad-brimmed felt hat and a white handkerchief, folded like a little shawl, loosely fastened around his neck. Omohundro wore moccasins instead of boots, and greasy deer-skin trousers with fringe along the seams. Around his waist was a belt in which was tucked a revolver and two butcher knives. Jack was "tall and lithe, with light brown, close-cropped hair, clear laughing honest blue eyes, and a soft and winning smile. Bill was dark, with quick searching eyes, aquiline nose, and delicately cut features, and he wore his hair falling in long ringlets over his shoulders."[19]

After several weeks of very successful hunting, Cody was interrupted. As he himself tells it, a "Chicago party—friends of General Sheridan—arrived at Fort McPherson for the purpose of going out on a hunt also. They, too, had a letter from the General requesting me to go with them. The Earl had not yet finished his hunt, but . . . I concluded to leave him and accompany the Chicago party." He explained the change of plans to Dunraven, and Texas Jack took Cody's place, but the "Earl seemed to be somewhat offended at this, and I don't think he has ever forgiven me."[20] Texas Jack guided well, however, and all ended favorably.

9

Limelight
1872-1874

1872 was a full year for Buffalo Bill. In addition to the much-publicized and glamorous hunts he had guided, his triumphant trip to New York, and his successful excursion into society there, he was also elected to the Nebraska legislature—or almost elected. He wrote:

> In the fall . . . a convention was held at Grand Island, when some of my friends made me their candidate to represent the Twenty-sixth District in the Legislature of Nebraska; but as I had always been a Democrat and the State was largely Republican, I had no idea of being elected. In fact I cared very little about it, and therefore made no effort whatever to secure an election. However, I was elected and that is the way in which I acquired my title of Honorable.[1]

In the later *Autobiography*:

> One day, in the fall . . . I returned from a scouting expedition, and as I passed the store there were a lot of men crowded in front of it. All of them saluted me with "How do you do, Honorable!" I rode straight to the general's private office. He also stood at attention and said:
> "Good morning, Honorable."
> "What does all this 'Honorable' mean, General?" I demanded. He said: . . . "[W]hile you were gone you were nominated and elected to represent the twenty-sixth district of Nebraska in the Legislature."
> "I said:

"That is highly complimentary, and I appreciate it, but I am no politician and I shall have to tender my resignation," and tender it I did.[2]

However, Cody presumably did not resign immediately, for as late as December 12, one newspaper was reporting: "Ned Buntline's hero, 'Buffalo Bill,' (Wm. F. Cody), having been elected to the State legislature, went to Omaha last week to 'brush up' ready for law-making. Some of the prominent citizens gave him a reception or banquet."[3]

And Cody did not resign simply because he was "no politician." Although the first count of the votes apparently gave Cody a majority of forty-four and the newspapers immediately began referring to him as the Honorable W. F. Cody, the decision was eventually taken out of his hands. A contest was filed in behalf of Cody's opponent, D. P. Ashburn, claiming that returns from a newly organized precinct had been erroneously sent to Lincoln, the capital city, instead of to Lincoln County; the count of the missent votes made a difference of forty-two in favor of Ashburn. Whether Cody originally intended to take his seat in the House the following year or whether from the beginning he meant to resign, we do not know. In any case, he did not protest the late count, and the seat went to Ashborn.[4]

The belief that Bill had been officially elected to the legislature long outlived him. Nearly seventy years later Judge Grant of North Platte stated, "Cody was a member of the Nebraska legislature at the time he went east to go on the stage, and many considered it a breach of trust."[5]

Walter Hoagland, another North Platte attorney, claimed: "I saw Buffalo Bill when he was in the legislature. He wouldn't stay down there because he wanted to give everybody a drink, and the state didn't think it had enough money."[6] This was probably said in jest, for Hoagland, who came to North Platte in 1884 at fourteen years of age, would have been only two years old in 1872.

The North Platte *Tribune*, in its Special Holiday Edition of 1897, stated that Cody was elected a member of the Nebraska legislature, representing the great cattle district, and was known as "the cowboy legislator."

Dr. George Kingsley, who accompanied the Earl of Dunraven on some of his hunting expeditions, wrote his impressions of Cody:

Buffalo Bill, as to face and feature, is a noble Vandyke stepped from its frame . . . one of the handsomest and the best built men I have ever seen. As for his manners, they are as perfect as those of the Vandyke would have been. . . .

Buffalo Bill has two styles of dress: the first, which is the one which he usually wears in the Settlements, is of beautifully dressed buckskin, decorated with fringes and lappets innumerable, and gorgeous beyond description. . . . [T]hen he, being a member of the House of Rrepresentatives of his State, thinks fit to assume, at times, a civilian and civilised garb—short black jacket, black pants, and thin kid side-spring boots, which makes him look like the aforesaid Vandyke nobleman trying to disguise himself as a steamboat steward.[7]

Delos Avery, in a 1944 Chicago newspaper feature aimed at debunking Buffalo Bill, wrote: "In 1872 Cody was elected to the Nebraska legislature, in which he was so obscure that most of his activities have been forgotten. He did answer a few roll calls but had no taste and professed no talent for 'lawmaking.' "[8]

Helen writes of this event in her brother's life that "He made no campaign, but was elected by a flattering majority,"[9] and then goes on to tell of his entry into show business. Ever since his return from New York, Cody had been getting letters from Edward Judson, urging him to come east, go on the stage, and play himself in some thrilling new plays which Judson would write and produce under his Buntline pseudonym. They would open in Chicago, the promoter wrote, then go on to New York, and there would be a lot of money in it for both of them. Remembering his earlier New York stage fright, Will had persistently refused.

Of this period of his life, Cody writes that, though tempted, "I remained undecided as to what I ought to do. The officers at the fort, as well as my family and friends . . . laughed at the idea of my ever becoming an atcor. That I, an old scout . . . should think of going upon the stage, was ridiculous in the extreme—so they all said."[10]

Shortly after the birth of the baby, Orra, Buntline wrote again, urging Bill to give the acting venture a try, for if he proved a failure, or did not like it, he could always return to his old way of life. Other matters also seemed to indicate he should go east. His sisters were both married and in homes of their own, and Louisa wanted to take her three children to St. Louis for a long visit in her old home. Cody was freer from responsibility than he had been in a long while. "Taking these and other things into consideration I finally resolved to resign my seat in the Legislature [the vote recount had not been completed at that time] and try my luck behind the foot-lights."[11]

Money, Louisa told Cooper, was the final persuader—money to send the children to "fine schools" and give them "everything" they needed.[12] The decision made, Bill resigned from his position as a U.S. Army scout and was paid off on November 30, 1872. He then sold his horses and "other effects." Louisa says they sold their furniture, even to the kitchen table which she herself had made; then she added that her husband not only resigned as a scout but "as a Colonel, as a Justice of the Peace and as a legislator."[13] This was laying it on a bit thick, because Cody had resigned as justice of the peace the previous June, and he did not acquire his rank as colonel until 1887.

While Cody was selling his horses and making arrangements to leave for Chicago, his friend and fellow scout Texas Jack told him he would like to go along. Since Jack had also been the hero of one of Buntline's stories, Bill figured he would make a good "star," too, and was glad to take him along. There was great excitement, says Louisa, "and when the stage pulled out one afternoon, late in 1872, there we were, piled in it, Will and Texas Jack, myself and the babies, bound for the adventures of the unknown."[14] Alas for romance: They went on the train, for the last eastbound stages had ceased to ply the valley road six years earlier, and Louisa was going only to St. Louis, her girlhood home.

Cody parted with his family in Omaha, where he put Louisa and the children on the train for St. Louis. He and Texas Jack were then entertained for a day or two by their Omaha friends; Cody, so the papers said, was a newly elected legislator on his way to Washington but would be back in time for the opening of the session in Lincoln. Their hosts were General Augur and the gentlemen who had taken part in "the last romantic buffalo hunt" a couple of months earlier.[15]

The scouts arrived in Chicago on December 12 and were met by Buntline, who had already advertised the show to open at Nixon's Amphitheatre the week of December 16. The show, as it was finally produced, was a mixture of imitation Indian chiefs, trappers, scouts, Ned Buntline as a temperance lecturer, and the stars, Buffalo Bill and Texas Jack. It bore the alluring title "The Scouts of the Prairie; or, Red Deviltry As It Is." Its script was the one Cody claims Buntline wrote in four hours, *after* the scouts arrived in Chicago; and the only professional in the cast was Giuseppina Morlacchi, a talented Italian.

On December 15 the Chicago *Times* heralded the coming attraction: "A sensational drama of the red-hot type, written by Ned Buntline, the prince of sensation-mongers, will be produced on to-morrow [Monday] evening. . . . The lovers of realistic romance will have a chance to gorge themselves in this highly flavored food. Mlle. Morlacchi, the danseuse and pantomimist, will appear as Dove-Eye, the Indian Maiden."

Two days later the *Times'* initial review of the play's opening was perfunctory: Nixon's Amphitheatre was "very well patronized" and the performance was "quite satisfactory" in its line. By Wednesday, December 18, the newspaper was taking more careful account of the play. Cody himself claimed the *Times* criticized the show by wondering what, if Buntline actually spent four hours in writing the play, he had been doing all that time.[16] The paper did not say that; what they did say was much worse, though they gave Bill and Texas Jack their due:

> They are the real attractions, not only as the heroes of the play, but as celebrities whose fame long ante-dates their appearance before the footlights. So when Buffalo Bill attempts a recitation, and accomplishes it as the schoolboy recites 'On Linden,' though its subject is of the most tragic character, the audience felt bound to applaud, and did it with a vim. On the whole, it is not probable that Chicago will ever look upon the like again. Such a combination of incongruous drama, execrable acting, renowned performers, mixed audience, intolerable stench, scalping, blood and thunder, is not likely to be vouchsafed to a city a second time, even Chicago.[17]

The reviewer was right on two major counts: the play was terrible, and the audience applauded with vim. But he drew the wrong conclusion. The show was popular; it was a financial success. It played to full houses; it made money for them all, just as Buntline promised. And it and similar plays were "vouchsafed" to city after city, again and again—even Chicago.

Part of the drama's success could be attributed to the fact that the cities of the U.S. at that time were intensely curious about a way of life involving Indians, buffalo, cowboys, and scouts of the plains, which extensive publicity about Buffalo Bill and his friends had made attractive and glamorous. But it was Cody himself who was more responsible than any other factor in the show's success. After all, where could be found another character as handsome and colorful or who counted among his personal friends so many millionaires, U.S. army generals, members of the nobility and royal families as Buffalo Bill, top scout and champion buffalo hunter of the plains?

From Chicago the show moved on to St. Louis where, on December 23, it opened in DeBar's Opera House. Will does not mention his wife's being in the audience, but it is reasonable to suppose she was, since she was in St. Louis and would want to see her husband in his new role. At any rate *she* says she was, and Cooper has her telling about it:

> With Arta on my lap, I sat in the audience, watching the performance, and waiting for Will to appear. At last, three or four Indians pranced across the stage, turned, waved their tomahawks, yelled something and then fell dead, accompanied by the rattle-te-bang of a six-shooter. Out rushed Will, assured himself that all three of the Indians were thoroughly dead, turned just in time to kill a couple more who had roamed on to the stage by accident, and then faced the audience.
>
> I was sitting in about the third row, and Will saw me. He came forward, leaned over the gas footlights and waved his arms.
>
> "Oh Mamma!" he shouted, "I'm a bad actor!"
>
> The house roared. Will threw me a kiss and then leaned forward again, while the house stilled.
>
> "Honest, Mamma," he shouted, "does this look as awful out there as it feels up here?"
>
> And again the house chuckled and applauded. Some one called out the fact that I was Mrs. Buffalo Bill.

When the crowd began to urge her to get on the stage, her husband joined in with, "Come on up . . . , you can't be any worse scared than I am." Someone placed a chair in the orchestra pit, hands reached to help, and she was boosted onto the stage, and Arta after her. Her stage fright plainly showed, and Will boomed, "Now you can understand how hard your poor old husband [he was twenty-six] has to work to make a living!" And again the audience applauded. After that, she says, whenever she went to see her husband's show, she chose a seat in the farthest and darkest part of the house. "But it did little good. For invariably Will would seek me out, and . . . call, 'Hello Mamma. Oh, but I'm a bad actor!' "[18]

The show went on to Cincinnati, where hundreds had to be turned away from the overflowing theatre every night. In Boston the gross receipts were $16,200 for one week, and in New York the house was again sold out at every performance. In view of all this it was disappointing to Cody, when the season closed in Port Jervis, New York, on June 16, 1873, and he counted his share of the profits, to find he was "only about $6,000 ahead."[19]

Louisa provides the clue as to why Will's share of the season's take was so slim. The money flowed in, she admitted, but—

Unheard extravagances became ours. And Will, dear, generous soul that he was, believed that an inexhaustible supply of wealth had become his forever. One night . . . we entered a hotel, only to find that the rooms we occupied were on a noisy side of the house. Will complained. The manager bowed suavely [and explained:] "The only way you could have absolute peace would be to rent the whole floor and, of course, you don't want to do that—"

"Don't I? . . . How much is it?"

The manager figured. Then he smiled.

"Two hundred dollars would be a pretty stiff price to pay for peace and quiet."

"Paid! . . . Now, let's see how quick you can make things comfortable for us. I've got a wife and babies and we're all tired."[20]

Although Cody does not mention that his family traveled with him that year, from Louisa's account it would appear they did, at least a part of the time, for she says she often took little Kit to watch his father play. Cooper has the whole family returning to Fort McPherson in the summer of 1873, in spite of having sold the cabin and all their posessions the fall before. It is more likely that Louisa and the children either remained in St. Louis or in the new home she says Will purchased for her in Rochester at the end of the first season.[21]

Buffalo Bill himself writes only that at the close of the season "Texas Jack and myself longed for a hunt on the Western prairies once more; and on meeting in New York a party of gentlemen who were desirous of going with us, we all started westward, and after a pleasant trip arrived at Fort McPherson."[22] The time spent on the plains was short, however, for the two scouts returned east before the end of August. Two reasons accounted for their early return. Texas Jack had fallen in love with Signorina Morlacchi and they were to be married soon, and the partners had to put together a new show for the coming season.

Omohundro and Morlacchi were married in St. Mary's Roman Catholic Church in Rochester on the last day of August, and preparations for the new show then went into high gear. Ned Buntline was not with the Buffalo Bill Combination[23] that second season, and his place was taken by Major John M. Burke, manager for Morlacchi. The show was almost exactly like the successful hodgepodge of the previous year, even to its name which merely substituted "Plains" for "Prairie."

W. F. Cody.

Louisa Cody.

   Wild Bill Hickok was invited to join the upcoming tour, as Cody knew his name would be a drawing card. Cooper has Louisa state that Wild Bill did not go east with them but arrived later, after the tour had begun, and came stumbling into the theater while Buffalo Bill was on stage, centered in the "limelight." Apparently Hickok had never seen a burning lime spotlight before; he called it "that white stuff that's floating all around" him and wanted to send right out for "five dollars' worth" to smear all over himself.[24]

Hickok had added considerably to his reputation since *Harper's Magazine* amazed its readers with his adventures back in 1867. He and Cody had met up again during General Sheridan's winter campaign of 1868-69 against the Indians; they were both members of the Carr-Penrose commands. Hickok had since been a deputy U.S. marshal, acting sheriff of Ellis County, Kansas, and the marshal of Abilene. Western and eastern newspapers had avidly followed his fortunes, and there is no doubt he was a drawing card for "The Scouts of the Plains.."[25]

Certainly, none of his partners wanted Hickok to leave the show. However, both Cody and Helen agree that he got himself out by over-playing his part and shooting too close to the legs of the "supers" who played Indians, inflicting powder burns that made them howl with anguish when they were supposed to be dead or dying all over the stage. Nonetheless, when he did finally part company with them at Rochester in March 1874, Cody and Omohundro each gave him $500 and a splendid revolver.[26]

Many years later D. J. Antonides, North Platte hardware merchant, reminisced:

> In New York, where I was raised, I saw Texas Jack and Buffalo Bill and Wild Bill. There had been several shows put on with real [professional] actors [playing the parts of Buffalo Bill, *et al.*] so nobody would believe these were the *real* scouts, but thought they were just more actors. But I saw them. The way it happened, our show was out before theirs was. We had gone to one on a neighboring street and we walked down that way. They had come out and were standing under a lamp post for advertising. They were dressed in regular citizen's dress and they were handsome. Texas Jack was a very handsome blonde fellow and Wild Bill was of a different build but good looking, and Buffalo Bill was always tops for looks. But we couldn't believe they were the real scouts. The funny thing about it was that, unlike the real actors, none of the scouts could memorize a thing. They had their parts written out for them, and the different things they could do, but it was no good. So they just "put on" about the things they did when they were scouting.[27]

In the main, Antonides was right, for Buffalo Bill and his partners never became very adept at their parts as set down in the script, but substituted plenty of shooting, noise, and action—and their audiences loved it.

In mid-May 1874 the Combination closed its second successful season. Texas Jack went to New England to spend the summer with his wife of less than a year; in August he returned west to guide the Earl of Dunraven on another hunt.[28] Cody returned west earlier also to serve as hunting guide. He was engaged in New York by "an English gentleman, Thomas P. Medley, of London. . . . He was a very wealthy man, . . . a relative of Mr. Lord, of the firm of Lord & Taylor, of New York. . . . He offered to pay the liberal salary of one thousand dollars a month while I was with him. . . . Of course I accepted."[29]

Dr. W. F. Carver, a dentist who had homesteaded on the Medicine near Paddy Miles, accompanied the Medley party from its starting point at North Platte and remained with it a few days. Cody writes that Carver had recently acquired considerable notoriety as a rifle shot. Old-timers on the Medicine claim that Ena Raymonde, a crack shot herself, was in love with the dentist and had taught him his shooting skills. This may very well have been, for Ena had also homesteaded near her brother, Paddy Miles, and Carver; that she was a skilled riflewoman is reflected in her diary entry for Friday, July 26, 1872: "Mr. Cody has *invited* me to *shoot* with him; says he hears I am a good shot, etc. But I don't know about shooting again. . . . I shoot because I love it; because I know I am a good shot; and because it is my pleasure! I am no stickler for praise. Never stoop to the *currying* of favors!"[30]

The hunting party broke up in North Platte in the latter part of July, and Buffalo Bill went to Fort McPherson, where he was at once hired, at $150 a month, to guide an army expedition commanded by Brevet Lieutenant Colonel Anson Mills to the Big Horn mountains. Its purpose was to make sure all Indians in the area hustled back onto their reservations; the expedition was successful, its purpose accomplished without bloodshed.

Cody completed his government expedition October 2. Texas Jack was still away on his hunt with the earl, so Bill returned to New York alone to put "The Scouts of the Plains" on the road for an abbreviated tour, with a substitute billed as Kit Carson taking Jack's place. *The Western Nebraskian*, noting Cody's departure for the East, declared, "No man more thoroughly enjoys the respect of western people than Buffalo Bill." The combination sustained another successful season, and Cody wrote: "I played my company in all the principal cities of the country, doing a good business wherever I went."[31]

10

The Black Hills
1875

By the Laramie Treaty of 1868 all the Black Hills region belonged to the Sioux, but rumors of gold in the mountains there resulted in Custer's 1874 expedition to ascertain the facts. The exploration party, made up of more than a thousand men, including ten companies of the Seventh Cavalry, two of infantry, scientists, miners, Indian scouts, newspaper correspondents, and even a band, left Fort Abraham Lincoln, Dakota Territory, on July 2. In August the news reached a waiting nation—there *was* gold in the Black Hills. The rush began at once, but during that summer and the following spring the military did attempt to keep the whites out, even to the extent of arresting would-be miners and burning their wagons.[1]

In the spring of 1875, the government, while still insisting that gold seekers stay out of the Hills, at the same time sent a military expedition north from the Union Pacific railroad to find and mark a more direct route for transporting supplies into "the locality in which the new Eldorado is located."[2] As early as March, Colonel Anson Mills, the officer Cody had guided to the Big Horns the previous summer, was awaiting wagons with which to outfit a trip from North Platte to Harney's Peak for the purpose of locating such a road.

Mills had been over the route in 1873 with cavalry troops and knew there was plenty of grass and water, but it is possible he had written to Cody about the proposed road-finding expedition, perhaps asking his advice on the best route to follow. At any rate, Cody must have known about it, for under the date of April 6 he sent the following telegram to railroad agent T. N. Shanks of North Platte: "A large party forming in Boston for the Black Hills to take route via North Platte. Are there any parties there who can furnish transportation for one or more hundred men at a guaranteed price? We are offered a $10.00 rate from Cheyenne and an $8.00 rate and one hundred pounds of baggage each, from Sidney. Answer by tomorrow."[3]

The word was quickly gotten "to the ear of the people," and within one hour from the time the message was copied off the wires an excited crowd had gathered at the courthouse. Charles McDonald, who had moved from Cottonwood Springs to North Platte in 1872 and opened a store, was chosen to lead the discussion. T. J. Foley, his competitor, wrote down the proceedings. The purpose of the meeting, of course, was to ascertain whether or not North Platte could make a better transportation offer than Cheyenne or Sidney.

Under flaring headlines, the North Platte *Republican* of April 10 reported the meeting:

TO THE GOLD MINES

BIG TALK ABOUT TRANSPORTATION

THE COURTHOUSE WAS CROWDED FULL. A SPLENDID GUARANTY ASSURED

The pros and cons relative to the city being the jumping-off point from the railroad to the Black Hills were thoroughly gone over. As far as the Platters were concerned, they were all pros. Once more golden transportation profits seemed to be within their grasp. [4]

The wide and treacherous Platte River and its forks had long been a barrier to all north and south travel in the state, but the railroad bridge, built in 1866, had turned out to be the means of giving North Platte a big advantage when the county, in 1870, had contracted with the railroad company to floor the bridge so that it could be used for wagon traffic. Thus, in 1875, North Platte had the only dependable wagon bridge across the Platte below the Black Hills country, and Cody had been quick to see the advantage for the town.

At that time, the main route to the Black Hills from the railroad was by way of Sidney, 125 miles on west of North Platte, then north fifty miles to the "Sidney Crossing," where all traffic had to ford the North Platte. Since the river flooded every spring, making it impassable for heavy freight wagons from the first of May to the middle of July, and dangerous and difficult at all times because of its quicksand bottom, their bridge, as it was pointed out at the meeting, made the whole thing "a cinch for North Platte," as far as easteners were concerned.[5]

Confident that by reason of their bridge their route was superior,

Union Pacific bridge
across Platte River.
(Picture taken from
North Platte town
end of bridge.)

T. C. Patterson, North Platte postmaster, suggested $7.50 would be a reasonable rate, as it was fifty cents under the nearest competitor's charge. But M. C. Keith advanced the argument that their rate could be even a little higher than the competition and still attract customers because the Sidney route required that additional 125-mile haul on the railroad before heading north to the mines. He also guaranteed to bring in a large number of mules from the west to haul the wagons. Ten dollars per one hundred pounds, he thought would be about right. Other leading citizens offered to put up money to help transport "the first installment of gold hunters."

C. H. Street declared "from this remote point [Boston] on our eastern boundaries comes this agreement that North Platte is *the* place. The good word will gather moss as it rolls westward from the Atlantic"; so he proposed that a list of names "of our best citizens" be attached to a rate guaranty and sent to Kimball, the Omaha agent who was handling the matter.

The guaranty, as finally put together, read: "We, the undersigned citizens of North Platte, Nebraska, will see that transportation will be furnished from North Platte to the Black Hills for one hundred or more persons with one hundred pounds baggage to each man for the sum of $8.00 each." The signers were Guy Barton, Charles McDonald, T. J. Foley, A. S. Senter, William Hinman, F. Fulton Gantt, H. R.

Ottman, T. C. Patterson, and others, all friends of Buffalo Bill.

The Western Nebraskian, on April 9, carried substantially the same information, with the added comment: "There is, perhaps, no one more competent to give intelligent advice respecting the most practicable route to the Black Hills than Buffalo Bill"; it also noted that "Captain Mills[6] and his company, based at North Platte, . . . has been ordered to examine the route from North Platte to the gold region and report as to its feasibility for the transportation of Government supplies." The troops were expected to leave any day now, as both the best route and the danger from Spotted Tail's Indians to anyone traveling it had not as yet been determined. Eager gold seekers from the East, however, the editor concluded, were not inclined to anticipate much difficulty from either the route or the red men.

Mills and his party of two other officers, sixty-two men, three laundresses, one wagon master, twelve citizen teamsters, two ambulances, ten wagons, fifteen days' rations, feed, wood, and three ladies, Mrs. Mills and the wife and the cousin of one of the other officers, set out upon their journey on April 16. They were to travel in a direct route from the east end of the railroad bridge to Harney's Peak, seeking the best road through the Sandhills for heavy traffic. There is no other route within 200-400 miles of the gold region that offers any assurance of getting across the North Platte River in the months of May, June, and part of July, asserted the *Nebraskian*.

The next few issues of the paper carried the reports sent back by the expedition. The findings must have been of interest to many besides the government officials, for strangely enough the great Sandhills region immediately northwest of Lincoln County was then almost as unknown as the mountains of the moon. Its fringes were, for the most part, forbiddingly dry, and most white people, fearful of getting lost in the endless rolling hills of what they supposed was a vast waterless waste, carefully steered around them.

Now and then cattle from the ranges established on the borders of the hills since 1869 had wandered into the region, or drifted in ahead of blizzards, and never been seen again. A few men, fleeing into the hills ahead of the law, had also disappeared from the ken of man. Most likely, so ran the tales, the bones of all lay bleaching in the sun of the treeless waste.

Mills' first report appeared in the *Nebraskian* of April 23, detailing the route followed. From the railroad bridge he had swung west up the north side of the North Platte River for ten miles, then north two miles, where he went into camp at "Emery Lake." On the seventeenth they had camped at the forks of the Birdwood, and the next day headed directly north through the hills, where they found the road sandier and traveling a little heavy. On the nineteenth they had to pull through a belt of about 200 yards of pure sand, very difficult for loaded wagons. However, they were now in a region of continuous valleys and lakes, and all was well. The first one hundred miles of the journey were behind them, and on the whole he considered the route a good one.

Although his dispatches do not mention it, he must have seen some of the cattle that had been "lost" in the Sandhills, for three years later (1878) cowboys from the Newman ranch on the Niobrara ventured south into the forbidding region to look for missing cattle—and found no less than a thousand head: wild, and most of them unbranded mavericks up to four years old. Although it was early spring, most of them were fat, proving the worth of the nutritious grasses on which the buffalo had fed well for generations. A year later (1879) Frank North drove a herd of cattle, gathered on the spring roundup and belonging to Cody and himself, from the head of Blue Creek, over in the Panhandle, east *through* the heart of the Sandhills to the ranch they had established in the spring of 1877 on the head of the Dismal. The shortcut shaved many miles off the long drive *around* the region.

North, too, found hundreds of lost cattle, some of them six- and seven-year-old steers, real old "mossy horns," and wild as deer.[7]

It is also interesting to note that the Indians, well aware of the abundance of wild game as well as grass and water for their ponies, had lived in high style in the Sandhills for many generations. When pressed too hard by pursuing cavalry, they frequently fled into the hills and "disappeared."

While Mills and his party were absent on their road-finding expedition, the merchants, Foley and Senter, received this brief letter which added further fuel to the gold fires: "Dear Sirs: Big excitement here. Parties organizing for the Black Hills. I am going to do all I can to get these parties to fit-out at North Platte; it will make business for the town. W. F. C." With the letter Cody enclosed several handbills, part of a supply being distributed in Boston for the purpose of calling meetings "to talk the gold question." Buffalo Bill was listed as one of the speakers.[8]

Immediately after the return of the exploring party, the officers and some of the townspeople met at the courthouse to discuss the road to the gold fields. The expedition must have come back by way of Blue Creek Valley, a more western route than the one followed on the trip out, for they report it a better road than the first. The *Nebraskian* of May 28 reports that "Buffalo Bill agrees the Blue Water route is best."

And there ends all mention of the superior road to the Black Hills. Apparently nothing more was done about developing a freighting route to the gold mines or putting their boasted bridge to use. The answer probably lies in a statement carried in the *Nebraskian* of July 23: "Although the government is still trying to keep miners out of the Black Hills, they are getting in. By the end of July one thousand will be hiding out there, waiting for the Hills to be opened to the whites."

That spring (1875) an expedition on its way to the mines had been intercepted by a strong military detachment near present-day Gordon, Nebraska, its twenty-nine wagons burned, and their owners escorted out of the country. Danger from the Sioux increased, too, as the summer passed and as the Indians saw the ever-growing possibility of losing their beloved Black Hills.

In view of such chaotic conditions it was only sensible that the North Platte merchants and freighters hold up for awhile. And by the next spring, when the rush to the mines could no longer be held back, other interests were already building a bridge "stout enough to bear the weight of a railroad train" across the river at the Sidney

Crossing. North Platte, as a jumping-off point for the Black Hills, was not to be.

As for Buffalo Bill, when his Combination disbanded for the summer, he went to his home in Rochester to spend some time with his family. Russell writes that it was probably the only summer of his life in which he remained quietly at home,[9] but the *Nebraskian* of July 23 states that he was to start for the Black Hills in a few days with ten men for a six-week buffalo hunt. Accompanying him were the New Yorkers J. F. Heckshier and Robert Adams of Beadle and Adams (the dime novel publisher), and several men and women of the Buffalo Bill Combination. Texas Jack was to go along. But nothing more can be found concerning the hunting trip. Perhaps it, too, did not come to pass.

It was well that Will Cody could spend that summer with his family, for it was the last in which they would all be together. He had always delighted in his children, and at last he had time to enjoy them, especially little Kit, now five years old. The little fellow wore his golden curls shoulder length, likely at the wish of his father, who had a small rifle made for him that summer and had his portrait painted, lifesize, with the little gun.

Ena Raymonde, the young lady from Georgia, who came to Cody country early in July 1872, six months too late to have taken part in the royal buffalo hunt, wrote in her diary on July 10 of that year: "I've spent one night with Mrs. Cody. . . . she has two charming little children. Kit Carson, the boy, is a handsome precocious little fellow . . . not more than three years old, or rather not three years . . . and just as keen as the little rascal can be! He gives promise of a future."[10]

At the summer's end Cody rejoined his partners in the Combination, Texas Jack and his wife. Major John Burke, who went where Morlacchi went, was, of course, their manager. "The Scouts of the Plains" was enjoying another highly successful season when it opened in Springfield, Massachusetts on April 20, 1876. Part way through the show Cody was handed a telegram informing him of the serious illness of little Kit. While waiting for his train he played out the first act, then sped to Rochester, where his beloved little son died of scarlet fever a few hours later.

Sister Helen, describing the harrowing death scene, says the child lived a day and a night after his father arrived. She goes on to tell how Kit had been kidnapped by gypsies a year earlier. "But Kit was the son of a scout," she writes, "and his young eyes were sharp. He marked the trail followed by his captors, and at the first opportunity gave them

Kit Carson Cody.

the slip and got safely home, exclaiming as he toddled into the sobbing family circle, 'I tumed back adain, mama; don't cry.'"[11] A rather remarkable feat for a child barely four years old.

Cooper, of course, wrings the last drop of tragic sorrow from the little boy's premature death. He has Louisa sending her telegram to Boston instead of Springfield, then telling little Kit that his daddy is on the way and will be with him at nine o'clock the next morning. The boy keeps murmuring "ten o'clock, ten o'clock." The long night passes. The mother listens for the whistle of the train that will bring the father home by nine o'clock. It does not come, the train is late. The minutes drag on, "Slower and slower and slower—a whistle, far away . . . the sound of hurried steps, the rushing form of a man who came into the room, his face white and drawn, his arms extended. As he knelt by the side of the baby we loved, the old clock on the wall struck ten!" Buffalo Bill takes his son in his arms, and "with the last stroke" of the clock his little Kit Carson was dead.[12]

Cody himself is the only one who lends dignity to the account of the heartbreaking loss. In a letter to his sister Julia, written at three o'clock in the morning, a few hours after his son's death, his sentiments are simple and tender as he struggles to understand why his gay little Kit had to be taken and tries to picture the boy in a bright and better world, "where he will wait for us." He reached home a few hours before Kit died, he wrote, and Lulu, worn out from her long vigil with the three sick children, is sleeping while he watches at the bedside of his little girls.[13]

11

Yellow Hair
1876

One of the most controversial of the many stories told about Buffalo Bill is the one dealing with the killing of Yellow Hand, son of Cut Nose, a Cheyenne chief. For years it has been hotly argued that Cody did or did not kill the Indian, and a profusion of proofs supporting both positions has been brought forth.

Historian Don Russell, after extensive research and careful sifting of records, reports, and stories on the subject, is convinced that Bill Cody did kill the young chief, whose correct name was Yellow Hair. The location of the killing and the manner in which it was done, as described by latter-day writers, are usually in error.

The spot where the Indian died is often described as the bank of War Bonnet Creek, a small stream in northwest Nebraska. Actually it was near Hat Creek, another small stream about forty miles north of War Bonnet. The Cheyenne's name was Hayowei, or Yellow Hair, referring to the scalp of a white woman he had taken; but a scout with the Fifth Cavalry, Baptiste Garnier or Little Bat, miscalled him Yellow "Hand" when reporting his death.[1] The instant notoriety that resulted, due to Buffalo Bill's part in his death, imprinted the name of Yellow Hand on the pages of history, where it remained. Later "historians" referred to him as "the noted chief," whereas he was really a very minor or subchief. Had anyone ever heard of him before his death, his name would not have been so garbled on the occasion of his departure for the happy hunting grounds.

The so-called "duel" between Cody and the Indian took place on July 17, 1876, and Cody was there because Colonel Mills had written him a number of letters urging him to come west to guide General Crook and his command into the Indian territory of Wyoming and Montana. Hoping in the excitement of another expedition into Indian country to somewhat forget his grief over his son's death, Cody made arrangements to close his show early. At a benefit performance at Wilmington, Delaware, on June 3, he told his audience he was through with play acting and was heading for the Indian wars out west on the plains.

When he reached Chicago, he learned that his old regiment, the gallant Fifth, was on the way from Arizona, also to join General Crook, and his old commander, General Carr, was in command. General Carr, too, wanted Cody for his guide and chief of scouts.[2] He hurried on to Cheyenne, where the Fifth had already arrived and where he was enthusiastically welcomed by the regiment.

Buffalo Bill signed on the payroll as scout on June 10. Had he been a few days earlier he would have been with Crook when he took the trail for the Rosebud and his resounding defeat there. As it was, he left Cheyenne for Fort Laramie with General Carr and his battalion on June 11. At Fort Laramie, on June 14, they were joined by General Sheridan and other officers. From there, with a company of cavalry as escort, Cody and Sheridan went on to the Red Cloud Agency while the Fifth Cavalry was sent out to scout the country between the Indian agencies and the Black Hills.

While Cody and Sheridan were at Red Cloud, Crook fought the battle of the Rosebud on June 17, and Custer and his men died on the Little Big Horn on June 25; but all of this was, as yet, unknown to the contingent at Camp Robinson, next to the old Red Cloud Agency. On July 1 Brevet Major General Wesley Merritt became colonel of the Fifth and took over command from General Carr. At dawn the next day, Merritt, with Cody as guide, marched the battalion closer to the Indian trail, after which the troops traveled about the country for six days, camping on Sage Creek in Wyoming on July 6. Early the next morning Cody came pounding into camp, bringing word of the Custer disaster. Four days later the Fifth was ordered to join Crook's command and at once set out for Fort Laramie. But early on the morning of July 14, General Merritt received a report from the commander at Camp Robinson that a thousand Cheyennes were planning to bolt the Red Cloud Agency.

Merritt at once turned back toward Rawhide Creek crossing, on the trail between Fort Laramie and Camp Robinson, hoping to get ahead of the Cheyennes and turn them back. This was on Saturday. By Monday night the troops had reached Hat Creek, after marching eighty-five miles in thirty-one hours. At first light the next morning, July 17, Cody, who had been reconnoitering, rode to a butte from which a soldier, Chris Madsen, watched the valley, ready to signal messages to Merritt's nearby headquarters tent. Cody told him to notify the command that the Cheyennes, encamped not far away, were preparing to move. At the same time Lieutenant King, commanding another hilltop outpost to the southwest, sent word the Indians were coming over a ridge from the southeast. By five o'clock Indians were in view across a three mile front, moving slowly, all unaware of the soldiers.

Meanwhile, the troops' wagon train of supplies had been coming up the trail in the rear of the marching cavalry. Just after the lookouts spied the Indians, they also saw the approaching wagon train; as quite a number of infantrymen were hidden in the covered wagons, the train was well protected, and the cavalrymen could remain hidden until the big body of Indians came nearer. At about this time, the Cheyennes saw the train and began to race about on various ridges and hilltops, watching its movement.

Cody, with two other scouts, had ridden up to Merritt's hilltop to watch. Suddenly thirty or forty Indians broke away from the main band and began scurrying about in great excitement. The cause of their activity quickly became apparent. Two horsemen, probably carrying messages to Merritt, were riding ahead of the train, unaware of the big band of Indians they would have to pass in order to reach the commander's tent. At this point seven Cheyennes dashed away to intercept the couriers.

Merritt's original plan to keep his troops hidden until the unsuspecting Indians were very near was now spoiled, for the two riders would have to be protected. Cody then suggested that they remain hidden until the last moment before the small band of Indians attacked the couriers, then he and seven or eight men would dash out and cut them off, thus maintaining the concealment of the main body of troops until time to charge the big Indian party. Merritt agreed.

With the two scouts and five or six troopers from Company K, Cody awaited the signal to charge, which was to come from Lieutenant King who, from his hill, was watching the approach of the seven Indians through binoculars. As the Indians dashed by in front of his hill, he shouted to Cody, "Now, in with you." The point at which Cody and his men intercepted the Indians was out of sight of Merritt's observation point, but army signalman, Chris Madsen, saw the meeting from his hilltop. In a manuscript written many years later, he described the scene he witnessed that morning:

> Cody was riding a little in advance of his party and one of the Indians was preceding his group. . . . Through the powerful telescope furnished by the Signal Department the men did not appear to be more than 50 feet from me. From the manner in which both parties acted it was certain that both were surprised. Cody and the leading Indian appeared to be the only ones who did not become excited. The instant they were face to face their guns fired. It seemed almost like one shot. There was no conversation, no preliminary agreement, as has been stated erroneously in some novels written by romantic scribes.
>
> They met by accident and fired the moment they faced each other. Cody's bullet went through the Indian's leg and killed his pinto pony. The Indian's bullet went wild. Cody's horse stepped into a prairie dog hole and stumbled but was up in a moment. Cody jumped clear of his mount. Kneeling, he took deliberate aim and fired the second shot. An instant before Cody fired the second shot, the Indian fired at him but missed. Cody's bullet went through the Indian's head and ended the battle. Cody went over to the fallen Indian and neatly removed his scalp while the other soldiers gave chase to the Indian's companions. There is no doubt about it, Buffalo Bill scalped this Indian, who, it turned out, was a Cheyenne sub-chief called Yellow Hair.[3]

Surprisingly but logically enough, a small Kansas weekly newspaper, the Ellis County *Star*, had more war correspondents in the field than the New York *Herald*, the Chicago *Times*, or the San Francisco *Call*, according to Don Russell, for most of the men in Companies A, B, D, and K were from Fort Hays; almost every week the *Star* carried long letters from the soldier-correspondents—Powers, Brown, or Mac—which the families of the Kansas men read to keep up with events in the field. Sergeant John Powers of Company A was riding in the wagon train that morning, and what he saw from the other side of the hill, after Cody crossed the ridge, was recorded in a dispatch from Fort Laramie, dated July 22 and printed in the *Star* on August 3. His story of the fight between Cody and the Indian leader is substantially the same as that told by Madsen.

Other official reports confirmed the facts related by Madsen and Powers, although without naming either Cody or Yellow Hair. "The Record of Events" of the Fifth Cavalry for June 30–August 31 states: "Early on the morning of July 17th, a party of seven Indians was discovered trying to cut off two couriers, who were on their way to this company with dispatches. A party was at once detached in pursuit, killing one Indian."[4]

Cody himself described the fight in a brief letter written to his wife from the Red Cloud Agency the following day: "We have had a fight. I killed Yellow Hand a Cheyenne Chief in a single-handed fight. You will no doubt hear of it through the papers. I am going as soon as I reach Fort Laramie the place we are heading for now send the war bonnet, shield, bridle, whip, arms and his scalp to Kerngood [a family friend who owned a clothing store in Rochester] to put up in his window. I will write Kerngood to bring it up to the house so you can show it to the neighbors. . . . I have only one scalp I can call my own that fellow I fought single handed in sight of our command and the cheers that went up when he fell was deafening."[5]

The above are the facts concerning the famous Yellow Hair fight. According to Cooper, Louisa told it somewhat as follows: For long, fearful weeks I knew only that Will was somewhere in the West, trailing Indians, and I daily lived in hopes of a letter from him and in dread of bad news from some other source. And then one day the expressman delivered a small box from Fort McPherson. It was from William F. Cody. I pried open the lid, and a very unpleasant odor caught my nostrils. I reeled slightly, reached for the contents, and then fainted. For I had brought from the box the scalp of an Indian. When Will came home again, he told me the scalp was Yellow Hand's and that he had killed him in a duel.[6]

Will then gives her and little Arta a lurid description of the fight, how he and the Indian were both unhorsed and had to finish the struggle with bowie knife and tomahawk. This is almost more than his little wife can take, so the tale ends with Will promising his Lulu that he will never scalp another Indian.

The *New York Weekly* published "The Crimson Trail; or, Custer's Last Warpath, A Romance Founded Upon the Present Border Warfare, as Witnessed by Hon. W. F. Cody." And Cody appeared on the stage in "The Red Right Hand; or, Buffalo Bill's First Scalp for Custer." In both the *Weekly* and the play the fight ended with the chief's dying in hand-to-hand combat with knife and tomahawk and Cody's holding the

Indian's scalp and war bonnet aloft and shouting, "The first scalp for Custer."

This dramatic version of the story was so widely told and believed that Cody apparently hadn't the heart to spoil it by telling the truth—and besides it was good for business, so he included the popular version in his first autobiography, published three years after the Hat Creek fight.

When Helen Cody Wetmore wrote her book in 1899, she drew her brother all of ten feet tall and added quite a lot of fancy embroidery besides; it was in her book that the fight first became a "duel." She writes:

> Here something a little out of the usual occurred—a challenge to a duel. A warrior, whose decorations and war-bonnet proclaimed him a chief, rode out in front of his men, and called out in his own tongue, which Will could understand:
>
> "I know you, Pa-has-ka! Come and fight me, if you want to fight!"
>
> Will rode forward fifty yards, and the warrior advanced a like distance. The two rifles spoke, and the Indian's horse fell; but at the same moment Will's horse stumbled into a gopher-hole and threw its rider. Both duelists were instantly on their feet, confronting each other across a space of not more than twenty paces. They fired again simultaneously, and though Will was unhurt, the Indian fell dead.
>
> The duel over, some two hundred warriors dashed up to recover the chieftain's body and to avenge his death.

Of course the rest of the soldiers then dashed up to rescue her hero brother as he swung the Indian's topknot and war bonnet and shouted, "The first scalp for Custer!" Helen also has Colonel Merritt's men killing three other Indians.[7]

Richard J. Walsh, who wrote *The Making of Buffalo Bill* (1928), declared: "Over what General Sheridan described as an almost totally unknown region of about ninety thousand square miles, the Sioux and their allies were supreme and aflame with hatred. There were twenty-nine thousand well-armed Indians at large in a country in which they knew every canyon and ford.

"To cut off the Cheyenne, who were riding to join Sitting Bull, . . . Colonel Merritt had to march his seven companies of cavalry eighty miles before the Indians could go thirty. He did it, and straddled the Indian trail at the crossing of Hat Creek." Walsh quotes Cody's 1879 autobiography of the fight, but adds: "It was not strange that the enemy picked on Buffalo Bill. . . . His comrades wore buckskin, corduroy or flannel so indiscriminately that officers and privates could hardly be told apart. Cody went into that fray all dressed up in one of his stage cos-tumes—a handsome Mexican suit of black velvet, slashed with scarlet and trimmed with silver buttons and lace. Why he should be wearing such regalia, far in the hills, at dawn, after an eighty-mile ride, when the regiment was in its working clothes, is impossible to explain, except as studied showmanship."[8]

At least Walsh was right on two counts: he put the skirmish on Hat Creek, and he hit upon the correct reason for Cody's spectacular dress that day. Russell agrees that he wore the vaquero stage outfit, and reasons that he had donned it very early that morning, knowing there was soon to be an engagement, so that, when wearing it on the stage the next winter, he could tell his audiences he was wearing the proper attire of a scout of the plains.[9] Or with dramatic flair he could truthfully announce to the audience that this was the very same outfit he was wearing during his most recent Indian fight.

Chauncey Thomas, well-known writer for *Outdoor Life* magazine, said he was the last to interview Cody just before he died. The doctors had told Cody "he would never see another sunset," and "he remarked to me, slowly but calmly, . . . 'when a man looks at his last sunset he can afford to tell the truth.'" "It was the End, and we all knew it. We talked at random, as all do, perhaps, at such times." Thomas asked Cody, "'What kind of a knife did you kill Yellow Hand with?'" And Cody replied, "'Just a big heavy bowie blade.'" Thomas adds that Will's sister, May Decker, in whose home he died, told him that she had heard her brother and Iron Tail talk of the Yellow Hand battle and that Iron Tail verified Cody's killing the chief.[10]

On the other side of the coin there is the story told by John Garnier, the mixed-blood son of Baptiste, or Little Bat, Garnier. Johnny Bat, as the son was usually called, claims that his father killed Yellow Hair. The chief challenged someone to come out and meet him with knives; Cody rode out, in spite of Little Bat's warning him that the Indian would cut him to pieces. So, to save Bill's life, Garnier had to shoot Yellow Hair, and he got him with a single shot.[11]

Another story concerning Little Bat's part in the death of Hayowei came by way of a letter from Norman Kelley, who wrote in 1927 that he had heard the story fifteen years earlier in his pool hall in Scenic, South Dakota. There Baptiste Pourier, or Big Bat, a scout with Crook, told how Little Bat and a man called Tate had been attacked by a small band of Cheyennes. They had dived into a buffalo wallow for protection and had managed to shoot two of the Indians, one of them Yellow Hand. A day or two later they met the Fifth Cavalry, and as they had often heard Cody say he wanted to scalp an Indian, they hunted him up and told him they had killed an Indian in full war dress near by. So Buffalo Bill had gone to the body and later came back wearing the war bonnet and other things.[12]

And then there is Jacob Blaut, a sergeant with Company I of the Fifth, who thinks he may have killed the chief; in one of his many tales of the affair he says definitely that he shot and stripped him, and that he and the other troops also killed eleven other Indians and captured twelve horses and a mule before the fight was finished. Another soldier, Jules Green, says Cody killed the chief but only because he, Green, chased him out of a canyon so Bill could fire the fatal shot into him. Still another man, Billy Garnett, or Billy Hunter as he was variously known, made the Denver *Post* on February 23, 1923, with his story of the duel; Cody and the chief fought with knives, he said, for more than an hour, and within sight of the garrison at Camp Robinson, thirty-five miles from the spot on Hat Creek where the army said Hayowei died.[13]

As the years went by, new accounts of the fight appeared in books and western story magazines. One is told by E. S. Sutton in an article entitled "Hero, Showman or Heel?" Sutton writes that he spent his boyhood in a small country village outside Denver, and that he *heard* Buffalo Bill say he did not kill Yellow Hand. Neighbor to the Suttons was an ex-bullwhacker, Gideon B. Beardsley, who was a good friend of Cody's. The scout, Beardsley told Sutton, had once saved his bull train from a surprise Indian attack. Years later, when the Wild West show came to Denver, the old bullwhacker took his young friend to see it, and during the afternoon they visited the tent of the great showman himself. And there, Sutton wrote, Beardsley asked, "Bill, just why have you permitted all of those belly-wash tales to circulate about the Yellow Hand duel and the killing of Tall Bull? You know they are darned hoss-feathers."

And Cody replied, "I never fired a shot in either engagement. I never scalped an Indian in my life. I have always been friendly with the old chiefs. To begin with, those were all *tall tales* tossed around campfires. We never believed them and never expected anyone else to. Then along came Buntline and other sensational writers; the public clamored for such tales, the yarns were published and now they are embalmed in history. Well, anyway, they were good advertising for the show!"

"My heart sank," wrote Sutton. "Watching Buffalo Bill enact his duel with Yellow Hand in the Wild West Show was disappointing. He had admitted the duel hadn't really taken place, when I wished so much in my boyish mind to believe in it!"[14]

Through research in later years, Sutton goes on, he learned that Cody had suggested to General Merritt that they trap the reservation-jumping Indians, and Merritt had deployed his troops accordingly. The general and Cody were watching the approaching Indians from a point of observation, wrote Sutton, "when two or three travelers (trappers or traders, probably) appeared in the valley. Fearing they would be attacked by Yellow Hand's band, some of the soldiers—without orders—moved out. As I recall it, Cody said a few shots were exchanged and Yellow Hand was killed by 'some red-neck sarge and scalped.' This is a far cry from the stories by Buntline," concludes Sutton.[15]

Indeed it is, for Buntline never wrote a word about Buffalo Bill and Yellow Hand. Buntline's first three tales in which Cody figured in any way were initially published several years before the Yellow Hair incident. His fourth, and last, published in 1885, was "Will Cody, the Pony Express Rider; or, Buffalo Bill's First Trail," a story of young Willie's pony express adventures.

Sutton then offers some information given him by Mari Sandoz, who told him she had a complete file on the engagement, gathered from military records, personal contact with Indians who were conversant with the affair, and personal research in various libraries. From all this, she concluded that after an exchange of a dozen or so shots between the soldiers and Indians, both sides ceased firing. "Yellow Hand, a young warrior who desired to win honors and prove his courage, then rode up and down between the Indians and the cavalrymen, challenging the soldiers to come out and fight.

"He continued to call them old squaws and dare them to meet him in combat. At length, one of the troopers, unable to withhold his anger, disobeyed Merritt's order to hold his fire and took a shot at Yellow Hand. The warrior's horse stumbled and fell to its knees. Yellow Hand stuffed his warbonnet under his belt and struck off towards safety. Another well placed shot killed the braggert. The trooper who downed Yellow Hand scalped him. We assume he took the warbonnet also. Cody paid him five dollars for the scalp that night, and it is presumed he came into possession of the warbonnet by similar means."

Mari Sandoz was not noted for presenting Cody in a credible light, but she must have known that such a medieval tourney-type battle, between opposing lines of foes, was completely foreign to Indian warfare, as Don Russell carefully points out.[16]

In contrast to the above comments on the Yellow Hair affair are those made by the Reverend George A. Beecher, rector of the Episcopal Church of our Savior of North Platte from 1895 to 1903, and later bishop of western Nebraska until his retirement in 1943. Beecher, who lived neighbor to the Codys in North Platte and was a close friend of Buffalo Bill's for many years, stated that Cody once told him he killed Hayowei, although he gave no details. He had then asked the minister if Mrs. Cody had ever shown him the Indian's scalp among the collection of curios in the big Cody house in North Platte. Beecher replied that he vividly remembered seeing the "mottled bunch of hair" when he and some friends had visited the home.[17]

The strangest version of all turns up in a letter written to Margaret McCann in the late 1920s when she was collecting material for a thesis on W. F. Cody. The writer, Robert Jenkinson Hicks, of Rochester, New York, said he lived on the same street as the Codys when Kit Carson was alive, and that "as I was the only lad on the street at this time, Kit and I became 'pals.' We were about the same age. Later on Ora, the second daughter, was born to Mr. and Mrs. Cody while they lived here." (Orra Cody was born in August 1872, at Fort McPherson.)

Buffalo Bill was in the show business with a company of scouts, Indians, and others, Hicks continues, and "among the cast . . . was Sitting Bull, Yellow Hand and other Indians I cannot now remember—as a boy I met them all. Colonel Cody's son, Kit Carson Elmore Jensen Cody, his daughter Arta and myself were made up to appear as little Indians during the campfire scenes while the performance was going on at the old Grand Opera House on South St. Paul street." (Hicks probably means Edward Judson, instead of "Elmore Jensen" as a part of young Kit's name. Cody had at first suggested naming the boy after Edward Zane Carroll Judson, Ned Buntline's real name, and had taught the child to repeat the entire string of names.)

Hicks goes on: "During one of these performances Yellow Hand was drunk. He was cautioned by Mr. Cody to stop drinking fire water under penalty. Yellow Hand resented this and cursed Mr. Cody in his language (Cheyenne) which Cody understood, and came to him for a fight after the curtain came down. He was immediately floored by Mr. Cody. . . . We youngsters in the rear of the stage were badly frightened." (The Sioux and Cheyennes have no curse words in their own tongues.)

When the season was over, Hicks wrote, the show disbanded and the Indians returned to their respective reservations; then the Indian uprising came on and Yellow Hand was the "chief in command, as I learned. The engagement brought Buffalo Bill and Yellow Hand face to face again. Yellow Hand never forgot nor forgave Mr. Cody for what he thought a gross wrong of years before on the stage in this city. This was no doubt the reason Yellow Hand challenged Mr. Cody to the hand-to-hand battle, as he (Yellow Hand) swore to kill Cody—as was reported by Mr. Cody to his wife, Mrs. Cody."

As the clincher to his story, Hicks adds: "Our families still resided on New York street. Kit Carson . . . had died and as we had been play-mates during the year and one-half [he lived there], Mrs. Cody would have me over to her house [because] she and the other children were very lonesome for Kit. It was in her side yard that she opened a wooden box about two and one-half feet long by one foot deep which had been sent here from the west by Mr. Cody. It contained all the items that Yellow Hand wore, plus his scalp, pipe and implements of war. Mrs. Cody and I picked up all those items, looked them over and replaced them into the box and then carried the package into the house, to remain there for further instructions from Mr. Cody. And she told me, I clearly remember, Mr. Cody killed Yellow Hand."[18]

It is quite possible that young Hicks did act in Cody's play during its engagement in Rochester. It would have been typical of Buffalo Bill to have his children in the show while it was in his home town, and any little friend of Kit's would surely have been included. There were no real Indians with the show at that time, but there may have been an altercation with one of the "made up" Indian supers, who played the parts of red men, which remained in the boy's memory. Furthermore, young Hicks could well have been on hand when Mr. Kerngood sent or brought the box of Yellow Hand gear to Mrs. Cody, and they might have unpacked and examined the things in the side yard. It is the kind of incident that would stick in the memory of a six-year-old for the rest of his life.

Under date of July 22, 1876, the gist of a brief notice in the *Western Nebraskian* is that there were 800 Sioux and Cheyennes bolting their reservation and that Buffalo Bill shot one. A week later the paper reported, "The Indian killed by Buffalo Bill was Yellow Hand, a young chief." Forty-one years later the North Platte *Telegraph* for May 24, 1917, under the headline, "Memorable Duel with Gun and Pistol Fought in Early Days A Matter of History of the West," related:

Following is an eye-witness description of the duel with knives between Colonel William F. Cody (Buffalo Bill) and Yellow Hand, chief of the Sioux Indians, which is accurately pictured in Essanay's current feature, *Adventures of Buffalo Bill*.[19]

On July 18, 1876, at Hot [sic] Creek, near Fort Robinson, Dakota, said Mr. Cross, Buffalo Bill, guiding General Eugene A. Carr and a detachment of United States troops drew up against the Sioux hordes. Yellow Hand, riding a yellow pony, rode out upon the crest of a high butte and signaled a bold challenge to Col. Cody, whom he knew, to settle their difficulties by fighting a duel. Before anybody could stop him, Col. Cody dashed out to meet the chief. Between the lines of soldiers and Indians the duel was fought. Cody fired the first bullet, which clipped a feather out of Yellow Hand's war bonnet. Shot after shot was exchanged, and finally the men, their ammunition exhausted, leaped from their horses and clashed with knives. Five minutes of fighting and Cody drove his knife into the Indian's heart. The next day Yellow Hand's squaw went over to the soldiers' quarters and in the presence of the officers cut off the third finger of her right hand. That was the supreme sacrificial act of a great chief's widow.[20]

Here not only is the chief mounted on a yellow pony and the duelists fire until they use up all of their ammunition, without scoring a hit, but artist Cross forgot to check to see who was in charge of the troops. The General that day was Merritt, not Carr.

To sum it all up, it would seem, to borrow from Don Russell, that no other Indian "died so often, in so many different places, by so many different hands," than did Yellow Hand, whose real name was Hayowei, Yellow Hair.

12

Rancher
1876-1882

Following the death of Yellow Hair and the surprise appearance of the troops from behind their hill, the 800 Cheyennes turned about and headed for the Red Cloud Agency, followed all the way by the Fifth Cavalry troops. Pursued and pursuers covered the thirty miles by evening, and it was not until then, Bill says, that he learned the Indian he killed was "Yellow Hand."[1] The next afternoon Merritt and his troops headed back to Fort Laramie.

After a very brief layover there, the Fifth marched to Fort Fetterman, arriving on July 25, and proceeding straight on to join General Crook's forces, encamped near the spot where Sheridan, Wyoming, now stands. From here on the movement was officially known as the Big Horn and Yellowstone Expedition, and Cody was employed as its chief scout at $150 a month. He continued with the campaign for several weeks, carrying reports and dispatches among Generals Crook, Miles, and Terry through rugged country swarming with hostile Indians.

By late August, however, the Indians had so scattered that Bill saw little prospect of any more fighting and decided to return east and see what he could do about organizing a new show for the winter—and so ended forever his employment as a government scout.

Cody and Texas Jack had come to a parting of the ways, and Jack and his wife, Giuseppina Morlacchi, with Major Burke, had organized their own combination for that season. Therefore, Buffalo Bill was on his own. In Rochester he looked up some old stage friends and put together a show founded on the events of the past summer on the plains, for all the East was titillated over the Indian wars in the West. A drama based on the so-called battle on the War Bonnet and billed as "The Red Right Hand; or, Buffalo Bill's First Scalp for Custer" was bound to be a winner.

The new show, as its star truthfully stated, "was a five-act play, without head or tail, and it made no difference at which act we commenced the performance. . . . It afforded us, however, ample opportunity to give a noisy, rattling, gunpowder entertainment, and to present a succession of scenes in the late Indian war, all of which seemed to give general satisfaction."[2]

From Rochester the "Red Right Hand" went on to New York, through the eastern and middle states, and then headed for the west coast. On the way, early in the spring of 1877, Cody stopped off in Sidney, Nebraska, where he met the North brothers, Frank and Luther, and there, according to Luther, Bill and Frank made arrangements to go into the cattle business together. While Cody was in California with his show, the Norths were to locate range for the cattle and build the ranch headquarters.

Sometime before the end of that year, a newspaper announced that Buffalo Bill was making his "farewell tour" as a theatrical star and would soon devote his life to being "a cattle dealer and gentleman farmer." At the close of the western tour the show would disband in Omaha and Cody would go to his ranch where "He now has 4,500 head of cattle, and hopes to have 10,000 by the close of next year."[3]

The newspaper seems to have been a bit premature, both as to Cody's (implied) ownership of any ranch or his retirement from the stage. Several writers have been mistaken about the date of Buffalo Bill's first ownership of land in Nebraska and the size of his holdings there. His sister Helen states that at the close of the season after he killed Yellow Hair, he "bought a large tract of land near North Platte, and started a cattle-ranch," adding that in partnership with Major North he already owned a ranch some distance to the north. There were 7,000 acres in the North Platte ranch, she wrote, with 2,500 acres in alfalfa and the same in corn. The ranch house, when "seen from the foothills, has the appearence of an old castle."[4]

Cooper has Louisa locate the North Platte farm "near the Wyoming line" and writes that Cody also "bought a tremendous ranch on the Dismal River in partnership with Major North." Another source pushes the date back even further by stating: "In the spring of 1870 Will homesteaded 3,000 acres at North Platte, Nebraska and settled down with his family near Fort McPherson, where he was employed as a scout."[5]

Still another writer claims "Cody owned many valuable tracts of land, as well as large herds of cattle. The land was presented to him by the government for his outstanding services as a scout during the many Indian skirmishes."[6]

Actually Cody did not own any land at North Platte until 1878, when he sent some money to banker Charles McDonald to buy land for him. On February 4, the banker bought 160 acres for $750.00 in Lincoln County.[7] The land had belonged to Morgan Davis and lay along the railroad tracks, south of Front Street and west of the barracks. There was a small house on it and some barns, but the rest was pasture where young Bill McDonald looked after eighty head of cattle for several summers, driving the herd out to the pasture in the morning and back to his father's corrals at night. A herd of fourteen antelope ran with the cattle one summer, he remembered many years later. For the next several years Bill sent money back to the banker, earmarked for the purchase of more land, but it was some time before the ranch attained its maximum size of 4,000 acres, most of it lying north of the railroad tracks.

Not one acre of land was ever presented to Buffalo Bill by a grateful government for any reason whatsoever, and he could not have home-steaded 3,000 acres for the simple reason that, at that time, 160 acres was the largest tract the U.S. government permitted any one person to claim by right of homestead. Neither did Cody or North buy any land on the Dismal. During the time they operated their ranch there, 1877-1882, all that part of Nebraska was open range, and the first man to put cattle upon any part of it, large or small, held it by the sim-ple right of first use. Although Cody and North claimed and used many miles of range land in McPherson, Grant, and Hooker Counties, they did not own one foot of the land, not even the ground where Frank North built a log ranch house, a sod stable, and a cedar pole corral while his partner was enjoying a most successful west coast tour.[8]

The location Frank North selected for the ranch was on the head-waters of the South Fork of the little Dismal River, deeper into the Sandhills than any rancher had yet ventured. In the valley where the Dismal comes to life, Frank found a well-grassed, well-watered region. The building site was about sixty-five miles north of North Platte, and there was no other white habitation between it and John Bratt's cow camp on the Birdwood, forty miles to the south.

The Dismal River country in the seventies was a paradise for cow-boys as well as cattle. Elk, deer, and antelope were everywhere; the lakes to the west of the ranch abounded with wild fowl of many kinds. The only drawback was Indians, slipping off the reservations and roaming the hills in small bands, running off a few horses wherever they could, killing a cowboy now and then.

In July, after paying off his company in Omaha, Cody met his partner in Ogallala, then the end of the Texas cattle trail. There they bought 1,500 head of cattle, hired a crew, branded out the herd, and drove it to their new range. Two of the crew were Texans, Buck and Baxter Taylor, both well over six feet tall. Buck, nineteen years old that summer and the taller of the two, was later to be famous as the "King of the Cow-Boys" in Cody's Wild West show.[9]

Bill spent most of the rest of the summer on the ranch, then made a quick trip to the Red Cloud Agency in August to hire some Sioux Indians for his new stage show, the first time he had used real Indians on the stage. With the Indians and his wife and daughters (where Louisa and the girls spent the summer is nowhere recorded), he went to Rochester, left Arta in a young ladies' seminary, and proceeded on to New York. There on September 3 he opened at the Bowery Theatre with a brand new show featuring bloody incidents from the "Mountain Meadow Massacre," whose perpetrator, the Morman John D. Lee, had been executed at the scene of the crime in Utah the previous March.

Although Louisa and little Orra traveled with the show for a part of that season, that type of life was not to Mrs. Cody's liking, and by February she was thoroughly tired of it. But the fact that she did travel with him for five months or more is interesting. When he paid off his troupe in Omaha the previous summer, there had been a disagreement between Louisa and Bill, due, according to his testimony in their divorce suit twenty-eight years later, to his kissing four of his actresses goodbye. Cody saw no harm in it, in fact took it for a compliment that the ladies, after six or seven months of the close association of the theater, still thought enough of him to want to kiss him goodbye. But Mrs. Cody took a dim view of the proceedings, and a rift developed. That she stayed with him through the winter and for the first time traveled with the show for any length of time is evidence that the rift healed by late summer—or that she distrusted her husband and felt compelled to accompany the show and keep an eye on him.

With little Orra, Louisa went to North Platte where, according to Bill McDonald, they lived in the officers' headquarters at the North Platte barracks while their new home, on the east edge of the newly purchased 160-acre farm and a block or so south of the tracks, was built.

Orra Maude Cody,
c. 1876.

Miniature replica of the Codys' first house in North Platte.

Of this first Cody home in North Platte we know little. Helen refers to it by its popular local name, "Welcome Wigwam," and says it "was built according to the wishes and under the supervision of the wife and mother."[10] Cooper, with his usual disregard of geography, locates it at North Platte "near the Wyoming line" and has Louisa declare: "Furnishings came all the way from Chicago and New York." The latter is possible, but he goes on: "The lumber [for the house] had been hauled across country, and there, out on the plains, we built a house that was little less than a mansion."[11]

Frances Fulton, who visited Welcome Wigwam for several days in 1883, said of it: the Cody's "beautiful home is nicely situated one-half mile from the suburbs of North Platte."[12] Years later, long after the house was gone, a life-long North Platte resident, George Macomber, described it as "an ordinary story and a half frame house with a small stable or shed on the back of the lot and a low white wooden fence around the yard."[13] By then, of course, many larger, finer homes had been built in the town, making the long-ago Cody house seem ordinary by comparison.

At the close of the season, the most profitable he had ever had, Cody returned to North Platte. Of the new home he wrote that Lulu had "personally superintended the erection of a comfortable family residence, and had it all completed when I reached there, early in May. In this house we are now living, and we hope to make it our home for many years to come. . . . One great source of pleasure to me was that my wife was delighted with the home I had given her amid the prairies of the far West."[14]

On his arrival in North Platte, Cody found the spring roundup for western Nebraska already assembled, ready to comb the vast region to the northwest to gather, sort, and brand the cattle ranging there. By 1878 the cattlemen of the area had organized a Livestock Association to maintain control of the roundups, set the starting dates, and establish the rules under which they operated. "Major North was awaiting me," Cody said, "having with him our own horses and men. Other cattle owners, such as Keith and Barton, Coe and Carter, John Bratt, the Walker brothers, Guy and Sim Lang [Laing], Arnold and Ritchie and a great many others with their outfits . . . were ready to start."[15]

That the ranch was more of a diversion for Buffalo Bill than a business is the consensus of opinion of most of his contemporaries. He himself stated, "As there is nothing but hard work on those round ups, having to be in the saddle all day, and standing guard over the cattle at night, rain or shine, I could not possibly find out where the fun came in that North had promised me."[16] Nevertheless, he made as much fun out of it as he could.

One ranchman, J. J. Douglas of Custer County, who knew Cody on those roundups, wrote of him, "Buffalo Bill . . . was a liberal fellow, never cared to lay up money, said he always believed in keeping it in circulation, always carried plenty to drink and smoke, and quite frequently set 'em up to the round-up." If he feared his original supply of refreshments might run short, he promptly sent a wagon to North Platte to lay in more.[17]

John Bratt also mentions Cody's hospitality at the ranch. There was always "something doing besides actual round-up work" when Buffalo Bill was there.

Some of the cowboys would take advantage of the Colonel's hospitality by going to his wagon and helping themselves to his cigars and sampling his liquors that had been brought along as an antidote against snake bites and other accidents. There would be broncho riding, roping, racing, riding wild steers, swimming contests, and sometimes a friendly poker game to see who would stand on night herd the longest. The cowboys were always glad to see the Colonel and the other cattle owners and foremen would vie with each other in showing him a good time, and would prepare special feasts . . . for him when he came to or near their ranches. Nothing was too good for Colonel Cody.[18]

During the few years he was in the ranching business, Buffalo Bill hosted numerous excursions to the Dismal headquarters for the entertainment of his family and their guests. One of the earliest of these must have taken place soon after the 1878 roundup broke up in mid-June. Miss Lottie Kocken, a North Platte friend of Arta's, tells the story:

Mr. Cody arrived in town with a party of five eastern men. He and Mrs. Cody at once organized a camping trip to the Dismal. In addition to the easterners, other guests included Mr. and Mrs. Frank North, their daughter Stella, and a group of Arta's friends. "Arta was twelve," Miss Kocken recalled, "fully matured, with great beauty and physical attraction inherited from both her parents." Lottie was thirteen, Kate Taffe and Stella North about fourteen. Seventeen-year-old Bill McDonald had been invited but didn't get to go as his parents thought the trip too long and dangerous.

Arta, Kate, and Lottie rode sidesaddles, Lottie on a horse named Sugar. Stella, who did not ride horseback, rode in a buggy with her mother. The young girls wore high-topped button shoes and black-ribbed cotton stockings. Their dresses, shoe-top length, were figured calico. Underneath they wore stiff muslin drawers and two petticoats apiece. Lottie wondered whether the horse or the girl was the most dressed up when each was mounted and her full skirts properly draped. For headgear they wore large white straw hats, anchored by elastic under their chins.

Mrs. North and Mrs. Cody, young women in their thirties, wore black cotton gowns with very full skirts and tight bodices buttoned down the front. Little Orra, six years old, was dressed like her mother and rode with her in a single-seated phaeton drawn by two handsome, spotted ponies. In addition to the ladies' rigs, there were two covered wagons, one for food and one to haul the tents, bedding, and baggage.

One cook and several helpers were in charge of the camp supplies.

The party stopped at noon to eat a hearty meal, then headed on across the treeless plains. The sun was hot, wrote Lottie, and the girls on horseback were soon quite well blistered. The matrons and the girls in the buggies fared better. When they came to the steep-banked, sparkling little Dismal, the girls had to hold their feet and skirts high while their horses crossed the stream.

They made camp that evening (she does not say where), put up the tents, and had supper. Bone weary, they went to bed early. Sometime during the night, Indians stampeded their horses. "We did not know what was to become of us then," Lottie recorded, "but the horses were finally found and we went on our way." One cannot help but wonder if the stampede of the horses was not one of Bill's little jokes, staged for the benefit of his eastern guests. Luther North, however, relates several instances of near trouble with roving bands of Sioux from the Rosebud Agency during this time,[19] but it seems unlikely that Cody would have taken the girls and women into the territory if there had been any serious danger.

Lottie writes that after they finally got on the road again, Mr. Cody sent Johnny Baker on ahead to notify the crew at the ranch that they would soon have company. In this she must be mistaken, for Johnny was only seven or eight years old at that time, a very tender age at which to be sent alone through twenty miles or so of empty, rolling, look-alike hills. Johnny may well have been with the camping party, however, for it is said that the lifelong friendship between the scout and the admiring boy began in 1878, and it would have been character- istic of Cody to invite Johnny to come along.

The courier was probably Cody's fifteen-year-old nephew, Will Goodman, who is mentioned in connection with some of the trips to the Dismal. At any rate, when the cavalcade reached the ranch their arrival was a surprise, for the advance rider had not shown up. A posse of cowboys at once rode off to hunt him up; it was getting dark by the time they found and brought him in, Lottie says.

The Codys and their guests maintained their own camp during the week they spent at the ranch. A carnival spirit prevailed all the while, with Buffalo Bill, the generous, genial host, organizing horse races, picnics, and target shoots to while away the pleasant hours. Everyone took part, even the young girls, and Cody shot a hole in a half-dollar with his rifle and gave the coin to Lottie for a souvenir of the trip.

In the evenings everybody gathered around the campfire; the cowboys joined them for singing and dancing, adding to the gaiety with their banjos, harmonicas, and jew's-harps. Cody and his boys told stirring cowboy stories, Lottie wrote, and the Colonel's favorite song was "In the Gloaming." He seemed never to tire of it.

The trip home was very tame: no Indians, no stampedes, no one lost. The other girls, worn out by the exciting week, put their saddles in the wagon and rode home in the phaeton. Only Lottie made the entire trip on her sidesaddle.[20]

Cooper has Louisa mentioning that Will came home at the end of the season following Custer's massacre and they made a trip to his great ranch on the Dismal. Helen goes into more detail about her visit to the ranch. She seems to place the time in the summer of 1878, and Cody states definitely that his sisters, Helen and May, came down from Denver to visit him that summer. She enlarges the ranch so much that it touches the Dakota line (it did not, of course, for all of huge Cherry County lay between the North-Cody range and the South Dakota border) but otherwise gives a plausible enough account of the trip.[21]

It is possible that Lottie and Helen are describing the same trip, for there are points of similarity, although Lottie does not mention Helen and May when she names the others in the party.

Luther North gives a brief account of another trip to the North-Cody ranch: "In the spring of 1880 Cody and his family came up to the . . . ranch . . . where a roundup was about to take place. One of the diversions was target shooting at fifty yards with rifles. Mrs. Timothy Coolidge . . . shot three times offhand and made three bull's-eyes with one of Cody's Winchesters. None of the men (Cody himself, Jason Backus, a market hunter, and John Hancock, an ex-buffalo hide hunter and cowboy) did as well. Anyone who could beat them was surely a crack shot." Luther later married the lady.[22]

Two years later, in the summer of 1882, Cody and his partner sold the Dismal River ranch to John Bratt for $75,000.[23] It was a good time to sell, for the days of the open range were about over. Since there was no land involved, only cattle, horses, some log buildings, wagons and harness, the price was a good one and showed a handsome profit for the few years spent in the business. It is also quite likely that those few summers spent on the big roundups had much to do with the beginning of the Wild West show, which followed close on the dissolution of the ranch.

13

Cody's Home Town
1877–1878

The town in which Mrs. W. F. Cody settled down to make her home
for the next thirty-five years was still a hustling frontier village in 1878,
a village of modest homes and dirt streets, with a few planks thrown
across the muddiest intersections along Front Street in the spring. By
then there were several "laid out" streets, with shops and houses more
or less lined up along them. Front Street ran east and west, parallel
to the railroad tracks. Spruce Street (now Dewey) stretched south from
the depot for some three blocks. Locust (now Jeffers), a block west of
Spruce, was the laid-out railroad crossing, but the townspeople crossed
the railroad right of way wherever they had a mind to.

There were few houses north of the tracks, and no trees anywhere
in the town, nor lawns or flowers in summer. A few of the homes, the
Barton house, the Dillon and Watts houses, and Mrs. Cody's new home
were a bit more pretentious than the rest, with picket fences to keep
wandering livestock out of the yards. Beyond Locust Street a few
houses sprawled west toward the mess halls, officers' quarters, barns,
and corrals that made up the barracks.

Three blocks south of the depot, between Locust and Spruce, the
two-story courthouse, topped by a tall, many-windowed cupola, loomed
impressively. Across the street to the east, on the corner of Fourth and
Spruce Streets, the high, narrow, new two-story schoolhouse reared its
twenty-foot belfry above the level prairie. Here Arta and Orra Cody
went to school for a few years. The previous November a fifteen-minute
earthquake, an extremely rare phenomenon in Nebraska, extending all
along the Union Pacific from Cheyenne to Omaha, had cracked the
lofty brick walls of the schoolhouse and frightened everybody in town.[1]

The damage was repaired by encircling the building with iron rods, but on days of high winds the walls vibrated so much that school was dismissed. Southwest of the schoolhouse and courthouse the open prairie spread away toward the river, providing an inviting space for wandering bands of Indians to camp for a few days every now and then.

Front Street, facing the railroad tracks, was lined with saloons, barber shops, blacksmith shops, and livery stables. Lined up on either side of Locust Street were grocery stores, the post office, Charles Mc-Donald's General Merchandise emporium, the McLucas jewelry, drug, and liquor store, a newspaper office, and the two-story McDonald residence. On Spruce Street and elsewhere about the town were four meat markets: Bratt's, Haight and Bogue's, Keith and Barton's, and Maggie Cohen's, the latter furnished with a meat block of solid oak weighing more than 1,200 pounds. There were two merchant tailors, A. O. Kocken and A. P. Carlson, two boot and shoemakers, Theodore Eirdam and John Neary, the latter an "anatomical shoemaker." Both made many a pair of fancy boots for Buffalo Bill.

Belton's hardware store advertised furniture, dishes, tools, machinery, lightning rods, pumps, chamber sets, tin ware, mattresses, etc., etc. Foley & Senter operated another big general store, the Star Clothing House, sold men's wear, and, in season, advertised "Star's medicated winter underwear." The Ladies Dry Goods Bazaar and Mrs. Gilman's Dry Goods Emporium supplied clothing, yard goods, and accessories for other members of the family. Blankenburg sold harnesses and saddles and made many of both for Cody's Wild West show; William J. Patterson built wagons, buggies, and rigs of all kinds. The Peale brothers, Ed and Frank, relatives of the noted Titian Peale, painted just about anything that needed or could be painted: railroad locomotives, wagons, buggies, houses. Charles Iddings operated a thriving lumber and coal establishment. A dozen doctors and lawyers attended to the medical and legal needs of the citizens. A Chinese laundry, just off Front Street on Spruce, thrived for a few years.

The foregoing is a cross section not only of North Platte as it was then but of most hopeful frontier towns of the period. As in other towns, barber shops, or "tonsorial parlors" as they were labeled, were numerous and often elegant. Early North Platte had half-a-dozen, and their individual popularity could be estimated at a glance by the size of the mug racks on their walls. When a local citizen or a traveling man who made regular stops had selected the parlor he preferred, he

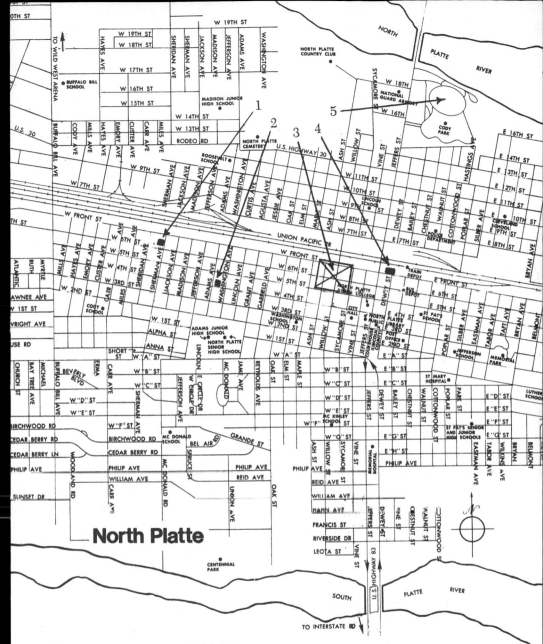

North Platte

Five locations important in Cody's life are
noted on a present-day map of North Platte:

 1 = first Welcome Wigwam
 2 = second Welcome Wigwam
 3 = army barracks
 4 = Union Pacific depot and hotel
 5 = Dillon race track

(Dewey Street was in Cody's day named
Spruce Street; present-day Jeffers Street was
Locust Street.)

deposited on the shop's rack his personal brush and mug, with his name lettered on the latter in gold.

Most of the mugs were lavishly decorated with the faces of pretty girls or the heads of horses, and the racks sometimes held extensive collections of art of this kind. The better shops sported decorative stuffed animals and birds, owls and eagles being the favorites, and offered an array of *Police Gazettes* with covers picturing ladies showing their stockings. The price of a haircut was twenty-five cents, a shave fifteen cents. Railroad men, drummers, land seekers, gamblers, and drifters made up a goodly portion of a barber shop's trade, and it was totally a man's domain.

Another feature of many tonsorial parlors was the public bathtub. One North Platte shop had five tubs. Bath water was heated on a coal oil stove in the "bathroom," and the used water ran through a drain pipe into the alley behind the shop. Freighters and men off the long cow trails, after many days on the road, made the barber shop-bath house their first stop in town. Often the man—bathed, barbered, and shaved—who sauntered out the door was scarcely recognizable as the one who had gone in, hidden beneath long hair, long whiskers, and many layers of dust and sweat.

The better shops advertised in the local papers. L. C. Boyer's Tonsorial Parlor boasted the "handsomest barber rooms in North Platte, the best three-chair shop in Nebraska, with two first-class artists in attendance." The Eureka Shaving Saloon, H. E. Cady, Prop., included a picture of its fancy lay-out, mug rack and all, in its advertisement; and in large letters Ottenstein's big shop advertised "Schampoos."

No one has left us the name of Buffalo Bill's favorite barbershop, if he had one. Quite likely he patronized any "parlors" that did good work, for he was particular, especially of his long hair. Years later, Edd Weeks, a classmate of Cody's youngest daughter, Irma, said: "It was a treat to see Buffalo Bill come into a chair with his hair folded up under his big hat, the way he usually wore it. It was sure interesting to see those barbers take the pins out of his hair. He wore more pins than any three women. His hair was very dark but was streaked with grey, and he was very proud of it."[2]

William Maloney, later a prominent North Platte businessman, related: "I first saw Buffalo Bill when he came into a barber shop on Front Street for a shoe shine. The colored shoeshine boy was out, and the proprietor told him, 'Here's a boy who can shine 'em for you.' So I said I'd try, and I did the job and Mr. Cody paid me fifty cents. Ten cents was the going price."[3]

Saloons were probably more numerous than any other kind of business in North Platte. There were at least seven on the three main streets of the town, and both drug stores and the general stores also sold liquor and wine. If half the stories told of Buffalo Bill and his drinking are true, he must have patronized all of them, although only a few are mentioned with any frequency by those who knew him. One belonged to Guy Laing, his rancher friend; it was a highly popular Front Street place, directly across from the depot.

Johnny Dugan, born in North Platte in 1868, said that when Cody came out of Laing's and got on his white horse, he and the other boys followed him everywhere he went in town. Telling of this in his old age, Johnny said proudly, "I have a picture of him that I got with tags or stamps from the Newsboy Tobacco Company. They used to put out pictures of actors and actresses, and you sent the tags to New York to get the pictures."[4]

There are several accounts of the large pictures of Cody that adorned two other one-time North Platte saloons, Charles Whalen's and Luke Healey's. Whalen, born in 1870, came to town as a young man and bought a saloon. "I had a fine big picture of Cody in my saloon on Front Street," he said, "but I forgot to take it when I sold the place to the Dugans."[5] Johnny confirmed that the picture was there when he and his brother, Jimmy, bought Whalen out. "But it was not an oil painting, as some say. It was an enlarged photograph and was a very fine picture of Cody in his younger days, with long curly hair and slightly bald above the temples."[6]

John Dick, born in North Platte in 1875, said: "Because Luke Healey was a friend of Buffalo Bill's, he had Cody's picture painted up in his saloon, but it was finally forgotten."[7] Another old-timer, Chancy Rogers, remembered that there used to be a beautiful picture of Buffalo Bill in Healey's saloon. "It took up about the whole wall and was painted right on the plaster. Luke used to be sheriff of Lincoln County, and he ran about the most orderly saloon that has ever been in this town."[8] Martin Federhoof also spoke of the big picture: "Mrs. George Minor was the artist and a damn good one. She went to Europe to study. There is an archway now, where the picture was, and I could show you some of the picture by peeling some paint off the wall."[9]

In addition to the liquor dispensers listed above, Adamson records the existence on the fringes of town of "brothels, gambling dens and unlicensed saloons that ran wide open all days of the week and hours

of the night." He also writes of Tucker's place, a notorious saloon on
the corner of Spruce and Sixth Streets, one block south of Front Street,
"much patronized by gamblers and questionable characters of both
sexes. Cowboys would ride long distances to have a 'good time' at
North Platte. They were a frolicsome lot . . . and it was not uncommon
for one or more to ride into a saloon, order drinks and in wild glee shoot
out the lights; or ride at a furious pace through the town, whooping
and yelling and shooting. Then, many a man died with his boots on,
and it was a question whether the law abiding feared white men or
Indians the most"[10]

During North Platte's first decade or so it had rival newspapers,
sometimes as many as three, all publishing at the same time and the
editor of each soundly castigating the others in almost every issue. On
one subject, however, they all agreed: something should be done about
the condition of the streets and alleys in the town, for as yet there were
no sidewalks except for the aforementioned intersection planks and
two brief stretches of boardwalk, one in front of the Nebraska House,
the other in front of Eirdam's shoe shop.

The streets were bad enough: ankle-deep in dry, choking dust in
summer, while four-horse teams could scarcely pull empty wagons
through the hub-deep mud in the season of melting snows and spring
rains; and ducks and mud hens swam in the sloughs interspersed about
the town. But the alleys were worse, and the papers frequently called
attention to their filth, especially during the first warm days of spring.

While the *Enterprise* pointedly requested "the gentleman who owned
the dog that died near this office to be kind enough to remove same,"
the *Republican* was observing: 'The hog in the alley back of this office
has now been dead for several months," or "the foulness of the air
caused by dead animals in and around the town [makes it] smell like
an 'offal' place," or "Old hoop skirts, wornout corsets, shoes, dirty socks,
old hats and underwear, tons of tin cans and old whiskey bottles, a half
ton of gunny sacks, 17 dead dogs, 1 horse, 3 cows and a bull, 7 hogs
and 11 pigs, one barrel spoilt pickles, about a thousand pounds of
sauerkraut and 7 boxes of rotten eggs compose a tithe of the nastiness,
rubbish and filth found in the alley in the rear of Front Street." After a
wet spell one July, the *Nebraskian* called attention to the "two greatest
nuisances in town, . . . the terribly muddy streets and a quacking
guinea hen." The editor recommended filling up the one and wringing
the neck of the other.

But life in the little town had its more pleasant side, too. As has been
mentioned before, horse racing was a highly popular sport in the valley.

The merchant, A. J. Miller, owned a number of fine trotters; so did Isaac Dillon and M. C. Keith. The whole town turned out for races, some of which were quite elite social affairs. Of course there were dinners, dances, and parties in the homes, or in the big Union Pacific hotel dining room if the gathering was too large for the family parlor.

By the time the Codys came to North Platte to make their home, Dr. Dick had installed a "beautiful silver-plated soda fountain" in his drug store at a cost of $200. There, at the elegant little tables with their twisted wire legs, both sexes and all ages could enjoy cooling beverages in the scented dimness of the long room. That the town, barely out of its swaddling clothes, stood on correct social procedure is attested to by Mrs. Thomas Patterson, wife of one of the attorneys, who said, "All social calls had to be made on a certain day, else there would be envy and some would say that 'so and so called on so and so before she did me.' "[11]

And when Buffalo Bill was in town, as one old-timer said, there was always something doing. Late that August, when he spent a few days at home before leaving for the East, the prime pastime was target shooting. On August 24, 1878, the *Nebraskian* reported that Mr. Cody had done some very fancy and difficult shooting at his place. There followed the first mention of Cody's shooting at glass balls, then the paper went on to say that upon running out of glass balls he "shot most of the potatoes from his garden on the fly. He intends to shoot glass balls on the stage when he starts his new season, and after more practice hopes to shoot against Dr. Carver." In the spring, Dr. Carver, called the "greatest of all living riflemen," had given a very fancy shooting exhibition in Omaha.[12]

Before he left for the East, Cody gave Dave Perry, a Front Street saloon keeper, a fine rifle. The rifle had been made for Cody by Frank Weston of Worcester, Massachusetts, and with it he had won numerous shooting matches in Maine and other eastern states.

Cody engaged Eddie and Charlie Burgess, North Platte brothers, to act in his new show. Eddie was to be the "Boy Chief," for he knew a great deal about Indians and had done some interpreting.[13]

The *Nebraskian* also mentioned that Mr. Cody owned a stallion, "Silver Clay," that had taken two premiums at a fair in Jefferson County, Kansas, and that the stallion was to be brought to North Platte the next year. This was evidence that Buffalo Bill was already planning the show place he meant to develop at North Platte, the show place with the handsomest house, the biggest barns, the finest blooded livestock in the country.

14

Plays, Real Estate, Rodeo 1878-1882

With the Burgess brothers as interpreters as well as actors, Cody hired a band of Pawnee Indians for his 1878-79 Combination and opened the season in Baltimore with the largest troupe he had ever put on the road. From Baltimore the show went to Washington D. C., and then south to Richmond and Savannah. When an outbreak of yellow fever turned them back, he headed his troupe for Philadelphia and the northeast.

Later in the season he had Colonel Prentiss Ingraham, well-known author and dramatist, write a play for him. The new drama, "The Knight of the Plains; or, Buffalo Bill's Best Trail," opened in New Haven and was an instant success. It was probably little, if any, better than its predecessors, and discriminating critics called it third-rate, sickly, even vile, but admitted that Cody himself was splendid in his part. Indeed, it seemed that Buffalo Bill in person was all that was needed to draw a full to overflowing house.

The play was so successful that Cody decided to take his troupe to California again, and did so early in 1879. At the close of his prosperous tour in the West, the *Western Nebraskian* of May 10 observed: "The Honorable W. F. Cody returned from California last Tuesday and was gladly greeted by his many friends." Three weeks later the North Platte *Republican* noted that Cody had ridden about town disguised in one of his stage costumes.

Following his little joke, Bill joined the spring cattle roundup, then in progress, returning to North Platte about the middle of June.[1] On the twenty-eighth, according to the *Republican, The Life of Hon.*

William F. Cody, Known as Buffalo Bill, the Famous Hunter, Scout and Guide: An Autobiography was just off the press, and the newspaper editor, James M. Ray, promised he would review it for his readers just as soon as he had time to read it himself.

Previous to the publication of his autobiography, Cody, pressed by the editors of the *New York Weekly*, the *Saturday Journal*, *Saturday Evening Post*, *Beadle's Half-Dime Library*, *Pocket Library*, and perhaps others, had written or at least signed several vivid stories about life on the frontier. There had also been the three book-length serials by Judson purporting to tell the adventures of Buffalo Bill, and the play written by Colonel Ingraham, who was also in the process of writing a serial, "Buffalo Bill, the Buckskin King," for the *Saturday Journal*.[2]

Cody's autobiography was published by Francis Edgar Bliss of the American Publishing Company of Hartford, Connecticut. It sold for $2.00 in cloth and $2.50 in leather.[3] Whether or not the author was in North Platte when the books arrived is not known, but that it excited the citizens of his home town is evident from reports in the local papers. For, true to his promise, editor Ray on July 12 published a long and highly favorable review in which he wrote, in part: Cody's "exploits as mule driver, Pony Express rider, hunter, trapper, soldier, scout, legislator and actor read more like fiction than reality, so many are the incidents and so rapidly do they crowd one upon another. . . . Buffalo Bill's life has been varied, exciting, fascinating and successful; his book . . . is just like him." The editor added that "Miss Arta Cody is canvassing the city to sell the book, a work which will meet with a ready sale wherever offered." Miss Arta was thirteen years old at that time but reputed to be a beautiful and well-matured girl at that age.

Bill Cody did not stay in town long, if he was there at all, for less than two weeks later he and his Combination were in Denver, playing to sell-out crowds, according to the *Republican* of July 26, which reported, "Buffalo Bill's show in Denver is a great success. Every inch of space was sold out and the aisles packed in spite of the heat." From Denver he went on to Cheyenne, where he made his "debut on August 2 and 3 in a double bill entitled *May Cody; or, Lost and Won*, and *Knights of the Plains; or, Buffalo Bill's Best Trail*."[4] Shortly afterward, he was back in North Platte making plans to organize yet another Combination and had sent an agent to Omaha to secure Indians for the 1879-80 season.

Two other *Republican* items of that 1879 August are of interest. During the week of August 9, Johnny Baker and some other boys

gathered wild grapes on the islands in the Platte River east of the railroad bridge. The boys had "hooked" a ride across the bridge on a departing freight huffing its way out of the yards. With the bridge so
near, trains did not pick up speed until after crossing the river. By the
same token, trains approaching from the east slowed down to a crawl
before rolling onto the bridge and whistling into town.

For this reason the town boys often caught rides to the east end of
the bridge, dropping off as the trains began to roll faster. After fooling
around awhile, swimming, hunting arrowheads, picking wild grapes,
they rode home on westbound freights. But this time Johnny, hampered
by the bag of grapes he carried, slipped and fell beside the track. A
wheel caught his foot and sliced off a portion of one heel. While the
wound was not serious, it was bloody, and all the boys were badly
frightened. A buggy, headed for the bridge, soon came along and took
Johnny to town, where doctors Longley and Dick trimmed up his foot
and saved most of it.

The same issue of the paper reported that a large number of friends
of the Cody girls enjoyed a birthday party at the Cody residence on
Wednesday. The birthday was Orra's; she was seven years old that day.
The paper does not state whether or not Buffalo Bill was on hand for
the party. As much as he loved children and all their activities, he was
surely there if it was at all possible.

That the Cody home was a popular gathering place for the townspeople, especially when Buffalo Bill was there, is evident from a statement made by Mary Sullivan Roddy: "The Codys used to have lots of
company in their house west of town, and parties. There wasn't any
cab service or buses or anything then, and my father, Patrick Sullivan,
the night switch engineer, used to run the engine up there to take
people to the parties, and when Cody was at home they flew a flag on
a tall flag pole in the front yard. As soon as he'd get home they ran up
the flag so his friends would know he was in town."[5]

For three more seasons W. F. Cody toured the East with his Combi-
ination, coining money as he played out his "soul-stirring, blood-curdl-
ing" dramas before packed houses. For, in addition to his ever-popular
Indians, he and his friends included some spectacular shooting exhibitions among the attractions offered on the stage.

At the close of his very successful season of 1881-82, Buffalo Bill returned to North Platte before the middle of June. That the homecoming
may not have been a happy one as far as family relations were concerned is indicated by a letter he wrote his sister Julia from Albany on

March 9; he asserts indignantly that he is "in a peck of trouble" because Lulu had gotten most of the North Platte property into her own name.[6]

Since his initial investment in Lincoln County real estate in 1878, Cody had been putting the profits from his show and cattle business into more and more land. William McDonald claims that Buffalo Bill frequently sent his father, banker Charles McDonald, money for the purchase of land to build up the ranch north of the tracks.[7] Mrs. Cody states in her *Memories*: "I added to his ranch, and attended to the thousand and one details of farming life that must be looked after, while he was away on the stage."[8] Cody, in his letter to Julia, wrote: "I have been sending money to her [Lulu] for the last five years to buy property, not dreaming but what she was buying it in my name. . . . I don't care a snap for the money, but the way she has treated me. My beautiful house. I have none to go to. Al and I will have to build another. I can't write more—to day."[9]

That Louisa was a shrewd businesswoman has been well proven, and not the least of her acumen is the fact that she did put the property she bought in her own name, for by this time she was well aware of her husband's impulsive generosity and his speculative tendencies. Accordingly, with the money Will sent her she purchased tracts of land in and around the town, and the North Platte *Telegraph* for April 14, 1881, reported that "Mrs. Cody is planning to erect several buildings soon."

Another reason why Louisa was careful to put all the property in her own name was that Will had for some time now been talking about and getting involved in a lawsuit over $15 million worth of property in the heart of Cleveland. On behalf of his sisters and himself he was suing for their rights in the land, which had once belonged to his grandfather. The suit would be expensive, and Cody was the only one to foot the bills. Although her husband was highly optimistic over the outcome, Lulu had no faith in his chances for success, and so put as much of the North Platte property out of his reach as possible.[10]

At the time Cody wrote his angry letter of protest, Julia and her husband, Al Goodman, were living in Valley Falls, Kansas, but all that winter he had been urging them to move to North Platte and take over the management of his ranch. A week later Bill wrote his brother-in-law, detailing plans he had made for Al to drive a hundred head of mares from Kansas to the ranch on the North Platte, where he was to settle in as manager.

On April 29, the last day of his current theatrical season, Will again wrote to Julia, who was still in Kansas, advising her that he would be home about the twelfth of May, after a trip to Cleveland to see about the lawsuit. That his quarrel with Lulu was by now full blown is shown by his statement to his sister: "I hear from Al [in North Platte] regular. He does all the writeing now Lulu has quit writing to me altogether."[11]

Several of Cody's biographers have written of his estrangement from his wife at this time and have intimated that it was of a permanent nature, and certainly his letter shows that he was very much put out with her. But he was not of a disposition to hold a grudge or hard feelings for long, and he loved his children very much. So, in spite of his declaration that he had no home to go to, he must have gone to Welcome Wigwam that summer, for his youngest daughter was born the following February, and he was on good terms with Lulu, or at least staying at home, the next spring before taking his first Wild West show on the road.

Bill's return to North Platte that summer was important for still another reason: it signaled the event that would reshape the rest of his life. At that period in our national history, and for a good many years to come, the birthday of our Republic was, along with Thanksgiving and Christmas, the most celebrated day of the year. Plans for its observance were usually made well in advance, and each year almost any given community tried to outdo all surrounding communities, as well as its own celebration of the year before, in observance of the day.

There are varying stories concerning the celebration planned for North Platte, that summer of 1882. Some say the town hadn't gotten around to making any definite plans for the Fourth before the Honorable W. F. Cody came home for the summer. Others say plans were already under way to do something big for the occasion but that the planners were waiting until Cody arrived to help them decide just what to do.

William McDonald, just turned twenty-one in June 1882, has probably told his version the most often. Nearly sixty years after that historic Fourth of July, he told the story that the town had been planning to celebrate the occasion with some horse races, but "that wasn't enough to suit Cody," who wanted to put on "something big," or try to. "They had sixteen buffalo down on the 'points' between the rivers," McDonald said, "and Cody rounded them up and put on an exhibition of riding them. And that was the beginning of his Wild West show."[12]

Twelve years later, when he was past ninety, McDonald remembered the story somewhat differently. He recalled that upon his return to

North Platte at the close of his stage season, Cody joined a group of men in Foley's store and asked what kind of a celebration was shaping up for the Fourth. When told there seemed to be little interest that year and nothing special had been planned, Cody said, "Oh, we ought to be more patriotic than that."

"In that case, you're nominated chairman of arrangements," one of the group promptly challenged Cody, who just as promptly replied, "I'll take it."

McDonald remembered Cody's taking him aside and saying, "I want to try something that's never been seen before. I want to show folks how we rope and run and tend cattle. Then I'll stage an imitation buffalo hunt and show them how I used to hunt and shoot buffalo. If it's a success, I'm going to call it Buffalo Bill's Wild West Show and Congress of Rough Riders."[13]

McDonald was partially anticipating developments by a full decade, for the last half of the famous title was not used until more than ten years later. It was true that many townspeople, even in the eighties, had never seen cowboys rope, brand, and handle cattle, but out in the ranch country local racing, roping, and bucking contests were regular Sunday affairs, where the "boys" gathered at one ranch or another to try their skills "just for the fun of it": to see who owned the fastest horse, or who could rope, throw, and tie a steer the quickest, or who could ride the toughest bucking broncs.

So Cody's idea had a good deal of merit, and a curious combination of events made it possible for him and his friends to put together an unusual program in time for the Fourth of July. To begin with, Bill knew that the big western Nebraska spring roundup would be pulling in on the long flat north of the river for its annual breakup of wagons and crews—the last time the outfits would so assemble, for with the year 1882 the big open-range roundups in Nebraska passed into history. There, within three miles of town, a score or more of wagons, some 200 cowboys, and 2,000 head of horses would be shedding the dust of hundreds of miles of range country by the end of June.

The site for the big show was also ready-made, for Isaac Dillon, nephew of Sidney Dillon, Union Pacific president, owned a private race track a little way north of the depot. His track was a good one, half-a-mile long and fenced all around with a stout six-foot solid board fence, and he was glad to put it at Cody's disposal for the day. Free-ranging buffalo herds were a thing of the past, of course, but a few animals were still available. The number ranges all the way from five to sixteen.

Some informants say they all belonged to M. C. Keith and were grazing that summer down at "the points," between the forks of the river. Others say they belonged to Cody, who kept them in the "park" he was developing at his ranch north of town. At any rate, Cody planned to use them and to gather a small herd of wild longhorn steers from ranges thereabouts.

Even though most of the men and horses from the great range country were to be camped at the town's back door in time for the Fourth, Cody wanted to make sure that every possible contestant and every family within a hundred miles or more knew about the big celebration. Well aware of the value of advertising in show business, he had the following announcement printed in the *Telegraph* for June 15, 1882:

4TH OF JULY CELEBRATION

ATTENTION ALL

All parties interested in a general celebration of the 4th of July in this city are requested to attend a meeting at the courthouse on the 17th at 8 P.M., for the purpose of arranging a program. By the request of I. Dillon, W. F. Cody, Anth. Ries, L. Eells, M. C. Keith, A. J. Miller, C. F. Groner, Chas. McDonald and others.

Out of his town meeting came the plan to print thousands of handbills and distribute them all the way to the state's borders, advertising the big free celebration—and something new, prizes in merchandise and cash to be awarded the winners of the races and other contests. No doubt Cody put up many of the prizes himself, but unfortunately, so far as is known today, almost a century after that first exciting rodeo,[41] not a single handbill survives to tell us anything more about it, and neither is there a known copy of any North Platte newspaper for the month of July 1882. All we have is a copy of the Omaha *Daily Bee* for July 7, which carried a most enthusiastic account of the day:

NORTH PLATTE

THE NATION'S HOLIDAY CELEBRATED

AT A LIVE AND ENERGETIC TOWN

A special reporter of the *Bee* left Omaha on the 3rd of July for North Platte, one of the most live and energetic towns on the U. P., arriving there on the morning of the Fourth.

The place was found alive to the importance of the occasion, and in full trim to celebrate the nation's anniversary.

At 10:30 there was a regular street parade, the programme having been duly arranged beforehand. The procession was a fine one, including the band, the G. A. R., a number of Sunday-school children, and a long line of citizens and visitors in carriages.

Hon. W. F. Cody acted as marshal of the day, ably assisted by Mr. Con Groner, the well-known sheriff of this county.

Mr. Cody was resplendent in a suit of white corduroy pants, black velvet coat of military cut, etc., and was strikingly handsome.

The procession was marched to the race track, . . . and a regular programme of speaking and singing was gone through with.

Following this came a most interesting feature of the day. Hon. M. C. Keith had four or five buffalo, one with a calf, which he turned loose and one of the boys lassoed and rode an animal for which he received $25. After this a Texas steer was turned loose, which was also lassoed and ridden to its great disgust.

In the afternoon there were trotting and running races, the horses entered being those of Messrs. J. S. Mitler, M. C. Keith, Ike Dillon and W. F. Cody. There were also running races of one hundred, three hundred and six hundred yards and a half mile race.

At night there was a fine display of fireworks and the G. A. R. ball, both of which were largely attended.

Notwithstanding the immense crowd, the utmost order and quiet prevailed, and not a single occurrence to mar the pleasure of the occasion was noted.

In the meantime, the roundup had pulled in on time and gone into camp north of the river. Other contestants from distant points began to arrive, and for two or three days before the Fourth the town was a lively place, with cowboys whooping it up in the streets and saloons and spending their wages as if there would be no tomorrow. By the third, wagons were plodding into town from all directions, bringing settlers from outlying farms and ranches, and tents were blossoming on the prairie all around.

Contemporary accounts of the events that took place inside the race-track arena on the afternoon of the Fourth are somewhat divergent. A. B. Snyder, ten-and-one-half years old at the time, rode up on the train with his older brother John from Maxwell, the village thirteen miles east, arriving a little before noon, too late for the parade. After a lunch of sardines and crackers, eaten while seated on bales of hay beside one of the livery stables, they walked from town to the Dillon place—across plank footbridges that spanned wide sloughs[15]—and joined the steadily growing crowd inside the arena. Snyder's story:

A little while ahead of the show Cody had some of the cowboys drive the buffalo, longhorns, and wild horses inside the fence, where they held them in one end of the long pen. The people stayed in the other end. There wasn't any seats for the people, nor a chute or anything for saddling or handling the stock. Cody wore a fancy outfit and rode a fine big bay horse, and went around shaking hands with everybody and making folks welcome. Every now and then he'd ride across the tracks to Guy Laing's saloon, and every time he came back he was a little jollier and his horse was stepping a little higher. When it was time for the show to start, he made a nice speech, telling the crowd what he was going to do and hoping they'd like it.

When Cody gave the signal to start, some of the cowboys rode into the bunch of scared wild stock and cut out a buffalo. They hazed him into the open section of the track, where everybody could see, and another cowboy lit out after him and roped, busted, and tied him. The boys roped and tied several steers and buffaloes, and then a small cowboy named West roped a big buffalo bull. The horse, a mighty fast little bay, stopped as soon as the loop sailed over the buffalo's head, but when that bull, scared and running like sixty, hit the end of the rope he popped it like a twine string and went right on. West hadn't even had time to jump off his horse, so he spurred the little bay and overtook the bull in about nothing flat. When he was even with it, he leaned over, got both hands full of buffalo mane, and slid off onto the old fellow's back. Then Nigger Johnson, one of Bratt's best cowboys, took a hand in the fun and loped out and jumped on behind West. That poor old spooked buffalo was doing some plain and fancy bucking and grunting, and everybody was having a big time, until he spun around and headed straight for the crowd. The ladies went to screaming, and the whole crowd was scattering like buckshot by the time some of the riders got there and hazed the buffalo the other way.

Everybody had fun at the show, Cody most of all, and it was such a success that he decided right then that a Wild West show would be a money maker. He went ahead that same year to put together the show that opened in Omaha the next May, and that went on to become the world famous Wild West Show and Congress of Rough Riders.[16]

Burr Murphy, whose father had settled near Brady, twenty-two miles east of North Platte, in the seventies, was a sixteen-year-old participant in the celebration. "Cody was magnificently attired," he wrote. "His boots, high and carved, were worth $125.00, the gift of a shoemaker in North Platte. He wore golden spurs which Duke Alexis presented him at the time he conducted the Duke on a buffalo hunt. He removed his big hat with a sweeping flourish and addressed the crowd, saying, 'If you'll all keep sober until four o'clock, then we'll all get drunk together.'" Murphy has a different version of the buffalo incident:

> I entered the buffalo roping contest with 18 others. One buffalo was loosed and all the riders together had to ride after it and rope and ride him. The first prize was $50 and the second $25. Three ropes descended on the buffalo's head. The first rope belonged to Oscar Moncey, a bad man from Sidney, the second to myself and the third to Henry Johnson, Mr. Keith's big nigger. Moncey's horse stumbled and he lost his chance to ride the buffalo. I slid onto his back and the nigger slid on behind me. So we got the two prizes.[17]

It was this double ride of a buffalo (although the next narrator says the animal was a steer) that seemed to stand out in the memories of these men when they recalled the celebration many years later. Erwin Bostwick, who had cowboyed in Nebraska since 1878, said he was on the big 1882 roundup and had "worked down to the points" with his outfit when he learned about the big doings. As he tells it, it was "Oscar Wilds who ran up and grabbed a steer, and Henry Johnson got hold of the steer by the tail and pulled himself up behind Oscar."[18]

George Macomber, another old-timer, said he saw Buck Taylor ride the buffalo at Dillon's race track that day, but does not mention a second rider.[19] Two other old-timers remembered the show this way, "Buffalo Bill had a cowboy riding a *saddled* buffalo bull. He was doing all right, too, when Nigger Jim spurred out and jumped on behind him." Memory must have been playing them tricks in recalling that the buffalo was saddled, even as it did in calling the Negro "Jim." Nigger Jim was another black altogether, Jim Kelly, who worked for Print Olive on his Loup River ranches.[20]

There are other variations in the story, told by men who were there but whose memories had grown dim with the years, or who, perhaps, confused that Fourth with other festivals of the early days. Snyder says there were neither grandstand seats nor shade of any kind, that the crowd sat or stood on the ground in one end of the enclosure. But Johnny Dugan, six or seven years old at the time, remembered a brush shelter and a few plank seats.[21] Murphy writes that Buffalo Bill led the contestants, of which he was one, on horseback to "the space before the grandstand" and faced the spectators to make his speech.

Snyder indicates that the only function of the steers and buffalo was to be roped, thrown, and tied by the cowboys. This was probably correct, for bulldogging and steer or bull riding is a practice of modern rodeos. So the buffalo-riding incident of that first rodeo was doubtless a whim of the moment, a stunt pulled by lighthearted cowboys on holiday.

McDonald said that Cody told him he was going to have some Indians in the celebration, for "I can get them and no one else can."[22] Sell and Weybright, in their *Buffalo Bill and the Wild West*, also mention Indians, as well as the holdup of a stagecoach, in the 1882 show, and state that Cody hired the Indians and bought the old stagecoach especially for that local show. No one else mentions either the Indians or the coach, and it is highly unlikely that either came on the scene until the next year, when it is known that Cody had both for his premier in Omaha.

Snyder and his brother went back to Maxwell on the evening train, so had no part in the evening's festivities; but Murphy wrote: "That night the town grew wild. Buffalo Bill threw down a handful of twenty dollar gold pieces on Tucker's bar[23] and said, 'Give the boys a good time.' There was shooting, but I was only sixteen years old, the youngster looking on. I stepped into the hotel and Oscar Moncey, mad, or showing off because he lost the prize money, fired each side of me until the sheriff relieved him of his guns." The *Bee* reporter must have been elsewhere at this time, or perhaps Murphy has confused the occasion with some other time. Murphy concludes his story of the celebration with a statement guaranteed to demonstrate that memory does play tricks on reminiscences: "The next year Buffalo Bill Cody was introduced to the stage by Ned Buntline." By then Cody had been on the stage for the past ten years, and his association with Buntline had been over for almost as long.

15
Where the Wild West Begins 1882 1883

Most writers and informants agree that the success of his Fourth of July show triggered the formation of the Wild West show W. F. Cody put on the road the next year. The idea for such shows was not new, however, and had even been tried before, on a smaller scale, but none had succeeded. Nate Salsbury, later Cody's partner in the show, claimed he had considered such a show as early as 1876, but had not tried to put it into operation. He says he had even decided that the entertainment he had in mind must have a well known "figurehead" to attract attention and had resolved to get Buffalo Bill as his central figure.[1]

Cody writes that he was the one who "approached" Salsbury with a proposition to join him as an equal partner.[2] Russell says the two had met in New York in 1882 and talked about a show of the Wild West type, and that Salsbury said he had "unfolded" the plan for the show to Cody, who grew very enthusiastic over it. But, as neither then had the money to "do the thing right," they agreed to defer putting the idea into operation for awhile.[3]

Several of the people who saw the show in North Platte on the Fourth have left recorded statements that Bill said, that day, he was going to put on the road next year a show like the one they had just seen, only bigger. In his own book, Cody strangely says nothing about the Fourth celebration. Bill Sweeney had been a drummer in the military band at Fort McPherson in its early days and later had taken up the cornet and become head musician in the band. When the post was abandoned in 1880, he settled in or near North Platte. After the Fourth of July show, when he heard Cody talking about putting together a wild west road show, Sweeney told him he would help out by organizing a cowboy band to go with it.[4]

Bill McDonald says that immediately after the Fourth, Cody told his brother-in-law, Al Goodman, to start buying wild horses for the show.[5] By this time Julia had joined her husband in North Platte, but Cody was unable to persuade them to stay and take charge of his ranch. Instead, they went back to Kansas soon afterward and did not return to North Platte to live until two years later. Even so, it is possible that before he left, Al did buy some horses for the proposed show.

One writer relates: "Old man M. C. Keetin [sic], one of our leading citizens, had just got together the last herd of buffalo that was ever raised near North Platte. He valued them above rubies, of course. . . . So as soon as we heard the government was going to buy them for breeding purposes, all the cowboys decided to have a farewell little round-up on Ike Dillon's ranch." After the Fourth, "Keetin turned to Bill Cody and said: 'Say Bill, I'd rather sell the buffalo to you than to the government. Why dont' you buy 'em, take 'em east with a lot of the boys and show the tenderfeet a real western show in the open air?' "[6]

Cooper, of course, has Louisa telling how, one evening in their big living room in North Platte, he told her of his plan to take the West to the East on railroad trains: Indians, horses, cowboys, buffalo, stage coach; they'd take it all and put on a show such as had never been seen in the East before.[7]

In his autobiography, Cody writes:

When the season of 1882-83 closed I found myself richer by several thousand dollars than I had ever been before, having done a splendid business at every place where my performance was given in that year. Immense success and comparative wealth, attained in the profession of showman, stimulated me to greater exertion and largely increased my ambition for public favor. Accordingly, I conceived the idea of organizing a large company of Indians, cow-boys, Mexican vaqueros, famous riders and expert lasso throwers, with accessories of stage coach, emigrant wagons, bucking horses and a herd of buffaloes, with which to give a realistic entertainment of wild life on the plains. To accomplish this purpose, which in many respects was a really herculean undertaking, I sent agents to various points in the far West to engage Indians from several different tribes, and then set about the more difficult enterprise of capturing a herd of buffaloes. After several months of patient work I secured the services of nearly fifty cow-boys and Mexicans skilled in lasso-throwing and famous as daring riders, but when these were engaged and several buffaloes, elk and mountain sheep were obtained, I found all the difficulties had not yet been overcome, for such exhibitions as I had prepared to give could only be shown in large open-air enclosures, and these were not always to be rented, while those that I found suitable were often inaccessible by such popular conveyances as street cars. The expenses of such a show as I had determined to give were so great that a very large crowd must be drawn to every exhibition or a financial failure would be certain.[8]

Cody has here apparently condensed the preparations of nine or ten months into the short span of time between the close of his Combination in April 1883, and the first performance of the Wild West in mid-May, less than a month later. For while his friends and "agents" were engaged in collecting the livestock and equipment for the show he envisioned, Cody was touring the East with his new stage show, "Twenty Days; or, Buffalo Bill's Pledge." However successful the show proved to be by the close of the season in April, a letter written to Julia on February 3 has a distinctly doleful and discouraged tone: "Dear Sister, your letter rec'd. found me still playing in poor luck. Money is awful scarce."[9] He goes on to mention the Cleveland suit, still dragging through the courts, and that Arta does not write to him any more, nor even answer his letters. But affairs must have improved, for it is said the show that season cleared in the neighborhood of $50,000.

Cody's family relations must have also improved by the end of his show season, for he went to Welcome Wigwam upon his arrival in North Platte. He brought with him his friend Jule Keen who had played the part of Hans the Dutchman in the stage show; Keen was to stay on with Cody for many years as treasurer of the Wild West.

Charles Stamp, a member of the town band that played for the Fourth of July celebration the year before, remembers that the band was practicing at the courthouse when Buffalo Bill got into town, and two or three prominent citizens came in and asked them to go up and serenade Bill at his home. The bandsmen went over to the railroad yards, three blocks away, climbed aboard a caboose, and rode up to the Cody house. "Cody came out and invited us in," Stamp said, "and showed us to a long table set with eats, drinks and smokes. He showed us his collection of Indian relics, firearms, etc. Then he said, 'I've done well in this show, but I've got something now that when I come back I'll have a barrel of money.' Then he went upstairs and brought Irma, his baby, down to show her off."[10] Stamp especially remembered that night, for it was the first time he had tasted champagne, and unaware of its potency he drank too much—for the first and only time in his life.

The baby, Irma, was born on February 9, 1883, and it is hard to believe that Cody, with his great love for all children and especially his own, would not have gone straight home to see his youngest child at the earliest opportunity. Even so, he could not have been home very long, for it must have been late in April by the time he reached North Platte, and by mid-May he was on the road again.

Whether or not Cody had to borrow money to start his first Wild West show will probably never be known. If he did, he probably borrowed it at the McDonald bank. According to Bill McDonald, Charles McDonald loaned him money at the beginning of most of his Wild West seasons, but he does not say he did so that first year.

One account says Cody borrowed $4,000 but does not say where.[11] Dr. W. F. Carver, his partner that first season, makes the figure half that. Carver and Cody had met in New Haven while "The Prairie Waif" was showing there that winter and had agreed to form a partnership. Of that meeting Carver wrote that Cody came to his home "down and out. I told him I was getting ready to bring out the Wild West Show, and gave me his solemn promise not to drink another drop if I would take him outdoors with me, and I agreed to do so. The result was that I invested $27,000 in the enterprise, and signed a note with him on the First National Bank of Omaha for $2,000, all of which I had to pay."[12]

It is doubtful if Carver put much if any money into the show. Always a braggert, he was often broke, or nearly so. During his early years in Nebraska he moved about a good deal, from town to town, practicing his trade of dentistry. Charles Stamp remembered him as a short-time citizen of North Platte and said that when he left, "he raffled his pony off. I bought a chance for three dollars, but I didn't get the horse."[13]

After Carver became a crack shot, he seems to have spent more time arranging shooting matches, doubtless accompanied by side bets, than he did attending to teeth. He began to advertise himself as the "Champion Buffalo Hunter of the Plains," a title he first laid claim to back in 1873. He boasted he had killed "in the neighborhood of 30,000 buffaloes," a number that would indeed have made him the champion, for if one allows him all of 1872 and 1873, more time than he gives himself, he would have had to kill 1,250 buffalo per month, or more than 41 per day.[14]

It cannot be denied that Carver was a notable shot, but he was not as good as he says he was. So far as is known, Cody first met him in the summer of 1874, when the dentist accompanied the Thomas P. Medley hunting party, of which Cody was guide, for a few days. They may have met occasionally after that, but Carver was in Europe on an exhibition shooting tour at the time of the Fourth of July Wild West celebration in North Platte. And certainly Cody was not "down and out" when they met in New Haven the next year.

The dentist had gone into show business for himself, giving shooting exhibitions in various American and European cities, but seems not to have been too popular in such circles, for Cody, still hoping to draw Nate Salsbury into his new venture, failed to do so because of Dr. Carver. "I was astonished in the Spring of 1883," Salsbury wrote, "to get a telegram . . . asking me if I wanted to go into the show . . . if *Dr. Carver did not object.* Of course I was dumbfounded and replied that I did not want to have anything to do with Doctor Carver who was a fakir in the show business and as Cody once expressed it 'Went West on a piano stool.' "[15]

Neither did Carver come to North Platte to help put the show together, being too busy, he said, with his own affairs at the time. Cody, however, had a good deal of help, his friends being as enthusiastic as he was over trying out the new show. John Burke came out to head up the show's staff and take care of the preliminary arrangements: the advertising, posters, and bills; the traveling and show schedules; the plans for feeding and caring for the show's people and animals.

McDonald says that while Cody was still on the road with his Combination, the North brothers and Goodman began rehearsing the Wild West show. He is probably mistaken about Goodman, who was still in Kansas; but Major Frank North certainly helped, and Luther may have, although he was at that time farming near Colville (later named Columbus), Nebraska and in his book does not mention having any part in the show. In addition to North and Sweeney and the band, others who took part in that first show were Buck Taylor, John Y. Nelson, Con Groner, and some of the Bratt cowboys.

William Levi (Buck) Taylor, the Texan who came to Ogallala with the first Cody-North longhorn trail herd in 1877, had drifted to Cody's ranch on the Platte and was on hand for the Old Glory Blowout, as the 1882 Fourth of July celebration came to be called. The 6'5" Texan was billed as the cowboy who could throw a steer by the horns or tail and tie him singlehanded, pick up a handkerchief from the ground while riding a horse at full speed, and ride the worst bucking broncs.

John Y. Nelson was the squaw man Cody had first met at Fort Mc-Pherson. He had guided Brigham Young to Utah in 1847 and had been a scout at the fort on the Platte when Bill was there. He had accompanied Cody on some of his tours with the stage show, and in the new Wild West show was to double as a stage driver and rider of wild horses, and also to throw glass balls for his employer to shoot. John had a full flowing beard, a Sioux wife, and five children. With his Indian family he was often in the forefront of pictures taken of the personnel of the big show.

Con Groner, a huge man, was billed as the "Cow-Boy Sheriff of the Platte." He had been sheriff of Lincoln County since the early seventies and was credited with helping break up Nebraska's notorious Doc Middleton outfit of horse thieves in 1879, although his part in that affair seems to be by reputation only.[16]

And finally there was Johnny Baker. Johnny, whose real name was Lewis, the same as his father's, was thirteen years old when Buffalo Bill organized his show. Still limping a little from the accident under the train wheels the year before, he was at his hero's heels every waking moment that spring, coaxing to be taken along with the show. Cody felt a real and deep affection for the lad, who was the same age his son Kit would have been, had he lived. Numerous old-timers say that Bill had wanted to adopt Johnny, but his parents, though they had seven children, didn't feel they could spare any one of them.

When Johnny begged Will to take him with the show, Will laughed and asked, says Cooper, "What would you do in a Wild West show, Johnny?" "Well, I could black your boots—and—and—make myself awful handy, replied the boy." "Will," to quote Louisa, "had taught him to shoot in the days in which he had played around our house—in fact, there never was a time when guns were not booming around there and Will was not shooting coins out of his children's fingers, while I stood on the veranda and gasped a remonstrance that the first thing he knew, he would have a fingerless family!"[17] Johnny became Cody's foster son and went along with the show, the beginning of a relationship that was to last to the very end of the Colonel's life.

The mechanics and labor of putting the show together and having it ready to roll by the middle of May must have been an enormous task, and it is unlikely there was time for any actual rehearsals of the whole show in North Platte. But a rehearsal was planned for Colville, Major North's home town, two or three days before the show was scheduled to open in Omaha on May 17.

Three accounts of the loading of the show at North Platte and its departure exist. Burr Murphy, the young man who claimed he earned first money riding the buffalo the year before, years later wrote that he was on the station platform when the show pulled out, "and all he [Cody] had for a start was a crated burro, a tall Irishman and a few Pawnee Indians."[18]

John Dick, son of the Dr. Dick who helped save Johnny Baker's foot, said:

> I was a kid about eight years old at the time. When he got ready to load out, he had a lot of cowboys and Indians and a lot of local talent from around here. They paraded through town to the stockyards, and the whole town was down to see them off. Bill Sweeney was director of the band. Ned Wheeler had a pair of elk he had broken to drive for the show. Abe Haner had trained a couple of Newfoundland dogs to drive to a wagon that he had fixed up like an emigrant wagon, with the bows on it covered with canvas. I remember that, because for years I wanted that team of dogs. The whole valley was excited when he left North Platte to start this career.[19]

Mrs. Maude Walker, daughter of Isaac Dillon, was not born until after the historic day of the show's departure from North Platte, but her father, who had helped Cody get the Wild West outfit together, had told her that it took "six boxcars and several passenger cars" to hold the people, livestock, and equipment. A large and excited crowd was there to see the show off, Dillon said, and to "hear the farewell words Mr. Cody spoke. In closing he said, 'I will not only exhibit my show in every state capital in the United States but also in Washington D. C. and some capitals in Europe.' At that, someone in the crowd said, 'That's a hell of a lot of wind, even from Bill Cody.' "[20]

The parade to the depot must have been colorful. Led by Sweeney's mounted cowboy band, it was made of of several unusual and unorthodox units. One was a Deadwood stagecoach. For some fifteen years, or since the coming of the railroad, stagecoachs had ceased to ply the valley roads, and already there were many people in the area who had never seen one. Cody had obtained his coach in Wyoming, where it had seen service on the Cheyenne and Black Hills Stage line in the seventies. It had cost $1,800 new, and Cody himself had ridden it on one of its regular runs in 1876; it had at one time been abandoned beside the road after an attack either by Indians or highwaymen near Indian Creek.[21]

John Hupfer, whose brother Joe was a member of the cowboy band, tells about a pair of elk in harness that used to pull a buckboard through the streets of North Platte. Whether these were Ned Wheeler's trained elk is not known, but they were likely part of that May day parade. John's father owned one of the town's saloons, often frequented by Cody and his friends. One time, John says, Cody and Buck Taylor had had too much to drink in his father's place, and someone from the ranch, driving the elk team to a spring wagon, came after them. They were loaded into the wagon, and the outfit headed for the ranch. At the railroad crossing a big dog ran out barking, and the elk ran away and straddled a telegraph pole beside the tracks. The jar "threw Bill and Buck both out, but it didn't hurt them at all, and I don't think they even woke up," John concluded.[22]

The engine that pulled The Wild West, Hon. W. F. Cody and Dr. W. F. Carver's Rocky Mountain and Prairie Exhibition (as it was billed), out of town was manned by road engine engineer, John Sullivan, brother of switch engine engineer Pat Sullivan, who hauled caboose loads of guests up to Cody's town house. And because he was at the throttle of that first Wild West special, Buffalo Bill gave him a lifetime pass to the show. The pass, treasured by John and by his family after him, disappeared only a few years ago.

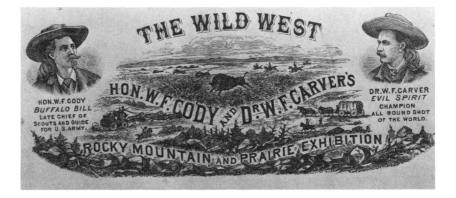

16

The Wild West Tours
1883

The Rocky Mountain and Prairie Exhibition went only as far as Columbus (then a prairie village called Colville), Major North's home town, on the first leg of its journey that was, in truth, to lead to all the United States capitals and to some in Europe as well. There it was unloaded for its dress rehearsal, and the entire outfit—cowboys, Indians, buffalo, elk, mountain sheep, wild horses, saddle horses, emigrant wagons, stagecoach, and all else—assembled in a suitable open space on the edge of town.

From the first, Cody insisted on absolute realism in everything connected with his show. The actors were genuine frontiersmen, and the acts were to be strictly in accordance with reality. Therefore, in his presentation of an Indian attack on the Deadwood stagecoach and the rescue by himself and his men, the only thing *not* permitted was killing and scalping. So, naturally, the four mules that drew the coach were wild and hard to handle, barely broken to the feel of the harness. The driver was Fred Matthews, one of the oldest and best-known drivers on western stage routes. His skill and courage had several times carried him safely through terrifying Indian attacks on the Plains.

Shortly before the rehearsal began, Major North and his Indians, all properly painted and feathered, took up their station in ambush behind a brush patch on the grounds. The cowboy rescue party was hidden from view on the far side of the arena. The stagecoach, waiting farther down the way behind the restive mules, was to be filled with very important persons, the mayor and the town council of Colville. The mayor, "Pap" Clothier, was popular, irascible, excitable, and handy with his fists, according to L. O. Leonard, who related the story of that rehearsal as follows:

"About 2 o'clock in the afternoon" the mayor and his councilmen arrived on the grounds, alighted from their rigs, and took position in front of the large crowd of spectators. As the Wild West Silver Cornet Band played "Hail to the Chief," Buffalo Bill, resplendent in fringed buckskins and sombrero, rode his "magnificent charger" out to receive and welcome the officials with flowery phrases. The mayor, all smiles and "visibly swelled up to the bursting point with pride at the distinguished honor accorded to him as chief guest and central figure" in the proceedings, bowed right and left.

Next came the Deadwood coach with "Sam Matthews"[1] on the high seat, his "immense flowing whiskers" waving in the breeze, his foot on the brake, and his gauntleted hands busy with the four lines and his long-lashed whip. With the best flourish he could manage with the faunching, wild-eyed mules, he brought the coach to a halt, and the mayor and his party climbed in. The spooky mules had already caught the scent of the ambush-Indians and were showing definite signs of insurrection.

As the band struck up "Hail Columbia," the coach hurtled off at a barely controllable gallop. While it made three fast circles around the half-mile track, the mayor and the councilmen smiled and waved from the windows. The crowd cheered and waved back, exciting the mules all the more. Then, as the coach passed the ambush for the third time, the Indians burst forth, shrilling their terrible war whoops and firing blank cartridges at the rig.

The excited spectators knew what was coming, "but the mules had not been advised of this part of the program, nor had they been trained to Indian massacre." So they bolted. Instantaneously Matthews had a full-blown stampede on his hands—a real runaway.

The Indians, excited to fever pitch by the initial success of their ambush, now became "delirious with . . . delight."

Sam, knowing he could not possibly stop the wildly frightened mules, concentrated all his skill and experience on simply keeping the lurching, swaying, bounding coach on all of its four wheels. As the runaway came by their hiding place, Buffalo Bill and his rescue party dashed out and tried to head off the mules and Indians. Instead, they only added to the noise and confusion, for the Indians forgot their instructions to retire from the attack at this point.

As the flying mass swept past the crowd again, the mayor stuck his head out the window, waved his hands frantically, and shouted, "Stop: Hell: stop—let us out." That was exactly what Sam was trying to do, but it was no use. The mob swept on around the track yet another time before the mules ran out of steam and, winded, were pulled to a heaving halt in front of the crowd. That the coach had not turned turtle was due entirely to Sam's skilled driving. But the enraged mayor, scared out of his wits, had no thought of that. Instead, as Major North and Buffalo Bill began cutting out bunches of Indians and heading them off the grounds, "Pap" leaped out of the coach and made for Buffalo Bill, ready for a fight.

At this point a young lawyer, Frank Evors, the town wit and jokester, climbed to the top of the coach and addressed the delighted spectators as follows; "Fellow citizens, it fills my breast with pride and swells my heart with joy to point to your view our noble mayor and city council. Look at them, gentlemen. They risked their lives . . . for your entertainment." But the unappreciative and purple-faced mayor now turned from his struggle to get at Buffalo Bill and swarmed up the near side of the coach, whereat Mr. Evors quickly climbed down on the other side and made his escape.

At this point Major North, his Indian war party safely under control, galloped up to Cody and remarked, "Bill, if you want to make this d—— show go, you do not need me or my Indians. . . . You want about twenty old bucks. Fix them up with all the paint and feathers on the market. Use some old hack horses and a hack driver. To make it go you want a show of illusion not realism."[2]

From Colville/Columbus the show rolled over the last eighty-five miles to Omaha for its scheduled big opening on May 17. Neither Bill nor his wife mentions the showing at Colville, though both describe the opening at the Omaha fair grounds, Louisa in Cooper's flowery prose, Cody more matter-of-factly. He writes, "In the spring of 1883 (May 17th) I opened the Wild West Show . . . in Omaha, and played to very large crowds, the weather fortunately proving propitious. We played our next engagement at Springfield, Ill., and thence in all the large cities, to the seaboard. The enterprise was not a complete financial success during the first season, though everywhere our performances were attended by immense audiences."[3]

Carver, also billed as "The Evil Spirit of the Plains," and Captain A. H. Bogardus, listed on the program as the Champion Pigeon Shot of America, joined the show in Omaha. An Omaha paper published (on May 20, 1883) an enthusiastic account of the show, providing us the best eyewitness version of its first performance now available. The arena parade here described is probably very much like the one Cody's friends saw in North Platte the day the show loaded out. This account differs from the Colville story in that the Deadwood coach is drawn by six mules instead of four. Perhaps Bill took the advice of his friend and substituted six well-broken mules for the four wild ones of the rehearsal, for the driver here seems well able to control all his steeds.

CODY'S CYCLONE

The "Wild West" Sweeps All Victorious Before It. Eight Thousand People Attend the Initial Performances, And Go Wild With Enthusiasm—The Races, Fights And Feats Of The Big Amusement Hit.

A clear day and solid streets at last smiled upon the opening performance of the "Wild West," a new show venture of "Buffalo Bill" and Dr. Carver. The patronage which the show would draw on its native prairie had been widely speculated upon by amusement managers, for Indians and cowboys, a large part of the attractions, are not a novelty in Nebraska. But the interest was great and fully 8,000 people, of all classes from frontiersmen to bankers were on hand at 2 o'clock yesterday afternoon at the driving park and after the first three or four acts the show was stamped with popular approval and it was evident that it was a "go."

THE OPENING PARADE

was the first feature and it was picturesque and well gotten up. A band of twenty pieces marched at the head, then came "Little Sitting Bull" riding on a pony and gorgeous in his war bonnet and paint; then three Pawnees on ponies; then three grown buffaloes and the baby buffalo, a frisky young thing; then a group of Omaha Indian squaws with papooses riding on ponies and led by their respective bucks; another group of squaws trailing an Indian wagon of hickory poles, the aboriginal baby carriage; next some forty Sioux and Pawnee braves mounted and in war paint; after them Honorable W. F. Cody ("Buffalo Bill") and Dr. Carver, who were cheered enthusiastically; then a party of cowboys; after them two strings of elk, who pranced about wildly and were with difficulty kept from breaking away and dashing across the grounds; then a pair of burros with packs, a dog team and a goat team driven by Indian boys, then the Monroe and Salisbury stage coach, which was attacked by road agents on the Black Hills run some years ago, drawn by six fine mules; and finally another band.

THE PERFORMANCE

was announced by "Pop" Whitaker, the noted caller for athletic games who is familiar to all patrons of sports in New York and who stood godfather to the new show with his accustomed elegance. The first [event] was a half mile dash for Indian ponies, in which there were ten starters. A big Sioux on an iron grey pony won. They rode like the wind and created much enthusiasm. Next was exhibited the pony express rider's method of carrying dispatches in which the riding and changing of saddle covers was done with startling rapidity.

Great interest was taken in the representation of the attack of a stage coach, and it was a thrilling scene, never equalled by an act in a hippodrome or theater. The coach started out with its load of passengers; the stage agent warned the driver against his dangers, and the six mules sent the vehicle rolling down the track. As the coach reached the last quarter, a band of fifty Indians emerged from a hiding place and set out in pursuit, yelling like demons. The driver whipped up his mules and the dust flew, but the Indians closed around the coach and the interchange of revolver shots made the secne exciting. Just as it seemed that the coach was captured "Buffalo Bill" and Dr. Carver, leading a party of scouts, came to its rescue, driving the Indians back, shooting and scalping them, and routing the discomfited savages from the road. The audience went wild with excitement, stood upon their seats and cheered and called for a repetition, but there was too much to follow on the program.

Next came a race between an Indian runner and a mounted Indian for fifty yards and repeat, which was applauded. Feats of shooting were the next acts. Captain Bogardus opened with a marvelous exhibition in breaking glass balls and pigeons after the English and American rules. "Buffalo Bill" and Dr. Carver followed in feats with the shotgun and rifle, concluding with shots [made] while riding at full speed. These exhibitions are beyond all rivalry, for the three best shots in the United States and the champion shot of the world were engaged in them.

"The Cowboys Frolic" with bucking bronchos came next, and then two fine Texas steers were turned loose and allowed to run wild within a circle of cowboys, after which they were deftly lassoed and thrown, and one daring cowboy rode a steer for a few yeards until the animal tossed him off. The final act was the "Buffalo Chase," in which the buffalo were liberated from the corral and set galloping over the ground, and they headed toward the crowd outside the grand stand, which began running away in terror; but the cowboys, who had control of the buffalo, turned them back into the corral, and the crowd thought they had been quite as near as was agreeable. A dash of the Indians around the grounds excited much enthusiasm and concluded the performance.

There was no mistaking the fact that the show was a success. The swiftest and most daring Indians, the most expert lassoers and riders among the cowboys, and above all Cody, Carver, Bogardus, and the best talent in every line to be had, deserved and won the favor of the people.

Mr. Cody and Mr. Carver rode up to the grandstand after the performance and Mr. Cody made a right manly speech, in which he said that he trusted the enterprise had pleased the people, and that he had aimed to make it "a thoroughbred Nebraska show," in which they should "hold the mirror up to nature." The speech was greeted with tremendous applause, and then the crowd dispersed.

A NIGHT PERFORMANCE

was given, consisting of Indian dances, the firing of rockets by Captain Bogardus, and other acts which could be given at night, the grounds being illuminated by blazing campfires. There was not a large attendance. Owing to the disappointment of many who were intending to go on Thursday and Friday, it has been decided to give a Sunday matinee this afternoon.

Whereas Cody wrote that the Wild West played its "next engagement at Springfield," Cooper has Louisa say it was Chicago, although she "can't remember the name of the place" where they showed; but it was "indoors, with boxes for prominent persons, [and] a tanbark ring." She goes on: "Our every cent was in that show now. It had cost thousands and thousands. . . . And if we failed in Chicago, we knew that failure would follow us everywhere." But the show was a big success and every seat was filled. "There was no worriment after that—our fortunes were made."[4]

Actually, the show exhibited next in Council Bluffs, Iowa, across the Missouri River from Omaha. There twenty-three-year-old Gordon Lillie, later known as "Pawnee Bill," joined the conglomeration as interpreter for the Pawnees. A native of Illinois, he had been seven years on the frontier by then and had been an employee of the Indian agency, due to his fluency in the Pawnee language.[5]

Walsh has Lillie describing the shock he experienced when he joined the show. The young interpreter explained that his mental picture of Buffalo Bill had long been one of a "fine looking man, well groomed, with a beautiful buffalo robe coat." Instead, the great man had been sleeping in some hay, his hair was matted, and he was drunk. "Cody was drunk every day for our first five weeks out," he added.[6]

Carver, too, later claimed that his partner "was dead drunk all summer . . . so we separated."[7] During their association in show business, Cody had trouble with both Lillie and Carver, and, although he never wrote unkindly of either of them, they both vented their spite on Bill by reciting exaggerated tales of his drunkenness.

From Council Bluffs the show went on to Springfield. Since fair grounds and race tracks of that period were not adequately lighted, the exhibition was limited to afternoon stands only. But wherever the Wild West went, it played to capacity crowds, and at the Aquidnuck Fair Grounds in Newport in mid-July Lord Mandeville rode in the Deadwood stage as it dashed into its Indian ambush and cowboy rescue, the first of many noble and royal personages to fill the venerable vehicle in the years to come.

Cooper intimates, through Louisa, that she accompanied the show through the entire season and returned with her husband to North Platte in the fall "to plan and scheme again, and to dream of greater things for the coming season."[8] Mrs. Cody and her daughters were quite likely present at the opening in Omaha, although no other writer mentions the fact, but they certainly did not travel any farther with the show.

For one thing, there was the frail health of the second daughter, Orra; and for another, the baby, barely past three months old. Mrs. Cody was not the type of mother either to drag a sickly child and a small baby about the country with a constantly moving tent show or to park them with nurses while she traveled with the show herself. And besides, marital relations between her husband and her were badly strained again that summer.

From Youngstown, Ohio, Will wrote on September 24 to his sister Julia, who was still in Kansas, that he had at last filed a petition for divorce against "that woman," and reiterated his declaration that "she has tried to ruin me financially this summer. . . . I could tell you lots of funny things how she has tried to bust up the horse ranch and buy more property [and] get the deeds in her name."[9] Furthermore, that Louisa and her three daughters were at home in North Platte in June of that summer is manifest by Frances Fulton's visit there at that time.

Miss Frances Fulton, a young lady of twenty or so, left her Pennsyl-

vania home in the spring of 1883 to come west with a "colony" of
friends. The entire party traveled via the Northern Pacific into northern
Nebraska, where most of its members filed on homesteads. Miss Fulton,
bent on exploring the wild frontier, went farther west than most of
her friends, as far as the raw cowtown of Valentine, then returned
alone to Omaha. From there she journeyed to North Platte by the
Union Pacific to visit Arta Cody.

Frances and Arta were "pen pals," although in the book she later
wrote of her adventures she does not say how or why they began
writing to each other. Of her trip on the Union Pacific she writes that
she spent Decoration Day in Fremont, where she boarded the train
for North Platte. At Grand Island the coach became very crowded, and
she saw an old gentleman "confidenced" out of $60. Later, when the
crowd thinned out and there was room enough to "turn the seat" to
make a bed, she lay down on the pocket where her money was and
went to sleep. At two o'clock in the morning the conductor wakened
her for the North Platte stop.

She had written Arta that she would arrive on that particular train,
she said, but had no idea it would arrive at such an "unreasonable"
hour. But Arta was there, waiting in the chilly spring night to meet her.
She greeted her guest with the simple, friendly words, "I am so glad
you have come, Frances." They went at once to the Cody town house,
where Mrs. Cody was also waiting up to meet their guest. Of her visit,
Miss Fulton wrote:

> Their [the Cody's] beautiful home is nicely situated one-half mile
> from the suburbs of North Platte. The family consists of three
> daughters: Arta the eldest, is a true brunette, with clear, dark com-
> plexion, black hair, perfect features, and eyes that are beyond
> description in color and expression, and which sparkle with the girl-
> ish life of the sweet teens. [Arta was sixteen.] Her education has
> not been neglected, but instead is taking a thorough course in board-
> ing school. Orra, a very pleasant but delicate child of eleven sum-
> mers, with her father's finely cut features and his generous big-
> heartedness; and wee babe Irma, the cherished pet of all. . . .
>
> It is not often that we meet mother, daughters, and sisters so affec-
> tionate as are Mrs. C., Arta, and Orra. Mr. Cody's life is not a home
> life, and the mother and daughters cling to each other, trying to fill
> the void the husband and father's almost constant absence makes.
> He has amassed enough of this world's wealth and comfort to quietly

Arta Cody,
1880.

Arta Cody,
1882.

enjoy life with his family. But a quiet life would be so contrary to the life he has always known, that it could be no enjoyment to him. . . .

To tell you of all the pleasures of my visit at the home of "Buffalo Bill," and of the trophies he has gathered from the hunt, chase, and trail, and seeing and hearing much that was interesting, and gleaning much of the real life of the noted western scout from Mrs. C., whom we found to be a lady of refinement and pleasing manners, would make a long story.[10]

It is to be regretted that Miss Fulton did not take time to write a "long story," as it would no doubt reveal much that is interesting about the Codys and their friends. She did, however, retell the tale of the Indians who ate Louisa's company dinner at Fort McPherson, as her hostess told it to her.

Miss Fulton concludes the account of her visit: "I left [Orra] a very happy child over the anicipation of a trip to the east where the family would join Mr. Cody for some time." The Codys had paid a visit to the grave of little Kit each summer since his death, and it must have been this anticipated visit Miss Fulton refers to, for Louisa and the girls did go to Rochester later that summer, probably in August, when the Wild West was in New York; quite likely the husband and father joined them there.

On August 16, Will wrote to Julia from Coney Island:

Darling Sister, I am now located at this place. have went to a big expense fitting up a place here—and as the watering season is about over it wont be worth much this year, but will be good for next. I am not much ahead on the summer in cash but I have my show all clear, and a fine place built here. I have over a hundred head of stock . . . ten head of fine race horses, the finest six mule coach train in the world and seventy head of good saddle horses—and the foundation laid for a fortune before long. The papers say I am the coming Barnum. . . . I am improving wonderfully in shooting, don't take a back seat from Carver or Roger. Tell Al I broke 87 glass balls out of one hundred thrown from a trap 21 yards rise with a shotgun riding a horse at full speed. I have broken 76 out of a hundred with a rifle horse running full speed. Our Cleveland suit didn't come off yet but it will. . . . Tell Al I have bought all of Lanchers Ranch, his milk ranch and all which gives me 800 acres more pasture and hay land. Write me Hotel Brighton, Coney Island, N. Y. Love to all, Brother Will.[11]

There is no mention here of any family trouble, nor did Frances Sims seem to find anything amiss when she wrote of her visit in June, yet it was on September 24 Will wrote Julia and Al that he had filed for divorce.

It can well be assumed that both partners to the Cody marriage were under a severe mental and physical strain that summer. In addition to the stresses of building up the big show and keeping it foremost in outdoor entertainment that first crucial season, there was the Cleveland lawsuit, still dragging through the courts, and the ever-increasing difficulties with the tempermental Dr. Carver. Because of less-than-efficient business management, the show was costing a good deal more than was necessary, and in spite of splendid attendance was barely making expenses. There is no doubt Cody was drinking too much that summer, probably due in part to his many troubles as well as to the constant presence of his many friends (within and outside the show) and guests who were always eager to bend an elbow with the popular showman. So, when further evidence of Lulu's acquisition of more North Platte property in her own name came to his notice, he decided to end their marriage.

Matters were no easier for Mrs. Cody at home. She was lonely for her almost-always-absent husband, and the failing health of her little daughter was a constant worry and heartache. She had numerous business affairs to manage, including the collection of rents from her town houses, and she may have been overseeing the management of the growing ranch north of the tracks, since the Goodmans had not yet moved there to take over its administration. Contrary to Cooper, she probably was not at all sure of the successful future of the unbelievably expensive Wild West show her Will predicted would make them all rich, but she was still certain of the failure of the Cleveland suit into which he was pouring so much money. No wonder, then, that she put all the money she could command into property he could not get his hands on to turn into ready cash.

While complaining that Cody had broken his promise and was drinking too much, Carver, the Evil Spirit of the Plains, was tipping too many bottles himself. Furthermore, the fact that the lion's share of the public praise and adulation went to Buffalo Bill did not sit well with the jealous and high-tempered Carver. Cody's reference to himself as the "coming Barnum" came from such reviews of the show as the one carried in the Hartford *Courant* calling it the best open-air show ever seen: "The real sight of the whole thing is, after all, Buffalo Bill, a perfect model of manly beauty. Mounted on his blooded horse, he rode around the grounds, the observed of all observers. Cody was an extraordinary figure, and sits on a horse as if he were born in the saddle. His feats of shooting are perfectly wonderful. . . . He has, in this exhibition, out-Barnumed Barnum."[12]

Carver, who considered himself a handsome man, and a better shot than Cody, could not accept this, and the two quarreled a great deal. (The fact that Bill was outshooting the doctor most of that season might well indicate that it was Carver who drank too much.)

When the show unloaded in Chicago's Driving Park for a four-day stand, October 17-20, Bill found Nate Salsbury playing in a Chicago theater and went to see him. According to Salsbury, Cody said he was through with Carver and would not go through another summer with him, not even for a hundred thousand dollars. Apparently some kind of an association was arranged between them, to go into effect as soon as Cody could cut himself loose from the Evil Spirit.

The Wild West was to travel on to Omaha and break up there a short time later, but before it left Chicago Cody was called home to North Platte by the death of little Orra. Frances Sims received a sorrowful letter from the grieving mother: "Orra," Mrs. Cody wrote, "my precious darling, that promised so fair, was called from us the 24th of October . . . and we carried her remains to Rochester . . . and laid them by the side of her little brother, in a grave lined with evergreens and flowers. When we visited the sacred spot last summer, she said: 'Mamma, won't you lay me by brother's side when I die?' Oh, how soon we have had to grant her request! If it was not for the hope of heaven and again meeting there, my affliction would be more than I could bear."[13]

Orra's death must have healed the breach between her parents for a time, for there is no more mention of a divorce for a number of years. At any rate, Cody returned to the show, and it quickly closed for the season in Omaha, where the two partners divided its assets equally. Walsh relates that they "flipped a silver dollar and chose in turn horse and horse, steer and steer, wagon and wagon." Cody was extra lucky in one toss, for he got the Deadwood coach.[41]

John P. Altgeld, later governor of Illinois, drew up the contract of partnership between W. F. Cody, Nate Salsbury, and A. H. Bogardus, the third partner in the show which they called "Buffalo Bill's Wild West—America's National Entertainment." From Omaha, Carver teamed up with Captain Jack Crawford, the Poet Scout, a veteran of the Civil War and an ex-scout about Cody's age, and took his share of the Wild West on a winter tour. Salsbury also toured that winter with his very successful Troubadours, a stage combination show. Cody went to Cleveland.

In a letter written to Julia and Al Goodman in late November, Will tells them he still has faith in their ability to win the lawsuit, but adds that it is costing him heavily, although even if he loses he will have the consolation of knowing he had done what he had promised his mother— that is, all in his power to take care of his sisters.

With only his prospects for the next season with the Wild West show as assets, Cody returned to North Platte. Whether he lived with Lulu in the town house that winter, or at the ranch, is uncertain. In any case, he was probably very busy putting the new show together. In a letter to Salsbury, written from North Platte on April 12, he said he had bought and paid for twelve head of new horses, five of them buckers, but was now out of money.[15]

Bill probably went to the Indian reservations himself to sign up the Indians for his show that year. That these "sign up" days were great occasions in the lives of the Indians is evident from a description attributed to Death Valley Scotty:

> The ceremony of selecting the Indians for the show became an annual spring affair, and when he could Cody selected the lucky individuals himself. The Indians, five or six hundred of them, would come to Rushville (a Nebraska town near the South Dakota border) where the selections were made, and they came in their finest buckskins, feathers, and beads. They were quite a sight in their gaudy finery. Only a small part of that number could be used, and the ones not chosen felt pretty bad about it. The government required the Colonel, or his representative, to post bonds that the Indians would be well fed while away and that they would be returned to the reservation in good health and a new suit of clothes.[16]

C. D. O'Kieffe, who lived in the area in the eighties, said, "I'll never forget seeing Buffalo Bill come each spring to get his braves. They left in paint and feathers and returned, after a year, in Prince Albert coats, Stetsons, patent leather shoes and long, well-groomed glossy hair."[17]

Con Groner, Buck Taylor, and Captain Bogardus continued with the show. Frank North joined for its second season. Seth Hathaway was the Pony Express rider. Bill Bullock, Jim Lawson, Bud Ayers, Dick Bean, Utah Frank, Bronco Charlie Miller, Montana Joe, and Blue Hall, top cowboys known from Texas to Montana, rode the bucking horses and headed the other cowboy acts. A new spectacle was the "Attack on a Settler's Cabin by Indians and Rescue by Buffalo Bill with his Scouts, Cowboys and Mexicans." This became one of the most popular acts in the show.

Of his work that winter, and the resulting new show, Cody wrote:

> Immediately upon forming a partnership with Salsbury we set about increasing the company and preparing to greatly enlarge the exhibition. Nearly one hundred Indians, from several tribes, were engaged, among the number being the world famous Chief Sitting Bull, and several other Sioux that had distinguished themselves in the Custer massacre. Besides these we secured the services of many noted plainsmen, such as Buck Taylor, the great rider, lasso thrower and King of the Cowboys; Utah Frank, John Nelson, and a score of other well-known characters. We also captured a herd of elk, a dozen buffaloes and some bears with which to illustrate the chase."[18]

Cody has included Sitting Bull in the list by mistake (he was often careless with dates), for the chief did not come into the show until the next year, 1885. A guest star he does not mention was Dr. Frank Powell, or White Beaver, referred to by Don Russell as his "drinking companion." Their friendship went back to Cody's arrival at Fort McPherson, already fifteen years in the past. The doctor was now practicing his profession in La Crosse, Wisconsin, when he wasn't engaged in show business. His act was exhibition shooting, a very popular type of entertainment at that time.

17

North Platte
1884-1885

The "vastly enlarged and reorganized"[1] Wild West opened in St. Louis, and two weeks later packed the Driving Park in Chicago with a crowd of 41,448 people for a single show. A month later it reached New York. Critics all along the way had proclaimed its excellence, with most of them praising the magnificent horsemanship of the Mexicans, Indians, and cowboys as the best part of the show.

However, the one-day stands proved expensive, and, in spite of the good crowds, by fall the show had not made much money. Hoping to do better, the partners decided to try playing in the south, where outdoor performances could be given all winter. The World's Industrial and Cotton Exposition was scheduled to open in New Orleans for a winter's run, and it seemed a good idea that while Salsbury took his popular Troubadors, a sure money maker, on the road again, Cody should put the Wild West on a boat, play down the Mississippi to cover expenses, reach New Orleans just before Christmas, and show there until spring.

At this point Pony Bob Haslam, Cody's old friend and the most famous of the Pony Express riders of twenty-five years ago, turned up in need of a job. With his usual generosity, Bill hired him and sent him out as advance agent to book shows and rent show grounds. Poor old Pony Bob, although eager to please, had no fitness for such work, and his blunders soon began to show up in greatly diminished receipts. The boat and navigator he hired at Cincinnati proved to be one of his biggest mistakes. Losses mounted as the decrepit tub chugged south. By the time they neared New Orleans, Cody saw that he'd better go on ahead and look into the arrangements his agent was making. At the Exposition city he hired a hack and headed through a pouring rain for the show grounds. The first man he saw there was traveling across the arena in a row boat.[2]

The worried showman had no sooner managed to rent a race track that, though muddy, was usable than he received a telegram informing him that the ill-fated boat carrying his show had collided with another boat and sunk in the Mississippi, near Rodney Landing. "In this accident," Cody wrote, "we lost all our personal effects, including wagons, camp equipage, arms, ammunition, donkeys, buffaloes and one elk. We managed, however, to save our horses, Deadwood coach, band wagon and—ourselves. The loss thus entailed was about $20,000."[3]

Almost in despair, Cody sent his now famous telegram to Salsbury, who, with his Troubadors, was playing at the Opera House in Denver: "Outfit at bottom of the river, what do you advise?" Nate wired back: "Go to New Orleans, reorganize and open on your date." Buffalo Bill proved equal to the emergency. "In eight days I had added to the nucleus that had been saved a herd of buffalo and elk, and all the necessary wagons and other properties, completing the equipment so thoroughly that the show in many respects was better prepared than at the time of the accident—and we opened on our date."[4]

Back in North Platte, the new Lincoln County *Weekly Tribune* (on January 24) informed the many interested friends of the big show that it was exhibiting at the New Orleans World's Exposition and "is reported to be drawing crowds in its usual mustard plaster style, while Johnny Baker, the Cowboy Kid, is now one of the leading characters and has seemingly taken the laurels from Con Groner, the Cowboy Sheriff, as Con is no longer starred."

By this time Frank North had rejoined the show. The previous July, at Hartford, as the Indians and cowboys were sweeping around the arena at full speed, North's saddle girth broke, throwing him beneath the galloping hoofs of the charge. Badly injured, he was hospitalized for months; now he was back, still ailing but game.

The weather, arbiter of all outdoor shows, turned against the big Wild West, completing the ruin that began with North's accident, Haslam's mistakes, and the sinking of the boat. For forty-four days it rained, never missing show time. There came a day when the ticket seller told Cody that they had better call off the show because there were only nine people. When told that they had paid for their seats, the showman proved his dedication to the great axiom of his kind. "If nine people came out here in all this rain to see us, we'll show," he said.[5]

In March the *Tribune* came out with the doleful report that the "Wild West didn't do as well as expected in New Orleans because of excessive wet weather, causing the show grounds, fitted up at a cost of several thousand dollars, to become a perfect mudhole, which had to be abandoned."[6]

In a letter to Salsbury in early March, Cody listed his assets: "about the same number of horses we had last summer . . . about twenty-five Indians in the saddle, 7 Mexicans and 8 cow boys." But some of the Indians were returning to the reservation to put in their spring crops, as required by the government, and he had sent Frank North back to Nebraska to get more Indians—and $5,000 if he could. In this letter he promised his friend that he would stay sober throughout the season ahead, but when it was over and the show laid up for the winter he intended to wash the bad taste of all his hard luck out of his system with "a drunk that is a drunk . . . [and] paint a few towns red hot."[7]

His good friend, Frank North, left on schedule for the Indian reservation but did not accomplish his mission. Never well since his injury, he became worse and hurried to his home in Colville, where he died on March 14. In addition to the loss of his valued friend and co-actor, Cody ended that disastrous winter $60,000 in debt. But he came out of it with two important new attractions in his show. One was Johnny Baker, who caught on with the public and was very popular as the Cowboy Kid, a crack rifle shot. The other was Annie Oakley.

A. H. (Roger) Bogardus, getting on in years and discouraged by the bad winter in New Orleans, asked to leave the show that spring. Since Johnny, according to his proud foster father, had been "shooting to beat L—breaks balls in the air like an old timer,"[8] Cody decided to star him that summer of 1885, in Bogardus' place.

Annie Moses Butler was twenty-five years old when she and her husband, Frank, with Sells Brothers Circus, played in New Orleans at the same time the Wild West was stuck in the mud there. Annie and Frank had then been married nine years, and all that time had played in stock companies and variety shows as Butler and Oakley, the last a stage name Annie had selected for herself, since she disliked her own surname of Moses; their act was built around Annie's amazing marksmanship with a rifle. When they visited the Wild West lot and indicated they would like to join the show, Cody and Salsbury discouraged them; they already had an abundance of shooting acts and no money to take on another, however good. When Frank offered to do their act, on trial, for three days, they were told to join the show at Louisville—and for the next seventeen years Annie was one of the show's greatest assets and most popular members.

That winter of 1884-1885, while Buffalo Bill was struggling in the rain and mud of the southland, North Platte was enjoying the blessings of winter's ice and snow—for the town would have been in trouble without its seasonal ice harvest, taken in January from lakes adjacent to the town. Two local dealers had each stored over a thousand tons in their icehouses, to be hauled through the streets the next summer and delivered a block at a time to the ice boxes of the town's kitchens. A butcher had "put up" 400 tons for use in his meat market, the brewery had likewise provided the wherewithal for cold beer on hot days, and the Union Pacific had stored vast quantities of the natural refrigerant in the company icehouse.

A heavy snow storm toward the end of the month brought out the town's sleighs, causing the *Tribune* to report "several fine turnouts on the streets enjoying the sport, among them Isaac Dillon, W. E. Beach [banker], B. I. Hinman [attorney], Dr. Duncan and Sheriff Bangs, Con Groner's successor."

From their home west of the now-abandoned barracks, Mrs. Cody and Arta witnessed a distressing incident that January: Mr. Dickinson, owner of a new livery stable in the town, came along with four loose horses he had just bought at O'Fallon's for use in his stable. "Arriving at the lane just above Mrs. Cody's, he waited for the east-bound passenger to pass, then put the horses into the lane, thinking he'd have time to get them through before the west-bound Overland came rushing through. But he miscalculated and the train came screeching down on him. The horses became frightened and took to the tracks. All were killed. They were valuable animals, two being worth $300."9

Arta Cody, just turned eighteen in December, had completed her education in eastern finishing schools and in Brownell Hall of Omaha, for years the state's most popular school for wealthy young ladies. At home with her mother that winter, she took a leading part in the town's social life. There is no doubt that she was both pretty and popular. Tall and well built, she had dark hair, large lustrous dark eyes, and a beautifully fair complexion like her father's. As Edd Wright, who came to North Platte in 1886, said many years later: "I used to think Arta was the prettiest girl I ever laid my eyes on. She was beautiful in the face and—well—she was just made right all the way round. She was fair and her eyes were big."10

Even at the age of twelve her poise and appearence had been so striking that sixty years later Erwin Bostwick, another old-timer, remembered an occasion in September of 1878 when a little celebration was going on in town and "Dr. Longley and his wife called on Arta to recite and she got up, a fine looking little girl, and spoke her piece and didn't seem a bit embarrassed."[11]

Mrs. Cody, well aware of the difficulties to be faced in rearing, single-handedly, the beautiful daughter of a famous father, had to be vigilant. When the story reached her that Sammy Van Doran, teenage son of a Front Street livery stable owner, had referred to Arta as "the buffalo heifer" before the usual lot of men and boys who hung about the barn, she promptly took steps. With her buggy whip in hand, she came down to the stable and ran Sammy down the street, taking payment from his young hide with every swing of the stinging lash.

By February diphtheria was raging in the town, and the editor of the *Telegraph* was urging that sanitation laws be put into effect. The alleys, he noted, were full of garbage and should be cleaned. Ducks still swam in ponds between the houses. Surface water, standing in puddles in the streets, should be drained; otherwise, the stench from the muddy streets would be terrible and loaded vehicles would be constantly stuck in them.

In April, Dr. and Mrs. E. F. Brady held a "Progressive Euchre" party in their home, thereby introducing a popular new card game to the local elite social set. Among the young people present where Arta Cody, Minnie Belton, Addie Cash, Kate Taffe, and Miss Groner. The gentlemen were Messrs. Hershey, Neely, Haines, McDonald (William), and Ira Bare. The latter, lately arrived from Pennsylvania, was the popular young bachelor editor of the *Tribune*, who could be depended on to give in the next week's newspaper a full and flattering account of the functions he attended.

As the weather warmed to the spring sun, a new building boom struck North Platte. Chief among the structures soon going up were the photographer's gallery and Lloyd's Opera House. The community had formerly depended on the "Union Pacific Railroad Photograph Car. J. M. Silvers, photographer. Stereoscopic Landscape Views of Notable Points on the Line of the Union Pacific Railroad Always on Hand." The car came into town twice a year and was shunted onto a sidetrack, where it stood as long as business was good. Now, with a gallery of its own, complete with "scenery" and magnesium flares, wedding pictures could be taken on the day of the nuptials and confirmation pictures at the time of the rites, not two, four, or six months later.

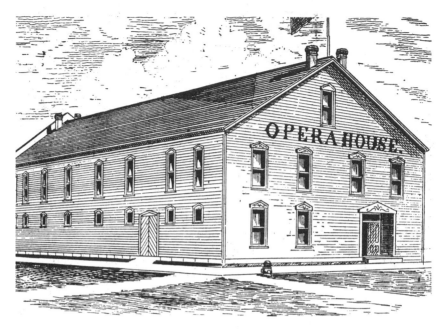

Second only to the depot, the new opera house would be the most imposing building in town. Magnificent for the time and place, it was 131 x 52 feet, with a 20-foot ceiling and a gallery that would seat a hundred people. On its main floor, in front of a movable stage, a thousand people could be seated. It was lighted with "Rochester lamps, big as pot-bellied stoves, that burned coal oil and pulled up and down on chains."[12]

An artist was imported from Chicago to design and paint scenery consisting of street scenes, a parlor, a kitchen, a prison, forest and garden scenes, three sky borders, and three sets of rock scenes. The stage was 35 x 51 feet and strong enough to hold up horses, if necessary. The drop curtain showed an elegant seacoast view, bordered by advertisements of the town's leading businessmen with a lifesize portrait of W. F. Cody at the top. Beneath the picture glowed the motto, "True to Friend and Enemy." It was the largest and finest hall between Omaha and Denver, declared the local newspapers.

Builder and owner of the opera house was Warren Lloyd. A native of New York state, Lloyd came to North Platte as an engineer with the

Union Pacific. In his middle fifties when he built the opera house, he was famous for his beard, the longest in town. It hung nearly to his knees and he took great pride in it, keeping it immaculately clean and well groomed. When combing it, said an old-timer, "he combed as far down as he could reach, then picked it up and finished it as one would comb a horse's tail. When he had it in good shape, he folded it neatly and buttoned his vest over it to protect it."[13]

A news paragraph, taken from the St. Louis *Republican* and reprinted in the *Weekly Tribune* on June 6, 1885, indicated that the rivalry between Cody and Carver got off to an early start that summer. After the breakup of their partnership in the fall of '83, the two had fought each other in print, and in court with libel suits, but when they jousted in the same town, each in his own arena, Cody seems to have won hands down. Proclaimed the *Republican*:

> The battle in this city between Buffalo Bill's *Wild West* and McCafferty and Carver's *Life on the Plains*, with Dr. Carver as the stellar attraction, was short and decisive and ended with Buffalo Bill as the decided victor. As an opposition against the *Wild West, Life on the Plains* with its cheap prices and poor imitations of the West was nowhere. Hon. W. F. Cody, with his original and justly called national entertainment of America, opened last Sunday at the fair grounds to more money than Carver and McCafferty played to during their whole engagement, and day by day the increasing crowds indicate a termination of the most successful engagement ever played in St. Louis by an outdoor entertainment.

On the same day the *Tribune* carried the flattering announcement of Buffalo Bill's triumph over his rival, John Burke was at the Standing Rock Reservation, signing up another noted attraction for the Wild West—Sitting Bull, the great Sioux medicine man. Two years earlier Sitting Bull had been taken on a tour of cities where, in St. Paul, he had seen Annie Oakley in her shooting act in a theater. He had then and there dubbed her "Little Sure Shot." After the show he had visited her, exchanged pictures with her, and adopted her into the Hunkpapa Sioux tribe as his daughter.

Sitting Bull had not enjoyed his first tour and was reluctant to sign on with Burke until, so it is said, the Wild West agent noticed Annie's picture in the chief's tepee and promised him that if he came with the show he could see Little Sure Shot every day. According to the contract, Sitting Bull was to travel with the show for four months at a salary of $50 a week and a $125 bonus. Five Sioux warriors and three women were to go with him, at lesser salaries. All were to have their way paid to Buffalo to join the show and home again at the end of the season.

Back in North Platte, Arta, on the Fourth of July, entertained her house guests, Grace Gregory of Talmage, Nebraska, and Nellie Anderson of Moline, Illinois, at a picnic at Burke's Grove. Other guests included her friends Lottie Kocken, Anna Cash, George and Carroll Hawkins, and Messrs. Cronin, Barnes, and Sanderson. In August Miss Cody enjoyed "the social gaieties at Colorado Springs, Manitou, and other mountain resorts." In late September she left for Chicago "to pursue a course of instruction in music and painting." She was gone one month.

At about the same time, Cody wrote to Al Goodman in Kansas, urging him even more insistently to come to North Platte to take charge of his ranch. It "is one of the finest in America to day," he declared, "And with you at its head to *Stay* we could make it the best by long odds of any ranch in America. . . . if you come . . . I want you to come for life—no more hoffing [hoofing] around the country." He reiterated his belief that he would win the Cleveland suit and added that Arta was coming to see him in St. Louis. (She probably stopped off there on her way home from Chicago.) He would be returning to North Platte by November 1, he concluded, and hoped to see the Goodmans there by then.[14]

Three weeks later the newspapers rejoiced in the homecoming of their most famous citizen:

The Honorable W. F. Cody, North Platte's Buffalo Bill, arrived in the city last Saturday and the flag which denotes his presence was raised at the ranches on his lands west of town. He was not seen by many as business occupied much of his time. He left Monday evening for Omaha to meet a party of Englishmen whom he will pilot on a hunt of six weeks to two months in the vicinity of Rawlins [Wyoming]. Con Groner, John Hancock, Johnny Baker and other members of the Wild West will be here next Sunday.[15]

Buffalo Bill, the far-famed scout and plainsman whose name has become household words in nearly every home in the U. S. by reason of his daring deeds, arrived Sunday morning and spent several days in visiting his family and looking over his fine ranch situated just west of the city. The briefness of his stay did not permit of the usual ovation tendered this gentleman by the citizens of North Platte, who claim him as their own hero, notwithstanding he spends much of his time on the road with his gigantic aggregation of western productions. After a several weeks' hunt, in company with distinguished English gentlemen, Mr. Cody will return to Chicago to take charge of his house show, which opens the season in that city November 2.[16]

During his brief stay in North Platte that October, Cody might well have found time to visit Wald and Wheeler's new saloon. The partners had put up the new emporium that summer, named it the Wild West, and opened it in time to welcome their illustrious townsman home from his triumphal tour. Termed "the finest saloon west of Omaha," it displayed "reminders of Buffalo Bill in its rooms."

Cody also welcomed Julia and Al and their five sons and two daughters and saw them settled in at the ranch. Previous to their coming he had employed one C. A. Dillon as ranch foreman. Just how long Dillon held the position is not known. Apparently he was not related to Isaac Dillon, and little is known of him beyond a few newspaper items:

In March his saddle horse, weary of waiting for him at a Spruce Street hitchrack, had broken his bridle and headed for the ranch "at a 2:17 gait. As a result Mr. Dillon walked home in a spirit not altogether Christian like." In June Dillon was busy making improvements at the ranch "calculated to make it more comfortable as a home and popular as a summer resort." A straight road leading from the south gate to the corral was nearly finished, "giving an opportunity to let the fast steppers spin if desired." And visitors could try out the "half-mile speed ring, constructed on scientific principles, than which there will be none better on these fertile plains." A fish pond was also under construction and was to be stocked with fish when completed. At Lincoln County's first fair, held September 30 through October 2, Dillon had exhibited cattle and horses from Cody's well-bred herds and had won several blue ribbons.

The fair, put on by the new County Agricultural Society, had been flamboyant and successful. The Society, organized at Isaac Dillon's office in the spring and promoted all summer by Ira Bare, had invested a great deal of ambition, money, and effort in the projected fair. By mid-July the premium list had been completed, and Bare was informing his readers that "No pains will be spared to make it [the fair] worthy of a county that is destined to take a first position among the great agricultural and stock counties of Nebraska. The Society has offered liberal premiums and been to large expense in purchasing and fitting up suitable grounds."

By September the Society had completed all arrangements and distributed a thousand copies of the premium list. All of western Nebraska was "earnestly invited to exhibit at this, our first fair, held in the midst of what was not long since termed the Great American Desert, and bring cattle, all kinds of stock and the products of the earth of every description [–] a bushel of potatoes, a bunch of onions, a few beets, a peck of any kind of grain [–] to show to the state and the world that the desert has vanished."

Bare was enthusiastic in his praise of the "largest exhibition grounds in the state, enclosed with a high board fence." Stables for horses and pens for cattle were ready, a "stand" had been built and a "speed ring" completed. An additional ten acres adjoining the fair grounds had been enclosed for the benefit of visitors from a distance who might wish to camp out.

Cody's ranch showed the prize Shorthorn and Hereford bulls, the best fat cow, and second-best yearling bull. The horse races, held the last two days of the fair, were "spirited." Three horses were entered in the half-mile free-for-all dash, "the event of the afternoon." C. E. Osgood entered "Blacky," J. Hunnell "Balley," and the Cody Ranch "Jack Rossiter." After holding the lead for most of the way, Rossiter fell back to second place behind Balley. The purse was $50. A. J. Miller, Isaac Dillon, and M. C. Keith had horses in the trotting races, where Keith won the first prize of $25. All in all, editor Bare concluded, "The fair exceeded the expectations of the most sanguine and was pronounced by all to have been a grand success. The barren wastes of former years have bloomed."[17]

This was no mere local chauvinism. The Omaha *Herald*, recognizing the progress in and around North Platte, sent a writer there the following month and devoted several pages of the newspaper to descriptions of North Platte, its homes, its businesses, and its people (including a review of the Hon. W. F. Cody's life up to that time), with drawings of buildings and streets of the town. The issue also carried a glowing one-and-a-half column account of Cody's ranch, "one of the finest on the American continent":

The waters of the great Platte flow through no prettier or more natural stock ranch. Nature in all her bounteous gifts or freaks never designed a place more fitting. The river skirts along the northeastern portion for four miles; in the southern portion [near where a fine new house would soon stand] a small overflowing creek, fed by a cool living spring, flows nearly through the center from west to east, dividing it into two parts. . . . On the south side the rich nutritious buffalo grass grows and furnishes food on which cattle grow fat in summer, on the north side a long, juicy wild prairie grass is found which when cut and cured furnishes a provender unequalled for cattle in winter. He has a tract of nearly four thousand acres here, the eastern portion adjoining the city's limits, which the rapid growth of North Platte is making very valuable.

Besides the ranch buildings which are three miles from the city, he has a residence one mile west of North Platte [the town house where Mrs. Cody lived]. Mr. Cody is a great lover of fine stock, and moreover a good judge of a horse or cattle as well. He takes great pride in his herd of 125 of the best blooded cattle, composed of Herefords, Shorthorns, Polled Angus and other high grades. His Hereford bull, Earl Horace, has a pedigree and was imported. Among the herd of 181 horses, most of which are thoroughbred, are some of the best ever brought out west.[18]

It is clear that C. A. Dillon had done a good job in building up Cody's ranch and in handling the livestock. It is not absolutely certain why Cody was so intent upon replacing Dillon with Julia and her husband. In any case, we do know of at least one problem revolving around Dillon. When Cody returned to North Platte in mid-October, he was faced with a civil law suit by David Cash, a local meat market proprietor, who was seeking to recover a meat bill run up by Dillon. Cody denied the foreman's authority to contract the bill (probably because Dillon should have butchered beef raised on the ranch); after a sharp legal contest, Cody was awarded the verdict *in absentia* early in the new year.[19]

18

Lloyd's Opera House 1886

The Wild West, with its many stellar attractions, had played to a million people that summer of 1885, and made a profit of $100,000, which had wiped out the losses incurred at New Orleans. During the latter part of the season, the show had made a successful foray into Canada, re-entered the States by way of Detroit, and closed in Colville (Columbus), before going into winter quarters in St. Louis.

Of course, all this was known in North Platte, and there is no doubt Cody thoroughly enjoyed the fame and success that attended him then and for many succeeding years as the star of the Wild West show. But it is also true that he regretted missing out on the summertime celebrations in his home town. That autumn, upon hearing his friends' enthusiastic descriptions of the fair just past, he made up his mind to have a part in the next year's exposition. If the Agricultural Society would set their dates just a few days later, he said, giving him time to close the season for his Wild West, he would come home for the fair, bring some of the Roman racing chariots used in his show, and put on a truly spectacular exhibition at the fine new fair grounds.

Cody also had plans for the new opera house, then nearing completion. Still in need of money to finance his big outdoor show for the next season, Cody had decided to go on the road for the last time with his "house show" or stage show, and John Burke had by then completed arrangements for its Chicago opening.[1] Cody's company that winter would be known as Buffalo Bill's Dutchman and the Prairie Waif Combination. For "his hometown, in which he takes great pride," Cody proposed to bring his stage show, "The Prairie Waif," to North Platte for the opening night of the Lloyd's Opera House.

Toward the end of November, Cody had returned from the Wyoming hunting trip with the visiting Englishmen, too late of course to make the November 2 opening of his Combination. But an actor named Matt Snyder had earlier been engaged to play the part of Buffalo Bill when Cody could not be with the show, and presumably Snyder had had to open the season in Chicago. Finally, on November 26, Cody departed North Platte to join his theatrical company.[2]

By then, and for the next month, editor Bare was kept busy reporting on the social happenings in his town. Mr. and Mrs. William Grady had given a Progressive Euchre Club party at which Arta Cody and Addie Cash won the first and second ladies' prizes. Messrs. Bare and Fitzgerald were high scorers for the gentlemen. A few days later Mr. and Mrs. Lester Eells hosted another club party—"light but tempting refreshments were served in abundance." And the season was off to a good start.

Arta Cody turned nineteen on December 16 and was feted with a surprise birthday party at her home that evening. "The guests were handsomely entertained by the accomplished young lady and a pleasant time was enjoyed by all. Card playing and dancing were indulged in and an elegant supper added conviviality to the occasion. Present were Misses Betty Graves, Anna Cash, Nora O'Connor, Anna Hawkins, Kate Taffe and Minnie Belton; Messrs. Streitz, Fitzgerald, Mitchell, Sanderson, Iddings, McDonald, Bare and Joe and Carroll Hawkins."

The following week Mr. and Mrs. H. S. Keith entertained six tables of Progressive Euchre, at which "the reporter noticed the beaming faces of twenty-four guests," including Arta Cody's and his own.

On Saturday, December 19, the Honorable W. F. Cody came in on Number One to spend Christmas with his family, and he was immediately involved in local politics.

Lincoln County was still renting and using the railroad bridge directly east of town, but a new bridge was badly needed. Watchmen were stationed at either end of the bridge to hold up wagon traffic when trains were due, but because of mixed signals, or no signals at all, there had been several near accidents on the bridge: wagons or buggies had almost been run down by trains, and a few head of loose livestock, wandering onto the bridge, had been killed. Furthermore, the railroad company did not wish to renew the contract and if forced to renew was sure to raise the annual rent. On December 23 an important town and county meeting was held to lay plans for building a new bridge across the North Platte River. Cody was "called to the chair."

"Mr. Cody briefly stated the object of the meeting and its importance. No sectional jealousies should prevent the hearty endorsement of an improvement so manifestly for the benefit of the whole people," the *Tribune* reported, and under Buffalo Bill's enthusiastic leadership the vote was unanimous "to devise ways and means to secure a successful [bridge] issue."

Cody also bore some bad news. Regretfully, the showman told his friends he would not be able to bring his "Prairie Waif" to North Platte until after the middle of February. However, he then set about helping them secure the "celebrated Milan Opera Company of Milan, Italy," with which to open their fine new opera house. A change of schedule had left the company with an unfilled date, January 15, 1886, and North Platte was conveniently on its route, halfway between Omaha and Denver. The town's newspapers were exuberant over this great good fortune, explaining that the Opera "is the finest and strongest organization now on tour in this country, and is the only one traveling and presenting grand opera in Italian. A superb chorus, magnificent costumes and a grand orchestra" would accompany Bellini's beautiful "La Sonambula" on the stage at Lloyd's Opera House on its official opening night. La Scala comes to North Platte!

The year ended with the marriage of Lottie Kocken to M. J. Cronin; the birth to Bill Tucker, proprietor of the town's most notorious saloon, and his wife of a son who was promptly named Cody Tucker; and the grand New Year's Eve party held in the new opera house.

The party, "tendered by the young ladies to the young men of the city, was in all respects the most elegant affair that has taken place in North Platte for several years." The south end of the opera house was used as a reception room and the floor covered with fine robes and velvet rugs. Furniture for the occasion was borrowed from the town's best homes and "formed a collection only seen in palatial residences in large cities. Large and elegant paintings adorned the walls and every nook and corner was filled with unique and ornamental bric-a-brac. It was a scene of luxurious magnificence and conspicuously hung over the entrance was the traditional sprig of a mistletoe."

Card playing and dancing entertained the young people until past ten o'clock, at which time the ladies escorted their guests to the supper table. Arranged on the big stage, the long board was laid with forty plates and a five- or six-course "collation" was served by hired waiters. "The ladies were arrayed in elegant and costly costumes, their bright faces wreathed in happy smiles. After supper the mazy whirl of the waltz resumed and continued until past midnight." The names of the guests, comprising North Platte's equivalent to New York's "four hundred," were as usual a part of the report of the "elegant" affair.[3] There is nothing, however, to indicate who squired Arta Cody to the ball.

Shortly after Christmas, Buffalo Bill rejoined his Combination in the East. Louisa also went east on an "extended trip"; she was doubtless making her annual visit to the graves of her children in Rochester. The couple may have gone together, and Arta possibly went with them, as her name is missing from the society news for some weeks after the New Year's Eve ball.

Lloyd's Opera House, on the other hand, was very much in the news all that winter. After the grand opening night, Ella Jane Mcade, a popular dramatic reader and artist; appeared there for one evening. Testimonials to her success, as given by banker W. E. Beach, the Honorable William Neville, and others were published in the following week's issue of the *Tribune*, and Mrs. J. H. Hershey was quoted as stating, "None that I have heard can scarcely equal Miss Meade"; but, alas, many seats for the performance remained unfilled, and the "entertainment did not pay expenses."

The "hops" held at the opera house by the local Terpsichorean Club must have done better, however, for they were continued, semimonthly, all that winter. The Odd Fellows gave a huge masked ball at the end of January, while "on the boards" for February were Maggie Mitchell and Hoyt's "Rag Baby"—"all good companies that will draw big houses if they keep the price below one dollar." They were, indeed, good companies, troupes that ordinarily would not have stopped in a prairie village of less than 3,000 souls, but partly because of Buffalo Bill, known to most of the players in the East, partly because of the fine new opera house, and partly because North Platte was one day's travel between Omaha and Denver, they stopped in Cody's home town.

Maggie Mitchell, appearing in a French play, "The Pearl of Savoy," did better than Ella Jane Meade, drawing a crowd of 500 and pleasing most of her audience, including editor Bare, whose only criticism was that her "abbreviated costume was hardly in good taste, at least for a country audience," and suggested that it would be better if she "adopted a dress more in accordance with the taste of American people."

None of the shows that played the opera house that winter, unless it was the Italian grand opera, created anywhere near the excitement caused by the coming of "The Prairie Waif." All through the forepart of the month, Cody's friends followed the progress of the "Waif" toward North Platte, where it was to show on February 20, a Saturday evening. Most of the halls where the show played in Nebraska, it was reported, were too small to accommodate the crowds that turned out. In Grand Island 500 people were turned away, in Hastings nearly the same.

By February 17 every chair in the opera house had been sold, and additional seats were put in. "No one need stay away for fear there will not be room," Bare assured his readers on Saturday morning. "The hall will hold fifteen hundred in a pinch, and we expect to see that number present."

The next week, in case there had been someone who had not been there to see for himself, the editor reported: "The Hon. W. F. Cody (Buffalo Bill) was greeted at Lloyd's opera house last Saturday evening by the largest audience that has gathered in that building this season. The company is a strong combination of excellent actors and presents *The Prairie Waif* with happy effect, Jule Keen, the Dutch comedian, bringing in enough fun to keep the audience in a roar of good humor. Mr. Cody is (now) on his way to California and is meeting with grand ovations at every stopping point. He expects to return to 'the states' by the first of May."

Whether or not Mrs. Cody and the girls went to the show is nowhere mentioned. That Arta was in North Platte at this time is shown by Ira Bare, who reported on February 20 that she and her girl friends had attended a dinner party at the home of Miss Betty Graves the week before. Their gentlemen friends had joined them later for "card playing and social converse." A week later Arta entertained the Progressive Euchre Club "in her usual charming manner," and Mr. Brown, the C.B.&Q. man, had had the misfortune on the way to the party to drive off the bridge, just east of the section house, and wreck his buggy very badly.

Two weeks later, at a church entertainment given at the opera house, Arta and her friend, Pauline Kocken, gave recitations. "Both young ladies have full, clear, round voices and, overlooking several inappropriate gestures, their respective recitations were exceedingly good," was the candid report of Mr. Bare.

For well over a score of years Lloyd's Opera House played an important part in the lives of the Cody family. Its floor was considered the best in the state, and all big parties and festivals were held there, including the annual Engineers May Ball, *the* social event of the year in North Platte. Amateur plays were frequently given there to well-filled houses, and it was the hub of all large public and private entertainments. Conventions, revival or "protracted" meetings, funerals, church suppers and bazaars, banquets, political rallies, drills, and graduation exercises—all gravitated to Lloyd's. Even the inaugural ball for one of North Platte's own was held there when M. C. Keith's grandson, Keith Neville, became governor of Nebraska. Neville was only a baby at the time of the big hall's dedication in 1886.

But the best times of all were the ones when Cody came to town and put on dances and floor shows and stage shows at the opera house. "Why, when Bill put on dances there, I've seen the floor so crowded with couples and sets that you couldn't squeeze another one on," said Edd Wright.[4] And Charles Stamp backed him up with, "When Cody had dances, it was a high old time for everybody, and he was always the center of everything."[5]

Another interesting Cody custom soon grew out of the appearance of road shows at Lloyd's. Half a century later, grey-haired men, who were boys in the heydays of the opera house, told about it. "When Cody was at home and word got around that a show was coming to the opera house, the town boys would begin to gather. Then some of the bigger boys would scout around and find Mr. Cody, who was usually in Guy Laing's pool hall, just off the barroom. The boys would let him know they wanted to see the show, and he'd make arrangements with the box office and the boys would line up at the window and be counted in. We never saw a ticket, but we saw all the shows, and Buffalo Bill paid the count. No one was ever turned away, and I'm afraid to tell you how many there would be of us. You wouldn't believe me if I told you."[6]

It made no difference who the boys were. Johnny Dugan, the half-Negro boy whose widowed mother eked out a living cleaning saloons, and many another poor boy who otherwise would never have seen any kind of a show, saw some of the best on the boards at the magnificent opera house because Buffalo Bill "paid the count."

19

Entertainment
1886

On February 14, 1886, Will Cody, the eternal optimist, wrote to sister Julia from Staten Island: "I think our poor days are over for I really believe the public now looks upon me as the one man in my business. And if they will only think so for a year or two I will make money enough for us all for our life time." It was good that he was doing so well with his Combination and that he had bright prospects for his Wild West for the coming season, for he had lost the Cleveland land suit and with it the dream of great wealth for his sisters.

In his letter he went on to urge Julia and Al not to be discouraged, and to assure them that a new house would soon be built on the ranch. "If I was pushed I could take up all my notes tomorrow," he continued, "so don't worry about me, but figure on a house and a *good one*. I want a parlor & a bed room with a bath room."[1] When he was home at Christmas time, he had seen the crowded situation at the existing ranch house, where in addition to her own family of nine, Julia was cooking for a dozen or so men. These latter included the ranch crew, cowboys in training for the Wild West show, and, a little later, Jule Keen, who recuperated from a broken arm at the ranch before rejoining the show. During most of the life of his Wild West, Cody often had one or more of his show people recovering from injuries or illness at the ranch.

On the day Cody was writing Julia from New York, his "Prairie Waif" was showing in eastern Nebraska, after completing successful engagements in Kansas City and Topeka. Matt Snyder must have been playing the part of Buffalo Bill in the "Waif" at that time, but Cody caught up with the show by the time it reached his home state and was with it when it played in Hastings, for the Hastings Gun Club invited him to shoot with its members while the show was in town. The club had some very excellent marksmen with shotguns, and some of them "did Mr. Cody up nicely"; but when that part of the meet was finished, Cody "caressed his rifle and showed them how to shoot" by breaking five balls out of six thrown from a revolving trap. He then gave one of the sports a silver dollar and told him to toss it into the air as high as he could. "The coin went up, Bill shot, and the coin, oh, where was it? After searching in vain it could not be found, the bullet having taken it in its embrace and carried it off. A reward is offered for its return to this reporter. This was as fine a display of marksmanship as has ever been seen in this neck of the woods."[2]

While in North Platte for the "Waif's" appearance at the Lloyd's Opera House, Cody visited with Al and Julia to help them plan the new house he wanted, and he and Al walked over the ranch grounds to decide where the fine new groves would stand. The Platte Valley today is so well-timbered, it is difficult to envision it as the treeless region it was when Buffalo Bill began to put his ranch together. There were few trees even in the town, and none at all on the ranch or on the wide expanse of grassy valley in between.

From trains passing by on the Union Pacific rails, passengers could see all the way to the river back of the ranch, and from the time of his first land purchase Cody had dreamed of a show place on the prairie north of the town. Instead of the narrow house and its adjacent buildings, he would have a palatial house, barns larger than any in the western half of the state, and a lake large enough for canoeing, all shaded by great groves of tall trees. In his mind's eye he could see how they would look from the passing trains, "a show place that would be the talk of the country." With the money he would send them, his beloved sister and her good husband would make his dreams come true.

The Goodmans were popular in North Platte. Lizzie, the eldest daughter, was an attractive young lady of sixteen. Will, the oldest son, helped his father on the ranch. Ed, about the same age as Johnny Baker, traveled with the show that summer. Josephine, the second daughter, and her younger brothers went to school in town, driving in from the ranch in a small, fancy two-seated carriage wth a fringed top.

As soon as the frost went out of the ground in the spring, Al Goodman started setting out trees and enlarging the lake from which the new groves would be irrigated. One of his helpers was eighteen-year-old Ernest Tramp, who was put to work with a team and slip, or "scraper," throwing up a higher dam at the lower end of the lake. One day an accident with the scraper knocked him unconscious and cut a nasty gash in his foot. Sixty-five years later, Tramp recalled: "Mrs. Goodman saw the team standing with their front feet up on the bank of dirt I had scraped up, and she thought something was wrong. So she came and picked me up and carried me into the house and laid me on the couch in the parlor. She got a piece of tobacco and chewed it and bound it on the wound to stop the bleeding. She was a fine woman, large and very good looking and motherly."[3]

In April, while Buffalo Bill was preparing to break up his Combination and quit the theater forever, one of his professional friends, Mary Anderson, created quite a stir by stopping off very briefly in North Platte. Celebrities in the town were not unusual, and all were appropriately dealt with by the enterprising newsmen of the place. During the decade of the eighties, incredible numbers of businessmen and land-seekers were flooding the West, wealthy hunters were still taking sashays to the plains, and prominent personages like Miss Anderson were traveling coast to coast. Travel was so extensive that the *Tribune* in late March stated that 7,200 people, an average of more than 40 per day, had signed the register at the Pacific House in the past six months, and the town's other three hotels were not far behind. The Pacific dining room was also the dinner stop for through passenger trains, and good-sized crowds of townspeople were in the habit of gathering at the depot to watch the evening train come in and see what important people might get off the cars and head for the dining room.

Miss Anderson arrived April 24 on Number Two, the eastbound evening passenger train. An admiring crowd quickly surrounded her table in the big dining room while the *Tribune* man interviewed her. The charming and popular actress was enroute east, following a most successful engagement on the Pacific coast. In her home town of Louisville, Kentucky, a theater had been named for her, and her stage career of the past seven years had been one of such uninterrupted success that, next to the great Lotta, she had accumulated more wealth than any other American actress. But what made the lady's stop in North Platte of especial interest to the community was the fact, as she charmingly informed the reporter, that she proposed to purchase A. J. Miller's horse ranch south of town. The ranch, she said, had been highly recommended to her by Mr. W. F. Cody, and she believed it would be a splendid investment as well as a delightful place to visit as often as her stage work would allow.

If the sale went through, she confided, she would put the place in charge of a relative and stock it with thoroughbreds, as she was passionately fond of horses. Well pleased with what she could see of North Platte and its surroundings, she would enjoy spending a month at the ranch as soon as it could be arranged. "You may tell your readers," she smiled from her window as the train pulled out, "that I am anxious to secure Mr. Miller's property and would like very much to become acquainted with the people of North Platte."

The week following the *Tribune's* glowing account of Miss Anderson and her intentions, the Hastings *Gazette-Journal* commented enviously: "North Platte is trying to start a boom by advertising to the world that Mary Anderson is negotiating for a stock ranch near that city. What with Buffalo Bill and Mary Anderson, North Platte is evidently going to be the Athens of Nebraska."

Not long before Miss Anderson stopped off at the Pacific, William Alstadt, correspondent for the Omaha *Post*, had visited the Miller farm to "write it up" for his paper. McNulty of the North Platte *Telegraph* had set up the interview for him at the Miller place, five miles southwest of town. Alstadt wrote a long and enthusiastic account of his visit to the 1,280-acre model farm. Out of 370 acres then under fence (barbed wire fencing was still an experiment in western Nebraska at that time), 270 acres provided grazing for Miller's 200 head of horses. The place already boasted splendid stables and corrals, but that afternoon they witnessed the laying of the cornerstone for still another stable, 103 x 34 feet. The reporter waxed lyrical over the merits of the "fine stepper, Tib, Lulu B, next to him in speed, and the great stud, Globe." A splendid five-month-old colt, "Buffalo Bill, showed every promise of as brilliant a future in the horse world as the gentleman whose cognomen he bore has had before the foot lights." He noted the herd of fine, fat Holsteins and Durhams, and "1,000 chickens of various breeds in the henery, as well as turkeys, ducks and guinea hens." There was a smokehouse and cellar and an elegant new stone residence in the course of erection.

It was this fine layout that Cody's actress friend contemplated purchasing. For some unknown reason the deal was not consummated, and there is no record that North Platte people ever again saw the charming lady who had wanted to know them better.

In April Buffalo Bill disbanded his stage troupe in Denver and came on to North Platte with his friend, Buck Taylor, for a couple of weeks of recreation, after which he would leave for St. Louis to reorganize

2d SILVER BENEFIT.

McClellan Opera House,   (1886)

One Night Only.

Saturday Evening, April 3d.

THE ONLY AND ORIGINAL

BUFFALO BILL

HON. W. F. CODY,

Late Chief of the Scouts of the U. S. Army,

and his MAMMOTH COMBINATION
in his great Sensational Drama, entitled,

"The Prairie Waif,"

Introducing the Western Scout and Daring Rider,

Buck Taylor, King of the Cowboys.

A Genuine Band of Pawnee Indians,

Under Pawnee Billy, Boy Chief and Interpreter.

24 First Class Artists.   New and Beautiful Scenery

Mr. Cody, "Buffalo Bill," will give an exhibition of fancy Rifle Shooting,
holding his rifle in twenty different positions, in which he is acknowledged preeminent.

Prices of admission as usual.   Reserved seats, one dollar,
to be had at Forbes & Stromberg's.

Advertisement from the Georgetown *Courier* in Colorado, where
Cody's Combination played on its return from the west coast.

"the only true and original Wild West show" for its summer season.
While he was at home, some unnamed person seems to have challenged
Cody and his company to a bucking horse contest. The *Tribune*, under
the headline "A CHALLENGE," carried Cody's reply, "I have a man in my
employ that I will bet against any man in Nebraska to ride any way
named and for any amount of money, the party who put the challenge
in the paper not excepted. As an evidence that I mean business, $25

have been placed in the hands of the editor of the *Tribune* as a forfeit. Buffalo Bill."

To this the editor added his own comment: "If the gentleman who has issued the challenge has any sand, our people will probably have the pleasure of witnessing a riding match soon in which the celebrated Buck Taylor may show his style. Buffalo Bill means business, as is evidenced by the forfeit he has put up."[4]

The contest was to take place at Scout's Rest Ranch the next afternoon, a Sunday, and a large and excited crowd of "pleasure seekers" was on hand to see the show. But as the afternoon waned and the challenger did not show up, the disappointed crowd began to mill about and grumble. "To fill the void, one or two scrub races were quickly gotten up, but were poor satisfaction to those present."[5]

Prior to 1886, Cody's ranch north of town went by no particular name, but when he built the new house that year he was hoping to be able to retire there soon and become a "gentleman farmer." In that anticipation he thought of the place as Scout's Rest Ranch and began to refer to it that way. Soon afterward, when he built the first big barn at the ranch, he had the words SCOUT'S REST RANCH painted on the roof in huge letters, even as they are today.

As usual, when Cody was at home, things were lively, with members of his troupe coming and going. This time, in addition to Buck Taylor, Major Burke, well-acquainted and popular in the town, stopped off for a few days enroute to St. Louis to reorganize the Wild West. But of considerable more interest to the townspeople was a newcomer, four-teen-year-old Lillian Smith, "The California Girl."

Cody had added Lillian to his troupe while in California with the "Waif" and billed her as "The Champion Rifle Shot of the World." When the show broke up in Denver, he retained her for his Wild West and brought her on to North Platte, where she was billed to give an exhibition of shooting with rifle, shotgun, and revolver at the opera house on the evening of April 20.[6]

In the next issue of his paper, editor Bare referred to the girl as "the best shot in the world." Her performance, he wrote, "bordered on the marvelous, breaking twenty glass balls in twenty-four seconds with a Winchester rifle, and twenty balls with a single loading rifle in fifty-four seconds. This is shooting as fast as an ordinary gunman can shoot his piece, to say nothing of taking aim at a fast moving target. A beautiful feat was breaking two balls with one shot as the balls swung past each other in the air."

Born in Mono County, California, Lillian had been riding from baby-hood and had started shooting at seven. In her first attempt at glass balls, she had made 323 successive shots without a miss and broke 495 out of 500, using a Ballard .22.[7] Wonderful as she was, the girl never made the impact on the public, nor on history, that Annie Oakley did.

Late in April, Cody shipped several carloads of horses that his men had gathered over the winter to New York for use in his show when it opened at Erastina Park for the summer. On the last day of the month, he, with Lillian and other members of the show, left for St. Louis where the Wild West would open a few days later. Soon after his de-parture, it was learned in North Platte that he would take the entire show to London in 1887 for Queen Victoria's great Golden Jubilee cele-bration. It had taken a surprisingly short time for Buffalo Bill to make good on the prediction he had issued from the steps of the train that had borne him from his home town that May morning in 1883.

While Cody was on his way east, Tony Denier, the Great Pantomimist, was negotiating with Warren Lloyd for a date at the opera house for his hit show, "Buffalo Bill Among the Indians." Bare, in reporting this bit of theater news, also complained about manager Lloyd's habit, common among theatrical companies, of "cutting" plays in small towns, "some to such an extent as to entirely destroy the effect. . . . Whether the audience be large or small, each individual is entitled to that for which he pays, and we are creditably informed that Cody and Maggie Mitchell were the only persons who gave us the full plays this season."

However, the season at the opera house closed on a pleasant note, with "the peerless soubrette, Patti Rosa, captivating all hearts with her performance in 'Zip' "; and with the "little trick mare 'Dolly,' the equine that skates on rollers," giving an exhibition on the stage. Dolly drew a large audience, and all agreed she was a clever horse, "but as to the merits of her skating there was a diversity of opinion."[8]

And that spring the long battle waged by the editors of the town's newspapers against the deplorable condition of the streets appeared to be bearing some fruits of victory. In May the city street commissioner posted the following warning: "Notice: All persons are hereby notified not to deposit manure, rubbish or garbage of any kind either in the streets, alleys or sloughs within the city limits under penalty of the ordinance of the city of North Platte." Fast driving on Fifth Street and other public thoroughfares was also banned by order of the mayor, and the city attorney was directed to draft an ordinance "nullifying the right of livestock to occupy sidewalks in preference to tax-paying citizens."

The reign of the Texas steer has passed into the shades of the past, and it is now proper for the people to assert and maintain their rights, editor Bare exulted. "It will be seen that you can't let your cows run on the sidewalks any more unless you want to contribute $5 for the public good."

None of the Codys spent much time in North Platte that summer. The great Wild West had settled in at Erastina Park for a long and successful summer run. Arta spent the early part of the summer in Iowa, visiting school friends, and Mrs. Cody and little Irma had gone east for awhile. Whether or not they saw Mr. Cody is not known. In July all the Cody womenfolk returned to North Platte. So did Con Cronor, the huge Cowboy Sheriff who had "severed his connection with the Wild West for the present." All were "warmly greeted" by their many friends. About the same time, word of the death of Ned

Louisa Cody,
c. 1886.

Buntline, "the discoverer of our own Buffalo Bill," was duly noted by the local papers.

Late in the month, as Mrs. Cody and her daughters were preparing to leave the heat of the Platte Valley for the mountain coolness of Manitou Springs, Arta entertained her friends at her mother's home in town. Ira Bare, still a most eligible and much-sought-after bachelor guest at such affairs, provided his usual flowery description of the party in the next issue of his paper:

> A very gay company of young folks assembled at the Cody residence Thursday evening in response to invitations extended by that pleasing and ever popular young lady, Miss Arta Cody, whose hospitality has accorded her such a high position in the estimation of North Platte people. The guests began arriving at nine o'clock and by half past the elegantly furnished compartments were full of happy hearts. . . . In response to waltz music, ladies attired in brilliant, airy costumes, conducted by gentlemenly escorts floated through the spacious rooms, while those not inclined to the mazy whirl enjoyed cards and other games. The party was a success throughout—at no time did the amusement lag or grow dull. At one o'clock the guests departed, having spent one of the most pleasant evenings of the season. In entertaining the company, Arta was ably assisted by her mother.

Out at the ranch, the big new house was going up at a rapid rate. Cody had left the planning of the structure to his sister, and she had chosen to pattern it exactly after the home of Judge W. S. Peniston, just completed at the corner of Fifth and Locust Streets. She even hired the same carpenter-contractor, Patrick Walsh. A well-known local builder, Walsh contracted to build the two-story, nine-room house, with numerous closets and pantries, at the same price as the Peniston house, $3,500, which covered all materials, plastering, and painting. Her brother was pleased with her choice and asked only that it be finished in six months, or by October 15 at the latest, and that the porches be ten feet wide instead of the customary six feet, as he thought nothing was nicer than a wide porch.[9]

Edd Wright, an eighteen-year-old Ohioan who had arrived in town only that spring, hauled the buff-colored rock for the foundation. "The railroad hauled it in [from Colorado]," he said, "three carloads of it and dumped it beside the tracks, straight south of the ranch headquarters, and I loaded and hauled it over from there."[10]

All through August, work went on briskly at the new house which was to be "a cozy residence costing in the neighborhood of $6,000 when fully completed."[11] The new figure included the carpeting and furniture, for Buffalo Bill had ordered Royal Wilton, the "latest style" in carpeting, for the downstairs front rooms and requested that all the furniture match it in elegance. Julia was to go to Omaha to select the furniture, but for himself he wanted "a side board [and] some nice decanters & glasses." These were to go in his bedroom upstairs, he said, where he wanted "a nice large bedsted & a nice bed . . . then if anyone gets full I can put them to bed."[12]

From the day the first course of stone was laid for the foundation, the road most often used for an evening drive or a Sunday afternoon spin was the one leading from town out to Scout's Rest Ranch. Everyone wanted to see how the new ranch house, "one of the handsomest residences in the western part of the state," was coming on. Interest in the country estate was even keener when it was learned that Cody had lately had his banker, Charles McDonald, purchase another 300 acres of land from the Ditch Company at $8 an acre, making "Bison William's ranch one of the finest properties in the state."[13]

The summer of 1886 was not only a great success for the Honorable W. F. Cody but the beginning of a long succession of victories and triumphs. At the show's opening in St. Louis, 40,000 people filled the stands. General W. T. Sherman was present on opening day at Erastina Park on Staten Island. Mark Twain saw the show two days in succession and declared it a "genuine" western exhibition, "wholly free from shame and insincerity." P. T. Barnum went to see it, the first time in forty years that he had gone to any show but his own, and had only words of praise.

Evening shows were held at Erastina; and twice a day all summer, except Sundays, the Wild West performed to capacity crowds of 20,000. Seventeen steamboats daily brought full loads of passengers to the island, and the Indians, cowboys, riding, shooting, and re-creation of the colorful Old West pleased them all. In July Buffalo Bill announced in the New York papers that he would give free tickets to all newsboys and bootblacks riding to the island on the first boat on a certain day. Fifteen hundred boys showed up and were given sack lunches as well as tickets. Cody made the boys a speech, urging them to go to school and Sunday school and do their best to be good citizens. From that day on, newsboys and bootblacks tagged him everywhere he went in New York, urging free papers and shines on him.

Other news from Erastina reached North Platte by way of letters from young Ed Goodman to his mother, Julia. In his letters he confided to her matters that he could not speak of on the show grounds. He was bothered by the way Johnny Baker was fooling his foster father:

> Johnie runs out very near every night with some of the boys and does not come in until 2 or 3 oclock in the morning and then half the time he is *drunk* but he gets sobered up by morning and Uncle Will does not know anything about it. . . . [B]ut you must not say a word so that Uncle Will will find it out for he don't know it and I would not have him find it out through me for anything. . . . Johnie & I make it all right [but] he is as big a gambler as there is in camp and there is a good deal of it going on. . . . Uncle Will never touches a drop I don't think I never hear of him doing so.[14]

This last statement is in accordance with most reliable reports of Cody's abstinence from alcohol during the show's activities. His sprees were on his own time, between seasons.

Later in the summer Ed wrote of his own difficulties with money: "I have hardly saved a cent . . . this whole season . . . and I can not see where it all goes to." Ed assured his mother that he neither drank nor gambled, and never would, and went on: "I am paying board now which is three dollars a week. The reason why I do that is because Uncle Will got mad at me a little and did that as a punishment for me. It was the only thing he could do and that was what he did. But he is all right now and as good as pie to me But I have to pay my board never the less."[15]

None of the Codys was in town when the *Telegraph*, on August 19, brought its readers the latest word on the exploits of its famous citizen:

> There seems little doubt now that our townsman, Hon. W. F. Cody, is the greatest showman on earth if judged by the number of people who go to see his show and their enthusiasm over the excellence of his entertainment, and there is no other fair standard to judge by. Barnum never had a daily attendance so large and so long sustained. Mr. Cody will keep his Wild West at Erastina Park till cold weather, and for this winter he has rented Madison Square Garden in New York City, paying a rent of $18,000 per month. As another incident showing the magnitude of Mr. Cody's operation, we mention that he has in preparation a book descriptive of the Wild West and has contracted for a first edition of 500,000 copies, a larger number for

a single edition than has ever been printed of any other book save the Bible. This book is for free distribution. Mr. Cody has promised that North Platte shall have at least one page in this book, which will be of great benefit to us in the way of advertising our resources. By the way, Mr. Cody has always been a great advertiser of our city and country.

When Mrs. Cody and her daughters came home from the mountains in early September, the town was in a buzz of preparation for the upcoming county fair. The latest word from Buffalo Bill was that he definitely would be home in time for the fair, and that in addition to the chariot races he would put on a twenty-five-mile horse race. Both, stated the *Tribune*, were "features never before attempted at a county fair." Telegrams were flying between North Platte and Staten Island, and when the showman advised the Agricultural Society that he could be in town by October 5, the dates of October 6-9 were promptly set for the fair. Cody, it was reported, had already placed an order with a local harness maker for the "peculiar harness" required for chariot races.

Plans, already in the making to give Cody a fitting reception on his arrival home, were given a boost when it was learned he had actually signed the contracts to take his show to London the following year. There are always those who refuse to believe in another's good fortune until it is down "in black and white," and the *Tribune* made it so on September 11:

> Contracts are signed and everything closed in black and white. Under the management of an English Syndicate he [Cody] is to go to London next season with his Wild West show to give two performances daily for six months, receiving one-third of the gross receipts, the company paying the expenses. Mr. Cody considers this the biggest deal he has ever made and something of its magnitude may be imagined when it is confidentially expected . . . that the receipts will run away above $600,000. Mr. Cody has made money this season but he will make barrels next year.

The papers did not spare the type as October approached. "Let everybody pull together," the *Tribune* urged, "and give Buffalo Bill the handsomest reception ever known in the city. North Platte has reason to feel proud of the world-wide reputation her honored citizen has received and should show her appreciation of him."

Even the Omaha *Republican* took notice of the showman's return by announcing that the "Hon. W. F. Cody will soon be roaming over the boundless prairies of Nebraska which he loves so well, and inhaling huge draughts of life-giving ozone that exhilarates but does not intoxicate."

With the big week at hand, each committee was outdoing all the others in preparation for the great banquet at which "the menu cards, to serve also as souvenirs, will be the handsomest ever used in this city and the supper will be on the same grand scale. Altogether, the affair will be worthy the guest and the hosts."

While the reception preparations were going feverishly ahead in North Platte, Cody was closing his show at Erastina, preparatory to moving it to Madison Square Garden for the winter. At noon on their last day in New York, the Pawnee, Sioux, and Commanche Indians who had been with the show all summer were eating their last dinner before leaving for their home reservations. All were decked out in new boots, pants, vests, and broad-brimmed felt hats. The night before they had performed a Medicine Dance in honor of their friend, Buffalo Bill.

They had planted an eagle feather in the center of the great tent and danced around it. No man dared touch the feather unless he had killed a man in battle and could prove it by someone present. "Rocky Bear, chief of the Ogalla Sioux, touched it several times, as did American Horse, the warrior chief of the Sioux nation. Lone Wolf touched the feather sixteen times and then plunged him arm into a large kettle of boiling water, from the bottom of which he took a beef bone."[16]

A full *Tribune* column, under the banner WELCOME HOME, described the reception tendered Cody by the people of North Platte as "the most pleasant and successful affair ever given in the city." That his friends were well aware of his importance is shown by the prelude to the account of the entertainment:

> Mr. Cody needs no introduction to the people of our city, of Nebraska or the United States. From the oriental to the occidental shores of this vast continent his name is of household familiarity and, as P. T. Barnum recently said, Buffalo Bill is known to more people by sight than any man living. The fame and reputation he has acquired has been well earned and merited. From the position of bull-whacker in the early days he passed through the various stations of wagon-master, pony express rider, government scout, stock raiser and actor until he stands today unrivaled as the greatest showman on the face of the earth.

During the period Mr. Cody has been before the people of the United States as showman, and as such gaining wealth and fame, he has not forgotten the fair city of the plains in which he first conceived the idea of presenting to the world a realistic and true representation of western life. In various ways he has shown recognition of the warm friendship and esteem for the people of our city and it was only fitting that they should tender him a reciprocation of that friendship in the shape of a banquet.

Mr. Cody having previously announced Wednesday morning as the date of his arrival, flags floated in the breeze in different parts of the city and an immense crowd together with the cornet band gathered at the depot to extend a welcome hand to their honored citizen. Stepping off the train, Mr. Cody was surrounded by personal friends and, after a general handshaking, was escorted into the hotel for breakfast.

At nine o'clock in the evening participants in the banquet began assembling at the Pacific hotel and by ten o'clock about eighty business and professional men awaited the opening of the dining room doors. Shortly after that hour Professor Klein's orchestra struck up a march and the party, headed by Mr. Cody, Mr. Hinman and Mr. Foley filed into the dining hall. To properly describe the decorations, the tables and the menu would require columns, and we can but say that never in the history of North Platte has the like been equalled. The most critical could point out no defects in the arrangement of the table or the cuisine.

Mr. Hinman delivered the address of welcome to which Mr. Cody responded in neat and fitting words, thanking the gentlemen present for the testimonial of their regard. Then followed responses to sentiments by Jule Keene, T. J. Foley, J. W. Bixler, Chas. McDonald, Major Walker, Dr. Dick and many others, all giving testimony to their and the people's high regard for the great and only Buffalo Bill. Late in the evening Mr. Cody, in reply to a request, gave a description of the performance which he will give at Madison Square Garden in New York this winter. The evening was one of solid enjoyment throughout, nothing occurring to mar the harmony of the occasion. About half past one, after bidding the famed guest goodnight, the party dismissed, everyone feeling that the hour for departure had come too soon.[17]

In part the Platters honored Cody because of his worldwide fame and popularity, and because they wanted the rest of the state to know they appreciated him, but mostly they were pleased to do it because they just plain liked Buffalo Bill.

Everybody's attention turned to the fair the next day. Practically every vehicle in the valley that had a wheel to stand on was pressed into service for the rest of the week to take visitors to the fairgrounds and back, making it a prosperous period for "Jehus, or people with rigs for hire."

Among the many out-of-town visitors at the fair were A. H. Fitch, solicitor for the Omaha *Bee*, and W. C. Thompson, a prominent citizen of Davenport, Iowa. Both had come especially to attend the Wednesday night reception, and Thompson, when called upon to make a speech at the banquet, said he thought the Platters were a little selfish in claiming Mr. Cody, as he was actually a native of Scott County, the county in which the speaker resided, and that the residents thereof laid claim to at least a portion of the honor which had been conferred upon the great Buffalo Bill.

Prominent among the milling crowds at the fairgrounds was the tall figure of the happy showman, overseeing the races, the dominant feature of the fair, and outdoing even the seventy-eight-pound pumpkin on display in the agricultural building. Everybody wanted to shake hands with the handsome Cody, to comment on his fine new home, looming up a mile to the northwest, or to talk about the north river bridge, soon to be built, which he had helped promote the year before.

The chariot races were scheduled for Friday afternoon, and the stores and schools closed so that all could go to the races. As the hour approached, the crowd began to gather at the starting point to watch the strange vehicles and their spirited teams assemble and maneuver for position. From town to the fairgrounds the road was lined with wagons, buggies, and carriages, all hurrying to the races, when a rider came racing from town, bringing word that Bangs Livery Stable was burning.

At the dread call of FIRE! most of the people already at the race track headed pell-mell for town, meeting head-on the crowd on the way out, which, of course, turned about and raced back in the wake of the others. As a result, almost no one saw the races that afternoon— and the stable burned to the ground anyway. Although everybody had done all they could, not only the big barn but several nearby buildings were destroyed, and the abutting rear end of the big opera house was badly scorched. When it was over and the sooty volunteer fire fighters learned that two teams had perished in the blaze, they took up a subscription and presented the cash to the emigrant who had owned the horses.

The Twenty-five Mile Race the next day at the oval track was well attended, and excitement was high. According to the rules, each rider could have up to six horses and must change mounts at the end of each mile, or oftener if he wished. Each rider was allowed two assistants to aid him in changing horses, although he must mount and dismount without help. The winner, S. M. Beardsley, who won the $75 purse by riding fifteen miles in thirty-seven minutes and fifty-three seconds before dropping out, beat the runner-up, Frank Wheeling, who retired from the race at the end of twelve-and-a-half miles.

The new house on the Cody ranch was finished just in time to welcome its owner home, and he expressed his satisfaction with it as Julia showed him through its rooms. A September freeze, however, had killed the leaves on the two-year-old trees, and the young saplings stood stark and bare—the only way Buffalo Bill was to see them for many a year.

For quite some time editor Bare consistently referred to the new dwelling as Mr. Cody's "palatial residence," and before he left for Denver on Thursday morning of the next week, Buffalo Bill gave a pleasant reception there for a number of his friends, including "several attorneys from abroad who were in attendance on court," entertaining them in his usual princely style.

Cody was back in town in time to attend an "elegant reception" given in his honor on October 21 at the home of Mr. and Mrs. T. J. Foley. The following evening he helped Julia and Al celebrate the birthday of their eldest daughter, Lizzie, with a party for forty guests. Bare wrote:

> The brilliantly illuminated mansion presented a very attractive appearance as viewed from a distance and as the carriages rolled up to the entrance the occupants were received by that prince of gentlemen, the redoubtable Buffalo Bill. When all the guests had arrived the orchestra struck up a waltz and for an hour or two the mazy whirl kept up. Card games and songs, and recitations by the funny Mr. Keen added much to the enjoyment of the evening. Miss Goodman received many handsome presents and many kind wishes. A superb supper was served and the party dismissed about two in the morning.

The day following the party at the ranch "the funny Mr. Keen" left for the reservation to engage new Indians for the Wild West show soon to open in Madison Square Garden. Vacation time was almost over. In a few days Buffalo Bill, too, would be on his way to New York and the heavy routine of "two-a-day" with the big show for the rest of the winter.

It was about this time that the editors of the Platte papers admitted they had been premature in rejoicing over an anticipated improvement in the state of the streets of the town. By now the city had several blocks of board sidewalk, and even a short stretch of brick walk in the business district, and the town council had finally gotten around to having Ordinance No. 53 drawn: "It shall be unlawful for any person to lead, drive, ride or permit any horse, mule, colt, cow or ox to go upon any sidewalk in the city of North Platte." Although the edict was to take effect immediately, enforcement had been so lax that one discouraged editor reported: "Grocers are still complaining of cattle eating vegetables on the sidewalks and from their delivery wagons." Apparently the city fathers were not too eager to gather in five-dollar bills for the public good, so the livestock still occupied the sidewalks, along with tax-paying citizens.

Shortly after Buffalo Bill left North Platte for the East, a well-known theatrical company, which normally played only in good-sized cities, stopped overnight to present its very popular play "On the Rio Grande" at the Lloyd's. Cody had met the manager, a friend of his, in New York and asked him to put on the show in North Platte as he passed through on his way to Denver. "A large crowd enjoyed the play and further efforts in this direction will be gratefully received by our people," observed editor Bare.

By Thanksgiving the *Tribune's* society columns were bulging with accounts of parties given by Arta and her friends. Arta entertained at her home just before Thanksgiving, Grace Stewart just afterward. A few evenings later the initial "hop of the season" was given by the Apollo Club at the Pacific House. The leading social affair the next week was a large party at the Foley's, followed by the first Progressive Euchre soiree of the winter. The final society note for 1886 took note of the departure of "the popular Miss Arta Cody," just after Christmas, to spend a month with friends in Lincoln and other eastern points.

20

To England
1886-1887

The Lincoln County *Tribune* on November 20 reprinted a long excerpt from the *New York Weekly*; under the heading "A Living Hero," it carried a glowing account of the reception given Buffalo Bill in North Platte on October 5. The *Tribune* also copied from the New York *World* a description of the preparations going on at Madison Square Garden for the opening of the Wild West:

The Indians to be used in the new Wild West at Madison Square Garden will arrive tomorrow and the cowboys, Mexican vaqueros and others will follow. The most extensive alterations are being made in the interior of the vast structure under the supervision of Buffalo Bill and Messrs. Steele Mackaye and Matt Morgan. The thousands who witnessed the Wild West on Staten Island last summer will be surprised at the difference in the style of the entertainment to commence on the 22nd in the Garden. About one hundred trained animals are to be utilized and the reorganized Wild West will present in coherent form the history of the conquest of the wilderness by the heroic pioneers of civilization. The perils begotten of the elemental forces of nature, as well as those entailed by the hostility of the Indians will be exhibited with a realism at once beautiful, terrible and humorously entertaining.

Buffalo Bill is the most enthusiastic individual about the Garden and declares this will be the culminating triumph of his career. It is claimed that the alterations alone will foot up to an expense of over $60,000. Mr. Matt Morgan has employed his artistic brush on

179

15,000 yards of canvas with startling results. In fact the whole exhibition will be on a scale of grandeur and magnificence.

Cody and Salsbury had indeed employed the best men in their fields to stage and direct the new show, "The Drama of Civilization," a wildly colorful collection of Indians, buffalo, cowboys, cowgirls, settlers, wagon trains, a stagecoach, a blazing prairie fire, a cyclone, the Pony Express, Annie Oakley, Lillian Smith, Johnny Baker, and Custer's Last Stand.

The show opened on schedule, and a week later Ed Goodman wrote his family they were turning people away every night, with seats costing from $.75 to $1.50 and standing room at $.25 and $.50. Even the boxes at $5.00-$12.00 each were always filled. After all, a show that was good enough to be invited to London for six months was surely worth seeing in its native land.

Late in the fall a letter nearly two columns long, signed by "Brick" Pomeroy and addressed to the editor of the *Tribune*, appeared on the front page of that paper, further exciting the Platters. Mr. Pomeroy, in London on business, wrote:

Buffalo Bill was more talked about than any other man in the world. Men ask me every day how he looks and acts; his size and habits; where he was born, how he came to have such a singular name; where and how he lives; where North Platte is and the kind of people there. All manner of questions are put to me simply because I am an American citizen and known to be one of the many friends of the great central figure around whom the Wild West will revolve while in Europe. . . .

A few nights since at a club Major John M. Burke . . . was surrounded by at least seventy-five prominent citizens who, for an hour or so, listened to some of the bright events in the life of Buffalo Bill, and descriptions of Isaac Dillon, Mr. Keith and other owners of cattle ranches in Nebraska; of A. J. Miller, of Buck Taylor and Con Groner, of Jule Keen and of old John Nelson, the white Ingomar of the Sioux; of little Johnny Baker, who will be the envied of the juvenile princes.

Pomeroy told of his visit to the grounds where the great American Exposition was to be set up, and described the adjoining tract of seven acres that under the direction of Major Burke was even then being readied for the Wild West show. About one hundred teams were at work smoothing and grading the grounds "so there will be a perfect soil and sod for the performers who will have millions to witness their maneuvers."

The grand stand will be covered and will easily accommodate 25,000. The private boxes for the royal family and the crowned heads and courts of Europe are to be modern and seats and conveniences for 40,000 people are being provided outside the grandstand. . . . Besides the tent headquarters and fittings for Buffalo Bill, there will be tents and offices for all the lieutenants and chief assistants. Also adobe houses for the Mexican cowboys, tents for the Texas cowboys, tepees, tents and lodges for the different bands of Indians; houses for the army of help that will be required, stables, wigwams for trophies and curiosities, buildings for refreshments, water tanks, telegraph and telephone offices and accommodations for reporters, artists and newsgatherers.

The whole was to be handsomely landscaped with streams, trees, and flowers. The grounds were surrounded on three sides by three railroad lines that "can set down or take up two thousand people per minute," and were accessible by cabs, carriages, and omnibuses. Pomeroy concluded that the average daily attendance was expected to be 60,000, although he thought the figure too low.

All of this convinced North Platte people that they, too, should see Buffalo Bill's "colossally realistic production" before it left its native shores. Therefore, early in the new year an excursion from North Platte to New York city was being "talked up." The plan was to get a party of forty or fifty persons and charter a railroad car for the trip. The main difficulty, according to the facetious editor, was whether the excursionists should be twenty men and their wives or forty men and lots of fun.

The excursion never got out of town, but every scrap of news about the show was eagerly received by the home town folks. They said it was "just like Bill," when they heard he had treated his Indians to a Christmas feast of stewed dog at the Garden, or when he entertained 10,000 school children at his show.

Early in February Mrs. Cody went to Lincoln to visit friends. Arta and little Irma joined her there a little later and went on to New York with her. Just what happened between Will and Louisa there can only be surmised. Probably the best clues are in a letter Ed Goodman wrote his father on March 17:

I received your letter this morning and am sorry to hear of Uncle Will's ——— [word deleted] What do you think about it anyway, and do you think the folks [probably Mrs. Cody and the girls] will go to Europe. I suppose Aunt Lue will do the same by me as she did with brother Will when he was there at N.P. that is she will turn the heart of Uncle Will against me if they make up again. As for me saying that about Aunt Lue that is like a good many more of her stories; as I never mention their family troubles to any one as no one in the Co. new any thing about there family troubles until she came and told it herself and every one knows it now and they come to me to find the full particulars but I do not tell them any thing about it at all but she told every one she saw here . . . one lady especially that lives at the Hoffman House maybe you have heard Uncle Will mention her name. a Miss DeValasco; and she tell me all about her all I knew and more too but I never made such a remark as she says I did she knows the whole family history better than I do for what Uncle Will told her and Aunt Lue she has got the whole thing down *pat*! . . . And I never said a *word* against Uncle Will for . . . he has always treated me right. Uncle Will knows that I would never say any thing about him behind his back that I would not say to his face. . . .

Well now I will make it all right I guess. I got $5.00 from Mr. Salsbury and that will keep me until Uncle Will gets here if he gets here by Sunday [March 20] and if he does not I will make it all right as I have plenty of friends in the Co.[1]

Mrs. Cody and her daughters returned to North Platte on February 27. Buffalo Bill closed his winter engagement on the twenty-second, although he was still playing to packed houses. On February 26, his forty-first birthday, he and Salsbury incorporated their Wild West by issuing one hundred shares of stock, of which they each held thirty-five. The remaining thirty shares were divided among three of their close friends.[2] The corporation held its first stockholders' meeting two days later, on Salsbury's forty-first birthday.

The following week Cody left for North Platte with two friends, Dr. Frank Powell and George Canfield. It must have been this visit home that worried young Ed, who feared his Aunt Louisa would "turn the heart of Uncle Will" against him if they made up again. It seems likely they had quarreled in New York, and certainly there was jealousy and bitterness between the women Cody loved best, his wife and his oldest sister.

While on his visit home, Cody had the pleasure of helping Al Goodman receive three imported thoroughbred stallions at his ranch. Their average cost, according to the *Tribune*, was $5,000 each, and they were "acknowledged by all to be the finest ever delivered in this part of the state. . . . Few, if any, ranches in the west have ever seen finer bred cattle and horses than are on Scouts Rest Ranch."

During that same week "several members of the Roland Reed Company, including the star himself, were the guests of Buffalo Bill on Wednesday afternoon, and there is no doubt they were royally entertained by the greatest showman on Earth."[3] Reed, a well-known comedian, and his company appeared at the Lloyd's in "Cheek" that evening and were acclaimed as among the very best.

While Cody was "resting up" in North Platte, two of his best friends were, as one newspaper put it, "committing matrimony" in New York. Nate Salsbury married Miss Ray Samuels. Colonel Bob Ingersoll, the notorious agnostic, a long-time friend of the groom, was one of the wedding guests. The other bridegroom was Buck Taylor, "famous cowboy and bronco rider and one of Buffalo Bill's old standbys." Buck married a pretty New York girl, "and it makes his old pards here stand cross-legged and whistle out of the corners of their mouths when they hear that the bride is worth $100,000." Other showmen, the *Tribune* editor added, had tried to get Buck away from Cody but failed, "and he goes to London with the Wild West."[4]

In the last few days before his March 17 departure for New York, Cody sent an agent to Pine Ridge to recruit the Indians he would take with him to England. "These favored Indians, before starting on their long journey, gave a farewell reception to the members of their tribe and bid them a sad adieu." For the Sioux believed that if any of their people attempted to cross the ocean they would fall sick, waste away, and die.

In August 1923 Tim McCoy was at the Wind River Reservation in Wyoming trying to persuade some of his Arapahoe friends to accompany him to England for six months in a promotional campaign for the movie "The Covered Wagon." Cody's Wild West had years ago provided ample experience of European travel for American Indians, but it had by no means cleared the way for McCoy and his proposal. Yellow Calf complained to McCoy:

It bothers me to go across the Big Water. I have talked with many Sioux who went over to this far country with Buffalo Bill. They tell me that when you take this big canoe it goes so far out onto the water that when you look back, there is no land and when you look ahead, there is no land. They also tell me that the land you will be going to is a small island. What is to prevent the big canoe from missing the tiny island and falling off the other side? No, . . . you ask too much of us.

Broken Horn grumbled: "You know, you get in that big canoe and pretty soon it goes up and down. You, also, go up and down. You throw up so much that you die. Then the white man throws you into the Big Water. How do you find the trail to the Great Mystery when you are at the bottom of the Big Water?"[5]

Buffalo Bill at all times had his western friends looking for good bucking horses and bronc riders, and when at home tried out both horses and men for possible additions to his show. This visit was no exception, and Otto Thoelecke, reminiscing more than half a century later, told how he had thought he might qualify for the show and get a trip to Europe: "So I mounted a horse that had been trained to perfection—not in the best way but the best in its way—bucking. There was a lot of applause, but I learned that it was for the horse, not me. So the horse went to Europe and I stayed home."[6] When such tryouts were held at the ranch, a big crowd always gathered to watch the fun.

Ever loyal to his adopted state and well aware of the favorable publicity that would ensue, Cody chartered the State Line ship *State of Nebraska* for the voyage to the Old World. Then, on his way east to help assemble and load the show, he was asked to stop in Lincoln so that Nebraska's governor, John M. Thayer, could appoint and commission him "Aid-de-camp on my staff with the rank of Colonel."

The title, of little value in the United States, sounded important abroad, and from then on Cody, formerly only "Honorable," was now legally a "Colonel," and was often so called. Cody's army officer friends followed through by presenting him with a jeweled sword, which further impressed the British press.

Yet further support was furnished Cody by his army friends. It was thought wise to collect letters of introduction for Cody to carry to England. Accordingly, John Burke called on the army officers with whom Cody had served. In less than two months he had secured complimentary letters from William T. Sherman, the only living four-star general in the United States; Philip Sheridan, commanding general of the army; Generals Crook, Merritt, Miles, and Emory; as well as many others of the highest ranking officers in the army, all generously praising their friend and former scout and guide. Of course, such endorsements were unnecessary, but almost no one on this side of the Atlantic fully realized the extent to which Buffalo Bill was already well known and highly esteemed in England. Not only had advance publicity for the Wild West and its hero engendered excitement abroad, but Cody's fame had preceded his arrival by years because he had successively guided so many British nobles on big game hunts in the American West.

Thus, armed with his new commission and with the letters made redundant by his reputation, Colonel Cody, with 83 salon passengers, 38 steerage passengers, 97 Indians, 18 buffalo, 10 mules, 10 elk, 5 wild Texas steers, 4 donkeys, 2 deer, and 180 horses, sailed from New York on March 31. Bill Sweeney's thirty-six-member cowboy band, wearing uniforms of grey shirts, slouch hats, and moccasins, played "The Girl I Left Behind Me" as the *Nebraska* weighed anchor before the cheering dockside crowds.

The Omaha *World* carried an unfavorable report of Colonel Cody's commissioning, to which the *Tribune* made the following cheerful rebuttal as the *Nebraska* sailed from our shores:

The *World* utters a deep groan because Gov. Thayer has seen fit to appoint W. F. Cody as a representative at the coming World's Fair to be held at London. Having been a resident of Nebraska since a boy, Mr. Cody has had an opportunity to witness its wonderful development and is thoroughly conversant with the needs of this great commonwealth. It is just recognition of the services Buffalo Bill gave the state while she was clothed in infantile garments and we are glad to know that the Governor appreciates the men who helped by deeds of valor to make Nebraska what she is. But then, the *World* wouldn't be happy if it didn't have something to kick about.[7]

At this point an odd story comes to light. It began back near the end of the Civil War when the United States sent a detachment of the army from Philadelphia to Pine Ridge, a newly organized army post in Dakota Territory. As the soldiers marched through the city to entrain for the West, a five-year-old boy on his way to school heard the army band, was fascinated by the martial airs, and fell in behind the soldiers.

At the outskirts of the city the troops became aware of the boy, who knew his own name, William Irving, but could not tell them where he lived. The men, probably in a hurry, did not bother to try to find his home but simply took him along with them to Pine Ridge, where he made his home with the officer in charge, as long as the detachment was stationed there. When they left the post, the lad stayed on, living with a white family who had another foster child, Ella Bissonett, the daughter of the Sioux chief Rocky Bear.

As William grew up he became one of the top bronc riders of the Pine Ridge. He later married Ella Bissonett, and their first son, Benjamin, was born about 1882. Bennie was about two years old when his father heard that Buffalo Bill was organizing a wild west show and planning to tour the East. Bronco Bill, as he was known by then, thought this might be his opportunity to go east and try to find his long-lost home and family.

With his wife and son the rider traveled by covered wagon to North Platte and joined the show at one of Cody's "tryouts" at the ranch, for Bronco Bill was also a top hand with a rope and spoke Sioux fluently. Eventually the show played in Philadelphia, and there Bill rode the city trolley until he spied his old home "which was a house with a sort of cupola over the front door with a rooster in it near the top."[8] When Bronco Bill went to the door, "the doorman refused to let him in, for he was dressed in the beaded buckskin jacket and leggins worn by western people in those days." He then asked for the lady of the house and she was called. When Bill asked her if she had once had a little boy who ran away from home, she stared at him for quite awhile, then said, "You are the one."

The two families were quickly united, and thereafter Bronco Bill and his family visited at his old home whenever they were in the vicinity. Bennie was five years old when the Wild West went to England, and he well remembered the rough crossing of the Atlantic. Almost all of the passengers were fearfully seasick, and the Indians were constantly feeling themselves to see if their flesh was shrinking away. Buffalo Bill, "sick as a cow with hollow-horn" himself,[9] had all he could do to keep them from totally giving way to their fears. After the third day at sea, when everyone had recovered enough to anticipate a safe arrival on the foreign shore, various entertainments were devised and the rest of the voyage was fairly pleasant.

On April 16, the *State of Nebraska* docked in England. Back home the *Tribune* was announcing that John Neary, North Platte shoemaker, "without a doubt the best in the state, has just completed the most elaborate and best pair of boots ever made in the state." Made to order for W. F. Cody, they were worn by him in his show in London that summer and were not merely for show but "intended for wear" as well. Neary had the fine boots photographed, and the pictures were on sale at many North Platte places, including the Pacific House.

Pacific House and Union Pacific depot, North Platte.

From the moment of its arrival at Gravesend, Cody and his show received wide and generous acclaim. Three trains transported the show from the port of London to the Midland station, hard by the exhibition grounds, where the show people set up camp the same day. The speed with which this was done amazed the Britishers, about whom Ed Goodman, in a letter home, said: "The working class of people are the slowest people I *ever* saw. . . . one good American man can do as much work as 4 English men."[10] By four o'clock that afternoon everything was done and the camp cooks were getting supper. As the concluding rite of the day, the flag of the United States was raised to the breeze while the cowboy band played "our national air [to] a storm of shouts and cheers . . . from the thousands that lined the walls, streets and house-tops of the surrounding neighborhoods." This was so gratifying that the Colonel had his band play "God Save the Queen." So "The Wild West and Bill Cody, of Nebraska, U.S.A., 'was at home in camp in London.' "[11]

21

London
1887

All of the major English newspapers carried vivid and lengthy accounts of Buffalo Bill, the Indians (especially Ogilasa, Red Shirt), the animals, and the huge camp. Very shortly a host of lords and ladies, many prominent globe-trotting Americans, and a number of well-known show people were flocking to the grounds. Among the latter were Henry Irving, England's leading actor who had seen the Wild West at Erastina; Ellen Terry, foremost British actress; Mary Anderson, who had eaten supper at the Pacific House and talked of buying A. J. Miller's ranch on the Platte; and Justin McCarthy, Member of Parliament and author of the melodrama that was later made into the musical "The Vagabond King."

Lady Randolph Churchill came to call at the camp, also Lord Ronald Gower, Lord Henry Pagett, the Grand Duke Michael of Russia, Lady Monckton, and scores of other titled people. As a result, the Colonel, who made a most favorable impression everywhere, was deluged with invitations to breakfasts, luncheons, dinners, garden parties, suppers, and midnight lay-outs. Busy as he was in preparing for the grand opening of his show on May 9, he managed to accept most of them, whereupon he was made an honorary member of many of the best clubs in the kingdom. He lunched with the Lord Mayor and his lady at the Mansion House, met the Prince of Wales at the Reform Club, and dined at the Churchills'. The list of such affairs fills two pages in his autobiography.

The arena was not nearly completed when the show went into camp, and to make matters worse the English spring had turned "backward":

cold rains soaked the grounds. Yet, in spite of the heavy demands on his time from supervisory as well as social duties, the Colonel found time to repay some of the lavish hospitality offered him by staging two outstanding entertainments of his own. On April 25 he received at his camp the Right Honorable W. E. Gladstone, former prime minister, Mrs. Gladstone, and a party of their friends, including Thomas Waller, Consul General of the United States. The cowboy band welcomed the visitors, and, in spite of the wet arena and uncompleted track, put on a partial show for them. Later Cody entertained them at a luncheon where he sat beside Mrs. Gladstone.

The Gladstone party went off so well that Cody and his people essayed an even more ambitious party on May 5, four days before the grand opening, by inviting Albert, the Prince of Wales, later King Edward VII, to a special performance. The grounds were still in "unspeakably bad condition," but the royal box was "handsomely rigged out with American and English flags," and the occasion was prudently used by Buffalo Bill as a dress rehearsal for the big show. The Prince and Princess came with their three daughters, Louise, Victoria, and Maude; and many "other high placed attendants on the assembled royalties."[1]

Buffalo Bill had worried much over this affair, but needlessly, as it turned out. For he found the Prince and Princess unassuming and friendly, and from the moment the yelling Indians "swept round the enclosure like a whirlwind" to the very end when Annie Oakley and Lillian Smith shook hands with the Princess, all went well. This last, termed by Cody a "small solecism" because the American girls shook the Princess' hand instead of kissing it, did not mar the occasion at all, as the lady likewise shook hands as if she enjoyed it.

The royal party then visited the whole camp. The dignified Red Shirt made a fine impression on the visitors, and while the ladies petted John Y. Nelson's littlest papoose the Prince went over to Cody's tent, where he was much impressed with the gold-mounted sword given him by his army friends. The Prince then insisted on visiting the stables where the company's 200 horses were kept. The Colonel was proud of the "apple-pie" order of his stables that muddy day and pleased at the interest Albert displayed in Old Charlie, the twenty-one year-old horse that had long been Cody's favorite mount.

In spite of the sodden grounds, the fact that the Pine Ridge Indians were all new and had never seen the show before, and that a hundred of the horses were fresh from the plains of Texas and had never been

The American Exhibition at Earl's Court, from *The Illustrated London News*, April 16, 1887. The *News* account described Cody's part in this "novel idea": "A large covered bridge, crossing the railway, leads from the main building [above, left page] eastward to the ground nearest Earl's Court Station, where will be located 'Buffalo Bill's' Wild West Exhibition [above, right page]. . . . This remarkable exhibition, the 'Wild West,' has created a furore in America, and the reason is easy to understand. It is not a circus, nor indeed is it acting at all, in a theatrical sense; but an exact reproduction of daily scenes in frontier life, as experienced and enacted by the very people who now form the 'Wild West' Company. It comprises Indian life, 'cow-boy' life, Indian fighting and burning Indian villages, lassoing and breaking in wild horses, shooting, feats of strength, and Border athletic games and sports. It could only be possible for such a remarkable undertaking to be carried out by a remarkable man; and the Hon. W. F. Cody, known as 'Buffalo Bill,' guide, scout, hunter, trapper, Indian fighter, and legislator, *is* a remarkable man."

ridden or shot over, when it was all over he could say to himself, "Cody, you have fetched em!" and cease to worry.

Back home the Nebraska newspapers kept their readers informed of Buffalo Bill's triumphs. The Omaha *Bee* reported the visit of William Gladstone and his wife who expressed themselves charmed with the Wild West's interest, weirdness, and beauty. The account went on, obviously picking up the story from a British paper:

> The most noticeable party of Americans seen at the theatre here in a long time was one at Drury Lane last night, made up of Buffalo Bill and some of his Indians and cowboys. They occupied half a dozen boxes and the Indians, being in their paint and feathers, created a great sensation.
>
> Some of the Indians had never been in a theatre before and none had ever seen anything like the performance, in which there is much brilliant spectacle and many ballet girls. At one point the scene is quite exciting and Buffalo Bill raised and gave the signal to the Indians who joined in the applause with a regular war-whoop that almost took the breath away from the Britishers.[2]

The non-admiring Omaha *World* had not neglected Cody either, but the Lincoln *State Journal* took up the cudgel in his defense:

> Some of the Omaha newspapers are trying to explain that, though 'Bison William' of the Wild West Show is a Nebraskan and is the accredited delegate from this state to the American Exposition in London, his show wasn't picked up in this state. This is a foolish impertinence. Of course it is a Nebraska show, and the lords and gentlemen and beef eaters to her majesty all agree that the Wild West is all of the exposition worth looking at.
>
> First thing we know Chicago and Kansas City will be sending secret circulars to England pretending that they are in Nebraska and that Buffalo Bill is a resident of their respective villages on the frontier. By the time the genial Cody gets through exhibiting in England the Briton's idea of America will be that it is a great big patch of paradise called Nebraska, with some outposts in a little section called New England and New York.

By May 9, the day of the grand opening, the Londoners had taken many members of the show to their hearts, especially Red Shirt, John Nelson's half-Indian papoose, Bennie Irving, and Annie Oakley. The popularity of Red Shirt caused the *Tribune* editor to observe that the chief had made such a profound impression on the royal family that "red flannel will undoubtedly be the fashionable fad in next season's dress" in England, and that the Wild West had awakened such great interest in Indian literature that Cooper's works were being extensively republished in London.[3]

Fortunately, the weather had changed, and sunny skies and balmy breezes ushered in the opening day of the show as Colonel Cody proudly ran up the Stars and Stripes to welcome the 20,000 people who streamed onto the grounds. Ed Goodman wrote home that the opening-day admission price was "$5 or 1 pound."[4] The London papers were almost hysterical over the show. *Sporting Life* concluded its review by noting that such a "vast concourse of the cream— . . . the *creme de la creme*—of society is seldom seen at any performance. The number of chariots waiting at the gates outnumbered those of Pharaoh, and the phalanx of footmen constituted quite a small army."[5]

Another long feature in an "influential London paper" described the show in detail, praised the shooting by Lillian Smith and Buffalo Bill, and marveled at the Pony Express, the attack on the Deadwood stage, and the startling feat of Mustang Jack, who covered thirteen feet with a standing leap, and then jumped over a horse that stood sixteen hands high. But to the Londoners the most novel part of the entertainment was the bucking horses. "No cruelty is used to make these animals buck," the reporter explained. "It is simply a way they've got."

In May, while the show was enjoying the plaudits of all England, "Mrs. Taylor, the daughter of a wealthy and influential New Yorker and the wife of the renowned Buck Taylor, came in from the west on a Saturday evening and spent Sunday at the Cody residence." Why Mrs. Taylor was not in London with her husband, or why she came into North Platte from the west, are matters for speculation. The following week, mid-May, Arta left for New York, where she was to take ship for England to join her father. There is nothing to indicate that Mrs. Taylor went with her, and, although an earlier news item had stated that Mrs. Cody would spend the summer in Europe with her daughters, she did not go either. Cooper has her say: "I was to stay at home and look after the business of the ranch, while Will was away [and] it was through [his] letters that I followed him on that trip."

Whether or not they were writing to each other then is not known. Cooper *quotes* from the exuberant letters the Colonel was supposedly writing her, but so much of the book is fiction that the letters also may be invented. With Al Goodman in charge at the ranch, Louisa probably had little if anything to do with its management, although she did have extensive properties of her own in the way of rentals to look after, and it is also known she did not enjoy extended trips away from home. At any rate, she stayed in North Platte with four-year-old Irma that summer.

Arta sailed on the *Arizona*, and on May 31 was listed among the passengers who gave a shipboard program for the benefit of a "sailors' orphanage." Miss Arta recited the 'Launching of the Ship,' which she no doubt rendered in her usual brilliant style." By June 18, when the above item appeared in the home town papers, Arta was in London, and editor Bare was predicting she would "win laurels in the swell social circles of England."

In the quarter century since the death of Prince Albert, Queen Victoria had attended few public entertainments, but on May 11, two days after the formal opening of the Wild West, Queen Victoria came to Earl's Court for the performance she had commanded. Benjamin Irving, recalling that performance in later years, described the parade that opened the extravaganza. Buffalo Bill rode at the head of it, he said, on a beautiful white horse. Bennie was next, on his well-trained little brown pony "Doc." Next came the cowboys, cowgirls (there were twelve women with the Wild West in London), Indians, covered wagons, stage coach, etc. Huge backdrops picturing a mountain and western scenery had been painted for the Earl's Court exhibition, and a concealed stairway led up the mountain side. Bennie rode his little horse up the stairway, looking to the audience as though he were riding over the mountain. On its summit he stopped and unfurled the American flag, which signalled the start of the show.

At the conclusion of the performance, Bennie was presented to the Queen. For this honor he rode little Doc up in front of her box and made the pony curtsey, whereupon "a man in a tall black hat lifted him off the pony and handed him up to the queen, who took him in her arms and hugged and kissed him."[6]

Much of the Wild West that year was made up of acts similar to the rodeo shows of today. Cody had three very fine bucking horses from Montana in London that summer. One was called "Midnight," one "Dynamite." The third was ridden for the first time at the Jubilee command performance. Bennie recalled that his father, Bronco Bill, made that ride, and the struggle between man and horse was long and spectacular. When it was over, the horse was named "Jubilee" on the spot. One bit of horseplay that intrigued showgoers was the placing of a

Bronco Bill Irving,
his wife Ella, and their
son Bennie,
1887.

silver dollar between Bronco Bill's boot sole and the stirrup before turning the horse loose; at the end of the ride the dollar was always still in place. No chutes were used in those days. Horses, often fighting savagely, were saddled and mounted in the open, then turned loose to do their worst with the rider on his back.

The Jubilee horse was a handsome animal, Irving said, and so valuable that he was treated the same as a race horse—that is, rubbed down and blanketed after each ride. As time passed he inevitably became gentle, and by the end of the London season was no longer a bucker.

Illustrating the popularity of the bucking horse part of the Wild West, and also the suspicions of the English as to the verity of the act, was a feature printed in the *Irish Times* in July:

Trump card of the cowboys is the bucking horse. Buffalo Bill has

In England, 1887. L-R: Albert Scheibel, secretary of the Wild West; Nate Salsbury; Keen; John M. Burke. Framed photo at right is of Annie Oakley.

twenty or thirty and at each performance invites anyone from the audience to try to ride one. Captain Byron Wood of the Royal Marines took the offer, saying he had "ridden and broken in similar cattle in Australia."

Colonel Cody did the honors at the "Welcome Club" which he kept open on the premises, and Captain Wood, properly primed with champagne, got astride "North Platte," one of the least vicious of the buckers and prepared to witch the world with his noble horseman-ship. But North Platte began curvetting and in about two minutes the gallant marine was buried up to his shoulders in earth and tan-bark. It was thought his neck was broken but, actually, he had lost only two front teeth and stoutly insisted on another try. He was so pressing that Buffalo Bill hadn't the heart to refuse.

He got aboard again but had hardly touched the saddle ere he was shot out of it and lit on his back twenty feet away. Shaken "but with his blood up," he insisted on a third try. This time he failed even to get on the bucker's back, for North Platte danced and jumped and shuffled and dodged and made arches and semi-circles and figures of eight to the extent that the Captain, quite baffled, let go the pom-mel, whereupon the mustang whirled and kicked him in the backside and sent him sprawling.

Quite a number of other first-rate English riders, all doubting the buckers were *real*, went down to Earl's Court to prove it, and were, without exception, bucked off, the best of them managing to last only about thirty seconds.[7]

Late in May, Fred Frederikson, North Platte citizen, returned from a visit to his former home in Germany. On the way back he had stopped in London to see Cody's show, he said, and there heard that the Queen was saying Buffalo Bill was the best-looking man she had ever seen. Years later Agnes Lawton Killen indirectly supported this statement with one of her own. Mrs. Killen, who made her home in North Platte in later years, was born in Leeds, England, and was seventeen when she and her family went to London to see the Wild West. "We were all so impressed with this fine-looking American gentleman on his beautiful white horse," she said. "My relatives kept saying, 'What a handsome man' and 'What a rider.' . . . People would look at him and bite their lips and say, 'My word!' "[8]

By June, along with reports that Buffalo Bill daily received bushels of letters from his fair admirers, that the Princess of Wales had ridden beside him on the box seat of the Deadwood coach, and that he was being toasted and feted all over London, came the first bad news from across the water. Under the headline BUCK TAYLOR SERIOUSLY INJURED, the *Tribune* gave the details:

> During the performance of the quadrille on horseback at the Wild West show this afternoon, the horse ridden by Buck Taylor became unmanageable and balked from his position in the figure, throwing his rider with terrific force against the cantle of the saddle on the horse next to him. Taylor fell to the ground and was at once taken to his dressing room. A physician examined his injuries and found that he had sustained a compound fracture of the thigh bone. The "King of the Cowboys" was at once removed to St. George's hospital. The horse used by Taylor was a new one, unaccustomed to the work expected of him.[9]

As soon as Buck was released from the hospital, Cody gave him a gambling concession on the grounds to occupy him until he was able to ride again. There is no mention of his wealthy wife during the emergency.

A week later editor Bare was concerned with some adverse publicity concerning Arta, who had spent a few days in New York on her way to England. The Omaha *Herald* was still jabbing at Cody and his family. "Some of the New York newspapers had fairly gone frantic over the beauty of Miss Arta," the *Herald* smoothly reported, before caustically commenting:

> A prophet has little honor in his own country and it is possible we have had a gem of purest ray serene dwelling among us and did not know it. . . . Miss Arta Cody, daughter of Buffalo Bill, is not the remarkably handsome person she has been represented to be by the New York papers. In place of being petite and slender she is quite stout and, though bright and intelligent, she has never been considered beautiful. There are many hundreds of Nebraska girls handsomer than she, but still it is pleasant to observe that the effete East is startled by her beauty.

A short time later the *Tribune* had to refute the claim of the Omaha *Republican* that Mrs. Cody, prior to her marriage to Buffalo Bill, was the widow of a Colonel Whitely of Kansas and that Mr. Cody had recently sued for and obtained a divorce from her. The facts, stated

Bare, were: "During the winter of '64-'65, Mr. Cody, while on detached service at St. Louis, became acquainted with Miss Louisa Frederici and in March, 1866, married her at the home of her parents in that city. No one here has heard anything relative to the divorce and the story is undoubtedly without foundation."

Apparently some Omahans were still disgruntled because Cody, former scout and plainsman, with little formal education and no prestigious ancestry, had been appointed by the governor to serve as Nebraska's commissioner and representative to the Queen's Jubilee and World's Fair in London. And no doubt some were unhappy that his Wild West was so completely eclipsing the rest of the American exhibition, which was a rather dull industrial display of "coffee-mills, stoves, Gatling guns, [and] liquid fish-glue."[10]

Certainly Arta Cody was attractive enough to cause a stir in any assemblage. And timely dilution of the *Herald's* unkind case against Arta appeared in a British publication and was reprinted in the *Tribune*:

Arta Cody.

Like other hard working men, Buffalo Bill finds delight in going out of town from Saturday to Monday. His favorite resort being the Oatlands Park hotel at Weybridge. To this quiet resort he has taken quite a fancy, and his commanding figure is becoming quite familiar to the habitues of the place.[11] Colonel Cody has lately been joined by his daughter, Miss Arta Cody, a young lady who inherits her father's handsome features and graceful bearing, and whose well-bred manners compare to her credit with the pork-packing prince hunters whose days seem to have departed. Indeed, the whole bearing of these quiet western folks in private life is a singular contrast to the blatant loudness of the American women who come here in search of notoriety, a goal which they attain, if ever, by the aid of stuffed corsets, pearl powder and bad language.

The Queen had so enjoyed her first visit to the Wild West that she commanded a second performance to take place on June 20 for her Jubilee guests. On this occasion a record number of royalty were present, including at least five kings, three crown princes, and any number of princes and princesses. It was on this day that the Deadwood coach, with Buffalo Bill as driver, carried the four kings of Denmark, Greece, Belgium, and Saxony and the Prince of Wales through the Indian attack, giving rise to the famous story of the "four kings and the Royal Joker" who rode with Cody that day.

In July Cody wrote to Al about his plans for a huge new barn at the ranch. In the same letter, again indicating that he and his wife were not corresponding, he wrote: "You say Lulu is going away [probably her annual visit to Colorado Springs]. Tell McDonald if she wants any money to let her have it." Louisa doubtless had enough money of her own, but the statement illustrates the manner in which Will always looked after his wife and his usual generousity when he was in funds, as he was that summer. For he adds: "I am running with such men as the Rothschilds now. I have been offered a million dollars for the Wild West providing I stay with it three years."[12]

In mid-August the Colonel sent his daughter and her cousin Ed Goodman on a six weeks' trip to the continent. "I am so glad Arta has taken such a liking to Eddie," he wrote his sister in North Platte.[13] No doubt he hoped that through the children the mothers might be brought to like, or at least tolerate, each other.

Two weeks later he wrote Julia that the cousins were having a grand time and that he had made arrangements at Brownell Hall in Omaha for Lizzie Goodman to enroll there in September, at his expense. Again he asked: "is Lulu at home and what does she say" Near the end of September he notified his sister that "Mrs. and Miss devolasco" would likely make a visit to the ranch, and he wanted her to give them a nice time and charge the entertainment bill to him.[14]

He had heard, too, that North Platte, long in need of a newer and larger hotel, was planning a first-class hostelry "if a bonus of $10,000" could be raised to underwrite its construction. According to the *Telegraph* of July 28, Cody had already subscribed a thousand dollars to the building fund. The rest of the townspeople, apparently, did not respond as well, for the hotel was never built.

Meanwhile the pace for Buffalo Bill went on as furiously as ever. The Wild West was playing to 20,000-40,000 people daily, and the Colonel was appearing twice a day in the show besides keeping an incredible number of social appointments. Said the *Tribune* of August 20: "All accounts agree that Buffalo Bill is the biggest man in England. At a recent reception where Mr. [James G.] Blaine, Minister [Edward J.] Phelps and other Americans of note were present, our own and only Col. Cody was the lion of the evening, the cynosure of all eyes. Blaine probably knows more about statescraft and such things than the Colonel, but he has never hunted buffalo with Grand Duke Alexis."

At this point the mother country's endless praise of his eminent fellow townsman caused editor Bare to comment in wonder: "A few years ago W. F. Cody was shooting buffalo and dodging Indians and playing 7-up and drinking bad whiskey in western Kansas. Then everybody called him Buffalo Bill. Now he is the social lion in London and Lords and Ladies are running over each other to get an introduction to him and they call him 'Colonel, the Hon. William F. Cody.' There is nothing wilder than this in any romance."

Perhaps the lionizing of Colonel Cody was carried too far. At any rate, some jealousy and disapproval developed. One London newspaper criticised Lord Beresford for inviting Cody, "chiefly famed as an adroit scalper of Indians," to the sacrosanct Coaching Club meet. Even James Russell Lowell, recently U.S. minister to the Court of St. James, wrote: "I think the true key to this eagerness for lions—even of the poodle sort—is the dullness of the average English mind." John Kendrick Bangs, editor of *Life* magazine, a humorous weekly, indicated that Lowell was something of a stuffed shirt and jibed that "Messrs. Blaine, Phelps, Lowell and Buffalo Bill, America's Big Four, are all [now] in London."[15] The month was August, 1887.

But at the same time Marshall P. Wilder, entertainer and author who was then in Europe, could say sincerely: "I must express my pride and delight, as an American, at the figure Bill cut in society. He fills a full-dress suit as gracefully as he does the hunter's buckskins, carries himself as elegantly as any English gentleman . . . , uses good grammar, speaks with a drawing-room tone of voice, and moves as leisurely as if he had nothing to do all his life but exist beautifully. . . . I ought to know, for [the English] have told me so themselves."[16]

As the London season drew to a close at the end of October, Cody could say: "from the day of opening our show in London until the close of our engagement . . . I had not missed a single one of the three hundred performances given." This, coupled with the many social events he crowded into his daily schedule, kept him "occupied nearly eighteen hours out of every twenty-four."[17]

During the six months at Earl's Court, thousands of people had visited him at his headquarters tent. The tent had two large rooms. The first was his parlor, with its floor covered with fine skins and robes and its supporting posts hung with many animal heads and horns. The bedroom beyond was furnished with a lace-covered bed and other fine furniture. Hot and cold water added to its comfort; a first-class hotel could hardly have been more elegant. The dressing table was covered all season with scented invitations, "stamped with armorial bearings," requesting the pleasure of Buffalo Bill's presence at various dinners, receptions, balls, and other affairs. On the mantelpiece were photos of the Queen and the Prince and Princess of Wales, Henry Irving, and many other notables of the time, all of whom had visited the Colonel there, some of them several times.

In spite of all this, the Colonel still found time that summer to turn some of his attention to affairs at home. With Al Goodman he had made plans for a huge barn at Scout's Rest Ranch. The foundation for the 148 x 70 x 40-foot structure was laid in early October; seven carloads of lumber were used in its construction, and its hundreds of rafters were sawed in the shape of gunstocks.

Also, late in the summer Cody sent to the North Platte board of trade a proposal that he secure a colony of a hundred English families of moral, industrious mechanics and farmers and send them to North Platte. If his proposal were accepted, he would build a hundred cottages on his property west of town to rent at low cost to the families. The town, in turn, would insure the colonists employment.

The *Tribune* heartily approved, since such a plan would generate a large amount of new business in town and would add a market for thousands of additional dollars worth of produce each year. But the proposal came to nothing. Some North Platte interests feared the colonist mechanics would endanger the jobs of resident workmen. Editor Bare disagreed. He could see only growth and good from such an influx, with the possibility of establishing new industries that would benefit everybody. His opinion did not prevail, and the idea died aborning. Time was to prove that most of the plans proposed by the farseeing Cody would prosper—but, owing to the overcautiousness of North Platte businessmen, many never materialized, such as his coloni- zation plan; and a few that did bear fruit benefitted the neighboring state of Wyoming, though even then, in some cases, *after* Cody's death.

That the frantic pace of the past months was telling on Buffalo Bill is shown in a letter he wrote to Julia on October 7. He did not believe the English climate agreed with him, he said, "and if I don't get my health back soon I will be tempted to leave it and come back to my own good country. . . . Oh how I would love to spend a month with you at the Ranch."[18]

Probably the knowledge that in only three more weeks he would have fulfilled his Earl's Court contract kept him going. At any rate, according to an account of the closing performance of the Wild West on the evening of October 31, he appeared in fine fettle. Stated a London theatrical journal:

Buffalo Bill was called upon for a speech and, prancing upon his old war horse, Charlie, who seemed to fully appreciate the impor- tance of the occasion, let off the following, straight from the chest, or perhaps I should say heart, for it was spontaneous, expressive and honestly delivered.

"Ladies and Gentlemen: You ask me to make a speech. I am no orator, but could I paint fully in the eloquence of expressive language the emotions I feel in saying good bye to London tonight, it would be the height of my ambition to do simple justice to the occasion and pay a final tribute to your kindness and my gratitude. In this expres- sion I may fail—in the feelings of grateful remembrance, believe me, I am heartily sincere. The stay of the Wild West in London has been attended by such genuine hospitality as to mark it a red letter epoch in the history of the world's amusements. The fast disappearing page of Western American pioneer history that we have the honor to portray consists simply of scenes in which we have all more or less participated.

"It is particularly gratifying that your perception has been such that you grasped the idea that I have been actuated by other than the absolutely sordid motives in transplanting a bit of American frontier history to the heart of this mighty metropolis, and glad I am that I can say that we have been met by a spirit of appreciation and cordial acceptance of our motives that will send us back to our western homes beyond the sea with hearts filled with kindness toward the English public. And believe me when opportunity occurs we will not fail to bear witness to your generous sympathy on our return.

"Personally, I dare not express myself fully for fear, in my exuberance, I might be misunderstood, but I have been overwhelmed with kindness, friendship and hospitality on every hand. Ladies and gentlemen of England, I owe you more than my most grateful remembrance can ever repay. But while my life shall last, the memory of this parting will live in my heart, and in conclusion I have but one sentiment to express to all—or rather two wishes to express—long life and general prosperity to you of Old England. Good bye and God bless you."[19]

Buffalo Bill did not do badly in his farewell speech. Not badly at all.

Also referring to the Wild West and the conclusion of its successful London season, the London *Observer* had this to say:

This week terminates the career of the Wild West exhibition at Earl's Court. After that it will, so far as London is concerned, be numbered among the wonders that were. The end of its phenomenal course of success as a show will not be greeted with unmingled regret by Mr. Cody and his company, for we dare say they will not be sorry to obtain a temporary relief from their daily toil.

What Mr. Cody, in his picturesque dialect terms "dust" has been gathered in beyond the wildest dreams of avarice. The fun of "the society racket," to use another of his expressions, must long ere now have palled on the jaded spirit of the overfeasted hero and his coadjudors, for whom an English winter can have no attraction. But since the exhibition of 1851 London has never seen a show that so completely took it by storm as this one.

Perhaps there never was a show, even in London, that was so sternly a matter of fact and owed so little of its attraction to stage effect and theatrical artifice. It was an honest effort to let people see, so far as could be done at Earl's Court, what the frontier life and adventure which they had read so much about was really like.

It seemed to catch the public humor at the very outset by reason of the honesty of its realistic methods, and so far as popularity was concerned, Mr. Cody's exhibition might have gone on exhibiting in London for the rest of his natural life.[20]

As it turned out, the presence of Buffalo Bill and his show in London was to have more important results than merely entertaining the English. As ambassadors of good will, the Colonel and his troupe had done a splendid job. On one occasion Cody, Major Burke, Broncho Bill (interpreter), and French Pete (cowboy artist) took Red Shirt, Flys Above, and some other chiefs to the Savage Club at the Savoy in London. Buffalo Bill and Red Shirt made speeches, and Red Shirt promised to send a peace pipe from his home in the West for the London Savages to hang on their dining room wall. Speaking in Sioux, he called the club members his brothers and thanked them for asking him to their lodge. The members were much impressed by his dignity.[21]

After his presentation to the Queen, the Sioux chief had pleased the English by an interview he gave a *Daily Mercury* reporter. He said that he and his young men had sat up all night talking about the "Great White Mother," that white men who had come from England to the Indian reservation had told him of the power of their queen, and that now they had seen her they all knew she was a wise woman. All the Indians in Dakota would come to them when they returned home to hear how they had seen this great woman. It had pleased their hearts that she came to welcome them "as a mother and not with all her warriors around her." Her face was kind and it pleased them, and all his young men had resolved that she should be their Great White Mother.

And all England had been amused by the chief's reaction to his visit to Parliament. "Red Shirt, the first American Indian ever to go inside the halls of parliament, accompanied by his interpreter and one of Cody's officials, visited the House of Commons and was introduced by Mr. Justin H. McCarthy. Red Shirt, who was in war paint, excited considerable interest among the members. Among others, he was introduced to Baron Henry DeWorms, who asked him what he thought of the British Parliament. He said he did not think much of it, laws being passed much more quickly in his country than in this."

22

Before the
Leaves Had Fallen
1887-1889

After they struck their tents in London, Buffalo Bill and his homesick company were not to see their homeland for another six months, for other English cities were insistent that the popular Wild West stop with them awhile, too. From London the show moved to Birmingham where, Cody said: "we met with a prodigious welcome from the screwmakers, the teapot turners and the manufacturers of artificial jewelry and 'Brummagem goods' in general."[1]

But it was November, and the weather, which had been unusually fine all summer, showed signs of breaking, indicating that it was time to get the Wild West into winter quarters.

While the show was at Birmingham, two of its cowboys were at Agricultural Hall, Islington, London, participating in a six-day race against two English cyclists. The racers competed for eight hours each day, and the cowboys used thirty horses, changing mounts every hour. The prize was £300. The average pace was about twenty miles an hour, and the cowboys won the race by two miles and two laps. The publicity was fine for Cody's Wild West.

Manchester, a city of about six million, was the final stop for the season, and during the preparations for setting up the show there, the Colonel and Arta made a hurried two-week trip to Italy. Cody and Salsbury had thought it might be possible to give an exhibition of their great Wild West in the Colosseum at Rome, but an examination of the ruins led to the abandonment of the idea.

At the Manchester-area race track, across the river in Salford, Cody and Salsbury had "the largest theater ever seen in the world" built for their show. Next to it was erected a building large enough to contain the tents and tepees of the entire troupe. The structures were heated by steam and lighted by electricity. The barns and stables already on the grounds housed all the animals. At a cost of $40,000 elaborate western scenery (painted by Matt Morgan) was contrived on 200-foot-long strips of canvas that were worked on drums thirty feet high.[2] A British newspaper sang praises:

> The theater, brilliantly lighted and well warmed throughout, is like nothing else ever constructed in this country. The seats, accommodating nearly ten thousand persons, are ranged in tiers, from the pew-like private boxes in front to a height of forty feet or so; and the distance from the extreme end of the auditorium to the back of the stage is so great that a horseman galloping across the whole area diminishes by natural perspective until the spectator is fairly cheated into the idea that the journey is to be prolonged until the rider vanishes in the pictured horizon. The illusion, indeed, is so well managed and complete, the boundless plains and swelling prairies are so vividly counterfeited, that it is difficult to resist the belief that we are really gazing over an immense expanse of country from some hillside in the far West. The pictures . . . are singularly beautiful in themselves.[3]

The Salford *Reporter* described the opening of the inaugural performance of Saturday afternoon, December 17:

> About a quarter past two the "Wild West Cowboy Band" entered the orchestra . . . and played an overture in excellent style, at the conclusion of which the Lecturer [Frank Richmond], speaking from an elevated point to the left of the stage, made an announcement. He said the entertainment was intended to pourtray certain aspects of life in America, and he claimed for it an educative as well as an entertaining purpose [—] to picture to the eye, by the aid of historical characters and living animals, a series of animated scenes and episodes, founded on fact, of the wonderful pioneer and frontier life of the Far West. . . .
>
> At once we are introduced to the whole of the resources of the establishment. The curtain divided and horsemen and horsewomen dashed into the arena, troupe after troupe, Indians, cowboys, American girls, and Indian women. The critical and expectant audience were somewhat taken with surprise. There was a sudden dash and

brilliancy about these entrances and exits. . . . After an introduction of the gigantic Buck Taylor, "the king of the cowboys," there was a pause. Then the name of Buffalo Bill himself resounded from the Orator's perch. Amid trumpet peals from the band and thunders of applause the hero made his appearance. He burst bravely into sight mounted on a long-tailed grey horse, galloped forward into the arena with many gestures, halted suddenly in front of the private boxes, from one of which he received a splendid bouquet, and then made a most impressive exit by forcing his horse backwards with surprising rapidity.[4]

Then followed the seven thrilling episodes of the show, from "the primeval forest" scene to "the grand climax, the attack on the Deadwood stagecoach, and an artificially produced cyclone or tornado, which is certainly impressive. The cyclone sweeps over the scene, carrying everything with it, and the curtain falls on the general wreckage. . . . Buffalo Bill has come, we have seen, and he has conquered."[5]

In Manchester the Colonel received many requests from the heads of schools and charitable institutions for seating space for their "waifs." His reply was always the same: "Let us know your numbers and come on Wednesday afternoon, . . . and we will fix you up for nothing at all, if we have to turn money away for you."[6]

While the show was in winter quarters, there occurred an episode that appeared as follows in the *Tribune* back home: "Recently a couple of Buffalo Bill's Indians filled up with a few glasses of ale and a bit of cold fowl and started out to daub the quiet old town of Manchester. They were run in in short order. It is quite probable a couple of Indians will second the motion to return to the U.S. early in the spring, where they can scalp settlers and Indian agents in peace and comfort."

It was well that the show people were so snugly under shelter, for Ed Goodman wrote his mother in January that "The winters in this country are the worst kind . . . slopy, wet, nasty, damp and many fogs." Salsbury, he added, was leaving for America the next week to make arrangements (at Erastina) for the show's return in the summer. At the end of his letter he asked his mother if she ever heard from Miss DeValesco, and if she might be coming back to North Platte in the spring.[7]

A month later he was writing that Uncle Will had been very ill with bronchitis and was terribly homesick besides. On March 4 Ed reported that although his uncle complained that the climate did not agree with him, he had gained eighteen pounds since he came to Manchester "and now ways 218 pounds in his light clothes. I believe it is only *home-sickness* that is the matter with him." The terrible weather, he added, accounted for the poor business they had had the past month.[8]

A week later the lad sent a cheerful letter off to North Platte. The weather was good and the show was playing to full houses. Best of all, Uncle Will had engaged a ship to take them home, and they planned to sail from Hull the first week in May. Then, in reference to a question asked in a letter just received from his mother, he wrote: "As for Arta being married I think they have it to soon. I would not be surprised if she married the man you speak of but she will not marry when we land in New York, She is a good and true girl and I am proud of her and she is deserving of a good husband and hope she will get one."[9]

Back in North Platte the *Tribune* announced: It is reported that Buffalo Bill is pining for his ranch in Nebraska and expresses himself in this way: "I want to come home. We are doing an immense business here, but the country cramps me and the climate chokes me. There is not air enough. If I start out to take a ride on my horse, just as soon as I get warm in my saddle I've come to the end of the island. If I get comfortably fixed in their damn railway coachs the guard announces that we've arrived. There isn't territory enough for the people. They tread on each other and their biggest country needs ventilation. You forget how to breathe here in six months. You're afraid of robbing some-body else of atmosphere."[10]

But, however much he longed for the abundant fresh air of Nebraska, the Colonel was enjoying the signal honors accorded him in England, where one evening "a magnificent rifle, decked in flowers and gaily adorned with ribbons" was presented him "by the artistic, dramatic, and literary gentlemen of Manchester." For the occasion a delegation of London's "*elite* of the metropolitan *literati*," some one hundred strong, came up to the show grounds to witness the ceremony. Afterward, Bill entertained all the celebrities at a camp dinner of fried oysters, beans, chicken, and a real "Indian 'rib-roast,' "[11]

A few days before the aggregation was to leave Manchester, the mayor of Salford announced that he had named three streets in his town for Buffalo Bill: Bill Street, Cody Street, and Buffalo Street.[12] All the newspapers made much of this distinction, and on April 30, when the Wild West gave its last indoor performance, the Colonel was all but buried in the flowers thrown by the audience when he made his entrance that evening. It was fully five minutes before the cheering subsided enough that the show could begin. The next afternoon Cody "was given a benefit by the race-course people"; it was held outdoors on the Salford race track arena, and nearly 50,000 people paid admission.[13] The following day the Colonel accepted a challenge to "an international ten-mile race between . . . English thoroughbreds and . . . American bronchos, for £500 a side." Tony Esquivel, one of Cody's Mexican vaqueros, rode the broncs. Each rider, without assistance, changed mounts every half-mile. Although the English rider took the lead at the beginning of the race, Tony won the meet by some 300 yards, using thirteen horses and chalking up a time of twenty-one minutes. The 20,000 spectators enthusiastically applauded both riders.[14]

Amid the cheers of thousands of well wishers, the Wild West pulled out of Windsor Bridge Station on the morning of May 4, bound for Hull, where they would take ship for home. All along the way crowds gathered to wave and cheer, and at Hull the throng was so great they had to send for a squad of police to open the way to their conveyances. The next day the big show gave its farewell performance in the open at Hull before an enormous crowd. By nine o'clock that evening the entire homesick troupe and all their effects, including the guns, jewelry, and other gifts given Buffalo Bill by his many admirers, were on board the *Persian Monarch*. Until the ship sailed at three in the morning, the faithful hosts lined the docks, cheering and singing.

Half-way to America, the happy, home-going show people were saddened by the sudden illness of Old Charlie, Buffalo Bill's best-loved horse. For two days his anxious owner stayed with him, giving him every care, but nothing helped. Old Charlie's death made headlines on both sides of the ocean. One feature stated that he was a half-breed Kentucky horse, that Yellow Hair "bit the dust" for him and his rider, and that he helped Cody earn his famous nickname when they ran down buffalo for a railroad crew. The first statements may be true, but the latter is certainly open to question. For Charlie, twenty-one when he died, was *born* in 1867, the year Cody supplied meat for the railroad and came to be known as Buffalo Bill.

The most moving of all accounts of the horse's life and death is the one his grieving owner wrote himself:

> When the Wild West went to Europe in 1887, old Charlie was the star horse. Nearly everyone in London got to know him and quite a number of the Royalty had a ride on his back. Among them was the Grand Duke Michael of Russia, cousin of the Grand Duke Alexis. He rode him several times and chased my herd of buffalo on him.

After closing our English Engagement we sailed for home on the Persian Monarch. I spent a great deal of my time below decks with Charlie. On the morning of May 14, 1888, I went down to see him and gave him some sugar. Less than an hour later my groom told me he was sick. I went down again and found he had a chill. In spite of all we could do he grew rapidly worse and at two o'clock in the morning of May 17 he died.

The death of a human being could not have excited more real mourning. Everyone had some reminiscence to relate of old Charlie's sagacity and many an eye was moist with tears. His burial was appointed for eight o'clock in the evening. I should have preferred to carry him home and bury him on the prairie, but this was impossible. During the day he lay in state on the deck, decently wrapped in a canvas shroud and covered with the Stars and Stripes. At the appointed hour the entire ship's company assembled. The band played "Auld Lang Syne," lights were burned and as the faithful creature glided gently into the water the ship's cannon boomed a last farewell to my consistent friend and companion of the last fifteen years.[15]

Early on the morning of May 20, the *Persian Monarch* steamed up from quarantine to Staten Island, the first time a great ocean steamer had ever landed there. The New York *World's* report would have made a press agent believe in Providence:

> The harbor probably has never witnessed a more picturesque scene. . . . Buffalo Bill stood on the captain's bridge, his tall and striking figure clearly outlined, and his long hair waving in the wind; the gayly painted and blanketed Indians leaned over the ship's rail; the flags of all nations fluttered from the masts and connecting cables. The cowboy band played "Yankee Doodle" with a vim and enthusiasm which faintly indicated the joy felt by everybody connected with the "Wild West" over the sight of home.[16]

A great crowd greeted the ship's arrival. Buffalo Bill, his daughter, Major Burke, Colonel Ochiltree, and others, along with several reporters, debarked and came up to New York on a tugboat, while Salsbury was getting the rest of the show settled at Erastina. Of his homecoming Colonel Cody said simply: "I cannot describe my joy upon stepping again on the shore of beloved America. . . . 'There is no place like home,' nor is there a flag like the old flag."[17]

Shortly before the show left England, Mrs. Cody had received "two elegant panel portraits of Arta "in *décolleté* costume and looking her sweetest."[18] In reporting receipt of the portraits, editor Bare had announced that Miss Cody would return home from Europe the latter part of May and that Colonel Cody would probably visit North Platte soon afterward. Arta, a celebrity in her own right after a year spent in Europe, did return home immediately, but her father, as much as he longed for his fine ranch at the forks of the Platte, remained on in New York.

The Wild West's opening at Erastina on Memorial Day was probably a "coincidence" engineered by Major Burke for publicity purposes, for Cody was able to share the honors of the day with the president of the nation and military heroes of renown. Cody, Salsbury, and 200 of the show's Indians and cowboys, "all mounted and dressed in their odd and fantastic garments," rode in the huge and popular Decoration Day parade in New York City. As the New York *Tribune* reported: "Buffalo Bill, dressed as a scout and mounted on a powerful young horse, rode with the staff of the Grand Marshal. He was received [all along the route] with shouts of applause."[19]

A little later the New York *World* proclaimed:

Buffalo Bill is probably the best known man in New York city. Wherever he goes he is recognized and pointed out by the crowds. His long waving hair and white sombrero assist materially in the identification. Yesterday afternoon Colonel William came up on a yacht from Erastina with Colonel Ochiltree and a party of ladies who had been taking a glance at the Wild West. The company landed at East 24th and was driven across the city in an omnibus. All along the route the east side children recognized the gallant scout and cheered him lustily. Some of them ran after the vehicle for entire blocks and shouted as they ran. Heads were popping out of windows, pretty girls paused to exchange glances and workmen with tin buckets nudged each other and said "That's him," as the bus rolled by. It was an ovation all along the line, and Colonel Cody bore it all with that quiet, gentle modesty which is so becoming to him. What a candidate for Vice President he would make to help out a chilly ticket.[20]

The Wild West had been booked at Erastina for only the month of June, but opening-day crowds were a good omen of success to come. The New York *Evening Telegram* of May 31 headlined: "20,000 People Welcome the Hero of Two Continents," and went ahead to record Major Burke's happy lament that "with 10,000 more at the gates who couldn't get in," they needed five more acres of land to accommodate the crowds. Attendance held up so well it was decided to remain longer, and the show stayed on until mid-August, playing to sell-out crowds the whole time. Near the end of July, Cody wrote his sister:

> I am feeling some better. . . . But I am tired out. . . . Two weeks from tomorrow we close here then go to Philadelphia and I am only going to give one show a day there, so I can rest of evenings. . . . I will be with you in October and take a whole month's rest, then I am going into into a new scheme—start a new show for the winter and one that nobody can get up immitations on. . . . I ain't even going to tell you & Al what it is till I spring it on the public in December.[21]

Late in October the Wild West closed for the winter at Richmond, Virginia, ending an uninterrupted season which had begun two years and seven months before at St. Louis. But before heading for North Platte, Cody and about seventy-five of his Indians visited Washington D. C., where the showman took the red men to visit the White House and see the House and Senate in action. Cody, Salsbury, and Burke explained to the Indians the meaning of all they were seeing, since only Red Shirt, Rocky Bear, and one or two others had ever been to the Capital. They smoked the peace pipe at the Bureau of Indian Affairs and called on the Great Father himself; President Grover Cleveland received the Indians in the East Room and was impressed with their majestic bearing as they filed by.[22]

From Washington the Indians returned to their reservation, and Cody, at long last, went home to North Platte. One account of his return says that for the first time he saw his ranch before the leaves had fallen from the trees. The *Tribune* states that he arrived home on November 6, election day, and received a warm greeting from all his friends, "and that means everybody in North Platte." For the first time in several years he was able to appear at the polls to cast his ballot.[23]

It is highly unlikely that frost had held off until November in the Platte Valley, but Cody must have been pleased with the young groves, their sturdy growth helped along by the buckets of water the younger Goodman children had carried from the pond back of the big house during dry spells. He was pleased, too, with the fine new barn which, as Bare described it, "looms up against the skyline like a mountain." Across its southern roof slope SCOUT'S REST RANCH had been painted in white letters four feet tall, readable from the trains passing on the tracks one-and-a-half miles to the south.

The big barn at Cody's ranch. Although this photo was not taken until a few years after Cody's 1888 visit (the T barn, in background, was built in 1891), it represents the sort of typical activity at the ranch when the Colonel was at home in North Platte.

W. F. Cody
and his sister
Julia Goodman,
c. 1888.

The changes in North Platte also must have pleased the Colonel, for during his absence the "brick block," the town's first, had been built between Fifth and Sixth Streets; and the waterworks plant had been completed, making it possible for residents to have running water in their homes. The city's postmaster-confectioner had introduced a new drink called a "milk shake," and brick sidewalks had at last spanned the downtown intersections. Farther out, a good many blocks of narrow plank walks, referred to by courting couples as "hug-me-tights," kept pedestrians' sole leather out of the mud in wet weather.

In honor of the Colonel's return, a group of townsmen had in September organized the W. F. Cody Rifle Club and set up a rifle range out at the fairgrounds. Judge Bixler had practiced so faithfully that by the time Cody arrived he had earned "an enviable reputation as a crack shot by shooting *a la* Buffalo Bill. That is, by standing with his back to the target and taking aim by means of a mirror."

Early in October the *Tribune* had noted H. S. Boal's opening of a real estate, loan, and insurance agency. "Mr. Boal, a Chicagoan, comes to this city full of vim and enterprise, characteristic of the people of Chicago," and Bare predicted the newcomer would gather a good share of business in his line. Later in the month, Horton Boal made the paper again with his first attempt at "riding broncs." Perseverance on his part and the help of a more experienced bystander had kept him in the saddle. Subsequent attempts were less successful.

Arta had spent the summer entertaining friends and house guests at her North Platte home, among them Mrs. Beck, the wife of George T. Beck of Wyoming. She had then visited friends in Lincoln and Iowa, but returned in time to welcome her father home in November.

On November 13, a week after the election, the Republicans held a Ratification Day parade and meeting to celebrate their victory. The business section of town, including the establishments of the Democrats, were handsomely lighted and decorated with flags and bunting. The reelected governor, John M. Thayer, was on hand for the event; all was in readiness for a big evening when the weather suddenly turned cold and threatening, and a strong north wind sprang up whirling clouds of leaves and dust into the air.

The long parade formed up anyway, lighted by huge flambeaus or torches, smoking and flaring in the wind. At its head, in full uniform and on a prancing charger, rode W. B. Risse, chairman of the Democratic Central Committee; the major was paying off a bet, his penalty for voting for Cleveland. Behind him came the "Lincoln County Bull

Team," a wagon load of Harrison Republicans pulled by a pair of well-broken bulls. Next came Governor Thayer in a carriage driven by Buffalo Bill, who was hosting the guest at his house. Stretched out behind them was a long line of dignitaries and other happy Republicans, some in carriages and buggies, some on horseback.

The signal for the parade to move off was the opening bars of a march, but when the horns just back of the governor and his escort blared forth, Cody's high-lifed team, already unstrung by the screeching wind and the shouting crowd, plunged wildly ahead onto Major Bixler's horse. The natty major, in command of the flambeaus surrounding the governor's carriage, was dealt a heavy blow in the back that almost unseated him. Order was eventually restored, and the parade struggled off over the laid-out course, fighting the wind and smothering dust. At its end everybody except Major Risse repaired thankfully to the opera house for the rest of the celebration.

Cody and the governor were seated among the other speakers on the stage, and the Colonel, when called upon to speak, was delightfully brief. He said he had been in many a tight place in his time, but he believed that to call on a good Democrat to make a speech at a Republican meeting was about the tightest. He had, however, he assured his audience, voted for Thayer.[24]

Whether Cody entertained the governor at his town house or at the ranch is not indicated, but a few days later he hosted Mlle. Rhea and her company at his big house on the ranch. The occasion was the presentation of "Much Ado About Nothing" at the opera house by the French actress and her troupe. The play was well attended and hugely enjoyed, with many people driving in from other towns to see it, but all had difficulty understanding Rhea's "imperfect English." In honor of his guests, the Colonel gave one of his famous Indian rib roasts and invited a number of his North Platte friends to the party.

A few days later, in the bitter cold, Mr. and Mrs. Cody, with Arta and a large party of friends, drove over to Wallace, across some twenty-five miles of rugged country. Included in the group were Major and Mrs. Haley, Mr. and Mrs. W. C. Lemon, Colonel Walsh, Guy Laing, Lord Boal, Judges O'Rourke and Bixler, a Lord Holbrooke, Diamond Dick, and others. Horton Boal, who came from a titled English family, was occasionally referred to as "Lord" by the local papers. Whether Lord Holbrooke was Boal's guest or Colonel Cody's is not known.

The occasion was a reception staged for Cody by the Cody G. A. R. Post of Wallace. Organized the year before while the Wild West was in England, the Wallace veterans had named their post for the "Man of the year, W. F. Cody," a signal honor which had required special permission from G. A. R. headquarters, since it was customary to name posts only for men who had lost their lives in some heroic action.

There was a great deal of singing and speech making at the meeting. Judge Bixler pleased everybody with the grand old army song, "I must and will be married/The fit is on me now." Colonel Walsh, Judge O'Rourke, and Professor Underhill were too worn from the long cold drive to say much, but Diamond Dick gave a rousing discourse on "Prohibition in the South Sea Islands." Diamond Dick (Dr. Richard Tanner) was a noted character of the plains. A sometime preacher-doctor and man of many callings, he was an old friend of Buffalo Bill's and had acquired his nickname because of the many diamonds he habitually wore—"shirt studs, tie pins and in every other possible place."

The Wallace paper noted that the two lords had the attention of every young lady present, and observed that "of Colonel Cody and his wife and daughter we can scarcely express our high opinion of their good sense, good looks and general American make-up. To Mrs. and Miss Cody belongs the honor of wearing the first diamonds ever seen on a woman in Wallace." The men wore black suits and tall silk hats.[25]

The banquet consisted, in part, of a whole roasted pig and a huge tub of slow-baked beans. The party-goers stayed all night in the little village of Wallace and drove home the next day, "the ride being a little long for comfort."[26]

The Colonel was no sooner home again than Governor Thomas Moonlight of Wyoming came down to spend a week with him. Cody held a reception for his guest, inviting in many of his North Platte friends. On December 11 a Mr. and Mrs. Blakesley of Ogallala gave a banquet and reception in honor of Buffalo Bill and the governor. The papers do not say how the Codys and their guest went up to Ogallala, but some twenty-five other Platters rode up on a freight train in the afternoon. After dinner all went over to the opera house (the skating rink on ordinary occasions) for a ball, which was attended by all of Ogallala. Speeches ended, the dancing began and lasted throughout the night. The Platters came home the next forenoon, no doubt by "special freight," having thoroughly enjoyed a "feast of reason and a flow of soul."[27]

The next evening Colonel and Mrs. Bentley and their daughter Kate entertained nearly one hundred guests, the cream of North Platte society, at the Pacific House, and the party "carried with it no little degree of flowery edge." When all the guests had been received and announced, the orchestra struck up and the dance began, with Colonel and Mrs. Cody leading the grand march into the ballroom. Many of the ladies were "*décolleté*," and the gentlemen who were not in full dress wore the conventional Prince Albert. Black waiters served cream and cake between dances, and after twelve numbers had been danced heavier refreshments were served.[28]

Hard upon the heels of the Bentley party, the Andrews Opera Company, a first-class troupe under the patronage of the Honorable W. F. Cody, presented the "Mikado" at the opera house. While in North Platte the troupe was "wined and dined at the Cody residence on Tuesday evening." The Codys then went up to Denver to visit friends. Newspaper reports of the social affairs of that period show that Horton Boal and his friend, George Field, spent the same span of days in the Colorado city; whether his visit had anything to do with Arta's is not now known.

The Cody family returned to North Platte for New Year's but left that evening for Omaha, where they spent a day before going on to Lincoln to attend the governor's inauguration. Buffalo Bill, as Governor Thayer's aide-de-camp, was expected to take part in the inaugural ceremonies. With Louisa, Arta, and Eddie Goodman, the Colonel arrived in Lincoln on the evening of January 2, 1889, and put up at the Windsor Hotel. Also at the Windsor that night was Governor William Larrabee of Iowa, his wife, two daughters, and official staff.

At 1:30 the next afternoon Governor Thayer, Governor Larrabee, Colonel Cody, their families, the judges of the supreme court and their ladies, and other prominent guests were taken in carriages through the streets to the capitol for the reception. Bands, uniformed companies of the Nebraska National Guard, the governors' official staffs, and a long line of old soldiers of the Union Army headed the big parade.

So many people turned out to see and meet the governors and the colorful Colonel Cody that it was only with the greatest difficulty the distinguished guests were shoe-horned through the crowds in the halls and corridors and into the reception room. There the reception line formed, with the Colonel and his ladies immediately below the governors and their families in the long line-up. So many people came (an estimated 4,000) that for two-and-one-half hours a steady stream filed down the reception line. Hundreds were still waiting to get in when it was announced that no more could be received as Governor Thayer's health would not permit any more handshaking. The guests were then requested to repair to another room, where the Grand March would form and the dancing begin.[29]

The Codys returned to North Platte, where, on January 9, the Boston Symphony and Orchestral Club gave a program at the opera house. It was most unusual for so prestigious a group as this "to stop at so small a city and it was only upon the personal solicitation of Mr. Cody . . . that the advance agent would consent . . . and then only upon [Mr. Cody's] guarantee. This will be a grand opportunity for our people to hear fine music, such as is seldom heard outside the largest cities," declared editor Bare, who appreciated good music. North Platte did not let the Colonel down, for the orchestra's seven members played to a "large and fashionable audience, every floor seat being taken and the galleries well filled. Mr. Nowell's violin solo was pronounced superb by local musicians." As usual, Colonel Cody had house guests, a Colonel Dennis Cunningham, who had presented him with an exceptionally fine horse, and a D. R. Roeder of Omaha being among them.[30]

From all of the above it would appear that Will and Louisa were on amiable terms during this period.

Sometime previously Cody had signed a contract to take the Wild West to Paris in the spring. Since he did not have to get the show ready for an American opening, he was able to prolong his stay in North Platte for a few more weeks. During this time the Buffalo Bill Hook and Ladder Company was permanently organized, officers elected, and uniforms ordered; this company was to be the "pink of the North Platte fire department." To help matters along, Colonel Cody, "with the liberality characteristic of the gentleman, presented the company with a check for $100."

It must have been during this extended visit home that Cody's tallyho arrived in North Platte; he had, no doubt, purchased the vehicle while in England and had it shipped home, for it is frequently mentioned as such soon after his return. Actually, it was not a tallyho, which is an open rig used on English fox hunts, but a British four-in-hand, a fourteen-passenger covered carriage with seats on top as well as inside. In North Platte, however, it was always called "the tallyho."

The big coach caused quite a sensation and was much used on special occasions, of which there were many in North Platte when its owner was around. The Colonel, who usually drove its four or six horses himself, used it for meeting trains and transporting his guests to and from the ranch or his town house, or for the convenience of his hunting parties.

Most of the tales about Cody and his tallyho have been gleaned from interviews with old-timers, made long after the rig disappeared from the city's streets. Said Edd Wright:

I liked to see Cody drive that big tallyho. He was a good driver, and I don't think anybody drove it but him. I've seen him take whole loads of people from the trains with that tallyho, and he was a picture driving it. There were a lot of gates to open between the ranch and the railroad and he had a man ride along to open the gates. He found the tallyho very convenient for hunting parties, too, and used to load his guests, who didn't feel up to riding the lively horses he kept available, into the big rig. I've seen him with the tallyho full up and twenty or so people on horseback, when they started out on a hunt.[31]

Mrs. Mary Roddy remembered how everybody ran to the windows to see the tallyho go by. "It was the only one in town, so we knew who was passing."[32] Mrs. Jessie Blankenburg Reynolds said she didn't remember it being used when Cody was away but that it was on the road a lot when he was at home. "I think he was the only one who had the flair for that sort of thing."[33]

The tallyho, with Cody at the reins, in front of Guy Laing's house.

Mayme Watts, eleven years old that winter and a close friend of
Josephine Goodman, told of the Colonel's taking the tallyho and gathering up a dozen or so children, Ada Kocken, the Conklins, his nieces
and nephews, and others and driving up and down the streets. He
carried some English hunting horns in the rig, she said, and he let the
children blow them as they drove along. She recalls that he had a
driver on those occasions, so that he could "stand in the middle and
direct the operation." After the drives they "always wound up out at
the ranch, where his private bartender, Jimmy Dugan, mixed drinks for
us. The Colonel always told Jimmy to use only the best of fruit juices
and no liquor in the punch for the children."[34]

Charles Whalen said: "Cody'd come to town every morning in that
big tallyho and pick up his mail and then come to my saloon. The boys
would see the tallyho drive up and they'd come and Cody'd buy two
or three rounds for them and read his mail and drink himself a cocktail.
He did that every morning for years whenever he was in town."[35]

Johnny Dugan, Jimmy's brother, remembered the days when there
were no trees in the valley and one could see all the way from the
ranch to the cemetery on the northwest edge of town. The Dugan house
was near the west edge of the cemetery, and he looked out the window
one day and saw "Cody and Nellie McHenry, an actress who had a
road show, coming afoot across the prairie. They had been out with the
tallyho and ran into an irrigation ditch and tipped over and smashed
up a little. Then they got thirsty and came on into town on foot, not
waiting to get the tallyho fixed up."[36] Hugh Gaunt's story was still
better:

> One time a bunch of chorus girls came to town to put on a show, and
> Cody took them all out to the ranch. He had to take them back the
> afternoon of the show, so we hitched up the horses and he got the
> girls all inside or on top of the tallyho. Then he looked at the check
> reins and told us to hook them up higher. [Tight reins made the
> horses hold their heads higher, a position that looked good but pre-
> vented the horses from seeing the ground.]
>
> The road from the ranch angled across to the cemetery, where
> there was a square turn. The snow had melted, then frozen in patches
> of ice, and the road was deep-rutted. We knew something would
> happen when they hit that square turn, with the reins hooked up
> like that, so three of us saddled up and took out after them. Sure
> enough, when the horses hit that ice-filled rut at the turn, the tallyho

upset. Cody got the girls out all right, but the tongue was broken. So he took the girls and went on afoot and left us to clean up the mess. But we all got comp tickets for the show that night.[37]

Louisa Cody's aging parents, Mr. and Mrs. John Frederici, had moved to North Platte to be near their daughter and her family, and the *Telegraph* editor noted that John, after forty-three years in America, in December 1888, took out his naturalization papers and became an American citizen.

Finally, the *Tribune* reported on the suit brought by Pat Walsh against W. F. Cody for the balance due him on the building of the mansion at Scout's Rest Ranch. The contract for the house, drawn and signed July 7, 1886, set the cost of building the new house and moving and repairing the old one at $3,900, to be paid in three equal amounts, with the final payment to be made when the work was completed to the satisfaction of the owner. The completion date, October 1, 1886, was now long past, and Walsh claimed he had not received a small portion of the last payment. Cody admitted this but said the work had not been completed even though he had given Walsh an extra two years in which to do it. Both parties asked for a jury trial. The jury, seeming to find some merit in the claims of each of the contestants, cut in half the sum sued for by Walsh, although finding in his favor. Both parties, commented the *Tribune,* are unhappy with the verdict.[38]

Scout's Rest Ranch house. Goodman children in front; their mother Julia (in dark dress) on porch.

23

Europe, Wounded Knee, Scout's Rest Ranch 1889-1892

The Wild West opened at the Exposition Universelle in Paris on May 19, 1889, and the grounds could not contain the immense crowds that thronged to see the American show. Sadi Carnot, president of the Republic of France, several members of his cabinet, and the American ambassador, Whitelaw Reid, saw the opening performance. The Shah of Persia also saw the show, as did former Queen Isabella II of Spain, who rode in the Deadwood coach.[1]

The famous artist Rosa Bonheur, then nearing seventy, came to see the show, and afterward spent many hours in its back lot during the seven months it was located there. Of the seventeen or more paintings she did of Cody, his Indians, horses, and buffalo, the most famous was the one of Buffalo Bill on his white horse. The picture, copied on posters, programs, and postcards, was soon familiar around the world. The original was shipped home to North Platte, where Louisa hung it on her parlor wall in company with the portrait of little Kit, proudly showing it to all who came to see it—and most of North Platte and the surrounding community did.[2]

The Colonel wrote Julia from Paris on July 5:

Yesterday was a busy day for me, first I went with the American Minister to the Tomb of General LaFayette then to the unveialing of Barthold's Statue, then to a reception & dinner we gave in camp— then the afternoon performance—then to the Legation reception— back for the evening show—then into my evening dress and to Minister Reids reception, turned in at daylight—and today I am off my feed—I am like you I can't stand so much as I used to and I am n~~ot~~

221

all well this summer. Now as we are getting old we must not kick at our breaking down, it can't be helped, but I don't want to break down until I get out of debt and ahead of the hounds for enough to take it easy.[3]

Cody was forty-six years old, but the pace he had maintained for so long was beginning to tell on even his stalwart body; the mention of debt and taking it easy was a refrain he was to sing often in the years to come.

That same month he cabled his wife that he had been decorated "with the badge of the Legion of Honor." The editor of the *Telegraph,* in commenting on this news, said he believed this was a distinction enjoyed by no other Nebraskan.[4]

The same issue of the paper reported a "Cottonwood Party" given at Scout's Rest Ranch by Miss Lizzie Goodman. This was a picnic under the cottonwoods, and graphically illustrates the rapid growth of cottonwood trees in locations to their liking. The trees, set out in the spring of 1886, in their fourth summer cast enough shade for a picnic. The Presbyterians held their Sunday School picnic in the young grove a little later.

But the big picnic of the season was the one held there to commemorate Al Goodman's fifty-fifth birthday. More than seventy men of the community gathered in the grove that late summer afternoon. Boat rides on "the pretty lake fringed with trees" were a part of the entertainment. Songs, sung by a men's quartet on the far side of the lake, drifted across the water. As the party progressed and the hilarity grew, many of the guests pulled off their coats and boots and ran foot races as they had not done in years. The exercise was a bit strenuous for men whose last races had been for Congress or a seat on the state supreme court bench, but served to give them good appetites for the fine dinner that followed. An after-dinner speech was delivered by Judge Bixler as he presented Mr. Goodman a handsome set of silver-ornamented carriage harness. As dusk settled over the valley, the assemblage smoked cigars on the velvety lawn and drank to the honoree's health and long life in "pure vintage De Pump 1889."

The velvety lawn, the lake, the trees, the great house and barn were Buffalo Bill's dream come true. And the dreamer, thousands of miles away in a foreign land, would no doubt have traded a dozen glittering palace dinners and badges of honor for the privilege of sitting on his own grass to smoke a cigar with his friends.

From Paris the Wild West set out in October on its tour: south of France, Spain, Italy, Germany. But trouble met the show in Barcelona where, with the rest of the city, it was quarantined for typhoid fever—or influenza or small pox, according to various accounts of the disaster. Frank Richmond, well-known announcer of the show, and several Indians died there. Other members of the show, including Annie Oakley, were very ill, and the financial loss was heavy.

Back home in North Platte, Cody had "lost" a daughter—and gained a son: Arta was married on November 27, 1889. But of course her father missed what must have been the most lavish wedding yet held in the town.

During the past couple of years, Will McDonald had married Minnie Belton in a very fashionable ceremony. In an event ranking high in the social season, editor Ira Bare had married Mollie Thompson, a young lady from "back East." Annie O'Hare, a quiet, dainty member of Arta's set, and Billy Baker, Johnny's brother, had seemed on the verge of joining the young marrieds; but when Johnny came home from the Wild West show, he persuaded Billy to go back with him for the next season. Billy tried the show, liked it, stayed on, and married one of the show girls. Annie lived for many years in North Platte but never married; her friends said it was because she never got over loving Billy.

What of Arta's romances? Unfortunately, little is known. Since her return from Europe in 1888, George Field, a newcomer from Chicago and the well-to-do owner of one of the town's lumber companies, had appeared regularly at her side, squiring her to balls, picnics, and parties. Whether or not she returned his ardent feeling for her is not known, but John Grant said he felt very sure of her.[5] Then Horton Boal, Field's best friend, came to town.

A Cody neighbor remembered an early fall day in 1889. Boal and Field were riding in the vicinity of Welcome Wagon when Boal's horse threw him. The Englishman's leg was broken; the injured man was carried into the Cody home and a doctor called.[6] Whether the two men were riding out to call on Arta or merely riding by, we do not know. Whether Horton replaced George in Arta's affections before his accident or afterward, we do not know. We do know that on October 9, 1889, the *Telegraph* reported two items: Horton Boal, on crutches, is "back at his office after breaking his leg five weeks ago"; Arta Cody has left for a visit to La Crosse, Wisconsin. By Thanksgiving the couple was married. Helen wrote: "It was impossible for the father to be present, but by cablegram he sent his congratulations and check."[7] The Grand Island newspaper reported: "H. S. Boal and Arta Cody were married at the Cody residence. . . . The young people left after the ceremony for Denver and points west. Among the presents was a draft from the bride's father, Col. W. F. Cody, for $5,000 and a deed to a cottage in which Mr. and Mrs. Boal will take up their residence after their return."[8]

Buffalo Bill was having his downs and ups in Europe. Released from quarantine in January 1890, the Wild West moved from Spain to Italy and opened in Naples on the twenty-sixth. The show reached Rome on the anniversary of the coronation of Pope Leo XIII, and the whole company attended the Vatican ceremonies. Walsh describes the event: "In full war paint and all the panoply the war chests afforded, the Wild West lined up along the corridor down which the Pope would pass. Cody, in dress coat with his long hair flowing over his shoulders—perhaps the only man who could ever wear such a combination without being ludicrous, towered a full head above the rest. His Holiness gazed intently at the great hero, and spread his hands in blessing."[9]

As the show moved on through Italy, the Indians did their war dances in the shadow of Mt. Vesuvius and wore their war bonnets while riding in gondolas in Venice. The Prince of Teano, still under the illusion there was some trickery about the western broncs, brought from his stud some wild horses that he said nobody could ride. The merry cowboys had them roped, saddled, and ridden in almost no time.

In northern Italy, Cody may well have unwittingly performed a cultural service. In Milan, Giacomo Puccini attended the Wild West and wrote his brother: "Buffalo Bill has been here. I enjoyed the show. They are a company of North Americans with some Red Indians and buffaloes. They perform magnificent feats of shooting and give realistic presentations of scenes that have happened on the frontier. In eleven days they drew 120,000 lire!"[10] While Puccini got his libretto for "La Fanciulla del West" from Belasco's play "The Girl of the Golden West," which he saw in New York in 1907, his real inspiration for the American West may well have come years earlier in Italy.

New storm clouds were gathering over Buffalo Bill's head. A rumor had gotten started that Cody and his partners were mistreating their Indians. The Bureau of Indian Affairs had looked into the matter, but in spite of ample proof that the Indians were well fed, well used, well paid, and happy, the rumors persisted in eastern American newspapers.

In addition, there was trouble in North Platte. As had so many Englishmen before him, Horton Boal hankered to manage a western ranch. Arta and her mother thought he should have charge of Scout's Rest Ranch and were taking steps to make it possible. Perhaps the old jealousy between Louisa and Julia had something to do with it, but whatever the cause, it was quite upsetting for Will Cody. To settle once and for all the stories of Indian abuse and to see what could be done about the family trouble, the Colonel decided to put the Wild West in winter quarters (in Alsace-Lorraine) and come home for awhile.

There is an expanded version of Cody's return and his motives. Tim McCoy remembers the "autumn evening in 1913" when three or four fellows were grouped around the Colonel at the Irma Hotel listening to him tell stories. In the fall of 1890, Cody said, he had been reading and hearing from visitors about "Indian troubles" back in his West—about the Ghost Dance popularity, about rumblings among the Sioux. Portents. In the Colonel's estimation things were going to be happening, so he returned to be in on them; it would be good publicity.[11]

Cody sent Major Burke on to Washington with the show Indians, planning to join them there in a short time and let the officials see for themselves there were no grounds for the tales of mistreatment. But when he stepped off his ship in New York, Cody was handed a telegram from General Miles, asking him to come to Chicago at once. Leaving Burke to take care of the Indian matter, he immediately boarded a train for Chicago, and a talk with the general.[12]

As had happened so often before, theft and dishonesty by white bureaucrats had robbed reservation Indians of the goods and supplies promised them by treaties, and the red men, hungry and despairing, had turned to the now-famous Ghost Dances as a means of restoring the days of peace and plenty. When the Sioux took up the ghost dancing, the whites in the area became fearful of an uprising and appealed to the government for help. Sitting Bull was believed to be at the core of the trouble, and General Miles, knowing of the friendship between Cody and the Sioux chief, asked the one-time scout to leave at once for Sitting Bull's camp, some fifty miles from Standing Rock Agency, and try to get the old man to come into Standing Rock and there await General Miles.

Cody, sure that if he could reach Sitting Bull in time he would listen to him, left at once on his mission. But others, chiefly Standing Rock agent James McLaughlin, felt this was the wrong action and went over Miles' head to President Harrison to have Cody recalled. The scout was headed off before he reached the chief's camp, and the end result was the death of old Sitting Bull on December 18, 1890, during an attempted arrest by Indian police. Cody always regretted what he considered the unnecessary death of the great Sioux Medicine Man. "If I could've talked to him," he said, "it wouldn't have happened."[13]

In the meantime, upon his recall from his mission, Cody had gone at once to North Platte. Julia had planned a Cody reunion at Scout's Rest Ranch for mid-November and had invited her sisters May, Helen, and Eliza and their families.[14] May had married E. C. Bradford; she and Helen lived in Denver; Eliza and her husband, George Myers, were probably still in Kansas. In her letter of invitation, Julia said she would let them all know when Will left New York for North Platte. When Eliza wrote that she did not have the money to come, her brother at once sent all she needed. Cody must have looked forward with pleasure to that reunion, but detoured through Chicago and sent on to the Standing Rock Agency, he did not reach North Platte until Deecmber. We do not know whether or when the reunion took place, but in any case Cody himself was soon called away again.

The killing of Sitting Bull had further upset the Indians on the reservations, and many had fled to the Bad Lands, where other frightened and rebellious bands were already hiding out. This state of affairs had resulted in the killing, on December 29, of Big Foot and many of his band at Wounded Knee Creek in South Dakota. Cody was at home in North Platte when the last sad chapter in the long tale of Indian warfare was enacted, but a few days later Governor Thayer asked him, as a member of his staff, to proceed to the scene of trouble and communicate with General Miles, who had come from Chicago. Cody was also to visit towns along the Fremont, Elkhorn, & Missouri Valley railroad and quiet the fears of the settlers in the areas adjacent to the reservation.

The Colonel carried out the commission and then went on to the Pine Ridge Agency, where Major Burke had just arrived with the Wild West Indians. The Indians had all testified to good treatment at the hands of the show's owners, and the government was satisfied that all was well. On January 16, 1891, with the surrender of the last of the truant Indian bands and the turning of nineteen Indian hostages over to General Miles, all hostilities were declared at an end. Buffalo Bill rode with the general that day, reviewing the troops who had taken part in the recent trouble. It was not only the end of the Indian wars but the end of Cody's service to his government.

At Pine Ridge, January 16, 1891. L-R, *standing*, Dent H. Robert of the St. Louis *Post-Dispatch*, Rocky Bear, Good Voice, Two Lance, Two Strike, W. F. Cody, Crow Dog, High Hawk, Short Bull, John M. Burke; *sitting*, Thunder Hawk, J. C. Craiger, American Horse, John McDonough of the New York *World*, Young-Man-Afraid-of-His-Horses, Kicking Bear, J. G. Worth.[15] *J. C. H. Grabill photo. Courtesy Library of Congress.*

Back in North Platte, the Colonel seems to have settled the family contest for the ranch, for the time being at least, and Al and Julia remained in charge there. But it was the end of March before Major Burke, in Washington, was able to secure signed contracts releasing a new contingent of Indians for service with the Wild West show. Nineteen of them were said to be the hostages taken by General Miles; they were sent to Europe with Colonel Cody as "punishment" for their alleged misdeeds.

Cody, out at the ranch, had signed on most of his riders, and all was in readiness to leave for Europe when Burke's telegram reporting the hiring of the Indians finally arrived, relieving the Colonel's extreme uneasiness in that respect. The Major arrived in North Platte on the heels of his telegram, and the next day the *Telegraph* announced that "a display of horsemanship will be tendered by the boys before they leave for Europe that is seldom equaled and never surpassed in any country." The riders "already here are famous in their respective districts and those who are to come are equally good."

Many tales are told of exciting times at the ranch when the Colonel was there, shaping up his crew of men and horses for the show. Ernest Tramp told of a horse called Black Jack and a rider he remembered only as Jim the Kid, a splendid rider.   Black Jack was a beautiful animal, but so vicious no one could handle him. He had to be fed and watered from the front of his roomy box stall in the big barn, as no one dared go into the stall with him. One day Jim the Kid said, "Colonel, I'm going to train this here animal so Annie Oakley can ride him in the show for you." And Cody said, "Jim, you leave that damned horse in the stall or he'll kill you."

There was a feed runway in front of the stall, with an iron plate along it. Jim sprinkled sugar on the plate every time he went near the stall. That's all he did, just sprinkle sugar there. At first the horse would snort and rear back whenever Jim came with the sugar, and sometimes blow the sugar away. But finally he began to stick out his nose, expecting the sugar. Then one day Jim held the sugar in his hand while the horse licked it up. One day Jim took Black Jack's water bucket in to him from the back of the stall. After that he got tamer and tamer, and one day Jim took him out of the stall to the wooden water trough in the yard. But the horse didn't know what the trough was, and he reared up and smashed it to splinters with his front feet.

You see, this horse was no ordinary bucking horse of the West. Cody had had him brought over from England with two other fine stallions, but they hadn't been able to do anything with this one. Of course Cody didn't know Jim was working with the horse, for he was downtown a lot, usually at Guy Laing's saloon, where he was the day Jim put the blanket on the horse. Later he worked the saddle onto him, everything slow and quiet. And finally one day he got on the horse out in the corral. This strain of English horse didn't know how to sunfish and twist like our broncs, but they'd fight and rear. Jim got him quieted and rode him.

Annie Oakley used to stay at the Cody ranch some, Tramp said, and she'd throw the glass balls for the Colonel to shoot. He had a race track there at the ranch where they practiced, getting ready for the show. Then one day Jim said, "Annie, here's your horse." So Annie was riding Black Jack when Cody came home from town, and he said, "What are you doing!?" and Annie said, "Ask Jim." And Jim said, "Colonel, you are going to take him to England, and Annie will ride him for you." And that is the story of the beautiful black horse Annie rode.[16]

The Colonel always rode a white horse, Tramp said. "I don't know where he got them, but think most of them were given to him. We had a half-gate at the ranch and a driveway leading straight south from the house. When Cody rode away, Mrs. Goodman would stand at the gate and say, 'Now boys, watch him!' And we always did. It was a kind of ritual. He never looked back. She often remarked about that, how he never looked back. She was so proud of him."

Under Goodman's management the ranch had become so well known for its good horses that buyers came from all over the country to deal for them. It may have been during this period of the Colonel's stay at the ranch that T. Koger Propst, with two or three helpers, came down from Merino, Colorado, to buy fifty head of horses. Happening to talk to Cody instead of Goodman, he said he'd heard they had good broke horses for sale and he'd like to see some.

After looking the herd over, he seemed disappointed. "These horses aren't very well broke," he told Cody. "Well, it all depends on what you call broke," Cody replied. "If they've been roped a time or two, *we* call 'em broke." Propst then told Cody he thought the asking price too high for horses hardly even broken to lead. "All right," said Cody, "I'll tell you what I'll do. You take the bunch and have your men work on 'em on the way back to Colorado. If they're *all* broke to ride by the time you get home, I won't charge you a cent. If not, you pay what I ask."

Propst agreed, took the horses, and started home. His men had a bad time with the broncs, but since Cody hadn't stipulated any time limit for the trip, he kept them at it—and when they pulled in at the home ranch three weeks later, the horses were well-broken to ride. Cody kept his word and Propst paid nothing for the horses.[17]

Another view of the Colonel as a horseman was told by Hugh Gaunt. Hugh's parents, Mr. and Mrs. Bill Gaunt, lived in the tenant house at the ranch and worked for Al Goodman. Hugh, at age eleven, was given the job of currying Cody's white horses. The Colonel would wear white gloves when he ran his hands over them to see if the job was well done. If they weren't spotless the boy didn't get his fifty cents for the job until he'd done them over.[18]

Whenever Cody was at home and had time for it, shooting matches were the order of the day, either at the ranch or on the firing range at the fair grounds. Hugh Gaunt said he used to throw glass balls for the Colonel to shoot at; Cody would be riding at full gallop around the ranch race track, but he never missed.

Several old-timers told the story of Cody's getting the two swans with one shot. A. B. Snyder, breaking horses at the ranch in March 1892, said Cody and an eastern friend were watching him work on the broncs when one of the Goodman boys came running to tell Cody a pair of swans had just landed on the lake. "The wind was blowing something fierce," Snyder said, "but Cody took his rifle and went to the lake. 'If I can get 'em lined up right, I won't need but one bullet,' he told his friend, and when the swans were lined up even, he fired his one bullet and got them both. The easterner had them mounted and took them home as a souvenir of the finest shooting he'd ever seen."[19]

George and Josie Goodman used to leave the team of spotted ponies they drove to school at Mrs. Linnie Breese's barn in town. The children often told her of the jokes they played on their Uncle Bill when he was at the ranch. One time they put a flock of decoy ducks on the lake and ran to tell the Colonel there was a bunch of ducks and would he shoot them a brace or two. They thought it great fun to watch him shoot at the ducks—and wonder why they went on swimming.

She recalled another time they told of tying a pair of deer antlers to a tree, with a blanket rolled up behind them for a body. They got him to shoot at the "deer" too. "Of course," said Mrs. Breese, "he let them think they were fooling him because he was having as much fun as they were."[20]

Cody loved a joke, whether he was on the receiving or giving end. Walter Hoagland told of the day the Colonel was shooting blue rocks with Joseph Hoagland, Walter's father, and some other friends. "Bill bet that he could outshoot anybody there. Someone took him up on it— and Bill lost. He did that several times, and by then everybody thought he was loaded to the guards and couldn't shoot worth a darn. Then Bill said he'd bet them all at once that he could outshoot them all, so everybody placed a bet—and that time he beat them all and took the whole pot."[21]

Nate Salsbury, in France with the show, had not been idle that winter. Aware that the persistent tales of mistreatment of the Indians might make it impossible to secure Indians for the 1891 season, he had undertaken to gather an aggregation of the world's finest riders, for all the world seemed to love colorful displays of horsemanship. By the time Cody finally crossed the ocean again, with the new band of Indians, Salsbury had engaged twenty German soldiers, twenty British and twenty U.S. cavalrymen, twelve Cossacks, and six Argentine gauchos. These, with the twenty Mexican vaqueros, the twenty-five cowboys and six cowgirls of former years, and the thirty-seven mounted musicians, made an astonishing assemblage of splendid riders. When Cody arrived with his hundred Sioux warriors, the partners were able to present an exhibition of horsemanship that for speed, color, and action would soon be the talk of all Europe.

The show now traveled from city to city in its own special railway train, unloading at each stop with lightning speed, setting up the vast camp, putting on a morning street parade, giving afternoon and evening performances, then packing, loading, and moving on to the next stop. In Germany the show's speed and efficiency at loading, unloading, and feeding the hundreds of people and animals was of special interest to the army officers. Annie Oakley noted that "at least forty officers of the Prussian guard [were always] standing all about with notebooks, [making] minute notes of how we pitched camp—the exact number of men needed, every man's position, how long it took, how we boarded the trains and packed the horses and broke camp, every rope and bundle and kit was inspected and mapped."[22] All this information would be translated into the rolling German field kitchens of World War I a quarter of a century later.

The show toured through Holland and Belgium, then into England again. In August a company was organized to play in English theaters during the winter months while the Wild West was in winter quarters and while the Colonel made a trip home to North Platte. All that fall his letters to Al and Julia had been increasingly homesick, filled with comments and queries about the ranch. Had they sold the colts yet? Who was the new governor? How were they coming with the haying? Did they need more money? Would they please send him the North Platte papers? He was nettled because newspapers in America were still "jumping" on him about the Indians, refusing to be satisfied that all was right in that respect. And he was heartsick over the situation concerning Arta and her husband and Al and Julia.

Arta, Horton, and Louisa all insisted Horton take charge of the ranch. Cody was opposed to it. For one thing, he had promised the ranch to Al and Julia for as long as they wanted to live there. For another, he did not believe his son-in-law had either the experience or ability to run so large an enterprise. In August he had written Al: "Boal is no man to run it. When you get to old to work you can ride around in a buggy & look after it." He wanted Goodman to build another large barn at the ranch, so there would be shelter for all the stock through the coming winter. He wanted the new barn painted white. "Then in the spring we could put a fresh coat of red paint on the Big Barn, and paint the House blue with green borders. . . . Red White & blue."

He also instructed Al to see that any grain on Mrs. Cody's place (the 160-acre farm where she had lived since 1878) was cut and her hay put up. "I often feel sorry for her," he wrote. "She is a strange woman but don't mind her—remember she is my wife—and let it go at that."[23]

And Al Goodman, good manager that he was, attended to everything. The new barn, called "the big T barn," was built that fall; and Mrs. Cody's crops, as well as those on the big ranch, were gotten in, in spite of a long spell of rainy weather at haying time. At Cody's urging, Al had continued to buy bulls from the best blood lines obtainable, so it had not been easy to write the news to Europe that lightning had killed two of the best in July, bulls he had just paid $500 apiece for.[24]

In November Louisa's home burned to the ground. Helen stated in her book that in November 1890, while the Colonel was on his mission to see Sitting Bull, "his beautiful home in North Platte, 'Welcome Wigwam,' burned." Far away on the plains to the north "Will received a telegram announcing that his house was ablaze . . . [His] reply was characteristic: 'Save Rosa Bonheur's picture, and the house may go to blazes.' "[25]

The *Tribune* gives the year of the fire as 1891. Not only the Bonheur but everything else in the house was saved. According to the paper and to numerous verbal accounts of the fire, it happened after this wise: The fire was first noticed about 8:30 in the evening by the engine crew of a freight coming in from the west. The engineer blew the alarm on his whistle, and it was taken up by an alarm from Box Twenty-three in town. The volunteer department responded promptly and made a run to the west with the hose carts, but the house was too far out, so the boys abandoned the heavy carts and ran on, unencumbered, at a good gait. Mrs. Cody and Irma were upstairs and did not know the building was on fire until the volunteers arrived, closely followed by most of the rest of the townspeople. It was clear from the first that the house could not be saved, although it burned slowly. So everyone turned to and helped carry out the contents, including the piano and a heavy sideboard.[26]

Many stories were later told of the spectacular burning of Welcome Wigwam. Mrs. Mary Roddy said all the fire hoses the town owned were connected and the switch engine pulled them up to the house, but there wasn't enough water to supply the line and it did no good.[27] John

Hupfer said he was assistant fire chief but they had only a bucket brigade and no water, so all they could do was move the furniture out and watch the house burn.[28] Edd Weeks said "it was the prettiest fire I ever saw. It burned slow between the walls, but we didn't have water to put it out, but we got the rugs and everything out while the fire ate down the walls."[29]

C. S. Clinton remembered the fire very well. "I was a charter member of the Buffalo Bill Hook and Ladder Company. We were all young fellows, and we were all out at Cody's ranch when we heard the alarm. We all had on our dress suits, Field and Boal and all of us, but we all went over and worked to put the fire out. There were no cleaning establishments in town then, so afterward we had to do our own refurbishing."[30]

Mrs. Jessie Reynolds, daughter of E. Blankenburg, the harness maker, said that after the fire it was told around town how the firemen carried out buckets of diamonds and jewels, pictures and treasures, tapestries and wall hangings, and all kinds of rich gifts that Cody had brought back from Europe.[31] And Mrs. Roddy recalled that the night of the fire her brother was wearing a fine onyx ring in a jeweled setting; as a member of the Hook and Ladder Company, he helped carry out the furnishings, and after it was all over he found his ring was gone. He never mentioned his loss to Mr. Cody, Mrs. Reynolds said; if he had, the ring would have been replaced.

The loss on the house was estimated at $5,000; the insurance coverage was only $3,000. Mrs. Cody moved into one of her other houses, and life went on as usual.

In December the Colonel wrote that he had "Hay fever or Grippe or something." He expected to come home soon, he said, as he was anxious to get to a country where he could see and feel the sun again.[32] Leaving the show in England, he did come home, early in 1892, but his visit must have been anything but restful, for the trouble between the Boals and the Goodmans came to a head as soon as he reached North Platte. As a result, Al and Julia resigned and returned to their former home in Kansas, and Arta and Horton moved to the ranch.

However, the show had to go on, and as usual during his winter visits to Nebraska, the Colonel bought more horses and signed replacements needed for the cowboy, Indian, and rough-riding acts. He had heard of a young rider down at Maxwell, thirteen miles east of North Platte, and in March he sent the following telegram to Bert Snyder, then twenty years old: "If you want situation with show come up on trial."

Snyder rode up to the ranch. There was quite a crowd of fellows there, he said. Some worked there, others were just riding through and stopped to visit—a normal state of affairs for the Cody ranch. When he rode up and introduced himself, Cody turned to one of his men and said, "Go get that bay horse. I want to see this fella throwed over the barn." While the horse was being brought up, the Colonel told him the hired girl had been bringing in the milk cows on the horse all winter, but he wanted Snyder to ride him and see if he had any action.

The horse was big and handsome. Snyder put his saddle on him and cinched it up, but left the back cinch rather loose. Cody, watching closely, said, "Bring that flank cinch up three or four notches." The cowboy did. "I never saw a horse make a higher, prettier jump than that one did when I yanked the cinch tighter," Snyder said years later. "But I had hold of the hackamore and I pulled him down and quieted him, easy enough."

Cody was enjoying all this, and now he said, "Get on him and spur him on the shoulders." Snyder stepped up in the saddle and spurred the bronc on the shoulders. He went just as high in the air as he had a few minutes before, but he was not hard to ride. So the cowboy kept spurring and the horse kept bucking, high and pretty, until Cody yelled, "That's good. Jump off."

"I had never jumped off a pitching horse in my life," Snyder said, "but I jumped off that one, lit on my feet, and stayed on them. I don't know how I happened to do it, but it sure tickled Cody." It was exactly the kind of spectacular performance that pleased the showman, and he rushed over and patted the bronc rider on the shoulder and started dragging him toward the house to sign a contract to go to England and join the Wild West show.

But Snyder, a practical young man, said, "All right, but what about wages?" Cody told him he'd pay him forty a month and his keep, and pay his way to England and back, which would cost sixty dollars each way. And Snyder replied, "Bill, I can't cut much of a figure in England on forty dollars a month; anyway I can get that in Wyoming any day. I ought to have sixty a month in England." Cody wouldn't agree to sixty, and Snyder wouldn't go for less, so the Colonel hired him to break forty-five head of broncs for his show Indians to ride. Snyder stayed on for three or four weeks, gentling the horses.

At the ranch, he said, the boys all ate in the main dining room at the big house but slept in a large room in the barn where they kept the broncs. While he was there, there was a big wedding at the ranch and quite a number of out-of-town guests came for it. The day before the wedding, the guests were all out on the big east porch, watching the young rider at his work in the big corral. The creek that fed the lake wound its way through the lower end of the corral, past the big T barn. Snyder, working above the creek on higher ground, brought out a bronc that had never been saddled before. He saddled and mounted, and the horse instantly stampeded down the east side of the corral, along the creek bank, up past the big north barn, and around again. He kept on circling the corral, his rider sitting him easily and waiting for him to run himself down—if he didn't slip into the creek as he tore past it. And that was what happened half a dozen circles later.

Wet and muddy, Snyder came out of the creek and went to the barn for his spurs. The Colonel didn't want the horses broken with spurs, but the bronc buster was wearing his when he got on the horse the second time. He kept the horse running until it had had all of that sort of thing it cared for, and all the while the wedding guests on the porch had been laughing, yelling, and cheering for their private little rodeo.

Snyder finished his job and went back to Maxwell. A little later he had another telegram from Cody. "Come up at once. Ready to load. Cody." It didn't say anything about more than forty a month, Snyder said, so he didn't go. Later, when he saw Horton Boal in town and the ranch manager wanted to know why he didn't come when Cody sent for him, he told him it was because he wouldn't pay him sixty a month. And Boal said, "Why man, Bill would have given you seventy-five a month if you had come when he asked you."

Whether he would or not, Snyder was never to know, but in later years he deeply regretted that he had not gone. The experience of seeing foreign countries he said, and being able to say, 'Yes, I was once with Cody's Wild West show," would have been worth the difference.[33]

24

Columbian Exposition, Other Business 1892-1893

Colonel Cody went back to Europe in the spring of 1892, taking the horses and other replacements for the show and leaving Horton and Arta in charge of Scout's Rest Ranch. The Wild West opened at Earl's Court in London, scene of its first European triumph; and its new acts, especially the colorful Cossacks, led by Prince Ivan Rostomov Macherdase, brought out large crowds.

Again Queen Victoria arranged for a command performance, and the show was held on the tennis court at Windsor castle on the morning of May 7. Afterward the queen presented Buffalo Bill with a magnificent signet ring.

Cody brought the show home in late October, after a European tour of some three years and four months, and spent the winter getting it ready to open at the World's Columbian Exposition in Chicago the next spring. Nate Salsbury had gone ahead to make arrangements with the Exposition officials for a concession for the Wild West on the fair grounds, only to be denied admission to the park. Quite likely the big show, with its vast camp-style living quarters for its people, would not have fit into the classic grounds that had been planned and laid out by the great park maker, Frederick Olmsted. Undaunted, Salsbury leased a fifteen-acre tract directly opposite the entrance to the fair grounds and put men to work grading, landscaping, and building a grandstand to seat 18,000 people. The show, billed now as "Buffalo Bill's Wild West and Congress of Rough Riders of the World," opened on April 3, 1893, four weeks ahead of the Exposition, with 500-600 men and women in the cast.

The Chicago papers devoted columns to describing and praising the show. They called attention to the additional transportation facilities necessary to carry "the fantastic numbers of people clamoring to get to the show," told how the Illinois Central had to extend the run of its special World's Fair train, and noted that the Elevated had to establish a station within a few feet of the entrance to the Wild West camp. The *Globe* summed it all up with its big headline: ALL ROADS NOW SEEM TO LEAD TO BUFFALO BILL'S BIG SHOW.

Twenty-five thousand people daily visited the show, with many coming so often the ticket sellers and takers became familiar with their faces. On May 1, the day the World's Fair opened, 130,000 persons visited the combined grounds of the two shows, and the Wild West had to stop selling tickets when its own enclosure began to overflow. When the Nebraska building opened on the fair grounds, Governor Lorenzo Crounse came to Chicago to ride in the parade, and Buffalo Bill rode with him. A reporter described him as "crusted with gold lace and, with the genius he usually displays in such matters, usurped a large share of the governor's glory and accepted the plaudits of the crowd with engaging candor."[1]

W. F. Cody. *Burke & Koretke photo, Chicago. Courtesy David R. Phillips.*

The "White City" of the Exposition was, indeed, beautiful and well worth seeing. And more than twenty-seven million persons did, in fact, see it between May 1 and October 30, but on June 18 the *Post* declared: "No other entertainment in the city can or does accommodate the half that daily visit the Wild West." "No other exhibition," said the *News* of June 17, "has received the plaudits of the people as has Buffalo Bill's Wild West." Several of the papers commented with high favor on the camp where the Indians, cowboys, Mexicans, Russians, Arabs, French, German, English, and American soldiers lived. Always open for inspection, it was the "cleanest, coolest and most comfortable resort, as well as one of the most attractive spots in or about Chicago, and visitors would do well to get to the grounds in ample time to spend an hour strolling about and studying the life and customs of these people."[2]

Exotic cavalry and foreign sights were not the only attractions during leisurely strolling. The life and customs of W. F. Cody himself drew much attention. Amy Leslie of the Chicago *Daily News* spent hours visiting in his tent with the Colonel, with Irma and Arta, and with his immediate show family.

> No such an engaging story-teller as Buffalo Bill figures in history or romance. He is quiet, rich in humor and mellow in his style as a bottle of old port . . . and not a dozen men I know have his splendid magnetism, keen appreciation and happy originality. He sticks to truth mainly and is more intensely beguiling than the veriest maker of fiction. . . . Everything reminds Cody of something else a shade better than the subject at hand.[3]

And horse racing was the subject at hand more times than not.

> Once a sleepy greaser matched a still more somnolent equine against the fastest horse Cody had on the ranch. The Mexican kept his steed in an old adobe house and let him graze around in a listless sort of style for a day or so. But the race day the horse appeared in pattern trim, surmounted with a dapper little jockey the like of which North Platte had never seen. Cody had all his money on his own horse and a glimpse of the opponent showed him that he had been watching the wrong horse doze about in the pampas. But they don't say much about those things out in that country, and Bill thought he would trot the race anyhow. After they had gone about half the distance and Cody had just caught sight of the jockey's chipper colors once in the heat the rider called out to him: "How much of

this do you want?" Bill yelled into the melancholy distance separating them: "I guess this is far enough."

Buck Taylor, who is one of those slow humorists in which the prairie abounds, sauntered out into the town one morning and found eight Colorado cowboys with champing broncos tethered to their iron wrists. "Whatcher calculate doin'?" lazily queried Buck. "Hoss race," was the portentous reply. "Whatcher conditions an sich in this hoss race?" asked Buck, with a smolder of sportive fire in his eye. "Goin' ter lead 'em down ter the two-mile tree and race back," volunteered a plunger. Buck looked at the outfit a minute and said solemnly, "Calculate to git back to-night?"

Out on the plains Pony Bob, Buffalo Bill and a congenial coterie of horsemen arranged a race for a considerable purse, even for those generous days, and made it free for all comers. Three days before the race a wild old man, with a covered wagon and team, drifted into the camp and incidentally remarked the evidence of sport. In the course of the day he offered to enter one of the queer animals dragging his covered wagon. Immediately the scent of the festive scout detected something suspicious and they delayed accepting the last entry until morning. That night when the soft Indian summer moon slid behind a convenient blanket of midnight the wary cowboys stole the old man's horse out of shelter and gave him a mile sprint under the blinking starshine. The horse trotted amiably over the ground in three minutes and they forgave the kindly gentleman for everything he had not intended, and they accepted him as a lead-pipe-cinch angel. The suspected entry was received with acclamations the next morning and nothing but money was staked against it during the interim. When the race was called the old man brought out his dusty nag and also, to the surprise and paralysis of the bettors, he began dragging from the covered wagon a sack full of toe-weights, quarter-boots and scalpers, with which he proceeded to decorate the three-minute "velvet" of the previous evening. With these levelers of speed the horse struck out and trotted in 2:40. Of course the untrammeled prairie trotter was outclassed and the emigrant carried away large accumulations of the golden dust staked against his traveling stable.[4]

The *Dispatch* noted that "those portions of the program most familiar to the public, . . . the attack on the Deadwood stage, the Pony Express, the Indian encampment, meet with the heartiest approbation and applause. The new troop of Arab horsemen, the Cossacks and the cavalry of the four great armies of the world, in a grand international musical drill, were magnificent." The *Tribune* said: "The dash and vim of Buffalo Bill's horsemen at the Wild West exhibition keep that place of amusement easily in the forefront of the World's Fair attractions. Up to date the attendance has increased steadily and there seems to be no reason why Colonel Cody should not duplicate his London success." At home in North Platte, the newspapers in May reported modestly: "Our people are glad to learn that Buffalo Bill is drawing immense crowds."

But if the people on the outside loved the Wild West, so also did the show people enjoy Chicago and the World's Fair. The Indians, especially, were fascinated by nearby Lake Michigan and spent hours watching its restless waters and riding on its boats. Most of all they loved the merry-go-round, riding its gay steeds for hours at a time. The *News-Record* of June 18 described an evening when fifteen painted, blanketed chiefs marched up, bought tickets, and solemnly mounted the painted ponies. When the machine started and the big calliope began to play "Maggie Murphy's Home," Chief No Neck held onto the bridle with both hands as his blanket floated out behind him. Then, as the horses whirled more swiftly, he let go a full-throated war cry, "Yip, yip, yi, yi, yip!" The others at once took it up and the tent walls billowed to the breeze. "The Indians," observed the *Record*, "seem to like being jerked around on a carousel. They prefer it to art galleries, and some people who are not Indians feel the same way."

The *Times* commented on the Indians' fondness not only for the merry-go-round but for peanuts, popcorn, and posies (buttonhole bouquets); they had, said the paper, lately spent all their wampum and gone broke on these delights. Glass canes, coconut fiber hats, and chewing gum also contributed to their penniless condition. But there was always another payday coming, and back on the reservation they would be far away from such pleasures.

Half a century later, an elderly woman in North Platte told of her visit to the World's Fair when she and her sister were little girls. Her father, who knew Buffalo Bill, took his family to visit at the Colonel's tent, and the showman asked the girls to do him a favor. He promised them all the candy they could eat if they'd ride on the merry-go-round with the Indians. The city people, he said, were afraid to get on the machine while the warriors were riding, but if they saw two little white girls, riding alone and unafraid, it would help. The girls were delighted to oblige. "Pshaw," the lady said, "we were used to Indians at home, so we rode with them and had a wonderful time."

At first the Wild West did not show on Sundays, but the demand was so great that it was soon showing seven days a week, twice a day, and the Illinois Central was running its special trains to the show grounds day and night, all week long. And then an unexpected publicity plum fell into the Colonel's hands, boosting the fame of the Wild West even more.

The previous winter, in Chadron, a western Nebraska cowtown, some horsemen began bandying about the idea of a thousand-mile endurance horse race: a race that would upset the record of fifty miles a day, for twenty days, set in France a few years earlier, and prove for all time that the speed and stamina of the western horse was the greatest in the world. Someone noted that it was about a thousand miles from Chadron to Chicago, and with the World's Fair going on there, why not run the race between the two towns and see the fair.

The idea quickly picked up enthusiastic backers. Chadron agreed to put up a $1,000 purse for the winner. When he heard of it, Cody, recognizing the built-in publicity angle, offered to add $500 and a fine saddle as prizes, on condition the race end at the entrance to the Wild West show. After some preliminary figuring, the planners set the time allowed for the race at thirteen days, which meant traveling an average of seventy-seven miles per day. Each man in the race was to start with two horses, riding one and leading one. He was to register himself and the horses at stated points along the road in Nebraska, Iowa, and Illinois. And each contestant was to come into Chicago riding one of the horses he started with.

To ride seventy-five miles in a day is not out of the ordinary, but to average that for thirteen days straight would test men and horses to the limit. The rider would not be mounting a fresh horse every relay and then riding without regard for the horse, but would have to conserve the horse's strength as much as possible. Also, a rider with a fresh mount under him can stand a long ride much better than he can on a jaded horse.[5]

Several men, including one John Berry, a Chicago & North Western Railway civil engineer, were appointed to lay out the route and set up the check points. On a bright June day the racers lined up in front of the Blaine Hotel in Chadron, and the starting gun was fired. No two accounts agree on all points in telling the story of the race, not even as to who fired the starting gun. Some writers list eight men in the race;

most say nine, including Doc Middleton, Nebraska's famous and popular outlaw, and John Berry, whose entry was contested on the grounds that he had helped lay out the route and so would have an advantage over the men who had not been over it. Berry, however, rode anyway.

All accounts agree that Berry was the first man to ride up to Buffalo Bill's show entrance, at 9:30 on the morning of June 27, after thirteen days and sixteen hours on the road. The rules stated only that "the first man across the finish line wins," and Berry was certainly the first. But one source relates that Berry, after the starting gun was fired, went to the Chadron depot, expressed his horses, and rode the train the first one hundred miles. For this violation he won only the saddle, while the purse was divided among the others who finished the race, with George Jones judged the speediest and awarded the largest share.[6] Another writer agrees that Berry shipped his horses part way and won the saddle but says the money was not awarded at all. Walsh says the money was divided eight ways and the riders and their horses exhibited in the Wild West show.[7] Some accounts claim another racer, Emmett Albright, also shipped his horses part way. Doc Middleton has been recorded as winding up with one horse, which he shipped into Chicago while he himself arrived comfortably by train, claimed his horse, and rode up to the Wild West tent, all fresh and chipper. One writer says that Berry and his horse, Poison, also won Buffalo Bill's first place money, which turned out to be only $175.[8]

The race was costly to the entrants, as each man sent a groom ahead by train to await his arrival at check points and feed and care for the horses while the rider slept a bit. Some sent pilots on ahead with a team and buggy to take care of any trouble that might develop. All along the way crowds of people—some in buggies, some on horse-back, some on bicycles—tried to follow the racers. Spectators everywhere cheered wildly as the racers passed.

One good horse was poisoned at one of the rest stops while its rider slept and its groom was absent for a moment. When the horse went down on the next lap, a veterinarian on a bicycle immediately took over and soon had the horse on his feet again, with a loss of only a few hours travel time. The race achieved national publicity when the humane society tried to stop it on the grounds of cruelty to animals. This was settled by promising there would be no cruelty or overriding of the horses, and by issuing an invitation to the societies to come along and oversee the race. This they did, and found that the ride involved no undue hardship for the horses.

The Chadron-Chicago horse race was one of the first of its kind ever staged in the United States, and its effects were far reaching. Not only did it result in a great deal of flamboyant publicity for Buffalo Bill's Wild West and the World's Fair, but it proved beyond question the value and staying qualities of the tough western horse, resulting in a strong demand for the breed in France and England, and the beginning of a substantial business in light cavalry horses between those countries and the Great Plains states.

Before the end of his season at the Chicago World's Fair, Will Cody found himself in real trouble with Louisa. Charles Whalen, of North Platte, who was with the show that summer, tells how it came about. Mrs. Cody, he says, came to Chicago to pay her husband a surprise visit. She went to his hotel and inquired for Mr. Cody and was told she would be shown to *Mr. and Mrs. Cody's suite*. Whalen excuses Cody by arguing, "It was only natural; any man would have done the same, the way women ran after him."[9] Back in North Platte, Whalen no doubt told the story, for Robert Week remembered, "It got out back here, and everyone knew about it."[10] Russell writes that Lulu, having heard rumors of her husband's association with an Olive Clemons, went to Chicago, and, though she found no Olive Clemons at "the house where he lived during the show season, . . . wrecked the place on general principles."[11] (This tale was told at the divorce trial some years later.) Walsh says the lady friend was the actress Katherine Clemmons, whom Cody had met during his first London engagement. He had been so impressed by her appearance that he promptly financed a stage tour through the provinces for her, and afterward brought her to the United States and spent $50,000 on a play for her. The play's failure took quite a bite from the Colonel's profits that year.[12]

Whichever woman, Clemons or Clemmons, or even another or none at all, was with Cody in Chicago, Louisa was definitely upset about it. Therefore, when Cody put the show up for the winter and came home to North Platte in November, he presented his wife a deed to the McKay mansion, the finest residence in town, a very handsome gesture of reconciliation.

George McKay, North Platte silk merchant and dry goods store owner, had built the great house in what is now the 1200 block on West Fourth Street, but was then a pretty meadow several blocks from the western edge of town. Soon afterward, Mrs. McKay's health failed and she could no longer manage such a large place. Mr. McKay, who after the custom of the times wore a long, full beard, had recently attempted to restore his greying whiskers to their original dark shade; the fact that the beard came out of the dye a violent green probably had no bearing on his decision to sell the mansion. But Buffalo Bill, loaded with the profits of his phenomenal season in Chicago, bought it for his Lulu.

The house was an ornate three-storied affair with inlaid parquet floors and a fine, open stairway ascending from the front parlor to a wide landing with a window above it, then on up to the spacious, many-bedroomed second floor. Downstairs, in addition to the big parlor, there was a den, or library, with a beautiful fireplace, and a large dining room. The kitchen was the huge old-fashioned kind, with a small "sitting room," much used by Mrs. Cody, opening off of it.

Welcome Wigwam,
the Cody town house
in North Platte.

Note stuffed buffalo in front of barn. The big barn or carriage house was not part of the McKay mansion when Cody bought the

Mrs. Cody and ten-year-old Irma moved into the new Welcome Wigwam, which was to be Louisa's home for the next sixteen years. She hung expensive Battenburg lace curtains at the downstairs windows, and the Bonheur and the life-size portrait of little Kit went on her parlor walls. Mrs. Robert Dean, who, prior to her marriage, worked for Mrs. Cody for several years, told of a very large painting "of a mountain scene with a deer" that could be seen from "the front, or entrance room, looking through three rooms." There were two other large pictures of Mr. Cody, she said, one painted with his hat off, showing his beautiful long hair, the other with his hat on.[13]

The third floor, a single large room, was used as a museum for many

home in 1893. The Colonel had the barn built soon thereafter; it burned in 1903, but the house stood for almost three decades more before it was torn down. Cody's tallyho is typically filled with guests; the Colonel is probably the driver.

of the mementos Cody brought or sent home from his travels. Almost everyone in North Platte must have visited that room at one time or another, and many left accounts of the things they saw there. Martin Federhoof remembered many Indian souvenirs, genuine Indian relics of all kinds, including a "dried scalp you could see had been stretched out flat, as the peg holes showed where it had dried back from the places that had been pegged."[14] This must have come from Yellow Hair. One of Irma's girl friends told of "a room you would call a study now, that her father kept his relics in. There was a rocking chair made of buffalo horns, and Indian things, scalps and furs and things."[15] Another mentioned trophy saddles, fine saddle blankets, and Indian trappings.

Whatever his welcome at home may have been that fall, the Colonel was received by the rest of the town with open arms. As usual, the band and practically everybody in town were waiting at the depot for Cody's train to come in. The band had been organized some years earlier by Nicholas Klein; a graduate of Heidelberg University, with a degree in music, Klein had come to America in 1878 to escape service in the Germany army. In the late eighties a North Platte girls organization had given plays and other entertainments to raise money to buy shirts and caps for the band members, the only "uniforms" they had ever had.

North Platte band that played at the Old Glory Blowout, July 4, 1882. Picture taken later but before the band's "uniforms" of shirts and caps had been purchased by the North Platte girls. L-R: *standing*, John Day, Charles A. Wyman, Charles Poole, Charles Shafer, Charles Monagan, Charles Stamp, Fred H. Johnston, Mike Sorenson, John A. Foster; *sitting*, Nicholas Klein, Charles Martin, Joseph F. Fillion.

When the train pulled in and the homecoming hero appeared on the steps of his special car, the band struck up its welcome. Charles Stamp, a member of the band, related years later:

As I recall it, Cody stepped into the street and made a little speech. He said, "Well, you boys' playing sounded pretty good, but it might sound better if you had new uniforms. I want each band man measured for a new outfit, the best possible, and send the bill to Buffalo Bill." I think the material was buff colored broadcloth, with the cape lined with satin. There were patent leather leggings and trimmings and a rosette of some kind with Buffalo Bill's picture on it, which was worn on the breast of each uniform. I think Cody paid $1,100 for the uniforms, though it might've been $900. Anyway, when the bill was presented to Cody he thought he was being charged for his fame and he went back to Chicago to the firm to get it straightened out. He had had enough experience in buying uniforms to know whether he was being held up or not. I think the bill had been about $1,300.[16]

Apparently Buffalo Bill was always willing to pay promptly for value received, but, as indicated by the lawsuits with Dillon and Walsh, he would not stand for any short-change deals or overcharges. It is, however, a fact that he bought the town band its first complete uniforms, but again there are many versions of the story.

Edd Weeks says the band had gone to a tailor's shop on the corner of Fifth and Spruce (now Dewey) to pick out some modest new uniforms, and while they were looking Colonel Cody came in and asked what they were doing:

We told him, and he said "Forget it, I'll take care of it." So Cody ordered the uniforms for us. Gordon Laing was our mascot. He was a little boy and his uniform was a small one, just like the leader's. North Platte has never had uniforms anything like those since and probably never will. They were the finest white broadcloth. The capes were lined with gold satin and were worn draped over one shoulder. The cuffs, collars, and front piping were of blue broadcloth. They had gold epaulets and gold braid, lots of it, across the fronts. The belts were red and gold braid on heavy saddle leather, with the gold initials GSCB, and a gold buckle.

The music rolls were of heavy saddle leather, white with gold braid, and the band initials in small letters. We fastened them to our belts, behind, and our leggings were black patent leather with two gold tassels and gold lacings. Each man had a pair of beautiful white gauntlets, and the helmets were silvered metal with what we called a "horse tail," or a white plume, screwed into the top. The front showed a metal buffalo head with a coronet around it. On the front of each uniform was a picture of Buffalo Bill in a frame of red and gold braid. The leader's headgear was a shako of white fur with two gold tassels. The leader and the mascot wore white leather leggings.[17]

Ed Keliher wrote that after Cody had listened to the band's welcoming serenade, he praised it as the best he had ever heard but said the group had the worst looking suits he had ever seen. So he told them to order the finest uniforms money could buy, and he would pay for them.[18]

In January 1894, the new uniforms arrived, and Cody was on hand to review the band in its new splendor. The *Tribune* enthused: "Talk about your poetry in pants. They are a whole quarto volume. The eighteen suits cost in cold clammy cash $835.05. . . . The uniforms for the drum majors, Fred Hartman and Gordon Laing, are a dream of beauty."

Mrs. Mary Roddy and John Baker agree in the main with these accounts, though Mrs. Reddy remembered a round thousand dollars as the cost; she also added the helpful explanation that the Gordon Silver Cornet Band was named for its mascot, Gordon Laing.[19] Gordon was Guy Laing's son and Charley Whalen's nephew; and Charley's brother, a one-armed man, traveled with the Wild West show and passed out programs. John Baker, grandson of the band leader, Nicholas Klein, remembers his grandfather telling him that Buffalo Bill bought the band its fine new uniforms, and Cody's only stipulation was that they wear his picture on the breast of each uniform.[20]

Charley Whalen himself says, cryptically, that "Cody never felt so good about those uniforms he got for the band. He felt he had been bulldozed into that by a certain individual here."[21] A story in the Lincoln *Courier* for September 21, 1895, may throw some light on the above statement:

> The Omaha papers say that one of the conspicuous sights of the street parades intended to enliven the nights of those obliged to remain in Omaha during the state fair was the Buffalo Bill brass band of North Platte, with their gorgeous uniforms, costing one thousand dollars, which were presented them by the Hon. W. F. Cody.
>
> There is a little story connected with this that is not uninteresting; everybody knows that North Platte idolizes Cody. His return home

Fred Weingand, 1894,
Gordon Silver Cornet Band member,
wearing new uniform
donated by Buffalo Bill.
Enclosed in the circle on the front of
the uniform is Cody's picture.

from his season's absence is always celebrated by a public demonstration of some sort. Last year the band was at the depot, and Cody was escorted to the opera house and given a banquet.

One of the things acquired by Cody during his life on the frontier, which he has not lost by association with the Prince of Wales, James Gordon Bennett, and "others" is a love of all kinds of drinkables, from beer to vermouth. A banquet at North Platte includes several courses of "forty rod" and by the time Bill had given "another evidence of our sociability" to all his home friends, he was so situated as not to care whether the band played Annie Laurie, or not. Then the job was worked.

It was suggested that the band was a fine one. It only needed new instruments, uniforms, music, etc. Cody told them to order a whole new outfit and send the bill to him. The order was telegraphed and in a few days the goods arrived by express C.O.D. The band fondly believed it was only necessary to add a Y to the C.O.D. and everything would be all right. But Bill professed entire ignorance of the whole matter and declined to become the victim of any such gouge game.

It looked as though the scheme had failed, until one bright band boy thought of the saying *similia similibus curantur*, like conditions produce like results. They tried it. Cody was caught down town, rushed into an adjacent dispensary and filled up on cowboy compound. Cody was reminded of his promise, remembered it perfectly, drew his check for the required amount, and "the band played on."

John Dick, son of F. N. Dick, North Platte's first railroad doctor, also took a jaundiced view of the Colonel's generosity. The town band met the train with a big torchlight procession, he said, "and Cody made the boys a speech and told them to order new uniforms. He said the price wasn't to be considered, to get the best, and the sky was the limit. They took him at his word. The uniforms were beautiful, and the band really put on the dog, but when the bill was sent to Cody he tried to renege. But he couldn't very well back out with his picture on the breast of each uniform."[22]

There is no doubt the Colonel paid for the fine new uniforms, and it is a fact the band wore them to Omaha for the first Ak-Sar-Ben parade in 1895 and won first prize for the best-dressed band, and second for its playing—and this while North Platte was still only a prairie village out in the middle of Nebraska. No wonder Omaha was envious!

The Colonel's generosity that fall, after the close of his World's Fair season, was almost endless. It was said that he had made "a cool million dollars"; it is certain he spent it freely. Robert Week declared that Cody came home with "barrels of money, and it was good for a five for a kid just to open the door to Guy Laing's saloon for him."[23]

Ed Keliher wrote that the same evening Cody told the band to order its new uniforms, he listed the names of all the churches in North Platte and gave each one $500.[24] Charles Stamp also remembered the same donations. John Dick, however, scales it down a good deal, and goes on to tell a tale: "The churches here put on a banquet to honor Buffalo Bill, but he got to celebrating and forgot to go. There was some bad feeling, and to smooth things over he gave them some money—I think it was fifty dollars apiece."[25]

Walsh raises the ante considerably: Cody "paid off the debts of the five churches and gave each pastor a year's living, [besides] buying uniforms for the silver-horned band and donating the cemetery and fairgrounds" to the city.[26]

The *Tribune* of November 4, 1893, noted: "Colonel Cody on Saturday last donated two thousand dollars to the religious organizations of the city, making W. H. McDonald custodian of the funds. In return the citizens gave a public banquet in his honor." There were six churches in the city at the time.

William McDonald related: "One night at a banquet in North Platte Mr. Cody planned to give some gifts to the churches. My father tried to keep all liquor out of the affair, but someone passed some to him in a teacup and he got pretty well 'lit up'—and over-generous accordingly. I handled all of the money, and gave two hundred dollars around to the churches; but on account of the liquor and the way it was handled, I kept some of the money back."[27]

Another old-timer said Cody not only gave every church in town $600 and bought uniforms for the band but also bought bloomer outfits and gaiters for the North Platte girls' drill team. Maude Dillon, daughter of Isaac Dillon and a lifelong friend of Irma Cody's, said the Colonel gave each of the churches $1,000 and presented every saloon keeper in the city with a fine gold watch and chain.[28]

But old Martin Federhoof topped them all with his bizarre tale. Cody, Lou Farrington, Dutch Snelling, and Bill Snelling, he said, were playing "freezeout" in Laing's place, and each of them took out $1,000 worth of chips. "In freeze-out, if you lose you can't buy more chips, you are just out. The game had simmered down to Cody and Farrington when a delegation of church women came in to get a donation. Bill said, 'Just wait till I finish this hand—if I turn my head this fellow will get a card out of the middle or off the bottom.' So they waited while he played his hand and won the pot, then he asked what they wanted. They said they had come for a donation to apply on their building, and he asked how far back they were. They said $1,700, and he wrote them a check for $2,500 and told them to get out, that a saloon was no place for ladies."[29] Federhoof may have known whereof he spoke, for he spent most of his life in one North Platte saloon or another. On the other hand, it is very unlikely that church ladies of that period would have entered a saloon, however worthy the cause they represented.

In the records of the North Platte Episcopal Church, under the year 1894, an excerpt from a letter written by a former rector, L. P. Mc-Donald, states: "Buffalo Bill this year contributed one hundred dollars to each church." This was also the year in which Mr. and Mrs. W. F. Cody had a huge and beautiful stained glass window installed in the sanctuary of the church in memory of their two dead children. Under

the rich-hued, life-size pictures of the little boy and girl are the in-
scriptions:

To The Glory Of God And In Loving Memory Of
Kit Carson Cody, Died April
20th, 1876, 5 years, 5 months.
Orra Maude Cody, Died October
24th, 1883.[30]

Of Cody's church donations, his sister Helen says only that he helped
build a church in North Platte, "a little temple," and that he was in
attendance one Sunday when the congregation attempted to sing "Oh,
for a Thousand Tongues." The organist, who played by "ear," started
the tune in too high a key and the people could not follow her. After
the second failure to get started, Will boomed out, "Start it at five
hundred, and mebbe some of the rest of us can get in."[31]

W. F. Cody (right) with Goodman family and guests in Scout's Rest dining room.

The Colonel's generosity that year also included Helen and his old friends Dr. Frank (White Beaver) Powell and Alexander Majors. In July, while the Wild West was in Chicago, Helen had married Hugh Wetmore, editor of the Duluth *Press*. At Helen's request, Cody purchased the *Press* for the couple and put up a fine new brick building to house it. Helen and her husband then built themselves a mansion at 620 Ash Street in Bay View Heights.

Some months earlier Cody had found the old employer of his youthful freighting and Pony Express days, Alexander Majors, living in poverty in Denver. The old man was attempting to write his memoirs, and the Colonel gathered the manuscript together and turned it over to Prentiss Ingraham, one of his own "biographers," for editing and paid $750 in printing costs. The book that resulted, *Seventy Years on the Frontier*, was published in Chicago that summer and sold at the Wild West show grounds.[32] The profits went to Majors.

From time to time over the years, Cody and Dr. Powell, contract surgeon at Fort McPherson when Cody arrived there in 1869, had been associated in various business enterprises, mostly having to do with patent medicines. Powell was also said to have been with Bill on his aborted trip to bring in Sitting Bull in 1890.

In 1893 the pair went into the manufacture of a roasted bran coffee substitute in La Crosse, Wisconsin, Dr. Powell's part-time place of residence. They called the concoction "Panamilt" and hoped to sell vast quantities of it to the Mormons, who did not use coffee. In August, Will wrote from Chicago to Julia, then living in Denver, urging her to try his new "coffee" and let him know what she thought of it. "Its creating a great excitement already we are getting orders faster than we can make it. And we are going to start a big factory or Mill where we can turn out thousands of pounds daily. I own one half interest in it. I am ashamed to tell you how cheap we can make it."[33]

The two partners also were associated in the distribution of a nostrum known as "White Beaver's Cough Cream, the Great Lung Healer," selling at fifty cents a bottle. In the mid-eighties, their cough cream advertisment, explaining that the medicine was made from ancient Indian herb preparations and would cure almost any respiratory ailment, was familiar to readers of the North Platte papers. Powell claimed membership in the Beaver clan of the Senecas through his mother, who was of Iroquois ancestry, and is said to have been given the name White Beaver by the Sioux, Rocky Bear. It was a name well suited to the lively patent medicine business of the times. No doubt it sold a good many thousand bottles of lung healer.

In 1923 a huge iron safe was discovered in a La Crosse junkyard, where it had lain for a quarter century or so. On the left hand door, beneath the name CODY, could be seen the time- and weather-dimmed picture of Buffalo Bill, mounted on his white horse. Below it was a painted buffalo head. On the right hand door was the name POWELL, above a picture of the doctor among his Indian friends. Below it was the faded painting of a white beaver. Investigation revealed that after the demise of the Cody-Powell partnership, the behemoth had been sold to the junkyard; it remained there until purchased in 1924 for $36 by a La Crosse machine shop. As late as 1956 it was still in use in the shop.[34]

W. F. Cody.
Courtesy
David R. Phillips.

25

Failures, Successes
1893-1896

Under Al Goodman's management, the ranch at North Platte had at
least been self-supporting most of the time, but, as Cody had feared,
Horton Boal was not the man to manage Scout's Rest. No doubt the
"hard times" and the financial panic of the mid-nineties had something
to do with it, and the fault may not have been Boal's to any great
degree. Certainly he tried hard enough to sell the ranch's large stock
of registered Cleveland Bay and Clydesdale horses; as he declared in
numerous letters written to prospective buyers in Omaha, Denver,
Portland, and other places, "we are prepared to dispose of [them] at
bedrock prices, away below what they are worth."[1] Although Boal may
not have been altogether to blame for the ranch's financial troubles,
neither could he get along with his neighbors as Al and Julia Goodman
had always done.

John Dick, who was not noted for getting along with the neighbors
either, tells of some of the difficulties he and Boal had:

Our ranch lay between Cody's and the river. The Cody hayland
could be reached easier by a cut-off through our place than by going
around by the county road, and we could get to town easier by going
through the Cody place than by the county road. After Boal ousted
Goodman as ranch manager, he posted "No Hunting" signs all over
the place. Our ranch was posted, too. I used to get on my horse and
go shoot prairie chickens. One day I flushed a bunch on our side of
the fence and they flew over it. I went right over the fence after
them [and Boal saw me] and got on his horse and ran me out. I
told him who I was, but he said there was to be absolutely no hunt-

ing on his ranch. So I got out. Two or three weeks [later] Cody came back from the east and brought a bunch of his friends to hunt. I got on my horse and waited for them. They flushed a flock of chickens and they flew over the fence onto my side, the hunters right after them. I told them to get out, that the ranch was posted and no hunting allowed. Cody said, "Why, Johnny, what's the matter?" And I told him. Boal was right there, [and when] Cody turned and asked him about it he admitted [it was so.] Cody fumed and said, "Absolutely Johnny Dick can hunt on my land as long as I own an acre of ground." But I didn't let the hunting party in any how.

The gist of the rest of Johnny's rather long story is as follows: Well, we kept some milk cows on a lot near town that is now West Fifth Street, and a few days later I started to town with a jag of hay for them, but when I got to Cody's ranch the gate across the road was shut and padlocked. So I had to turn around and go to town by the county road. It was haying season, so the next day I went out and padlocked our gate. I did it while Boal's hay hands were in to dinner, and when they came out and found the gate locked they were going to tear it down and go through anyway. But I was waiting for them, and I told them I had put that lock on to stay, so don't tear it down. Then they said they'd just take the fence down, and I told them they'd better not touch it. So they went after Boal. He was going to go through the fence, too, but I told him I didn't think he'd better. Then Boal went to town and told Mrs. Cody about it. She went straight to my father, Dr. Dick, and talked to him about it. I happened to come in just then, and father asked me if I'd locked that gate. And I told him why. He said to Mrs. Cody, "Well, that's the story," and let it go at that. So Mrs. Cody said they would either give me a key to their padlock or take it off altogether, if we would leave our own gate open. And that's the way we settled it.[2]

Apparently there was a heavy mortgage against Scout's Rest Ranch. Whether it was taken out after Horton Boal took over management, or before, we do not know, but on August 19, 1893, he wrote Rodney Dennis of Hartford, Connecticut, to inquire if he would make a rebate on the interest if the note and mortgage against Cody were paid the next month. The following week he wrote more letters offering "big bargains in stallions, as our registered stallions are to be sold regardless of the times. This is a bad time of year to sell, and a very bad year, but we will dispose of them at prices to suit the times." On the last day of the month, Boal wrote again to Dennis:

Yours relative to payment of W. F. Cody's loan received. I thought, considering the condition of the money market, that your company would be glad to receive $25,000 and allow a reasonable rebate. Please consider this as confidential, but I wish to say that, knowing Colonel Cody as I do, if it is possible I should like very much to have you make some proposition for accepting the money not later than September 20, for he now has considerable cash on hand and is besieged on all sides by parties who wish to make this or that investment, which will tie up any surplus effectually in a short time. I would be pleased to hear from you further on this matter.[3]

Boal was right when he wrote of the "parties" who besieged the Colonel with investment schemes. Some of the plans, though valid and worthwhile, involved large cash outlays and were slow to pay off. Such were his Wyoming projects and his plan to irrigate his home ranch.

Cody's work as a scout and leader of hunting parties had frequently taken him into the grandly scenic Big Horn country of Wyoming, where he had seen striking possibilities for its development. U.S. citizens became travel- and entertainment-conscious at the same time that transportation facilities were being improved and extended, and they began to travel about the country to see its wonders. The Rocky Mountains attracted many, and Cody, ever looking ahead, saw good returns for the man who invested in reliable transportation to the mountain parks and lakes beyond the railheads.

The Colonel was instrumental in interesting officials of the Burlington & Missouri River railroad and the Sheridan Land Company in building a huge hotel in the busy town of Sheridan, following completion of the railroad to that Wyoming point in 1892. Such a hotel would provide a fancy way station for tourists and for wealthy eastern sportsmen bent on hunting big game in the mountains. By the May 1893 opening date of the historic Sheridan Inn, Buffalo Bill had had two stage coaches shipped by train from Deadwood to Sheridan. One was a six-horse coach, the other a four-horse outfit. At the same time he had a large livery stable built near the Inn. Although Cody did not own any part of the hotel, it is said that he bought the furnishings for the luxury establishment, which boasted steam heat, running water, bathrooms, and electric lights. The water was pumped from a well in the basement to a huge tank on the top floor, thus providing pressure to carry it to all parts of the building. Power for the lights came from a threshing machine boiler and dynamo in the backyard and was provided only from dark until midnight, when the dynamo was shut off; lamps and candles in each room took care of those needing after-hours illumination.

George Canfield, former proprietor of the old Canfield House in Omaha, and a close friend of Cody's, came out to manage the Inn, and the best of help was brought in from Omaha and other Nebraska cities to work in the many-gabled building. Only the finest foods were served there, and the enormous saloon, with its magnificent carved wood-back bar, was known as the most respectable in town.

During the next two decades, Colonel Cody was frequently the genial host to large parties at the Sheridan Inn, and many tales are told of those fantastic days. He entertained many notable people there, and transportation was always by one of his coaches, with Cody himself often handling the lines. Old-timers said he insisted on having the wildest teams hitched to the coach, which he then drove about town, stopping now and then to buy drinks for his guests. And whenever he came into a saloon he treated everybody in the house and paid with twenty-dollar bills.

Sometimes, said Sherman Canfield, son of the proprietor, the Colonel would get up early and come downstairs at the Inn to have a drink with the elder Canfield—and that was the only time he would ever take a drink on the house, when no one was around. Bill bought bucking horses for his show, the worst outlaws to be found in the country, and had them tried out on the vacant space in front of the hotel. While expert cowboys rode, or failed to ride, the broncs, the Colonel and his guests sat on the wide veranda, enjoying their own private rodeo.

From the Inn, too, Cody and Canfield took coach loads of guests on hunting parties about the country, sometimes to George Beck's ranch in the Becton country; after chasing coyotes with hounds, they would return to the Beck ranch house to drink mint julips made in water buckets.[4]

The Colonel had never given up his dream of sharing the wide open spaces of his beloved West with people from the crowded areas of the world, or for making something truly different in the way of settlement of his Scout's Rest acres. As he saw it, irrigation was the means by which he could bring this about. Accordingly, in January 1894, in partnership with his old friend and fellow ranchman, Isaac Dillon, he purchased two hundred acres of land west of his ranch, thereby gaining access all the way to the North Platte River for the irrigation canal he proposed to dig through his valley holdings.

As originally planned, the ditch was to be twelve miles long, and

600,000 cubic feet of water per second were to be taken from the river to irrigate some 12,000 acres. The ditch, completed in 1894, cost Cody and Dillon $10,000, and in the end irrigated a total of about 4,000 acres. A January 1894 column in the *Telegraph* revealed Cody's plan; under the headline CODY TURNED QUAKER, it read:

> A recent telegram from New York City says that Buffalo Bill is at the Hoffman House and there are wild rumors that the Colonel, after all his stormy career, is about to become a quaker. "I am free to confess," he said, "that I have had dealings with Philadelphia Quakers. They are excellent people, the very salt of the earth. I have been negotiating with them to start a colony on my ranch.
>
> "I own four thousand acres of fine land there. It is rich soil, well watered, wild grasses grow luxuriantly and peace is everywhere. My intention is to divide this land into small holdings of forty to eighty acres each. A Quaker family will occupy each holding. Each tenant will build a house of frame or brick and cultivate his holding for ten years. My idea is to establish a community of interests and to keep the property forever in control of the Quaker sect.
>
> "At my own cost I am to construct an irrigation ditch large enough to furnish each tenant water for his holding. I will thus, I hope, have five hundred Quakers about me."

Many stranger things have happened, concluded the *Telegraph*. Why should not Buffalo Bill become a Quaker if he sees fit?

By November 1893, Horton and Arta had left Scout's Rest Ranch. Whether Cody had to relieve him as manager, or whether Horton realized he was not the man for the position and removed himself, is a matter for speculation. At any rate, Horton and Arta went to La Crosse for the winter, and Bill was urging Al Goodman to return to the ranch as manager. Goodman came back in time for Cody to accompany General Miles on a hunting trip to the Southwest.

Whatever the circumstances attending the Boals' departure, family relations seem to have remained cordial, for Louisa, Will, and ten-year-old Irma spent Christmas with them in La Crosse, and Horton returned with his father-in-law to help lay out the course of the Cody-Dillon irrigation canal. During January, the Colonel contracted with the Oxnard Sugar Company of Grand Island to raise that next summer one hundred acres of sugar beets, a new crop for Lincoln County; he also ordered twenty or more sets of extra-heavy work harness made by a local harness maker, Henry Yost, for use in digging the canal.

Arta Clara Boal,
1893.

Before the end of the month, Cody went up to Sheridan to purchase
some ranch property and make arrangements to send all of his stock
not needed at Scout's Rest and in the construction of the irrigation
canal to the Wyoming range, thus making room at North Platte for
his Quaker colonists. Then he headed for New York to arrange for the
opening of his 1894 season there.

Early in the new year, Al Goodman was kicked in the face by a horse.
The injury did not seem unduly serious, and he went about his duties
as usual. But after a month or so, he became very ill with what his
doctor called inflammation of the brain. Julia had refused to return to
Scout's Rest to live, and Al was there alone at first, except for the
numerous ranch hands and a housekeeper-cook. A *Tribune* report of
his illness records that he was being cared for in Mrs. Cody's home
in town and that Julia and William, the oldest Goodman son, had come
down from Denver to be with him. In spite of numerous references in

Cody biographies to the hard feelings existing between Louisa and the Goodmans, it appears that she opened her home to them in time of need.

Al recovered, and Julia returned to Denver with her son. Cody, after attending an irrigation convention in Omaha in March, shipping several carloads of horses to New York for use in the show, and going up to the Pine Ridge Agency to sign up his contingent of Indians for the summer, took his family to Sheridan for a pleasant visit. Arta may have accompanied her parents and sister, as she had come down from La Crosse at about that time. Whenever the Codys were in Sheridan they put up at the Inn, and "a good time was had by all." Old-timers there remember them as a strikingly handsome family.

From a near millionaire in the fall of 1893, Cody tobogganed to near bankruptcy the next year. The nation was still suffering from the widespread drouth of '93 and the continuing money squeeze, and none of the Colonel's many investments had paid off. Hail had severely damaged his irrigated crops in the Platte Valley, and the national shortage of money had ruined his plans for the Quaker colony and caused the failure of his coffee substitute business. In Sheridan he had "loaded up with a big force of help, provisions & expecting several big excursion partys," which did not come because of the Burlington railroad strike.[5] There was no sale for horses, and Helen was unable to rent any office space in the big building he had built for her in Duluth. He had laid out large sums of money for a great covered grandstand, seating 20,000 people, at Ambrose Park, South Brooklyn, New York, where the Wild West performed twice a day, all summer, for fifty cents general admission.

In a despairing letter to Julia, who was still in Denver, he wrote on July 18, that the show was costing him $4,000 a day, attendance was poor, due to the hard times, and he was in the "tightest squeeze" of his life. "I am not sleeping well now—do nothing but think and try to plan some way out of it." Even so, he devoted a part of his letter to commiserating with his sister over her own poor health and urging her to come back to the ranch: "the house is there no one in it but Al—As you are not able to work, you must not cook for anyone but yourself, [or] you can board with the men. Al keeps a woman cook."[6]

However difficult the summer had been, Bill came home in October, full of plans for the future and apparently his usual genial self. In advance of his coming, he had written Al to "rig up the tallyho teams and get the dogs ready" for a hunt, because he was bringing some New

York guests, one of them a son of Jay Gould. Of course, the townspeople, with the resplendent band and the Cody Guards, were on hand
when Cody's special car came in.[7]

A few months earlier, in spite of some dissension, a company of
Nebraska Home Guards had been organized in North Platte, and Governor Lorenzo Crounse and several officers of the State Guard had
come out from Lincoln to muster in the fifty members. The ceremonies
had taken place in Lloyd's Opera House, followed by a banquet and
"eloquent speeches." The company was titled the "W. F. Cody Guards."[8]

In connection with an announcement of the coming hunting party,
the *Tribune* had modestly predicted it would "probably create a little
life in town for a week or so." No doubt it did, for the Colonel's local
hunting parties were famous far beyond the Platte Valley. Old-timer
Otto Thoelecke used to tell of the season he worked at Scout's Rest,
when Dillon was foreman. Dillon had put him to training thirty-five
dogs for a hunt Cody was planning for some Englishmen and partner
George Beck of Wyoming. He was also to exercise forty head of saddle
horses and keep them fit for visitors to mount, whether they stayed
mounted or not. On the day of the hunt, Thoeleke and other hands got
about twenty guests mounted, temporarily, put the rest in the tallyho,
and set out. Riders were strewn along the way, causing many delays,
and the hunt was not a howling success, as a hunt, but everybody had
fun.[9]

There is frequent mention of Cody's hounds in these old tales. Some
highly pedigreed dogs had been given to the Colonel by some of his
English friends, and since hunting dogs were popular in the Platte
Valley anyway, the introduction of the superior breeds had given new
impetus to the sport. Always generous, Bill had made the services of
his fine male dogs available to the community, and in a few years' time
there were in the region a good many hunting dogs named Cody.

Colonel Cody was busy all that winter, attempting to pull his affairs
into shape and get himself out of his financial difficulties. He spent
considerable time in Sheridan, expanding his interests there. Louisa
and Irma accompanied him on some of his trips, as Horton and Arta
were living in Sheridan that winter. He also made numerous visits to
Denver. He held meetings in North Platte for the purpose of organizing
a sugar beet company and building a factory there; he had interested
a Chicago banker in the project, and Beach Hinman, Charles McDonald, John Bratt, and other Platters were planning to come in. By
January the sugar company was tentatively organized, with a capital of

$250,000, after which it sank without a trace.

Busy as he was with his many enterprises, Buffalo Bill still found time to entertain numerous groups of his friends of the stage-show days. During one week in January 1895, he hosted two stage companies at the ranch and showed them about the town in the tallyho.

Compounding Cody's troubles was the illness of his partner, Nate Salsbury, who, from the autumn of 1894 on, was unable to take an active part in the management of the big Wild West show. Much as he disliked doing so, in January Bill had to ask Salsbury to sign his note for $5,000 to keep his credit good and open the show that spring.[10] In addition, Cody had to make still another deal with James A. Bailey, of Barnum and Bailey, to provide transportation and local expense money in return for a share in the profits.[11] Bailey furnished railroad cars for the show and laid out an itinerary that would carry the outfit over a 9,000-mile route of 131 stands in 190 days. Strenuous as the schedule was, Cody took pride in the fact that his was by far the biggest show on the road that season, requiring fifty-two railway cars, ten more than Barnum and Bailey used and fourteen more than Ringling Brothers.

In March the Kearney *Hub* interviewed Cody and brought forth the following animated report:

> Kearney people are always interested in the ventures and adventures of Buffalo Bill, nearly as much so, in fact, as are his own people of North Platte. They are proud of him as a Nebraskan, and equally so as a showman and entertainer who has given pleasure to all the big guns at home and the big wigs and crowned heads abroad.
>
> Buffalo Bill will open his Wild West Show at Philadelphia April 22, with the largest show that has ever been put on wheels. There will be six hundred people in his company and six hundred animals. His portable grandstand will be largest ever built and will seat 18,000 people. . . . Few people supposed that his Wild West venture would ever pan out as an average success, much less the great proportions it has attained, and at the same time make its originators both rich and famous.
>
> Not content, however, with his laurels, won with his great exhibition and delineation of the old frontier life, Mr. Cody has planned another great original enterprise of as great, if not greater, magnitude than the first. The new enterprise will be located on permanent grounds in Ambrose Park and will be a grand exposition of the history of American slavery. This is certainly unique. The show will be com-

posed of one thousand Negroes who will every day present, in tableaux and human panorama, the entire history of American slavery. These tableaux will present the Negro as a savage, a slave, a soldier and a citizen. The best Negro talent in the U.S. will be employed in this great show and everyone knows that the colored man is strictly in it when it comes to entertainment.

Mr. Cody said "Negro humor and melody will in this show reach the acme of perfection, as we have engaged a large company of the most celebrated colored opera and jubilee singers and each and every member of the aggregation will possess musical talent, so that the grand chorus of one thousand voices will be a thrilling performance." Imagine one thousand Negroes, in varied costumes, parading and singing in one great wave of melody, those old plantation songs. Scenes descriptive of the ante-war period will be presented, showing the plantation with cotton pickers at work and the various other phases of plantation life, even the auction block and the whipping post will be faithfully shown.

This grandiose plan, of course, recalls the letter Will Cody wrote to Julia in July 1888, from Erastina, in which he mentioned "a new show—one nobody can get up an imitation on": the one he wouldn't even reveal to Al and Julia until he was ready "to spring it on the public."

Buffalo Bill's dream, as actually carried out by the ailing Salsbury and Lew Parker, long-time stage manager for the Wild West and a veteran of minstrel shows, fell far short of the plan Cody had outlined for the *Hub*. The show, called "Black America," employed 300 blacks who traveled in fifteen railway cars.[12] Although both Cody and Salsbury had high hopes the show would recoup their fortunes, it did not "take" with the audiences of its day and died a slow death by autumn. Perhaps it was ahead of its time.

From New York in mid-April, Cody wrote to Al again, urging him to bring Julia back to North Platte. "I will give you a five or ten years contract to run that place if you will take it," he offered. "I will agree to any kind of a proposition you can suggest—to board the help, yourselves, or pay Julia a salary to look after the boarding of the men." Al's health was no longer the best, and Cody, in his eagerness to keep his brother-in-law in charge, wrote, "You can ride around and superintend everything, and no one can keep a lot of men moving better than you can. You are the man for that place. You built it. . . . Where could you find a better place?"[13]

So Julia, who had sworn never to return to Scout's Rest Ranch, capitulated, and in May her husband went up to Denver and brought her and their three youngest sons back to the ranch. Although she now had a woman to help her with the work, Julia was still a busy person. As she wrote in her diary: "We had so much company in the Big House it kept us all busy all the time. Brother would write me that some of his friends would be there at such a time and Al would have to go in rigs down to the North Platte Depot and bring from six to twelve for me to wait on and entertain—and they would stay from one week to months."[14] All this in addition to the score or so hired hands employed at the ranch in haying and other busy seasons.

By June Buffalo Bill was in the midst of a sharp "show fight" with Ringling Brothers. As he described it, such a fight was a lively affair, and a costly one, for "newspaper advertisements and bill boards and brainy men to write" came high. His share of the contest would cost him $15,000, he wrote Al, but Ringling's would be $60,000, and Cody was winning—and making big profits, besides, from his barnstorming tour.[15]

The Philadelphia *Public Ledger*, the Holyoke *Daily Transcript*, the Rochester *Herald*, the Washington *Post*, and others lauded Buffalo Bill and his company to the stratosphere. They described the show in detail and declared that Barnum and Bailey and all other huge shows did not compare in interest and entertainment with Cody's Wild West. The *Daily Transcript* stated "with absolute truth that nothing ever gave so much satisfaction in Holyoke"; the *Herald* reported that at Rochester the crowd was so great over 5,000 people were turned away.[16]

At Duluth, in the plant he had bought for his sister, the Colonel had 60,000 copies of the *Press* run off to distribute to his show patrons. North Platters were happy over a four-column advertisement for their town appearing in the paper. The Washington *Post* said half the retired army officers in town saw the show in the capital city and that the War Department seemed to have taken the day off for the same purpose. When Buffalo Bill himself rode in at the head of the Congress of Rough Riders, his old army friends gave him a great ovation and presented him with a laurel wreath four feet in diameter, tied with red, white, and blue ribbons. Cody slipped the wreath over the shoulders of his big sorrel horse, which had been given to him by General Miles after the affair at Wounded Knee, "and a handsomer pair than the man and the horse would be hard to find."

While Black America was losing money for Cody and his partners, the Wild West was making it; just as well, for the Colonel was spending it as fast as it came in. He was sending Al money to pay for an extension on the Cody-Dillon ditch and for other ranch expenses.[17] With partners George T. Beck and Horace Alger he was negotiating with the state of Wyoming, under the new Carey Act, to build a huge irrigation canal from the South Fork of the Shoshone River out across the Big Horn Basin-acres of his new ranch, the TE. Expenses and equipment for their Shoshone Land and Irrigation Company were to take huge bites of his income for the next few years.[18]

After he put the show up for the winter, Cody divided his time between his Wyoming and Nebraska ranches. In February he sent his nephew, Henry Goodman, to the TE with 140 head of horses from Scout's Rest. In March he bought 1,200 head of horses in Lincoln County and sent them to Wyoming to work on the Shoshone canal. The following month he shipped grain to Billings, Montana, from where it was hauled out "to feed his ditch horses at work up in that country." At about the same time he sent fifteen blooded greyhounds, with an attendant, in a railroad box car to his Big Horn ranch. Some of these dogs, the *Telegraph* noted, were priced as high as $1,000 each. The hounds were shipped west in preparation for a big deer hunt the Colonel was planning for a party of "English nabobs."

But the big talk in North Platte that winter of 1895-96, was the coming Irrigation Fair. Someone had suggested that Nebraska, just coming into recognition as an irrigated state, should have a state irrigation fair; this in addition to the state agricultural fair at Lincoln. The idea caught on, meetings were held, committees named, and North Platte was selected as the site for the first state-wide gathering. With some 200 miles of canals and many miles of laterals already in operation in Lincoln County, the site was a logical choice. By the time these details were settled, Buffalo Bill was back in North Platte, and the fair committee, anxious to present the best possible fair, hastened to ask the Colonel for suggestions. His reply outdid their wildest expectations: "If you fellows will get out and hustle until fall, I will bring my entire show here for the opening day and we will see if we can't make this fair a success."[19]

The announcement immediately sparked state-wide interest in the fair. The Grand Army of the Republic, then an organization of many thousand members, decided to hold its big state reunion there the same week, and was eager to know the date. On May 3, Cody, traveling with his show in the East, wrote W. G. Park of the North Platte committee:

I am really proud of our townspeople to think they are going to wake up and do something for their own interest. You say it would be some advantage to be able to advertise the Wild West from the start. As it now looks like the Lincoln County people are really going to try to get up a decent fair, I will do my part. You may advertise the Wild West for October 12. Although it is a big run for my two trains from Omaha to North Platte, when I could play a much larger town directly on the route, and will cost me $5,000, I will do it. I advise that work on the buildings begin at once and I hope the Fair will be a great success.[20]

The Colonel's letter had the desired effect. North Platte got busy. But by July a controversy had arisen. Bill wanted to bring in one of the presidential candidates of that year to open the fair. The committee and some of the townspeople did not care for the idea. "This is not the occasion for the booming of any political candidate. It [the fair] is held for an entirely different purpose," they stated.

Years later, Jack Hayden wrote that Buffalo Bill was staunchly supporting McKinley that summer and while in town for the fair made a political speech on Front Street, denouncing Bryan and his platform.[21] North Platte newspapers of 1896 do not bear this out. A Cody letter in July urged manager Park to secure Bryan to open the big fair in October; he was backing Bryan, he stated, but was against his free silver policy. "I have been a Democrat for forty years, but I don't like some of the party's moves."[22]

When told of the committee's reluctance to invite a candidate, Cody wrote Park: "I don't suppose you would accept a watermelon on a twenty-foot pole." He went on to urge him to "let the Boy Orator of the Platte" open the fair, as they would be having a future U.S. president in their midst if they did. And if they invited Bryan, Cody wanted to have him as his guest in North Platte. "I appreciate," he added, "that everyone will have to keep open house or there will not be room enough in town to take care of the visitors."

No candidate was invited to open the show, and E. L. Seeberger, secretary of the fair committee, took care of the housing problem by arranging with Wolf Brothers of Omaha to furnish all the tents, cots, and camp stoves needed to accommodate visitors. By late September the new Womens Building and the bandstand at the fair grounds had been completed; the grandstand was extended fifty feet by the addition of bleachers. Many Platters then pitched in to help clean and spruce up the grounds, which were "very tastefully arranged with a floral hall, amphitheater, half-mile race track, ample stalls and stable room and a ten-acre lake which supplied water to *rapify* the grounds and serve as an example of proper irrigation." From Buffalo County on west, large agricultural exhibits were coming in, and there was no question but that Nebraska's first Irrigation Fair would be a grand success.

As a final touch to their preparations, the fair officials had ordered a life-size statue of Buffalo Bill in his scout's attire. This was to be furnished by Ritner and Swan, North Platte marble cutters, at a cost of $800, and set up at the entrance to the fair grounds in time for the opening.

In early September, Cody's advertising manager, a Mr. Gardiner, arrived in North Platte to arrange for covering the city and county with flashy billboard posters advertising Buffalo Bill's complete Wild West Show and Congress of Rough Riders, to stake out the site of the show, to make arrangements for feed and water at the grounds, and to look after all other details. Gardiner and his men were taken to the ranch in the tallyho, and while there a Mr. Allen in the party told a reporter he had often heard Colonel Cody express pride in his home town, and that after visiting North Platte, he thought such pride commendable.

A little later Mrs. W. H. Broach, wife of a local photographer, returned home from a visit to Battle Creek, Michigan, where she visited the Wild West as the guest of Colonel Cody. He had assured her, she said, that "he would positively be showing in North Platte on Monday, October 12, afternoon and evening, and that he expected to give the people of his hometown the best exhibition he had given any place."[23]

On September 25:

> Colonel Cody's advertising car came in . . . on No. 1 and a score of men have been busy all day in billing the city and the country surrounding. Some very nice advertising matter was put up and it will not fail to draw a big crowd to the Wild West exhibition. Mr. H. Harlow Gunning is in charge of the car. Mr. Gunning made this office a pleasant call and said that the people of this city and vicinity should understand that Colonel Cody will give exactly the same exhibition here, down to the smallest detail, as was given at the World's Fair, without the difference of a man or horse in number or kind.[24]

Until the return of Mrs. Broach with her first-hand assurance from Buffalo Bill himself and the actual posting of the town, there seem to have been skeptics in the town—a few folks who did not believe Cody would really bring his great show to North Platte.

The tented city, prepared for the Civil War veterans and other visitors, was set up in a large open space four blocks west of the present Jeffers Street viaduct, north of the railroad tracks. The Union Pacific piped water to the grounds and furnished stacks of old ties for campfire fuel. Most of the visitors came by covered wagon, following the old Oregon Trail and dallying along the way to hunt prairie chickens and quail. Most of the G.A.R. wagons stopped for the night at old Fort McPherson National Cemetery, where the old soldiers formed firing squads and saluted their honored dead.

On Sunday morning, October 11, all vehicles were moving toward North Platte. Near Sioux Lookout, a rugged peak a few miles east of town, someone started singing "John Brown's Body." The tune was quickly taken up all along the line, echoing from the hills like rolling thunder. For hours a solid line of wagons crossed the long wooden bridge across the river directly south of the town. Many wagons carried large flags floating above the canvas tops, making a picture not unlike a sea of sailing ships topped by waving Stars and Stripes.

By noon the streets of the town were jammed with wagons, buggies, and carriages, with more coming in on every road. It was said afterward that by sundown upwards of 4,000 wagons were parked among the tents, making up a camp never before equalled in size in Nebraska.

In the meantime, the Wild West was on its way to North Platte. Helen says she joined her brother in Omaha after the Saturday night performance there. She writes that the Union Pacific officials had promised to make special time on the run from Omaha to North Platte, but when they awoke Sunday morning they found the trains had been held up for several hours. At the next station double-headers were put on, and they began to make up time. A little later the Lightning Express, the "flyer" to which all other trains gave way, was sidetracked so the Wild West trains could go by.

The trip was a continuous ovation, Helen wrote. Every station was thronged, and Will was obliged to step out on the platform to make a bow as the train thundered by and the people cheered. Due to the lateness of their arrival, they reached North Platte about the middle of the usual church service hour. Even so, "the entire population" was at the station to welcome Buffalo Bill and his show, the ministers having dismissed their congregations and accompanied them to the station.

The tallyho, drawn by six horses, was there to take Cody and his family to the "home residence," whichever one that was, and they drove through the town preceded by one band and followed by another. One, no doubt, was the Wild West cowboy band, the other the town band. At the end of the drive both bands united "in a welcoming strain of martial music."[25]

The show unloaded west of the depot, next the showgrounds, and by nightfall everything was in order there. Then the cowboys from the outlying ranches hit town from all directions, their ponies' hoofs pounding the streets as the frolicsome riders shot out the kerosene street lights[26] while officers of the law looked on tolerantly, for this was holiday and no one was going to be stuffy about it. One group rode their horses into Guy Laing's saloon, where some of the patrons lifted the piano onto a pool table so one of the riders could sit on his horse while he pounded out a few tunes, accompanied by some of his fellows on jews-harps and mouth organs. Then Buffalo Bill strode in, laid $200 in bills on the bar, and told Guy to give the boys a drink—and so the fun went on.

The big parade took place the next morning under sun-washed, blue October skies. The Colonel headed the march, driving a spirited grey Arabian team to a high-seated carriage with a footman on a stool at the rear. Mrs. Cody and Governor Silas Holcomb followed in the Deadwood stagecoach. Thirteen-year-old Irma, who had come home from her school in Omaha, probably on the show train with her father, rode a beautiful white horse in the parade. Arta was there, too, having come down from her Wyoming home two weeks earlier to stay until after the fair.

The great concourse of vehicles, mounted cowgirls, and hundreds of horsemen, the world's best, advanced up North Platte's dusty streets to the stirring music of the show's three bands, with the world famous cowboy band out in front. Years later, Chancy Rogers recalled standing on the street that day watching the oncoming parade. Beside him stood the old Medicine Creeker, Paddy Miles, who had taken part in the Duke Alexis buffalo hunt twenty-four years earlier. The Colonel, handling his prancing greys with a firm hand and bowing right and left to his friends on either side of the street, recognized Paddy, halted his team, and invited his old friend to get in beside him. Grinning, Paddy did so, telling Bill to go on with the bowing and he (Paddy) would just go along for the ride.[27]

The Union Pacific ran special trains from all the towns on its line that day, bringing in spectators by the thousands. At thirty-minute intervals other trains shuttled from the depot through the G.A.R. campground to the fair grounds, and all the show-goers streamed past the handsome statue of Buffalo Bill as they entered the gates.

Buffalo Bill statue,
North Platte.
(Water might have flowed out of
the opening beneath Cody's hand.)

In later years, long after the old fair grounds were purchased by the Union Pacific Company as a site for its great ice plant, and after the monument had toppled and broken to bits, one old-timer said the statue had also been a fountain, "and we used to drink out of Buffalo Bill's hand."[28] John Little said "it was never used for a fountain because there was no water up in that part of town, except a couple of pumps."[29] Since the Union Pacific had piped water to the grounds for the duration of the fair, the statue could have, and may have, been used as a kind of drinking fountain on that one occasion.

Sister Helen wrote that the Wild West had visited her town of Duluth for the first time that summer. On that occasion Buffalo Bill had bet his sister a fur cloak against a silk hat that in October his little home town of 3,500 would turn out a larger crowd than would Duluth, a city of 65,000. Helen accepted the wager, knowing her brother did not expect to win. In North Platte, when the tent man asked if he should stretch the full canvas, Cody replied, "Every inch of it. We want to show North Platte the capacity of the 'Wild West,' at any rate."

As she watched the immense crowds pouring into the grounds, Helen began to worry about her "sure thing" bet. Hurrying to the ticket-seller to ask how matters stood, she was told, "It's pretty close. Duluth seems to be dwindling away before the mightiness of the Great American Desert." Her story of the North Platte exhibition ends there, except to say that over 10,000 attended; she mentions nothing about winning the fur cloak.[30]

At admission prices of fifty cents for adults and twenty-five cents for children under nine, a local paper reported that "Buffalo Bill took in twenty thousand dollars from the people who went to see his show." Correspondent Hayden recalled the attendance at "more than eighteen thousand" for the two performances.

That there was a goodly crowd is attested to by the reminiscence, forty-four years later, of Ray Langford, North Platte banker. Langford was one of the ticket sellers that day. As he described it, the fair board had set up several "little buildings resembling privies, with so much change, and they gave us each a revolver and locked the door and left us to sell tickets. There were so many people, and such a jam of the mob, so many people went away without picking up their change. At first I took a lot of pains to help them get their change, but it got so I was putting in as much time trying to get their change back to them as I was in selling tickets, so I began to pay more attention to my job as ticket seller. We were well paid and with the additional change I found myself flourishing when the show ended."[31]

William Sander, who attended the big show, remembered his experience in buying a ticket as follows: "I was in the line going by the ticket window at one of the booths. I handed the ticket seller a five dollar bill for tickets for me and my girl. The young man in the window handed me my tickets, but when I tried to wait for my change he yelled, 'Move on, move on, you're holding up the line.' The people behind me, a long line of them, were pushing and shoving, so I had to go on without my change."[32]

More than forty years after the great Irrigation Fair, with its many races, contests, and attractions, the men and women who saw it all seemed to remember only Buffalo Bill and his big show. Earl Brownfield, fifteen at the time, said: "There were three performers there whose like you'll never see again: Annie Oakley—the world has never seen such a wonderful lady marksman as she was; Johnny Baker—the

Johnny Baker.

W. F. Cody and his sisters, mid-1890s. L-R, *standing*, Helen Wetmore, May Bradford; *sitting*, Eliza Myers, the Colonel, Julia Goodman.

world's best shot and a fine performer; and Cody himself—the most out-standing of all. He rode on a dead run and had an Indian with him to throw the balls up for him to shoot, and he seldom ever let one get away from him."[33]

Landon Reneau, who had seen the Wild West twice in Chicago at the World's Fair, saw it again in North Platte at the Irrigation Fair. By then, he said, it was rumored that Cody's "rifle was loaded with buck-shot instead of bullets, but I didn't care; I couldn't have hit the side of a barn with either one, the way he was going around that arena."[34]

Girls and women who saw the show were especially interested in Annie Oakley. "How I did admire her,' said Mrs. J. R. Baskins. "It was the first time I had ever seen a woman in mannish attire, and I was rather shocked, . . . but I would've given anything if I could rope and ride and shoot as she did. But what I remember best is Buffalo Bill on his white horse, riding out from the big tent to greet the crowd and tell them how much he appreciated the recognition they were giving him. Then he dismounted and led his horse, walking through the crowd and shaking hands with friends and all the children. His handshake was hearty and his voice friendly. Irma was just about my age and she was with him, happy to be with her much-admired father."[35]

Another 1896 show-goer said of the great crowd: "I don't know where all the people came from, but they came. I knew of one family that drove a hundred miles with a team and wagon to see that show." Another remembered that pretty Ann O'Hare, Billy Baker's former sweetheart, was invited to ride in the stagecoach when it made its dash around the arena ahead of the war-whooping Indians. Still another said he thought the best part of the show was a square dance put on by horses and riders. "That was the most artistic act I ever saw. Cody was a fine horseman, one of the best, and the horses were beautifully trained. They went through that entire dance as if they were dancers on a floor, except that they had a large stage."[36]

It goes without saying that Cody's show people did their level best to put on the finest exhibition of their careers for his home-town folks. Certainly Johnny Baker did, for it was his home town too, and he was the boy who had made good in a mighty big way. The town "cheered and applauded him uproariously for his fancy shooting."

And when the evening performance was history, Hayden said, the Colonel visited the G.A.R. headquarters tent at the campground to register in with the other veterans and then to walk among the blazing campfires, greeting old comrades and making new friends.

26

On Tour
1896-1898

From North Platte the big show backtracked to Hastings, Nebraska, and then to Lincoln, and from there to St. Joseph, Missouri, where Buffalo Bill was arrested and charged with putting on his show without a license. The Wild West Company had a license for a sideshow, for which it had paid $20. A license for a circus exhibition cost $250, but Cody declared his show was not a circus. A continuance of the case was granted to give him time to engage counsel, and he stated publicly that he would take the case to the highest court in the land before he would buy a license for a *circus exhibition*. Nothing more was heard of the case, and a short time later the Colonel put the show in winter quarters, after traveling more than 10,000 miles that season of 1896 and making 132 stands.

After having been a "life-long Democrat," Cody switched parties that fall and voted for McKinley. And by January it was known in North Platte that the town's favorite citizen would be among the most honored guests at President McKinley's inauguration. Each U.S. Senator had the privilege of naming two men from his state to attend the president-elect on that occasion, and Nebraska's Senator W. V. Allen had named Colonel W. F. Cody as one of his choices. "The Senator could not have made a better selection," the *Telegraph* declared, "and the appointment is an honor to Nebraska and North Platte, as well as to Colonel Cody."

In the meantime, since presidential inaugurations did not take place until March 4 in those days, the Colonel was busier than ever with his many enterprises. With George Beck and others he was deeply involved

275

in the Big Horn Basin project, where they had laid out the town that was to be known as Cody. In August they had secured the Cody post office and had Ed Goodman appointed its postmaster. They had put up a hotel, and a store and several saloons were flourishing. Propelled by the money poured in by the Colonel, the Cody canal was snaking its way into the Basin.

In February a new little newspaper, the *Shoshone Valley News*, published at Cody, Wyoming, reported:

> We understand that we are soon to welcome to our mountain wilds the charming wife and lovely daughter of the renowned Colonel W. F. Cody. We truly hope Mrs. Cody will be pleased with the country and we extend to her a welcome to our hearts and homes. It has been often said that her untiring efforts and unselfish devotion to Colonel Cody has enabled him to reach the highest rounds in the ladder of fame, and indeed we scarcely ever see a popular man where there is not the hand of a devoted wife or mother helping guide him on the road to greatness. Mrs. Cody is a lovely lady in every sense of the word. She is beautiful, too, of the darkest brunette type, and she is intellectual and kind hearted to all.

The above, reprinted in a North Platte paper, may have been somewhat surprising, and confusing, to a few of the Codys' North Platte neighbors, and certainly so to the Colonel's biographers, who have long believed that Will and Louisa were at swords' points or, at best, barely tolerating each other during most of the years of their marriage. However, a careful examination of a wealth of home town records over the years seems to largely bear out the comment of the *News*.

By this time Colonel Cody was twice a grandfather. A daughter, Arta Clara, had been born to Arta and Horton on November 7, 1890, in North Platte, and a son, William Cody Boal, in March, 1896, in Wyoming. That the Codys were proud and loving grandparents is evident from the many visits exchanged between the two families during those years. In fact, the whole family seems to have been very close at this period. The local papers carry frequent mention of Mrs. Cody's visits to her daughters, Arta in Wyoming and Irma at school in Omaha, and both girls usually came home to North Platte whenever their father was there.

The summer of 1898 was another long, triumphal tour for the Wild West. The show opened in New York in April, capturing the city by storm, according to the papers, and outdoing even its former successes

W. F. Cody and his sister Helen examining manuscript pages of her biography of him, *Last of the Great Scouts*. Taken in New York by Gessford & Van Brunt, probably in 1898, prior to the book's 1899 publication.

there. Eastern newspapers once again were filled with ecstatic descriptions of the exhibition. The New York *Telegram* summed them all up in its own concluding statement, "All over the world there are circuses and museums and side shows and red lemonade, but there is only one Buffalo Bill."

Later in the summer, as the show toured the central states, the St. Louis *Globe-Democrat* published an interview with Major Frank Powell, Cody's old friend, White Beaver. Why Dr. Powell thought it necessary to embroider his story as he did is perplexing; certainly neither the Colonel nor Johnny Baker needed it. After rambling on about the way things were in the early days of the West when "men had to nail down their hair to keep it on," Powell said, "I remember once that Colonel Cody and I came to a ranch where the owner and his wife had been murdered by Indians and the house set afire. As we neared the place a little boy, crying, came running to meet us. Cody took the boy with him, cared for him and has had him with him ever since. I expect a great many St. Louis people remember him, as he was with Colonel Cody during his tours. His name is Johnny Baker."

The home town paper reprinted the outlandish tale, then declared, "Colonel Cody ought to lasso Major Powell and place him on exhibition in his side show as the biggest liar God ever let live. . . . Johnny Baker's father, old Lou Baker, is living today right here in North Platte. So is his wife, and devil an Indian ever scalped either of them."

Tim McCoy, the real Wyoming cowboy from 1909 on and the famous Hollywood cowboy of the 1920s and 1930s, had his "initial exposure to the West" during Buffalo Bill's tour of the midwest that summer of 1898. McCoy remembers the day, July 16, when Cody's Wild West came to Saginaw, Michigan. Young Tim was thrilled with the show— "a fantastic spectacle"— but double thrilled when he got to meet his hero. Tim's father, as Saginaw's chief of police, took him to Buffalo Bill's tent after the show. Years later, McCoy recalled:

> He sat in his tent, holding court in a dark cutaway coat. His shirt was trimmed with the kind of long collar worn today, only he was wearing them then. Around his neck was a four-hand tie, half a size larger than is fashionable now, and in that tie was a stickpin with the three feathers of the Prince of Wales, given to him as a token by the Prince when he was touring England. . . .
>
> Cody was the most impressive man I had ever seen, unmatched either before or since. As someone once said, he was the "greatest one-man tableau that ever lived."[1]

The Spanish-American War was in progress that summer of 1898, and Cody had expected, and hoped, to take an active part in it. In April he had offered his services to General Nelson Miles, commander of the U.S. Army. The general had at once appointed him to his staff, on standby orders, and Cody had shipped two of his best horses to Washington for his own use whenever Miles should send for him. Preparations for war seemed to move at a snail's pace, however, and many weeks passed before any U.S. troops sailed for Cuba. In the meantime, Cody's show went on, with the popular addition of two "great guns, each drawn by six powerful horses, thundering across the arena at full gallop with their drivers and cannoneers hanging on like monkeys." Not until late July did Miles himself reach Cuba. Within a few days it was apparent that the "summer war" was almost over and there would be no need of Colonel Cody's services.

That was also the year of Omaha's great Trans-Mississippi Exposition, and on August 31 Nebraska honored her favorite son with a recognition and an ovation that has probably never been equalled. Well in advance of the date, it was proclaimed as "Cody Day," and Buffalo Bill had arranged to bring his Wild West to Omaha, to play on the same spot on which it had held its first performance fifteen years earlier.

The Lincoln and Omaha papers outdid themselves in reciting the wonders of the occasion. Senator John M. Thurston, Governor Holcomb, and four ex-governors were present to honor the Colonel. Twenty-four thousand people came to pay their respects that day, thirteen thousand of them in the evening. When Buffalo Bill rode into the arena at the head of his brilliant cavalcade, the crowd surged to its feet as one and gave voice to wave after wave of cheers. Dismounting at the grandstand, the handsome old scout took his place among the dignitaries and his old friends of the frontier days in the box seats.

Governor Holcomb paid eloquent tribute to the guest of honor and his long service to Nebraska. Senator Thurston was next, with a speech so laudatory that it must have kept the Colonel blushing. And then an old man stepped forward and was introduced as Alexander Majors, founder of the famous Pony Express; he made a moving and sincere speech, recalling the days when he first knew Cody. Helen has the old plainsman say:

> "Forty-three years ago this day, this fine-looking physical specimen of manhood was brought to me by his mother—a little boy nine years old [he was eleven]—and little did I think at that time that the boy that was standing before me, asking for employment of some kind . . .

was going to be a boy of such destiny as he has turned out to be. . . .
I remember when we paid him twenty-five dollars for the first
month's work. He was paid in half-dollars. . . . He tied them up in
his little handkerchief, and when he got home he untied the handkerchief and spread the money all over the table."[2]

"And I have been spreading it ever since," Cody put in. Many
Nebraskans knew how true this was, but few knew that Majors himself,
old and broke by then, lived on an allowance paid him regularly by
Buffalo Bill.

"Bless your precious heart, Colonel Cody," Majors said as he sat down.
Cody concluded the speaking with a most appropriate speech of his
own, followed by wild cheering and "The Star Spangled Banner"
played by the assembled bands.

The Omaha *Herald* scarcely seemed able to find words properly
descriptive of Cody Day. One reporter wrote of the evening crowd:
"Thirteen thousand people gathered within the megatherium canvas
walls. As early as seven o'clock, long before the evening breezes had
had much chance at tempering the fierce heat that sunken Phoebus
had left in his wake, the crowds were a sea of seething, sweltering
humanity. Hundreds and hundreds were turned away."

The Lincoln *State Journal* devoted a long column to the life of
Buffalo Bill, stating: "The day when the Wild West show left North
Platte for the East has been given a prominent place in the history of
the town, and all dates count from that day"; they added:

Colonel Cody is a Nebraskan. Back in the sixties he drifted north
from Kansas and finally stopped to make his home at North Platte.
He has never left that home. He has business interests in the Big
Horn basin, has owned a factory or two in Wisconsin and started a
large weekly newspaper at Duluth, but his allegiance to the western
Nebraska town has never changed.

When he visited his hometown two years ago with the show the
welcome received would have turned most men's heads, but Cody
is too big for that. He simply gathered his friends and fellow citizens
around him, thanked them for the ovation, gave them all complimentary tickets to the show, and at the performance put on a few
special acts for the benefit of the homefolks. He had a crowd such
as he had rarely seen at his show in larger cities; old-time cowboys
rode for two hundred miles to see Cody, and people from near and
far turned out to see the show.

From Omaha Cody brought his show to North Platte again for a single afternoon performance on Saturday, September 3, after which he went on to Denver for the fifth and to Colorado Springs for the eighth. Again, all of western Nebraska turned out for the North Platte show. "Colonel Cody is very dear to the hearts of the people of North Platte and adjacent territory," said the *Telegraph*, and went on to set down these interesting statistics: The mammoth tent covers eleven acres of ground, the grandstand four-and-one-half acres. The working arena is 70,000 square feet in area. The tent-wall canvas stretches for 22,750 yards; 1,104 stakes and twenty miles of rope hold the massive tents together. The show's electric plant is valued at $15,000. Sixty men are employed in the cook tent alone.

On its way to North Platte the show gave two performances in Grand Island. "No *crowd* was ever seen here until today," stated the newspaper. "The people came by team, by train, on horseback, on wheels and on foot from every direction, and kept coming until there was such a jam in our streets that one could scarcely move."[3]

Arta had come down from her Wyoming home in time to go to Omaha with her mother on Monday. The two ladies picked Irma up at her school and met the Colonel when he came in with his show that night. All three came west with Cody in his special car and, according to the *Telegraph*, accompanied him on to Denver on Sunday.

From Colorado the show swung south. Later in September, Mrs. Cody was called to Kansas City by a telegram informing her that her husband was seriously ill with typhoid fever. Walsh writes that a month after Cody Day in Omaha, Buffalo Bill fainted three times during a performance. Numerous speculations were rumored: he suffered from a cold or typhoid or a nervous breakdown; he was broken hearted because Katherine Clemmons was in love with Howard Gould; he was too drunk to stay on his horse.

By October, however, The Colonel was home again for another of his peculiar rest periods, in which all he had to do was "visit his family, look after his extensive interests, shake hands with all his friends and recuperate his health."[4]

27

Irma
1890-1900

From all accounts left by those who knew her in her childhood, Irma Cody was a harum-scarum youngster. Dora LaBille, daughter of John LaBille, the butcher, was a year older than Irma. Dora recalled:

She was my good friend, and we had lots of fun together. She had a little two-wheeled cart and a shetland pony, and she'd pick up some of us girls, a whole cart full, and we'd just sail down the street. She wore a middy blouse and skirt and a sailor hat, and that hat would be back off her head and she'd get hold of those lines and we'd tear around the country. My mother bought me a pony, to, and we'd ride together. There wasn't anything Irma was afraid of, and she was a better rider than I and never had to hold on to the saddle horn, as I did, to keep from falling off. Oh, she was a tomboy if ever there was one.

I often went to Irma's home with her and she'd have me stay all night. I always thought Mrs. Cody was cross. She used to get after Irma a lot and just give her the dickens. I liked Irma and didn't think she deserved it. Oh, she had a lot of life and was chock full of the old Nick, all right. One time Professor Garlich got up a play, "Goldilocks and the Three Bears," that was to be put on in Lloyd's Opera House. Irma had a leading part and was to do a "skirt dance," and there were fairies that danced. But that Irma! She was so mischievious and noisy at practice that the professor got so mad he threw his cane at her and told her to go home and not come back. But she was back the next day, as brazen as you please, and she played her part just fine.[1]

Edd Weeks, another of Irma's classmates, also remembered. "She played her violin in Professor Garlich's orchestra," he said, "and never got very hot with her music, but she was sure full of the dickens."[2]

Mabel Davis said: "When I went to school with Irma, there were three of us who were her special chums, Maude Dillon, Jessie Bullard, and myself. Almost every week the four of us would go to the home of one or another of us and spend the weekend together. Mr. Dillon was a great man to want children to have a good time, and he would pop corn and entertain us. And in the winter, when Buffalo Bill didn't have his show on the road, Irma used to have parties at the ranch and bring some of her father's Indians in to see us. Then her father would take us on his knees, two on each knee, and tell us they wouldn't hurt us and not to be afraid."[3]

Martin Federhoof, son of North Platte's early "Tenderloin" district, had more lurid memories of the youngest Cody daughter. "That Irma was wilder than a goldurned coyote. On the way to school me and her used to try to beat the Catholic kids to a brick pile, and we'd get on that pile and fight the other kids. And that Irma could fight—goldurn, she could fight like a boy, and she'd fight any boy or anybody. She hit me with a brick one time, and I've still got the scar, here by my right eye."[4]

Another classmate of Irma's was Hettie Schmalzried, whose father, Fred, owned a cigar manufacturing plant in North Platte and made, advertised, and sold the "Buffalo Bill" cigar, She remembered one of Irma's spankings: "We went to the old frame Washington School in the 600 block on West Third, and Irma got into trouble at school one day. Her mother came and got her. She took her out in front, where she'd left her buggy standing, and spanked her right there; then she put her in the buggy and took her home."[5]

When Irma was fifteen her mother entered her at Brownell Hall, in Omaha, no doubt hoping the elegant young ladies' finishing school could polish a few rough edges off her tomboy daughter. But when at home, the girl, impulsive and as "full of the dickens" as ever, made things lively for herself and her friends, and once again the big house on West Fourth Street was the scene of gay parties and dances, as it had been in Arta's teenage years.

On one occasion, Irma, coming home unexpectedly from Brownell Hall, decided to take a party of her friends on a drive but had no carryall at hand for the purpose, since her mother, when alone at Welcome Wigwam, kept only one old buggy horse in the town house stable. But

Opposite page: Irma Cody. *Above:* W. F. Cody and his daughter Irma, c. 1893.

Irma, in too much of a hurry to wait for a team to be brought in from the ranch, borrowed Harrington's grocery delivery wagon, loaded in her companions, and set off. Mrs. Mary Roddy had good reason to remember that day. "The streets were muddy," she said, "and I had bought a lot of groceries at Harrington's, but Irma had the delivery wagon for her party. It went by full of young folks, all standing up in it, and if they weren't having a time."[6]

John Grant, a young lawyer a few years older than Arta, who usually attended the big Cody parties, said: "There was nothing snobbish about the Cody girls. They would speak to anyone and made no distinction between rich or poor, well-to-do or well-dressed. It was all the same to them; they were friendly with everybody. I used to dance with the Cody girls. I had two good legs then and I could dance. The Cody girls were good dancers, too, and made friends with everyone."[7]

As the Cody girls grew up, they grew away from their childhood friends, although this was not so much the fault of Arta and Irma as of the friends themselves. Jessie Blankenburg, the daughter of the Colonel's harness maker, explained it best: "As a little girl I was at the Codys' house a good bit, but my parents were very strict and did not approve of the way Irma was raised. She could do things I was not allowed to do, and we drifted apart."[8] Linnie Breese, another childhood friend, added: "It seemed to me the Cody girls' clothes and affairs and their out-of-town friends set them apart from other young folks their age here."[9]

After Irma went away to school, North Platte saw comparatively little of her for awhile. In the summertime she spent a few weeks traveling with her father and the Wild West, or with her mother, visiting at Arta and Horton's Wyoming home. She frequently visited school friends in Omaha and Iowa, or brought them home with her. But when she was at home, Welcome Wigwam rang with merriment while she entertained her house guests and old friends. The fact that some of the latter did not accept her invitations because they did not think their clothes suitable was not Irma's fault. Rich or poor, it was all the same to her. She was friendly with everybody.

By 1899 Irma was a handsome girl of sixteen. Like her mother, she was tall and well built, with a wealth of dark hair. That summer, it appears, the family took every opportunity to be together that the Colonel's schedule would allow. In March, Arta came down from Wyoming to visit her parents before her father left for New York, late in the month, to open the Wild West in Madison Square Garden.

Louisa Cody and her daughters Irma (left) and Arta, c. 1897.

The Trans-Mississippi Exposition had been so well received the year before that it held over into 1899. The second summer, under the title of The Great American Exposition, the management again urged Cody to bring the Wild West back for a grand finale. Mrs. Cody went down, so that she and Irma could spend a Sunday with him there, and on Monday General Miles joined the party, as the next day was "General Miles Day" at the fair.

Irma and her mother then spent several weeks in the East, visiting in "Boston and other points in Massachusetts." Following her last year at Brownell Hall, Miss Cody toured the East with her father and the show, returning to North Platte late in June to stir that little city to its very roots with her social activities. For Irma was having house guests, a Miss May Conrad of Grand Island, Morris O. Johnson of Chicago, J. Kendrick Johnson of Louisville, Kentucky, and Florence Turpie and George Leikert of North Platte. The party was to begin with the arrival of the guests on the last Monday in July and last two weeks.

The party opened with a tallyho ride on Monday evening; a dozen Platters, including A. Searle, C. B. Smith, and H. G. Barnard, were

invited to go along. The next day Irma and her guests drove down to
Fort McPherson to picnic. The fort had been abandoned some years
back and its buildings sold and moved away, but the National Cemetery, established there nearly thirty years earlier, was a tranquil spot
of green lawns and rows of small white grave markers, shaded by tall
old cottonwoods. The drive home in the dusk and the early moonlight
was pleasant, too, retracing the old Oregon Trail along the foot of the
rugged canyons past tall, grim old Sioux Lookout peak, past the
mouths of brush-filled gulches where Indians had once attacked and
burned stagecoaches and wagon trains, back to the comfort and
security of Welcome Wigwam.

On Friday evening Irma gave a huge dance, and on Saturday she
took her guests to Lexington, sixty-five miles east, to see Ringling
Brothers circus. The following is an account of the dance, as given
in the *Telegraph*:

> One of the largest social events that has occurred here for some time
> took place at the Cody mansion last evening, one hundred and forty
> guests participating in the party given by Miss Irma Cody in honor
> of the five guests she is entertaining during her two weeks house
> party. The ability Miss Cody possesses for making an affair of this
> kind pleasant for everyone is well known, and the party of last eve-
> ning added to the laurels she has achieved in the past as a hostess
> and entertainer. The interior of the house was tastefully arranged
> for the reception of the guests of the evening, while a number of
> innovations in the shape of tents and canopies had been prepared
> on the lawn.
>
> Miss Cody was assisted in receiving by her guests of honor, while
> six children, Iona Neir, Helen Hershey, Laura Letts, Mamie
> Edmonds, Florence Stamp and Herold Hershey, all attired in elf-
> like costumes, served punch and lemonade with becoming grace
> throughout the evening. Ice cream and cake were served at eleven
> o'clock.
>
> The dancing began about half past nine on a large pavilion in the
> front yard, music being furnished by mandolin and guitar. While
> part of the guests lost themselves in the pleasures of the mazy waltz
> and the flying quick step, others sought quiet nooks, hammocks or
> swings, which were to be found on every hand, and passed the time
> in pleasant conversation. There was abundant provision for general
> enjoyment and the guests threw away no opportunities. Miss Cody's

party will long be remembered as one of the most enjoyable social happenings ever to occur here.

It is a little surprising that Irma and her guests made the train to Lexington and the circus the next morning, but the *Telegraph* says they did.

The main event of the second week was a reception and dance given in honor of Irma and her house guests by Mr. and Mrs. C. M. Newton for seventy-five young people. The Newton lawn was gaily illuminated with Japanese lanterns and acetylene gas lights scattered about. Almost the entire front yard was spread with canvas for dancing. The porch was decorated with lights, and settees were cosily arranged upon it. Inside, the rooms were adorned with cut flowers, potted plants, and palms. "Small tables and chairs were to be found on all parts of the lawn, where couples or quartettes might sit and whisper pleasant nothings into each other's ears. There were many hammocks, occupying corners where other pairs of young people reclined and held their sub-vocal conferences."[10]

Following the hour-long reception, music and dancing were the order of the evening. Punch was served in the dining room by another group of children, Irma Clinton, Della Durk, Gordon Laing, the little band mascot, and Geraldine Bare, daughter of *Tribune* editor, Ira Bare.

The dancing party was followed by a camping party the next afternoon. Irma and her guests rode out to the Turpie ranch, the home of Florence Turpie. The ranch was several miles south of town, and that night the party camped in the hills, well out of sight of any habitation of man. The next day was spent riding to hounds in search of coyotes. Whether or not any coyotes were sighted or run is not stated.

Irma and guests spent the balance of the week resting, and when the out-of-town visitors boarded the train on Saturday, headed homeward, Irma rode "a portion of the way" with them before saying goodbye.

Another of Irma's parties was a picnic to Lamplaugh's lake, six miles north of town; this affair was given to honor another Cody house guest, Miss Leona Robinson of Lincoln. Some thirty-five young people left the city in carry-alls and carriages to spend several hours "in the enjoyment of a moonlight excursion." The party got underway about seven-thirty on a Thursday evening and reached town again early on Friday morning. An orchestra accompanied the revelers and played delightful music on the shores of the lake. Dancing was the principal amusement of the evening, but some of the couples enjoyed boat riding and wandering through shadowy nooks and dells. One young man hung a hammock between two trees, but before he could invite his girl to sit in it with him, heartless comrades had cut it down. Josephine Goodman and her brother Finley were among the guests at all of Irma's parties that summer. All of the picnics and camping parties were most capably chaperoned by older married couples.

Before the summer's end Irma went down to Columbus, Nebraska, on the invitation of Professor E. A. Garlich and a Mrs. Chambers, to spend a few days. While she was there, her hosts gave a dance in her honor. Apparently her old music teacher had forgiven her for raising "the dickens" in his classes a decade earlier.

Early in September, Irma, Arta, and their mother joined Colonel Cody in Omaha for a brief visit. The Wild West must have been scheduled to show there again that fall, the third time in as many years, for the Omaha *Bee* carried this interesting announcement: "In the morning, after the parade, John Baker and Miss Olive Burgess, of Holyoke, Massachusetts, were united in marriage in the parlors of the Merchants Hotel in the presence of a few invited friends."

According to the *Bee*, Buffalo Bill was not at the wedding because Johnny "couldn't screw up his courage to the point where he could announce the event to his patron." No explanation for Johnny's reluctance to tell his foster father of his marriage has yet been found. Johnny had been married some years earlier to the daughter of Jule Keen, treasurer of the Wild West Company. Following the birth of their second daughter, Mrs. Baker had died and Johnny had taken the baby girls to his mother in North Platte.

Following the wedding, the new Mrs. Baker returned to North Platte with Irma and Mrs. Cody to spend two weeks at Welcome Wigwam. The *Telegraph* reported her to be "a lady of charming disposition" and predicted that Johnny's friends would all agree that he had done well in choosing a life partner.

At the end of Olive Baker's visit, all the ladies went down to Omaha. From there Louisa Cody accompanied her guest to Kansas City, where the bride joined her husband and the Wild West. Arta and Irma went on to New York where "Miss Irma was to attend Mrs. Brown's school on Fifth Avenue."

28

Cody, Wyoming 1899-1903

In 1899 W. F. Cody, at fifty-four years of age, had been the star of his own great show for seventeen years. His tall figure was still arrow-straight, his eyes as clear and far-seeing as in his youthful scouting days on the plains. As always, he was looking ahead and pouring the profits from his phenomenally successful show into an ever-increasing number of vast, far-reaching enterprises.

Before he went off to New York to open his show that last season in the old century, he "renewed the kindly feeling and brought forth words of cheer" from his North Platte friends with a big entertainment at his town house. The fifty guests, all North Platte businessmen, were met at the door of Welcome Wigwam with a most cordial greeting by the Colonel, Mrs. Cody, Arta, Irma, and May Bradford, Cody's widowed sister. After a splendid supper, the guests spent their time smoking, visiting, and "viewing the beautiful pictures, Indian curiosities, cowboy paraphernalia, souvenirs and relics of foreign countries gathered by Colonel Cody in his travels. These occupy and decorate the walls and ceiling of the entire third story of the residence. He presented each guest with a fine glass paper weight containing a picture of Colonel Cody and General Miles on horseback on a hill overlooking the badlands during the Indian trouble at Wounded Knee."[1]

The Wild West that season featured sixteen veterans from Teddy Roosevelt's contingent of Rough Riders and included a lively re-creation of the battle of San Juan Hill, a spectacle that proved immensely popular, especially with the social and hunting sets of the big cities. Before the summer's end, the show played in Washington, D.C.; there the Colonel's old friend, J. H. Peake, one-time editor of the North Platte *Enterprise*, visited Cody's tent. The Colonel promptly invited him to come to Cody, Wyoming, and publish a new *Enterprise*. Peake accepted and on August 31 brought out the first issue of the Cody *Enterprise*, boosting the new town as enthusiastically as he had boosted North Platte back in 1874.

Home again in February 1900, Cody sat in on a meeting of North Platte citizens at the courthouse to discuss the building of a big new schoolhouse. Everyone agreed that a new building was necessary, but there was great diversity of opinion as to where to locate it. The building then in use was near the center of town, and some citizens still favored that site. Cody argued against it. Build it farther out, he urged, else the school will soon be surrounded by business houses. Votes for the old site at the corner of Fourth and Dewey won—and within a short time the new big red brick building was hemmed in on all sides, and almost smothered, by busy business streets.

From the school meeting the Colonel went directly to Wyoming to attend to business there. He had turned down a $400,000 Mormon offer for all his Big Horn Basin holdings. Shortly thereafter traces of gold and copper were found on his lands, and he was busy organizing a million dollar mining company. He was also getting up a petition to be sent to Congress, asking that a road be built from Cody to Yellowstone, a much shorter route into the Park than any existing. And, of course, he was still pushing his enormously expensive irrigation project in the Basin.[2]

When he went east again in March to put his show on the road, one of his first acts was the purchase of a new private railroad coach. His former car, the one originally owned by P. T. Barnum until his death in 1891, had burned in winter quarters in New Haven in February. The magnificent new car was the palatial coach in which Adelina Patti had made her last tour of the American continent. Cody's friend, H. H. Hake of the Omaha Merchants Hotel, reported that "Colonel Cody is as tickled over his new car as a boy over his first pair of long pants."[3] It was in this fine new coach that Irma traveled with her father later in the season.

That fall a marksmanship contest was held by the Buffalo Bill Gun Club at the North Platte Athletic Park. Known as the Buffalo Bill Handicap, it was a large and much-advertised meet. Naturally, Buffalo Bill supplied the trophy, an "elegant gold and silver cup standing thirteen inches high, of solid silver inlaid with gold." Mrs. Cody had selected the cup, showing "excellent taste," and its inscription read,

"Presented to the Winner of the Buffalo Bill Handicap, North Platte, Nebraska, September 5, 1900, by Col. W. F. Cody (Buffalo Bill)." The beautiful cup was on display in the window of C. S. Clinton, jeweler.[4]

On the day of the meet, the Colonel was, of course, far away in the South with his show. He was home, however, in time to cast his vote for the Republican presidential candidate, McKinley; again, Louisa met him in Omaha and rode back to North Platte with him. His balloting attended to, Bill and his wife made an extended visit with Irma in New York. As McKinley's inauguration neared, North Platte was boasting: "Small as North Platte is compared with some of the great cities of the country, she generally manages to have some part in any great performance, and she has those, too, who can take a part with credit to themselves and honor to the town. At the inauguration of President McKinley our own and only Col. W. F. Cody will head the parade."[5] Four days later the same paper announced: "Our illustrious townsman, W. F. Cody, who has been with his family for a day or two, will go east tonight on his way to Washington, where he will lead the inaugural parade March 4."

For a few days in the summer of 1901 the Right Reverend George Allen Beecher was a guest of the Colonel and his show in Chicago, and in Davenport and Washington, Iowa. It was typical of Cody to invite his friends to travel with him as long and as far as possible, and to make their visits lively and entertaining. Reverend Beecher and his family had moved to North Platte in 1895, after he was called from Sidney, Nebraska, to pastor the Episcopal Church of Our Savior.

In his autobiography, the minister does not say just when he first met Cody, but he tells *how* it came about. He was sitting in his front room one afternoon when "a strikingly beautiful livery, such as I had never seen before," passed smartly down the street. He rushed to the gate and watched the vehicle turn in at the Cody residence, a few blocks beyond the rectory. It was the Colonel and his daughter, Irma, driving a team of thoroughbreds. Beecher wasted no time in paying a call, "and our acquaintance developed into a lifelong friendship. . . . I learned to respect the man for his virtues and to be patient with his faults. Most of the latter were surface irregularities which developed upon the fringe of his better self as the result of long continued relationship with those who proved false friends and jealous critics. It is always easier to criticize than to praise. I know he was never guilty of betraying a friend, and that he never placed a false advertisement in any department of his famous show."[6]

In Davenport, Cody asked the minister to ride with him in the street parade and to go with him afterward to the home of Colonel and Mrs. Nutting who were giving a porch luncheon for him (Cody). As the parade began to form, the Colonel and his guest stepped into a graceful spider, and Cody headed the famous span of white Arabian stallions toward the head of the column, in front of the mounted cowboy band. As they were making their way through the immense crowd that had already gathered, an old man with his wife on his arm stood in front of the prancing team and waved his cane to stop them. Cody pulled the team up quickly, bringing the procession to a halt, and the old man shouted, "Willie, I knew your father and mother here near Davenport and my wife knew your mother and sisters. Now go ahead, we'll see you again." The Colonel at once handed the reins to Beecher, pulled a book from his pocket, and wrote the old couple a pass to a private box at the show that afternoon; then he went on through the cheering crowd, rising every little way to remove his hat and bow "in the most graceful manner."

The Nuttings, old-time friends of Cody, came for their guests in a handsome closed carriage, but the journey to their home was almost like a second parade, Beecher said, for everyone seemed to recognize the Colonel. At the show that afternoon, the minister occupied a "place of honor" with the Nuttings; and the happy old couple who had held up the parade were nearby, "having the time of their life." That night, after the evening performance, both Cody and Beecher were guests of Robert Law, president of the Burlington, Cedar Rapids & Northern railroad, at his Burlington home. At daylight next morning, Law transported his guests in his own private car to Washington, where the show played that day.

Johnny Baker's family were members of Beecher's church back home in North Platte, and the rector had often gone hunting with Johnny on his visits home. In Chicago, between shows, the guest had the pleasure of shooting targets with Johnny and with Annie Oakley, in the empty arena, and of running up a "creditable score."

That autumn, soon after his return to North Platte, the Colonel called at the rectory to invite Beecher to be his guest on a big game hunt in Wyoming. The minister met his host at Sidney the next Monday morning, where they boarded a train for Alliance, Nebraska. As soon as the crew and passengers heard that Buffalo Bill was aboard, Beecher wrote, they began to file through the car to greet him. It was amazing, he added, to see the Colonel stand and greet so many of the long line by name and ask about their families, their livestock, and other matters.

At Alliance they transferred to a mainline train for Sheridan and Cody, and near the western edge of the state two Indians joined them for the hunt. At this point Cody told Beecher he had to send some messages; he would be back as soon as he could. Would the minister please take Iron Tail and Black Fox to the diner and order food for them? When they were seated in the diner, the Indians made known, by signs, that they were very hungry. While Beecher was wondering what he should order for them, Bill Sweeney, leader of the cowboy band, leaned across the aisle and told him to "order some meat with a bone in it." So he ordered "a porterhouse steak for four." While they waited to be served, Cody returned to the car and sat down at the table. "Imagine my embarrassment," said Beecher, "when the waiter brought a full-sized porterhouse for *each* of us." I was thinking, he added, of the size of the bill for the meal, but I soon learned that "was a very small consideration," so far as the Colonel was concerned.

With the food before them, Cody asked the minister to say grace, which he did, and then remembered the first time the Colonel had made a similar request. During Beecher's first visit to the show he had spent the nights in Cody's private car, where Jule Keen and Johnny Baker also lived. When the four sat down to breakfast the first morning, Keen picked up his knife and fork, but the Colonel said, "Wait a minute, Jule." Turning to the minister, he said, "Mr. Beecher, we show people are a sort of roughneck outfit, but we are mighty glad you're with us and we respect what you represent. Will you just—open the ball?"

Both Beecher and Johnny had blushed beet red, but the minister said grace, as he knew that was what Cody meant. When he finished, the Colonel said, "Mr. Beecher, I didn't ask you right. I couldn't think of the word."

"Oh, that's all right," Beecher said. "We usually say 'Will you say Grace?'" 'With a disgusted look on his face, Cody exclaimed, "Oh Hell, that's what I meant."

"There was not the slightest intention on his part to be irreverent or profane, and I honored the man who asked me to say Grace at the showmens' table, even though he 'couldn't think of the word,'" Beecher said.

On the train to Sheridan, however, after the blessing, Iron Tail put his hands up to his face and began to laugh heartily. Then he and Cody held a conversation in Lacotah, after which the Colonel told Beecher the Indians had ridden a hundred miles to meet the train, and Iron Tail thought it remarkable that a young, white-faced tenderfoot like this one had known exactly what they most wanted for breakfast, especially since they had not eaten since the day before; it had so tickled him he could not get his pallet fixed to eat it. When they did start eating, they ate everything in sight except the dishes, and for dessert had a whole pie apiece, ice cream, cake, and several cups of coffee. Iron Tail then gave the large minister the Indian name "Oglala Tonka," or Big Sioux.

The big game hunt was not the sole cause for the trip west that November. Another very important reason was the opening of the new town of Cody, Wyoming. Colonel Cody had been instrumental in getting the Burlington to build a branch line from Sheridan to Cody. The first passenger train over the rails, bearing Cody, Beecher, Sweeney, the two Indians, and several other friends, rolled into Cody City the morning of November 12, 1901.

Most of the young town's one thousand inhabitants were at the station to greet the founder and his party. Closely following Cody's train came a special from Billings, Montana, bringing Wyoming Senator C. D. Clark (who had defeated George Beck for Congress in 1890), Congressman Frank Mondell, the Billings band, and a large number of Buffalo Bill's friends. It was a beautiful autumn day, in spite of the high wind that lashed the town raising clouds of Wyoming dust. Undaunted, the mayor of Cody, elected only the night before, swept up with a buckboard and a fine team, hailed the Colonel into his rig, and led the parade, which had already formed.

Reverend Beecher was invited into an old Concord stagecoach drawn by a half-broken six-horse team. It seemed that every man and boy in the crowd was firing some sort of weapon. When the minister spied a small boy clinging to his mother's skirts and crying in terror, he remarked that all those guns were scaring the little fellow to death; the driver of the stagecoach broncs replied, "'Taint the guns the boy's afraid of, it's the band."

After the parade, a great barbecue was served on the edge of town, with everyone taking part. That evening a big meeting was held in an unfinished store building. The mayor made the flowery address of welcome. Cody responded, and all the other notables also made speeches. "It was a characteristic opening day for a new town in which scarcely a building was completed," stated Mr. Beecher.[7]

The North Platte papers, understandably, had little to say regarding Cody's opening of his new town in Wyoming. The *Evening Telegraph* for November 9 noted briefly that the railroad had just been completed to Cody and that the Colonel said he had relinquished his *legal* residence in North Platte, "of which we can justly mourn. He still retains ownership of his North Platte and Lincoln County property. Our best wishes will ever be with Mr. Cody." Another North Platte paper carried these few lines: "The town named Cody, after our own William, in Wyoming was opened Tuesday with great ceremony. On the arrival of the first train, on which were, among others, Colonel Cody and Reverend Beecher, the band burst into patriotic music and the procession arranged beforehand started. The noise and excitement was tremendous and probably no city in the west ever had such a day. A grand ball in the evening finished the day's ceremonies."

For nearly a quarter of a century the city at the forks of the Platte had been "Buffalo Bill's home town." Now that it was, in a sense, losing that distinction, its newspapers were not about to boost its most prominent citizen's new town any more than it could help. The Colonel's Platter friends did wish him well, however. The night before he left for Wyoming, they gave a "smoker" for him at the Commercial Club.

Beecher's story of the big game hunt that followed the opening of Cody is interesting for several reasons. The large party of hunters was transported to the TE ranch, thirty-five miles southwest of Cody, the next day. Beecher describes the great log cabin with its huge stone fireplace across one end, and notes that as in Cody's Nebraska homes it was decorated with posters, showbills, pictures, and souvenirs of the Wild West and its travels.

The guests slept on the floor in sleeping bags furnished by their host. The next morning Beecher was mounted on one of Cody's finest horses, Prince, which had not been ridden since General Miles had used him the year before. When the hunters came to the fork of the Shoshone River, the Colonel halted the entire party and explained that he planned to build a public road through that very place to Yellowstone Park. Then, taking an axe, he blazed several trees and announced that here he intended to build an inn. Turning to Beecher, he told him he was going to name it "Beecher Inn."

Before mounting his horse again, the Colonel translated what he had just said into Lacotah for Iron Tail's benefit. The Indian made a vehement reply, and Cody told the group Iron Tail had said it should be called "Pahaska Inn." Since that was the Colonel's Indian name, meaning "Long Hair," the minister immediately said that Iron Tail had the right idea. And that, he says, was the way the famous inn at the forks of the Shoshone on the highway from Cody to Yellowstone Park got its name.[8]

That year of 1901 had its griefs and trials, too, as so many of Buffalo Bill's remaining years were to have. His "Brother Al" had been ill with a kidney ailment for two years and was not getting any better. When, in January 1901, he became too sick to oversee the ranch any longer, even from a buggy, Julia moved into North Platte to give him better care. In March, Cody wrote his brother-in-law from New York, expressing his pleasure in receiving a letter written by him, the first in many months. He went on to urge both Al and Julia to be ready to go to DeMaris Springs, a place of "God healing waters," near Cody, as soon as the railroad was completed. He would arrange for transportation and for lodgings, and they must plan to stay at least three months.[9]

Another letter to Al in June promised him he need have no worries for Julia, that he would see to it she always had a big rocker and could take it easy. But Al was never to bathe in the "healing waters." He died in October, before the railroad reached Cody. The Reverend George Beecher held the funeral services in North Platte, but the Colonel, far away in the South with his show, could not come home to be with his sister. He did, however, write her a letter of loving sympathy and encouragement, assuring her that she should never want for anything as long as he was able to look after her.

Five years earlier, Cody had also been unable to attend, in Denver, the funeral of his other brother-in-law, Ed Bradford, although Al, Julia, and Louisa had gone. Sometimes the Colonel must have wondered if the game was worth the candle, for the Wild West had made him miss so many events that he must have wanted, with all his heart, to attend. And with each passing year it became more necessary that he keep the show going and that he make his daily appearances in the arena. For, exciting and tremendous as the show was, Buffalo Bill was still the heart and soul of it all. If he did not appear at every performance, smiling and bowing, the audiences felt they had been cheated, and so badly did he need his share of the daily proceeds, he could not afford to risk any slackening in attendance. For all of his many enterprises demanded money, huge amounts of it, to keep going.

Nate Salsbury, still ailing and unable to travel with the show, worried about Cody's spending. The irrigation project in Wyoming, he insisted, was being handled in a way that made him sick to his stomach, and too many people were cheating the Colonel in too many ways.[10] The mining company in Wyoming had come to nothing, as there was not enough gold or copper to pay to mine it. In the meantime he was going ahead with his plan for Cody as the jumping-off place for Yellowstone Park. In addition to his newspaper there, he was building the Cody Military College and International Academy of Rough Riders and had opened his big Buffalo Bill Barn, with coaches and rigs for hire.

The government was building "Cody Road," at a cost of $50,000, from Cody town to the east entrance of the Park, where Pahaska Inn was going up rapidly. Halfway between Pahaska and Cody, the Colonel was establishing another hostelry, Wapiti Inn, and at Cody he was about to build still another beautiful hotel. As soon as Cody Road was completed, he intended to be ready to put a line of stagecoaches in operation over it, to and through the Park. And he had only his share of the profits from the Wild West with which to finance all his projects.

At this time Cody estimated that in addition to the people in his show he was employing more than 4,000 men. He wanted, he said, to be known "as a pioneer and developer of civilization," rather than only as a scout and showman.[11]

To add to his burdens and worries, the Wild West train suffered a damaging wreck in October of that year, its third in less than two years. The first had occurred near Detroit in July 1900, when the first section of his train, twenty-four cars and the caboose, was struck in the rear by a freight, hoisting the caboose on top of a sleeping car full of employees; one man was killed and several severely injured. The second, near Louisville in June 1901, had resulted in the deaths of several horses and the smashing of the Colonel's private buggy. This last one, less than four months later in North Carolina, entailed the heavy loss of over one hundred show horses, including Old Pop, Cody's personal mount. No lives were lost, but Annie Oakley was so severely injured she was hospitalized for many months and was never again able to appear as the World's Champion Lady Shot of Buffalo Bill's Wild West.

In his many letters to Julia, Will Cody often let down the bars and told her his troubles—financial, domestic, alleged poor health, and all— often, no doubt, in somewhat exaggerated form, the better to spark a full measure of her motherly sympathy. Even while showing a smiling face and cheerful attitude to his public and assuring one and all that he had never felt better, he would write Julia that he was suffering from overwork, chills, nerves, hay fever, grippe, sleeplessness, and other ailments, but usually ended by advising her to say nothing to anyone about it.

Now, again, he brings up the matter of a divorce. In March 1902, he wrote his sister from New York that he could no longer go on living "a false lie" with his wife, that he could see no future for himself and Lulu together, only a life of misery for both, no happiness or content- ment unless they divorced. He said he would offer her all of the North Platte property and an annual income if she would give him a "quiet legal separation." If not, "then it's war and publicity."[12] As Arta was visiting in North Platte at that time, he told Julia he wished she would talk to her, probably to try to persuade her to agree that divorce was best for both her parents. But again he cautioned Julia to say nothing about his domestic troubles to anyone else.

Julia wrote and asked her brother's advice about mortgaging her home in North Platte, and he urged her to sell and move to Cody. She was just the person to "mother" for him the new hotel he was building there, just the someone who would love and care for it as he would himself. He intended to furnish the building in such a "fine and costly" manner that he could not rent to just anyone. He was sending a man from New York's Hoffman House, where he was then putting up, to be the head cook and line up a professional staff of uniformed waiters. Julia could oversee everything, do the buying, "over look the chamber maids," and run things in general. The hotel, he promised, would be a home for Julia, her daughter Josephine, and her son Walter (the boy born after she and Al left Scout's Rest back in 1891). Josephine lived with her mother and little brother in North Platte and taught in the city schools; that May, according to a *Telegraph* story of the eighth, she won a city-wide popular teacher contest, with nearly twice as many votes as the runner-up, Professor J. C. Orr.

All that spring Cody's letters were brimming with enthusiasm for the new hotel, which he was naming after his youngest daughter, Irma. By then his sister Eliza was dead and May and Helen widowed. As he had cared for the two younger girls in their youth, he now intended to provide for them in their later years. They too, he said, could live at the hotel, and Nellie (Helen) could be the treasurer and bookkeeper, also a "Friendly night clerk." Josie could get a position in Cody as a teacher, and he was writing to the president of the school board to arrange it; she could stay at the hotel "till she gets married."[13]

As he had written Julia years before about his private bedroom and bar at Scout's Rest Ranch, so now Will wrote her that he wanted a pri- vate parlor and two bedrooms, with bath and closet, reserved for him; but since he would be there very little for the next three years (the Wild West was to be in Europe during that time), Julia and Helen could use the suite for their own quarters. He hoped to open the hotel early in September; he had already bought a farm ten miles from Cody and had a man and wife there to raise chickens, make butter, and grow vegetables for the hotel. He had even bought for the unbuilt building more than 200 "etchings from the paintings of artists like Fred Remington," and the very best of furniture; there would be a piano for the parlor and another for the dining room. "I tell you . . . I will make it [the hotel] the talk of the West," he exulted.[14]

He was pleased, too, that he had found the right manager, "one without a wife—I don't want any wife to be bothering you." This bothering-wife remark may well have been prompted by Cody's thinking of the wife of Johnny Boyer, the foreman of the Cody farm south of the ranch headquarters at North Platte, the "Davis farm" that had been the first land owned by the Codys; Mrs. Boyer hated Louisa and likely included Julia in her circle of dislike. Or the Colonel may have had in mind his own wife, for Julia and Louisa did not get along much of the time. By the end of May, Will was arranging transportation for his sister to Cody by way of Rawlins, where she could visit friends who had hotel interests. There she could learn all about buying groceries, cooking, serving, wages, how often sheets are changed, how many rooms one maid takes care of, the whole bit.[15]

But before the gala opening of The Irma, tragedy befell the family: out in Sheridan, in late October, Horton Boal killed himself. From items in the North Platte newspapers of 1901 and 1902 it seems that Arta was spending a great deal of time visiting in North Platte or traveling in the East. Their daughter, Clara, was in a girls' school in Denver, and little Cody Boal was with his grandmother Cody at different times. There are two somewhat similar stories about the manner of Horton's suicide, though mystery still surrounds his death. Sherman Canfield, whose father, George, was the first manager of the Sheridan Inn, wrote that Horton and Arta often stopped at the Inn during the years they lived on the ranch at Slack, Wyoming, near Birney, Montana. Horton used to stay there for several days at a time, he recalled, and seemed to be a very nice, pleasant, neat-appearing person, but he did not like to be introduced as Buffalo Bill's son-in-law. Sherman went on:

> One morning about nine, Horton came down to the bar, and he and my dad had a drink together and talked for a long time; then they had another drink, and Boal bought a bottle of brandy, as he said he had a lot of letters to write and wanted a bottle in his room. Along

about three that afternoon he was missed, and someone went to his room and knocked on the door. They could smell chloroform, so forced his door open and found him dead on the bed with his face in his shoe, in which he had placed the chloroform. By his bed was a gun and a note, which said he used the chloroform instead of the gun because it was Arta's gun and he did not want to shoot himself with that. He asked in his note that his saddle horse follow the hearse to the cemetery and be shot over his grave.[16]

Elsa Spear Byron, member of a pioneer Wyoming ranch family and a lively historian in her own right, says the suicide did not take place in the Inn, although she is familiar with that tale. Horton, she says, took his chloroform, wad of cotton, and rubber shoe to a big cottonwood beside the railroad tracks several blocks from the Inn, and there put himself to sleep forever. Elsa says nothing about a note, but agrees with Canfield that his horse did follow the hearse, saddled and with his boots turned backward in the stirrups; but the authorities would not allow the horse to be shot, although Arta requested it because it was her husband's last wish.[17]

Both Canfield and Mrs. Byron mention the enormous crowd that came to the funeral, but other details usually gleaned from newspaper accounts are unavailable because newspapers from that period are missing.[18] Speculations can be pieced together from earlier and later snippets. There were always the rumors whispered years ago in North Platte concerning some kind of scandal in Arta's life; they focused around handsome Dr. Charles Thorp, woman's physician and surgeon, who came to North Platte in the 1890s and became very popular there.[19] Dr. Thorp was friendly with the Boal family; "shortly tongues began to wag [and] the doctor was forced to seek other fields. [In 1901] Mrs. Boal came to St. Anthony hospital [in Denver] for treatment and her case came under the supervision of Dr. Thorp, who was acting house physician there."[20]

In September 1902, North Platte was informed that "Mrs. H. S. Boal will go to Kansas City Thursday, where she will make her future home."[21] This certainly suggests a rift between Horton and Arta. The following month Horton took his own life.

Because Horton stood to inherit a small fortune from his mother, money problems seem clearly ruled out as a possible motive for his suicide.[22]

Immediately after the funeral, Arta moved to North Platte. She brought with her many lovely pieces of furniture, a great deal of silver, china, glassware, pictures, mementos, and souvenirs of all kinds given her by her father or collected during the year she spent in Europe and during her marriage. All were stored at Welcome Wigwam.

Two weeks after the funeral, Colonel Cody, Arta, and her two children went up to Cody for the previously scheduled opening of The Irma. Irma Cody was already there, helping her Aunt Julia and cousin Josephine put the finishing touches to the handsome two-story brick hotel with its sixteen-foot-wide porches. A thousand engraved invitation cards, ornamented with a gold buffalo, had been sent out for the party.[23] A North Platte newspaper, *The Independent Era,* published an account of the Colonel's welcome at Cody on Saturday, November 14:

> The town of Cody put on its holiday attire, business houses were decorated with flags, bunting and portraits of Colonel Cody, and the whole country turned out to demonstrate to the founder of the town the heartiness of the welcome afforded him.
>
> Colonel Cody's beautiful hotel, The Irma, was the center of attraction and presented a gala appearance, reflecting great credit on Manager Decker and Mrs. Goodman. Meeteetse's [Wyoming] fine cornet band and orchestra enlivened the happy occasion with plenty of fine music. At 11:15 a reception committee and two or three hundred citizens drove to the depot in carriages to greet their distinguished friend and benefactor. As the train rolled in the band played HAIL TO THE CHIEF, and judging from the enthusiasm on every hand, the Colonel could not doubt the sincereity of his reception from his old comrades and neighbors.
>
> Colonel Cody appeared in the best of health and spirits. He was accompanied by his foster brother, Dr. Franklin Powell of St. Paul, and Professor N. Lehnen, a leading mining expert of the northwest. The journey from the depot to the town, about a mile and a half, was a continuous line of greetings, music, and a general good time. Only one circumstance marred the day's program. That was the enforced absence of Mayor J. E. Edwards, who was confined to his home with a broken leg.
>
> Upon arriving at the Hotel Irma, the procession halted and the Hon. H. S. Ridgely, formerly of North Platte, ascended the steps and delivered, in a most cordial manner, the address of welcome to Colonel Cody and his friends. Space forbids that we give in full the

hearty words of greeting, but in brief, Mr. Ridgely extended in the name of the mayor a free and hearty welcome and said the people of the new country fully appreciated the honor of the Colonel's influence and the fact that a man of world-wide fame had chosen to make his home among them. By the energy, pluck, courage, integrity and capital of Colonel Cody the railroad has been brought into the Big Horn basin, a flourishing town founded, irrigation ditches built and the waters of the Shoshone caused to depart from their natural bed ... and brought out across the sunburned plains and deserts ... converting them into fine fields of waving grain.

Mr. Ridgely further said that Colonel Cody will not only go down in history as our great scout, our great Indian fighter and our great showman, but he will also be mentioned as a great state builder as well. At the close of the address of welcome, Colonel Cody responded in his usual fluent and happy manner, assuring his old neighbors and friends that these home comings were the red-letter days of his life. Dr. Powell was also called upon for a speech, and did not disappoint his listeners, being ready with pleasant and witty remarks.

The afternoon was occupied by pleasant social affairs and at nine the beautiful dining room of the Irma was cleared and a most enjoyable dancing party was in progress until midnight, the inimitable Meeteetsee orchestra furnishing the music. At eleven o'clock lunch was served, at which time Mr. Ridgely announced that on Thanksgiving night Colonel Cody would hold "open house," to which everybody and their friends would be most welcome.[24]

During that same evening, the Colonel announced the engagement of his daughter, Irma, to Lieutenant C. A. Stott, stationed at Fort Mackenzie, Sheridan, Wyoming.

Nowhere does anyone mention Louisa Cody. Emma Seifert recalled: "At this time Mrs. Cody was at their home at North Platte."[25] One can only wonder as to her feelings.

The fact that Cody "appeared in the best of health and spirits" speaks well for the man's remarkable constitution.[26] He was fifty-six years old and had just completed his most wearing and arduous season. The show had toured coast to coast, making the largest number of stands in one season in its history. His sick partner, Salsbury, was failing fast, and the suicide death of his son-in-law must have left its mark. The estrangement from Lulu and the impending divorce also must have had some effect on him, and he was facing a long tour with his Wild West show in Europe.

With the new day, Buffalo Bill and his friends, Dr. Powell and the other "old scouts," headed for the TE and a big game hunt, the "rest" he had looked forward to all season.[27] In the party was a Boston *Herald* reporter, Charles Wayland Towne, who wrote a highly embroidered account of the opening of The Irma.

The hunting party came home on December 6, and on the fifteenth the Colonel sailed for England with his show. In London, Cody and Bailey were notified by cable that Nate Salsbury had died at his New Jersey home on Christmas eve. The show opened on schedule the day after Christmas, with all flags at half-mast and the banner carried by the cavalry draped in crepe.[28]

29

Yellow Ribbons, Red Ink 1903

On Tuesday, February 24, 1903, Welcome Wigwam was the scene of a brilliant military wedding, that of the Codys' youngest daughter Irma to Lieutenant Clarence Armstrong Stott, of the Twelfth U.S. Cavalry.

Ray Langford, the young ranchman who had sold tickets at the Irrigation Fair seven years before, wrote the wedding invitations. His father, superintendent of Lincoln County schools for many years, had made his young son practice Spencerian penmanship as other parents made their children practice the piano. As a result, Ray wrote an almost perfect Spencerian hand, and Mrs. Cody engaged him to come to her home and write the invitations. "I don't remember how many I wrote," Langford said years later, "but there were several hundred of them, and she paid me one dollar apiece for them"—enough to increase the Langford cattle herd by quite a few cows that spring.[1]

The house was beautifully decorated with jonquils, palms, ferns, and flags, which were held in place by bands of yellow ribbon of the true cavalry shade. The ceremony was performed in the library, where the walls were hung with pictures of some of the most famous generals: Miles, Commander of the U.S. Army, and Grant, Sherman, and Sheridan. Prominent among them was the famous picture of Colonel Cody painted and presented to him by Rosa Bonheur.

A large silken flag was artistically held afloat to form a background while the bridal party stood under a canopy of smilax. A statue of Colonel Cody stood nearby. Overhead were hung crossed sabres and also the figure 12, denoting Stott's regiment. The sabres were the first two used by him: his non-commissioned officer's weapon and the one he first used upon becoming a commissioned officer.

At noon the ushers, Platte White and Edwin Goodman, marched down the winding stair and removed from the posts the ropes of smilax. Proceeding to the library door, they stood facing, forming an aisle to the altar where the impressive Episcopal service was to be read by Reverend George Allen Beecher, assisted by Reverend Edward Dunning Wood, rector of the Church of Our Savior.[2]

The bridal party followed, led by Master William Cody Boal, the ring bearer. A miniature soldier, he wore the uniform of a second lieutenant of cavalry and carried a sabre. The ring was tied to the sabre hilt with a yellow ribbon. He stood at attention and saluted the groom as he approached, attended by Lieutenant Ferdinand A. Fonda of the Twelfth Cavalry, and took his place at the altar.

To the strains of the Mendelssohn wedding march came the maid in waiting, Arta Clara Boal, followed by the bride, walking alone. She was met by Dr. Franklin Powell, who gave her away, acting proxy at the request of Colonel Cody, who was in Europe. The bride was beautiful in a gown of white Irish lace with sash and trimmings of white liberty and satin chiffon. Her delicate tulle veil was worn thrown back from her face and was wreathed with natural orange blossoms. Her only jewel was a pearl crescent, a gift from the groom.

The maid in waiting, a niece of the bride, wore a dainty white French batiste and valenciennes lace over white taffeta, with ribbons and sash of white liberty gauze. She carried upon her left arm a large bouquet of jonquils and ferns, tied with a wide yellow ribbon, the streamers reaching nearly to the hem of her skirt. The groom and his best man wore full dress uniforms of the army, and the clanking of their sabres and spurs made music which thrilled the hearts of those present.

As soon as the blessing was pronounced and while the newly wedded couple received congratulations, a male quartette sang the soldier song which had been sung at the time of the announcement of their wedding in Cody the past autumn. Messages and cablegrams were then read, including a long one from Colonel Cody, expressing his regret at being absent but wishing all joy and happiness to his daughter and his new son.

Before the buffet luncheon was served, a table covered with a silk flag and decorated with asparagus ferns tied with yellow ribbons was brought in and placed before the bride. Lieutenant Fonda and Master Cody Boal stood at attention while Lieutenant Stott, in a gallant and soldierly manner, presented his wife with his sabre, with which she cut the cake in half. Afterward, the guests were presented with bits of the cake in white boxes adorned with tiny flags and tied with yellow ribbons. The guests were entertained with music and song, the accompanist being Jessie Bratt (daughter of John Bratt), a girlhood friend of the bride. Miss Bratt also played the wedding march, fulfilling a promise made long ago.

The Independent Era continued:

The bride was born in North Platte and has always made her home here. She has traveled extensively and will make an ideal army wife. She is fond of outdoor sport, is a good horsewoman and will be able to follow her husband wherever ordered. Lt. Stott is a native of Pennsylvania, the son of the late Colonel W. W. Stott, who served through the Civil War. His forefathers were military men who won many laurels in the Mexican and Revolutionary wars. He, too, anxious to win a name for himself, enlisted in 1900 and, after service in the Spanish war, was a volunteer in the First U.S. Cavalry which was ordered to China. He saw service during the Chinese troubles, the Spanish war and the Philippine insurrection. While in the Philippines he won his commission . . . and remained there two years, returning to America last August with the Tenth Cavalry. As he prefers active service, he is transferring to the Twelfth Cavalry, now under orders for foreign service.

Lt. and Mrs. Stott, amid showers of rice and good wishes, left in the afternoon for Ft. Clark, Texas, where the Twelfth will be stationed until mid-summer, when they will report for a two years tour in the Philippines under command of Colonel William C. Forbush, an old family friend who was stationed near here, years ago, when Colonel Cody was chief of scouts with the Fifth Cavalry. The bride was becomingly attired in a black tailor-made traveling suit and wore a large black hat of tucked silk, ornamented with wings. On her handsome fur muff was a large bunch of violets, fastened by a seal pin, a facsimile of those she presented as parting gifts to her attendants.

Lt. and Mrs. Stott were the recipients of many costly and beautiful gifts from many parts of the world. There were many beautiful costumes worn by the ladies present. Mrs. Cody wore a handsome gown of black lace over white, with white chiffon trimmings, and the diamond locket presented her husband by Queen Victoria.[3]

Simple as it was, Irma's wedding must have cost her father a considerable sum, what with orange blossoms, roses, and other hothouse flowers in Nebraska in February, and so many expensive lace gowns. Arta did not take part in the wedding, probably because she was still officially in mourning for her late husband.[4]

In later years, the neighbors remembered other details of the elegant affair. Mrs. Mary Patterson, widow of Judge Patterson and a guest at the wedding, said that Stott "looked at Irma as if he adored her."[5] Mrs. Mary Wyberg, who was not at the wedding, had a spicier tale to tell:

> I didn't know the Codys well, although we lived only a few blocks apart. The wedding was at noon and the day turned warm. They had hired carriages to go after the guests, and the horses went slopping along the streets, throwing slush with their hoofs and the carriage wheels. After the wedding, after most of the guests had gone, the bridegroom and some of the men were off in a room smoking, and Irma came in and took a cigar and sat down and crossed her legs and smoked with them. I guess some of the guests were really shocked, and the new bridegroom too.[6]

More amusing is the anecdote told by Geraldine Bare—"Cubby" to her friends back then. As Clara's best friend, she was present at the wedding with her parents, Mr. and Mrs. Ira Bare. Some of the guests were from Omaha, she said, along with officers from Fort Russell and others from out of town. All of these were to stay for a big dinner at Welcome Wigwam that evening. After Irma and her lieutenant left for Texas, Cubby and Clara spent a good deal of time in the kitchen, getting in the way of the busy kitchen force. The attraction was a huge crock of maraschino cherries, the first the girls had ever seen and the first to be served in North Platte.

Arta came in early in the evening, fed the little girls a quick supper, and sent them upstairs to bed. From the top of the back stairs, the pair watched their chance, and while the main course was being served and the kitchen was empty, they flew down the steps, dipped into the crock for double-handsful of cherries, and fled back to their bed. Hours later, when the guests had gone and Arta came upstairs to look in on the girls, she took one glance and screamed. By the dim night light she had mistaken the cherry juice that smeared the girls' faces and bedclothes for blood—and thought they had been murdered in their sleep.[7]

Probably few if any of the guests at Irma's wedding knew that Colonel Cody was planning for a divorce, but a letter he wrote to

Julia from Manchester, England, on April 12 reiterated his intentions: "I think when Lou and Arta sees I am determined—they will agree to a mutual seporation. Lou likes to be boss. She loves to be the whole thing—And if I give her all the North Platte property, and money besides, she will take it. She will be a rich woman. And her own boss."[8]

Cody was bombarding his sister with letters all that spring, long letters advising her what to do at the hotel and telling her what he planned to do. For some reason letters from America were not getting through to him, and he was frantic for news from home. He complained: "no one tells me—who we owe or how much. I have sent $6000 & I know I did not owe that much." The Burlington would be running daily Pullman trains to Cody that summer, with tourists for the Park, he told her, and the government wagon road to Yellowstone was to be finished by July 1.[9]

Already the Colonel wanted to build an addition onto The Irma. Julia told him there was not enough business to warrant it, but he insisted there soon would be and intended to go ahead. He also warned her against allowing any gambling in the hotel. He had turned down a fellow who wanted to put in a gambling concession, he said, and was determined not to permit any hotel profits from that source.

Previous to his departure for Europe, Cody had purchased a large mining estate in Arizona, and his hopes of riches from that source were high. He had, of course, sunk vast amounts of money in mining machinery and wages, but had as yet received nothing in return. On March 13 he wrote from London that he had been "on an awful strain waiting to hear from our gold mine—And when the cable came that we had struck the vein we had been tunnelling for for seven months night and day I assure you it was a relief. . . . I presume Arta is with you," he went on. "It's perfectly right she should know something of my affairs. [Julia must have been wondering and asking how much of the Colonel's business she should reveal to Arta.] Do you have milk from the cows at the barn, does Christy [the farm manager] bring eggs? I like to hear of these little things. You can use water out of the irrigating ditch, . . . have it filtered—And it will save that normous expense of hauling water."[10]

While Buffalo Bill may have dreamed too big for his time, the grasp he had of all the details, both large and "little things," in his many enterprises is amazing—especially when, so much of the time, he was not even in the U.S. From mid-March on, for awhile, his letters were exuberant. He was so confident of the eventual success of his mine that he called himself a "millionaire" and was already spending the anticipated fortune. He was promising his sister a new house of her own, advising her to get it started right away, "on 90 days time," and he would send her the money soon. He told her to buy additional Cody town lots, also on time, and he would pay for them with profits from the mine—profits now delayed because of the necessity to build a mill to process the ore. If she could just "run that dear old face" for a little while longer, she would be rich and could "sit around and give orders, & look nice" and have her own carriage with a driver.[11]

Julia had evidently welcomed Arta's help with the business in Wyoming, for near the end of March Cody acknowledged Arta's cable that the books, statements, hotel, ranches, and everything were all right. However, Julia was still balking on the addition to The Irma, and the Colonel was gently scolding her for her lack of faith in Cody town. "I am a broad gazer," he reminded her, "And I am willing to back my judgement. I expect to let the contracts for the addition this week."[12]

Besides a complete absence of black ink on the mining books, business was poor in England too; Cody, though hoping for a big summer after they left London, wanted to "quit the show business for ever." As soon as the mine began to pay off, he told his sister, they both would work only when they felt like it. It was a little tough, he observed, for a bonanza king to be hard up—"a busted Millionaire."[13]

And so it went all that season. In one letter Will would encourage Julia with good news and the assurance that it would not be long until the gold would be flowing and he would be helping the poor and the churches and making all his relatives and faithful friends happy. In the next he would report delays: snow storms that set them back in the mine development or problems in completing the mill on schedule. The old couple who ran the hotel farm wanted to quit, and he was letting them go, but intended to see that they never came to want, for he liked them.

Then there was trouble with Nellie (Helen). "It's a real shame the way Nellie is treating me," he wrote Julia. "After all I have done for her. Try and coax her not to be in Cody when I am there." Louisa must have been involved in this family squabble, too, for Will is urging Julia not to resign from the management of The Irma. "I would not give Lulu the satisfaction of your going away for the blamed hotel," he wrote. "I want you to be on the porch to greet me when I come." And then adds, "I have heard indirectly that Lulu did not sign the deed for Cody View to Nellie. If Nellie is there tell her not to worry for I will own it after Lu and I have a settlement."[14]

Cody View was the mansion Helen and her newspaper husband, Hugh Wetmore, had built in Duluth after the Colonel bought the paper for them and put up the fine business building which Helen failed to manage profitably. When the bills for construction of the house came due and the contractors threatened to sue for their labor and materials, brother Will, as usual, had come to the rescue and paid off. He did, however, take the precaution to have the deed made out to Louisa, with the stipulation that the Wetmores have lifetime occupancy. In gratitude to her brother for saving her home, Helen had named it Cody View.[15]

In June 1901, Irma had gone to Duluth to attend the wedding at Cody View of her cousin, Mary Jester, Helen's only daughter, to Robert Allen. Since then Hugh Wetmore had died. Now his widow wanted to sell her home, but Louisa refused to deed it over to her. No doubt she figured Will had wasted enough of his wealth on Helen's impractical business ventures.

In June, Cody was still frustrated about the divorce. He complained to Julia, "I have written Ridgely time and again for what he is doing about the divorce but he don't answer." The next day he wrote again, in reply to a letter just received, "My Dear Poor Tired Sister, Don't you think for a moment you are going to be turned out of my house. I gave every thing at North Platte up to Lulu, now she want to run me out of Cody its all Lulu work . . . and I won't stand for it. I have just cabled Ridgely you remain. . . . No one shall put you out of my house. God bless you, Brother."[16]

H. S. Ridgely, the former North Platte attorney who had delivered the address of welcome from the Irma Hotel steps a few months before, had stayed in Cody, at the Colonel's request, to look after his many interests there and to advise Julia in her management of the hotel.

When he failed to effect a settlement with Louisa, Will managed a reconciliation with Helen by giving her his interest in the Cody *Enterprise*. "She can do what she pleases with it," he declared. "I am not agoin to quarrel with her ever again. . . . If she comes to the hotel take good care of her and charge bill to me." He concluded that almost bitter letter to Julia with these words, "Well, it's war now. I got the first cross letter to day that Arta ever wrote me. But I am going through with it [the divorce]. I think I am entitled to be at Peace in my old Age. And I surely can't have it with Lulu. And she will be happier too."[17]

All during the summer, the Colonel admitted to Julia that he was very tired and did not feel well. Certainly he had reason enough for weariness and despair. The show did not do as well as expected in Europe (some said Bailey had taken it there so his own circuses would have a clear field in the U.S.), the mine was still gulping cash, The Irma was not making expenses, and there was as yet little income from irrigation in the Big Horn Basin. In addition, Helen quarreled with Judge Peake of the *Enterprise* and went back to Duluth in a huff. And Louisa refused to cooperate by giving Will a quiet divorce.

Julia was still at The Irma to greet her brother on the porch when he made his quick trip home in November. May was there, too, and he assured them both that affairs were bound to better the next year, promised May to build her a new house as soon as he could get to it, urged Ridgely to get busy on the divorce proceedings, then hurried up to the TE for a few days' rest. The hunting season was over by the time he reached his mountain retreat, so he actually spent a few quiet days there, then hastened back to England.

No one mentions that he saw either his wife or Arta, and by then Irma and her husband were in the Philippine Islands, where the lieutenant was to be stationed for two years.

30

Louisa
1904

As knowledge of the Cody divorce proceedings made the rounds, the people of North Platte began to "take sides"; the affair became "personal," dividing friends and even families. William Sweeney's sisters are a case in point: Mrs. John Baker's sympathies were with Mrs. Cody, Mrs. Mary Elder sided with the Colonel.[1]

Many of the townspeople laid the Cody troubles to the jealousy between Louisa and her sisters-in-law. Some said the Colonel's sisters were to blame, that they had gotten the "big head" over their brother's fame and success and thought his wife wasn't good enough for him. Others thought the Colonel didn't take his wife with him as much as he should have and that she was jealous over the attention he paid his sisters and the money he gave them. Still others said Buffalo Bill tried to take Lulu with him, but she got jealous over attentions paid him by the showgirls and tried to "bust up the Wild West."

There may be some truth in all these allegations. Certainly Cody was handsome, famous, and (sometimes) wealthy, and both Louisa and his sister Julia loved him unselfishly and devotedly. Both thought what they did for him, or tried to do for him, was for his own good. Louisa, by buying a great deal of North Platte property in her own name, hoped to protect her over-generous husband from himself and arrange matters so that he would someday have a fortune to fall back on. Julia worked hard at the ranch, and later at The Irma, to see that his friends were taken care of in a style and manner reflecting well on his hospitality, and to provide for him a pleasant home where he could come to "rest" and entertain between shows. The love of his other sisters,

314

May and Helen, seems less unselfish, especially that of Helen, for she too often appeared to base her affection for her brother on the extent of his largess to her.

And then there were the whispers about a woman, "the mother of Cody's son." Charles Whalen said: "I never heard anything about an illegitimate daughter of Cody's, because it was a *boy* born to this woman. But Cody never married her. The woman finally told him to get a divorce and marry her—or else. It drug out several years, but Cody never intended to divorce his wife, but that woman kept after him."[2]

Dora LaBille Ketchum said: "It seemed she [Mrs. Cody] was afraid he'd marry one of them things that wanted him just for his title, but she didn't turn him loose."[3] Ella Drake told of stories that "got out that Cody was in love with a younger woman traveling with the show."[4]

The people mentioning this matter were understandably reluctant to talk about it, even though the principals were long dead. Some still felt deep affection for the Codys and considered talk of the old scandal disloyal to their memories; others hesitated because, as one man said, "That boy of Cody's was well regarded and well known here, though he doesn't live here now."

One wonders what Louisa Cody's thoughts and feelings were during this period. In her *Memories* she does not once mention the divorce or any other serious domestic trouble. No letters from her have come to light. However, most of her contemporaries in North Platte, who in later years told what they knew of those troubled times, said they believed Mrs. Cody loved her husband through it all.

In the early years of their marriage, there had been some lean times when Louisa had to help out. After both were in their graves, there were some who liked to tell that Buffalo Bill's wife had to take in washing and sewing at Fort McPherson to keep food on her table. These were the people who said that Cody was out of work most of the time and cadging on his friends. One North Platte woman even told how her father had paid the doctor bill when the Cody son was born and had bought Mrs. Cody $50 worth of groceries besides.

That these stories are untrue is proven by the post records, which show that Cody was continuously on the government payroll there from May 1869 to December 1872, when he resigned to begin his stage career. The records also show that the post doctor delivered the baby, as Cody and his family were entitled to the free services of the resident physician, the same as any other men on the government payroll.

There is as little truth in the "taking in washing" story, but Louisa did do sewing for pay during her husband's scouting days. She loved to sew, as attested by the fancy outfits she made for Will, and she was an expert needlewoman, the result of her convent training as a girl. In those days, when good dressmakers were scarce and in great demand on the frontier, it was only natural that she accommodate her friends among the officers' wives at the post by sewing for them.

The fact that Louisa was sometimes low in funds, even after Will went on the stage and was making good money, was largely due to his romantic and improvident ways. Lottie Kocken, the girl who rode her horse all the way to the Dismal and back on the Cody excursion in 1878, wrote years later that during his travels with his stage show, he would send his wife a big bouquet of roses when he didn't have time to write. And Mrs. Cody, "who was of a practical turn," would remark that he sent her roses when she needed money more.[5]

Jessie Blankenburg Reynolds also remembered Mrs. Cody's saying that "Willie just couldn't hold onto money, for he was a grand spender, and she had had to fix it so he couldn't mortgage everything."[6] Another neighbor told that an acquaintance once asked Mrs. Cody where she got the money to buy all the houses she owned, and Mrs. Cody laughed and said, "Oh, when Will comes home I go through his pockets."

Katherine Clemmons certainly cost the Colonel plenty, and the other women in his life from time to time must have been expensive, too. The showman's friends excused him for this by explaining that women continually "ran after" him, making it difficult for him not to notice them. When Cody was touring with "The Waif," said Miss Kocken, a woman named Lydia Donniel, or Danniel, played the part of the waif; according to home-town rumor, she was very much in love with him, "which was only natural because he had an abundance of physical attraction."

It was only "natural," too, that Mrs. Cody should resent his attentions to other women. And her resentment, coupled with his anger over her investing the money he sent her in property held in her own name, may have fueled the fires that finally led to Cody's determination to sue for divorce.

Beata Cox, a North Platte girl who sewed for Louisa from 1896 until 1907, and became a close friend of her employer, said the loss of little Kit Carson was the cause of it all. Beata said Mrs. Cody never mentioned their dead son but once, when she told her that Willie had gotten wild and "fast" after Kit's death and she began finding other women in their bedroom. Because of this she would not travel with him anymore, "but it never would've happened if our boy had lived. He wanted a son to carry on his name, and there wouldn't have been any trouble if Kit had lived." And then after Arta's first husband died, Beata continued, Mr. Cody wanted to adopt Cody Boal, but Arta wouldn't hear to it. She said the name of Boal deserved to be carried on the same as that of Cody. Mr. Cody did Mrs. Cody shamefully, Beata concluded, "but she was loyal to him and loved him more than most women nowadays love their man."[7]

Louisa may have had to learn through the *Era* of her husband's injury at Manchester, England, in April 1903, when his horse reared and fell backward on him, spraining his foot so badly he had to make his arena entrances in a buggy for two weeks. Or perhaps Arta and her father were still communicating, for it was not until July that she wrote him the "cross" letter.

Louisa had other worries and responsibilities besides the pending divorce suit. C. E. Salisbury, who had followed Al Goodman as foreman of Scout's Rest Ranch, had taken ill and gone home, leaving her to manage the ranch, as well as the numerous houses and farms she owned. Her grandson, six-year-old Cody Boal, was with her most of the time, and she also had the care of her aged father, John Frederici.

"Cubby" Bare, Clara's friend, who was often at the Cody home, remembers how good Mrs. Cody was to the old man. He loved waffles, she said, and Mrs. Cody often made them for him, cooking them in an old-fashioned waffle iron on top of the big coal range in the kitchen, where the family ate all their meals, except when the Colonel was at home or they had company. Mr. Frederici, Cubby said, had a very long beard which he doubled up and tucked inside the waist band of his trousers, and they had quite a time trying to keep the waffle syrup out of the old man's whiskers.[8]

In July, however, Louisa managed to get away long enough to go to San Francisco to bid Irma and her husband bon voyage when they set sail for the Philippines. Little Cody accompanied her. It may have been from the *Era*, too, that Mrs. Cody learned, in December, that the Colonel had purchased from the Nate Salsbury estate Nate's interest in the Wild West, making Cody and James Bailey equal co-owners in the company. Or perhaps Arta told her when she returned from New York on the Friday before Christmas. A few hours later, the fine carriage house back of Welcome Wigwam burned to the ground.

When the Colonel bought the McKay mansion in 1893, he had immediately erected a two-story carriage house and barn back of the big house. Ray Newman, who tended the barn for Mrs. Cody around the turn of the century, described it as a large structure with several box stalls on the ground floor next to a big harness room where many sets of fancy harness hung along the walls on long carved pegs. A pair of glass doors divided the harness room from the carriage room, which housed the big tallyho, half a dozen buggies, and a handsome two-seated phaeton. Above the stable room was a good-sized haymow, and next to it a two-room apartment intended for the use of the stableman.

Since Ray, sixteen years old when he took charge of the stable, lived down the street a few blocks with his parents, the upstairs apartment was unused, and it was there that Arta had stored her household furnishings after Horton's death. After school and on Saturdays, the lad worked for Mrs. Cody, who used her buggy nearly every day, except when the weather was bad. Also each morning he hustled over to the barn to feed, water, and harness her horse and hitch it to the buggy. He left the outfit tied to a hitching post near the house, and if the day was cold or wet he blanketed the horse.

The horse was an odd-looking old white animal with long whiskers, which stuck out in all directions from its nose and hung in a sort of goatee from its chin. But it was Mrs. Cody's favorite steed and she would drive no other. Though quiet and gentle, it had one unbreakable habit—if it ever got loose it would go straight to the ranch, two-and-a-half miles away. Then someone had to walk there and get him, as no other horse was kept at the town house, unless Colonel Cody was at home. After he had to go after the horse a time or two, Ray was careful to see that it was well tied.

Mrs. Cody drove the old horse to her "everyday" buggy to attend to her business affairs or to go downtown. On Sundays she drove one of the fancy buggies to the Episcopal church or to call on friends. After school Ray came back to the house to stable and feed the horse and put the buggy inside. On Saturdays he worked all day. Since the streets were not paved, the vehicles used during the week were either muddy or dusty, and he had to clean and polish them, grease the wheels, clean out the stable, dust and polish the harness, and see that everything was in order in the carriage room.

Mrs. Cody always had him in for the noon meal on Saturdays, and the boy enjoyed the time spent in the big house, not only because he was hungry and the food was good but because Mrs. Cody was a good talker and very friendly. She talked mostly of Buffalo Bill, he said, and it was plain to see that for her "the sun rose and set in W. F. Cody." She told Ray the Colonel was always good to her, and she laughed about the time, years ago, when he wanted her to go buffalo hunting with him and she had protested, saying she couldn't shoot a buffalo. But he said there was nothing to it, you just pointed the gun and pulled the trigger. So she went with him, and when they came up with the buffalo, she pointed the gun and pulled the trigger, and sure enough the buffalo went down. She didn't know until years later that Buffalo Bill had shot the buffalo for her.[9] "Oh, she thought the world of 'Willie' and admired him so much," Ray said. "If she wanted to make any changes around the place she always waited until she could talk to 'Willie' first."

On certain Saturdays she collected her rents, and on those days she had Ray go along to drive and wait in the buggy while she went in to visit with her tenants and get the money. Sometimes he drove her out to the ranch to see how things were going there, and she often mentioned how much the ranch was costing her, what with salaries for the help and all; said she often had to use her rent money to pay the ranch expenses, but she didn't seem to mind. She was a very able-bodied woman and always seemed cheerful. She paid Ray by the hour, and paid well, very good wages for those times.

The Newman home was quite near the house where Al and Julia Goodman lived for a time, on West Third Street, near the old Washington School, and Ray was also very fond of the Goodman family. Mrs. Goodman was a wonderful woman, he said. Ed Goodman was a fine man, too, and pretty Josephine was a popular teacher in the town schools. Ray was no longer stableman when the fine barn burned in December 1903, but he said he felt an almost personal sense of loss in its destruction.[10] As told by the *Era* of December 24:

About three o'clock in the afternoon the fine barn on the Cody property in the west end of town was found to be on fire. An alarm was immediately turned in, and the firemen, accompanied by a goodly portion of the citizens, rushed to the scene. A high wind was blowing from the northwest and it was with great difficulty that the residence was saved. The nearest hydrant was too far distant to be of much service and a bucket brigade was formed to fight the fire. Blankets, rugs and carpets were saturated and used to protect the house. The barn was entirely destroyed, the loss being partly covered by insurance. Many valuable relics of Colonel Cody's and all the furniture, china and bricabrac belonging to Mrs. Boal were a total loss. It was only by the determined efforts of the firemen that the residence was saved at all, it being badly blistered and once on fire.

After all the Codys had done to equip and support the local fire department, it was ironic that the equipment did not include a nearby hydrant.

A little over a week later, on New Year's Day 1904, Arta married Dr. Charles Thorp. Again there is a disappointing scarcity of local news coverage, but we know that it was a small wedding in Denver, at her sister May's house; Arta's father was present.[11] Beata Cox, the Cody seamstress, tells of making Arta's trousseau for her second wedding:

> I was nine weeks making it. Arta was a beautiful woman, kind and fine, with beautiful eyes and a fine form. I loved to sew for her and she and her mother were always doing nice things for me. Arta wanted me to come and stay with her after she was married, and be her companion, but her mother said, "Why Arta, that wouldn't be right. Beatie has her poor old frail mother to take care of and mustn't leave her." So I promised Arta that I'd come to visit her in June.[12]

But "Beatie" never made that promised visit, for Arta died a month after her wedding.

Arta and her new husband had gone at once to Spokane, Washington, where Dr. Thorp had been appointed surgeon for the Northern Pacific railroad. Just before the end of the month, Mrs. Cody received a letter from her daughter, telling her that an operation for "organic trouble" would be necessary, that it was of a critical nature, and that she (Arta) had grave doubts as to her recovery. Mrs. Cody had quickly packed a bag and, with little Cody, hurried to the depot. While she was waiting for her train, she was handed a telegram informing her of Arta's death. Louisa and Will accompanied Arta's remains to Rochester, where she was buried beside her little brother and sister.

On her return from New York, Mrs. Cody gave the local "fire boys" a check for $100, with her compliments, for their heroic work on the occasion of the fire that destroyed the carriage house. But early in March the fire alarm again shrilled its summons, sending the department to Scout's Rest Ranch where some haystacks were on fire. In spite of the high wind, the flames were soon under control, and only a few tons of hay and some fences were lost. The *Era*, observing that Mrs. Cody was having bad luck with fires that spring, congratulated her that her loss was no heavier. The congratulations were premature, however, for a few days later:

> About four o'clock, with the wind blowing at forty or fifty miles an hour, a fire alarm was turned in and the fire department and nearly every available citizen responded to fight a prairie fire which had reached the Cody ranch and threatened to come into town. The large T barn was completely destroyed and the machinery shed, in fact every building on the place except the horse barn and the residence, was ablaze. Only by the greatest effort were these saved, the flames at one time coming within six inches of the barn. All the farm machinery and about four hundred tons of baled hay were burned. The total loss will not be less than $6,000 and may reach $10,000. About two-thirds is covered by insurance. The fire is said to have started on the Dick ranch, west of Cody's. A heavy rain began to fall about six o'clock and the flames were finally extinguished.[13]

Before the end of that disastrous March, the Colonel filed his suit for divorce and gave his deposition; he was sailing for Europe before the trial, which was set for April in Cody. In North Platte, feeling waxed hotter and hotter as the various factions argued the merits of the case; in many instances, townspeople quit speaking to each other. A friend of Mrs. Cody's referred to H. S. Ridgely, who had been in town "looking up evidence in the case," as "that dirty, low-down lawyer who tried to get me to talk about Mrs. Cody; but when he started his string of lies, I said there wasn't a word of truth in it, so he saw he wasn't going to get anything out of me."[14] In Colorado it was reported that "the people of that state censure the Colonel considerably."[15] Nation-wide, newspapers had a field day with the famous case.

Soon after Arta's death, according to Beata Cox, Horton Boal's sister came to get one of Arta's children; she let Mrs. Cody have her "choice," so Louisa let her take the girl and Cody stayed with her.[16] Welcome Wigwam was now a lonely house. The Colonel no longer came home at all, Arta would never come again, her pretty little daughter would return but once, and Irma was in the Philippines. Only Louisa, her old father, and little Cody lived in the big house. But still, the neighbors said, Mrs. Cody seemed cheerful and matter of fact, putting a good face on the whole sad affair.

31

Cody vs. Cody
1904-1905

In April 1904, the Denver *Post* announced that W. F. Cody, in his suit for divorce, had charged his wife with "nagging." His testimony, as given at the St. James Hotel before Notary Public W. F. Wolff, was principally along lines of incompatibility rather than of cruelty. One of the statutory grounds for divorce under the laws of Wyoming was that one of the partners should make the marriage relation "intolerable." According to the *Post*:

> Buffalo Bill claims that Mrs. Cody began making things intolerable for him even in the earlier days of their wedded life and has kept it up. His testimony was in the nature of an autobiography. He sketched his own career, his successes and his failures. In the early days on the plains there were many of the latter. "She grumbled and kicked," he said, "and took me to task because I didn't make good, although I was doing my best. When things finally came my way she found something else to kick about." Aside from the charge that his wife tried to poison him when he was ill three years ago, Colonel Cody's testimony was not severe against his wife. He told of many petty quarrels and related many instances of her alleged ill temper. "It has been nag, nag, nag," he said, "it has worn me out and I want to get away from it."

In April, John Boyer, foreman of Cody's North Platte farm, his wife, and several other witnesses went up to Cody; Buffalo Bill, with seventy-five Indians, was on his way to Europe. The witnesses, advised that the trial had been postponed until June, came home again. One postponement followed another until November when Cody, back in the states again, filed an amended dictation for divorce in Sheridan. The charges against his wife were the same as before, only in more specific form. He reiterated the charges of attempted poisoning, intolerable indignities, and a regular and systematic course of ill treatment of himself from 1878 until the present, and added that his wife had declared he was the cause of Arta's death. Louisa had refused his reconciliation offer, threatened to denounce him at their daughter's grave, and had threatened his life, declaring she would "fix" him.[1]

It is interesting to speculate how much of this the Colonel actually said and how much was imputed to him or intimated by his attorneys.

Mrs. Cody's attorney, W. T. Wilcox, went up to Cheyenne in January 1905 to file his client's answer to the Colonel's charges. He also filed a motion that the taking of testimony, which had been set for the last day of the month, be postponed indefinitely, as Mrs. Cody's eighty-seven-year-old father was dying in North Platte and she could not leave him. After argument, the first trial date was set for February 14 at Cheyenne.

Mrs. Cody's answer to her husband's charges, as reported in the *Telegraph*, was not sensational, as had been expected; it merely detailed the life of the couple during "their married state."[2] An item in the same paper two weeks later was more hopeful for gossipmongers. Under the headline, WE'RE LIABLE TO HEAR NAUGHTY THINGS, the squib noted that Mrs. Cody had denied attempting to poison the Colonel or submitting him to indignities, but made "a countercharge of his infidelity" to her.

The following week Ridgely spent several days in North Platte, taking depositions, and Cody went to Omaha, where his deposition was taken in rebuttal of Mrs. Cody's. The deposition was taken at the Merchants Hotel, where Cody had the bar opened and everybody treated to a popular new drink called the "Horse's Neck." Wesley Wilcox, Mrs. Cody's attorney, was present, and said the drink was a mixture of whisky and lemon and that everybody there was drinking Horse's Necks.[3]

The celebrated divorce case of Cody vs. Cody came on for trial in the Cheyenne district court on February 16 before Judge R. H. Scott. The courtroom was well-filled and interest intense. The Colonel, attended by attorneys Ridgely and Stotts, and his friend Dr. Powell, was there. Mrs. Cody, still at her sick father's bedside, was represented by her attorneys, Wilcox and Halligan. The case got under way, with

Mrs. John Boyer the first witness called.

John Boyer had gone with Cody on his first tour of Europe. On his return he had met and married a Mrs. Agnes Temple while the show was in winter quarters in the South. Some Platters say that Mrs. Temple had also traveled with the show before she met Boyer, though not as a performer. Soon after their marriage, the Boyers had come to North Platte to live on Cody's farm. Mrs. Boyer had a handsome young son, Charlie Temple. The Boyers had no children.

In 1896, N. E. Trego, a cowboy on the Cody ranch and a long-time friend of John Boyer's, married May Wilson in the parlor of the Boyer home, a neat frame house about a half-mile south of the ranch. May Trego, who knew Agnes Boyer well, says that Agnes and Mrs. Cody were on the best of terms at that time and that she never heard her speak a disparaging word of Mrs. Cody. Mrs. Trego had often gone with Mrs. Boyer to the Cody town house, and the pair had been very friendly.[4] In view of such cordial relations between them in the nineties, Mrs. Boyer's testimony comes as a surprise, for she testified that Mrs. Cody was quarrelsome, frequently "got on the rampage," and made things unpleasant for Cody and his friends.

The first sensation "was sprung" when attorney Ridgely asked the witness if Mrs. Cody ever attempted to poison the Colonel. Mrs. Cody's counsel objected, but Mrs. Boyer got in a very emphatic "yes" before he could complete his objection. After a legal hassle, Mrs. Boyer was permitted to tell how Mrs. Cody gave the Colonel doses of "dragon's blood" in his coffee and tea. She got the dragon's blood from a gypsy and gave it to him because it made him helpless; he would then sign papers and do other things she wanted him to. She had, for example, given it to him on the evening of a big banquet given for him on his return to North Platte from Europe. It always made him awfully sick, she said.

Mrs. Cody once put the drug in his coffee, the witness went on, but she (Mrs. Boyer) changed the cups so Mrs. Cody drank it, and it made her very sick. She testified that she had tried to get Mrs. Cody not to give the Colonel the drug, saying it might kill him, and Mrs. Cody replied that she didn't care if it did, that she would either rule or ruin him. One time out at the ranch Mrs. Cody gave him some of the stuff in a cup of "Garfield tea," and when the Colonel was carried off to bed, the witness said she told Mrs. Cody that if Buffalo Bill died she would report the matter to the authorities; the two then had a big quarrel and had never been friends since.

Mrs. Boyer also testified that Mrs. Cody always kept whisky, wine, and beer in the house and was a habitual drinker herself. The first time Mrs. Cody had ever called on her she had told Mrs. Boyer that her husband was immoral with any woman he met, it didn't make any difference who she was. She also swore that Mrs. Cody was often rude to guests and had once had one of her children drop the piano lid on a lady guest's hand. She had driven her husband's guests out of the house by discharging the servants, appearing in old, dirty wearing apparel, and telling the guests they had made her a lot of trouble and she hoped they would never come to her house again, all the while using forceful and unbecoming language. Sometimes, she said, Mrs. Cody's language was too profane to repeat before gentlemen, much less ladies, and she had known her to get so drunk she had to be put to bed. Mrs. Cody had also told her about the time she had gone to Chicago to the World's Fair and "cleaned out" the house where Cody was keeping Viola Clemons.

"Wasn't it Katherine Clemmons?" asked the counsel.

"No," said Mrs. Boyer.

On cross-examination, Mrs. Boyer had to admit that Mrs. Cody really gave the dragon's blood to her husband to make him love her. She also admitted that the Colonel sometimes got drunk and that on two occasions when he was drunk, Mrs. Cody gave him the drug; when he was in such drunken condition, he acted the same as when drugged. She said the Codys often quarreled. She admitted telling a neighbor that Mrs. Cody had "never tried to poison the Colonel, but only gave him the powders to try to get sway over him."[5]

Another witness called was Mrs. H. S. Parker of Cheyenne, whose husband had been Cody's train master at Fort McPherson and in 1901 was manager of Scout's Rest Ranch. Mrs. Parker testified that she was very intimate with Mrs. Cody, who told her that "just for spite" she had poisoned some stag hounds presented to the Colonel by the czar of Russia.

Years later, Hugh Gaunt told the following tale of the poisoning of the royal hounds. Mrs. Cody, he said, claimed to be clairvoyant or a spiritualist or something. "One day she said the spirits told her to destroy a flock of turkeys belonging to the woman who was the mother of the boy of Cody's. This woman lived out there close to the ranch. Well, Mrs. Cody put strychnine on some liver and stripped it into little chunks and threw it to the turkeys. Some of us were out exercising the hounds, and they smelled that liver and lunged into the turkey flock.

So the hounds got the liver and it killed every one of them."[6]

Mrs. Parker went on to testify that Mrs. Cody had horsewhipped Irma and "burnt a scar in her face with a lighted match." On cross-examination she admitted she had never seen the scar, but went on to tell that Mrs. Cody often consulted fortune tellers, particularly one in Battle Creek, Michigan, and another in Denver, and paid them to answer her questions. The Battle Creek prophet had told Mrs. Cody that the Colonel had already lived five years too long.

And then came the sensation of the day. When cross-examined as to the names of women Mrs. Cody said the Colonel had been intimate with, Mrs. Parker named the late Queen Victoria of England and the present queen, who had been the Princess of Wales when Cody was first in Europe. She also named Katherine Clemmons, now Mrs. Harold Gould.

A Mrs. C. P. Davis of Cheyenne then testified that she was a seam-stress in the Cody home in 1893 and that Mrs. Cody had told her of the Colonel's infidelities and that she had cruelly whipped Irma with a horsewhip.[7]

Next came May Bradford, Colonel Cody's sister, to tell what had happened at the time of Arta's death. She testified that her brother sent his wife a telegram, asking her to bury all the differences, and that Mrs. Cody wanted to send a reply charging him with the murder of their child but was persuaded not to. Instead, she sent a telegram accusing him of breaking Arta's heart. As a result, she said, on the train to Rochester the Codys traveled in separate parties and did not speak.[8]

Walsh writes that Arta wrote her mother, " 'Oh papa, why did he do it? My heart is broken over it.' Three days later she died. In her grief Mrs. Cody cried that Arta had been killed by her own father."[9]

No doubt her parents' pending divorce had hurt Arta deeply, but her grief probably had little effect on the final outcome of her illness. Arta had not been in the best of health for some time, and it was while a patient in a Denver hospital that she met Dr. Thorp again and re-sumed her romance with him. Beata Cox, in telling of her making Arta's trousseau, added: "She hadn't been well while she was at home. Something was the matter with her stomach, and the doctor she was marrying was going to have an investigation of her ailment after the honeymoon."[10]

At the Auditorium Hotel in Chicago, May Bradford went on, Mrs. Cody created a scene and en route east threatened to denounce her husband at the graveside, saying, "I will bring you Codys down so low the dogs won't bark at you."

By the end of that day, those who had listened to the testimony were deducing that international complications might arise as a result of the Parker statement that Colonel Cody had been intimate with the two English queens.

Dr. Frank Powell, star witness for Cody, testified that he too tried to reconcile the Codys. At the Powell Hotel in Rochester, he said he told Mrs. Cody the Colonel wanted to make up and that she refused. "When I carried her refusal to the Colonel," Powell said, "he was all broken up, as he had ardently hoped for a reconciliation."

On cross-examination, attorney Halligan changed somewhat the picture painted by Dr. Powell. "For how long," he asked the doctor, "did Colonel Cody want to be reconciled?"

"For all time," replied Powell. ·

"Now, did you know that Mrs. Cody telegraphed the Colonel saying she was willing to be reconciled for all time, or *not at all?*"

"Yes."

"And did you know that Colonel Cody had telegraphed her, wanting a reconciliation *only* while burying their daughter, Arta?"

"Yes," admitted the doctor; he also added that Mrs. Cody's actions at the grave were most ladylike.

"And didn't you know," asked Halligan, "that Mrs. Cody still desires a reconciliation?" (At this, Colonel Cody, who had been sitting quietly gazing out the east window into Ferguson Street, turned around with a look of surprise on his face, but said not a word.)

"No, sir," said Dr. Powell.

"Would you communicate it to the Colonel if you did?"

"No. I think this affair has gone far enough," replied the witness in a very emphatic manner.[11]

From all this, one has the feeling that Louisa Cody must have been very much alone on that trip to Rochester and at the graveside of her daughter. If Dr. Powell and May Bradford, and perhaps others who stood to benefit if she was out of the picture, had not been there, and if the eyes of the nation had not been upon them, Will and Lulu might very well have bridged their differences in their love for one another and their grief over their dead daughter. But Cody had made public some serious charges in his suit, just filed, and Mrs. Cody had been deeply hurt by those same charges. In addition, she understood that the Colonel wanted to make up only until the funeral was over, then go on with his suit.

s. George Vroman, the final witness for the plaintiff, testified that when Cody's niece, Lizzie Goodman, was married, Mrs. Cody wouldn't let the Colonel go "but played cards with him that evening and fixed his liquor so that he had to go to bed."

Major Lester Walker was the first witness called for Mrs. Cody. The major had only complimentary remarks to make of both the Codys. Mrs. Cody, he said, was never rude or insulting to the Colonel's guests. She always prepared lavish entertainments when she knew he was coming home with guests, and hired extra help for such occasions. "The Colonel was a generous entertainer, and whenever he came to North Platte we met him with a band and he would take a large number of us to his home and Mrs. Cody was always an admirable hostess and always acted a perfect lady."

When John Boyer, husband of the witness who had painted Louisa in such dark colors the day before, was called to the stand by Mrs. Cody's attorneys, "he made a sorry spectacle of himself." On direct examination, he had made of Mrs. Cody a veritable virago, but on cross-examination he frequently contradicted himself. He said he had worked for the Codys nine years, and admitted he had never heard the Colonel say an unkind word about his wife nor permit anyone else to. He said he had seen her take a drink of gin once, then admitted that he had had one, too, and had then followed the trail to the pantry and had several more. He said Mrs. Cody had used profane language to him when he had disputed over ranch affairs with her, but could remember no specific times or occasions. His testimony was definitely of more help to Mrs. Cody than to the Colonel, the reporter summed up.[12]

Colonel Cody was called to the stand by attorney Halligan for the purpose of identifying some fifteen or twenty letters written by him to his wife in past years. Attorney Wilcox then began to read from one of the letters: "Dear Lulu—I am delighted to find how well you are running the ranch. I never dreamed that you could do it. There are so many different—different—" The lawyer hesitated, having trouble deciphering the Colonel's attractive but difficult handwriting. Cody, in the witness box, quickly stood up. "Here, let me read that for you," he said. "That may be the one I wrote while in the saddle." He took the letter and, with considerable dramatic effect, finished it: "There are so many difficulties in business for a woman, but I am sure you can handle the job. June and July will be busy months for you and then I want you to come east and make me a long visit. Affectionately, Papa."

Cody returned the letter to attorney Wilcox with a smile. In another, written from the Hoffman House on October 5, 1900, the Colonel told his wife she was to be the supreme boss at the ranch and to notify foreman Boyer to obey her. Another referred to some trouble she was having with Boyer, in which she had to order him off the place. Still another advised her to fire "the would-be fighting Mrs. Boyer," and a later one said she was justified in discharging her. In explanation of these letters, the Colonel said they were in answer to one from Mrs. Cody listing Mrs. Boyer's offenses. "I don't recall now what they were, but they must have been pretty rocky," he said.[13]

Mrs. Boyer, who had listened closely to all this, moved uneasily in her seat and cast a reproachful glance at the man in whose behalf she had given such sensational testimony. What emotions passed over her as she heard this remark can be imagined.

Attorney Wilcox, reminiscing thirty-five years later, spoke of the day he read the Colonel's letters at the trial. In one of them, he said, Buffalo Bill had referred to his wife as the "Queen of Alfalfa of the North Platte Valley," no doubt in admiration of her management of the big ranch with its vast acreage of alfalfa. "The Colonel's reading of the letters was very touching," he added.[14]

The testimony brought forth by numerous other witnesses was much in Mrs. Cody's favor: that she did not use intoxicating beverages herself, was firmly against their use by others, did not use profane language, always spoke affectionately of her husband and appeared to take great pride in him, and usually called him "Willie" and he called her "Mama."

Major M. C. Harrington, who had moved from North Platte to Denver in 1902, and Charles Iddings, North Platte lumberman, declared Mrs. Cody to be a shrewd and capable business woman, more efficient in that respect than her husband. Harrington said that even after the Colonel filed for divorce, Mrs. Cody had told him she hoped to live happily with her husband in the future and that she would forgive "all charges he has made against me except the poisoning charge—and that broke my heart."[15]

A Mrs. Neir testified that Mrs. Cody "was ever kind and genial with Irma." The last witnesses called were two women who had known Mrs. Cody well in North Platte. Miss Edith Colvin of Billings, Montana, stated that at Christmastime 1901, Mrs. Cody got up at midnight to meet her husband's train and was "over-joyed to have him at home again." The Colonel brought her a fine purse containing a fifty dollar bill as a gift; he stayed at home for eleven days, and relations between the two were very cordial. Miss Colvin, with Mrs. Cody and Irma, had then gone up to Denver with the Colonel to see him off on his travels again. At that time, said the witness, there was no indication of trouble in the family. Mrs. Cody, she added, always had photographs of the Colonel prominently displayed in her house, including one in her bedroom.

Miss Nan Corn, the final witness, said she had been a guest at Irma's wedding, and on that occasion saw Mrs. Cody refuse to drink; on other occasions when she had been in the home, she had never seen her drink intoxicating liquor nor heard her use improper language. Other witnesses for Mrs. Cody, including Mrs. John Baker, who had gone to Cheyenne for the trial, were not called to testify. The judge apparently concluded there was such a wealth of testimony in the defendant's favor that there was no use in prolonging the trial.[16]

In connection with the banquet given for the Colonel on the occasion of his triumphant return from the Chicago World's Fair (not from Europe), Mr. Iddings stated that Cody drank a great deal and was unable to respond to a toast given for him. Another witness, Arthur McNamara, who had helped arrange the festivities, testified that Bill was "quite full" and unable to give his speech. Early in the course of the banquet, he said, the Colonel asked for a cup of coffee; the chef, thinking he needed a bracer, gave him whisky in a teacup. (William McDonald refers to this incident.) Cody drank it and soon became sick.

Others testified that Colonel Cody was very sick at the banquet, but said it was because Mrs. Cody had given him a drug before he left home. If the drug was to keep him from drinking, as some thought, and he drank anyway, it was not surprising that he was very ill.

At the conclusion of the preliminary trial, Judge Scott announced that Mrs. Cody would make her deposition in North Platte on February 28, that Colonel Cody would be given until March 6 to make his affidavit in rebuttal, and that the formal trial would be held on March 20 at Sheridan. No oral testimony would be used at this trial, the case going to the court on briefs and depositions, and neither of the Codys would be present.

The *Telegraph* ended its long report with this statement:

Some decidedly sensational testimony will be given by Mrs. Cody on the 28th, when the charges of infidelity she has made in answer to Buffalo Bill's suit will be elaborated upon. The deposition will be taken behind closed doors and the Colonel, in his rebuttal affidavit, will deny in toto every allegation of wrong-doing made by his wife. It is generally accepted that the name of Miss Bessie Isbell, Buffalo Bill's handsome advertising agent, will be mentioned frequently by Mrs. Cody . . . as Miss Isbell is directly named as co-respondent. It is understood that Mrs. Cody's detectives have traced the actions of Cody and Miss Isbell over nearly the entire U.S. during the time they have been on too friendly terms.[17]

The testimony, as published in the *Telegraph* on March 2, again did not fulfill the promise of "sensational testimony." Attorney Halligan took the deposition, and in answer to his questions Mrs. Cody told of her forty years of marriage to W. F. Cody. Of their years at Fort Mc-Pherson, she said, "We were poor in those days and I did what I could to assist in supporting the family by taking in sewing." She went on to tell of Cody's years on the stage, of living in Rochester, and then the move to North Platte. "From then on," she said, "we bought other property . . . with earnings from the Colonel's show business."

In reference to the banquet, she was questioned as to whether she had administered a drug, or a liquid, to her husband that would injure him. She said she had not but that she had "doctored him and given him medicine for his little troubles when he drank."

"Did you ever administer 'dragon's blood' for the purpose of making the Colonel love you more and other women less?"

"No, sir, and I don't know what dragon's blood is. I never saw any and never heard of such a thing."

Louisa also denied ever giving the Colonel anything to make him sick, or that she had ever poisoned him. When asked if she had ever told Mrs. Boyer that she drugged him to get him under her control so that he would sign papers, or if she had ever, in Mrs. Boyer's presence, given him a drug to overpower him, she denied it emphatically. She said it was possible that Mrs. Boyer had seen her give medicine to Cody when he was ill.

When asked if she had poisoned Cody's dogs, she said she did not do so intentionally, but that she had told the men to put out strychnine for rats, which were bad in the harness room and granary, and that some of the dogs got the poison. She had felt as badly about it as he did, she said. Asked if she had ever punished her children, she replied, "Yes, whenever they needed it." But when questioned about using a buggy whip on Irma, or burning her face with a match, she answered indignantly, "No, I never used a buggy whip, and I know nothing about the match affair. I did use a small riding whip occasionally, when the children were especially bad."

In answer to a question about any trouble with Mrs. Vroman, Mrs. Cody said the Vroman boys were always into mischief and had shot the weather vane from the roof of her house. When she protested, "Mrs. Vroman naturally stood up for the boys."

Louisa denied using either liquor or profane language, and when asked, "Do you still love Mr. Cody?" she replied, "Yes, he is the father of my children and I love him still."

"Do you desire a reconciliation at ths time?"

"Yes, I do, but I think the Colonel ought to retract the poisoning accusation."

"Would you be glad to see him now?"

"Yes, I would gladly welcome him home."

"Did you ever tell Mrs. Boyer the names of any women with whom you thought the Colonel was intimate?"

"No, sir."

On the subject of the funeral trip to Rochester, the attorney asked, "Did you ever send him a threatening telegram in connection with the matter?"

"I wired him I thought he had been the cause of breaking Arta's heart."

"Did Colonel Powell come to you at Rochester, or at any place, and ask for a reconciliation with Colonel Cody?"

"No, sir."

Mrs. Cody then told of her husband's homecoming on Christmas, 1901. "The Colonel appeared very glad to see me," she said. "He embraced me as he came from the train, and kissed me." Her face took on a look of pleasure as she remembered that happy event. She mentioned the purse and the fifty dollars, and told of his visit at home, and of how he embraced her and bade her an affectionate farewell, kissing her as he stepped aboard the train that Christmas night. "And that was the last I heard from Colonel Cody, either by letter or by word of mouth," she said sadly.[18]

The Halligan deposition describes a solid-gold, diamond-studded brooch about the size of a hen's egg, with a locket in the center. The jewel had been presented to Colonel Cody by Queen Victoria on the occasion of his 1892 visit to England. On his return to the states, he had given it to his wife, who, said Halligan, had always prized it highly, wearing it whenever she appeared in public. On the back of the brooch, "engraved in a dark green stone inlaid in gold, appeared the inscription 'Her Majesty, Queen Victoria, to Colonel W. F. Cody, June 25, 1892.' In the center of the jewel, under a hinged lid of gold, was a very fine portrait of the Queen."

"The object of the defense in offering the brooch in evidence is to show that Mrs. Cody was proud of her husband, then and now, that she was proud to think the queen of a great nation had presented him her picture in a locket. It is figured by both the counsel for the defendant and plaintiff that submission of the locket, together with auxiliary testimony, will go far toward clearing up the atmosphere that was befogged by the sensational testimony of Mrs. Parker at Cheyenne last week."[19]

The alleged poisoning case that keeps turning up in the testimony is interesting. The Colonel, during one of his periods of disgruntlement with his wife, may have been sincere in suspicioning that she once tried to poison him. More likely he tried to capitalize on rumors of such an incident when he needed additional support to bolster his weak suit for divorce.

Most of the rumors that circulated in North Platte for many years had to do with a can of tainted salmon rather than an actual attempt at poisoning. Dan Muller, who claims to have lived at the ranch as a ward of the Codys, tells the story thus: Mrs. Cody lived out at Scout's Rest Ranch. Buffalo Bill was at home, getting ready to take the show back to Europe. Mrs. Cody had been down with a cold and wasn't feeling very well, so the supper she fixed one evening was mostly out of cans—salmon, beans, and the like. The three of them, Mrs. Cody, Dan, and the Colonel ate it in the kitchen. Mrs. Cody didn't feel like eating, Dan didn't like salmon, so Mr. Cody ate most of the fish.

Soon after the meal, Dan found "Uncle Bill" moaning in his room. "I'm dyin' Dan," he groaned. "That woman has finally done it." Dan called Mrs. Cody, who sent one of the men to town for the doctor and hurried to give the sick man an emetic of mustard and hot water. Later, when the doctor told Cody he would have died if his wife hadn't given him the right treatment so quickly, he insisted that she had tried to poison him. Why was he the only one to get sick? Why didn't Dan and Lu get sick, if it were the salmon? Dan says he left for Europe still believing his wife tried to poison him.[20] It is more likely that the so-called poisoning was actually a rather severe case of ptomaine.

Among the many reporters and journalists who covered the trial was

Arthur Sears Henning of the Chicago *Tribune*. His first dispatch, headlined "Buffalo Bill" At Last Stand on page one, included:

> Intrenched in a legal fastness and surrounded by a band of brave attorneys, who know every byepath of the Wyoming divorce laws, the hero of the thrillers of two generations started today to fight his way to marital freedom. . . . The colonel declares he is seeking to escape the indignities and insults from which he has suffered for thirty years, and that he feels free to attempt it now that his children are married.
>
> Mrs. Cody, . . . surrounded by another brave band of attorneys, is determined to fight to the last ditch, for she asserts the colonel wants the divorce only in order to marry another woman.[21]

The filing of the suit was attended with tragedy, Henning continued. "Oh Papa! Why did he do it?" moaned his daughter, Arta, who had just been married. "Three days later she died—of grief, 'twas said. [This is probably where Richard Walsh found his information for his book, published twenty-three years later.] Mrs. Cody was to deny later the charge that she accused Cody of causing the death of their daughter. She testified that she had sought a reconciliation with her husband at Arta's funeral but that Cody refused it."

Henning described Cody as appearing at the trial in a buff-colored Newmarket coat and a black slouch hat of the most romantically wild and western cut. His long hair was tied in a knot behind. In connection with the charge of "poison" at the banquet, Henning writes that Mrs. Cody's lawyer asked Mrs. Boyer if it wasn't true that Louisa was only trying to sober her husband up for the dinner, as he had been drinking all day. Mrs. Boyer thought not, and said Mrs. Cody's only concern had been three "lady guests in the house [who] were paying too much attention to the colonel."

At mention of Katherine Clemmons' name, Henning says Cody "twisted his imperial and cast a mirthful sidelong glance at the women who daily accompanied him to court." This would intimate that the Colonel came to court surrounded by his bevy of admiring feminine friends. No doubt the women were there in swarms, but if Cody hoped to make a good impression on the judge it hardly seems likely he traveled in the midst of a female coterie. Perhaps Henning, already well-known and later to be chief of Washington correspondents, was only spicing up his copy a bit. He goes on to report that "Cody was compelled to take the stand and identify and read the affectionate letters he had written his wife up to 1900."[22] Wilcox and the *Tele-*

graph's reporter say the Colonel *offered* to read the letters.

On the day Mrs. Parker testified that Mr. Cody had had improper relations with the queens and with Mrs. Howard Gould, Judge Scott had immediately directed that their names be stricken from the record. "I regret," he said, "that the names of innocent parties have been dragged into the case. Counsel should have known that the court has the right to rely upon their good faith that the answers to questions propounded will not reflect upon the dignity of the court. . . . [T]he answers here are so manifestly unjust, preposterous, false and brutal they will be expunged from the records."[23]

On March 23, the district court at Sheridan refused Colonel W. F. Cody's petition for divorce. At the same time, Judge Scott requested Mrs. Cody's attorneys to amend their answer in the case by striking out those sections which dealt with Cody's conduct in Chicago and his early excesses at Fort McPherson (which had not been proven). When this was done, the court found entirely in favor of Mrs. Louisa Cody.[24]

Arthur Henning wrote that Judge Scott found the charges on both sides unwarranted and required that the Bessie Isbell charges against Cody also be stricken from the records. The judge said that the poisoning charge was not sustained, that Mrs. Cody had merely administered remedies for intoxication, and that Cody's inability to speak at the banquet was due to his intoxication. He believed that she took pride in her husband and his success: kept his statue in her hallway, hung his portrait by a famous artist in her bedroom, entertained his guests cordially. Finally, Mrs. Cody did not use profane language.[25]

Colonel Cody at once stated his intention to appeal. His attorneys argued the case before a Cheyenne judge in May, insisting they had new evidence. When this court denied him the right to a new trial, he said he would take the case to the supreme court.[26] In the meantime he went back to Europe to take his show on tour again.

In a cable to Dr. Frank Powell, Cody directed that his appeal in his suit for divorce be immediately withdrawn. "This was done at the earnest request of his only living child, Irma, the wife of Lt. Stott. . . . It is known to their friends that no reconciliation has been effected between Cody and his wife. The dismissal . . . is not the result of any change in their relations, but the result of the efforts Mrs. Stott has been putting forth to bring her parents together."[27] Mrs. Cody would continue to make her home at Welcome Wigwam; the Colonel would remain in Europe for a year or two, then return to the United States and to Cody.

On March 10, Mrs. Cody paid her real estate taxes—not due until May 1—in Lincoln County on 1,200 acres of land and numerous houses assessed in her name, and on 700 acres assessed to the Colonel. The total amounted to more than $600 (making her one of the largest tax payers in the county), which she paid in "cold cash."[28] The rest of that year, following her father's death in November 1905, she entertained guests, enjoyed a visit from Irma, and, with young Cody Boal, visited friends in Denver.

And so we are left to wonder: Why did Buffalo Bill want a divorce? He would not disown or "divorce" his sisters, for he loved Julia devotedly, and he had promised his mother that he would always care for his sisters. Since they seemed to need his support to the end of their lives, he must have felt an obligation in that direction. Did he hope, then, that by "paying Lulu off" and not having to deal with her anymore, he could escape the wrangling in which these four women seemed to keep him embroiled? Or was there another woman in the shadows, putting pressure on him to divorce his wife and marry her? Or had he actually fallen in love with a woman young enough to give him the son it was said he wanted so badly—perhaps the young journalist Mrs. Cody had named as correspondent? Two authors claim he had a candidate for Mrs. Cody No. 2 in Katherine Clemmons,[29] but she had married Howard Gould several years before Cody sued for divorce and remained married to him until 1909.

Whatever the real reason for the divorce attempt, its results and aftermath were unhappy in many ways. The Colonel had deeply hurt his family, tarnished his own reputation, and caused friction between his friends. It was a long time before some of the divided townspeople spoke to each other again, or ceased to blame Buffalo Bill for the grief he had brought his wife and daughters, or Louisa for not letting him go.[30]

32

Woes
1905-1909

A serious aftermath of the divorce trial was a projected Masonic trial, to be held for the purpose of ejecting Colonel Cody from the Masonic ranks. Cody was aghast. He had been a charter member of the lodge organized at Fort McPherson in 1869 and had risen through all the degrees to the thirty-third. In Manchester, England, in 1888 the Prince of Wales, Grand Master of the Free Masons, had presented him a gold watch from that order. And now his own lodge brothers at home proposed to put him out because of the publicity of the divorce trial.

By then, of course, Cody was in France, but Julia and her daughter Josie wrote letters to the wives of the home town Masons, to Judge Grimes of North Platte, and to a "brother McIlvain." Their efforts were successful, and the trial was never held. That was welcome news to the Colonel, for he had trouble aplenty on his hands that summer of 1905.

Even though Lulu was no longer a member of the family circle, the constant jealous strife among his sisters continued to distress him. Helen had quarreled with May, and "Brother" was trying, by letter, to get them to make up; whereupon Helen turned on him, accusing him of no longer loving her because he wrote more letters to the other sisters than he did to her.

Julia, finding the management of The Irma too much for her, had moved into her own big house (which the Colonel was paying for) and was taking in boarders, while Louis Decker had taken over as manager of the hotel. Helen then left Duluth for good, came back to Cody, and, as her brother put it, "listens to gossip. then jumps on me with ten page letters." She accused the Colonel of leaving Julia with a mortgaged home to pay for; Cody begged Julia to "give her the facts, before she tells it all over town. She says I spend thousands of dollars more on others than I do on My Sisters—brings up the old Peake trouble again—and goodness knows what all. . . . When I see a letter from her among my mail, I shake & tremble like a leaf."[1]

Although it had cost Cody and Bailey $150,000 to winter the show in England, the season had started off well, with attendance so large they often had to turn away almost as many (17,000) as they seated. Later the crowds thinned.

Further, disease supposedly broke out among the horses. Charles Griffin, who was with the Wild West in Europe, later wrote that the show left Paris on June 4, and shortly afterward glanders broke out among the broncs. The French government placed veterinarians with the show, presumably to help eradicate the disease; forty-two horses were taken out and shot in one day. When the season closed at Marseilles, only about a hundred broncs were left, two hundred having been killed since the outbreak of the disease. To placate the authorities, the remaining saddle stock was killed and all their bright trappings burned.[2]

But that winter, after his return to North Platte, Bill Sweeney told his family a different story. When the first horse died in Chartres, he said, the head cowpuncher, knowing French meat markets sold horse meat for human consumption, peddled the carcass to a local butcher. A French meat inspector happened to see the horse, and, upon examining it, declared it infected with glanders. Although this highly contagious disease sometimes affects man, the diagnosis did not prevent the diseased carcass being sold for meat; but it did result in the authorities coming down on the show, charging it a big fee for a permit to leave town, and ruling that government veterinarians must stay with it for the remainder of the season.

By the time they reached their next stop, word of the contamination had preceded them and the city authorities were waiting, hands out, with a firm demand for another fee in return for permission to set up. The city's butchers were on hand, too, to collect the horses condemned that day by the government men. This went on, Sweeney said, until the show went into winter quarters and the partners were heavily in debt. Sweeney insisted that he did not believe any of the horses had had glanders but that the whole thing was a neat racket worked by the French.[3]

Colonel Cody, in a July letter to his niece, Josie Goodman, said only that he had had some bad luck, "the glanders broke out in my stables—And I had to Kill some horses. And lost two towns."[4]

Beata Cox, the Cody seamstress, remembered a Nebraska reaction:

I was at Codys while Mr. Cody had his show in Europe and there was a terrible outbreak of the hoof and mouth disease. The show was put in quarantine and Mrs. Cody used to get the most heart-breaking letters telling of this and that fine horse that had to be destroyed. She would stand in front of that painting of Mr. Cody on that fine white horse [the Bonheur painting] and cry and cry. "Oh Beatie," she used to say, "I know it has taken the heart out of him to lose that horse." I used to feel so sorry for her. She felt bad about the loss but it was what he was going through that made her feel worse.[5]

Implicit in Beatie's story is that Will was writing to Lulu. Was he? Were they reconciled? Probably not. The explanation must be that the Colonel was writing to Irma at this time, and she brought or sent the letters to her mother from Georgia.

Along with the Wild West's other woes, the worst weather in many years plagued the show that summer. In August, at Thouars, France, lightning struck one of the horse tents, instantly killing four horses, two of them the magnificent white Arabians the Colonel drove to his private carriage. Four days later, at Orleans, a frightful storm completely demolished the big tent, injuring scores of people. It rained eight of the ten days they played at Bordeaux.[6]

Also in August, Cody was forced to fight another dog-eat-dog battle with J. A. McCaddon, similar to the struggle he had had with Carver twenty years earlier: "he jumped in ahead of me. . . . And tryed to take my route away from me. Well I followed right behind him. And billed and advertised the same towns he did. And kept it up until I broke him. . . . And Maccaddon had to steal out of the country or go to jail," Cody wrote his sister. "That, with my horse troubles no wonder I am thin. But I won the fight But it was an expensive one."[7]

In spite of his troubles and losses, Will was still sending his sisters money, $500 to Julia to pay on her house, $300 to Helen, although he had to borrow the money in both instances. He was urging Julia to beg Helen to leave him alone for awhile. "When she gets financially embarraced which happens often, I raise the money in some way to help her out. . . . My *brain* is nearly gone thinking how I can tide over my financial trouble."[8]

George Beecher was a guest of the show again that summer, and if he knew anything of the Colonel's financial difficulties he does not write of them, other than to mention the "disease which spread among the horses," causing heavy losses. Since his earlier visits with Cody, the minister had been called to Omaha as dean of Trinity Cathedral. In June, Dean Beecher had received a letter from Johnny Baker, asking him to pick up his oldest daughter, ten-year-old Della Baker, and bring her to Paris. Enclosed was a round-trip ticket for the minister and a one-way ticket for the little girl.

Johnny's wife, Olive, met the two in Paris and traveled with them to Lyons, where Cody and Johnny were stationed with the show. "I was given a beautiful horse, with a silver mounted saddle, to use every day as I liked," wrote Beecher, but unfortunately tells little more of his visit until time to leave for home two weeks later. On a hot day, at the close of the afternoon show, he told Johnny and his family goodbye, then went to Cody's tent.

> He was sitting alone on his locker, trying to keep cool. He was think-ing of the home folk. He knew that I would see them long before he would. Irma, . . . in Fort Oglethorpe, Georgia, . . . had written her father for some money to purchase a thoroughbred to drive tandem in her dog cart, as some of the army people were doing at that time. . . . Handing me a package carefully wrapped, [the Colonel] said, "I will be grateful if you will send this to Irma. It is $250.00 in gold for the new horse she wants. You know, Mr. Beecher, a lieutenant's salary is not very large, and dog cart tan-dems are rather expensive." I shall never forget this picture of the Old Scout, reaching out this message of fatherly affection for his daughter far away. . . . I don't believe I ever saw anyone more homesick than Colonel Cody was when he bade me goodbye.[9]

Reverend Beecher was taken to the station in the Colonel's own car-riage, where he found twelve or fifteen of the cowboys at the entrance. They had "chipped in" and bought the minister his ticket to Paris and, of all things, a big bouquet of roses. As he told them goodbye and boarded the train, they gave the big reverend "several old-time prairie yells" as their parting blessing. This gave the other passengers the impression that he was a very important person, a reputation he en-joyed all the way to Paris. And at the London dock he received mes-sages from almost every homesick member of the show.

Cody was heavily in debt when he and Bailey put the show in winter quarters at Marseilles and the Colonel headed for the TE for a brief visit. Johnny Baker went on to Omaha to buy horses to replace those killed in France and arrange their shipment to Europe. Before the end of January 1906, they were all back in France, breaking out the new horses and getting the show ready for its March 4 opening.

Young Henry Goodman accompanied his uncle back to Marseilles, and on March 5 Cody wrote Henry's mother to tell her what a great ride her son had made on Two-Step the night before. Two-Step was a Colorado horse, sent to Europe by John W. Kuykendall, a prominent cattleman. "The others are good," Cody wrote Kuykendall, "but Two-Step is the hardest horse to ride I ever saw. He is a world beater."[10]

The opening week, which ended at Nice on March 10, was the biggest opening week, financially, in the history of the show.[11] From there the four trains carrying the Wild West went to Genoa, Italy, where thousands were turned away on opening day. The triumphal tour continued, recouping some of the previous year's losses. The king and queen of Italy and a number of nobles visited the show in Rome, where the king commanded a private performance for the next day and presented Cody many fine gifts. Booth Tarkington came to see the show the following day.

While they were in Italy, Vesuvius erupted, a lurid backdrop for the great Wild West, and Buffalo Bill promptly sent $5,000 to the "sufferers" in the damaged villages, and $1,000 to San Francisco, which had just been shaken down by the great earthquake.[12] The Colonel's delight with the show's unqualified success that spring was dealt a severe blow with the death of Bailey on March 22, leaving him no level-headed business partner on whom to depend. He still had Johnny Baker and Major Burke, hard-working and faithful, who would be with him to the end, but neither was capable of handling the complicated business of the vast enterprise as efficiently as Bailey had done.

In Budapest, where the crowds were still enormous, a local society for the prevention of cruelty to animals accused the cowboys of using "nails, thorny chains, knives and straps to induce his horses to buck." Representatives of such societies followed the show all through Hungary, threatening to close it down. In Vienna, when asked about these alleged practices, Buffalo Bill looked at his inquirers scornfully, then turned his back.[13]

The show went on through Germany, Belgium, and a number of countries to give its last European performance in Arles, France, on

October 30, 1906. It had been a long, difficult season, though a triumph both financially and artistically, and the entire homesick company was glad when it was over.

Every member, including the Indians, had already stocked up on trunksful of clothes, souvenirs, and gewgaws. The show broke up immediately. Colonel Cody, Jule Keen, Johnny Baker, Bill Sweeney and the cowboy band, the Indians, and the balance of the show people sailed for America the next day. All of the saddle stock, except the top buckers and some of the draught horses, were sold to a Brussels firm. The rest of the Wild West paraphernalia was shipped to New York. Buffalo Bill's Wild West would not leave its native soil again.

After the successful season just ended, Cody should have been in better circumstances, but the death of Bailey had thrown his affairs into turmoil again. Among Bailey's estate papers was a note for $12,000, signed by Cody, who said he had paid it when the show was doing well in London many months earlier. No doubt he had, but Bailey had neglected to release it, and the Colonel was careless about such details, always trusting to the honesty of the men he dealt with. Now the Bailey heirs not only demanded payment of the note but took over the mortgaged Salsbury share as well, leaving Cody only a one-third interest in the show. With his other debts, he now had a burden he would never manage to unload.

From the Bailey Building in New York he wrote Julia on November 23, "I am very busy as I have no partner I must put the show together alone. . . . I am at my desk every morning at 8 30 and work all day. And office work is not my fort."[14] He did, however, manage to get to Wyoming for a short visit at Christmastime, after which he hurried back to New York to prepare the Wild West for its Madison Square Garden opening.

Among the numerous dinners and social affairs he still had to find time to attend was one that tickled the folks back home in North Platte. Late in March, the "Huckleberry Indians" entertained him at a dinner at the New York Athletic Club, where the committee in charge thought it a good idea to play an April Fool joke on the Colonel. Small boxes of "pasteboard huckleberries were placed in front of each banqueter at just the right moment to make the trick go well." Everybody around Cody fell into the trap and tried the fruit, but no one let on, munching away at the berries as if they were delicious, until the guest of honor drew his box toward him. After one close squint, Cody said, "My eyes aren't as good as they were fifty years ago, but I can still 'smell Injun' as well as ever." When the Colonel donned the head-dress of the tribe, Comptroller Metz said, "he was the picture of Tecumseh."[15]

During all his years with the Wild West, Cody had always had a working partner: Carver, Salsbury, and then Bailey. Now he was alone except for the Bailey estate representatives, who were more of a trouble than a help to him. Nevertheless, in preparation for the opening of the show on April 23, 1907, he made a brave announcement to the public: "After nearly five years absence in foreign lands my foot is on my native heath again and I desire to let my friends and patrons know that the Old Scout is still alive and active, and with the same fidelity and sense of duty to the public will be found in the saddle twice daily, rain or shine, at the head of the ORIGINAL and the ONLY morally and RIGHTFULLY entitled 'Wild West and Congress of Rough Riders of the World.' "[16]

In mid-April, when a hundred Sioux Indians—men, women, and children—passed through Norfolk, Nebraska, on the Great Northern, en route from Pine Ridge Agency to join the Wild West, the Norfolk *News* observed: "It seems remarkable that the people of the east will pay good money year after year to see these sons of the plains do their cheap antics. But the show always draws big houses and pays large dividends."[17]

After its long absence, the Wild West truly seemed as popular as ever. Its stirring scenes included the battle of Summit Springs and the always exciting stagecoach holdup, old favorites of past years. New was "The Great Train Holdup and Bandit Hunters of the U.P." This act was patterned after the numerous train holdups that had plagued the Union Pacific since the Sam Bass episode in September 1877. A very real-looking steam locomotive pulled its string of cars into the arena, where it was held up by the bandits, who uncoupled the engine from the coaches, robbed the express car, and blew open the safe. The passengers were then lined up and relieved of their cash and jewelry, but at this point the famous U.P. Bandit Hunters dashed in on horse-back and captured or shot the outlaws.

While he was running the 1907 show, Buffalo Bill was helping turn out articles and write another book, *True Tales of the Plains*. "I work every day in my tent," Cody said, "and two hours before I leave my private car I spend with my secretary, dictating. That's the way I write stories. Sit down and talk them off."[18] This in addition to wrestling with countless management and financial problems of the show and his other businesses. The stories he "talked off" to his secretary were probably for the series of articles, "The Wild West in Europe," published in the *Sunday Magazine*. Walsh and Russell agree that John Burke's hand was heavy in the articles and the book, and Russell suggests that other press agents also contributed to the writing.[19]

That year, too, Walsh says, the old Katherine Clemmons scandal surfaced again when Howard Gould sued the actress for divorce, claiming she had had improper relations with Cody. Gould also offered the Colonel $50,000 to testify against her at the trial;[20] Cody, of course, refused and denied he had ever behaved in an unseemly way with Katherine. And this at a time when $50,000 would have bailed him out of debt with the Bailey interests. Gould was unable to prove anything at all against Cody, or to win his suit for divorce, either.[21]

Dan Muller's account of the Cody-Clemmons affair is interesting, mostly because it is all highly improbable. Since most of the rest of his book is fiction, this part probably is, too. Although the actress had married Gould before ever Cody applied for divorce, Muller writes: "It is possible that the Colonel's fiasco at getting a divorce had discouraged her . . . and the Gould millions beckoned attractively. While the show was in London she came out to the show grounds a lot with him and I saw her when I visited Uncle Bill at the Savoy."[22] Again, while the show was touring the states in 1907, Muller says she kept turning up at odd places on the route, even though Gould's detectives were following the show.

To protect the Colonel and his lady-love, Muller writes, "I often stayed until late at night in the hotel corridor to guard against their being taken by surprise." He also mentions a fight between the Colonel and Fred May, in which Cody knocked May unconscious with a single blow. Katherine was the reason for the altercation, he says, although neither gentleman mentioned the lady's name to the press. Walsh, in his book, published twenty years earlier, also mentions the fight; Muller may have borrowed the incident to liven up his tale of Cody's love life. Dan also places himself in the Colonel's bedroom when he tells of Gould's attorneys coming there with the $50,000 offer for testimony that would compromise Katherine. Mr. Cody, Muller said, told the attorneys "to get the hell outa here." He adds that Cody was subpoenaed when the case went to trial, and on the stand denied intimate relations with the actress at any time.

None of the North Platte newspapers mentions any of this. Evidently they had had enough of Cody's marital troubles and did not propose to help keep such scandals going.

Cody Boal.

In the summer of 1905, following the close of the Cody divorce suit, Lieutenant Stott and Irma had been transferred to Fort Oglethorpe, Georgia. In July of 1906, Irma and her husband's sister visited Mrs. Cody at Welcome Wigwam. The following November and December Mrs. Cody and Cody Boal visited Irma and the lieutenant in Georgia. In June 1907, the Stotts were stationed at Fort Des Moines, Iowa. In September, Mrs. Cody and her grandson visited her daughter in Des Moines. No hint here (unless in the last instance, where the lieutenant is not mentioned in the North Platte newspaper account) of any rift in the Stott household.[23]

In the many 1940s interviews, North Platte neighbors barely mentioned the Stotts, but there were suggestions of marital troubles and of suicide. Mrs. Mary Patterson said of the Stotts' marriage, "They were in the South, where Irma became quite gay and disaster overtook them and they parted." Martin Federhoof said, "She married an army man and he killed himself." A note attached to a batch of old photos of Irma and her children bears the single notation, "Lt. Frederick Stott died during the divorce action."[24]

Official army records indicate that Lieutenant Stott died of pneumonia on December 16, 1907, in White Horse, South Dakota; within a week his personal effects were turned over to his widow at Fort Des Moines.[25] In January, Irma moved her household goods from Fort Des Moines to North Platte, intending to make North Platte her home.[26] She spent the rest of the month visiting her father in Cody, Wyoming, then left for an extended stay in Omaha. On March 3, Irma returned to North Platte, and on March 16, 1908, she married Frederick Harrison Garlow, the son of a prominent Omaha family. Whether there was indeed a divorce action initiated prior to Lieutenant Stott's death we do not know. In any case, the Garlows took up residence at Scout's Rest Ranch immediately after the wedding. Fred became manager, and the old mansion again became a lively home. The local paper tells us that on April 24, Mrs. Fred (Irma) Garlow entertained the Wednesday Afternoon Club at Scout's Rest Ranch; the members were taken out to the ranch in Mrs. Garlow's carriages and returned to town the same way.

Saturday, March 10, a week before Irma's second marriage, was "the day North Platte became famous," according to one of the few surviving copies of the *Telegraph* of early 1908. The headline proclaimed:

RACERS COME AND GO
ARRIVE IN THIS CITY AND STOP FOR DINNER
VISIT CODY RANCH, THEN START ON RECORD BREAKING RUN
TO SIDNEY AND CHEYENNE.

Beginning at 11:40 A.M. all the telegraph instruments started up a mighty chattering and news ceased until they had sent to north, east, south and west a message of 10,000 words which should proclaim to the world that North Platte exists and that it has been found by Montague Roberts and Explorer Hanson in the great Thomas Flyer.

Great crowds gathered on Dewey street, thronging the sidewalks and obstructing the road long before time for the appearance of the American car. The Locomobile carrying the Denver news party, which had been in the city four days awaiting the racers, started at 10:15 to meet the racer. At 11:25 word was telegraphed from just south of town that the autos were in sight. At this the "syron" set up its mournful wail and all the engines in the roundhouse and yards joined with their shrill whistles. This kept up until the Great American Car, preceded by the Locomobile and the Omaha pilot machine came to a stop at the Western Union Telegraph office at

12:10. As they drove up the street all the people set up a great shout and filled the street behind the cars, following to the telegraph office and then to Salisbury's stable, where the pilot car and the Flyer were run inside and the doors shut while the occupants of the car went to dinner at the Pacific House. Before they returned the people were allowed to file into the stable, "inspect the autos, write their names on the flags and look for something loose to carry away with them."

As Monte Roberts came out of the hotel with Cody Boal, who was a special guest at dinner, he asked to ride the lad's pony, tied in front of the hotel. He was photographed on the horse, then climbed into his machine. Before starting the long, hard run to Cheyenne the machine was "gassed" at Fillion's, the only local gasoline supply "station," after which it proceeded to Welcome Wigwam. There both Irma and young Cody were photographed with Roberts and Hans Hanson, Arctic explorer. The racing party made one more stop, at Scouts Rest Ranch, to take a picture of the Cody statue, then buckled down for the run west, arriving at Julesburg, eighty miles on west, at 6:15. At 7:30 the car left for Sidney, forty miles away, on its first night run. They arrived three hours later.

This, of course, was the occasion of the famous *first* automobile race across the United States. Cars were still a distinct curiosity in the West, and night driving was a daring venture. Only three years earlier a picture had been taken of Colonel Cody at the wheel of a Ford Model

K in front of the Colorado state Capitol in Denver. The car, a topless model, belonged to Charles Hendy, Jr., of Denver, son of the Hendy who had been hospital steward at Fort McPherson when Cody was there. The 1905 ride had been Cody's first. The Roberts-Hanson trip was, in its time, almost as exciting to the nation as the first trip to the moon would be some sixty years later. That North Platte was singled out for a stop and photographs was due to the prominence of the Cody family. Thus, its claim to a day of fame.

Two months later it was announced that Buffalo. Bill's Wild West would make two stands in Nebraska: at Omaha on August 28 and in Grand Island the following day. The show trains passed through North Platte in the night, on their way to the August 31 stand in Denver, but the Colonel made no attempt to see any of his friends. No doubt he had not forgotten that Ira Bare had given him quite a scoring in the *Tribune* at the time of the divorce trial, ending his remarks with the words, "Shame on you, Mr. Cody."

Irma and Fred, however, had gone to Omaha and spent a week with the Colonel, traveling on to Denver with him; and a number of Platters rode down to Grand Island to see the show there. Shortly afterward, Sells-Floto brought their show to North Platte and created quite a local sensation in town by inviting Mrs. Cody, her family, the Garlows, and young Cody to be the honored guests of the owners, Tammen and Bonfils of the Denver *Post*.

Although Buffalo Bill was staying away from North Platte, Irma saw her father again in January 1909, after he had put the show up for the winter in Memphis on November 19. She and her new husband had planned to meet him in Denver to attend the annual Denver Stock Show as Cody returned from what was probably his first personal visit to his Arizona mines. But a last-minute wire from the Colonel changed the plans; instead, he met the Garlows in Omaha, after which they all went to Cody, "where a big hunt had been set up for the showman and his friends."27 The hunt and the partying lasted until mid-February.

That winter of 1908-09, Cody, still deeply in debt and struggling to meet his bills, decided to team his show with that of "Pawnee Bill" Lillie. Gordon W. Lillie had replaced Major Frank North as interpreter with the Pawnee Indians on the Wild West's inaugural season back in 1883. Since then Lillie had put together several shows of his own. Most had failed completely. In 1904 he had enlarged his show, named it Pawnee Bill's Historic Far West and Great Far East Show, and toured with it until 1907. At the close of that season he had sold his trains and wagons and played the summer of 1908 at Wonderland Park, Boston. It was this show, made up of elephants, camels, Arabs, and other "Far East" peoples and acts, that he united with the Wild West.

The important thing was that he put money into the show, paid off the Bailey heirs, and made Cody an equal partner—the new partner's share to be paid out of the show's earnings, after which he would receive his half of the earnings in cash. In spite of the merger, the great show was still far more "Wild West" than "Far East," still mostly Buffalo Bill's own unique show.

One new act was added: football on horseback. As a Platter who saw the show in 1911 described the game, it was played with a ball about four feet in diameter. The horses would rear and strike the ball with their feet, attempting to put it across a line before the defenders could turn it back. After the first game, the riders dismounted and the horses played a game by themselves, in which Colonel Cody's white horse always put the ball over the goal line.[28] Russell writes that the game was played with Indians and cowboys as opponents and that on signal the horses rushed forward and struck the ball to the right or left with their chests.[29] Harry Webb, a cowboy with the Wild West, said: "Football on horseback between cowboys and Indians [was] little less than murder."[30] The act was exciting and popular.

The show started in the East, as usual, and came west again, to Columbus, Nebraska, where its wild chaotic dress rehearsal had been held twenty-six years earlier. "Colonel Cody is always mindful of the men who assisted him in winning fame for his Wild West show during the early years of its existence," declared the Columbus *Telegram* in announcing the visit of the show. "Frequently it is his custom while playing towns in which those men made their homes to conduct special ceremonies in their honor."

Four of the original members of his show had made their homes in Columbus: Major Frank North, now twenty-four years dead; Captain Fred Matthews, driver of the runaway mules on that rehearsal day; George W. Clother; and George Turner. The first three named were buried in the Columbus cemetery. Only George Turner was above ground to welcome the Wild West back to its starting point.

According to the *Telegram's* description of the return, a *real* crowd had never been seen in the town before. Long before time for the performance to begin, the roads to the show grounds resembled a flowing river of humanity. The train from Spalding came in with passengers crowding the platforms and the coach tops; several freight cars had been hitched on behind, and they were all packed full of people. The Norfolk train presented the same appearance an hour later. Six hundred railway tickets were sold at Humphry, and at Platte Center the over-loaded train pulled out leaving forty people behind. At the show grounds the tent could not accommodate the great crowd; ticket sales for the afternoon performance ran well over 10,000.

The show unloaded at night, as usual; the next forenoon was given over to the memorial service Colonel Cody and his company held for his old friends at Major North's graveside. Twenty-five different na-tionalities from the show's personnel filled the carriages that made up the long, long procession traveling from the show grounds to the cemetery, where hundreds of people waited at the gates. With slow, marching steps the horses followed the long, straight road to the burial ground. In total silence the riders, adorned in the costumes of their twenty-five different countries, dismounted from the carriages. The entire company, including the befeathered and painted American Indians, marched four-by-four behind the tall, erect figure of the old Colonel to the graveside of his friend.

Johnny Baker was there, of course, and Major Burke and Irma and her husband. All stood bareheaded as Dean George Beecher read the scripture and conducted the brief service. Colonel Cody, his long white hair blowing in the wind, gave a short and heartfelt eulogy to the major, "the truest friend I ever had," and brushed away the tears as he finished. Johnny Baker then gave the signal for Captain Sweeney's cowboy band to play "Nearer My God to Thee," and Captain Devlin and his famous troupe of zouaves fired three rounds over the graves. The old showman then silently placed flowers on the graves of his three friends, and a cavalryman sounded "Taps" as many a tear was wiped away.[31]

Following the Columbus stand, the Colonel dared to venture nearer home and came on to Kearney, only a hundred miles from North Platte. Mrs. Nicholas Klein and Mrs. John Baker, mother and sister of Captain Bill Sweeney, went down to see the show and visit with Bill. A good many other Platters went, too. The resentment against the Colonel was wearing thin.

33

Scout's Rest Ranch 1909

The Howe family came from Liverpool, England, to North Platte in May 1909, and moved into a house at 521 East Fifth Street, almost directly across from the "poorhouse." The manager of the poorhouse at that time was a cousin of Mr. Howe's, Mrs. Emma Pulver, who had encouraged the Howes to come to North Platte. One week after their arrival, eighteen-year-old Alice Howe met Louisa Cody.[1]

Alice, the eldest of eight children, was raking up the yard in front of their new home when a buggy drove up to the poorhouse across the way and a large lady got out. In dismounting, the lady caught her long skirt on the buggy seat and was "hung up" in an embarrassing position. Alice hurried across the street to ask if she could help. The lady was grateful for her assistance, and together they disentangled the skirt. The lady explained that she had stopped on her regular visit to the poorhouse with a hamper of fruit, cakes, candy, and magazines for the inmates. Alice helped her unload the hamper and carry it in, explaining in her turn that she was Mrs. Pulver's neice. Alice then went along to help carry and distribute the gifts.

Mrs. Cody took an immediate fancy to the pretty blonde English lass, and before she left that afternoon she asked Alice if she would be interested in living at Scout's Rest Ranch and helping her daughter Irma care for the baby she was expecting shortly. Alice was interested and her mother was willing. Irma and her mother, with their usual lavish hospitality, at once invited Alice out to the ranch to visit until the baby came.

From the first, the young woman enjoyed life at Scout's Rest. Mr.

McClennon and his wife were foreman and cook. There were two hired girls, a fat one and a thin one, who helped with the kitchen and house work. The number of men varied with the season: several at all times and more during haying and other busy seasons. Mrs. Cody and Irma were always friendly with the help, Alice said. Fred Garlow, while something of a martinet with his men, was well-liked by most people. He was a gentleman though, Alice said, never demeaning himself by doing any of the actual ranch work—very different from Al Goodman, the first manager.

Alice was a guest at the ranch for nearly a month before the baby arrived. Irma, a large woman anyway, was huge during the last stages of her pregnancy and could not get around very well, so enjoyed having the English girl there to keep her company. The baby, little Jane, was born at the ranch on June 30, 1909, with Dr. Daniel Quigley and nurse Zella Van Brocklin, a tiny woman, in attendance. Mrs. Van Brocklin "lived in" at the ranch for a month or so after the confinement, caring for Irma and helping Alice with the baby.

As soon as Irma was up and about again, she and her mother and Fred began to plan some extensive remodeling of the big ranch house. Their ideas included complete modernization, electric lights, indoor plumbing, a furnace, and the addition of several rooms. Since the Garlows entertained a great deal and often had house guests for days at a time, the additional room was badly needed. While the building and remodeling were going on, Fred, Irma, Alice, and the baby moved into town to stay with Mrs. Cody.

Irma was an emotional woman who cried easily, Alice said, and one summer evening she began to weep. When her mother asked her what she was crying about, she sobbed, "I'm homesick for daddy. If he won't come to see me I'm going to see him." " 'Well then, why don't you!' her mother said, for she always tried to cheer Irma up," Alice recalled.

"I will," Irma said. "I'll write to him tomorrow and see where we can meet him." Since the Colonel kept her supplied with itineraries for his show, she could always reach him by letter. But, strangely enough, she received a letter from her father the next morning, inviting her and her family to meet him in Omaha the last week in August, when the Wild West would be coming to Nebraska. He was eager to see his new grandchild, the letter said, and he would be entertaining a number of his old friends at the same time and holding a memorial service for Major North and his other former show members when they reached Columbus.

While the packing and excited preparations for the week-long visit were going on, Louisa took Alice aside and said to her, "Tell Will I still love him and I wish he'd come home." There was so much sadness in her eyes, Alice recalled years later; but before Fred and Irma, baby Jane, Alice, and Cody Boal left the house, Mrs. Cody whispered to Alice, "No, don't tell him anything. He'll come home when he gets ready."

The party put up at the Henshaw, Omaha's finest new hotel, where Colonel Cody had taken a suite for all of them. Others who came from North Platte to visit the Colonel and stayed at the Henshaw were Dr. Quigley and his wife; Emil Seeberger, president of the First National Bank, and his wife; Mr. and Mrs. Joe Stone; and Lester Walker, son of old Major Walker, and his wife, daughter of Isaac Dillon. Dean and Mrs. George Beecher of Omaha were also members of the group.

The Colonel was "simply wild" over baby Jane, Alice said, and held her whenever she was awake. He spent every possible moment of the week with his family and in entertaining them and his friends. He gave a fancy cocktail party for Fred and Irma one evening, and on another took them all to dinner and then to a theater, where he had taken three boxes for his guests. In one of them he sat with Fred and Irma and his grandchildren. "We had the baby in her basket between the Colonel and me," Alice said. "He was so proud of young Cody, too. He'd put his arm around him and hug him and say 'Cody, you're getting to be a fine boy and your grandfather is proud of you.'"

The Colonel spent two or three days in Omaha with his family, commuting across the river to Council Bluffs to take his part in the show there, then returning to the Henshaw to enjoy his guests. The nights were far gone before the family took to their rooms, and the forenoons were spent lounging about in pajamas and robes. Mr. Cody, Alice said, wore a nightshirt almost as long as a nightgown (ankle length in those days), and a long nightcap with a pointed top and a tassel on the point.

One morning, while he was holding the baby on his lap, she caught hold of the tassel and pulled the cap off. He had his long white hair pinned up in a knot on top of the bald spot on his head, and it all fell down; he looked so funny and was much embarrassed, but the young nurse smoothed his tresses down neatly and put his cap back on for him.

From Omaha the family went on to Fremont with the Colonel in his private car. In Fremont they were the guests of old family friends, the Evans, who had a magnificent home with a wide porch running the full length of the house. The porch was lovely with potted ferns and palms and luxurious furniture, and there Mrs. Evans did most of her summer entertaining. "We had a gay time in Fremont," Alice recalled, "with several porch parties given by Mrs. Evans in Irma's honor, and the Colonel taking us all to the show as his guests."

When the show moved on to Columbus, the Beechers, the Garlows, Alice, and Cody Boal accompanied it. There all of them except Alice and the baby rode in the carriage procession to the cemetery for the memorial services. Upon their return to North Platte, Mrs. Cody quickly found an opportunity to ask Alice, "Did Will mention me at all?"

"In a way he did, and in a way he didn't," Alice said. "You see, I told him you said you still loved him and wanted him to come home."

"Oh! Did you tell him that? And what did he say?"

"He said, 'Tell her I'll be home one of these days,' and the tears came to his eyes. Mrs. Cody said, 'Really!' right quick—and didn't mention it again."

Immediately after his return to North Platte, Cody Boal, his cousin, Walter Goodman, and Charles Dixon, son of a prominent North Platte jeweler, went down to Kearney to enter the Military Academy there. Back in 1904, Colonel Cody had written Josie Goodman that as soon as little Walter was old enough, he wanted to send him to a military school. Now, no doubt, he was paying the bills for both Walter and Cody. A month later Mrs. Cody was praised by her Sunshine Society for bringing in a "splendid variety of boys' clothing," the outfits young Cody would no longer need. The clothing was divided among three families, the *Telegraph* noted, and all the little boys were pleased.

How many times Louisa Cody had had to perform that sad chore. Long ago she had packed away little Kit's things, then Orra's, then Arta's, then pretty Clara's, and now young Cody's. True, Clara would soon come home again for one brief visit, and Cody Boal would come often, but the lad the grandmother had loved and nurtured through his little-boy years was now a teenager, almost a man.

Alice remembers that Mrs. Cody's face, in repose, "had so much sadness in it." This is understandable, in view of the many sorrows in her life: the deaths of three of her children, the tragic end of two sons-in-law, the lovely granddaughter she had not been privileged to see grow up, and the husband she loved but who never came home any more.

Clara Boal's last homecoming occurred about the middle of that

December. It had been six years since the pretty schoolgirl left North Platte for a new way of life with her wealthy Chicago relatives. She returned a tall, lovely young lady of nineteen, lively and gay, as her mother had once been. All of North Platte was eager to see her again, for it was known that she had gone to school in Paris, as well as to the best schools in the United States. Her grandmother and her aunt Irma were extremely proud of her, and on the first Tuesday evening of her visit "gave one of the most delightful parties ever given in our city in her honor."

The beautiful Cody home was ablaze with lights and Christmas decorations and warm with welcome and hospitality. Evergreen wreaths and Christmas bells, holly and mistletoe filled every space. Bouquets of white carnations and ferns graced the mantles, and a huge vase of red carnations centered the great dining room table. The evening was spent in an informal way, with music and the renewing of acquaintance between Clara and twenty-six of the young friends of her girlhood.

The next day Mrs. Cody showed her granddaughter off to fifty of her own friends at a "perfectly appointed tea." Assisting were Cody Boal, Irma, her best friend, Maude Walker, and three of Clara's former friends. Miss Boal left for Chicago two days before Christmas, and the next word of her was the news of her marriage on January 7, 1910, in Trinity Chapel, New York City.[2] Her grandfather, Colonel Cody, was present to see the nineteen-year-old girl wed to a forty-year-old Franklin Hamilton Benn, wealthy English lumberman. The couple sailed for England the next afternoon. The pair had met while Clara was attending school in Paris, it was said, and Clara would henceforth make her home in a "finely appointed" English mansion.

The Garlows, with the baby and nurse Alice, moved back to the ranch as soon as the house was livable, leaving Mrs. Cody, for the first time, alone in the big town house. A woman who loved company and someone to talk to, she soon found her aloneness a burden she could not bear. Daily visits to Irma were not enough, and the nights were too empty. When she learned of a fifteen-year-old farm girl who needed a place to work for her board and room while going to school, she took her in.

Mable Hankins said, long afterward, that there was really very little for her to do at Welcome Wigwam, as Mrs. Cody was a good cook and housekeeper. "She really just wanted company, somebody to talk to. But even with me there she was still lonesome, so before Thanksgiving she decided to close the house and go live with Irma and her family.

But she was so good to me, and I loved her and did not want to leave her," Mable said.[3] And so, after sixteen years in the fine town house, Louisa locked its doors and moved to the ranch.

The remodeled mansion at Scout's Rest was larger by five rooms, several hallways, and a large back porch. As Alice Howe described the house, the front door opened into a wide vestibule from which a curving stairway ascended to the second floor. On either side of the vestibule, wide-arched openings led into the parlor on the left and the den, with its big bow window, on the right. The far side opened into the dining room, a long room taking up most of the width of the house. Doors opened from both the dining room and the parlor into the front bedroom at the west end of the dining room. A short hallway, that in the original house had led from the dining room past the kitchen door, had been extended on to the new kitchen, built across the north end of the house. The old kitchen then became the hired hands' dining room. This hallway, called the butler's pantry, was twenty-two feet long by four feet wide, with its outside wall completely taken up with cupboards in which china, glass, and silver for the two dining rooms were kept. All the food and all the changes of china for the elaborate dinners served in the big dining room had to be carried the full length of the long hallway.

There had been three large upstairs bedrooms in the old house, and two smaller rooms, used for either bedrooms or storage. Four more rooms and two hallways were added. Mrs. Cody moved into the big southwest-corner front bedroom, which had a door opening onto the balcony above the wide front porch. The southeast-corner bedroom, above the den and twin to Mrs. Cody's room except for its bow window, was a guest room, as was the big room next to it. The Colonel had used one of these when he used to come home to the ranch.

Of the new rooms, the large one above the kitchen became the "bunk room," accommodating six hired men. The bedroom next door belonged to the foreman and his wife. Next to that was a room shared by the two hired girls. One of the new hallways led from the southeast front guest room, past the second guest room, and on to the bunk room. The other hallway was built on a slant, past the doors of two other bedrooms, to its juncture with the first hall. Because of the slanting hallway, the room beside it was strangely shaped, with none of its four walls the same length. This odd room had various uses: a bedroom when needed or for extra storage space. Narrow back stairs led from the back bedrooms to the kitchen.

Between the twin front bedrooms a steep, narrow enclosed stairway ascended to the cupola, a square room with a window in each of its four sides, perched atop the tall house. It has been told that here Irma spent the last month of her third pregnancy before her second son, Bill, was born; the weather was very hot, and the four windows assured a cooling cross-draft across her bed. There are two good reasons why this is just another of many myths about the Codys. First, according to Alice, Irma was too large at this time to have gotten up the narrow stairway; second, Bill was born in January, a month when Nebraskans have no difficulty keeping cool. The only times Alice remembers the cupola being used for any purpose was when someone went up to look over toward town to see if expected guests were on the way.

When she first stayed at the ranch, Alice slept in the queer trapezium-shaped room. Soon Mrs. Cody, who had become deeply attached to the English lass, had a pair of narrow beds put into her own room, with a little lamp table between them, and asked Alice to move in with her. When Irma weaned the baby and installed her in the nursery, one of the little rooms across the hall, Alice could share Mrs. Cody's room and still be near the baby. The other small room, directly across from Louisa's door, became the "jam room," where she kept the generous supply of jams, jellies, and pickles she loved to make but did not want the hired girls helping themselves to at will.

The ranch house, while nicely furnished, was not as elegant as the town house, Alice said, but comfortable. The parlor was the most pretentious, with its red-rose-patterned Axminster rug, big piano, heavy bookcases and chairs. A long, wicker "fernery" filled the lace-curtained front windows; and two large photographs, one of Buffalo Bill on his white horse and one of Queen Victoria, hung on the walls.

Adjoining the front bedroom used by Fred and Irma, was a large bathroom, and next to it the big closet where Irma kept her fine wardrobe. Fred Garlow, who enjoyed frequent nips, liked to keep a good supply of wines and whiskeys handy. Aware of his mother-in-law's objection to liquor, he kept the domestic waters calm by putting his supply into gallon jugs and lining them up along the wall of Irma's closet, only a few steps from the dining room. Mrs. Cody was told that the jugs contained "dip" for use on the ranch livestock. However, the idea of keeping the dip in the same room with Irma's lovely clothes did not please her either, and one cold day she told Alice she wished "Fred would get that old dip out of there." Alice, who knew what was in the jugs, thought fast and said, "Oh, it would freeze and be ruined if they took it outside now, and that would be an awful waste of money."

"Well, maybe you're right," Mrs. Cody assented, "but it does look like he could find some other place for it."

Installation of the new furnace had done away with the massive base-burners that had formerly heated the parlor, den, and dining room; and with the little heating stoves in each of the upstairs bedrooms. The four-horsepower engine and dynamo that made up the new ranch lighting plant had likewise eliminated the battery of kerosene lamps, both plain and fancy, that had lighted the ranch house. The nineteen-room house was now, as the *Telegraph* noted, "one of the coziest suburban homes in western Nebraska."

In those days, Alice said, there was no door in the wall between the den and the main dining room (as there is now), and the den wall was covered with a magnificent display of pistols, some of them ivory-handled and very fancy. A huge elk head looked down from a second wall, and another of the long, wicker ferneries stood in the angle of the lace-curtained bow window, which looked out on the creek and the big T barn, before the latter burned.

Life was always pleasant and lively at the ranch, as Alice remembers it. The regular "family" was made up of the Garlows, Mrs. Cody, the foreman and cook, two hired girls, and six or more hired men; with Alice, a minimum of fourteen souls, but few days passed that neighbors did not drop in or that Irma and her mother were not entertaining guests. Mrs. Cody and the Garlows were always having people in for large dinners, small dinners, card parties, club meetings, luncheons, and teas. They frequently had out-of-town guests, and when Cody Boal came home he usually brought friends along.

The tree-shaded lake was the popular spot in summer, Alice said, not only with guests and friends from town but with everyone at the ranch. During the summer, Irma and the cook made up a six-gallon crock of root beer one week, and the same amount of ginger ale the next. The cook daily baked cakes and made up great baskets of sandwiches, and every fine evening the food was carried to the lake. Everybody on the ranch took part in the picnics, the hired help and any of their families or friends who might be there. Often they topped off the supper with a big freezer of homemade ice cream, and afterward experts with jews-harps and mouth organs made music while the rest sang. "We were just like one big family," Alice recalls, "and everybody had fun."

Bridge at Scout's Rest Ranch. *Courtesy Nebraska State Historical Society.*

Another of Alice's memories of Mrs. Cody is that she was always busy. "She loved to sew and made little Jane so many lovely clothes that Irma had to tell her the baby could never wear them out before she outgrew them." She turned out dozens of lovely tea aprons, and whenever Irma had a tea party she brought out one for each of the friends who helped her serve and after the party told the delighted ladies to keep them. She made pretty things, usually blouses, for Alice and the hired girls, too, gifts they wore with pride and pleasure.

When the cook had left the kitchen in mid-afternoon, Mrs. Cody took over and made jelly, or baked pound cake, her favorite delicacy. The cakes she kept in a little covered box on the wide ledge outside her bedroom window, and after she and Alice had retired to their room at night, she cut them into wedges for snacks.

Despite the near half-century difference in their ages, the young woman and the older one were very close during the two years Alice spent at the ranch. "We used to shampoo each other's hair," Alice said. "My hair was long, and she would put it up on rags for me at night, so it would hang in long, pretty curls the next day." Mrs. Cody's hair was long and heavy, and she wore it in great coils on the top of her head. One summer night, as the two sat in their rocking chairs on the balcony, eating pound cake, a bat swished by too close to Mrs. Cody and became entangled in her hair. "What a time we had, getting that poor, scared bat out of all those coils of hair!" Alice exclaimed.

After they had gone to bed, Mrs. Cody would talk on and on, mostly about her absent husband. Sometimes she would sigh and say, "I wonder who Will has in his arms tonight?" And once, when Alice was brushing her hair for her, she asked, "What would you do if you had a husband like mine?"

"I'd tell him to go to the hot place," Alice replied firmly.

"Do you mean Hell?" Mrs. Cody asked.

"Yes, that's what I mean," the girl replied.

"Oh, I couldn't do that," Louisa protested. "I love him too much."

"And she did love him," Alice insisted sixty years later. "She loved him an awful lot. And she used to say if it wasn't for wild women and whiskey he'd be at home where he belonged."

And then there was the ouija board. Mrs. Cody loved her ouija board and put a lot of faith in it. She had several friends in town who liked the board, too: Mrs. Joe Stone, Mrs. John Baker, and Dr. Quigley's wife. They'd have little parties, with tea and cakes, while they played the ouija board. Irma, however, had no use for the board and tried to discourage her mother in its use. To avoid an argument, Mrs. Cody would order the carriage, take Alice and the baby along, and go out for a ride. They always ended up at one of her friend's homes for a session with the board. Until the baby was weaned, they always had to be home in time for her next feeding, and often Irma would ask where they had been. Mrs. Cody would take a new spool of thread out of her handbag and say, "I had to get this." Sometimes she really did stop for the thread, Alice laughed, but usually she put the thread in her bag before she left home.

One time in their room, Alice and Mrs. Cody were sitting with their finger tips on the little planchette and the older woman asked ouija if Will still loved her. The planchette spelled out "y-e-s," and she threw the board to the floor in anger and disgust. It had been nearly eight years since that Christmas of 1901, the last time she had seen her husband or heard directly from him. No wonder she found it difficult to believe the board.

After almost two years with Mrs. Cody and the Garlows, Alice left them to marry a young carpenter, Arthur Arzt, whom she had met while the remodeling was going on. All of this had been foretold by the ouija board. Alice has always retained a warm affection for the family, and her memories of them are happy ones. She even has the silver dollar the Colonel once gave her to buy ice cream cones for herself, Cody Boal, and baby Jane. She used her own money to buy the ice cream and kept the dollar.

34

Reconciliation
1910-1911

Colonel Cody closed his 1909 season in the South, put the show up for winter, and met Fred and Irma in Omaha in late November for the Corn Show celebration. He was back in New York City for the wedding of his granddaughter in early January, then in Omaha again for another meeting with the Garlows shortly afterward. From there he went to Wyoming, and possibly on to his mines in Arizona.

On another windy day in March 1910, three calls for help were sounded to battle a raging prairie fire, which, if it had not been checked by the desperate efforts of almost every man in the neighborhood, would have wiped out the Cody ranch. However, the excitement attendant on the big fire was as nothing to that generated by the news that Buffalo Bill was finally coming home.

For the last two or three years, the home town newspapers had been mentioning the Colonel in warmer and warmer tones, indicating that antagonistic feelings against him were fast fading. In blazoning the impending homecoming, the *Telegraph* of March 24 announced that Lowell's band would "meet the train and greet him with joyous music."

Calvin Lowell, Lincoln County's musical deputy sheriff, had put together a fine cowboy band, which was called on to play for all important occasions—and this was one of top importance, no doubt about that. The Colonel came in from Wyoming on the ten o'clock train on a Saturday night and was greeted by the band, in full uniform, and several hundred Platters. The band struck up as soon as the train entered the railroad yard, and as the cars came to a stop west of the depot the crowd let go with a lusty cheer and kept it up until Cody appeared on the platform of the rear coach. Standing there, the Old Scout swept his big hat from his snow-white head and bowed his thanks to his old friends.

Irma was waiting at the car steps to accompany him to her carriage, parked at the far east end of the long depot-hotel building. Putting his arm about his daughter, the Colonel walked the whole distance with his head uncovered, indicating the deep emotion that stirred him at this homecoming. Most of the townspeople were hoping—and expecting—that a reconciliation between Louisa and Will would result from his visit. Certainly Irma had planned for it. With her mother in residence at the ranch and her father spending two days there, it would seem that her hopes might be realized. That they were not is explained by Alice Howe.

Mrs. Cody had so longed to have her husband come home, and had talked about it on many of those nights when she and Alice had visited from their beds. "But do you know," Alice said, "when he got there she wouldn't see him! She wouldn't come out of her room at all, even had her meals sent up; and when Mr. Cody came and knocked on her locked door and pleaded with her to let him in, she wouldn't. So he went away again without seeing her."[1]

On Sunday afternoon Fred and Irma hosted a huge barbecue at the ranch in the Colonel's honor, and that evening had more than a hundred of his old freinds in for a grand reception, some of them men who had been with him on scouting and hunting expeditions forty years ago. At the height of the party a telegram from the New York *World* was handed to Cody: "Your friends read with interest today of your welocme home. What were the sensations of home-coming after ten years absence? A sentiment from you would be appreciated by thousands of newspaper readers who have followed your career as a national figure in American life. Please answer at our expense."[2]

In his reply, written before the guests and co-signed by North Platte's mayor, T. C. Patterson, he told briefly of his royal reception and said he was at that moment happy with upwards of 150 friends about him. Toward the end of the evening, the Colonel made a little speech, expressing his pleasure in the occasion and his pride in the way North Platte had grown in the past ten years. The town lacked only one essential, he declared, and that was a large hotel.

Since the days when he had tried managing his first hotel at Salt Creek, Kansas, Cody had been interested in such establishments. Nearly twenty years later he had helped develop the luxurious Sheridan Inn, followed by the building of his fine Irma Hotel and other inns on the Yellowstone Trail. That none of them made him any money had not dampened his enthusiasm for hotels, and he closed his speech by announcing that he expected, shortly, to build a $50,000 annex to The Irma.

On Monday afternoon the Colonel was entertained at an open reception at the Commercial Club, and in the evening he was the guest of the Five Hundred Club at a theater party. Afterward, with young Cody Boal, who had been home from military school for the weekend, he boarded the late train for New York and Madison Square Garden.[3]

Back in 1905, Cody had written his sister from France that he planned to retire in 1910, when he would be sixty-four, "The age all my old Army friends retire."[4] Attempting to hew to his self-set deadline, in May 1910 he addressed a vast audience at the close of the Madison Square Garden engagement and made his "farewell" speech:

I have determined to retire from active service at the expiration of a final and complete tour of the American continent, following a series of farewell exhibitions which I hope to give in the next two years. I shall permanently abandon the arena and seek to enjoy some of the fruits of my labor, which I feel I have earned during a long life of activity on the frontier, in the field during the Civil and Indian wars, and as a provider of the most approved drama of our national history.

Out in the West I have my horses, my buffalo, my staunch old Indian friends, my home, my green fields—but I never see them green. . . . My message to you is one of farewell. However, it is my earnest desire to once more salute from the saddle my millions of friends and patrons, and I take this opportunity to emphatically state that this will be my last and only professional appearance in the cities selected, as no return dates will be given. It is my purpose to leave the active management of the exhibits I have created in the hands of my partner, Major G. W. Lillie, "Pawnee Bill" . . . who will continue the enterprise . . . but without my presence in the saddle.[5]

One writer noted that at the conclusion of this speech, when the old plainsman, as erect as ever in the saddle, said, "God bless you all—goodbye," there was not a dry eye in the Garden.[6] Two more years with the show meant that he would be sixty-six at retirement, but the news that Buffalo Bill would soon leave the arena packed the stands at every stop for the rest of that season.

Russell relates that on July 28, 1910, the Colonel and Lulu were reconciled—that while the Wild West was touring the area, Cody Boal persuaded his grandfather to come to North Platte, and when he arrived, the family contrived to leave the two alone together in a room; when they came out, all—or most—was forgiven.[7]

According to the *Telegraph*, it happened a little differently. There is no doubt that Cody Boal and his Aunt Irma were bitterly disappointed when the hoped-for reconciliation did not take place in March. Just what the fourteen-year-old lad said to his grandfather on that night train ride to Kearney, where the boy got off to return to school, is not known; nor what Irma may have said to her father before he left, or written to him afterward. But on April 14 the *Telegraph* proclaimed:

> MAY SPEND THEIR OLD DAYS TOGETHER. There are many who will be pleased to learn that Colonel and Mrs. W. F. Cody are to be reconciled to each other. It reads just like a romance! In a letter last week, written to Mrs. Cody, the Colonel asked to be forgiven for the past and is desirous of spending their "old days" together, as he terms it. In reply, Mrs. Cody says she is willing, but some things must be understood between them if they are to be happy together. There are thousands of people who will be highly pleased over the reconciliation.
>
> It is Colonel Cody's desire that Mrs. Cody, Mr. and Mrs. Fred Garlow and young Cody Boal . . . accompany him to New York where he opens his Wild West show at Madison Square Garden this month. The reconciliation was not effected while he was here visiting his daughter, notwithstanding reports throughout the country in the daily press, for they never met during his short stay. No doubt much credit is due their daughter, Mrs. Garlow, in bringing about the reconciliation, at least this is the opinion of this writer. . . . The many friends of Mr. and Mrs. Cody, here in North Platte, will be greatly pleased when they are once more settled down together, and the *Telegraph* joins in the congratulations, and wishes them many happy days together.[8]

No doubt Irma had done some persuading on her mother, too, for Mrs. Cody had been receptive when the Colonel's letter arrived, though there is no further mention of the conditions she wanted understood in order for them "to be happy together." But quite likely one of them concerned the Colonel's drinking.

William McDonald stated often that Cody entirely left off drinking alcoholic beverages during the last nine years of his life. When he "set 'em up" for others after his sixty-fourth year, or was offered a drink himself, he always took lemonade, McDonald said. The Colonel's abstinence was due, in part, to his doctor's orders, but Mrs. Cody may also have had much to do with it.

At any rate, the reconciliation meeting took place in June, as soon as Cody Boal's spring term at the Kearney Military Academy was over and Louisa and the boy could join the Colonel and the show in Buffalo. The Wild West toured on through New York state, Pennsylvania, Ohio, Michigan, Indiana, Illinois, across the northern states to Montana, into British Columbia, back to Washington and down the west coast, across Texas, and closed at Little Rock on November 15.

Mrs. Cody was still traveling with the show in August when Omaha's cowboy mayor, Jim Dahlman, old friend of the Colonel's, came to North Platte to deliver a speech in his campaign for governor. Riding in an automobile with the reception committee, which included Fred Garlow, he was escorted to the courthouse by the cowboy band. After introducing Dahlman, the chairman read the following telegram from Milwaukee: "I am very sorry I cannot be with you today to welcome Mayor Dahlman to Scouts Rest Ranch. Mrs. Cody joins me in extending to him and friends our hearty congratulations. Although a Republican myself, knowing the sterling qualities possessed by Dahlman, I believe it for the best interests of Nebraska that the people elect him their next governor. W.F.C."[9]

In his turn, Democrat Dahlman said: "I am proud to be in the home town of that neighbor of yours who has made himself not only a national but an international reputation. He is big, he is broad-gauged and honest, true to his friends, and I am glad to express these sentiments in the presence of his daughter and son-in-law."

A letter from Cody, datelined August 19, Fergus Falls, Minnesota, to the McDonalds, his North Platte bankers, indicates the pressures under which he still worked, as well as the precarious state of his financial affairs. He began by apologizing for not answering the bank's request for payment of certain notes. He had left the statements in the inside pocket of a vest he had taken off, he explained, and only yesterday had found them again. By then Mrs. Cody had left for home, but if her signature was needed on the notes, which he wished extended, he would get it from her as soon as possible (at long last they seem to be in agreement on these matters), or he would put up additional security. Ever the optimist, he added:

> Now, as things are coming my way, and if they keep on coming, I'll be making deposits instead of borrowing. And when that time comes I surely won't forget you. And before another year ends I am going to [make] North Platte get a move on. I have some original ideas in regard to waking the old town up. As we are once more established in Welcome Wigwam, I will be there more. I've always loved that old town and believed it had a good future, and believe it still. My ideas about how to boost the town may make some of you have heart failure. But it can be done."[10]

A few days after Cody Boal and his grandmother reached home, following their long tour with the show, "a party of North Platte boys, including Johnnie Burgman, son of the head Union Pacific trackman, visited their friend Cody at the ranch. Imbued with the spirit of the West, a show was organized and the boys were playing at it hard when Johnnie tripped on a rope and fell, breaking his arm."[11] From the time Cody, at the age of three, came to live with his grandmother, he and his friends had played among the souvenirs on the top floor of Welcome Wigwam—the silver-mounted revolvers, fancy belt buckles, bows and arrows, and the great, gaudy Wild West show bills—even as Irma and her friends of the previous generation had done. In the summers, they had put on many a Wild West show in the big, shady backyard, wearing the Indian headdresses and moccasins and brandishing the tomahawks as they ambushed each other.

Russell Langford, son of the young man (later a banker) who had penned Irma's wedding invitations, was another of Cody Boal's friends. When Cody came home from military academy and demonstrated how he could jump up, cross his legs, uncross them, and come down facing in the opposite direction, his friends were filled with envy. "But when I tried to do it," Russ said, "I almost crippled myself for life."[12]

Cody Boal's best friend of the North Platte years was Johnny Baker, Jr., (no relation to the Johnny Lewis Baker who traveled with the show as Buffalo Bill's foster son). Johnny's grandmother had known Louisa Frederici (Cody) in St. Louis, and the two women were fast friends all their lives. His uncle was Bill Sweeney, leader of the Wild West cowboy band. His mother, the former Inda Sweeney, and Arta Cody were the same age, and Johnny was just two weeks older than Cody. When the two little boys played at war in the big town house trophy room, Cody would don the little officer's suit and sword he had worn at Irma's wedding and conduct himself in snappy military style. After Mrs. Cody moved out to the ranch, young Cody often came up from Kearney for weekends, which the two boys spent together at Scout's Rest.

Irma was a big, handsome woman, Johnny said, while Fred was a rather small, short-tempered man. The Garlows bought their first automobile at this time, a high-wheeled black Buick with about as much brass work as an ocean liner. Fred wanted the brass trim shining at all times, so often kept Johnny and Cody at work polishing it. Weary of the endless job, Cody one day bought a can of black Jap-a-lac enamel, and he and Johnny painted the brass work to match the rest of the car.

"Fred sure worked us over good for that," Johnny said, "and we had to work all the next day taking the paint off."[13]

On August 30 of that year, the two Bills set up in Billings, Montana, 120 miles north of Cody, for a one-day stand. To honor their distinguished founder, an army of a thousand citizens went up from Cody to see the Colonel and his show. The Wild West had made cowboy bands famous, it seems, for the delegation was headed by the Cody cowboy band, which played a concert in the street in front of the Northern Hotel, where the Colonel was putting up. From the porch of the hotel, the delighted Old Scout invited all the Cody folks to gather in front of his private tent on the show grounds at one o'clock so he could thank them properly for coming all that way to see him.

Louisa rejoined the show in California in October, staying with it until it headed across Texas on its way to Little Rock for its final show of the season on November 15. From Little Rock the Colonel went directly to his Arizona mines, which seemed about to return some of the wealth he had poured into them. As proof, he sent his wife a bracelet made of gold from the Campo Bonito mine, and specimens of gold and copper quartz from the same source. Mrs. Cody put them all on display in jeweler Dixon's window, and all of North Platte was quite excited.

On his way home from the mines, the Colonel stopped off at Pawnee, Oklahoma, for the grand opening of Pawnee Bill's palatial $75,000 bungalow, which was fiilled with furnishings and ornaments worth another $100,000. The party lasted a week, and guests from all over the world came to partake of the Major's hospitality.[14] Cody's next stop was Omaha, where he told friends and reporters that the year just ended was "the most prosperous I have had since I went into show business. From the time we opened in Madison Square Garden there wasn't a serious accident the whole season." The show grossed a million, and the profits were $400,000. It was his last great season. He reached Scout's Rest Ranch a week before Christmas, and from there, on December 22, he wrote to Julia, who had moved to Lincoln, where the Colonel had put Walter in another military school: "Dear Julia, . . . I found every one well & glad to see me here. . . . Cody (Boal) came last night [from military school in Culver, Indiana]. He looks fine in his new Uniform. . . . No little stranger yet but expect one any day now. . . . I am haveing a good rest this week. I did not know I was so tired until I got a chance to rest."[15]

The "little stranger" was Irma's second child, which had not yet arrived when the prospective grandfather left Christmas night for Cody, Wyoming; nor yet two weeks later when he went on to his mines again. On the way to Arizona he stopped off in Denver, where, as in all cities that he appeared, he was at once surrounded by reporters. When one asked if he came to Denver on special business, he quipped, "How can you get anywhere without going through Denver?," then added, "I have many friends in Denver, and I'll probably buy some machinery for my mines while I'm here." And there went his profits from the 1910 season—down the shafts of the Oracle mines.

Cody was at the mines when Frederick Harrison Garlow was born at the ranch on January 19, and still there when he received a telegram that his sister, Helen Wetmore, was dying in Pasadena, California, where she had gone to visit her daughter, Mary Jester Allen. In spite of all the grief she had caused him, he left at once, traveling by horseback, stage, train, and automobile from the isolated mines to his sister's bedside. He won the race with death by a few hours and remained with her until she passed away on February 8. He buried her there, returned to the mines for a short time, and was back in North Platte by March 6, his forty-fifth wedding anniversary.

Despite all the rifts and turmoil of those forty-five years, the marriage now seemed on a more solid footing than ever before. At that, few marriages in "show business," then or now, have done as well, or any better. To show the pleasure of family and friends in the old couple's reunion, Fred and Irma entertained at dinner, Sunday and Monday evenings, in their honor. Covers were laid for fourteen on Sunday and for twelve on Monday. Each dinner was served in seven courses, the decorations were cut flowers and ferns, and the tables sparkled with cut glass and silver.[16]

This was the kind of thing that utterly delighted the Colonel, and his spirits were high as he displayed gold nuggets (one weighing several ounces) from his mines and some of the gifts given him by the crowned heads of Europe: a handsome watch from the king of Italy; a locket, enclosing her picture, from Queen Victoria; a scarf pin from the Prince of Wales; and many others. The guests were the Codys' oldest friends. Among them were the McDonalds, who had so often helped finance the show; J. J. Halligan, who had pled Louisa's case in the divorce trial, and his wife; Judge Grimes, who had helped avert the Masonic trial, and his wife; Major and Mrs. Walker; editor Bare and Mrs. Bare; and Colonel Getchell, superintendent of the Oracle mines.

On the afternoon preceding the Sunday dinner, Colonel Cody had proudly stood sponsor at the christening of Frederick Harrison Garlow. Two days later he left for New York. On his way through Omaha he was interviewed about the possibility of his running for the U.S. Senate from Arizona. He stated that he would do so if statehood were granted Arizona that year.[17] Across the country other headlines flashed: in Philadelphia, "Senator Buffalo Bill"; in Arizona, "Buffalo Bill for the Senate"; in Washington D. C., "Buffalo Bill Belongs in Senate"; in New York, "Col. Cody Not Shying at Senatorship Job."[18]

Cody wrote Doc Waddell in March: "I am just back from my mines in Arizona. I have two quartz mills running, pounding out the values. I am working forty mines, getting out ore for the mills. I am president of two companies, and own controlling interest in both. I like the mining game. It's as exciting as the Wild West show." Waddell printed the letter in his column in *The Show World* and added the prediction that Arizona would send Cody to Washington as its first senator.[19]

In North Platte the *Telegraph* reported that Col. W. F. Cody had established his residence in Tucson, Arizona, as the people there proposed to run him as their candidate for the U.S. Senate as soon as the territory was admitted to the union. It would certainly be fitting, editor Kelly said, if Colonel Cody rounded out his career by becoming the first senator from the new state. But Arizona did not become a state that year, and Buffalo Bill did not become a senator.

35

Farewells
1911-1913

The Wild West began its 1911 farewell tour at Washington D. C. on April 17, with an exceptionally good show in which Buffalo Bill was shooting almost as well as ever. At the afternoon performance, fifty balls were thrown into the air as he galloped around the arena, "and not one was missed by the old scout as the applause from thousands of hands and throats followed him."[1] Cody called the opening "splendid," with two immense houses, and said that President Taft would attend the performance the next day.[2]

One successful "farewell" performance followed another until May 24, when a major train wreck near Lowell, Massachusetts, strung the show all over the landscape. Elephants and buffalo stampeded, burros ran wild; Indians, Cossacks, and Arabs hunkered in nearby fields while the cowboys lassoed the livestock. Some of the animals and their keepers were imprisoned in the wrecked cars, several with severe injuries.

Colonel Cody's private car was a part of the wrecked second section, but it was Cody who, with Johnny Baker's help, brought order out of the chaos. Realizing that it would take hours to clear the track and proceed by train, Cody arranged for the immediate care of the injured, then lined up the rest, animals and people, and led them by "foot caravan" down the highway to Lowell, where he opened the afternoon show right on schedule.

The show went on up through New England, across New York, and into Ohio, Indiana, Illinois, and Iowa. A typical advertisement (this one in *The Show World*) insisted upon the Colonel's leave-taking:

"Positively Last Personal Appearance in Chicago. . . . July 15-23," and the magazine later reminded its readers of "the announced farewell appearance of Col. William F. Cody (Buffalo Bill), in the saddle."[3]

Scores of cities observed Buffalo Bill's last visit by presenting him with fancy "loving cups," so many that he was almost crowded out of his private coach. When it was learned in May that the Colonel would also pay a farewell visit, "in the saddle," to North Platte on August 19, the town's enthusiasm knew no limits. One newspaper, disregarding the fact that only a few years ago there had been many Platters who sang a different tune—and probably some who still did—now stated that "this city with its loyalty and never tiring devotion, which has done so much to spur the great old scout on to bigger and better things," was eagerly looking forward to his visit. "In this, his final engagement, Buffalo Bill will bid you goodbye in person; he wants to gather just once more with those old time friends that are left. He wants to shake hands for the last time and tell you . . . that he will soon be with you again—but next time [after 1911] without the trappings of Buffalo Bill, merely as the man, one that is loved the world over, the honorable William F. Cody."[4]

For days the home town papers reviewed in detail the Colonel's life and accomplishments and urged everybody to "get busy" and make the occasion one never to be outdone or forgotten. Again and again Platters were reminded that their town had been the birthplace of the whole Wild West idea, "where the baby of his brain was born."[5] One editor reminded his readers that thousands of visitors would come to North Platte to see the show, so all owners of property, vacant lots included, were urged to clean up all ashes, garbage, and manure from their premises and alleys.

Neither was Buffalo Bill's home town remiss in the matter of a loving cup. It was ordered early and put on display in Dixon's window for more than a week before the show arrived. On July 17 the first Wild West advertising car pulled in to placard the town. Ten days later

the second rolled in and put up more "highly illuminated lithographs."[6] By the time the third car departed, a week before show day, the town had all but disappeared beneath the blizzard of posters and advertising.

Six years ago, during Irma's army-wife days, her father had sent her the money to buy a "horse and tandem." This summer he sent her a new Buick automobile, which "she was driving with the skill of an experienced chauffer" by the time the show arrived three weeks later. Scout's Rest was jammed with family and visitors as show day drew near. Both Mrs. Cody and Cody Boal (who had joined his grandparents as soon as school was out) came home ahead of the show trains. Five weeks ahead of the show's arrival, the Colonel had sent the two young daughters of Louis E. Cooke, his general agent, to North Platte to be Irma's guests at the ranch. The aging Major Burke came in on Friday, the day before the show, as did young Frank Winch. Both visited the ranch and possibly spent the night there.

Winch, "a much sunburned young fellow with snap and ginger in every move," was the general press representative for the Wild West show. He was also the playwright-author who the previous winter had dashed off the book *The Thrilling Lives of Buffalo Bill and Pawnee Bill*. This was the book that ended with the Colonel's moving farewell speech in Madison Square Garden in May 1910, and was published in time to be sold for a dollar a copy at every stand the show made in 1911.

In his huge Model 16 Buick, gaily bannered with the names of the two Bills, Winch had driven more than 21,000 miles since leaving New York on April 2, part of the time through "Iowa gumbo up to the hubs and over," he said. In the performance of this feat he admitted to the use of four tire chains and seventy-five feet of one-inch manila rope on each front wheel. On Friday afternoon he spurted into town and drove through the already-crowded streets to the *Telegraph* office, "attracting as much attention as a circus parade." Within ten minutes he was busy on the forms and makeup of the four-page extra section that came out with the Saturday *Daily Telegraph*—pages replete with pictures and stories of Buffalo Bill and Pawnee Bill; pictures showing Buffalo Bill shooting glass balls from the back of a galloping horse, killing his last buffalo, and fighting the battle of Summit Springs. A half-page spread on the back told the story of Pawnee Bill, his talents and accomplishments, and built him up as the successor to Buffalo Bill and the Wild West when Cody retired.

Without question, the largest crowd ever in North Platte up to that time poured into town on Friday and Saturday, August 18 and 19. Julia Goodman came up from Lincoln for the show, and every town for miles around was emptied of every citizen who was not bedfast. They came by wagons, trains, and automobiles, three hundred of the latter by actual count.

At the tiny town of Maxwell, thirteen miles east, 400 people bought tickets to North Platte on the morning train. Another train, pulling out of Hershey, the same distance to the west, carried 900 people into North Platte that forenoon; every inch of space from the coal car to the rear platform was crammed with humanity. Parents who stood in the packed aisles hoisted their little children to the tops of the seats to keep them from being smothered.[7]

A goodly crowd was on hand in the small hours of the morning to see the two forty-seven-car show trains pull in and unload south of the tracks and about a mile west of present Dewey Street, on land owned by the Codys. At 1:30 that afternoon every business house in town closed its doors, and clerks and proprietors joined the thousands hurrying toward the show grounds on foot and by wagon, carriage, and auto.

Frank Winch says 40,000 people were on the grounds that day. Monday's *Telegraph* said 20,000, with 16,000 paid admissions for the afternoon and many turned away to wait for the evening show. The *Tribune* reported all of the show's 16,000 seats filled and 2,000 seated on the grass between the stands and the roped-off arena. Some said they did not think the Colonel made *any* money in North Platte, the way he gave out passes to the show.

Promptly at 2:00 the Rough Riders of the World were introduced: the Indians, cowboys, cavalrymen, cowgirls, Bedouins, Mexicans, Arabs, Cossacks, and all the other nationalities; when these had taken their places, Buffalo Bill entered the arena, amid thunderous applause, and dashed down the line to take his place at the head of the cavalcade. Amid the deafening cheers, the Old Scout lifted his hat and bowed. Then Mayor Patterson stepped into the arena, and the Colonel's white horse bowed down on one knee as the mayor presented North Platte's $200 loving cup and made an appropriate speech about the love and esteem felt for the Colonel by his "home folks." "With this token of their love will go their prayers for your long life and happiness," the mayor concluded.

Deeply touched, the old showman accepted the cup and thanked North Platte for its testimonial which, he said, "I prize more than gold or silver. It will ever remind me of the deep debt of gratitude I owe to you, my dear friends, and when the time comes that I retire I shall again make my home among the old friends and neighbors I have known so long and love so well." When the Colonel finished speaking, the mayor filled the loving cup with water and Cody drank to the health of all the vast audience.[8]

The rest of the show pulled out that night for points west, but Colonel Cody stayed over Sunday so that he and Mrs. Cody could attend a dinner given in their honor by Mr. and Mrs. J. J. Halligan. He joined the show at Cheyenne the next morning. His family placed four of his loving cups, one of "especially beautiful design and great value," in Dixon's window, then followed him west, joining the show in Denver and traveling with it for a week. While the Wild West made a wide loop through Wyoming, Colorado, and Kansas, Mrs. Cody, the Garlows, and Cody Boal joined it for short visits at various times.

It was on this tour that Cody had his confrontation with "Buffalo Bill" Mathewson. There are, Don Russell says, "several versions, but the most definite is that of Frank Winch, press agent for the Buffalo Bill show."[9] As Russell summarizes Winch's account, which Winch wrote eighteen years after the encounter, William Mathewson of Wichita, Kansas, vociferously claimed to be the *original* Buffalo Bill, a nickname acquired a decade before Cody ever shot buffalo for the railroad. Mathewson wrote Cody an irate letter and announced that when Cody and his show came to Kansas (the end of August), "I aim to tell you to your face that you are using a title that doesn't belong to you." To stave off unfavorable publicity, Winch went to Wichita. "He found that Mathewson was hard up," Russell says, "and had recently sold a cherished rifle, which Winch recovered and presented to 'the original Buffalo Bill' in Cody's name. That broke the ice, and when the show arrived, Winch brought Cody and Mathewson together. The quarrel evaporated, and . . . Cody arranged to take care of Mathewson's needs unknown to the recipient."[10]

A contemporary story finds Colonel Mathewson much less angry and much better off financially, and does not mention any letter from one Colonel to the other. A Wichita newspaperman interviewed Mathewson before Cody brought his show to town; his picture of Mathewson is of a healthy, generous eighty-one-year-old man who "does not and never did worry about the matter in the least, even though he feels that he has been very much imposed on." Mathewson insisted that "the name of Buffalo Bill was tacked onto me before Bill Cody knew the difference between a buffalo and a jack rabbit," but he did not seem to begrudge Cody his fame. Mathewson said: "I don't care what Cody has said or done, for my friends know where and how the name of 'Buffalo Bill' was given to me and if he has been successful in commercializing my reputation, I can only say, 'He is welcome.'" And as for being hard up, the newspaperman reported that Mathewson "can now write a check for close onto a hundred thousand. . . . So it is apparent . . . that it is not through the want of notoriety that the claim [to the title Buffalo Bill] is made."[11]

Throughout 1911 newspapers in the cities where the Wild West showed all carried the same "farewell" speech Cody had given in Madison Square Garden in 1910. Even the paragraph at the head of the speech began the same: "In an interview given today, Col. W. F. Cody (Buffalo Bill) made the following statement as to his desire for retirement after the present tour ends. This visit here will positively be the last time Buffalo Bill will be seen in a local arena." The only difference was in the name of the editor appearing on each announcement. The one in the *Telegraph* was under A. P. Kelly's byline, yet editor Bare quoted Cody: "A great many people have the impression that this is my last season with the show; this is not a fact, as I will remain in the saddle and at the head of the organization until November, 1912. Then my partner, Major Lillie, and John Baker, both men who started with the Wild West in 1883 and who are now with it, will continue the exhibition. Then, my dear friends, I am coming back to the old home to be one of you." This, of course, squared with Cody's 1910 farewell speech when he referred to the exhibitions he would give for "the next two years."

In Kansas City on September 4, several reporters questioned the Colonel as to his plans. According to the Kansas City *Journal* his answer was: "Yes, I'm going to retire all right. I am getting along in years now and some people have got the impression that because I look robust and healthy this 'last tour' business is only a ruse; but they'll see. Buffalo Bill is getting tired of moving from place to place, turning every day into a regular Fourth of July." When asked if it was true that he had given a free show at North Platte, he replied that he had taken in $8,500 there, and that his old friends had been pleased to show their regard for him by paying the regular price, fifty cents, to see his show.

The show did fairly well until it reached the South, where it ran into four weeks of rain and suffered heavy losses. Even the Arizona mines had suffered from weeks of rain and cloudbursts that had washed out roads and bridges, delaying the installation of the new machinery and holding up work on the ore railway. The Colonel was weary and discouraged, and wrote Julia of the sleepless nights he spent worrying over raising money to outfit the mines.[12]

The old showman's retirement seemed a fact, however, when he played the closing engagement in Richmond, Virginia, on November 1. The next day newspapers across America made it official. "COLONEL CODY RETIRES. Col. W. F. Cody, 'Buffalo Bill' to all the world, retired from public life tonight."

But for Buffalo Bill there was to be no retirement yet. When he and Major Lillie totaled up the year's business, the profits came to only $200,000. It was not enough. Cody's share would not pay his debts and support his many enterprises. His mines were not showing enough profit that he could afford to take a chance on quitting the show. Also, Pawnee Bill, who realized the tremendous drawing power of "Buffalo Bill," both the name and the man, insisted that he make the circuit one more year. Cody agreed, but was upset when he learned they would be showing in some of the bigger cities where he had made *positively* his "last appearance" the year before.

However, he put the best possible face on the matter, and the New York *Sun,* under the headline CODY'S SECOND FAREWELL reported on December 19 that the Colonel would make another farewell tour next year because "I got to say farewell all over the country. When I showed in New York last fall it *was* positively my last appearance in New York. But I haven't said farewell in Brooklyn and a lot of other cities. And now I'm going out to my ranch at North Platte and see my wife and daughter and grandchildren."[13]

By this time Mr. and Mrs. Cody were great-grandparents, for their granddaughter, Clara Benn, had had a baby son in September. In January 1912, Fred and Irma had their third and last child, William Joseph.

During the week he spent in North Platte at the close of 1911, the Colonel gave a buffalo dinner at Scout's Rest for his closest friends, the buffalo being a gift from Major Lillie, who kept a herd at his Oklahoma ranch. The guests were transported to and from the ranch in a large bobsled, drawn by teams of fine horses raised on the place. The next day Cody hurried back to New York to negotiate for more new machinery for his mines. This was the second time Cody had paid for ruinously expensive machinery for the mines. The first had not been the right type and could not be used. On his way west again, Mrs. Cody and Cody Boal joined him at North Platte and accompanied him on to

Arizona, where they stayed until April 1912.

Walsh writes· that the mines, like the Wyoming irrigation project of earlier years, were not properly managed; Johnny Baker, after a visit to one of them, reported he had found only four men working although there were thirty-six names on the payroll.[14] On the advice of his "experts," Cody had laid out wagon roads and then built railroads, had installed a water system, and had bought more and more machinery—for always the million-dollar payload was there, just beyond their reach. Estimates of the fortune he spent on the Oracle vary from $300,000 to $500,000. Whatever it was, it was enough to break him.

William Sweeney and his Wild West cowboy band, 1912.

The Wild West did not do so well in the season of 1912. Audiences were smaller, and the profits dropped to a mere $125,000. That fall the Colonel had 116 acres of the first land he had ever owned at North Platte—the tract on which he had built the first Welcome Wigwam and where he had set up the Wild West show the year before—platted into town lots and acre tracts. The streets in the new addition were named after the old officers under whom he had once served: Sherman, Sheridan, Miles, Carr, Custer, Emory, Hayes, and Mills. The project was in charge of Fred Garlow and young Charley Temple, the handsome son of Mrs. John Boyer, Cody's chief witness in the divorce trial.

The Colonel himself was in Arizona when the land went on sale, and the sixty-seven lots sold on the opening day brought a telegram of congratulations from the former owner. But at $75-$150 a lot, with terms of $10 down and $5 per month, or a ten percent discount for cash in full, the lots, even had all of them sold that winter, would not have made much of a dent in Cody's debts.

To help out, Mrs. Cody that fall sold the big town house, which had stood empty since her removal to the ranch three years earlier. The purchaser was Mrs. Harriet Welch, widow of a pioneer ranchman, Samuel Welch; she had long admired the great English-style house with its front and back parlors, and floors inlaid with maple, oak, and walnut. The sale price was $10,000.[15]

During the three years he had been with Lillie, Cody had annually used his share of the show's profits to reduce his debts and finance his mines, while Lillie paid the costs of keeping the aggregation in winter quarters. Each spring Lillie collected his partner's share of the winter costs from the company's first earnings. After the bad season of 1912, Lillie did not feel able, or disposed, to continue the arrangement and asked Cody to raise his share, $20,000, before the show went on the road in 1913.

Cody was seeking a loan of that amount when he went to Denver in November 1912, to visit his sister, May Decker. While there, he met Harry Tammen, co-owner with F. G. Bonfils of the Denver *Post*. When Tammen learned of the Colonel's need, he promptly loaned him the $20,000 for six months. With the money in hand, Cody left for New York, where he visited with a reporter from the New York *Clipper*.

The Colonel sounded cheerful, even enthusiastic, as he described his plans for the coming year. "I will not be in the saddle," he said, "but I will be with the show and appear at every performance. It will be my pleasure to meet my friends and introduce Major Gordon Lillie as my successor." Once more, he said, there would be street parades (a practice discontinued some years earlier), and he would receive officials, reporters, and his friends in a special office tent beside the main entrance. He would no longer make his entrance to the arena on horseback, as he had done for twenty-nine years, but would ride in behind a pair of spanking bays in a fancy phaeton with driver and footman in full livery. Also, he told the reporter, "It may interest you to know that I will participate in the inaugural parade next March, representing the states of Nebraska, Wyoming and Arizona. I have taken part in many inaugurals, but I am looking forward to this as being one of the most pleasurable in my career in this and other lands. With me will be Indian chiefs from Nebraska, Indians, cowboys and ranchmen from Wyoming and miners from Arizona."[16]

Mr. and Mrs. Cody spent Christmas of 1912 in Arizona. On their return to North Platte in late January, they stopped in Denver, where
another honor was accorded the Colonel. Denver was making plans to
hold a summer-long pageant, called the Last Grand Council of Indians,
in 1915. Three hundred representative men of Colorado held a meeting
at the Brown Palace Hotel, Denver's finest, to urge Colonel Cody to
take charge of the pageant, and that evening he held his audience spellbound as he described the history of the West as he had known and
lived it. When he had done, a man said, "One had the sensation of having finished a university course in American history."

The Last Grand Council of Indians was to be a vast living panorama
of the Indians of the United States, coming together in a historical
assembly to celebrate the opening of the Panama Canal. In the pageant
he envisioned, Cody intended to bring to Denver members of every
Indian tribe, and as many as possible of the old generals of the Indian
wars still above the sod. He also reminded his audience that "an idea
without a dollar was like a soul without a body," and one million dollars
was subscribed to the council fund that night.[17] Colonel Cody, ever
optimistic, could not then foresee that he would not be both wealthy
and retired by 1915, able to devote his time and money to the Last
Great Council.

Back in North Platte Cody was still hopeful that his mines would
soon be "heavy producers."[18] But with his Eldorado still in the future
and the mines at the moment barely paying expenses, he had to find
some immediately usable cash. In February 1913 he left for Canada to
attempt to sell mining stock to some of his relatives there. The relatives
were interested, and in June he reported to Julia that they had organized a syndicate and sent an engineer to Oracle "To Expert" the mines.
The engineer's report had been "excellent," he wrote, "And the Cana-
dians will finance and take over the properties if we can come to terms.
I'll sure come to terms."[19] Nothing more is heard of help from the
relatives.

On his return from Canada, the Colonel learned that he was about
to become a part of the Sells-Floto circus. Whatever the wording of the
agreement he had signed when he borrowed the $20,000 from Tammen,
he probably did not dream he was agreeing to some sort of an alliance
with Tammen and Bonfil's Sells-Floto show; but Tammen, apparently a devious crook of the first order, had tied him up hard and fast.
The *Telegraph* announced that Colonel W. F. Cody had, at the office
of the Denver *Post*, signed a contract to appear in conjunction with

Sells-Floto during the season of 1914 and thereafter. It would seem that his name was the price he paid for the $20,000 loan, for he had nothing else with which to pay it.

Russell says Cody was so badly in need of money at the close of the 1911 season that he sold his Scout's Rest Ranch to Lillie for $100,000. Of this, $80,000 went to Mrs. Cody and $20,000 toward his $30,000 debt to Lillie, the remainder of that obligation being covered by a $10,000 mortgage on the Irma Hotel; this deal had made the Colonel a half owner in the show again.[20] The sale of the ranch must have been known only to the Codys and Major Lillie, for North Platte knew nothing of it until February 1913, when the *Telegraph* announced it in a few stark lines:

COLONEL CODY WILL SELL RANCH

The following dispatch was sent out from Omaha to the eastern papers yesterday: The State of Nebraska learned with regret today that Colonel W. F. Cody intended selling his famous old ranch, "Scout's Rest," located near North Platte and containing three thousand acres. Scout's Rest is the place Buffalo Bill has called home since the early days of Indian fighting. For years it has been the main point of interest in the state for all travelers. Princes, Russian dukes, English lords and noted globe trotters have been entertained there. The value of the ranch is estimated at $100,000.[21]

An April 10 item listed a James M. Hamilton of Chester, Pennsylvania, as the purchaser, and stated, "the deal was closed this week . . . and the consideration was $100,000." No doubt the news of the sale had to come out when Lillie sold an interest in the ranch to the mysterious Mr. Hamilton. A Mr. E. Botsford moved in as manager of the ranch as the Garlows moved out, leaving that same month for Wyoming to take over management of The Irma and Cody's other interests there.

In June 1913, the Wild West's advertising car No. 1 went through North Platte on its way to Denver to bill the circus there. Before another month should pass, the two Bills would heartily wish that neither car No. 1 nor any other part of the show had gone anywhere near Denver.

36

Where the
Wild West Ends
1913-1914

Colonel Cody kept his promise, made the fall before, and at his opening performance in Convention Hall in Philadelphia made his arena entrance seated in a trap behind a team of high-lifed horses. It was the first time in thirty years that he had not gone before his public in buckskins, mounted on his favorite horse. From now on he would shoot no more glass balls from the back of a racing pony, and he told his audience, "I feel bad about this, but I decided to dismount before Father Time bucked me out of the saddle."[1]

A featured member of the Wild West that season was Goldie Griffith. Goldie joined the show in New York, as the leader of the cowgirl contingent. Years later an old-timer said of her, "She was a heller in skirts, half man, but all woman, and pretty, and she could ride better than half the men in Nebraska."[2]

As Buffalo Bill had announced the fall before, the Wild West was putting on street parades again, but when the aggregation prepared to parade down Fifth Avenue, as it had done in former years, the city fathers opted against it—too many automobiles using the great thoroughfare now. So, on opening day, Colonel Cody and all his mounted show people—cowboys, cowgirls, soldiers, Indians, and Congress of Rough Riders of all nations—pranced their steeds down the avenue, and there was not a thing the officials could do about it, for there was no law against "sight-seeing" and no ordinance against doing it on horseback. That was also the day Goldie rode her horse all the way up the steps of Grant's Tomb, to the wild cheers of a gathered crowd.

Goldie not only rode top bucking horses but took part in some of the

wildest acts in the show. In the thick of the action in one scene, someone fired a blank in her pony's ear; he belted across the Garden
toward the Fourth Avenue exit, sending Goldie crashing, spurs over
curls, into the front-row boxes. To the audience it looked like the end
for the pretty cowgirl. She was carried off to Bellevue Hospital and
patched up; two days later she was back in the arena and in the saddle,
where she said her marriage vows with Harry Walters, a handsome
Wild West cowboy.

In a show such as the Wild West, involving hundreds of people and
horses and a great deal of noise and fast action, accidents were frequent, and it was a miracle more of them were not fatal. On another
occasion, it was Goldie again who was badly injured. It would not have
happened, she said, if she had stayed on top of a horse, but she let
herself be talked into riding the Deadwood stagecoach in the popular
holdup scene; she, of course, rode up front with the driver. When, in
the mad escape from the Indians, the front wheels hit a rut, the coach
upset, strewing passengers all over the arena. Several went to the hospital, with Goldie in the worst shape of all. It was said that Colonel
Cody cried when told of her condition, but she came back to ride with
the show until its final performance.

Annie Oakley, during her years with the show, had spent her spare
time embroidering. One of her pieces of handiwork was a large square
pillow top. She had had forty of her friends write their names on the
silk, which she had then embroidered in dainty colored stitches. (This
pillow, donated to Scout's Rest by R. Langford, is on display there.)

Among the wedding gifts Goldie and Harry received was a Sears,
Roebuck sewing machine. In *her* spare time Goldie whipped up things
for everybody in the show, even shirts for the cowboys.

All of the show people, especially the Indians, liked Colonel Cody,
Goldie said, for he never "bawled anybody out," nor would he allow
anybody else to do so. In fact, she said, the old Colonel worried and
fussed over his show people like a mother hen. When the weather was
cold and wet he had his striker, an Indian named Carlos Miles, mix hot
toddies in the big silver punch bowl Queen Victoria had given him.
All who came to his tent on such days were given a cupful to keep them
from taking cold. The toddies were very good, Goldie remembered,
and she and some of her friends used to wish it would rain more often.[3]

It rained too often for the good of the show that season as it headed
south; cold and freezing drizzles reduced attendance, and high winds
blew the canvas down. In Knoxville, the Colonel was ill and missed

several shows. The price of cotton had gone down, too, and the South was too poor to support the show. It lost money at stand after stand.

While the Colonel was ill in Knoxville, an incident of interest to North Platters took place in Bristol, Tennessee. The show's doctor was called to examine the sprained hand of a teamster. As soon as he looked at the injured member, the doctor knew it did not belong to a man. The secret then came out. The teamster was attractive twenty-year-old May Shaffer, a ranch girl from near North Platte. Her sweetheart, Leonard Sasseen, was a leading cowboy with the show, so Miss Shaffer had applied for a place in the cowgirl troupe. When told the show didn't need a cowgirl but could use a teamster, she and her lover had worked out a disguise so perfect that she had been driving an eight-horse team for ten days before the accident to her hand. The doctor called Pawnee Bill and explained matters. The good-natured showman then gave her the cowgirl job she wanted, and that day she rode beside her beau in the arena, to the great delight of all the show people.

The Wild West headed north again and by July 1 was in Chicago, where the United States Printing and Lithograph Company had its home office. Although this company held a $16,000 note against Cody and Lillie for 1912 printing of posters and advertising, the management, due to its high regard for Colonel Cody, had contracted in December to furnish another $50,000 in advertising for the 1913 season. By July 1 the company had furnished printing to the value of $40,000, while still holding the $16,000 note for 1912.

Adolph Marks, general counsel for the lithograph company, called on Lillie to remind him that nothing had been paid on the account and to inform him that his company was prepared to attach the show for the debt. Lillie, Marks said, agreed to send $10,000 on account if they would let the show run for two more weeks. "We felt friendly to Colonel Cody," Marks said later, "and didn't want to embarrass him."4

W. F. Cody in his spider phaeton, Wild West arena, Julesburg, Colorado, 1913.

So the show continued on its way, pulling into Denver to keep its July 21 booking there. While the whole season of 1913 had been a series of mistakes and disasters for the Wild West, its biggest mistake was in going to Denver at all—and its greatest disaster befell it there.

When the show trains passed through North Platte on July 19, Bill Sweeney invited his sister, Mrs. John Baker, and her daughters, Jessie and Helen, to come up to Denver on the twenty-first. "I'm afraid the show is about done for," he said, "and if you want to see it one more time you had better come up." The ladies accepted the invitation, and when Buffalo Bill saw them coming across the show lot, he hurried out to meet them. "Just you wait here," he told them, "and I'll go find Willie for you." Sweeney saw them seated in the tent for the evening performance, told them to come to Cody's private car after the show, then hurried to take his place at the head of the cowboy band.

The blow fell at the close of the performance. Walsh says the Colonel saw the sheriff and his men come onto the lot and, guessing why they came, sent one of his men sprinting for the treasury wagon to save the day's receipts. The sheriff got there first.[5]

As the crowd left the tent, Sweeney, unaware of what was taking place out front, escorted his sister and nieces to Cody's car. The Colonel had just arrived, all broken up over the loss of the day's take because it meant he could not pay his show people or even buy food for them and the animals. By the next day they all knew the full extent of the disaster. The show people's trunks had been attached, too, along with everything else; they had left only the clothes they were wearing.

Lillie could have saved the show by dipping into his private funds. This he refused to do because he knew Cody, under the terms of his contract with Tammen, would be with Sells-Floto the next year anyway. Instead, Lillie immediately fled to New Jersey, where the show was incorporated, to file a petition in bankruptcy. There, before he could accomplish his own filing, he was served with an involuntary petition in bankruptcy against the Buffalo Bill Wild West and Pawnee Bill Far East.[6]

According to Adolph Marks, who exonerated Colonel Cody from any blame in the affair and bitterly denounced the stand taken by Major Lillie, the Colonel's hands were tied because he had deeded his only negotiable property, the North Platte ranch, valued at $100,000, and the Irma Hotel, worth $75,000, to Major Lillie. Cody was willing to transfer these securities to the lithograph company, but Lillie absolutely refused to make any such settlement. Since leaving Chicago, the attorney said, the show had taken in at least $30,000, yet Lillie had not paid the $10,000 he had promised, nor any other sum to settle the huge printing debt.

In Denver, where Marks had again called on the partners, Lillie had admitted his default and asked for another day's delay, which had been refused. Marks had then offered to defer collection of the whole account for two years if Lillie would transfer the mortgages on the Cody real estate to his company. "But Lillie holds Cody's estate and Lillie seems to mean to keep it," the attorney said.[7]

Even so, the partners had not looked for the axe to fall quite so soon, and the foreclosure had caught them totally unprepared. This is where Tammen came in. No doubt the Denver *Post* owners had not counted on the summer of such high losses, but when it turned out that way, Tammen had seen his chance to put Pawnee Bill's show out of competition with his own and had joined forces with the lithographers to send the sheriff in without warning to serve an attachment on everything in sight. Tammen now owned Buffalo Bill *and* his title to the Wild West show.

Cody's first and greatest concern was for his people and animals, left penniless and shelterless by Tammen's action. What little cash he could command he used to help them, and when a sympathetic friend sent him $500 he also spent that on them. Goldie said a place was found in a stable in Overland Park for the horses, then most of the show people soon had to move in with them and sleep in the hay, wash out their clothes at night, and wear them again the next day.

This day-to-day existence went on for some time, since few of the stranded had money for transportation home, and Cody could help them but little, though he investigated every possible source to raise the necessary cash. The members themselves took jobs wherever they could to earn "eating money" or fare home. Goldie wrestled a male partner at the Denver Auditorium and contributed her share of the proceeds to the community kitty, helping keep the wolf from the stable door.

Some of the Indians, it was said, had to sell their show costumes to get back to their reservations, although Adolph Marks claimed he had arranged to send them home. In either case, their return was complicated, so Goldie said, by their habit of raiding city dumps, where they picked up old pans, tinware, and other treasures, all of which they insisted on taking with them.

When it was known that all of the show's belongings—tents, seats,

animals, wagons, the Deadwood coach, the Colonel's phaeton, everything—would go under the auctioneer's hammer on September 15, the
troupers began drifting away, taking other jobs, or going home. Some
earned their fare home, others had relatives who could help them, but
one group had to do it the hard way. This was a company of Boy Scouts
who had been traveling with the show since it left Chicago. Broke,
they headed for home on foot, giving exhibition drills in the towns
through which they tramped and taking up collections to buy food.

During the third week in August, the troup stayed all night in North
Platte, put on their drill, then headed for Chicago. Days later the
"Buffalo Bill Boy Scouts" made Omaha, footsore, haggard, and worn
(for August is a hot month in Nebraska) but still doggedly determined
to reach home base. The following week the Omaha *Bee* reported a
communication from Boy Scout national headquarters advising the
public that the Buffalo Bill show refugees walking to Chicago were
not Boy Scouts at all. "What of it?" the *Bee* wanted to know. "What is
the difference between a Boy Scout and a scouting boy when it comes
to such straits?" Near the end of October, North Platte's Mayor Evans
received the following telegram: "We, the Buffalo Bill Boy Scouts, arrived in Chicago October 14 on our walk from Denver to this city. We
wish to express our appreciation for kindness shown us while in North
Platte." (Chicago newspapers did not cover the scouts' arrival.)

As for Cody himself, although his show was gone, along with his
North Platte ranch and the Irma Hotel, he was "not down and out."
At sixty-eight years of age and deeply in debt, he was already making
plans to start over. In a letter to an old friend, Tom Foley, he wrote:
"I am not down and out. . . . Although I regret the scandal and publicity . . . I will soon be on the road with a new and better show, under
new management with unlimited capital. While the new show is being
organized I am going to Cody . . . to see for the first time in the summer that empire in bloom."[8]

With Louisa, who had remained in Denver, standing by him through
the whole trying ordeal, the Colonel did go to the TE in early August.
He was back in Denver, however, on the day of the public auction of
the possessions of the Two Bills Wild West show. A good friend,
Colonel Bills of Lincoln, Nebraska, tells the touching story of that heart-
breaking affair:

> I met my old friend, Colonel Cody, in Denver a short time before the
> sale of his effects. He seemed rather downhearted and I suggested

an automobile ride to the sale. The Colonel replied that he didn't care to go. I further questioned him and he said he could see everything else in the show sold but he couldn't bear to see Isham, the faithful horse that had carried him for over twenty years, sold to strangers.

His eyes glistened with tears as he spoke and I did not urge him further to go with me. I met him again, soon after the sale, and he asked, "Has Isham been sold?" I told him he had and he wanted to know the buyer's name, and said he hoped he would treat the old horse kindly. So I told him I was sure Isham would be treated with kindness by none other than his master of twenty odd years. When the Colonel realized that I was the purchaser and that I was giving Isham to him, he broke down and tears fell from his cheeks. His simple words of thanks were worth more to me than the trouble it took to buy the horse for his old master.[9]

The trouble Bills referred to came about because Carlos Miles, the Colonel's old striker, was bidding against him for the horse. Carlos had sold his saddle and other personal effects so he could bid the horse in and give him to Cody. Neither man had known the other's purpose, and when Carlos had to stop at $150, all he had, he is said to have muttered, "If the man who bought that horse don't give him back to Colonel Cody, I'll steal him tonight and take him back myself."

Cody was not to spend much time on his ranch after all, for many who saw a chance to make money on his name and fame were soon camping on his TE doorstep. Vaudeville managers made him offers. He refused them all, including one from London at $2,500 a week; he replied that $5,000 was his price. Then Tammen wrote to offer him a part in a moving picture.

This new entertainment was becoming popular across the nation and was one of the reasons why attendance at tent shows was falling off more each year. Perhaps movies was the medium *he* should take up, Cody thought, and immediately envisioned a series of great historical films, showing on celluloid what he had attempted to show with his Wild West acts. He could re-enact the Indian battles he had known: the fight with Yellow Hair, the battle of Summit Springs, the Wounded Knee affair.

Whether his optimistic statement, issued only a week after his Wild West was closed, that he would soon be on the road with a new show and unlimited capital was merely whistling in the dark or whether he was already planning to make and show motion pictures, is an un-answered question. At any rate, the *Telegraph,* ever his staunch sup-porter, was announcing three weeks later that Cody had not "ridden his last roundup" nor done any of the other *final* things credited to him by eastern newspapers. Instead, he was to appear in an entirely new role the next year and would be traveling with Sells-Floto, personally con-ducting a historical pageant of early Wild West scenes that would appeal to children and all lovers of fairy tale lore.[10]

Or perhaps Tammen and Bonfils were the source of the "unlimited capital" he spoke of. At any rate, they approved his plan for the his-torical films, and the Secretary of War consented to the use of army troops in the pictures. General Miles, retired, was happy to take part, and the Secretary of the Interior agreed to the use of Pine Ridge Indians. The Essanay Film Company of Chicago was to do the filming for the "Colonel W. F. Cody (Buffalo Bill) Historical Picture Com-pany."

Broadcast by the newspapers as "the greatest film ever made, a last-ing pictorial history of these early campaigns to hand down to pos-terity," the shooting got under way in Wyoming. Old-time cowboys and the same Indians who fought the palefaces played their parts in the streets of Cody in the last days of September 1913. Johnny Baker, "a pillar of strength to 'The Old Man,'" was on hand as director; with Ted Wharton, noted producer, to side him, the new company was prepared "to combine education with its mission in fact and realism."[11]

The goal of "fact and realism" becomes somewhat suspect in the light of the description of the first "great drama" filmed at Cody. The scene was laid in front of the cabins on East Sheridan Avenue that in the days of the town's youth were occupied as a hotel, a saloon, and a post office. Ted Wharton of Essanay directed activities, and Cody, George Beck, Sheriff Dahlman, and others were the actors. Signs were placed on the buildings as they appeared in the early days: Hotel de Dego; Salune, Last Chance, Tom Purcell, prop; and Cody Trading Co. and Post Office. A number of men were loafing in front of the saloon when a cowboy and a cowgirl rode up and were warmly welcomed by Mrs. J. M. Schwoob, landlady of the hotel. Just then Colonel Cody and George Beck drove up in a buggy and alighted, carrying surveying in-struments. As the two men approached the saloon, the bartender pitched a man into the street. As he rose he pulled a gun. Colonel Cody grabbed his arm, the gun discharged, and Sheriff Dahlman rushed in and placed the man under arrest. Carlos Miles acted the part of the gunman and all characters performed their parts like born actors.[12]

The scene here enacted seems patterned after nickelodeon "westerns" already showing in almost every town in America, and was filmed during the Park County fair, then going on at Cody. Adding a fillip to the whole affair was the presence of Prince Albert the First of Monaco, who had come to Wyoming to visit Cody and, if possible, shoot an American bear. At Cody's request, Prince Albert formally opened the fair; the shooting of the big movie scene on "old Sheridan street" followed, after which Buffalo Bill and Fred Garlow conducted the prince and his party to Torrent Creek for the big hunt. Fred Garlow bagged a large elk, as did the prince, who also got his bear. "The big brown bear I shot has been skinned and the hide will adorn one of my rooms at Monte Carlo," said the prince to reporters upon his return from the Big Horns. "It took only one shot and the rifle I used belonged to Colonel William F. Cody. We had a grand time in Wyoming. . . . I like the personalities in the West. Men are real out there. I like Colonel Cody more than I can say." The prince also liked Wyoming and Nebraska. He announced that he hoped to return the following year for another hunt, and returning east "in his private car" he "stopped off in Broken Bow" in order to file application for a homestead somewhere on the third of a million acres of public land in central Nebraska which opened for settlement in October 1913.[13]

From the Prince Albert hunt Cody went on to Rushville, Nebraska, where the equipment and people for the re-enactment of the battle of Wounded Knee were assembled. The Chicago & North Western railroad had hauled several carloads of materials, including fifty cameramen and their apparatus, into the town, while Cody and Colonel McCune, his old Wild West show manager of Indians, were busy engaging the necessary Indians and securing government consent for their participation in the play battle. Among the soldiers and officers taking part: Col. Marion P. Maus and Generals Frank D. Baldwin, Charles A. King, Jesse M. Lee, and Nelson A. Miles. Several of the original Indian chiefs, including Short Bull, No Neck, and Woman's Dress, were also there.

Louisa, who went to Pine Ridge with her husband, describes the gathering at Wounded Knee. "Over the hills they came, in wagons, on horseback; . . . from the far stretches of the Bad Lands . . . the old Indians who once had fought against Buffalo Bill. . . . By the hundreds they gathered, each to come forward at sight of the tall, straight man whose long hair now had turned from black to white, to take his hand and exclaim: 'How kola! Waste Pahaska!'" Hello, Good Pahaska.[14] Cooper writes that they camped that night in the cold moonlight and sang their wailing death songs. Tepees were set up exactly where they had been on the day of flaming carnage almost twenty-five years earlier; it was difficult for the old warriors, and the young ones, too, to listen to the death songs as they looked up the hill to the long grave where the frozen bodies of 156 men, women, and children of their tribe had been flung that December day, and not think thoughts of revenge.

The old Indians know the futility of such thoughts, but not so the young ones. All the rifles used in the re-enactment of the battle were to be loaded with blanks; but suppose, said the young men, they loaded theirs with live ammunition. During those first few seconds of gun play, their grandfathers would be gloriously avenged. But word of the plot got to the old chiefs, and by the time the sham battle was fought, all the ammunition used was sham, too.

The Indians had been alarmed at first, when the Hotchkiss guns were set up and the battle arrangements laid out, fearing they, like their forefathers, were to be massacred right there. But when a merry-go-round was set up they forgot their fears, straddled the horses, and rode as earnestly as if they were on fleet ponies.

Cody had declared that all the scenes were to be absolutely true to life, and General Miles was even more insistent. To please him, everything had to be moved into the Bad Lands, miles away, in order to play out some acts exactly where they had originally occurred. Also, because he had had 11,000 troops in the field years ago, he ordered the cavalrymen on hand (some say 300, others 600) marched past the cameras until 11,000 had passed the lens. After the first few repeats, the cameramen, to save film, surreptitiously closed the lens, although the troops continued to march.

No particular parts were given out for the pictures; the participants were simply told to re-enact the parts they had played in the original battles. Three great campaigns were filmed in the jerky flicks of the period: the battle of Summit Springs; the Custer fiasco, terminating in the shooting of Yellow Hair at Hat Creek; and Wounded Knee. People from fifty miles around came to watch the filming, and frequent reports were sent back to the North Platte papers for the information of the home folks, who were quite excited about it all. The filming in South Dakota was finished in time for the Colonel to make a quick trip to New York, probably in connection with his new moving picture business. From his room at the Waldorf Astoria, he sent Julia, now back in Cody, ten shares of his mining stock, assuring her it would be "worth par value some day."[15]

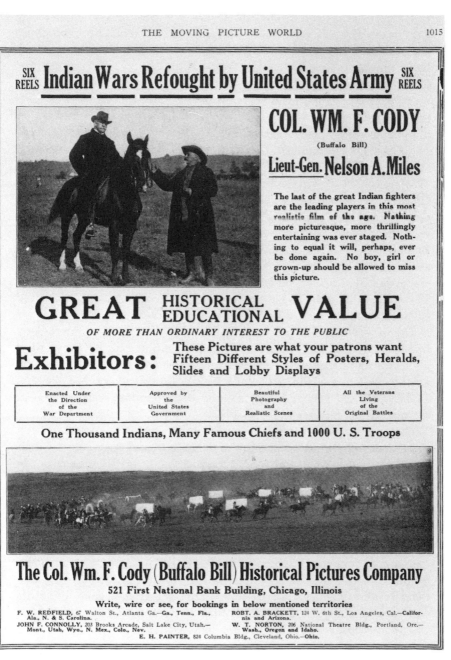
Trade journal ad from November 21, 1914 issue. *Courtesy Library of Congress.*

When his grandparents and the Garlows moved to Wyoming, Cody Boal moved into the John Baker home so he could finish his high school education with his best friend, Johnny Baker. The Colonel, on his way back from New York, picked Cody up and took him on to Wyoming for Christmas with the family. The Garlows, as enthused as Colonel Cody over the epic of "The Indian Wars," subleased the Irma Hotel to an eastern man and moved to Omaha, where Fred was to handle the promotion of the films. The Colonel himself went to Washington, where, on February 27, 1914, he premiered "The Indian Wars" for members of President Wilson's cabinet and the Congress at the New Home Club.[16] From Washington, Cody made a brief tour with his pitcures, showing them in Chicago, in the American Theater in Omaha, and then in Denver.[17]

By April, Cody was in California, fulfilling his contract with Tammen by appearing in the show now billed as the Sells-Floto Circus and Buffalo Bill's Wild West Show—Two Big Institutions Joined Together at One Price of Admission. The admission price was a quarter; Cody's wage was $100 a day, plus forty percent of the receipts over $3,000. This year, although he led the parades in his buggy, the tired old Colonel was required to introduce the show from the saddle.

The show was in Santa Cruz on April 18, the day the horse herd Cody had spent years in building up to one of the finest in the West went under the hammer in the North Platte stock yards. The show toured on up the coast to Canada, and while it was showing there, May 13 and 14, Fred Garlow was running the eight reels of Indian war pictures in the new Keith Theater in North Platte.

The circus closed in Texas in mid-October, and Cody went directly to Denver, where his sister May and her husband took him to their home. He had been ill throughout the last weeks of the season, partly because of worry over his ever-pressing debts. A few days of rest put him on his feet again, but while he was sick Tammen called on him and persuaded him to sign a new contract.

The Colonel had not been happy with his niggardly share of the profits of the 1914 season, and when he was himself again he was appalled to find that his new contract gave him an even smaller cut. Seething with anger and disappointment, he went up to the TE and there killed a big buck deer by moonlight, a feat that gave his spirits a lift and convinced the invincible old marksman that he was a long way from being a has-been.

37

Pahaska, Farewell 1915-1917

On his sixty-ninth birthday, Colonel Cody was entertained by the Cody Club of Cody, Wyoming. Sixty-nine guests were invited to the banquet given in his honor at the Irma Hotel. After drinking the toast proposed to him, the Old Scout, standing erect and clear-eyed, gave a long and moving speech of appreciation.

He seemed rested and fit when the nightmare show season of 1915 began in Texas on April 13. By the end of May they had had only four sunny days, but his wife was with him and enjoying the tour. In a letter to Julia, written on Louisa's seventy-second birthday, May 27, Cody still insisted that in spite of the show's bad luck, he was feeling better than he had in years. The admission price was shortly to be raised to fifty cents, he said, and he would then begin to make more money, and the weather was bound to get better, too.[1]

That the Sells-Floto show was really a circus, a long step down from the Wild West exhibition Colonel Cody and Major Burke had so long managed with dignity and aplomb, is shown by the publicity that attended the show's coming to North Platte that June. On the tenth, the *Telegraph* announced that "the most modest man in the world came to town today. Proof? None is needed. He admits it himself." Several paragraphs of near ridicule extolled the "the greatest show ever put together." This modest fellow, Al Butler, special agent for Sells-Floto, seems the sort of man who would go blithely along with Tammen's dishonest conduct of the business.

But for Cody, their old friend, the Platters' affection and respect was undiminished. As the circus rolled into town on Sunday afternoon, the up-and-coming young Charley Temple, now secretary of the Chamber of Commerce, and other friends whisked the Colonel out through the Cody Addition, where most of the lots had already been sold and new houses were springing up all over the landscape. Charley then entertained his guest and a dozen of his pioneer friends at a dinner at his home, and from there he was carried off to the Elks Club for a smoker attended by more than a hundred Elks. Ira Bare, his long-time *Tribune* friend, was there; and Major Walker, of the old Fifth Cavalry; and many other old-timers. The reminiscing lasted far into the night. The Colonel was shown a handsome gold medal, emblazoned with his own likeness, which each member was wearing to the national Elks convention in Los Angeles in July.

The next morning the town turned out, full force, to watch their old neighbor lead the parade (two miles long, so the posters said) down Dewey Street, doffing his big hat, smiling, and bowing right and left from his prancing horse. Every seat in the big tent was filled that afternoon. As in times past, Colonel Cody paid his old home town sincere compliments in the address he made from the saddle, and was soundly cheered in return.

The next issue of the *Tribune* carried a half-column tribute to Cody, written by John E. Evans, register of the U.S. land office in North Platte. Evans had listened carefully to the review of history that had passed before him in the reminiscences of the old scouts and plainsmen at the Elks' smoker. From their conversation he had written his review of Cody's life on the plains and through the glittering years on the stage and with the Wild West show. Western Nebraska, he concluded, owed Cody much. He had played a leading part in developing the Platte Valley and had pioneered the opening of the Big Horn Basin. "From eastern Kansas, through Nebraska, Colorado, and now in the heart of Wyoming, Colonel Cody has blazed a trail and builded monuments that will stand as testimonials of his sagacity, his energy, his liberality and his honesty."[2]

From Kansas City, a few days later, came a letter written to Ira Bare on July 4: "My first duty on this national day," Cody wrote, will be to thank my old friends of North Platte for the kind hearted reception given me by the men and women I have always loved and respected." He added that the Evans write-up was being published in all the metropolitan papers; he wanted the "world to know that old friends are the best."

In late August, the Colonel wrote Julia a despairing letter: "Everything I attempt to do goes wrong." Tammen had assured Cody, after the sheriff's sale in Denver, that his $20,000 debt was paid in full. But Tammen later wrote Cody that "Lawyers and thieves had gotten away with all the [sale] money" and he still owed the $20,000.

"I have two buyers [for my tungsten mine] and Tungstun is five times higher than it ever was," Cody continued to wail to Julia, "but I am so unlucky nothing comes my way. . . . I expect to pull off a big hunt this fall but I am in such bad luck that might fall down—

"I am very tired and nervous and discouraged. . . . Such things won't let me get well."[3]

Then the honest old Colonel found that the circus was doubling its admission price by the dubious method of advertising a twenty-five-cent show and then holding.up its patrons for the extra quarter *after* they were on the grounds. Cody threatened to quit.

The big show tent was old and its ropes rotten. Cody worried about that, too, genuinely afraid it would go down in a storm and kill scores of women and children. His threat to leave the show brought Tammen to see him in Lawrence, Kansas, where the unscrupulous Denver man told Cody he would sue him for $100,000 if he broke his contract. Cody stayed, but he was bitter about it. The show closed the season in Texas, after 366 performances given in 183 days over a route of 16,878 miles. "And with Gods help I haven't missed a performance," Cody wrote. But he had to cut out the Wyoming hunt. Although business had been good for many weeks and he figured the show owed him $18,000 for his cut of the profits, he was unable to collect. But at last he was rid of Tammen, and he and Louisa could go home.

It is interesting that Courtney Ryley Cooper was the Sells-Floto press agent that season. Did he visit Louisa in the Cody tent those summer days and take the notes and reminiscences that, four years later, were published as *Memories of Buffalo Bill?* If so, it seems that with Buffalo Bill there, too, he would have checked the accuracy of many of the statements he made in that work and attributed to Mrs. Cody.[4]

In spite of wide publicity, the western moving pictures failed to garner the big profits originally anticipated, and the Garlows had given up the movie business, along with their Omaha residence, and returned to The Irma. Here Will and Louisa came for a rest at the end of the 1915 season, but the Colonel had no sooner greeted his family and friends than he set to work on new plans to raise the funds he needed so badly.

Louisa Cody, daughter Irma Garlow, granddaughter Jane, 1916.

Fred and Irma Garlow and children, Jane, Freddie, and William.

With Fred Garlow he began turning the TE into a dude ranch or "summer resort second to none," as the *Enterprise* termed it. Cody had had such a plan in mind for several years. Pioneers in the dude ranch business were already making big money, as much as $40,000 a year, right there in the Wyoming mountains, and Cody needed cash in amounts such as that.

Fred was to build additional houses and cottages among the pines around the TE ranch house, and by the first of the year several guests had booked reservations for the summer of 1916, among them the noted actor William Faversham. Circulars announcing the opening of the TE to tourists were floating about in North Platte that spring, along with the news that the old Colonel was going on the road with a new Wild West show of his own in a short time.[5] Apparently he was actually going to carry out his promise, made from horseback in the arena in North Platte the past June: since that city had given birth to the first Wild West show, he hoped, if he lived, to start another and greater show from the same town.

However, the new Wild West the Colonel had in mind involved the Miller Brothers 101 Ranch show of Oklahoma. He had hoped to raise the money to buy the show outright. Failing that, he "hired out" to the company on a contract similar to the one he had had with Sells-Floto— $100 a day and one-third of the profits over $2,750, a good deal for the old showman.

While waiting for the opening of the season, Cody went to his nephew's (Julia's son, George) home in New Rochelle, New York, that winter of 1915-16, to begin writing a series of autobiographical articles for *Hearst's* magazine.[6] Under the title "The Great West That Was: 'Buffalo Bill's' Life Story," these were published from August 1916 to July 1917. Two posthumous spin-offs resulted from these *Hearst's* articles. In 1920 they were gathered together into a book and published as yet another Cody autobiography.[7] A few years later Universal Pictures Corporation mined the series for movie serials.[8]

In February 1916 the Colonel set out on a three-week tour of eastern cities with his own moving pictures, "The Indian Wars." The theme of his accompanying lectures was "preparedness," for war was raging in Europe, and the prospects were strong that the United States would soon be involved.

And here Tammen showed up again, attempting to claim a share in what he made on the tour and threatening to sue if he used the Buffalo Bill Wild West title for his new show. One of the Essanay partners talked Tammen out of pushing his claim on the former, and Cody paid him $5,000 to drop his claim on the latter.[9]

Buffalo Bill liked the Miller Brothers show. Johnny Baker was with him again as arena director and Major Burke as press agent. His share of the money was paid promptly—one week he made $4,161.35—and he still lived and traveled in a private car with a valet.[10] But his debts

W. F. Cody and his wife Louisa, 1916.

crowded him ever closer, and he often had to draw his salary in advance to keep ahead of his creditors. He had been forced, or persuaded, to sue both Lillie and Sells-Floto, and the expenses were heavy.

In spite of his insistence to the contrary, his health was failing, and he often had to be helped onto his horse behind the scenes. The man who had once leaped on and off a bronc, racing at full speed, now had not the strength to pull himself into the saddle of a gentle, standing mount.

To complicate matters even more, cold, rainy weather dogged them for weeks, followed by hot, sticky days and an epidemic among children that paralyzed business. All three of the show's owners, Colonel Joe Miller, George Arlington, and Edward Arlington, were ill and hospitalized for long periods that summer. But day after day the old Colonel, once on his horse, rode out as proudly as ever—and even shot glass balls from the saddle that final season.

Although he headed the parade in his buggy, the Colonel proudly wrote Julia in early October that he had not missed a parade or a performance the whole summer, and that his stories in *Hearst's* magazine had created more of a demand than the publisher could fill. William Randolph Hearst, he added, wanted him to write a book about his show life, including his tours of Europe and the royalty he had met.[11]

On October 26, Cody wrote his sister from North Carolina, that he was feeling fine and investigating two or three deals for a show next season, for "now that my health is good, I must get to makeing big money." The show would close in a few days and her brother planned to stop at May's in Denver for four days; then he would be seeing her, he told Julia, in Cody "about Nov. 21st."[12]

But those last weeks had taken a toll far greater than he realized, and the Colonel left the train in Denver too ill to go any farther. May sent for Louisa, Irma, and Julia, and they hurried to his bedside. However, a few days' rest, coupled with sheer determination, had him on his feet again in a week or so, and he went on to Wyoming.

The various accounts of Colonel Cody's last weeks are contradictory and confusing. Walsh writes that he went to Chicago to try to raise $100,000 from his rich friends to buy his own show for the next year. Failing in this, he turned to a professional money raiser who would work on a ten percent commission on stock sold to the public through newspaper advertising. Leonard and Goodman have it that he left Cody on his way east, stopping off in Denver to see May, and was taken suddenly ill there.[13] A clipping from a North Platte paper, dated only "December, 1916," states: "Colonel W. F. Cody passed through this morning enroute to New York, where he goes to make arrangements for organizing the show he will put on the road next season." The next word of him from North Platte, dated December 23, announced that Cody, who had been very ill for several days in Denver, "at one time being reported near death," is now much improved in health.[14]

Whatever the facts concerning his business trip east, he returned to Denver and became ill at the home of his sister May. Again Louisa,

Julia, Irma, and Fred hurried to his bedside. Several days later he
seemed much improved, and his doctor, J. P. East, advised a trip to
Glenwood Springs, Colorado, to try the healing waters there. Julia, Dr.
East, and a nurse made the trip with him; the others returned to Cody
and to the Garlow children, aged eight, six, and four.

The Colonel stood the trip well and seemed somewhat improved the
next day. But two days later, Dr. East, convinced that he was beyond
help, took him back to Denver and again sent for the family. On January 8 it was announced that Cody was dying. During the next two days
almost hourly bulletins on the old Colonel's condition went out from the
Decker home. Boy Scouts, eager to be of service, kept vigil on the
porch. Telegrams, letters, and phone calls came from everywhere.[15]

The *Telegraph,* under the big headline, COLONEL CODY IS DYING IN
DENVER, told how it was in North Platte:

A hush hung over the streets this morning, such a hush as is known
only in a city when some great disaster is pending. Sad faced men
and women gathered in little groups and talked in subdued tones,
now and then seeming to stop and listen as though waiting for the
end of something unknown. It was as if they listened for, yet feared
to hear, the galloping of the pale horse that would bear the grim
reaper on his final journey. For North Platte's most famous and most
beloved citizen is dying in Denver. . . . Colonel W. F. Cody, "the
greatest plainsman the world ever knew," is calmly awaiting the
end—watching the sands of life's hourglass run out.

There are also differing accounts of Colonel Cody's last hours. Louisa
speaks only of her *last* meeting with him, after his return from Glenwood Springs. She mentions his bravery, how he tried to cheer the rest
of them, the many times he said, "I wish Johnny would come." Johnny
was on his way, speeding westward from New York, but he did not
arrive in time to see his beloved foster father alive.[16]

Mrs. Foote wrote that Cody "lived again his yesteryears" in panto-
mime during his last days.[17] Several of his biographers state that after
he learned he was dying, he said: "Let's forget about it and play high
five."[18] Cody Boal wrote: "We played a game of high five and I remember when I played as his partner, his opponents sluffed a trick to
him, and even in his weakened condition he called them on it. He was
always a square shooter and demanded fair play."[19] Louisa said he
played a game of solitaire.[20]

Russell records: "On the afternoon of January 9 he was baptized and received into the Roman Catholic church by Father Christopher V. Walsh. . . . Mrs. Cody no doubt urged this decision upon him."[21] But Mrs. Cody attended and supported the Episcopal church all her years in North Platte. Mrs. Leonard wrote that just before the Colonel went east on the December business trip, he told Julia: "When I come back, I want you to have your preacher come over here. I want to talk to him about the next world for I feel my time is coming soon. I know that your church suits me."[22] Julia's church was the First Presbyterian of Cody; W. O. Harper was its minister. Cody had also been a close friend and admirer of Episcopalian George Beecher, the big "Bishop of the Great Plains."

Cody Boal wrote: "During his last illness the house was full of reporters from all the news syndicates, asking numerous questions pertaining to his life, experiences and personal affairs, and elaborating on any scrap of news available."[23]

Many sources relate that the sick man, when told he had no more than thirty-six hours to live, calmly directed his family to let the Elks and Masons take charge of his funeral.

Buffalo Bill died at 12:05 in the afternoon on January 10. Joseph Bona, of the Olinger Mortuary in Denver, says he was called to the Decker home at 2932 Lafayette Street about one o'clock. He embalmed the body in the bedroom where it lay; Bona said he found a man of unusual appearance, tall and straight, with fine, big veins that made the embalming so easy he was finished in about two-and-one-half hours. The young mortician later told how impressed he was by the telegrams and messages streaming in from all over the world: from the king of England, the kaiser of Germany, President Wilson, governors, generals, senators, friends from everywhere.[24]

Along with the news of the Colonel's passing came the announcement that he was to be buried on top of Lookout Mountain, above Denver. This was a surprise to everyone, for it was common knowledge that Cody had long ago picked his burial site—on Cedar Mountain, above the town of Cody, where he had piled stones on the exact spot. In the spring of 1902 the Colonel had written Julia about the Wyoming location: "I have got a mountain picked out big enough for us all to be buried on."[25] A few years later he wrote in his will:

It is my wish and I hereby direct that my body shall be buried in some suitable plot of ground on Cedar Mountain. . . .

I further direct that there shall be erected over my grave, to mark

GONE TO JOIN THE MYSTERIOUS CARAVAN

BOYHOOD'S GREAT IDOL

Famous political cartoonist J. N. "Ding" Darling drew this tribute to Cody; it appeared January 11, 1917, on the front page of the Des Moines *Register*. Two years later, upon the death of Theodore Roosevelt, Darling repeated the Cody-drawing motif for his TR cartoon, which turned out to be Ding's most reproduced work. *Courtesy University of Iowa Library.*

the spot . . . a monument wrought from native red stone in the form
of a mammoth buffalo, and placed in such a position as to be visible
from the town, . . . that it may be a constant reminder . . . that it was
the great wish of its founder that Cody should not only grow in
prosperity and become a populous and influential metropolis, but
that it should be distinguished for the purity of its government and
the loyalty of its citizens to the institutions of our beloved country.
I give to my executors the sum of ten thousand dollars for the cost
of the monument and its erection and to carefully keep the ground
around it in proper order.[26]

However, in the final pages of her *Memories*, Louisa wrote that whereas
long ago at Cody her husband had told her he wanted to be buried on
Cedar Mountain, "where the last rays of the sun touched the hills at
night," now, on his last day on earth but one, he had changed his mind
and wanted to be buried on Lookout Mountain. "It's pretty up there.
. . . You can look down into four states," he said.[27]

Most of Cody's friends and biographers questioned the decision to
change the burial place. They saw in it the devious hand of Harry
Tammen, who was said to have paid Mrs. Cody $10,000 for the priv-
ilege of choosing the grave site. Since Louisa paid for the funeral, she
had the right to name the site; but whether or not Tammen pursuaded
her, in her bereavement and grief, to let her husband be buried on
Lookout Mountain, or whether the Colonel had really changed his
mind, will likely never be known.

Certainly the Denver *Post* lost no time in capitalizing on the famous
man's death by announcing that he would be buried on Lookout, on a
site donated by Mayor Speer and Park Commissioner Milburn and
considered the most beautiful spot in North America. A more distinguished honor was never conferred on any man by an American mu-
nicipality, said the *Post*, and a superb monument would be erected by
popular subscription. The drive to raise the monument funds soon
became known as the "pennies from schoolchildren" campaign, with
no child permitted to contribute over five cents.

As a *Time* staff writer observed twenty-nine years later, on the occasion of Colonel Cody's one hundredth birthday anniversary: "Denver's
mayor Robert W. Speer was out to claim him. Buffalo Bill, dead and
enshrined, would obviously be a greater civic asset than Buffalo Bill
alive with one foot on the Albany Hotel bar rail."[28] Substitute Tammen
and Bonfils for Mayor Speer's name, as the moving spirit behind the
plot to keep Buffalo Bill in Colorado, near Denver, and the comment

is true—even though Cody for nearly ten years had not had his foot on a bar rail, at least with an intoxicating drink in his hand.

Immediately after Colonel Cody's death, the Colorado legislature passed a resolution permitting his body to lie in state in the Capitol rotunda from ten to twelve o'clock on Sunday, January 14. The city of Denver, in conjunction with the Masons and the Elks, was planning "a monster memorial for the West's most famous character," and the funeral would be held in the afternoon in the auditorium of the Elks' lodge at Fourteenth and California Streets.[29]

North Platte quickly ordered a suitable floral tribute, and some thirty members of Palestine Commandry No. 1, the local Knights Templar organization of which the Colonel was a member, made plans to charter a special railway coach and attend the funeral. By the next evening the number planning to go to the funeral had dropped to a score. Thirteen sir knights actually went, riding up to Denver on the midnight train.

Colonel Cody's body was taken from the Decker home, where it had lain in state for three days, to the Capitol building on Sunday morning, and the doors were opened to the public at ten o'clock. An estimated 25,000 people, many, many of them children, filed by the bronze casket beneath the golden dome, above which floated the U.S. flag at half mast. Troopers from Fort Logan formed lines through which the people passed. At twelve o'clock, the hour set for closing the casket, the crowd was still pouring in. They were then held back while the family bade the Colonel farewell. Johnny Baker was with the family, and following them came the delegation of Knights Templar from North Platte. Next to pass the bier was a large number of old cowboys. The guard of honor at the casket included members of the Colorado National Guard, the Pioneer Society, the Elks, and the G.A.R.

The public was then admitted for another twenty minutes, after which the funeral procession from the Capitol to the Elks' home lined up to follow the casket on its horse-drawn caisson. Among the distinguished citizens following in motor cars were the governors of Colorado and Wyoming, the lieutenant governor of Nebraska, Elks from Kansas and New Mexico, and Masons from North Platte. Seventy cowboys walked in the procession. Two of them led a riderless white horse, with stirrups reversed and the Old Scout's pistols hanging from the saddlehorn.

Several writers say the horse was McKinley, the Colonel's last mount. Cody Boal says the horse was Isham. Actually, the nameless white horse came from a Denver livery stable, merely window dressing for the funeral of the man who had striven always to keep everything about *his* show strictly *real*.

Several thousand people brought up the rear of the procession, trudging determinedly in the cold wind, many of them to stand for two hours outside the building waiting to get in for a glimpse of the body before it was taken to Olinger's to be placed in a crypt until summer. Numerous eulogies were delivered at the funeral service, which was presided over by the Elks' chaplain, the Reverend Charles H. Marshall, pastor of St. Barnabas Episcopal church.[30] Joseph Bona said Father Christopher V. Walsh, the Roman Catholic priest who had baptized Cody six days earlier, said the funeral mass.

Before the end of the month, the *Telegraph* announced that Cody, Wyoming, was planning to erect a life-size statue of Cody, a monument to cost $25,000 and be located on one of the principal street corners in the town. House bill No. 50 had already been introduced, providing for a state appropriation of $10,000 to start the fund.

Nebraska determined not to be outdone in the matter of a monument to her most famous son. On January 31, the directors of the O L D highway called a meeting to change the name to the "Buffalo Bill Trail." This portion of the first trancontinental highway, stretching from Omaha to Denver, had just been laid out and named the "Omaha, Lincoln and Denver highway," or O L D for short. What better way to honor Buffalo Bill than to name the great new road for him. The proposition met with an enthusiastic reception, and it was proposed to introduce a bill in the legislature to secure $25,000 to put up suitable markers for the trail. Originally, it had been suggested the above amount be appropriated to "throw in" with Colorado, Wyoming, and Denver in the erection of the "superb monument" the Denver *Post* had in mind—something to cost around $100,000. Wyoming's appropriation had been funded by February 1. Nebraska's bill apparently died aborning. No more was heard of it.

Grosset and Dunlap, publisher, was busy on a new edition of *Last of the Great Scouts*, this time with a foreword and an afterword by Zane Grey.

The Essanay Film Company was even faster at work, letting no prairie grass grow under its feet. Within *days* after Cody's death, they had stories and ads in the trade papers (e.g., *The New York Dramatic Mirror*, January 20, 1917; *Motion Picture News*, January 27, 1917) about a new feature film, "Adventures of Buffalo Bill." Whether they had this in the works prior to Cody's death is not known.[31]

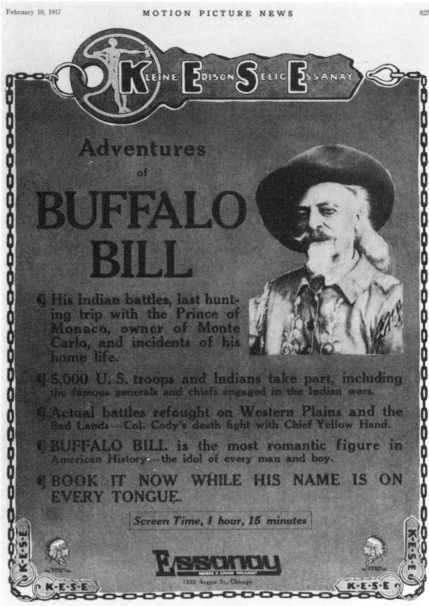

Trade journal ad. *Courtesy Library of Congress.*

By June, Tammen's burial site was ready, with a grave blasted out of the solid granite on the mountain top. Again it was estimated that 25,000 people toiled up the seven-and-one-half miles of looping mountain road to see them "press the earth over the sleeping form of Pahaska. It was the most impressive, the most notable funeral ever witnessed in America. No president could have been more honored by the presence of thousands. To Nature and to God, this afternoon, we Americans of the West surrendered Pahaska to his final slumber. Pahaska, Farewell." So wrote Gene Fowler for the Denver *Post* on June 3, 1917.

The procession did indeed "toil," at a pace no faster than a man could walk, Joe Bona said; and many did walk, although there were 3,000 motor cars in the cavalcade as well.

The Masons had charge of the burial. The younger John Baker, who went to the service with his friend, Cody Boal, said he and Cody rode to Denver on the midnight train with some "higher up Masons," including six Knights Templar who were to act as Honorary Escort at the burial:

> The Olinger mortuary had a car waiting at the depot for Cody and me, and it took us to the Albany Hotel where Mrs. Cody and the Garlows had a suite. We had breakfast with them, and then we went to the mortuary with Fred. That was about 10 A.M.
>
> They had Mr. Cody in that big bronze casket in a crypt in the wall and we saw them slide the casket out and put it on a stand. Joe Bona said he [Cody] had been as good a specimen as you could ask for, almost perfect preservation. Back at the Albany they had limousines for all the funeral party. Mrs. Cody, Judge Wall[32] and Cody and I rode in the first car. The second car had the Garlow family and the third the Colonel's sisters, Julia Goodman and Mrs. Decker, and her husband.
>
> Everybody attached to the funeral seemed to be Masons. They all wore the white lambskin aprons: the car drivers, the policemen at all the intersections from the mortuary to the west edge of Denver. On the way to Golden and on to Lookout Mountain, there were more Masonic policemen at every major intersection, or where anyone might need directions, or be asked not to cross the funeral procession on the road they call the Lariat Trail now. I don't know where they found so many Masons.
>
> When we got to the top of the mountain it was a little after noon

Courtesy Denver Public Library, Western History Department.

and Mrs. Cody was very tired and she rested awhile. At that time there was a pavilion on top of the mountain and she rested in that. There was a dining room and we had lunch there, before the service. Mrs. Cody was such a thoughtful lady and she said if all those people had come to pay their respects to the Colonel's memory, they should get to see him if they wanted to, and she told them to open the coffin.

So they let the people go by the open, glass-topped casket and it was hotter than seven hundred dollars that day. So they put a big umbrella, one of the great big ones like they use at beaches, over the casket to shade it. The casket was standing on the framework they use over an open grave and the people passed along in two lines, one on each side of the coffin. Mr. Cody was dressed in a regular business suit and he looked very nice.

Some things have been written about six of Buffalo Bill's old girl friends sitting in a front row at the burial, and that one of them stood up and shaded Mr. Cody's face with a little fancy parasol. There were chairs for the family, but I didn't see anyone I thought would have been there because she was an old girl friend of the Colonel's. And there was the big umbrella shading the casket, like I said.[33]

Cody Boal and Johnny Baker, Jr. were twenty-one years old that summer of Buffalo Bill's burial on Lookout Mountain.

38

Bunk and Fact

The grave marker, quickly erected above the grave on Lookout Mountain, was to be only a forerunner to the $100,000 monument planned by the Denver *Post*. It read: "In Memoriam. Colonel William Frederick Cody. 'Buffalo Bill.' Noted scout and Indian fighter. Born February 26, 1845, Scott County, Iowa. Died January 10, 1917, Denver, Colorado. At rest here by his request."

An outsize controversy at once arose over the last sentence, for many refused to believe the Colonel had wanted to be buried anywhere but on Cedar Mountain in Wyoming. Scores came forward to state that Cody himself had often said so, and Goldie Griffith said he had taken her and several others to the spot on horseback in 1913 and told them he was going to sleep there some day, overlooking Cody.[1]

There was argument, too, over what form the fine permanent marker should take. The *Post* speculated on this in its editorials, and the Boulder *Camera* responded: "Why not let the Denver *Post* proprietors determine the kind of shaft to erect over Buffalo Bill. He was their meat. It was they who brought him down, after a gallant career, by breaking his proud heart. Why should not the shaft be crowned with a miniature 'Red Room'[2] bearing this device: Abandon hope, all ye who enter here."

Perhaps it was resentment over Tammen's and Bonfils' apparent abduction of the body that caused the project to fail, but the $100,000 fund did not get far off the ground, and no monument other than the original native stone marker with its bronze plaque was erected at the tomb.

While a number of North Platte folk were in Colorado for Cody's burial, others were at work on the town's first memorial for him. The year marked Nebraska's semicentennial as a state, and the town celebrated with a giant birthday party, June 26-30. The chief event of the occasion was the two-day re-enactment of the battle of Summit Springs. Some 200 actors were used in the lively show, which "faithfully followed every detail of the famous battle."

The drama began with the Indians making camp, getting supper, and stomping out a few war dances. As the camp settled down for the night, Buffalo Bill was shown discovering the village and giving the signal that brought troops down on the sleeping Indians. The slaughter was general and the camp was burned. In the hand-to-hand combat between Buffalo Bill and Tall Bull, the chief was killed; one of the two white women prisoners was rescued, while the other died under Mrs. Tall Bull's tomahawk. "Great care was taken to do justice to the impersonations of Colonel Cody, General Carr and Major Walker and no expense was spared."

In October of that same year, the North Platte city council voted unanimously that "to further the remembrance of Colonel W. F. Cody the North Side City Park be named Cody Park." This beautiful ninety-acre park lies just east of the old Cody ranch along the North Platte River. It extends south to Fourteenth Street and includes the portion of the old Dillon ranch where the 1882 Fourth of July celebration was held. Until 1927 the only trees in the park were the few wild ones that grew along the river. Since that time thousands of elms have been planted and winding roads laid out among them and around the large artificial lake. Today much bigger cities can well envy North Platte its fine Cody Park with its many shaded picnic tables, barbecue fireplaces, ball diamonds, tennis courts, children's amusement area, wild animal zoo, and swimming pool.

Other than this, although various memorials were proposed from time to time, for years North Platte did nothing more to perpetuate the memory of its most famous citizen.

Meanwhile, Cody, Wyoming, was busy collecting $25,000 for its own memorial to its founder. The fund resulted in a fine twelve-foot bronze statue depicting the Colonel as a scout reining his mount along the old South Fork Trail in Wyoming, scanning the ground for Sioux pony tracks. The statue was designed and cast by Gertrude Vanderbilt Whitney of New York, who attended to every detail with great meticulousness, even to traveling out to the TE ranch in the fall of 1923 to select the horse to be used as her model for the statue. The horse, Smokey, a fine black saddler born and raised on the Colonel's Wyoming ranch, was shipped to New York in a special car. While in Cody, Mrs. Whitney selected the spot for the statue, a wind-swept mesa near where the Cody Museum was later to be built.

In 1924, during Cody Stampede Days, July 3-5, Jane Garlow, Colonel Cody's fourteen-year-old granddaughter, unveiled the splendid memorial. An unknown poet caught the special significance of the monument in the following verses:

I am riding to the mountains,
Riding westward on the trail;
Where adventure leads I follow
Fair the day or fierce the gale.

All my friends rode on before me,
All the scouts that I once knew;
Buffalo have almost vanished;
Indians are meek and few.

I, Pahaska, ride forever.
On old Brigham, swift and wise,
Westward to unbranded mountains
Where the untamed eagle flies.

Missing from the unveiling ceremony were most of those who had been closest to Colonel Cody. Major John Burke had survived his best friend by only thirteen weeks, dying of pneumonia on April 12 in Providence, Rhode Island. In October, William Sweeney, Wild West bandmaster for twenty-nine seasons, crossed the last divide in a Minneapolis hospital, following a gallstone operation. His sister, Mrs. John Baker, Sr., brought his body back to North Platte for burial. Irma Cody Garlow and her husband, Fred, passed away within four days of each other in October 1918, victims of influenza. Both were buried in Cody. Late in October 1921, Louisa Cody succumbed to a heart attack.

Meanwhile, Denver and Tammen had lost no time in capitalizing on the possession of all that was mortal of Buffalo Bill. By the fall of 1921, Pahaska Tepee was in operation on Lookout Mountain, hard by the old showman's grave. A rustic structure built of giant lodgepole pines, it was in charge of Johnny Baker and housed the hundreds of souvenirs he had gathered during his years with the Wild West.

Johnny, a fine showman in his own right, was sincere in his desire to

Cody's grave and Pahaska Tepee museum atop Lookout Mountain.

keep alive the memory of his beloved foster father by displaying the saddles and guns Buffalo Bill had once used, the splendid relics given him by his Indian friends, and the famous paintings that had once graced the Cody homes. The paintings included "King Edward's Visit to the Wild West Show in London in 1903" and Pappacena's "The Scout" and "Buffalo Bill on White Horse Scouting a Trail," painted in 1889.

The grave and the big lodge proved immensely popular, just as Tammen had foreseen, and the city of Denver made a handsome profit on the concession as hundreds of thousands of visitors filed by the grave and visited Pahaska Tepee. Soon it was said that Lookout Mountain was as popular a mecca for tourists as the tombs of Washington and Grant. So popular, indeed, was Buffalo Bill's burial place that Cody and North Platte became ever more wrathful over letting the bonanza get away from them; mutterings and threats seeped back to Denver. In alarm, the powers in charge there hastened to forestall any attempts at body snatching by weighting their gold mine—the bronze casket—down with several tons of concrete and iron.

Johnny personally kept green the memory of Pahaska until the spring of 1931. On April 22, while a snowstorm whipped the summit of Lookout Mountain, Johnny Baker died in a Denver hospital. Old Bishop Beecher, on a crutch and a cane, traveled to the mile-high city to preach his old friend's funeral sermon; and Johnny's wife, in accordance with his last wishes, had his body cremated before she went back to Lookout Mountain to keep the lodge open that summer. The following January she carried Johnny's ashes back to Rochester, to be buried in Mount Hope Cemetery near the graves of Arta, Orra, and little Kit, where, since the deaths of Buffalo Bill and Louisa, he had come in the winters to place flowers on the three graves.

In the spring of 1928, Cody, Wyoming, opened its Cody Memorial Museum, a large log building modeled after the TE ranch house. Filled with Cody furniture, pictures, and family belongings of many kinds, it stood near the Whitney bronze, and soon proved almost as important a tourist attraction as Pahaska Tepee on Lookout Mountain.

By this time, however, the fad of debunking heroes had taken over, and a host of writers were busy tarnishing the reputations of almost all of America's great, from George Washington on down. Bill Cody did not escape, but where he was concerned there were always two extreme camps. One took Buffalo Bill stories as the veritable truth, the other called them barefaced lies. The reality lay somewhere in between.

As one of his friends said, he was a man of his times and we should not sit in judgment on him. Few men of this or any other century were ever beset with so many temptations, and living in a show window as he did for so many years, his sins were bound to be almost an open book to the public. There were men in his town, high-placed men, who committed worse deeds, but because they hid behind a churchly facade, died respected and admired by all except the few who knew their sins but dared not tell them openly.

By the forties, the debunking was in full flower. In 1946, the *American Mercury* and the *Reader's Digest* published an article written by Stewart Holbrook, who argued that the power of publicity had turned a simple prairie scout into an immortal symbol of our western frontier. Holbrook was off the track, for Buffalo Bill Cody was never a simple man. Without the publicity he would still have left a lasting impression on all who saw or knew him.

Holbrook gives the major publicity credits to John Burke and Edward Judson, "a couple of homemade press agents without whom Cody would have been merely an entry in the yellowing files of U.S. Fifth Cavalry records." He goes on to repeat the old mistakes of 4,280 buffalo shot in eighteen months and of the hero-hunting Ned Buntline being turned down by Major North, resulting in the "discovery" of Buffalo Bill. He dwells on Cody's daily "habit of getting swacked at show-time" and being unable to hit the glass balls, even with sizable charges of buckshot. He concludes with the popular tale of the six mistresses at the burial, one of them holding her "antique black parasol over the glass-topped coffin all through the long service, gazing at the still hand-some face of the Prince of the Prairie."[3]

The same year *Time* magazine carried a column claiming that of all U.S. heroes "almost none [had been] so artificially contrived," that nearly all the Buffalo Bill legend "sprang straight from the brain of a raffish scribbler known as Ned Buntline." Between Buntline and "Ari-zona John" Burke, the writer alleged, "no buffalo was left unskinned, no redskin unscalped and no maiden unavenged west of the Missis-sippi." He then gives his own raffish account of Cody's burial and the weighting down of his coffin with fifteen tons of scrap iron and con-crete.[4]

"Uncle" Lee Casey, in his "History of the World" column for chil-dren, called Buffalo Bill a charming fake. Uncle Lee claims to have wept with Cody over the passing of his show. "We felt so bad," he wrote, "that we could scarcely drink our bourbon." He goes on to tell the children that Buffalo Bill was never a colonel, save for a casual commission from a governor of Nebraska that anybody could get if he could carry a precinct. Also, he was never a scout, much less chief of scouts. His fight with Yellow Hair didn't happen but was an invention of Ned Buntline (who never mentioned it at all). He allows that Cody did shoot some buffalo, "with about as much risk as your daddy would take if he chose to shoot his neighbor's dairy cows." Uncle Lee men-tions the burial, too, but scales the concrete and scrap iron down to two-and-one-half tons.[5]

E. S. Sutton in his "Hero, Showman or Heel?" claims Cody told him he did not kill Yellow Hair. Sutton has Sitting Bull, "a sick man return-ing home after the failure of the Wild West Show in Europe," telling him that Buffalo Bill had never killed an Indian, except in self defense, and had never scalped one in his life.[6] Sitting Bull of course, was never in Europe with the Wild West, and it did not fail there.

Soon writers were claiming that Cody never rode for the Pony Express, never amounted to anything as a stage driver, and was not present at the battle of Summit Springs. The main argument against his riding for the Pony Express was that he was only fourteen in 1860, the year the famous Express originated. However, in those days it was not unusual for boys of that age to be employed on business of that kind. Keenness of eye, strength, ability, and endurance were more important assets than another year or two of age. Light weight and courage were also essentials, and some three dozen other lads little older than Cody rode Pony Express.

An example of the Pony Express debunking is a feature by a columnist who signed herself "Millie." She wrote derisively: "Much malarky has been ground out about Cody as a rider with that famed shortlived outfit. Bill Cody was only a boy of fourteen. Nevertheless he did establish a tenuous connection with the Pony Express firm as a carrier carrying messages between the freight wagon trains operated by the founders (Russell, Majors and Waddell)."

Millie gives all the credit for the Wild West show to Nate Salsbury, "a theatrical manager who had outlined the plan for such an extravaganza to Cody in 1882." Immediately enthusiastic, Cody decided to try it. "The first effort," she wrote, "a comparatively modest affair, was given during the July 4th celebration in North Platte. The program included riding and roping by cowboys, Indian pony races and exhibition shooting. The piece de resistance was a thrilling abortive holdup of passengers in an authentic stage coach. Around this time little orphan Annie Oakley, a crack shot, joined the cast."[7] There were, of course, neither Indians nor a stagecoach in the 1882 celebration, and Annie Oakley, who was not an orphan, did not join the Wild West (which was first produced the next year) until two years later.

Another *Rocky Mountain News* writer, David Brand, described Buffalo Bill as "a boy who never grew up," and wrote that his wife was "probably as emotionally immature as her husband." He detailed the "messy" hearing in Cheyenne and enlarged on the possibility that there had been something to the Queen Victoria testimony. There had been rumors in the 1890s, he said, that Bill had received letters from the queen indicating a strong attachment, and the old New York *World* had elaborated on the story; Bill had denied it and the U.S. government had denied it, but the tale kept spreading, Brand concluded.[8]

Janice Holt Giles, in her *Six Horse Hitch*, quoted a man who told her that Cody did drive stage for about a year but was a "show-off and not a very skilled driver." He was, instead, "a whip cracker . . . and none of the boys who knew him in his younger days was surprised when he took to circus driving. It was just about all he could do. What did surprise us was how that hard drinking peacock had the business sense to make three months on the Pony Express and a year on the Overland pay off so well. My! My!"[9] Does one detect the greenish tinge of envy here?

In 1916, Luther North, in his *Man of the Plains*, stated flatly that Buffalo Bill did not kill Tall Bull because he did not reach the battle scene until well after the fight was over; rather, Luther's brother Frank was the hero of that occasion.[10] All subsequent Cody writers repeated Luther's version; from then on the belief grew that Major Frank North was the real scout and Indian fighter and Cody only a faint imitation.

However, *My Life With Buffalo Bill*, a book written by Dan Muller and published in 1948, is the strangest of all the Cody books. A Los Angeles *Times* review of the book stated:

> The one man living who really knew Buffalo Bill has now written a splendid biography, illustrated by himself, of the old scout and showman. Dan Muller was taken into the Cody household when he was nine. Buffalo Bill raised the boy, who was later to become his secretary. Dan Muller tells the truth about W. F. Cody, dispelling all the cheap stories surrounding the man.
>
> Never glossing over the fact that "Uncle Bill" dissipated his health and earnings by too great an addiction to whisky, Muller shows the old man fighting like a frontiersman against enemies in the show world, notably the Denver duo, Bonfils and Tammen. Good reading and flavorful, a story that needed telling and has been well told.[11]

This is all very well—except there is little truth anywhere in the story, at least in the portions concerning the Codys. Dan has himself arriving at Scout's Rest Ranch in 1899. Since Buffalo Bill was on the road with his show at the time, Mrs. Cody, "Aunt Lou," took him in and mothered him. Dan described the ranch house as having a large parlor with a fireplace across most of one end and a long first-floor hallway with bedrooms opening off each side; the fourth door down was the one to Dan's room. The second door led to Irma's room, the third to "Uncle Bill's," and the last to Aunt Lou's. This is very interesting in view of the fact that the Scout's Rest mansion had only one downstairs bedroom. There was no long hall with four doors opening off it and no fireplace in the entire house.[12]

Even more fascinating is Aunt Lou's living at the ranch from 1899 until 1905, as Muller has it; she did not go there to live until 1909. At the time Dan says he arrived at the ranch, Julia and Al Goodman were living there. After Al became ill, in January 1901, he and Julia moved into North Platte and a hired overseer, under Mrs. Cody's supervision, took charge of the ranch.

In 1905, just after the tainted salmon incident, which the Colonel insisted had been an attempt to poison him, Dan claims he went to Europe with Uncle Bill and the Wild West show. He says Aunt Lou kissed him (Dan) goodbye on the ranch house porch; she then told her husband she would not be living at the ranch when he came home. By then, actually, the Codys had not spoken to each other for four years, since the Christmas of 1901, and the divorce trial was almost over.

Dan also has Colonel Judson (Ned Buntline) visiting Scout's Rest in February 1900, and the three of them, Muller, Cody, and Judson, traveling together on a train to Chicago. Russell reminds us that after 1873 Cody had no connection with Buntline, except for his fourth book, *Buffalo Bill's First Trail; or, Will Cody, the Pony Express Rider* (published in 1888; serialized earlier, in 1885, in *Beadle's Weekly* under title "Will Cody, the Pony Express Rider; or, Buffalo Bill's First Trail"). Even more conclusive is the fact that Buntline died in Stamford, Connecticut, on July 16, 1886.

My Life with Buffalo Bill is almost pure fiction. Muller's greatest disservice to the man he claimed to love and admire is his exaggeration of the Colonel's drinking habit. Also, nowhere does he mention Cody Boal, who lived with his grandparents during most of the time Dan says he (Dan) was at the ranch. Neither did Cody Boal, when interviewed in 1954-1955, remember ever meeting Dan Muller.[13] Dan's description of the ranch house more nearly fits that of Welcome Wigwam, where there *was* a large fireplace, although all the bedrooms were on the second floor. It would seem that Dan might be putting himself in Cody Boal's shoes and switching the locale from the town house to the ranch. The rest is town gossip and imagination.

As the years passed, anyone who had known Cody or had a part in his show was sought out by writers, for *any* story about the famous showman was salable, even an occasional yarn that more or less praised the Colonel. Such was the tale related by Alfred Heimer to Jack Keenan of the Billings *Gazette* in 1934. A long story, it told how Heimer had been major domo of Cody's private car for eight years; it, too, is marred by many inaccuracies, whether attributable to the teller or to the writer. It states that Major Burke, Cody's publicity man, first met the

Colonel in *York*, Nebraska, where the twenty-eight-year-old buffalo hunter was stationed as an army scout. York is in eastern Nebraska, where there was no need for army scouts in Cody's time. Heimer also claims that until 1893 the Wild West show was given on *stages*, like other theatrical performances.

Heimer, although he revered the man, made much of Cody's temper and claimed that Burke and the Colonel were "inflammably jealous" of each other. He says that he signed on at Bridgeport, Connecticut, to take care of Cody's car, and that on the fifty-mile run to New York he and the cook were fired three times by the Colonel; "it was a rare day when he didn't get his walking papers at least once." Everybody else on the show was fired with equal regularity, he assured Keenan.

By 1934, Heimer said, many writers were exaggerating the Colonel's drinking, picturing him as seldom sober and often too drunk to perform. All lies, the old major domo said, for only twice in the eight years he was with Cody did he drink so much he could not perform, and both times he had been practically kidnapped by old friends: once by G.A.R. comrades and once at a reunion of old scouts. In fact, stated Heimer, Cody was opposed to any drinking by show people and eventually dropped his French dragoons for using too much liquor.[14]

Most vicious of all the Cody debunkers were Dr. W. F. Carver, his one-time partner, and Herbert Cody Blake of Brooklyn, New York, perhaps a distant relative, although not listed in the Cody family directory. Carver, in letters and a booklet, stated that "no western man ever took him [Cody] seriously and he was considered by every westerner to be the poorest shot on the plains."[15] There is much more in the same vein, indicating that to the day of his death in 1927, the "Evil Spirit of the Plains" (Carver) never forgave his partner for the sin of being the more popular showman.

Blake seems to have made almost a profession of reviling Cody, branding him "liar," "humbug," and other derogatory terms. He states positively that Bill did not ride Pony Express, shoot in the Comstock contest, or kill Yellow Hair. His clincher is: "I know enough—not printed—to hang Bill Cody if alive, and had my mother had a .45 on her in 1886 she said she'd have shot Bill when he knocked Louisa down in front of a hotel. Drunk as usual." This Blake wrote in a letter to Margaret McCann, who had evidently written to him for information on Cody; personally unacquainted with the lady, Blake adds to the end of his letter: "I'd need to know approximately your age, or if married, in case I wrote you much referring to Bill Cody. It's not for the ears of extreme youth."[16]

After the publication of Don Russell's fine and carefully researched *Lives and Legends of Buffalo Bill* in 1960, thirteen years passed before another major work on Cody appeared. This was John Burke's *Buffalo Bill: The Noblest Whiteskin*. Almost nothing new came to light in this book, for the author, although he lists it in his bibliography, evidently did not read Russell's book or do any serious research of his own. Instead, he merely rehashed all the tired old myths and misinformation of the many previous Cody "biographies." Although Burke claims his work is not a "demolition project," as Cody was a "lovable man," he goes right ahead to paint his subject as one of the greatest whisky tipplers and woman chasers of his time and, of course, ends his tale with the six old "Camilles" facing Louisa across the bronze casket.[17]

But, in spite of his detractors, Buffalo Bill's fame went right on growing. Iowa and Kansas took steps to preserve and publicize his birthplace and his boyhood home. Wyoming and Colorado continued to advertise and enlarge their memorials.

Platters talked from time to time of doing something more. At one time the North Platte Women's Club tried to raise $2,000 to purchase Welcome Wigwam from Hershey Welsh, with the object of restoring and preserving the mansion as a Cody museum; the town was not interested enough, and in 1930 Dr. Charles Heider, Sr. bought the house, tore it down, and built a "modern" residence on the same site, using some of the original materials in its construction. In February 1936, aging Ira Bare lamented editorially:

> The town of Cody is planning a celebration on February 26 to commemorate the birthday of Buffalo Bill, who would have been ninety years old on that day. Though Colonel Cody made Lincoln County and North Platte his home for a much longer period of time than in any other place, and made the town of North Platte almost a household word in every city, town and crossroads in the U.S. as well as in continental Europe, this city has never made a move to in any way perpetuate his name or erect a memorial to him. North Platte in its earlier years was indebted in many ways to Col. Cody; he did much toward starting this city on its way toward reaching its present importance and modernity; certainly we have been lax in our appreciation of him.

Less than two years earlier, the link of Transcontinental Highway 30, the first paved all-weather road across the nation, had been completed in Lincoln County. So now North Platte arose and erected a handsome arch across the pavement at the west edge of town. A wide metal frame supported the huge words NORTH PLATTE, with a larger-than-life-size, colored portrait of Buffalo Bill between the words. Handsome square brick pillars on either side of the pavement bore the arch aloft.

A few years later it was necessary to widen the highway, and the arch came down, to be relegated to oblivion.

The years went by, and North Platte was finally stirred from its indifference to Buffalo Bill by the news that Twentieth Century-Fox was making a spectacular picture of the life of W. F. Cody, starring Maureen O'Hara as Louisa and Joel McCrea as Buffalo Bill. This was to be an accurate history of the life of the famous scout, the largest technicolor picture yet released by Fox; and there was a possibility that if North Platte made a determined enough effort, the world premier showing might be held there. At this, North Platte citizens and their friends pulled every string they could lay hands on, proclaiming their pride in Colonel Cody. In the end, on April 11, 1944, they shared the world premier with Denver. The movie, based on an original story by Frank Winch, was admittedly magnificent, but its accuracy was on a par with that of the books by Buntline, C. R. Cooper, Ingraham, Helen Wetmore, and Muller. Winch's story was so "original" that people who knew better shook their heads in wonder when, for instance, the Cody's first child was born in a cave along the trail somewhere out on the lone prairie.

Charlton Heston played Buffalo Bill in Paramount Pictures' 1953 fictional movie "Pony Express."

In 1976 United Artists released Dino De Laurentiis' movie, "Buffalo Bill and the Indians; or, Sitting Bull's History Lesson," based somewhat on Arthur Kopit's controversial 1968 play "Indians." The movie starred popular Paul Newman but was not a critical or commercial success.

On May 4, 1951 attention focused briefly on North Platte and Buffalo Bill when the president of the Woodmen of the World Life Insurance Society, Farrar Newberry of Omaha, on behalf of the society presented a large granite and bronze memorial monument to the town, county, and state. The plaque read: "To honor W. F. Cody, American scout and showman, Pony Express rider, champion buffalo hunter, Chief of Scouts, member of the Nebraska National Guard, legislator elect— known and loved throughout the world as Buffalo Bill." The handsome monument was erected on the northeast corner of the courthouse square, where it stood for fifteen years. It was overturned and broken by vandals in 1966, and was not re-erected.

Now and again over the years there had been talk of purchasing Scout's Rest Ranch and turning it into a museum. For, even though the Codys had not lived there since 1913, passengers from the East, limbering up on the depot platform while their trains changed crews and engines, continued for years to ask if the famous ranch could be seen from the train. Sometimes transcontinental passengers laid over a train or two and drove out to see the ranch. But nothing came of the museum talk, and in 1927 all that was left of the ranch was purchased by ranchman Henry Kuhlman, who moved his family into the big house and, with his many sons, went on to make history and a fortune with Polled Herefords.

In an interview in December 1939, Mrs. Kuhlman said she had had many North Platte callers who had told her so much about Buffalo Bill's drinking and woman chasing (but apparently nothing about his many benefactions to the town) that she was disgusted with him, although she supposed "he did contribute something here in the early days." She said that a North Platte woman had come one day and told her of the Codys' domestic trouble. "So I thought that was probably right," she said, "and I repeated it to another woman who came to call, and she said, 'Yes, I guess I was the cause of part of their trouble. I was supposed to have been his daughter.' So I didn't tell *that* story anymore," Mrs. Kuhlman concluded.

More years passed. Travelers still came to the town, hoping to see Buffalo Bill's home, or homes, and eventually the place woke up to the monetary value of their one-time foremost citizen's fame. After all, Wyoming and Colorado were coining money with their Cody memorials. So at long last the community decided to do something. Obviously, the thing to do was buy and restore the famous ranch buildings. The price, burgeoning with the years, was now $75,000 for the house, barn, and the twenty-five acres of land. By then the house was in such a sad state of disrepair that the Kuhlman's had built a new home farther west; the old mansion stood empty, its floors falling in, its roof leaking, and its plaster peeling. Restoration costs would come to three times the purchase price, and help was plainly needed. When the state agreed to provide half the initial $75,000, the county set about raising the other half.

The Lincoln County Historical Society spearheaded the collection drive and in 1960 matched the state's share, whereupon the site was purchased and made a state park. The state legislature appropriated funds for the restoration, and when the last shingle had been replaced, the last nail driven, and the last strip of wallpaper smoothed on, Buffalo Bill himself could not have told it from the ranch that had been his pride and joy in the 1880s. Many of the same trees, set out nearly ninety years earlier and grown to giant size, shaded the trim white mansion and the great red barn, and velvety lawns spread away on all sides. The lake was gone, but Scout Creek still gurgled its way through the grounds as it had done in Colonel Cody's day. In June 1965, the park was dedicated to the memory of Buffalo Bill.

Due to their considerable headstarts, Pahaska Tepee and the Cody, Wyoming museum had collected most of the best Cody memorabilia; yet it was surprising what a wealth of furniture and artifacts came flowing back to Scout's Rest Ranch, largely due to the untiring efforts of the park's enthusiastic superintendent, George LeRoy.

When the Nebraska Game and Parks officials undertook to restore and develop the ranch as a tourist attraction, they also envisioned a recreation of the great Wild West and Congress of Rough Riders, the show to be enacted on the ranch grounds every evening of the summer months. The state appropriated the money to build a large stadium, and construction got under way in 1969. Shortly afterward, Montie Montana, Jr., a second-generation California showman, heard about the goings-on back in Nebraska. Now it happened that Montie, the son of a well-known western roper and showman, had long wanted to emulate the great Buffalo Bill and put together a Wild West show of his own. Therefore, in May 1971, he signed a contract with the state of

Nebraska, giving him the right to use the title, "Buffalo Bill's Wild West and Congress of Rough Riders of the World" (to which the state claimed ownership), and requiring him to bring the show back to North Platte every summer for five years.

The young showman secured private financial backing, put together a show of seventy performers (only three fewer, it was said, than Buffalo Bill started with in 1883), and was soon on the grounds with his livestock and show people. He had real Indians, a genuine stagecoach, several buffalo, horses, covered wagons, and authentic costumes for his Cossacks and the other members of his Congress of Rough Riders. Associated with him were numerous professionals, including Tom Blackburn, well-known western author and script writer, who wrote the narration for the show; Mary Wills Doss, former head costume designer for Samuel Goldwyn's studio in Hollywood; and Jack Royce, whose parents had performed in the original Wild West show. Jack, a Hollywood actor, was Montie's arena director. Bill Hammer, wearing his own mustache and goatee and a long-haired wig, played the part of Buffalo Bill. Other big-name professionals handled the music, lighting, and narration—all in all, an impressive and expensive cast.

In true Buffalo Bill style, the grand opening (on July 31, 1971) was preceded by a gala downtown parade and a balloon ascension. That evening, a stone's throw from Scout's Rest Ranch, the state's governor and numerous other important officials occupied the best seats in the big grandstand as the re-activated Wild West got off to a good start. The show did well that first season, showing during August to more than 60,000 people, including many from foreign countries. In September, Montie took his show on tour, with bookings in Phoenix, Los Angeles, San Diego, Salt Lake City, Seattle, Vancouver, Canada, and other cities. But in Phoenix, where the show drew an opening crowd of 4,000, disaster struck with true Buffalo Bill dramatic impact. Ringling Brothers brought suit against the show and its backers for using the name "Buffalo Bill's Wild West and Congress of Rough Riders," claiming to be the sole owner of the famous title, and stopped the show with a temporary restraining order. The action forced Montie into court to defend his right to the title—and it bankrupt the show, which was what the circus firm had set out to do. Montie won the right to use the name but lost his backers and his show.

As had happened to Buffalo Bill back in 1913, all the show's belongings, including the stagecoach, were sold at auction. Though staggered by the blow, the young showman set to work straightening out the company's tangled affairs, at the same time promising North Platte he would be back in 1972 with another show. With the help of some Platters, he raised new backing, put together another show, and in good Buffalo Bill tradition came back for a repeat performance that summer. His 1973 show, both bigger and better, ran for five weeks. It came back again in 1974 (July 13-August 18), but auto gasoline shortages cut attendance so drastically that the show went bankrupt.

In 1959, Nebraska inaugurated a Hall of Fame in its beautiful Capitol building. A famous Nebraskan was to be elected to one of its niches every other year. Up to 1966, four Nebraska greats, George W. Norris, Willa Cather, General John J. Pershing, and Father Flanagan, had been selected for the hallowed spaces. 1967 was Nebraska's centennial. The Lincoln County Historical Society thought it fitting that W. F. Cody be the 1967-68 selection. The Colonel was chosen over William Jennings Bryan, J. Sterling Morton, Major Frank North, Edward Creighton, Red Cloud, and others. But since the legislature had neglected to provide any funds for busts of those elected, it was now up to Lincoln County to raise the $2,250 needed to pay for the larger-than-life bronze bust, which was cast from an original plaster sculpture made from life in Germany in 1892. By 1969 the bronze was finished and paid for, and on June 12 a Lincoln County group, including a number of men and horses from the county Sheriff's Posse, went to Lincoln for the unveiling. Buffalo Bill would have enjoyed the parade, led by his very look-alike "stand-in," Charlie Evans, on his white horse, Snowball; the Sheriff's Posse, marching band, and carloads of dignitaries made their way down the street to the imposing north entrance of the Capitol. There , in the great hall north of the rotunda, the bronze was unveiled, to take its place near Cody's old friends, Bryan (chosen 1968-69) and Pershing.

On the pleasant Sunday afternoon of June 19, 1977, a thirty-three-foot bronze equestrian statue of Cody, "The Legend of the Westerner," was unveiled in the Freda Hambrick Gardens on Persimmon Hill, the home of the National Cowboy Hall of Fame and Western Heritage Center in Oklahoma City. Dean Krakel, managing director of the Hall, conceived the idea of the statue years ago; it was designed by Oklahoma City sculptor Leonard McMurry, and donated by Hall board members Mrs. Nona Payne of Pampa, Texas, and Jasper Ackerman of Colorado Springs, Colorado. Taking part in the dedication ceremony, in addition to the above-named, were William F. Cody III, grandson of the famous Plainsman, and Joel McCrea, star of the 1944 movie

"Buffalo Bill" and former Cowboy Hall of Fame board chairman.[18]

On July 4, 1977 a bronze of Buffalo Bill, "The Plainsman," was erected in the foyer of the Cody Museum; the sculptor of this splendid statue of Cody, on foot, with his hat in one hand and his rifle in the other, was Bob Scriver of Browning, Montana.

Yet another heroic-size statue memorializing the renowned scout and showman may be the proposed bronze planned by Friends of Buffalo Bill, Inc. This North Platte organization began in 1978 to raise $175,000 for a large likeness of Buffalo Bill, mounted, doffing his hat in his famous "Farewell Salute." The sculptor chosen is Ted Long, young North Platte rancher, already well-known for his realistic western bronzes and his fine oil paintings of Indians and western scenes; the model will be Charlie Evans and his white horse Snowball.

Odd stories connected with Buffalo Bill keep turning up. Back in 1910 there was one about a woman from La Porte, Indiana, who, with her ten-year-old child, arrived in North Platte by train. She said she had seen in the movies that Buffalo Bill and his cowboys were always willing and anxious to help women and children. So she had spent all her money for a ticket to come visit them, expecting to be the Colonel's guest and have a good time. She was deeply disappointed when the city fathers explained that such pictures were a snare and a delusion, then bought her a ticket and put her on an eastbound train.[19]

A 1911 account re-told the story of Colonel Cody's purchase of the fine uniforms for the Gordon Silver Cornet Band. However, in the eighteen years that had passed since the uniforms were new, their cost had grown to $1,000 *apiece*, they had been made in Paris, and they came packed in miniature trunks, each bearing the name of its owner.[20]

Interesting, too, are the stories told about Scout's Rest Ranch. A popular one has it that the ranch was winter quarters for the whole show and that elephants were kept in the big barn during the winter months. And there are those who believe the cupola on top of the house was the lookout from which Buffalo Bill watched for Indians; when he saw some coming, he ran downstairs, got under the house through the trapdoor in the kitchen floor, and shot them through the openings in the stone foundation. All this in spite of the facts that elephants would perish in unheated barns in Nebraska's winter cold and that the ranch house was not built until 1886, several years after the last hostile Indians had left the Platte Valley.

True, however, are items relating to the International Order of Red Men that flourished in many cities around the turn of the century. The lodge at North Platte named itself Pahaska Tribe No. 10 and claimed the Colonel as a member.

It is also true that Cody helped organize the prestigious Showman's League of America in Chicago, March 15, 1913, and was its first president. (Its membership consisted of performers from all classes of tent shows, a form of entertainment which reached its peak about that time.) In the magnificent million-dollar museum at Cody there hangs a photograph, some 3 x 4 feet in size, of the dinner tendered Mr. Cody by the League on that occasion in the La Salle Hotel. A huge poster of Buffalo Bill hangs on the wall of the ornate and well-filled ballroom, back of the head table, where the new president sits with twenty other dignitaries. (A companion photograph shows Cody at the sumptuous dinner given for him by Rodman Wanamaker, America's merchant prince, at Sherry's in New York on May 12, 1909.)

It is true that hundreds of thousands of people yearly have visited the three main memorials to Buffalo Bill: his grave and Pahaska Tepee on Lookout Mountain; the splendid museum at Cody, near the life-size statue, "The Scout," where he rides on forever in bronze; and his beloved ranch at North Platte. At the latter place, in the theater partitioned off in a corner of the big barn, one of the earliest movies made in America is shown—jerky, fascinating flicks taken in 1898 by the great Thomas Edison himself of Cody's Wild West show in Madison Square Garden.

It is also true that in 1968 Colorado and Wyoming ended their fifty-year-old feud over the old showman's burial place when, with an exchange of smoke signals between Lookout Mountain and Cody, the spirit of Pahaska was transported on a riderless white horse from its tomb to the site on Cedar Mountain where, so many believe, he really wanted to be buried.

It is true that the 328-feet-high dam (in 1910 the highest in the world) across the Shoshone River, near Cody, is named for Buffalo Bill, the man who first envisioned the barren Wyoming prairies blossoming like a garden under irrigation—and did something about it.

And, at long last, in North Platte today, in addition to Scout's Rest Ranch, Cody Park, and the reincarnated Buffalo Bill's Wild West show, a hotel, a school, and a tourist camp are named for W. F. Cody. A radio station uses the call letters KODY; there is a Buffalo Bill Avenue, the Fort Cody trading post, a Buffalo Bill chapter of the Kiwanis Club, and a Buffalo Bill Corral of the International Westerners. An organization known as the North Platte Cody Scouts confers the rank of colonel upon worthy citizens. A colonelcy is not lightly given, and far more nominees for the rank have been turned down than have been accepted; national celebrities as well as local citizens have been made members of the Cody Scouts.

Back in 1963 a Lincoln County ranchman, Charlie Evans, was tapped for the part of Buffalo Bill in a Fort McPherson pageant. To "make up" as the famous scout, Charlie grew a mustache and goatee and let his hair grow long. In hip boots and beaded buckskin jacket, he looked so much like the original Buffalo Bill that the local high school asked him to officiate at all home football games. Mounted on Snowball, he waits beside the hometown goal posts, and each time the North Platte team makes a touchdown he races around the field, firing his revolver. He leads the annual NEBRASKAland Days parade and heads the Grand Entry for the nightly performance of the Wild West show.

It is probably true that more pictures of Buffalo Bill have been made and sold than of any other man in history. Charles E. Stacy of New York, Cody's personal photographer, said in 1932 that he alone had sold more than a million of the pictures he made of the Colonel during his Wild West period. His post card pictures still sell by the thousands in "Cody country."

It is true that the *World Book Encyclopedia* listed W. F. Cody with the famed scouts Boone, Carson, Crockett, and Bridger. And that Golden, Colorado, celebrates "Buffalo Bill Day," Denver celebrates "Buffalo Bill Week," Leavenworth, Kansas, celebrates Buffalo Bill Cody Days, and Nebraska celebrates "Buffalo Bill" month, all in August. Each June, North Platte also puts on an "Old Glory Blowout," commemorating the world's first rodeo, the July Fourth celebration gotten up there by Buffalo Bill in 1882.

It is true that three days after the Colonel's death, his old friend, Congressman F. W. Mondell of Wyoming, read several paragraphs into the *Congressional Record,* eulogizing him and his contributions to the development of Wyoming; the reading was interrupted several times by hearty applause from the floor. It is also true that the Boy Scouts of America were so named because of Mr. Cody. Artist Dan Beard had organized a society of scouts he called Sons of Daniel Boone. Later, after he came to know Buffalo Bill, he and Robert Baden Powell re-organized the society into the Boy Scouts, patterned their activities after the life of a plains scout, and adopted as part of their uniforms the sombrero and neckerchief, such as Cody wore. In 1946, on the cen-tennial of Buffalo Bill's birthday, a troop of Boy Scouts formed the guard of honor at the Lookout Mountain tomb as Chief Blackhorse laid a wreath on the grave, while other Indians, Denverites, and mounted cowboys looked on, and a nationwide radio hookup carried Cody stories. The observance ended with a great ball at Denver's Windsor Hotel.

In the middle 1950s, North Platte's mayor, C. J. Frazier, received a letter from Essen, Germany; addressed only to "The Mayor of the Home Town of Buffalo Bill," the letter was delivered.[21] In 1965, when Mr. and Mrs. Merlin Garey of Edison, Nebraska, visited the Holy Land, the first thing they saw when they alighted from their bus in Nazareth was a theater marquee advertising a Buffalo Bill movie.

In 1968, in a nationwide contest, pictures of Buffalo Bill's Ranch State Historical Park appeared on millions of Kellog's cereal boxes as part of an Old West Trail promotion campaign.

In the latter years of his life, Colonel Cody had conceived the idea of organizing the many members of his family into a "co-ordinated society" but died before the organization was completed. In 1924 his niece Mary Jester Allen, of Cody, called a meeting of all the family members she could reach and "co-ordinated" them into The International Cody Family Association. Its purpose: "to perpetuate for all time the name and memory of Colonel Cody and to assemble in genealogical form the records and data of the Cody family." The first president was Arthur Cody of Chicago, and the first "annual reunion" was held the next year. The association has come to number well over 2,000 members from all over the world, and reunions are held in the U.S. and Canada. A magazine, *The Review,* is published every year on Buffalo Bill's birthday at Kissimmee, Florida, keeping the members up-to-date on all Cody data. In this manner the Codys carry on for their famous ancestor.

39

Epilogue

Strangely, of the many persons who have written of Buffalo Bill, few ever visited his home town and talked with any of the people who knew him longest and best, his friends and neighbors in North Platte. Don Russell was one who did, but by the time he arrived, in the late 1950s, it was too late to visit with any of Cody's contemporaries except ninety-year-old William McDonald.

Fortunately, however, between 1939 and 1941, a team of interviewers talked at length with most of the men and women, still around, who had known the Cody family. These interviews, preserved in historical files, have been invaluable in the compilation of this book.[1] Also, most of Cody's biographers have largely ignored his wife and daughters, in effect, as one writer observed, relegating them to the quiet backwaters of North Platte; therefore, it is interesting to see what the neighbors had to say about Louisa, Arta, and Irma.

Although the Cody girls had been educated in exclusive eastern schools and had traveled over most of the United States and some foreign countries, they were welcome members of North Platte's social life when at home. Mrs. Cody, too, though well traveled in America, was an active member of the Wednesday Afternoon Club and like organizations of her home town. At home in their ornate Welcome Wigwam they entertained lavishly and often; and after the Goodmans moved from Scout's Rest, they sometimes held social affairs there, as when Mrs. Cody entertained the members of the Episcopal choir there, transporting her guests to and from the ranch in two large wagons.

Whenever the Cody girls gave dances, picnics, and skating parties, there were always rigs and teams available from the Cody stables to carry the guests, no matter how many; also, all types of new entertainment were to be found at the Cody home ahead of anywhere else in town. When Irma, as a young girl, became the first owner of a phonograph, it was worthy of an item in the newspaper.

That Mrs. Cody and her daughters were popular and well liked is attested to by many of their neighbors. Edward Keliher, often a guest of the Codys during Irma's time, said: "Both Irma and Mrs. Cody had the rare ability of making every guest feel that *he* was the one most welcome, and we all left their parties in that spirit."[2] C. H. Stamp thought Mrs. Cody a fine woman. "She belonged to a mother's club that my wife belonged to. She was just as common as we were and we called her 'Ma Cody.'"

John Little said she wasn't afraid to work, that she used to drive out to the ranch to see how things were getting along. She didn't put up a big front, and to see her driving along you'd think she was just a common farmer's wife. She was nice to work for." Linnie Breese recalled visits to Mrs. Cody at the town house. "The last time I saw her she was ironing veils. She had a lovely complexion and always wore a veil when she drove out to the farm."

Beata Cox, the Cody seamstress, said Mrs. Cody and Arta were fine people to work for. "I had lovely materials to work with there. The lace and silk alone for one dress for Arta cost $40. I made Clara Boal's clothes when she went away to boarding school, and I made shirts for Mr. Cody, too, of satin that cost $18 a yard. I suppose it was imported. He was a large man and the sewing on many things he bought was rough. They could get what they wanted by having it made.

"One time when I was there the phone rang and Mrs. Cody called, 'Oh, Beatie, come quick.' I ran downstairs and she said, 'I want you to talk on the telephone.' Somebody said, 'Hello, how are you and how is your mother?' It was Irma. She had called her mother from the Philippines and Mrs. Cody wanted me to have the thrill of talking to her there. She said I could tell my girl friends that I had talked clear to the Philippines on the telephone. I was a poor girl and that was a luxury. Mrs. Cody knew, too, how much I wanted to paint and she used to say, 'Beatie, when we get rich we will go to Europe and study art.'"

Louisa, too, had a love of art and for some time was a member of a china-painting class in North Platte, attending faithfully and turning out numerous creditable pieces of delicate china.

Of those interviewed, only old Martin Federhoof, who as a boy had played in the trophy room at Welcome Wigwam, had unkind words for Mrs. Cody. "Mrs. Cody was the goldangest, squirreliest old no-account, no-good crank that any woman could be," he said. Others, who as children had known Mrs. Cody, had only pleasant memories of her. "Mrs. Cody used to give me dolls at Christmas time, when we lived on one of their farms," said Mrs. Elmer Crawford.[3]

William Chase, born in North Platte in 1886, said he was a poor boy who lived in a shack next to the livery stable. "Mrs. Cody was always feeding me," he said, "and I used to go to the ice house where the Union Pacific workers would be icing the trains. They'd break off pieces for me and I'd run to Mrs. Cody with them and she'd give me a nickel. By the time I was nine I'd made enough to buy a rifle that hung in the hardware store window. It cost $3.60."[4]

Mrs. Hettie Mesmer, daughter of Fred Schmalzried, who manufactured the Buffalo Bill cigar, told of the time she played the part of an Indian maiden in an operetta the Episcopal church held at Lloyd's Opera House when she was a small girl. As everyone else did on similar occasions, she went to Mrs. Cody to be outfitted for her part from the Indian articles in the trophy room. "She dressed me up in everything I needed, and I admired her so very much."[5]

Many Platters recalled Louisa's addiction to ouija boards and spiritulism. Beata Cox said she used to write letters to someone in Paris who claimed to read her horoscope for her. At the time Will Cody was trying to get his divorce she relied heavily on the monthly readings, "and no one could tell her there was nothing to them," Beata stated. Johnny Baker, Jr., also spoke of Mrs. Cody's belief in mediums, Gypsies, and fortune tellers. "And she could sure write with that ouija board. Many times I've seen her play it with my mother. She'd ask it, 'Does Daddy love me?' and things like that, and it would spell out y-e-s. But she was a wonderful person. Lots of hoboes came to her house, and so far as I know she never turned one away. She used to stash money away all over the house. When she needed cash in a hurry, she would reach into the flour bin or someplace and get some. I knew her as well as I knew my own grandmother [Mrs. William Sweeny, Sr.], and when Mrs. Cody died my mother went up to Denver for her funeral."[6]

As a boy, Johnny often played in the top-floor trophy room and well remembered the scores of loving cups of all shapes and sizes given to Colonel Cody in the cities where he presented his farewell shows.

Geraldine Bare Munger, another of the youngsters who played in the big room at the top of Welcome Wigwam, remembered dressing up in the Indian headdresses and other things. "We'd wear them outside, with the feathers dragging on the ground, and put on shows of our own. And Mrs. Cody believed in dreams and had ways, dream books and the like, of telling what they meant. Clara Boal and I and some of the other girls used to make up dreams to tell her, and she'd look them up and tell us what they meant. In the wintertime she'd take us to the ranch to skate on the frozen lagoon, then we'd sit around a big bonfire and eat and sing."

So much for the opinions of those who actually knew Louisa. Sell and Weybright, who did not know Mrs. Cody, wrote in their *Buffalo Bill and the Wild West* that she displayed a quick, sharp temper all her life, was moody and resentful, distressed by her husband's "tall stories," highly volatile and emotional, exceptionally beautiful but with the vanity of a spoiled daughter.[7] Chauncey Thomas described her as "a constant millstone around his [Cody's] neck. . . . He wanted freedom for years, but she would not give it to him."[8]

Some of the Cody friends said that if Louisa had traveled more with her husband they might have gotten along better; but Louisa, when asked by Alice Howe why she didn't, said somebody had to stay home to look after the children (her daughters and, later, Cody Boal) and keep them in school. "But," said Charlie Whalen, "Mrs. Cody was always waiting for William to come home."

Irma was something like her father when it came to pride in the horses and rigs she used. Young George Hanna came down from the north Sandhills country while Fred Garlow was ranch manager and hired out to break some horses for him. "When that was done," George said, "they gave me a kind of choreboy job. Part of it was looking after Irma's horses [she rode a lot] and her driving outfit. If her tall bay driving horse, or the rig, had a speck of dust on them she'd send me back to the barn for an oiled rag to polish things up a bit."

In the spring of 1913, when Mrs. Cody and the Garlows were ready to move to Cody to make their home, the North Platte Elks Club gave a huge farewell banquet and dance in their honor. Professor Garlich (who had once thrown his cane at Irma) and his orchestra furnished the music and "regret was general over the removal of these worthy people," according to the *Telegraph*. The day following the ball, Fred and Irma left for Cody to take over the management of the Irma Hotel, and Mrs. Cody went east to join her husband and the show in Philadelphia. She later returned to Cody, where she once more waited for William to come home.

The hotel was not doing so well and economies had to be practiced. Irma was usually in charge, and friends who patronized the hotel said she presided regally at the desk. Thirty years old when she moved to Cody, she was a very large but stylish-looking woman. Dressed in black satin, she made a handsome appearance as she presented the register to her guests and rang loudly for the bellboy. When no boy appeared, she explained apologetically that he must be busy, then invited the guests to carry their own luggage up the one flight of stairs. It was the same for hot or cold water for the rooms: the ever-busy bellboy would not show up and everybody carried his own. Hotel stationery for that period listed the Irma as run on "The American plan only, rates $4 and $5 per day."

In October 1918 Fred and Irma fell victims to influenza and died within four days of each other. Mrs. Cody, of course, took their three small children into her home to love and care for. A short time later she legally adopted them.

Louisa's last brief appearance in the spotlight came in June 1920, when she traveled to Philadelphia to champagne-christen a steel cargo shop. Named *Cody* in honor of Buffalo Bill, the ship was the eleventh built for the U.S. government.

In concluding *Memories,* Cooper in 1919 quoted Louisa as follows: "And now, up here in Cody, I face the sunset. My children are gone. . . . I am alone, my life lived, my hands folded. . . . it will not be long now . . . until the time shall come when I am with the children I loved, and the man I loved—on the Trail Beyond."[9]

The "time" came fairly soon. In 1921 she became ill with organic heart disease. After several severe attacks she seemed to be getting better, then died suddenly on October 20, 1921, at her home. Johnny Baker in Denver and Cody Boal in North Platte were the first to be notified. Speculation began immediately as to where she would be buried. Would it be possible to lay her beside her husband on Lookout Mountain, or must she go to a lonely grave by herself? May Decker, quoted in the Denver *Post,* said: "Hopes that Mrs. Cody might be buried by the side of her husband cannot be realized. It would be necessary to blast the grave out of solid rock and this could not be done without working great damage to Colonel Cody's burial place. She probably will be buried at Cody."

But a letter Louisa wrote to Johnny Baker a few days before her death changed all this. Johnny had visited his foster mother often during her illness but was in Denver at the time of her sudden death. In the letter, which arrived after she died, she expressed her wish to be buried beside her husband, and Johnny said that it should be granted, as he saw no reason why a place could not be made for her in the tomb on Lookout Mountain. On November 1 she was buried above the concrete layer that covered Buffalo Bill's coffin. Her one-time attorney, W. T. Wilcox, said it would be a satisfaction to Mrs. Cody to know that she is lying in the same grave with her husband, whom she must have truly loved.

Walsh, in his *The Making of Buffalo Bill,* stated that Cody's debts went on for years after his death, that his estate remained in a tangle, and that his will was only a bit of paper leaving everything to his wife—and "everything" was barely enough to care for her until her death.[10] Mrs. Cody's own will seems to refute this.[11] When her assets were appraised and evaluated they came to $95,000. She left one dollar to Arta Clara Boal Benn, of London; $5,000 to Cody Boal of North Platte; the balance to be divided equally between Jane, Fred, and William Garlow, "my grandchildren by blood and by adoption," when they attained their majority. In the meantime the children were to be cared for in the Cody home by an aunt and uncle, Mr. and Mrs. George Wallacker.

In the summing up from his neighbors' comments, Buffalo Bill also does quite well, as shown by the following statements, taken from the old interviews:

Charlie Whalen: "I first met Mr. Cody in '87. He was a friend of everybody's, the kind of a man that if he made friends with a four-year-old the child would never forget him. When he made his appearance in a crowd, he spoke to everybody. There wasn't a man, woman, or child that he knew or ever met that he didn't speak to. He was a man I called a gentleman, drunk or sober, a real leader. His manners were perfect, and he was quiet and courteous under any circumstances. His personal appearance was striking, and he always attracted a crowd wherever he was. He was a great man and I always had a great love for him."

C. H. Stamp: "Buffalo Bill was a beautifully built man. He was about twenty-five the first time I saw him, and I knew him from then until he died. He was one of the finest men I ever met."

Vaughn Hinman: "He was a handsome man, a way above common, and very courteous. Even when he was drunk he was never a rowdy."

Jimmy Dugan, the half-Negro: "I never saw a bad trick out of the man in all my life."

Dr. D. T. Quigley, the Cody family physician: "There were many admirable things about Colonel Cody. He was a fine figure of a man, a bright, keen, courtly, and considerate gentleman with the finest instincts. Of coure he was human, like the rest of us, but he treated people with consideration and good will. He thought a great deal of his children and grandchildren."

C. W. Yost: "He gave lots of money away. Nobody ever went hungry around him. If a man asked for a dollar he was as likely to give him ten. He was a great man."

John Hupfer: "He was a grand fellow, and the best looking man I've ever seen. He liked to drink and some didn't like him because of that, but he was never a ruffian at any time."

Edd Wright: "They said he was a man who had gone from Indian squaws to the princesses of Europe. I don't suppose that was ever said of any other man."

Hugh Gaunt: "There was never another man lived as popular as he was. It wasn't his fault that women went crazy over him."

Although not a North Platte resident, A. J. Bath of Columbus, Ohio, was with the Wild West show in his youth. Many years later he wrote of Cody: "I thought him the most valuable asset of the United States to foreign lands, and I stand by the conviction that there has never been his equal, with or without portfolio." Following Cody's death, Hugh D'Arcy, veteran actor, wrote: "I first met W. F. Cody in Louisville in 1878, while he was in his border play. He was the handsomest man I ever saw in my life and he was notably generous, a gentleman through and through." Charles E. Stacy, Cody's personal photographer, said the Colonel came to his South Brooklyn studio many times to sit for pictures, but only once in his later years would he have his picture taken with his hat off. "It wasn't hard to guess the reason; my friend was getting a little bald, and was always proud of his long hair. He was handsome as a god, a good rider and a crack shot."[12]

Other little glimpses into Colonel Cody's personality are to be found in the following comments: Lottie Kocken related that when guests came to Welcome Wigwam for the first time, Cody always showed them the portrait of little Kit and, with tears in his eyes, introduced the boy with: "This is Kit Carson Edward Judson William Buffalo Bill No. 2 Cody" and explained that he had taught the lad to say his name that way as soon as he could talk.

Johnny Baker Jr., who, with his friend Cody Boal, had spent some time with the show, recalled the crowds who always came to Cody's office tent on the grounds to shake his hand and have their pictures taken with him. He kept a uniformed doorman at the tent opening to announce visitors, Johnny said, and no matter who was outside, from a mayor to a shabby woman with a baby, the Colonel would smooth his mustache, stand tall and straight, and tell the doorman to "show 'em in." He greeted everyone the same. William McDonald, who loved to talk of his association with the famous showman, often told how when Cody was in Europe and cabled the McDonald bank for £3,000 sterling, or about $15,000, to bring the show home the next year after the glanders outbreak, he had wired the money right back. When some of his associates had demanded, "What do you have to hold [collateral]?" McDonald said he replied, "I've got this cable. With Cody that is enough."

The comments of North Platte's feminine contingent are quite as interesting. Said Julia Siebold, foster daughter of Mrs. A. W. Randall, Lincoln County's first cattle queen: "I don't like to hear these disparaging things said of Mr. Cody. He was a brave man. He did drink—but show me the man in those days who didn't! He was a perfect gentleman and the most magnificent horseman I ever saw. I remember seeing him come riding to our ranch on a splendid black horse. His manners were princely, and when he rode up he bowed as few men in this country could."[13]

Mrs. Charles Clinton, wife of the town jeweler, stated: "Colonel Cody was one of the handsomest men I ever met. His pictures do not flatter him." Mrs. Mary Roddy said: "I think Buffalo Bill did more to put North Platte on the map than anyone else who ever lived here. He was a romantic figure, with the carriage of nobility, and so courtly. His manners were beautiful; when introduced to a lady he would take off her glove and bow from the waist and kiss her hand, and women everywhere went for it. They had nothing in Europe to beat him."

Mrs. Kate Woolsey, daughter of the town's first school teacher and for many years children's librarian in North Platte, remembered that the Colonel always called on her mother when he came to town. Though only a small girl, she thought him a very handsome man and was impressed by his beautiful manners and his long, curly hair. Zella Van Brocklin, assistant at the births of Irma's children, said simply: "Mr. Cody was the finest man I ever knew."

Mrs. Jessie Blankenburg Reynolds, daughter of the leading harness maker, said her father had learned his trade in Germany, was an artist at the business, making his own designs, and that Cody was one of his best customers. "He always bought the best and was no quibbler when it came to fine and showy harness and saddles. His orders were very large and he paid handsomely. We all admired him a great deal, though we did not always approve of some of the things he did."

Several of his old friends mentioned Cody's complexion, unusual for an outdoorsman in that even in his old age it was as beautiful and clear "as the skin of a pampered woman's face." Both Charlie Whalen and C. W. Yost remembered his erect carriage. Said Whalen: "One Decoration Day the Grand Army of the Republic veterans paraded here. The old fellows marched along, all pretty well stooped and bent— getting up in years—but Cody towered head and shoulders above the rest of them, straight as a ramrod. He marched along as if he wasn't more than thirty, but his hair was white. He was way above the average, physically and every other way." Yost said the last time he saw him was at the funeral of Judge Elder. "He walked from the house across the tracks to the Presbyterian Church and then to the cemetery, and he was as straight as an arrow, even at his age, a striking figure of a man, head and shoulders above the rest."

On the other side were the few who made "disparaging" remarks, most of them actuated by envy more than anything else. John F. Pell said: "Yes, I knew Cody, but by gol I can't say much for him. He was a cheat. One time I seen him playing cards in a livery barn between Fifth and Sixth Streets. He was trying to skin an old man. Some of us fellows watched him and we always said we ought to of locked him in there. The old man accused him of cheatin' and Bill called him a liar. The old man got up and invited him to take a lickin', or give one, and old Bill took to his heels. He was always shootin' off his mouth. Wasn't anything to him but a windbag. Th' fellows that used t' be at th' fort never had much use for Cody."[14]

Slightly more favorable to Buffalo Bill is the tale told by John's brother, Harry Pell: "Cody was a pretty man, a ways off, but close up he was coarse and ugly. He was a big-hearted man and a big crowd used to follow him from one saloon to another and he'd set them up. He would ride up to a saloon, and if a boy was settin' on the sidewalk he would throw the reins to him and whatever change he happened to get hold of, a dollar or a half dollar, he'd throw it to him.

"He was a rounder and he had no grit. One time when old man Cash was running the Pacific Hotel, Cody and him got into it on the street. Cash hit Cody, and Cody took out of there. [Cash and Cody were involved in a lawsuit in 1885, but no such altercation as this is mentioned elsewhere.] One time my uncle, Edd Myers, sold him a gun and waited and waited for the money. One day he struck him for it, and Cody hemmed and hawed. My uncle was a rough man, so he took off his coat and said, 'I'll show you how to cut the buckwheat,' and Cody didn't stay around. I knew Frank Grouard in '95 at Sheridan, Wyoming. He had been chief of scouts at Fort McPherson. Cody was a scout but he wasn't chief of scouts."[15]

Colonel Cody's other male detractor was John Little, who did not know him personally but only repeated stories told him by two old men who had homesteaded near the fort: "They never had much good to say about him. They said he used to like to get in big with some fellow that thought he was rubbing shoulders with the real thing and be a good fellow and buy the drinks until he got a believer made of him. He got in with some rich Englishmen that way. But from what I heard there were fellows that knew him that said he never did much real scouting and never did kill but one or two Indians. He managed to get assigned as chief of scouts and got the glory for a lot of work the other fellows did. He about broke all his friends with his show. He was always borrowing money, but I don't know as he was so good at paying it back."[16]

Buffalo Bill's female downgraders based their opinions largely on his drinking and his association with dance hall girls. Said Ada Breternitz, daughter of a saloon keeper and the first white girl born in North Platte: "I never could see anything in him. My earliest recollection of him is seeing him so drunk he could hardly sit in his carriage." Mary Elder, sister of band leader Bill Sweeney, told her interviewer that she probably wouldn't want to print what she would have to say about Buffalo Bill: "I've seen him sit out in front of Dave Perry's saloon, holding two of those fast girls from the old Square Top[17] on his lap." (Mrs. Elder's sister, Mrs. John Baker, Sr., was one of Cody's staunchest friends.)

When the interviewer attended a meeting of a North Platte writers club, she gleaned the following comments from the members: "One would hardly care to build a memorial to so drunken a sot as we remember Buffalo Bill to have been." "I did not know him, but in the interests of temperance it seems the least said of such a character the better." Only Mrs. John Dick took his part: "You couldn't blame Cody. He was no worse than the other men. They all drank. But everybody admired him. He was a fine looking man and you couldn't help liking him."[18]

Tales of Cody's capacity for hard liquor vary as much as others told of him. Jessie Blankenburg Reynolds stated: "I've heard he and his cowboys would ride into the saloons, line up at the bar, and drink their whiskey sitting on their horses. I wouldn't put it past him. Few men, then or now, had the vitality and love of life that he did." John Dick declared: "Heck, I've seen him treat a whole saloon full of men, then walk out of that one and treat the same in another place." Charlie Whalen recalled a time when the Colonel came downtown with his friend, Beck, of Montana, and stopped in at Guy Laing's saloon: "The place was full and Cody wanted to treat everybody, so he and his friend stepped behind the bar and helped Guy and his two bartenders set up the drinks. When they'd had all the fun they wanted, they came out from behind the bar and Cody paid the bill."

In the summer of 1882 it is recorded that Cody held a reception each evening for a week at Guy Laing's place. His friends from the Niobrara to the Republican and from Sidney to Plum Creek flocked to North Platte, and conviviality reigned supreme from eight in the evening to seven in the morning. Each night the Colonel threw a dozen or more $20 gold pieces on the bar to pay for his party.[19]

J. L. Ketchum told how Buffalo Bill and one of Louisa's relatives, a man named Frederici, used to put on a "William Tell act": Cody would shoot an apple off Frederici's head. "One time I guess he had a little too much liquor and grazed the old man's neck. It left a scar, and he always carried his head to one side afterward. He used to talk about it and show the scar."

James A. McCann, who had traveled with the Wild West, boasted that he used to go with Cody after the performances to help him keep his social engagements, "because I could handle the liquor better." The stories of Buffalo Bill's drinking had become so exaggerated by 1968 that the *Masonic Tribune* published this statement: "He became a heavy drinker in later years and was often lifted onto his horse for his triumphal entry into the circus ring. Even with shells loaded with fine shot, he had difficulty hitting the targets."[20]

William McDonald, however, told of meeting Cody and two other friends in Omaha on the Fourth of July in the closing years of the showman's life. "We decided to go to a bar and wet our whistles, and when the bartender asked the Colonel what he'd have, he said, 'lemonade.' The others wanted to know 'how come?' and Cody said, 'Gentlemen, I haven't drunk hard liquor for three years. Oh, in my time I've drunk enough to float a battleship, but since I've quit I feel better."

Joseph Stone, a North Platte druggist for many years, also spoke of Cody's "later years, when he was on the wagon. He became very fond of orange ice cream sodas and would come into my place and say, 'Joe, fix me up some of that goop with orange in it.'"

Several old-timers have told that the Colonel was thoroughly intoxicated on the occasion of his 1913 appearance with his show in North Platte: lying drunk in the weeds near the show grounds, lying drunk on some bales of hay in the animal quarters, too drunk to hit the glass balls when he rode into the arena that afternoon. Of these stories Mrs. Mayme Watts Langford said with lady-like disgust: "Yes, I know they said he was intoxicated when he rode into the arena, but I said, 'Well, he knows more drunk than half the rest of us know when we're sober.'"

I myself remember Cody's appearance in the ring that afternoon, how straight he sat in the saddle as he rode his white horse up to a tubfull of water just below the section where we sat. Dismounting, he took off his big white hat, dipped it full of water from the tub, and held it for his horse to drink; with a graceful sweep of his arm, he emptied the hat, then filled it again and drank from it himself. Bowing deeply, he replaced his hat, mounted, and galloped away.

One of the times when Colonel Cody failed to handle his liquor with aplomb was the $5-a-plate dinner given for him at Lloyd's Opera House in the early years of his rise to fame. Said Mrs. Mary Patterson: "It was a huge affair and very brilliant, and he had to go and get drunk. He tried to give a talk, and Mrs. Cody kept trying to push him down into his chair." In telling of the same incident, Martin Federhoof said Mrs. Cody kept pulling on her husband's coattail, and Cody said, "Don't do that, Mama," too drunk to know she was trying to get him to sit down.

In summing up it would seem that Buffalo Bill's good traits far outweighed the bad, and of the good his generosity is most often mentioned. His neighbors say he ran his own medicare program and made jobs for his crippled or handicapped friends. Charlie Whalen's brother, a one-armed man, traveled with the show and passed out programs. Guy Laing's one-armed brother was an usher. After the hippodrome rider fell from his three horses and struck his head on a stake, causing fainting spells, Cody made a job for him, too. The list goes on.

It was said he was always taking young fellows under his protective wing. Faye Simmons was one of his proteges, a seventeen-year-old North Platte lad who drove for Cody when he was in town. Faye's mother was a widow who kept a cow and sold milk to her town neighbors for a bit of income. One morning when his employer told him to "hitch up," the boy said he had to go home and haul some hay for his mama's cow. Cody replied, "You hitch up, I'll take care of mama's cow." When Faye went home he found the little corral so full of hay that the cow had to be tied outside.

Hugh Gaunt, who as a boy had curried and groomed the Colonel's horses at the ranch, later tried farming near North Platte but was "eaten out" by grasshoppers. He had hoped to make enough money to build a house and get married but had to give up his plans and go into his father's blacksmith shop as a helper. About this time he met Buffalo Bill, who asked him how he was getting along. When he told his sad tale, Cody handed him $200 and told his to go ahead with his house. In those days $200 would build a very decent small house. Said Gaunt: "I thought Buffalo Bill was one of the squarest men I ever knew. If he saw anybody in trouble he stopped to help, no matter where he was."

Joseph Baskins, one of the kids who had often "lined up" at the old opera house as a guest of Buffalo Bill's, later became a bellhop at the new Palace Hotel on Front Street. "One day," he said, "Cody and Sam Morant [a local rancher] came into the washroom. They were wearing white Stetson hats and soft, high-topped dress boots. I'll never forget how fine they looked. They had me polish their boots, and when I finished Cody asked, 'How much?' I said twenty cents, and he threw me a dollar and they walked out, with Sam telling Cody he'd 'get even' over town. Later on, I was working at the laundry, and I got eight of his shirts to do in one afternoon. They were made by a fellow in New York by the name of 'Budds,' and they had collars made right on the shirts, with bosoms to match."

In the early '80s Charles Bergstrom came to North Platte from Sweden and got a job as blacksmith on the Union Pacific. He soon had saved enough money to send for his wife and three little daughters but was unable to find a house for them. Cody heard of his plight and told him to go ahead and send for the family; he would see that he had a house. By the time the family arrived, Cody had one of the little houses Louisa owned ready for them.

Shortly afterward another newly arrived Swedish family pulled into town in a covered wagon. Bound for western Nebraska and a homestead, they had to stop over to await the birth of a baby. When they too couldn't find a house, the Bergstroms took them in, making four adults and seven children in the cottage. Cody came by every few days to see how they were and if the children were warm and had enough to eat. By the time the baby arrived the host family had decided to go on west with their new friends. So Bergstrom hunted up his landlord to pay the rent, but Cody would not take a cent for anything. "Keep the money and use it for the kids," he said.[21]

Indeed, Colonel Cody was at his finest when dealing with children. For years the village boys vied with one another to hold his horse and run his errands. "I'd hold his horse in front of the post office or saloon," said Johnny Dugan, and when he came out he'd reach in his pocket and give me whatever he got hold of, even a dollar." Said Edd Weeks: "One time I only went two blocks and he gave me the $5 gold piece he pulled out." Otto Thoelecke recalled that Cody frequently paid fifty cents for an errand when ten cents was the going wage. Even better than running errands and getting overpaid was being hoisted onto the saddle behind Buffalo Bill for a canter down the street on one of his fine horses.

When a little girl, Mrs. Mary Roddy once helped sell chances on a doll for a Catholic fair held in the old Unitarian Hall. The doll was a beautiful thing, dressed all in blue satin. Buffalo Bill was in town, and someone told her she should ask him to buy a chance. She did, and he asked her how many she had left. She told him twenty-eight, and he said he'd take them all and she could put *her* name down for every one of them. "Oh, I wanted that doll so much," she said, long years later, "and I had twenty-eight chances to win, but Emma Alsteadt, a girl with only one chance, won it." Incidentally, it was Emma's father, butcher Alsteadt, who, in his German-accented English, called Buffalo Bill "Beef-a-lo Bull," to the great amusement of the whole town.

It is said that one time when his show train paused in North Platte for a few minutes on its way west, the Colonel came out on the rear platform of his private car to greet the crowd gathered to welcome him. He was followed by two helpers carrying a half-bushel container of coins. He announced that he was going to scatter the money in the street for the kids, and he wanted the grownups to keep hands off.

In the towns where he showed, the Colonel hired boys to pass out hand bills advertising the show, and paid them with free tickets to the performances. Frequently kids too young to be hired would hunt him up on the grounds to tell him sad stories about passing out hand bills—and then not getting paid for their work. Bill would listen with a twinkle in his eye, then give the boys free tickets. With his approval,

Bill Sweeney and Johnny Baker used to watch for boys attempting to sneak into the show. One would take one side of the tent and one the other, grab the kids as they wriggled under the canvas, and march the poor scared youngsters around to the front entrance, then take them in and put them in good seats. They did this at every show for years, for neither Sweeney nor Baker had had a dime, as kids, and they knew how it felt. The old Sioux chief, Red Fox, who travelled to Europe with the show in the '80s, said that he and other show employees also "booted poor kids under the canvas into the show tent."

Small fry who saw Buffalo Bill in his show never forgot him, but George "Rusty" Shiltz had more reason than most to remember him. The Shiltz family had lined their wagon up at the side of the street in Cheyenne to watch the parade go by, the parents in front, the kids in the back of the wagon. Buffalo Bill pranced by on his horse, followed by the rest of the parade, but when the caliope came by it scared the Shiltz team and away they went, "with us kids too scared even to yell. Then here came Buffalo Bill alongside on his horse and grabbed our team and stopped 'em."

Fred Elliott, who came to North Platte as a boy in 1881, wrote: "We soon discovered that Mr. Cody was the top ranking citizen of the town. He gave me the first money I ever earned, for holding his horse in front of the post office." Six years later his English-born parents took the family home to visit. The Wild West was playing in London at the time and they went to see the show. Afterward they called at the Colonel's tent. "Mr Cody showed us every courtesy and invited us to dine with him in his private mess tent. Arta was there, and Annie Oakley and Johnnie Baker."[22]

A typical Cody story describes a chance meeting in Omaha between the Colonel and four of his friends from Broken Bow. Cody at once invited the four to go to dinner with him at Maure's, the city's finest restaurant. On the way, he stopped at a fancy gent's furnishings store to buy half a dozen fine white silk handerchiefs and give one to each guest. A little farther down the street they stopped in at a furrier's where Bill was to pick up an overcoat he had bought. When the proprietor brought out the beautiful astrakhan coat, Cody tried it on, then said to one of the four, a man of about his build, "George, I can't tell how this looks on me. You put it on and let me size it up on you." George put the coat on, and his host said, "It looks so good on you I want you to keep it. I'll buy another like it for myself." As a result of such open-handed hospitality, Cody's several days of visiting in

Omaha ran his expense account into the thousands of dollars.[23]

Said Chief Red Fox: "The Colonel was such an 'easy touch' he would freely give away his last dollar, and if he reached in his pocket and didn't find anything he'd just holler for Johnny Baker to bring some more money."[24]

Edward Keliher, who operated an ice cream parlor in North Platte from 1910 to 1913, said that whenever Cody was in town he would bring Irma into the place and say, "Ed, a box of your finest candy for Irma." Then, if there were any other women or girls in the shop, off would come that big sombrero and, with a sweep and a bow, he would say, "And will you ladies accept a box of candy from Colonel Cody?"[25]

His kindness extended to *everyone*. The *Tribune* for March 31, 1888, reported that Mrs. Little Chief, wife of one of the Pine Ridge Sioux, had died in New York on Monday. She had taken sick in England and begged to go home to die. Cody had at once put her and her husband on a steamship bound for home, but she lived only to reach New York.

Colonel Cody was one of the early backers of the Red Cross Christmas Seal project. In 1914 he had, along with the citizens of Cody, Wyoming, purchased 22,500 of the little stamps. The town's population was then about 1,200, which meant that the Cody people used about twenty stamps per capita. The next year Bill and his friends bought even more, for they had agreed that every piece of mail leaving the town should bear a Red Cross seal.[26]

Although he often gave generously to churches, Cody was not a church-going man, a fact which worried his sister Julia. In 1901 he answered a letter from her, in which she had pleaded with him to accept Christ, by assuring her that he would never pray openly to God in church on Sunday then cheat his neighbor in a horse trade on Monday, and that he would wrong no man knowingly and would always restrain vice and wickedness when he could, and help the poor and needy.[27] He later wrote Julia: "trying to live on earth as God would be pleased to have me live. I slip up some times then I ask God's forgiveness. And try again."[28] Indeed, the tone of his letters to her in those last years indicated a decided change in his outlook on life and religion, for he often mentioned their "saintly mother," who had lived a consistently God-fearing life.

A man born thirty, fifty, or a hundred years too soon, Cody was one of those rare individuals who saw far ahead of his times. This faculty caused him to back projects that although they broke him were sound and eventually came to fruition in a big way, as did irrigation in both the Platte Valley and the Big Horn Basin. On other matters, too, he foresaw the shape of the future, as when he told Washington reporters in 1913 that we would one day be at war with the Japanese and that "airships" were bound to play an important part in our future wars.[29] And here is Cody on "Women's Liberation." When asked by a prominent member of the Sorosis society, "Do you believe that women should have the same liberty and privileges that men have?" he replied, "Most assuredly I do."

> I've already said they should be allowed to vote. Why, of course, if a woman is out earning her living she keeps up with what is going on in the world, and she knows the best man to vote for. Men have their clubs and I say let the women have theirs, too. Women are so much better than we are that they don't take to our kind of clubs, but if they want to meet and discuss financial questions, politics, or any other subject, let 'em do it and don't laugh at them for doing it. They discuss things as sensibly as men do, I'm sure, and I reckon know just as much about the topics of the day.
>
> One thing gets me. You take a single woman earning her living in a city and the average man looks at her suspiciously if he hears that she lives alone. That makes me tired. A woman who is capable of financiering for herself is capable of taking care of her morals, and if she wants to take an apartment and live alone, where she can do her work more quietly, or have things her own way when she comes from business, she has just as much right to do so as a bachelor. If a woman is a good woman she will remain good alone; if she is bad, being surrounded and overlooked and watched and guarded and chaperoned by a hundred old women in a boarding house won't make her good. This applies to society as well as to working women. There are bad women in every walk of life, but most women are good. What we want to do is to give our women more liberty than they have. Let them do any kind of work that they see fit, and if they do it as well as men, give them the same pay. Grant them the same privileges in their home and club life that men have, and we will see them grow and expand into far more beautiful and womanly creatures than they are already.[30]

In 1967 David Brand, the *Rocky Mountain News* writer who had once described Cody as "the boy who never grew up," was asked to do another feature on the perennially popular Buffalo Bill. He decided a picture and story on the room where the Colonel died would be about right. The house at 2932 Lafayette street had been sold to a Mrs. Donald Tooke in 1938, and when Brand called Mrs. Tooke to ask her if he might take a picture of the room she said, "What will be in it for me?" The reporter explained that this was history and would be above anything like mere money. But she said she didn't see any use in letting a photographer come in unless she got something out of it. Wrote Brand, "Thus does history treat its heroes. And when the flicker is reduced to a spark we come to our senses. But then it is too late and we mourn over the ashes."

A few of the Platters interviewed in the '40s were also "mourning over the ashes." Beata Cox Dean said sadly: "It hurt me to see their old house [Welcome Wigwam] torn down, and I never could understand why North Platte allowed the Cody treasures to be moved away from here." (In 1912 the Colonel had offered to the city of North Platte his entire collection of Indian relics, one of the finest in the West, and many articles collected during his trips abroad. When the city fathers *could not find a place* to store the priceless collection, the Cody family took it with them to Cody, Wyoming, the following year.)

Joseph Baskins echoed Beatie's sentiments when he said: "Cody was connected with every social and community activity here, and I find myself among those who feel that we as a community have fallen far short in honoring a great man, whose time and effort to build up, in fair weather and foul, was given to us without measure."

So ends this story of William F. Cody—Buffalo Bill, that unique, picturesque personality, without precedent, without successor.

Notes

Most "unidentified" newspaper clippings are in my personal files. (N.S.Y.)

Chapter 1   Fort McPherson

1 Stella Adelyne Foote, *Letters from Buffalo Bill,* 34.
2 Ruby Wilson interview with Frank Boyer, May 13, 1940. W.P.A. project.
3 There was presumably yet another trader ensconced then at Cottonwood Springs, someone who years later would figure large in the Buffalo Bill lore—William A. Comstock, he of the famous Cody-Comstock buffalo hunt contest. (See below, Chap. 2.) Although local histories and reminscences do not mention Comstock (his stay may have been brief), the census taker found him there in June 1860. (John S. Gray, "Will Comstock, Scout," *Montana the Magazine of Western History,* July 1970, 7.
4 Louis A. Holmes, *Fort McPherson, Nebraska,* 73, 76.

Chapter 2   Nebraska, Marriage, Buffalo Hunter

1 W. F. Cody, *Story of the Wild West,* 432; Don Russell, *The Lives and Legends of Buffalo Bill,* 35.
2 Musetta Gilman, *Pump on the Prairie,* 39.
3 Lucille Morris Upton, "50 Years Ago in Springfield," weekly column in unnamed newspaper.
4 Cody, *Story,* 481.
5 Louisa Frederici Cody and Courtney Ryley Cooper, *Memories of Buffalo Bill,* 3, 4.
6 Ibid., 40-47.
7 Writers and historians often misname this railroad, an understandable confusion because of its name changes, which ran as follows: 1855-1863, Leavenworth, Pawnee and Western railroad; 1863-March 3, 1869, Union Pacific Railway, Eastern Division; 1869-1880, Kansas Pacific; 1880-present, Union Pacific. Cody himself remembered correctly when just before his death he told Chauncey Thomas: "They called me 'Buffalo' Bill because I had that buffalo contract with the U.P. and got down over 4,250 for meat." (Interview quoted in Zane Grey's

Afterword to 1918 edition of Helen Cody Wetmore, *Last of the Great Scouts,* 328.)

8 Cody, *Story,* 492-93.
9 Cody bought Brigham from a Utah Ute Indian and named him after the Utah Mormon leader Brigham Young. For more on Cody's celebrated horses, see Agnes Wright Spring, *Buffalo Bill and His Horses.*
10 Cody, *Story,* 496.
11 November 26, 1867.
12 Russell, *Lives,* 87.
13 Cody, *Story,* 495-97.
14 Russell, *Lives,* 88-89.
15 Cody, *Story,* 511.
16 Cody and Cooper, *Memories,* 122.
17 Cody, *Story,* 507.
18 Ibid., 508-11.
19 John S. Gray, "Will Comstock, Scout," *Montana the Magazine of Western History,* July 1970, 13-14; Ida J. Ipe of Youngstown, Ohio, a distant relative of Comstock, has also done extensive research on her ancestor but has been unable to document the Cody confrontation (correspondence, 1977 and 1978). Cody himself roughly dates the contest late spring 1868; Mrs. Cody suggests a fall 1867 date. For a closer examination of the dating problem, the location problem, and the general documentation problem, see the summary analysis prepared by Joseph W. Snell of the Kansas State Historical Society (7-page typescript, at Society).

Don Russell presents the only "hard" evidence in the Cody-Comstock case when he reports on the empty bottles found at one presumed contest site (*Lives,* 93; this information came to Russell in a September 6, 1957 letter from Edward M. Beougher, attorney from nearby Grinnell), but he treats it with what appears to be proper tongue-in-cheekness; after all, the old beer and champagne bottles could well have been the festive celebration remains from any 19th-century luxury hunt by some wealthy hunter and his entourage.

20 Gray, "Comstock," *Montana,* 14. Cooper's poster lists Fort Sheridan as the site of the Shooting Match, but there never was a town or a military post in Kansas by that name, although there was a Sheridan town; however, the railroad did not reach Sheridan until August 22, 1868, *after* Comstock was killed by Indians August 16.
21 Cody and Cooper, *Memories,* 155.

Chapter 3   Scout

1 James T. King, *War Eagle,* 101.
2 Don Russell, *The Lives and Legends of Buffalo Bill,* 107.
3 See Ruby Wilson's biography (forthcoming) of Frank North for more on the Pawnee Scouts; Wilson also presents different interpretations of Cody's role as scout at the battle of Summit Springs, of the killing of Tall Bull, and of what happened to Tall Bull's horse.
4 Post records, quoted in Louis A. Holmes, *Fort McPherson, Nebraska,* 38.
5 Cooper, with typical mis-sequence, places the Summit Springs battle months too early, but he does, ironically, incorporate into his book which is rife with exaggerated stories an account of Cody himself correcting an exaggerated story. Lulu had, so Cooper says, read a St. Louis newspaper report of the Summit

Springs affair in which her husband had led the charge on the Indian village; Cody saw the Cheyenne chief, Tall Bull, holding the captive Mrs. Weichel "by her hair"; Tall Bull "was just raising his tomahawk, when suddenly sounded the rush of hoofs and the banging of a gun in the hands of Buffalo Bill, with the result that another renegade had traveled to the happy hunting grounds." When Lulu showed Will the newspaper story, he told her the only thing wrong with it was it was not true: he did not rescue Mrs. Weichel. But he did get "a wonderful horse" out of the scrap. He then told Lulu how he shot Tall Bull (after killing two other Indians who were shooting at him) so he could capture and claim the chief's fine horse. (Louisa Frederici Cody and Courtney Ryley Cooper, *Memories of Buffalo Bill*, 154-55, 158)

6 Russell, *Lives*, 130n2; see also 154n7.
7 Luther North, *Man of the Plains*, 113-18.
8 Russell, *Lives*, 139, quote from *Blake's Western Stories*.
9 North, *Man*, 117.
10 W. F. Cody, *The Life of Hon. William F. Cody*, 260-61; Russell, *Lives*, 143-44.
11 From an account of the battle, written many years later, by Major Leicester Walker of North Platte. The original manuscript, in pencil, is in possession of his great granddaughter, Mrs. Richard (Beverly) Smith, Fort Collins, Colorado. By his North Platte friends, Major Walker was often called Lester, the name he gave his son. The "Major" may have been honorary.
12 Captain George F. Price, *Across the Continent with the Fifth Cavalry* (a regimental history compiled by its adjutant from official records), 138-39; Russell, *Lives*, 137; W. F. Cody, *Story of the Wild West*, 583.
13 Jessie Morant interview with William H. McDonald, December 20, 1939. W.P.A. project.
14 The post office, located in one end of the post trader's store, was merely a tall cupboard with some three dozen little boxes or pigeon-holes in its upper section and with shelves, concealed by doors, below. Built by an enlisted man who had been a cabinetmaker "back East," the humble piece of furniture had furthered the exchange of letters from many a homesick soldier and civilian to the girls they had left behind. (From it, in 1867, Brevet Major General George Armstrong Custer had mailed tender letters to his Elizabeth while he laid up at the post for a few days.) This piece of furniture is now preserved in the Western Heritage Museum in North Platte.
15 Cody, *Story*, 590.
16 North, *Man*, 118.
17 Ruby Wilson interview with Mrs. Mary Elder, March 20, 1940.
   In her *Memories*, Cooper has Lulu referring to the "wagon train from Cheyenne, bearing the furniture that Will had ordered." Why Will would have ordered furniture from Cheyenne and why it would have come by wagon train is mysterious indeed. Cheyenne, barely two years old and still a rough frontier hamlet, hardly compared with Omaha as a market place. The latter, founded in 1854, was quite a city by the time Cody needed furniture for his cabin at Fort McPherson. One also wonders, *if* Will went to Omaha to meet Lulu, why they did not order the furniture while they were there. Most amazing of all is that the order came by wagon train, when the Union Pacific, with its daily trains, had been hauling freight to McPherson Station and North Platte for the past two years. Louisa goes on to tell how worried Will was because one parcel had not come with the rest of the order. Finally, he rode horseback to Cheyenne, "for more than a hundred miles away," to get it himself. (It was well over two hundred miles to Cheyenne from the post.) When he returned, she found it was wallpaper he had gone after. He then tried to paper the cabin walls himself, but

made such a mess of it that he finally gave up, saying he was "more of a success as an Injun killer." Lulu's earlier description of a detail of construction may unwittingly help explain Will's lack of success as a paperhanger: "Will [had taken] a number of tents which had been condemned, and with these the walls had been lined, after a chinking of mud had been placed against all the logs." (Cody and Cooper, *Memories*, 160-64, 161)

18 Frances Sims Fulton, *To and Through Nebraska*, 158-59.
19 A number of writers, Cooper among them, have made the mistake of placing Dunraven in the West in 1869. Actually, in 1869 Lord Adair and his bride sailed to the U.S.A. as their honeymoon trip; he *intended* to hunt in the West, but "just as he thought of heading westward, he had a sunstroke in Virginia and so he returned to Ireland with Florence Elizabeth. He did not get back to the United States until the fall of 1871. . . . His father had died recently and he was no longer Lord Adair but the Fourth Earl of Dunraven." (Marshall Sprague, Introduction to 1967 edition of Dunraven's *The Great Divide*, ix; see also Dunraven, *Past Times and Pastimes*, vol. I, 67)
20 Richard J. Walsh, *The Making of Buffalo Bill*, 157.
21 Russell, *Lives*, 160-61.
22 Cody, *Story*, 595. In telling this story in his book, Cody refers to a buffalo hunting guest on hand for the race, "George Boyd Houghton, of London—the well-known caricaturist." (594) The correct name is Arthur Boyd Houghton, and a better description of him would be artist-journalist (with occasional stings of satire) for the British weekly *The Graphic*.
23 Cody, *Story*, 603.
24 Morant interview with McDonald, December 20, 1939.

Chapter 4   The Platte Valley

1 Captain Eugene F. Ware, *The Indian War of 1864*, 70-71.
2 John Bratt, *Trails of Yesterday*, 61. See also Nellie Snyder Yost, *Call of the Range*, 32-33 and note.
3 Charles M. Clark, *A Trip to Pike's Peak*, 52.
4 Ruby Wilson interview with Charles Stamp, January 10, 1940.
5 Don Russell, *The Lives and Legends of Buffalo Bill*, 169.
6 "Autobiography of Hester Ann Rogers Brown, 1835-1924," *Bits and Pieces*, October 1969, 6.
7 There had been criticism about the construction of the Union Pacific railroad, and Lieutenant Colonel James H. Simpson was in North Platte to examine and report on the matter. Simpson, formerly (prior to the Civil War) for over two decades with the Corps of Topographical Engineers, U.S. Army, was at the time superintendent of railroad construction, Department of the Interior. On Christmas Eve 1866 he penned a letter to the Washington *Chronicle* praising God, the westward spread of Christianity, the progress of the Union Pacific, and the new town on the Platte. Letter reprinted in Silas Seymour, *Incidents of a Trip through the Great Platte Valley*, 124-25.
8 *Fort McPherson Centennial Booklet*, 36.
9 Ibid.
10 D. S. Tuttle, "Tales from Old Timers—No. 4," *Union Pacific Magazine*, July 1923, 35. Tuttle's service was presumably brief, for he adds: "I should gladly have had *full* services there had I stayed over Sunday [but] we left North Platte at 10 a.m. on Whitsunday (June 9)." (emphasis added)

11 Archibald R. Adamson, *North Platte and Its Associations*, 27.

12 Ibid., 31.

13 W. H. Miles, *Early History and Reminiscence of Frontier County*, 10.

14 Adamson, *North Platte*, 30-32.

Chapter 5   Pleasures

1 Ruby Wilson interview with Mrs. Mary Elder, June 13, 1941. Similar baby-swapping stories were standard fare for years among Plains folklore. Owen Wister in *The Virginian*, for instance, has his protagonist perpetrate just such a baby switch at a frontier dance (Chapter X); Wister concludes: "To-day you can hear legends of it from Texas to Montana." (Chapter XI) True.

2 My interview with Mrs. Randall's foster daughter, Mrs. Julia Siebold, North Platte, 1945.

3 *Fort McPherson Centennial Booklet*, 30.

4 Louisa Frederici Cody and Courtney Ryley Cooper, *Memories of Buffalo Bill*, 196-205.

5 Mary H. Hebberd, "Notes on Dr. David Franklin Powell, Known as 'White Beaver,'" *Wisconsin Magazine of History*, Summer 1952, 306.

6 Helen Cody Wetmore, *Last of the Great Scouts*, 175, 180.

7 In addition to exchanging yarns, Cody must have also, in his brief time with Marsh, taught him something of buffalo hunting, for two years later when Marsh was on another expedition in Kansas, he rode into a buffalo herd, "ready to shoot," he wrote, "in the exact manner my first guide, Buffalo Bill, had taught me long before." (Charles Schuchert and Clara Mae LeVene, *O. C. Marsh*, 129)

8 Wetmore, *Great Scouts*, 175.

9 Ibid., 180.

10 Ibid., 185.

Chapter 6   Justice of the Peace, Cody's Favorite Hunt

1 Don Russell, *The Lives and Legends of Buffalo Bill*, 169.

2 In 1866 old Shorter County had been reorganized and renamed Lincoln County. The following year the county seat was removed from Cottonwood Springs to the new town of North Platte and a new set of county commissioners and other officials elected. There is no existing record of Cody's appointment as a justice of the peace, but convincing evidence that he actually served in that office is found in the minutes of the County Commissioners Court for June 1872, in the entry noting his resignation as a justice of the peace at Cottonwood Springs. See Ira L. Bare and Will H. McDonald (eds.), *An Illustrated History of Lincoln County, Nebraska and Her People*, vol. I, 53.

3 W. F. Cody, *Story of the Wild West*, 604.

4 Helen Cody Wetmore, *Last of the Great Scouts*, 180.

5 Louisa Frederici Cody and Courtney Ryley Cooper, *Memories of Buffalo Bill*, 207.

6 Cody, *Story*, 605.

7 Cody and Cooper, *Memories*, 210-13.

8 Cody, *Story*, 609.

9 Ibid.

10 Ibid.

11 [Henry E. Davies,] *Ten Days on the Plains*, 29.
12 Ibid., 25-26. The "brilliant drama" Davies refers to was Fred G. Maeder's play, "Buffalo Bill, **the** King of Border Men," adapted from Ned Buntline's serialization of the same title, which began December 1869 in the *New York Weekly*. (Davies' citation of the *New York Ledger* is an error, though an understandable one, inasmuch as both were story weeklies popular at the time.)
13 Cody, *Story*, 609-10; W. F. Cody, "Famous Hunting Parties of the Plains," *Cosmopolitan*, June 1894, 139.
14 Ibid., 140. Even the most famous buffalo hunt of all time plus the Dunraven hunt and the Chicago party yet to come did not dim Cody's happy memories of the first of the hunts that fall of 1871; some years later, commenting on the Grand Duke Alexis' expedition itself, he added: "But I cannot say that, personally, I ever enjoyed anything more than the New York party." (Ibid., 140)
15 Cody, *Story*, 616-17.
16 Ibid., 619.
17 Ibid. Some writers date the Earl of Dunraven's Nebraska hunt in 1871, in which case it would have to have come during these late fall (or early winter) weeks when Cody "had little to do," or during August prior to the New York party's hunt and the Chicago party's hunt. Don Russell correctly reminds us that Cody "was careless with dates," but in the Dunraven case—and for other reasons which I suggest below (Chap. 8, note 16)—I take Cody at his word: "In the fall of 1872 the Earl of Dunraven . . . came to Fort McPherson." (Ibid., 640) Therefore, I have Cody ending the fall of 1871 on his leisurely note.

Chapter 7   Grand Duke Alexis

1 W. F. Cody, *Story of the Wild West*, 619-22.
2 Don Russell, *The Lives and Legends of Buffalo Bill*, 176-77.
3 William McDonald interview in North Platte *Telegraph-Bulletin*, January 13, 1958.
4 Ibid.
5 Bayard H. Paine, *Pioneers, Indians and Buffalo*, 23.
6 Omaha *Weekly Herald*, January 17, 1872.
7 Ibid.
8 McDonald interview in North Platte *Telegraph-Bulletin*, January 13, 1958. An identical menu was, according to one Cody autobiography, served to General Sheridan and the New York party during their hunt in September 1871. Maybe such dinners were standard fare on distinguished visitors' hunts. Or perhaps McDonald's memory played tricks on him and switched hunts. Just as likely, this illustrates the problem of recollection and certainty in all of Cody's autobiographies, but especially in this posthumous one, published in 1920. During the winter of 1915-1916, Cody, at his nephew's home, had written a new autobiography "that appeared serially in *Hearst's International Magazine* from August, 1916, to July, 1917, under the title 'The Great West That Was: "Buffalo Bill's" Life Story.'" (Russell, *Lives*, 276) Cody's accounts were edited and rewritten before they appeared as the serial articles. Three years later the *Hearst's* articles were published as a book, though again not without further editing. (It "contains many blunders that Bill could not have made." [Ibid.] Therefore, although Cody himself wrote what served as the basis for this autobiography, other writers' hands shaped (and misshaped) the final product. Let the title of the book symbolize the book's confusion: The outside cover of the book carried

the title *Buffalo Bill's Life Story: An Autobiography;* the title page called it *An Autobiography of Buffalo Bill (Colonel W. F. Cody);* the running heads throughout the book at the tops of the text pages read "Buffalo Bill's Own Story."

9 Cody, *Story*, 626-28.

10 Helen Cody Wetmore, *Last of the Great Scouts*, 198-99.

11 W. F. Cody, *An Autobiography of Buffalo Bill*, 235-36.

12 Louisa Frederici Cody and Courtney Ryley Cooper, *Memories of Buffalo Bill*, 215. The thrilling Buntline tales actually appeared only in Cooper's or Louisa's romantic imagination, for at this time only *one* Buntline tale had appeared, that had been almost two years previous, and although Buffalo Bill appeared in the title, the tale scarcely dealt with anything Cody ever did in real life. Cf. above, Chap. 6, note 12.

13 Cody and Cooper, *Memories*, 216-17. That this story is only a bit of wistful vaporing is borne out by the simple fact that the Duke did not go to Fort McPherson. All on-the-spot accounts of the movements of the hunting party have the visitors arriving at North Platte, going directly to the camp at Red Willow, and returning directly to North Platte after the hunt. A number of writers (e.g., Archibald R. Adamson, *North Platte and Its Associations*, 208) besides Cooper have perpetrated the misconception that the caravan left the train at McPherson Station, less than four miles from the fort, drove to the post, and from there went to the Red Willow camp. It *might* have happened this way, except for a bridge. In all likelihood, the officials responsible for the safety of the Russian prince were hesitant to risk his royal neck on the narrow, shaky, railless log bridge across the Platte at McPherson Station, especially when straight south of North Platte a fine new steel bridge with side rails and a plank floor had just been completed by the county at a cost of $30,000.

14 Ruby Wilson interview with Mrs. Ray C. Langford, January 23, 1940.

15 W. H. Miles, *Early History and Reminiscence of Frontier County*, 22-23. William H. Palmer was the son of a Georgia plantation owner, but because of a serious infraction of the law there, he left Georgia, changed his surname to Miles, drifted north to the Medicine in 1870, and settled there. In Nebraska he was generally known as "Paddy."

16 [William W. Tucker,] *His Imperial Highness the Grand Duke Alexis in the United States of America during the Winter of 1871-72*, 184, 186, 189.

17 Ibid., 188.

18 Ibid., 189, 190.

Chapter 8   Celebrity

1 Louisa Frederici Cody and Courtney Ryley Cooper, *Memories of Buffalo Bill*, 218.

2 Don Russell, *The Lives and Legends of Buffalo Bill*, 180.

3 Cody and Cooper, *Memories*, 218-19. The "Colonel's gold braid" was a bit premature (or, more likely, a case of Louisa's poor memory or Cooper's exaggeration): Cody was not a colonel until commissioned by the Nebraska governor fifteen years later.

4 W. F. Cody, *Story of the Wild West*, 634. (Cody misspells Freligh's name.)

5 Ibid., 636.

6 W. F. Cody, *An Autobiography of Buffalo Bill*, 247.

7 Ibid., 248. Cody had his share of troubles with formal wear; for another early 1870s clawhammer duds story he tells on himself, when General Sheridan invited him to a ball at Riverside in Chicago, see Chicago *Daily News*, June 26, 1893, 4.

8 Cody and Cooper, *Memories*, 221.
9 Post medical history, August 15, 1872: "3 P.M. Mrs. Cody, wife of Mr. William Cody, Post guide and interpreter, delivered of a daughter."
10 However, forty-four years later the medal was taken away from Cody because at the time of his "gallantry and intrepidity" he had been a *civilian* employee of the Army and not an Army man himself. On April 27, 1916, Congress approved an act which provided a symbolic pension to honorably discharged medal recipients—$10 per month for life after the medal holder had reached the age of sixty-five; this was "to give the Medal of Honor the same position among the military orders of the world [especially England and France] which similar medals occupy," as urged by the Medal of Honor Legion which had lobbied for over two dozen years for such legislation. Some persons also had been troubled that perhaps the Medal of Honor had been too loosely given in years past; therefore, part of this April 1916 act called for a review of all previous medal recipients to determine genuine eligibility. A total of 2,625 cases was considered, and by February 15, 1917, 911 names had been "stricken permanently from the official Medal of Honor list" (in the words of the June 3, 1916 Army reorganization bill which defined new criteria for the medal and created a review board). Of these 911 medals, 864 involved a group case from 1863: they had been given to one Civil War regiment—part (555) represented a clerical error, the others (309) did not meet 1916 criteria. This left forty-seven scattered cases, of which Cody's was one. Another of the forty-seven was that of Mary Walker, a Civil War surgeon and the only woman ever to receive the honor. (*Medal of Honor Recipients 1863-1973*, U.S. Senate Committee on Veterans' Affairs, Committee Print No. 15, 93d Cong., 1st Ses., Washington, D.C., October 22, 1973, 8-10.) A decade later, Congress by special act gave the Medal of Honor to Charles A. Lindbergh for his clearly civilian act of flying solo across the Atlantic; his "military" qualifications were his earlier (1924) enlistment in the U.S. Army Air Service Reserve and his enlistment (1925) in the Missouri National Guard.
11 For dating of the Omaha party hunt, see Louis A. Holmes, *Fort McPherson, Nebraska*, 47; Holmes also mentions a U.S marshal and surveyor general as members of the party. For an interesting 1879 sidelight on Judge Dundy, see Virginia I. Armstrong (comp.), *I Have Spoken*, Appendix, 164-78.
12 Cody, *Story*, 643.
13 Ira L. Bare and Will H. McDonald (eds.), *An Illustrated History of Lincoln County, Nebraska and Her People*, vol. I, 368-69.
14 Ibid., 368.
15 Cody, *Story*, 642.
16 Everyone agrees that Dunraven was at Fort McPherson in 1872; the dating problem is whether this was his first or second visit. Cody himself suggests 1872 was the first (*Story*, 640), but we cannot rely upon him for dating. (See above, Chap. 6, note 17) Herschel C. Logan, in his biography of Texas Jack, says outright: Dunraven "first visited Fort McPherson in 1872." (*Buckskin and Satin*, 120; Logan's footnote at this point cites Dunraven's autobiographical *Canadian Nights*, but actually Dunraven is no more helpful than Cody in pinning down dates, for in his opening words to *Canadian Nights* Dunraven lets us know how unconcerned he is with accurate dating: "Years ago, it matters not when. . . .") Louis A. Holmes seems to agree with Logan's 1872 date (also implying that the Dunraven hunt followed the Omaha party). In detailing events at the fort, Holmes would surely not have skipped 1871 if the earl had been there that year too; rather, he concludes: "The Earl was so pleased with the success of the hunt that

he expressed a determination to do so again as soon as opportunity afforded [1873?]." (*Fort McPherson, Nebraska*, 47-48) Dr. George Kingsley, Dunraven's hunting companion, wrote many letters home when he and the earl were in the West; his daughter collected them into a book published years later but unfortunately chose to drop most of the letters' dates in their printed versions. Nonetheless, she says her father was at Fort McPherson for his hunt (by implication his *first* hunt there) when he was forty-six years old; this would have been 1872. (George Henry Kingsley, *Notes on Sport and Travel*, 124) Buffalo Bill says his guiding of the Dunraven party was interrupted by the arrival at Fort McPherson of a group of Chicago businessmen who also had (as had Dunraven) a letter from General Sheridan asking that Cody guide them on their hunt; this could not have been 1871, if it were after October 8, for that was the date of the Great Fire in Chicago, and no businessman from that devastated city would likely have gone off for a fall of fun—and Sheridan wouldn't have had time to sit around in his office pointing out mounted elk heads to Dunraven and writing letters to Fort McPherson: Chicago that fall was under martial law and Sheridan was "ruling" the city, amidst much controversy. Therefore, if Dunraven were in Nebraska in 1871, it would have to have been August or very early September.

On the other hand, Don Russell dates Dunraven's first Nebraska hunt with Cody 1871 (*Lives*, 3rd printing, 166: a correction from the 1st and 2nd printings, which dated it "probably in 1869," 165) and his second 1872. (Ibid., 188) And Marshall Sprague is clear and detailed about Dunraven's two Nebraska hunts: 1871 and 1872. (*A Gallery of Dudes*, 150, 153; see also Sprague's Introduction to 1967 edition of Dunraven's *The Great Divide*, ix-xi) Unfortunately, documentation by Russell and Sprague is as slim as that by Logan or Holmes. Sprague writes that he must have had good reasons for his 1871 and 1872 dating, but his files are not now, at this late date, accessible for detailed verification. (letter, March 1978) Russell says Brevet Lieutenant Colonel Anson Mills led the military escort for the earl on the second Nebraska hunt in 1872 (*Lives*, 188), but Mills himself dates his Dunraven escort 1873. (*My Story*, 153)

What about the communiques from General Sheridan to Fort McPherson authorizing the Dunraven party and the Chicago party hunts, requesting Cody as guide? They would date the hunts, but, regretably, a search (though less than thorough) of Sheridan's correspondence at the National Archives failed to turn up copies of either communique or any reference to either hunting party.

17 Earl of Dunraven, *Canadian Nights*, 52.
18 Ibid., 53-54.
19 Ibid., 56.
20 Cody, *Story*, 640.

Chapter 9   Limelight

1 W. F. Cody, *Story of the Wild West*, 643.
2 W. F. Cody, *An Autobiography of Buffalo Bill*, 256.
3 Unidentified Nebraska neswpaper clipping, December 12, 1872. Graff Collection, Newberry Library, Chicago, Illinois.
4 Don Russell, *The Lives and Legends of Buffalo Bill*, 191.
5 Jessie Morant interview with John Grant, January 19, 1940. Grant, a graduate of the College of Law at the State University of Iowa, did not come to North Platte until 1896, twenty-four years after the election; though he was a good friend of Cody's, he was not around at the time the election was held.

6 Ruby Wilson interview with Walter Hoagland, December 6, 1939.
7 George Henry Kingsley, *Notes on Sport and Travel*, 134, 135, 136. Kingsley adds a comment that gives us, even with all his other praise of Cody, a different and humorous picture of our hero: "For some inscrutable reason he delighteth to hunt in this particular rig, adding thereto, however, a white Texan sombrero, which, when the leaves thereof are tied tightly down by a handkerchief knotted under his chin, assumes a prudish and poke-bonnet-like appearance which entirely unprepares you for the noble face and flashing eyes which suddenly appear at the end of its tunnel when he turns the apparatus end on towards you." (136)
    Who was Kingsley and what was he doing in Nebraska? He was a consummate sportsman and world traveler. Dunraven "followed the custom of British aristocrats by taking along his own doctor, George Henry Kingsley. Kingsley was a brother of Canon [Charles] Kingsley, the *Water Babies* author, and an uncle of Rose and Maurice Kingsley who [helped] found the resort of Colorado Springs at Pikes Peak and [give] it the English tone that caused it to be nicknamed 'Little London.' " (Marshall Sprague, Introduction to 1967 edition of Dunraven's *The Great Divide*, ix)
8 Delos Avery, "Buffalo Bill: The Story of a Reputation That Ran Away with a Man," Chicago *Tribune*, March 26, 1944, Graphic section.
9 Helen Cody Wetmore, *Last of the Great Scouts*, 204.
10 Cody, *Story*, 644.
11 Ibid., 645.
12 Louisa Frederici Cody and Courtney Ryley Cooper, *Memories of Buffalo Bill*, 231.
13 Ibid., 233.
14 Ibid.
15 Omaha *Daily Herald*, December 5, 1872.
16 Cody, *Story*, 651.
17 Chicago *Times*, December 18, 1872, 3.
18 Cody and Cooper, *Memories*, 248-50.
19 Cody, *Story*, 652.
20 Cody and Cooper, *Memories*, 251-52.
21 Ibid., 257. Helen says her brother bought the Rochester home and moved the family there in 1874. (Wetmore, *Great Scouts*, 226)
22 Cody, *Story*, 652.
23 "During most of [Cody's] decade on the stage, his productions were advertised as the 'Buffalo Bill Combination.' A combination was a traveling theatrical troupe organized primarily to present one play, although at least one other play was usually held in reserve for emergencies. Thus a combination was distinguished from a stock company, which offered a repertory of frequently changing plays and might remain indefinitely at the same theater. The Buffalo Bill Combination usually disbanded in late May or June, and often was an entirely new organization the next fall. Cody spent most of his summers guiding hunting parties or returning to his old occupation as scout. This kept alive the tradition that he was still the plainsman he depicted—and he was. On several occasions his summer experiences gave him material for a new play." (Russell, *Lives*, 204)
24 Cody and Cooper, *Memories*, 256. Sister Helen, however, put *both* Wild Bill and Texas Jack with her brother in Chicago for the opening of the show the year before, and writes that Cody had a hard time talking them into going at all. So, according to her account, the tour of 1873-1874 was Hickok's second season with the show, and by then he was tired of the whole thing and wanted out. The manager refused to release him from his contract, she says, and he had to figure out a way to break it. Helen was wrong; Hickok was *not* in the first

season, even though Cody's *Autobiography* also says so ("Together we made the trip to New York. . . ." 258). See Joseph G. Rosa, *They Called Him Wild Bill*, 247-51; Russell, *Lives*, 277.

25 That Hickok had national "star quality" worthy of commercial exploitation in connection with Cody is underscored by the fact that in his 1869-1870 serialization, "Buffalo Bill, the King of Border Men," Buntline had included Wild Bill Hitchcock (sic) as Cody's best friend. Then, in the first season (1872-1873) of the Buntline-Cody-Omohundro stage play tour, before Hickok himself joined the Combination, Buntline sometimes introduced Wild Bill (played by some handy actor) as a character in "The Scouts of the Prairie." Finally, when Hickok did actually join this band of actors, he occasionally got a kind of billing that overshadowed Buffalo Bill and Texas Jack. For instance, one program sheet for "Buffalo Bill, the King of Border Men" (which the Combination alternated with "The Scouts of the Plains" that 1873-1874 season) carries a "Facts about the Scouts" section but devotes so much space to Hickok as to leave little room for material on Cody and Omohundro. (Rosa, *Wild Bill*, 253)

26 Ibid., 259. For a longer discussion of why Hickok left the Combination, see Rosa, *Wild Bill*, 255-61, 266.

27 Wilson interview with J. Antonides, June 12, 1940.

28 This is the expedition Dunraven describes in his book *The Great Divide: Travels in the Upper Yellowstone in the Summer of 1874.*

29 Cody, *Story*, 654-55. Rosa is skeptical of Medley's credentials and thinks he may well have been "in fact a Chicago saloonkeeper." (*Wild Bill*, 263n3)

30 Ena Raymonde manuscript diary. (emphasis hers) Nebraska State Historical Society, Lincoln.

31 Cody, *Story*, 656.

Chapter 10   The Black Hills

1 For detailed treatments of the Black Hills gold rush, see Donald Jackson, *Custer's Gold: The United States Cavalry Expedition of 1874* and Watson Parker, *Gold in the Black Hills.*

2 *The Western Nebraskian* (North Platte), April 9, 1875.

3 North Platte *Republican*, April 10, 1875.

4 A year earlier North Platte had experienced the excitement and frustration of an abortive attempt to freight goods north. In 1874 Major Leicester Walker, North Platte cattleman and banker, secured a contract to freight government supplies to the Indian agencies on the Nebraska-Dakota border. While Cody was in town that summer, Walker sought him out and inquired about the best route through the hills to the agencies; Bill told him what he knew of that vast and little-known region of Sandhills to the north. On August 1, 1874, the North Platte *Enterprise* announced that the first freight train would start the following Monday, "when about forty ox teams will be loaded out as the first section." A similar section would load and begin the next week. The town was excited over the venture, which promised to develop into quite a freighting business. On August 8 the *Enterprise* was still booming "the one million pound freight contract" that would likely employ all the surplus teams between North Platte and Grand Island. But no freight had yet left the town. Finally, at the end of August the first ten wagons departed for the agencies; James Kerr "yoked and hitched about forty yoke of wild Texas steers in two and one-half hours and drove them nine miles the same day without breaking any necks or doing other material

damage." (*Enterprise*, August 29, 1874) Walker calculated one month for his wagons' round trip, but time and the Sandhills undermined his optimistic estimate: the train pulled into North Platte the second week in October. Another shipment left that same week for the agencies, but nothing more is known about the success or failure of this train—or of Walker's entire venture. His 1874 contract was probably fulfilled, but the route proved too slow and difficult for a paying freight business.

5 For discussion of other early Nebraska routes to the Black Hills, see Harold Hutton, *Doc Middleton*, 40-41, notes 2 & 3, rear endpapers map.

6 Mills was by assignment captain, Third Cavalry, and was referred to as Captain Mills by Cody and local writers.

7 Nellie Snyder Yost, *Call of the Range*, 90, 91, 96, 97.

8 North Platte *Republican*, April 23, 1875.

9 Don Russell, *The Lives and Legends of Buffalo Bill*, 212; Cody also states that he spent the summer of 1875 at Rochester with his family. (W. F. Cody, *Story of the Wild West*, 656)

10 Ena Raymonde manuscript diary. Nebraska State Historical Society, Lincoln.

11 Helen Cody Wetmore, *Last of the Great Scouts*, 211.

12 Louisa Frederici Cody and Courtney Ryley Cooper, *Memories of Buffalo Bill*, 262-64.

13 Stella Adelyne Foote, *Letters from Buffalo Bill*, 13.

Chapter 11 Yellow Hair

1 Don Russell, *The Lives and Legends of Buffalo Bill*, 215.

2 W. F. Cody, *Story of the Wild West*, 658.

3 Russell, *Lives*, 226.

4 Ibid., 229.

5 Ibid., 230 and note 22.

6 Louisa Frederici Cody and Courtney Ryley Cooper, *Memories of Buffalo Bill*, 267-70.

7 Helen Cody Wetmore, *Last of the Great Scouts*, 217. For meaning of "Pa-has-ka," see below, Chap. 28, note 8.

8 Richard J. Walsh, *The Making of Buffalo Bill*, 190-91.

9 Russell, *Lives*, 231-32.

10 This paragraph is from two sources: Zane Grey's Afterword to 1918 edition of Wetmore, *Great Scouts*, 330, where Grey quotes from Thomas' *Outdoor Life* articles; and letter from Thomas to Margaret M. McCann, March 19, 1929. Nebraska State Historical Society, Lincoln.

11 Margaret M. McCann, "The Life of William F. Cody with a Criticism of the Sources" (M.A. thesis, University of Nebraska, 1929), 90.

12 Russell, *Lives*, 233.

13 Ibid., 234.

14 E. S. Sutton, "Hero, Showman or Heel?" *Frontier Times*, Summer 1961, 37. Wyoming pioneer cowboy Tom Hood also reported about the Yellow Hair encounter: "Cody wasn't in sight, and never claimed to be there. . . . He told me he wasn't within five miles of the place. . . . Cody . . . let the story go on for advertising purposes." (John R. Burroughs, *Guardian of the Grasslands*, 190n24)

15 Sutton, "Hero, Showman or Heel?" *Frontier Times*, 37. Sutton adds that he had seen "among the papers" of F. M. Lockhard, publisher of a Kansas country newspaper, "the Buntline story of the Yellow Hand fiasco."

16 Russell, *Lives*, 232. In fairness to Sutton, it should be added that he played fair with Cody by concluding his *Frontier Times* article: "Buffalo Bill does not need all of that phony goldwash [the killing of Yellow Hair] to make him an outstanding hero. There is plenty of solid silver underneath after the goldplating is rubbed off to qualify him for a place in the West's Hall of Fame."

17 George Allen Beecher, *A Bishop of the Great Plains*, 118-19.

18 McCann, "Cody."

19 The eyewitness in the *Telegraph's* account was H. H. Cross (1837-1918), celebrated painter of Indians and animals; Cross was eighty years old at the time of the newspaper story.

For details on "Essanay's current feature" film mentioned here, see below, p. 405; Chap. 37, note 31.

20 From "Project 71" file, Scout's Rest Ranch, North Platte.

Chapter 12   Rancher

1 W. F. Cody, *Story of the Wild West*, 678.

2 Ibid., 689.

3 Don Russell, *The Lives and Legends of Buffalo Bill*, 256.

4 Helen Cody Wetmore, *Last of the Great Scouts*, 219.

5 Stella Adelyne Foote, *Letters from Buffalo Bill*, 10.

6 Fred Elliott, Jr., manuscript written c. 1960, now in possession of his daughter, Bernice Elliott, Omaha, Nebraska.

7 The south one-half of the northwest one-quarter and the north one-half of the southwest one-quarter of Section 32, Township 14, Range 30. Warranty of Deeds, Book B, p. 31. Lincoln County Courthouse, North Platte.

8 One of the earliest visitors, perhaps the first, to the ranch was George Bird Grinnell: "In the summer of 1877, in response to an invitation from Luther H. North, I went out to western Nebraska, to visit him. That spring, I think, William F. Cody and Frank North had gone into the cattle business. . . .

"The ranch when I reached it consisted of a couple of tents stuck up on the edge of the alkaline lake which was the head of the Dismal River. On this lake a pair of trumpeter swans had a nest. The sand hills roundabout abounded in antelope and deer. There were some elk in the country, and one or two little bunches of buffalo." (Autobiographical manuscript, 78, 79. Connecticut Audubon Society, Fairfield. This is the typewritten material referred to as "MEMOIRS" in John F. Reiger [ed.], *The Passing of the Great West*.)

9 Cody and North branded with an NC connected. (Harry E. Chrisman, *The Ladder of Rivers*, 219)

For more on the Taylors, especially Buck, see Russell, *Lives*, 305-06; Harold Hutton, *Doc Middleton*, 248n6, 250n22, 250n23.

10 Wetmore, *Great Scouts*, 221. This home was located in what came to be, after the town of North Platte grew over the years, the center of the block (west side) on Sherman Avenue, just south of West Front Street. Front Street was so named when North Platte began because it fronted the railroad tracks; it ran the length of the town, parallel to and south of the tracks. At the time the Cody home was built, the west edge of town extended only a little way beyond the barracks on Sycamore Street, which was right "downtown"; this would have left about a half mile of vacant land between the edge of town and the Cody home.

11 Louisa Frederici Cody and Courtney Ryley Cooper, *Memories of Buffalo Bill*, 278, 279.

12 Frances Sims Fulton, *To and Through Nebraska*, 158-59; cf. below, Chap. 16.
13 Ruby Wilson interview with George Macomber, April 6, 1940.
14 Cody, *Story*, 690, 692.
15 Ibid., 691.
16 Ibid.
17 Solomon D. Butcher, *Pioneer History of Custer County*, 9.
18 John Bratt, *Trails of Yesterday*, 278-79.
19 Luther North, *Man of the Plains*, Chap. 10.
20 In her seventies, Lottie Kocken wrote her life story, and this Dismal River story
   is taken from this manuscript autobiography, now in possession of her niece,
   Mrs. Bruce Snyder, Paxton, Nebraska.
21 Wetmore, *Great Scouts*, 241-46.
22 North, *Man*, 282.
23 Ibid., 279.

Chapter 13   Cody's Home Town

1 *The Western Nebraskian*, November 18, 1877.
2 Ruby Wilson interview with Edd Weeks, January 1940.
3 Wilson interview with William Maloney, October 10, 1940.
4 Wilson interview with Johnny Dugan, January 25, 1940.
5 Wilson interview with Charles Whalen, January 1940.
6 Wilson interview with Dugan, January 25, 1940.
7 Wilson interview with John Dick, November 1939.
8 Wilson interview with Chancy Rogers, October 1940.
9 Wilson interview with Martin Federhoof, May 1940.
10 Archibald R. Adamson, *North Platte and Its Associations*, 42-43.
11 Wilson interview with Mrs. Tom (Mary) Patterson, March 1940.
12 *The Western Nebraskian*, April 13, 1878.
13 Ibid., August 24, 1878.

Chapter 14   Plays, Real Estate, Rodeo

1 *The Western Nebraskian*, June 14, 1879.
2 This serialization ran from November 1879 to February 1880. Don Russell, *The
  Lives and Legends of Buffalo Bill*, 269. In Chap. 20 of his book, Russell analyzes
  at length the books, stories, and articles written *by* Cody and the many others
  written *about* him. Unraveling the complications of who wrote what and when
  was not aided even by Cody's family. Sister Helen indicates in her book that her
  brother's autobiography was published in 1877, and that she, by then a widow
  dependent upon him for support, had undertaken the agency of the book for the
  state of Ohio; she writes: "But I soon tired of a business life, and turning over
  the agency to other hands, went from Cleveland to visit Will at his new home
  in North Platte." (Helen Cody Wetmore, *Last of the Great Scouts*, 223) Since
  the home was not built until 1878, nor the book published until 1879, her visit
  had to be later than 1877.
3 Russell, *Lives*, 271.
4 Ibid., 263. The phrase "double bill," used by the critic Russell quotes, is perhaps
  misleading; in fact, Cody played one play August 2 and the other August 3, as
  a way of getting some of the same audience to return for a two-day stand.

5 Ruby Wilson interview with Mrs. Mary Roddy, January 24, 1940.

6 Stella Adelyne Foote, *Letters from Buffalo Bill*, 18.

7 North Platte *Telegraph-Bulletin*, June 7, 1952, Margaret Brown interview with William McDonald.

8 Louisa Frederici Cody and Courtney Ryley Cooper, *Memories of Buffalo Bill*, 280-81.

9 Foote, *Letters*, 18.

10 Legally, Louisa could not operate entirely independently in her financial dealings, because while a married woman could buy and own property in her own name in Nebraska during the 1870s and 1880s, said property automatically became the property of the husband also. However, neither party could mortgage or sell the property without the other's signature or written consent; therefore, William F. Cody could not mortgage or dispose of any of the Louisa-purchased, jointly-owned property without his wife's consent. Louisa felt this was adequate protection for her.

The Cleveland suit itself can perhaps best be explained, though lengthily, by quoting from an Omaha(?) newspaper of May 13, 1882. It appears that a reporter interviewed Cody as he passed through town on his way home to North Platte, thereby giving us as close a summary as we have of Cody's own version of the situation:

"Bill has recently struck a bonanza for himself and the Cody family generally, and he has assurances of able lawyers that his claim to valuable real estate in Cleveland is well worth fighting for, and if he wins the suit he will realize an immense fortune—several million dollars. He began an active investigation into the claims of the Cody family to certain Cleveland real estate some months ago, and it has resulted in his bringing a suit . . . for its recovery. He stopped in Cleveland on his way home for this purpose.

"The facts in the case are that in 1832 Philip Cody, senior, moved from Canada to Cleveland, Ohio, and located on lands in Cleveland and adjoining the city. He was regarded as quite a wealthy man in those days. His family consisted of seven children, among whom were four sons, Elijah, Isaac (who was the father of Buffalo Bill), Philip, junior, and Joseph. Three of these brothers—Isaac, Philip, junior, and Elijah—moved to Iowa in the days of the early settlement of that state, Joseph remaining at Cleveland with his father.

"In 1838-9 Philip Cody, senior, begin to show signs of insanity, and in 1843, 1844 and 1848, his property was sold and deeds were given to the purchasers, the deeds purporting to have been made by him.

"The brothers Elijah and Isaac, who were then in Missouri, knew of the sale that had been made of the homestead, but did not realize their portion of the father's estate. Philip Cody, senior, died in 1850. Philip, junior, meantime had returned to Cleveland and secured his share of the property. Elijah and Isaac remained in the west, where their children were born and grew up. These children were not aware that they had any claims to the property in Cleveland until the death of Joseph Cody in Cleveland in 1880. On his death-bed he made a statement to the effect that there was property coming to the heirs of Elijah and Isaac Cody. This led to an investigation which proved that the deeds to the property in question, which were given in 1843, 1844 and 1848, were made while Philip Cody, senior, was demented, in which condition he had been since 1839, and furthermore that they were not only forgeries but have been proven so by the fact that Philip Cody, senior, was demented, and that Joseph Cody got the old man to sign the deeds while he was in that condition.

"The lands to which the Cody heirs lay claim comprise fifty-five acres of Euclid avenue, one of the principal thoroughfares of Cleveland. Their claims seem to be so strong that the property owners cannot sell with any safety or make any improvements. Two parties, who are in possession of a large part of the disputed property, offered Buffalo Bill, while he was in Cleveland, the sum of $300,000 to settle the suit so far as they were concerned, but he refused to do so.

"The suit proper is against 113 different parties who now occupy the land, and was begun on the 10th of this month.

"The attorneys for the Cody heirs are Senator Teller of Colorado, Hutchins, Kimball, Johnson & Co., of Cleveland, Adams & Butcher, of Cincinnati, Jarvis, of Toronto, and Phehan, of Kansas." (Nebraska newspaper clipping, May 13, 1882; no location, but probably Omaha. Graff Collection, Newberry Library, Chicago.)

11 Foote, *Letters*, 19. All quotations from the Foote volume are verbatim, thus retaining the spelling and punctuation of the original letters.

12 McDonald speaking at a special meeting of the Lincoln County Historical Society, September 9, 1940, held to honor the early settlers of the county. Several old-timers spoke at this meeting, and their reminiscences were recorded by Ruby Wilson, whose original transcript is at Nebraska State Historical Society, Lincoln (copy at Lincoln County Historical Society, North Platte).

13 North Platte *Telegraph-Bulletin*, June 7, 1952, Brown interview with McDonald.

14 North Platte claims the world's first rodeo was held there, and for its 1982 centennial a book is in preparation documenting this controversial claim and also telling the stories of all the successive rodeos held there.

15 The Dillon place was in a low area, and water stood over much of the land in the spring; ducks often swam between the buildings. Plank footbridges extended in all directions, from one high spot to another, with dryer knolls between.

16 As told me by my father, A. B. Snyder, in 1948.

17 Burr Murphy manuscript, in possession of his nephew, Milton Murphy, North Platte.

18 Bostwick at Historical Society meeting, 1940. See above, note 12.

19 Wilson interview with George Macomber, April 11, 1940.

20 For details about Jim Kelly, see Harry E. Chrisman, *The Ladder of Rivers*.

21 Wilson interview with Johnny Dugan, January 25, 1940.

22 North Platte *Telegraph-Bulletin*, June 7, 1952, Brown interview with McDonald.

23 Tucker's saloon was a notorious place that operated for years on the corner of Sixth and Spruce (now Dewey) Streets. During the summers when lawless Ogallala was the end of the Texas cattle trail, Bill Tucker also ran another saloon, The Cowboy's Rest, in that town.

Chapter 15   Where the Wild West Begins

1 Don Russell, *The Lives and Legends of Buffalo Bill*, 288-89.

2 W. F. Cody, *Story of the Wild West*, 695.

3 Russell, *Lives*, 289.

4 Ruby Wilson interview with Mary Elder, March 20, 1940. My interview with Johnny Baker, Jr., North Platte, October 1968; this Johnny Baker is no relation to the Johnny (Lewis) Baker who became Cody's foster son.

5 North Platte *Telegraph-Bulletin*, June 7, 1952, Margaret Brown interview with William McDonald.

6 Richard J. Walsh, *The Making of Buffalo Bill*, 216-17.

7 Louisa Frederici Cody and Courtney Ryley Cooper, *Memories of Buffalo Bill*, 81-83.

8 Cody, *Story*, 693-94.

9 Stella Adelyne Foote, *Letters from Buffalo Bill*, 19.

10 Wilson interview with Charles Stamp, January 10, 1940.

11 Fairfield (Iowa) *Ledger*, August 23, 1958; interview with Mrs. Calvin Lowell and Mrs. Maude Walker.

12 Letter from Carver to Thorp, February 16, 1927. (Raymond W. Thorp [ed.], "The Letters of Doc Carver," *Outdoor Life-Outdoor Recreation*, April 1930, 89)

13 Wilson interview with Stamp, January 10, 1940.

14 Charles R. Nordin, "Dr. W. F. Carver," *Nebraska History Magazine*, October-December 1927, 346.

15 Russell, *Lives*, 289. For explanation of the piano-stool crack and for evidence that Carver was not without some virtue and show business savvy, see Nellie Snyder Yost, *Call of the Range*, 106.

16 Harold Hutton, *Doc Middleton*, 264n3.

17 Cody and Cooper, *Memories*, 285-86.

18 Burr Murphy manuscript, in possession of his nephew, Milton Murphy, North Platte.

19 Wilson interview with John Dick, November 1939.

20 Fairfield (Iowa) *Ledger*, August 23, 1958; interview with Lowell and Walker.

21 Russell, *Lives*, 295.

22 Wilson interview with John Hupfer, March 18, 1940.

Chapter 16   The Wild West Tours

1 Leonard, in his article, uses the name Sam Matthews; however, when Don Russell refers to this rehearsal (and cites Leonard), he uses the name Fred Mathews. (294) When queried about this, Russell replied (conversation, November 1977) that in his original research he concluded, with Agnes Wright Spring's help, that Leonard had probably intended Fred instead of Sam; however, this was not a definitive conclusion, Russell said, adding that his (Russell's) spelling of Mathews was even less definitive. A newspaper columnist who signed himself The Light Touchman interviewed our stage driver in 1887 and called him Fred Matthews. (*Topical Times*, September 10, 1887) A Wild West show poster had it Fred Mathews. (Jack Rennert [ed.], *100 Posters of Buffalo Bill's Wild West*, 33)

2 L. O. Leonard, "Buffalo Bill's First Wild West Rehearsal," *The Union Pacific Magazine*, August 1922, 26-27.

3 W. F. Cody, *Story of the Wild West*, 694. Actually, although announced for May 17, the show's opening was postponed until May 19 because of rain. (William E. Deahl, Jr., "Nebraska's Unique Contribution to the Entertainment World," *Nebraska History*, Autumn 1968, 194)

4 Louisa Frederici Cody and Courtney Ryley Cooper, *Memories of Buffalo Bill*, 290-91.

5 Don Russell, *The Lives and Legends of Buffalo Bill*, 296-97. Frank North did not accompany the Wild West during its first season. His wife was ill (she died later that year, 1883), and he was also due to serve in the state legislature; therefore, he returned home after the show's Omaha opening. This is why Cody needed Lillie as North's replacement in interpreting for the Pawnees.

6 Richard J. Walsh, *The Making of Buffalo Bill*, 229.

7 Russell, *Lives*, 293.

8 Cody and Cooper, *Memories*, 295.

9 Stella Adelyne Foote, *Letters from Buffalo Bill*, 21.

10 Frances Sims Fulton, *To and Through Nebraska*, 154, 153-54. (Two obvious typos/misspellings from the 1884 book have been corrected in this quote.)
11 Foote, *Letters*, 20.
12 Walsh, *Buffalo Bill*, 228-29.
13 Fulton, *Nebraska*, 159-60.
14 Walsh, *Buffalo Bill*, 231.
15 Ibid., 232.
16 Unidentified newspaper clipping.
17 Robert Phipps, "Nebraska Scene," Omaha *World-Herald Sunday Magazine*, March 19, 1950, 2C.
18 Cody, *Story*, 697-98.

Chapter 17   North Platte

1 W. F. Cody, *Story of the Wild West*, 698.
2 Richard J. Walsh, *The Making of Buffalo Bill*, 241.
3 Cody, *Story*, 699.
4 Ibid.
5 Don Russell, *The Lives and Legends of Buffalo Bill*, 309.
6 *Lincoln County Tribune*, March 7, 1885.
7 Walsh, *Buffalo Bill*, 243, 244.
8 Ibid., 245.
9 *Lincoln County Tribune*, January 31, 1885.
10 Ruby Wilson interview with Edd Wright, January 30, 1940.
11 Wilson interview with Erwin Bostwick, September 8, 1940.
12 Wilson interview with Martin Federhoof, May 1940.
13 As told me by my father, A. B. Synder.
14 Stella Adelyne Foote, *Letters from Buffalo Bill*, 21, September 28, 1885 letter.
15 North Platte *Telegraph*, October 22, 1885.
16 *Lincoln County Tribune*, October 24, 1885.
17 Nellie Synder Yost, North Platte *Telegraph*, Family Weekend section, August 15, 1969.
18 Omaha *Herald*, December 6, 1885.
19 *Lincoln County Tribune*, January 9, 1886.

Chapter 18   Lloyd's Opera House

1 Shamokin (Pennsylvania) *Citizen*, November 17, 1886.
2 *Lincoln County Tribune*, November 28, 1885.
3 Ibid., January 2, 1886.
4 Ruby Wilson interview with Edd Wright, January 30, 1940.
5 Wilson interview with Charles Stamp, January 10, 1940.
6 Jessie Morant interview with Joseph Baskins, January 1940.

Chapter 19   Entertainment

1 Stella Adelyne Foote, *Letters from Buffalo Bill*, 22.
2 Hastings *Gazette Journal*, February 20, 1886.
3 Ruby Wilson interview with Ernest Tramp, October 1940.

4 *Lincoln County Tribune*, April 17, 1886.
5 Ibid., April 24, 1886.
6 Ibid., April 17, 1886.
7 Don Russell, *The Lives and Legends of Buffalo Bill*, 318.
8 *Lincoln County Tribune*, May 8, 1886.
9 Foote, *Letters*, 24.
10 Wilson interview with Edd Wright, January 30, 1940.
11 Unidentified North Platte newspaper clipping.
12 Foote, *Letters*, 24-25.
13 *Lincoln County Tribune*, August 28, 1886.
14 Foote, *Letters*, 26.
15 Ibid., 27.
16 *Lincoln County Tribune*, October 2, 1886.
17 Ibid., October 9, 1886.

Chapter 20   To England

1 Stella Adelyne Foote, *Letters from Buffalo Bill*, 27-28. (Presumably Foote deleted the word in the opening sentence; in her book it reads: "Uncle Will's ——————X What . . .")
2 Frank C. Maeder, Milton E. Milner, William D. Guthrie.
3 *Lincoln County Tribune*, March 19, 1887.
4 Ibid.
5 Tim McCoy and Ronald McCoy, *Tim McCoy Remembers the West*, 1-2.
6 Thoelecke at Historical Society meeting, 1940. See above, Chap. 14, note 12.
7 *Lincoln County Tribune*, April 2, 1887. In addition to commissioning Cody a colonel, Governor Thayer at the same time (March 8) had officially appointed him "Commissioner for the State of Nebraska to the American exhibition to be held in London."
8 O. B. Waddill, *Saddle Springs*, 63, 64.
9 W. F. Cody, *Story of the Wild West*, 704.
10 Foote, *Letters*, 30.
11 Cody, *Story*, 712.

Chapter 21   London

1 W. F. Cody, *Story of the Wild West*, 726.
2 Reprinted in the Gothenburg *Independent*, May 4, 1887.
3 *Lincoln County Tribune*, May 11, 1887.
4 Stella Adelyne Foote, *Letters from Buffalo Bill*, 30. Ed added: "they *expect* 20,000 people and if they come that will be $100,000." This special admission charge was clearly for opening day only. A British laborer in 1887 made roughly 1 pound per week; therefore, though he could ill afford to attend the Wild West's opening, he could attend later for the regular prices: one shilling to four shillings (c. $.25 to $1.00).
5 Cody, *Story*, 734.
6 O. B. Waddill, *Saddle Strings*, 64.
7 Julia Cody Goodman's scrapbook of newspaper clippings. Nebraska State Historical Society, Lincoln.
8 Jessie Morant interview with Mrs. Agnes Killen, December 1939.

9 *Lincoln County Tribune*, June 4, 1887, from London dispatch to Omaha *Herald*, June 1, 1887.
10 Reporter in a British newspaper, as quoted in Don Russell, *The Lives and Legends of Buffalo Bill*, 336.
11 Cody's "favorite resort" had a venerable history. In 1538 Henry VIII acquired the Oatlands estate and built there a palace, which over a century later was torn down so the stones and bricks could be used in building the Wey Navigation Canal and its bridges. New buildings were later constructed. At the end of the eighteenth century the Oatlands mansion burned down, having been home for more than a hundred years to various ladies and lords, duchesses and dukes, the most recent before the conflagration being the brave old Duke of York who "had ten thousand men" and "marched them up to the top of the hill" and "marched them down again." In the next half century the estate house was rebuilt and often remodeled. In 1856 the Oatlands Park Hotel came into existence; it operates still today, providing fine, four-star accommodations. Cody found it a handy retreat, only about thirteen miles (as the crow flies) southwest from Earl's Court. (Information provided by Mrs. Avril Lansdell, curator, Weybridge Museum, Weybridge, Surrey, England, and by Joseph G. Rosa.)
12 Foote, *Letters*, 31.
13 Ibid.
14 Ibid., 32.
15 Russell, *Lives*, 334-35.
16 Ibid., 336.
17 Cody, *Story*, 749.
18 Foote, *Letters*, 33.
19 Reprinted in *Lincoln County Tribune*, November 26, 1887.
20 Reprinted in *Lincoln County Tribune*, November 5, 1887.
21 Huddersfield *Daily Chronicle*. The irony of the situation is not entirely lost even when we are reminded that the club was named after the British poet Richard Savage.

Chapter 22   Before the Leaves Had Fallen

1 W. F. Cody, *Story of the Wild West*, 748.
2 Ibid., 750; Don Russell, *The Lives and Legends of Buffalo Bill*, 339.
3 From *Sunday Chronicle*, as reprinted in Cody, *Story*, 751.
4 Salford *Reporter*, December 22(?), 1887. (Provided by J. L. Shirt, librarian, Local History Library, Salford Central Area Library, and by Joseph G. Rosa.)
5 Ibid.
6 Cody, *Story*, 756.
7 Stella Adelyne Foote, *Letters from Buffalo Bill*, 33.
8 Ibid., 34.
9 Ibid.
10 *Lincoln County Tribune*, February 25, 1888.
11 Cody, *Story*, 757.
12 The street renaming was presumably temporary and for "show," because today there are no street names in Salford honoring W. F. Cody.
13 Cody, *Story*, 762. Cody's "On Monday evening May 1st" is one of his date errors; Monday was April 30.
14 Cody, *Story*, 763.
15 Aurora (Nebraska) *Register*, June 14, 1888.

16 Helen Cody Wetmore, *Last of the Great Scouts*, 254.
17 Cody, *Story*, 766.
18 *Lincoln County Tribune*, May 5, 1888.
19 New York *Tribune*, May 28 and 31, 1888.
20 Reprinted in the *Lincoln County Tribune*, June 23, 1888.
21 Foote, *Letters*, 35.
22 *Lincoln County Tribune*, October 13, 1888.
23 Ibid., November 10, 1888.
24 Ibid., November 17, 1888.
25 Ira L. Bare and Will H. McDonald (eds.), *An Illustrated History of Lincoln County, Nebraska and Her People*, vol. I, 168.
26 *Lincoln County Tribune*, November 24, 1888.
27 Ibid., December 8, 1888.
28 Ibid., December 15, 1888.
29 *Daily Nebraska State Journal*, January 4, 1889.
30 *Lincoln County Tribune*, December 22, 1888, January 5, 1889.
31 Ruby Wilson interview with Edd Wright, January 30, 1940.
32 Wilson interview with Mrs. Mary Roddy, January 24, 1940.
33 Wilson interview with Mrs. Jessie Reynolds, January 11, 1940.
34 Wilson interview with Mayme Watts Langford, January 23, 1940.
35 Wilson interview with Charles Whalen, January 1940.
36 Wilson interview with Johnny Dugan, January 25, 1940.
37 Wilson interview with Hugh Gaunt, February 6, 1940.
38 *Lincoln County Tribune*, December 8, 1888.

Chapter 23   Europe, Wounded Knee, Scout's Rest Ranch

1 Don Russell, *The Lives and Legends of Buffalo Bill*, 350; North Platte *Telegraph*, May 22, 1889.
2 The painting now hangs at the Buffalo Bill Historical Center in Cody, Wyoming.
3 Stella Adelyne Foote, *Letters from Buffalo Bill*, 35-36.
4 North Platte *Telegraph*, July 17, 1889. It is puzzling that no other documentation can be found to support this *Telegraph* story. Nowhere in Cody's autobiographies or biographies is the award mentioned. Further, the curator of the National Order of the Legion of Honor in Paris was queried: "the Archives of the Chancery of the Legion of Honor show no proof that William F. Cody . . . was awarded the Legion of Honor while in Europe, in 1889." (letter from Georges Fieschi, Consul General of France, Chicago, Illinois, May 4, 1978)
5 Jessie Morant interview with John Grant, January 19, 1940.
6 Ruby Wilson interview with Mary Patterson, March 1940.
7 Helen Cody Wetmore, *Last of the Great Scouts*, 262.
8 Grand Island (Nebraska) *Daily Independent*, November 30, 1889. No North Platte newspapers seem to have survived for the period, roughly, November 1889 through March 1890; therefore, local news about this important event, Arta's wedding, is scant indeed. Record of the marriage, however, was found in the yellowed pages of the old record book of the Episcopal Church of Our Savior in North Platte. The officiating minister was George Jenna, rector of the parish; the witnesses were George Field and Betty Graves. George, so John Grant said, sought solace for his broken heart in a bottle; whether true or not, he was Horton's best man at the wedding. At any rate, unlike Annie O'Hare, *his* heart had mended enough by 1895 that he could wed another.

Meanwhile, Horton and Arta were quickly establishing for themselves a fine reputation as entertainers in the community; the April 11, 1890 *Telegraph* reported that Mr. and Mrs. Boal hosted twenty guests to a Loto party for Horton's sister, Edna, of Chicago.

9 Richard J. Walsh, *The Making of Buffalo Bill*, 279.
10 Letter of April 24, 1890, in Giuseppe Adami (ed.), *Letters of Giacomo Puccini*, 62.
11 Tim McCoy and Ronald McCoy, *Tim McCoy Remembers the West*, 100-01. Skeptical that I might be misreading McCoy's reminiscences at this point, I queried him specifically about his understanding of what Cody said that day back in Wyoming; McCoy replied that he had *no doubt* in his mind that desire for publicity was a major reason for Cody's returning then to the U.S. "It would," Cody said, "give the show a goosing." (McCoy letter, January 8, 1978) Even Cody's own Major John Burke wrote a line that *might* be interpreted to support this notion: "He came at a great expense from Europe to reach the field in the Ghost Dance Campaign." (Wichita *Eagle*, August 20, 1911).
12 In McCoy's account, Cody recalled about his meeting with Miles: "We were in Chicago, enjoying the considerable hospitality of the Parker [sic] House. It was November 24. . . . [T]he general wrote out an order on the back of the Palmer House's wine card. With that, I was off to Injun country." (McCoy and McCoy, *McCoy*, 101, 103)
13 As told me by my father, A. B. Synder. To McCoy's group Cody used stronger words, especially about " 'those goddamned stupid *Indian agents*'—he spat the words— . . . 'those stupid, panicky *Indian agents!* . . . [t]hose monkeys.' " (*McCoy*, 101)
14 Foote, *Letters*, 36.
15 Some name spellings have come from Oliver Knight's *Following the Indian Wars*. Identifications have been made from captions for a similar photo in Robert M. Utley's *Last Days of the Sioux Nation* (334), from caption for a related photo in Russell's *Lives* (406c), and from Grabill's notation in lower left of photo. However, since not everyone appears in each photo and since there are seventeen men pictured in the photo used here but only sixteen names in Grabill's notation box, two identifications are less than definitive—Craiger and Worth. Furthermore, other photos in Utley's book raise questions about identification of two Indians— American Horse and High Hawk: on p. 320 American Horse appears in another picture but does not look much like the American Horse in Utley's p. 334 picture; the same problem occurs in comparing the High Hawk pictures: p. 331 vs. p. 334.
16 Wilson interview with Ernest Tramp, October 1940. Don Russell (*Lives*, 321, 332) mentions a James Willoughby, known as Jim Kid, who was a crack bronc rider as early as 1884, was associated with the Wild West in 1886, and later married Lillian Smith. Perhaps this Jim Kid was the same person whom Tramp called Jim the Kid or simply Jim.
17 Story told me by T. Koger Propst's nephew, Amos Hehl, North Platte.
18 Wilson interview with Hugh Gaunt, February 1940.
19 Nellie Snyder Yost, *Pinnacle Jake*, 47-51.
20 Wilson interview with Linnie Breese, February 1940.
21 Wilson interview with Gaunt, February 1940.
22 Courtney Ryley Cooper, *Annie Oakley*, 236.
23 Foote, *Letters*, 37-38.
24 North Platte *Tribune*, July 22, 1891.
25 Wetmore, *Great Scouts*, 266.
26 This sideboard is now on display in the restored ranch house at Scout's Rest Ranch.

27 Wilson interview with Mrs. Mary Roddy, January 24, 1940.
28 Wilson interview with John Hupfer, March 18, 1940.
29 Wilson interview with Edd Weeks, February 1940.
30 Wilson interview with Charles S. Clinton, February 28, 1940.
31 Wilson interview with Jessie Reynolds, January 11, 1940.
32 Foote, *Letters*, 40.
33 Yost, *Pinnacle Jake*, 47-50.

Chapter 24   Columbian Exposition, Other Business

1 Richard J. Walsh, *The Making of Buffalo Bill*, 302. It was not *all* plaudits and parades for the Wild West; there was one parade they missed: "After raking in all the loose currency in the old country and being made a lion of by the crowned heads of Europe, it must strike Buffalo Bill as a pretty good joke to have it declared that his show is not dignified enough to take part in the parade at the World's Fair on Illinois Day." (Chadron *Citizen*, August 31, 1892)
2 Chicago *Post*, June 18, 1893.
3 Chicago *Daily News*, June 26, 1893.
4 Ibid.
5 Nellie Snyder Yost, *Boss Cowman*, 192.
6 Ibid., 193.
7 Walsh, *Buffalo Bill*, 303.
8 Bernard Schuessler, Omaha *World-Herald Magazine of the Midlands*, October 15, 1972, 8-9. Two recent treatments of the race offer a broad consideration of the many disputed questions: origin of race, distance traveled, number of riders, division of prize money, etc. See William E. Deahl, Jr., "The Chadron-Chicago 1,000-Mile Cowboy Race," *Nebraska History*, Summer 1972; Harold Hutton, *Doc Middleton*, Chap. 15.
9 Ruby Wilson interview with Charles Whalen, January 1940.
10 Wilson interview with Robert Week, January 1940.
11 Don Russell, *The Lives and Legends of Buffalo Bill*, 432.
12 Walsh, *Buffalo Bill*, 306.
13 Wilson interview with Mrs. Robert Dean, February 5, 1940.
14 Wilson interview with Martin Federhoof, May 1940.
15 Wilson interview with J. L. Ketchum, January 1940.
16 Wilson interview with Charles Stamp, January 10, 1940.
17 Wilson interview with Edd Weeks, February 1940.
18 Letter to me from Edward Keliher, Omaha, January 22, 1970.
19 Wilson interview with Mrs. Mary Roddy, January 24, 1940.
20 Told me by Johnny Baker, Jr., North Platte.
21 Wilson interview with Whalen.
22 Wilson interview with John Dick, November 1939.
23 Wilson interview with Week.
24 Letter to me from Keliher, January 22, 1970.
25 Wilson interview with Dick.
26 Walsh, *Buffalo Bill*, 307. This quotation is a good example of how stories can get out of hand. The facts about the fairgrounds and the cemetery are as follows: The site for the fairgrounds had been purchased from the Codys several years earlier. The land for the first cemetery (five acres) was obtained from an early settler, Franklin Peale, at $20 per acre; later, in 1884, an additional ten-acre extension was purchased from Mrs. Cody.

27 Jessie Morant interview with William McDonald, December 1939. A few years
   later at the Cody divorce trial, May Bradford testified that her brother had
   promised in his banquet speech to "give $200 to every church in North Platte and
   $50 to every other in the county." Cody himself, commenting on that night,
   said: "Yes, I made a pretty good speech. . . . But I went a little too far. That
   church business cost me a pretty penny. They began putting up churches to get
   the money. They even built several log churches in inaccessible parts of the
   county and touched me for $50 each." (Chicago *Tribune*, February 18, 1905, 4)
28 Told me by Maude Dillon.
29 Wilson interview with Federhoof.
30 This beautiful window was saved and reset into a new building erected a few
   years ago.
31 Helen Cody Wetmore, *Last of the Great Scouts*, 274-75.
32 Russell, *Lives*, 279.
33 Stella Adelyne Foote, *Letters from Buffalo Bill*, 41.
34 La Crosse *Daily Times*, June 20, 1956.

Chapter 25   Failures, Successes

1 Copies of Horton Boal's letters are preserved in their original leather-spined,
   hard-bound Letter Book in the archives at Scout's Rest Ranch.
2 Ruby Wilson interview with John Dick, November 1939.
3 Boal's Letter Book, Scout's Rest Ranch.
4 From interviews and clippings on file at the Sheridan Public Library, Wyoming.
5 Stella Adelyne Foote, *Letters from Buffalo Bill*, 42.
6 Ibid., 41, 42, 41.
7 Following the death of P. T. Barnum in 1891, Cody bought the circus magnate's
   private car, which he used thereafter as his traveling palace while his own show
   was on the road. Since Barnum believed in the showiest and best for himself, one
   can imagine that the coach was something very special indeed.
8 North Platte *Telegraph*, November 25, 1893. The State Guard was the Nebraska
   division of the National Guard. The Home Guards were local units of the Nebraska National Guard. The North Platte Home Guard unit's official designation
   was Company E, 2nd Regiment, Nebraska National Guard, but it was popularly
   referred to locally as the Cody Guards. The State Guard was subject to call for
   any state need—riots, etc.; they might also be called up, with other state units,
   for national service. The Home Guard could be quickly mustered for local needs
   or crises—fires, tornadoes, riots, etc.
9 Thoelecke at Historical Society meeting, 1940. See above, Chap. 14, note 12.
   Thoelecke's memory is slightly off, because Dillon had been discharged three
   years *prior* to the tallyho's arrival in North Platte.
10 Richard J. Walsh, *The Making of Buffalo Bill*, 309.
11 Don Russell, *The Lives and Legends of Buffalo Bill*, 378.
12 Walsh, *Buffalo Bill*, 310.
13 Foote, *Letters*, 42.
14 Ibid., 43.
15 Ibid.
16 These and other accounts were copied from the eastern newspapers and printed
   in the North Platte newspapers.
17 Foote, *Letters*, 44.
18 At his Wyoming ranch, Cody branded with a TE connected, **Ŧ** , which brand
   the Colonel acquired from Mike Russell when he purchased a herd of TE-branded

horses from this South Dakota friend. (Manfred R. Wolfenstine, *The Manual of Brands and Marks,* 29) In Nebraska, at Scout's Rest, Cody branded with a clay pipe outline, , "on both sides on cattle and left shoulder on horses." (Recorded August 8, 1879, at North Platte, in brand record book; copied from book by Ruby Wilson, October 1940. See also North Platte *Nebraskian,* November 14, 1885.)

For details about Cody's initial involvement with Beck and Alger; about early problems of money, construction, and settlers; and about Cody's and Salsbury's 1897 additional canal project, see Kristine Haglund, "Buffalo Bill Cody Country," Chicago Westerners *Brand Book,* October 1975, 41-43.

19 North Platte *Telegraph-Bulletin,* undated feature by Jack Hayden.
20 North Platte *Semi-Weekly Tribune,* May 12, 1896.
21 North Platte *Telegraph-Bulletin,* undated feature by Hayden.
22 North Platte *Telegraph,* July 1896. It is likely that Hayden, in writing his recollections of the fair, recalled that Cody was opposed to Bryan's platform and assumed he did not like Bryan either. The matter is mentioned here simply to point up how often stories about Buffalo Bill contradict each other.
23 North Platte *Telegraph,* September 12, 1896.
24 Ibid., September 26, 1896.
25 Helen Cody Wetmore, *Last of the Great Scouts,* 283.
26 The electric light company had failed and gone out of business in 1895.
27 Wilson interview with Chancy Rogers, October 1940.
28 Wilson interview with Edd Weeks, February 1940.
29 Wilson interview with John Little, February 1940.
30 Wetmore, *Great Scouts,* 284.
31 Wilson interview with Ray Langford, January 8, 1940.
32 My interview with William F. Sander, North Platte, 1973.
33 Wilson interview with Earl Brownfield, December 1939.
34 Jessie Morant interview with Landon Reneau, December 1939.
35 Morant interview with J. R. Baskins, January 1940.
36 Wilson interview with Dr. Scott Wisner, February 1940.

Chapter 26   On Tour

1 Tim McCoy and Ronald McCoy, *Tim McCoy Remembers the West,* 17.
2 Helen Cody Wetmore, *Last of the Great Scouts,* 286.
3 Grand Island *Republican,* September 2, 1928.
4 Unidentified North Platte newspaper clipping, October 1898.

Chapter 27   Irma

1 Ruby Wilson interview with Dora LaBille Ketchum, January 1940.
2 Wilson interview with Edd Weeks, February 1940.
3 Wilson interview with Mabel Hatch.
4 Wilson interview with Martin Federhoof, May 1940.
5 My interview with Hettie Messmer.
6 Wilson interview with Mary Roddy, January 1940.
7 Wilson interview with John Grant, February 6, 1940.
8 Wilson interview with Jessie Reynolds, January 1940.
9 Wilson interview with Linnie Breese, February 1940.
10 North Platte *Telegraph,* August 7, 1900.

Chapter 28   Cody, Wyoming

1 North Platte *Semi-Weekly Tribune,* March 20, 1899. The names of all fifty guests were listed at the end of the news column. The paperweight photo was one taken by the Deadwood photographer, J. C. H. Grabill; see Don Russell, *The Lives and Legends of Buffalo Bill,* 406b.

2 For details about the Colonel's Wyoming mining ventures; see Kristine Haglund, "Buffalo Bill Cody Country," Chicago Westerners *Brand Book,* October 1975, 43.

3 North Platte *Telegraph,* May 25, 1900.

4 Ibid., September 7, 1900.

5 Ibid., February 19, 1901.

6 George Allen Beecher, *A Bishop of the Great Plains,* 112-13.

7 Ibid., 117-18, 120-21.

8 Ibid., 121-24. The Sioux gave Cody the name Pahaska, or Long Hair. Although Cody himself in his autobiographies spells it Pa-he-has-ka (or Pa-ho-has-ka), his biographers have used the Pahaska spelling. Sioux linguists say that, actually, for accuracy and to better indicate the nasals, it should be spelled Pehin Hunska.

9 Stella Adelyne Foote, *Letters from Buffalo Bill,* 47.

10 Richard J. Walsh, *The Making of Buffalo Bill,* 327.

11 Ibid., 322-23.

12 Foote, *Letters,* 49.

13 Ibid. Josephine, or Josie as her family and friends called her, did go to Cody to live. She had not been long in Wyoming before she met a young forest ranger, Harry Thurston, whom she married; Thurston later became supervisor for the Shoshone Forest Reserve.

14 Foote, *Letters,* 50.

15 Ibid. There is some confusion about *who* managed the Irma Hotel *when.* Clearly Cody had in mind during the months preceding its opening that his sister, Julia, would be the manager. In his letters to her he wrote in this vein; furthermore, the course of instruction he set out for her in Rawlins was surely that for a manager. Yet Cody also expressed satisfaction about finding the right manager— "one without a wife." Presumably this was unmarried Louis Decker, for in describing the opening of the hotel in November, a Cody newspaper gave credit for its "gala appearance" to "Manager Decker and Mrs. Goodman." We can only assume that Julia was apprehensive about undertaking full management responsibilities and therefore welcomed Decker; perhaps the intention, then, was that they *jointly* manage the hotel. Who carried the title? We don't know. In any case, Decker was soon gone. We learn from a Cody letter that in March 1903 Julia was managing The Irma with the help of "Mr. Welch . . . a good hotel. man." (Foote, *Letters,* 54) But that did not last, and Julia clearly felt burdened. In June the Colonel was writing Julia that he "will send Louie Decker for Manager," and by July Decker had arrived and assumed the managership. Decker later (1906) married Bill Cody's widowed sister, May Bradford. *When* Decker left Cody town and *why,* and what he was doing during the period before he returned to be manager (again) of The Irma, is not certain, though presumaby he went to England with Buffalo Bill in the spring of 1903. (He is known to have been employed with the Wild West.) Perhaps the hotel was running smoothly, and Cody and Julia felt she could manage it alone. What about the man whom Cody hired away from the Hoffman House in New York to be head cook and manager of waiters at The Irma? With his experience in a fine hotel back east, he could surely have been called upon for managerial advice. Yes, but he was not around; Emma Hagenow tells why: "Colonel Cody had engaged an expert chef from New York City. This man was seized with such

a terrible homesickness a few days after his arrival at Cody, that he boarded the east-bound train the night before the opening and disappeared." (See note 25 below for details of the Hagenow reminiscence.)

16 From Sherman Canfield file (clippings, transcripts of interviews, etc.) at Sheridan Public Library, Wyoming.

17 My interview with Elsa Spear Byron, June 21, 1972.

18 No newspapers for late October 1902 can be found in North Platte or Sheridan. According to the Sheridan Cemetery Association, Horton Boal was buried on October 29.

19 An 1897 Special Edition of the North Platte *Tribune* lists the town's most prominent business and professional persons; among the latter is Dr. Charles Thorp, and a picture is shown.

20 Newspaper clipping (source unknown) datelined Denver, January 8, 1904 (the week of Arta's second marriage); clipping in a scrapbook made by Nettie McDonald and kept in the McDonald family until 1972, when it became the property of the Lincoln County Historical Society.

21 North Platte *Telegraph*, September 16, 1902.

22 The McDonald newspaper clipping (see above, note 20) also reported that Boal's daughter Clara would probably inherit her father's share of a $4 million estate in Chicago, an estate that had belonged to Horton's mother, who died a few days *before* her son's suicide.

23 Foote, *Letters*, 50, 51.

24 The North Platte *Independent Era*, November 29, 1902, took its account from the Cody *Stockgrower and Farmer.*

25 Emma Seifert, of Lincoln, Nebraska, enrolled at the University of Nebraska in 1876, but dropped out in her sophomore year to marry Lincoln musician August Hagenow, who at one time or another was band leader at the university, one of the founders of the Lincoln Symphony, and director of other music groups. Emma played the violin in the Hagenow orchestra and ensemble. Colonel Cody engaged this orchestra to play at the opening of The Irma. "We were treated royally coming, going, and while there," she remembered. "Colonel Cody supplied a coach and driver and we were taken to see some of the magnificent sights of the immediate neighborhood. . . . Our party was sent home in the enjoyment of the private car of Ex. Gov. Savage." Two decades later Emma went back to the university and received her B.F.A. She put many of her memories of the old days into papers for an English 6 course; her reminiscences here are from one of those papers, supplied by her niece, Emma Jo Seifert Knight, of Lincoln.

26 Don Russell writes that Buffalo Bill, resplendent in white tie and tails, was, on orders from his doctor, not drinking, and in deference to him the old scouts also abstained. (*Lives,* 428)

27 Foote, *Letters,* 51.

28 Walsh, *Buffalo Bill,* 329.

Chapter 29   Yellow Ribbons, Red Ink

1 My interview with Russell Langford, Ray's son, 1973.

2 Rev. Beecher moved to Kearney, Nebraska, as rector of St. Lukes, January 1, 1903, but returned to North Platte to officiate at Irma's wedding.

3 North Platte *Independent Era*, February 26, 1903, front page.

4 At the turn of the century, the customary period of mourning for a member of the immediate family was at least one year.

5 Ruby Wilson interview with Mary Patterson, March 5, 1940.

6 Wilson interview with Mary Wyberg, January 15, 1940.
7 My interview with Geraldine Bare Munger, 1970.
8 Stella Adelyne Foote, *Letters from Buffalo Bill*, 55.
9 Ibid., 52.
10 Ibid.
11 Ibid., 53.
12 Ibid., 54.
13 Ibid., 54-55.
14 Ibid., 56.
15 Duluth *Herald*, July 29, 1969.
16 Foote, *Letters*, 56.
17 Ibid., 57.

Chapter 30   Louisa

1 My interview with Johnny Baker, Jr., October 1968.
2 Ruby Wilson interview with Charles Whalen, January 22, 1940.
3 Wilson interview with Dora LaBille Ketchum, January 1940.
4 Jessie Morant interview with Ella Drake, January 6, 1940.
5 Lottie Kocken manuscript; see above, Chap. 12, note 20.
6 Wilson interview with Jessie Reynolds, January 11, 1940.
7 Wilson interview with Mrs. Robert (Beata Cox) Dean, February 5, 1940.
8 My interview with Geraldine Bare Munger, 1969.
9 Cf. Louisa Frederici Cody and Courtney Ryley Cooper, *Memories of Buffalo Bill*, 136-14.
10 My interveiw with Ray Newman, 1968.
11 *Rocky Mountain News* (Denver), July 23, 1970.
12 Wilson interview with Mrs. Dean.
13 North Platte *Independent Era*, March 10, 1904.
14 Wilson interview with Cora Finn, December 21, 1939.
15 North Platte *Telegraph*, April 14, 1904.
16 Wilson interview with Mrs. Dean.

Chapter 31   Cody vs. Cody

1 Omaha *Bee*, November 24, 1904.
2 North Platte *Telegraph*, January 26, 1905.
3 Wilcox at Historical Society meeting, 1940. See above, Chap. 14, note 12.
4 My interview with Mrs. May Trego, March 22, 1973.
5 North Platte *Telegraph*, February 23, 1905; Cripple Creek *Times*, February 17, 1905.
6 Ruby Wilson interview with Hugh Gaunt, February 6. 1940.
7 North Platte *Telegraph*, February 23, 1905.
8 Ibid.
9 Richard J. Walsh, *The Making of Buffalo Bill*, 331.
10 Wilson interview with Mrs. Robert (Beata Cox) Dean, February 5, 1940.
11 North Platte *Telegraph*, February 23, 1905.
12 Ibid.
13 Ibid.
14 See above, note 3.
15 North Platte *Telegraph*, February 23, 1905.

16 My interview with Johnny Baker, Jr., October 1968.
17 North Platte *Telegraph,* February 23, 1905.
18 Ibid., March 2, 1905.
19 Ibid., March 4, 1905.
20 Dan Muller, *My Life With Buffalo Bill,* 132-36.
21 Chicago *Tribune,* February 17, 1905.
22 Arthur Sears Henning, "Charged Insults and Poison Plots," Chicago *Daily Tribune,* January 8, 1954. This is one in a series of his memoirs; it recalls Henning's coverage of the Cody divorce trial and quotes from his 1905 dispatches to the Chicago *Tribune,* although his own quotes are almost but not quite verbatim: a few insignificant changes in spellings and omissions of words.
23 North Platte *Telegraph,* February 23, 1905.
24 Ibid., April 6, 1905.
25 Chicago *Tribune,* February 17, 1905.
26 North Platte *Telegraph,* June 1, 1905.
27 Ibid., undated clipping, on file at Scout's Rest Ranch.
28 Cozad (Nebraska) *Tribune,* March 10, 1905.
29 Muller, *My Life,* 139, 141; John Burke, *Buffalo Bill,* 234-36.
30 The farcical impression the highly publicized accounts of the trial left on many is probably well summed up in these lines, written by S. W. Gillitan and published in the Baltimore *American* during the trial:

The Cody Divorce Case

("She drove away my friends," said Buffalo Bill, in testifying against his wife. "When they were no longer welcome, it was no longer my home.")

When Stumped-His-Toe, with war paint on, came in one day to lunch
And murmured that no human gore was mingled with the punch,
She drove him out! And when Hot Dog and Crippled Cow arrived
And chopped the furniture because of booze they were deprived,
She made a scene, until they felt that there was something wrong,
And shortened up the contracts we had made for twice as long.
And when Black Crow had scalped the cook—although 'twas done in play—
She carried on just dreadful till I coaxed the brave away.

The Man-Who-Feared-His-Horses came one night at half-past one
And gently waked us from a sleep with his unerring gun;
I rose to let him in to stay the balance of the night;
But she, the captious hussy, had hysterics in her fright.
One time a bunch of cowboys, with their chaps and ponies came
And woke me at 2:45 to join a little game;
They only fired three vollies and let out a whoop or two;
But wifey got so nervous that she knew not what to do.

And once when Mangy Bill, the scout, got restless in his sleep
And rounded up the servants like they'd been a flock of sheep,
And shot the pendants, one by one, from off the chandeliers,
This woman grew hysterical—I scarce could calm her fears!
Then Leather Leg and Poodle Face set out one night to tell
The story of the battle field on which poor Custer fell;
She stood it fairly well until they tried to illustrate
The war-whoops, then she fainted—warn't she a pretty mate!

She even raised a row the time I had some companee
Come in to spend the evening and rehearse my show with me;
She said the bucking ponies sure would ruinate the rugs,

And all the punchers had to go, and take away the plugs;
She said the baby fretted through the "battle of San Juan,"
And not a smidgen further would she let the play go on!
Now, judge, I want my papers, for I have to make amends
To those my wife has driven away from our home—my gentle friends!

Chapter 32   Woes

1 Stella Adelyne Foote, *Letters from Buffalo Bill*, 65-66.
2 Charles Eldridge Griffin, *Four Years in Europe with Buffalo Bill*, 67-68. No news of the disaster was published in the U.S.A., Griffin said. After the first horses were shot, he wrote a long article for the American press, but when F. B. Hutchinson, the show's manager, read it, he said, "Charles, the least said about this the better."
3 My interview with Johnny Baker, Jr., October 1968.
4 Foote, *Letters*, 64.
5 Ruby Wilson interview with Mrs. Robert (Beata Cox) Dean, February 5, 1940.
6 Griffin, *Four Years*, 63.
7 Foote, *Letters*, 65.
8 Ibid., 66.
9 George Allen Beecher, *A Bishop of the Great Plains*, 156.
10 North Platte *Telegraph*, May 1906.
11 Griffin, *Four Years*, 73.
12 Foote, *Letters*, 67.
13 North Platte *Telegraph*, August 1906.
14 Foote, *Letters*, 68.
15 North Platte *Telegraph*, April 18, 1907. The Huckleberry Indians was/is a men's social club; it still meets today at the New York Athletic Club.
16 Unidentified North Platte newspaper.
17 Reprinted in North Platte *Telegraph*, early May 1907.
18 Richard J. Walsh, *The Making of Buffalo Bill*, 334.
19 Ibid.; Don Russell, *The Lives and Legends of Buffalo Bill*, 276.
20 Walsh, *Buffalo Bill*, 334.
21 Russell, *Lives*, 436-37.
22 Dan Muller, *My Life with Buffalo Bill*, 139.
23 Newspapers of the area for this time period are very scarce today, and other information is scant, making it difficult to piece together what happened between September 1907 and March 1908.
24 This packet of photos was sent to Scout's Rest Ranch in 1959; the note accompanying the photos was signed by a Mrs. John Fredericks.
25 Office of Surgeon General report, National Archives, RG 94; see also for summary of Stott's army career and for photo of Stott, RG 94, AGO.
26 North Platte *Telegraph*, January 21, 1908.
27 Ibid., January 20, 1909.
28 Jessie Morant interview with Mrs. J. R. Baskins, January 5, 1940.
29 Russell, *Lives*, 449.
30 Harry E. Webb, "Buffalo Bill: Saint or Devil?" *The Roundup*, January 1974, 5.
31 Columbus *Telegram*, September 7, 1909.

Chapter 33   Scout's Rest Ranch

1 Most of the material used in this chapter was told me in 1972 by Mrs. Alice Howe Arzt, North Platte.

2 An unidentified newspaper clipping describing the wedding states that the bride was born on the Crow Indian Reservation near Pass Creek, Montana, but this is a mistake; the Boals were still living in North Platte at the time of Clara's birth. It was her brother, Cody, who was born on his father's ranch north of, Sheridan, at which time an unknown writer penned the following verse and sent it to Horton and Arta:

Of all the fine babies that were born in the west,
Why that of the Boal's was acknowledged the best.
He weighed full eight pounds and looked like his pa,
At the same time he closely resembled his ma.
The fame of this infant quite passes belief,
And the head waters of Pass Creek hail him as chief.
He is the joy of his mother, the pride of his dad.
When his grandfather was told he nearly went mad.
We will fill up our glasses and drink to the boy,
May his life in the future know nothing but joy.

3 My interview with Mable Hankins, 1969.

Chapter 34   Reconciliation

1 My interview with Mrs. Alice Howe Arzt, 1972.
2 North Platte *Telegraph*, April 2, 1910.
3 Ibid.
4 Stella Adelyne Foote, *Letters from Buffalo Bill*, 63.
5 Reprinted in North Platte *Telegraph*, September 1910.
6 Frank Winch, *Thrilling Lives of Buffalo Bill and Pawnee Bill*, 224.
7 Don Russell, *The Lives and Legends of Buffalo Bill*, 435.
8 The newspaper owner-editor, A. P. Kelly, and his wife were long-time friends of the Codys.
9 North Platte *Telegraph*, August 1910.
10 Letter from W. F. Cody to Charles McDonald; property of S. F. Diedrichs, North Platte.
11 North Platte *Telegraph*, August 1910.
12 My interview with Johnny Baker, Jr., October 1968.
13 My interview with John Baker, Jr., October 1968.
14 Winch, *Thrilling Lives*, 208-09.
15 Foote, *Letters*, 70.
16 North Platte *Telegraph*, March 11, 1911.
17 Omaha *Bee*, March 24, 1911.
18 Foote, *Letters*, 71.
19 *The Show World*, July 15, 1911; accompanying the articles are four pictures of Cody at his Arizona mines.

Chapter 35   Farewells

1 Washington *Star,* April 18, 1911.

2 Stella Adelyne Foote, *Letters from Buffalo Bill,* 72. Major John Burke says that in addition to President Taft and Generals Leonard Wood and Nelson A. Miles, "thirty-five retired generals whom he had guided and fought under saluted him on his farewell appearance in Washington." (Wichita *Eagle,* August 20, 1911)

3 *The Show World,* June 24, 1911, July 22, 1911. The magazine added: "Among advertising people it has been common talk for the past week or ten days that not in years have the Chicago newspapers carried as much interesting press stuff for an amusement attraction as they have for the Two Bills' show. Each comment of this kind has been a new laurel for the veteran Major John M. Burke, Col. Cody's personal representative and associate for years, and Frank Winch, the clever young purveyor of 'stories' who is this season officiating as general press representative for the show." (4)

4 North Platte *Telegraph,* May 1911.

5 Ibid., June 15, 1911.

6 Ibid., July 28, 1911.

7 With my parents and little brother, I came into North Platte on this train from Hershey; my brother and I made the trip perched atop a seat back.

8 North Platte *Semi-Weekly Tribune,* August 1911; North Platte *Telegraph,* August 24, 1911.

9 Don Russell, *The Lives and Legends of Buffalo Bill,* 91. See also Frank Winch, "Buffalo Bill—Frontiersman," *Ace-High,* First April issue 1929.

10 Russell, *Lives,* 91-92.

11 Emery E. Hardwick, "Which 'Buffalo Bill' First Got the Famous Name?" Wichita *Eagle,* August 20, 1911.

12 Foote, *Letters,* 73.

13 North Platte *Telegraph,* December 21, 1911, reprinted from New York *Sun.*

14 Richard J. Walsh, *The Making of Buffalo Bill,* 339.

15 Jesie Morant interview with Hershey Welsh, December 27, 1939.

16 North Platte *Semi-Weekly Tribune,* December 6, 1912, reprinted from New York *Clipper.*

17 North Platte *Telegraph,* January 23, 1913.

18 Ibid., July 31, 1913.

19 Foote, *Letters,* 74.

20 Russell, *Lives,* 451. A thick sheaf of copies of the old deeds and mortgages pertaining to the portion of the original land on which the buildings stand is on file today at the restored ranch house. These show that Cody bought Section 19, Township 14, Range 30, for $640 on July 15, 1880. Three years later Mrs. Cody mortgaged it to Charles McDonald for $2,500; that was the year Buffalo Bill first went on the road with the Wild West show. The debt was paid and the big ranch house built by December 1888, when the Colonel mortgaged it for $21,000. At that time he was building the big T barn and preparing to take the show back to Europe the following May. Throughout Cody's ownership, the ranch house was seldom free of debt. A $25,000 mortgage was taken out in 1893, while Horton Boal was manager. Three years later, on December 27, 1896, William Cody mortgaged the ranch to Louisa for $85,000. She probably had some money saved, and no doubt borrowed the rest on her other property, including Welcome Wigwam. This, then, must have been why $80,000 of the sale price of the ranch went to Louisa in 1911; she used it to pay off her own mortgages.

21 The dispatch telescoped time: Scout's Rest was not built in the *early* days of Indian fighting; and Russian dukes appeared in the state only in the singular, and then prior to the ranch's existence.

Chapter 36 Where the Wild West Ends

1 North Platte *Telegraph*, April 19, 1913.
2 Ibid., October 9, 1967.
3 Ibid.
4 North Platte *Telegraph*, July 31, 1913.
5 Richard J. Walsh, *The Making of Buffalo Bill*, 341.
6 Another account gives a slightly different version, advancing further questions about Lillie's role: Bankruptcy proceedings were brought July 28 in New Jersey "by Frederick W. Biddle of Philadelphia, who has a claim for $3,800 for board and provisions; Nathan W. Perry, of Denver, whose claim is $342; and Charles Anderson, of Denver, with a claim of $36.

    "The nominal amount of two of the claims gives color to the report that the proceedings were brought with the assent of Pawnee Bill, who . . . waited in Trenton to be served with papers. . . .

    "C. Clinton Cook was appointed receiver and Henry D. Oliphant was made referee." Major Lillie "has been an intimate friend of Receiver Cook." (*New York Dramatic Mirror*, August 6, 1913, 17)
7 North Platte *Telegraph*, July 31, 1913.
8 Ibid.
9 Ibid., September 4, 1913.
10 Ibid., August 26, 1913.
11 Ibid., October 2, 1913, reprinted from Cody *Enterprise*.
12 North Platte *Telegraph*, October 2, 1913, reprinted from *Northern Wyoming Herald*.
13 Chicago *Inter Ocean*, October 15, 17, and 16, 1913. For a few details about Prince Albert's alien status and about this particular land lottery distributing the public lands of the North Platte forest service or the Fort Niobrara Military Reservation, see Everett Dick, *The Lure of the Land*, 295-96.

    For an interesting series of six photographs depicting Prince Albert in Cody town, accompanied by Buffalo Bill, presenting a gift rifle to Crow Chief Plenty Coups, see David R. Phillips (ed.), *The West: An American Experience*, 150-51. The Prince Albert hunt was also filmed, and portions of this movie were about 1915 incorporated into a revision of the Colonel's Indian Wars movie; see below, Chap. 37, note 31.
14 Louisa Frederici Cody and Courtney Ryley Cooper, *Memories of Buffalo Bill*, 306.
15 Stella Adelyne Foote, *Letters from Buffalo Bill*, 74.
16 Washington *Post*, February 27, 1914, 14; February 28, 1914, 2.
17 North Platte *Telegraph*, April 11, 1914. See below, p. 405; Chap. 37, note 31.

Chapter 37 Pahaska, Farewell

1 Stella Adelyne Foote, *Letters from Buffalo Bill*, 76.
2 North Platte *Semi-Weekly Tribune*, July 2, 1915.
3 Foote, *Letters*, 76.
4 C. R. Cooper also had a similar opportunity to interview Cody two years earlier when, as correspondent for the Denver *Post*, he covered the shooting of the Colonel's 1913 Indian Wars film.
5 North Platte *Telegraph*, January 4 and 5, 1916, February 11, 1916.
6 Foote, *Letters*, 78, October 2 letter.
7 Don Russell, *The Lives and Legends of Buffalo Bill*, 276-77, 462. See also above, Chap. 7, note 8.
8 "Fighting with Buffalo Bill," 1926, ten episodes; "The Indians Are Coming,"

1930, twelve episodes; "Battling with Buffalo Bill," 1931, twelve episodes. *(Motion Pictures, 1912-1939: Catalog of Copyright Entries)*

9 Foote, *Letters*, 77; Russell, *Lives*, 461.

10 Richard J. Walsh, *The Making of Buffalo Bill*, 356.

11 Foote, *Letters*, 78.

12 Ibid.

13 Walsh, *Buffalo Bill*, 358; Elizabeth Jane Leonard and Julia Cody Goodman, *Buffalo Bill: King of the Old West*, 284.

14 North Platte *Telegraph*, December 23, 1916.

15 Leonard and Goodman, *Buffalo Bill*, 285.

16 Russell, *Lives*, 470; Walsh, *Buffalo Bill*, 359; Louisa Frederici Cody and Courtney Ryley Cooper, *Memories of Buffalo Bill*, 324-25—all agree that Baker was not there when the Colonel died on January 10. And the *Telegraph* of January 12 reported that Johnny Baker went through North Platte on January 11, on his way from New York to Denver to attend Cody's funeral. However, Cody Boal, who had hurried from North Platte to Denver in answer to his grandmother's telegram, says Johnny was there: "Toward the last, when he [the Colonel] had lost the power of speech, he used Indian sign language to make his wants known to Johnny Baker." (William Cody Boal, *My Grandfather, Buffalo Bill*, small booklet with unnumbered pages)

17 Foote, *Letters*, 79.

18 Henry Blackman Sell and Victor Weybright, *Buffalo Bill and the Wild West*, 256.

19 Boal, *My Grandfather*.

20 Cody and Cooper, *Memories*, 324.

21 Russell, *Lives*, 469. Father Walsh, assistant at the Cathedral of the Immaculate Conception in Denver, reported that Cody was "in complete command of his faculties, that he said he had never belonged to any religion and had never been baptized. But he had always believed in God. He knew he had only a short time to live and he wanted to die in the Catholic faith. He made a perfect response to the necessary questions. Father Walsh baptized him at 5 P.M. . . . in the home of his sister, May Decker." (William E. Barrett, "Baptism of Buffalo Bill," manuscript at Scout's Rest Ranch; printed in article of same title, *Catholic Digest*, September 1960, 103)

22 Leonard and Goodman, *Buffalo Bill*, 284.

23 Boal, *My Grandfather*.

24 North Platte *Telegraph*, January 11, 1966. Joseph Bona died in February 1978, at 90 years of age; his obituary, more than six decades after the event, still tied his reputation to Buffalo Bill's burial. (Chicago *Sun-Times*, February 12, 1978)

25 Foote, *Letters*, 50.

26 Sell and Weybright, *Buffalo Bill*, 255.

27 Cody and Cooper, *Memories*, 324.

28 *Time*, March 4, 1946.

29 North Platte *Telegraph*, January 18, 1917.

30 Russell, *Lives*, 470; Sell and Weybright, *Buffalo Bill*, 257. Weather and grave preparations dictated postponement of the actual funeral until June.

31 This "Adventures of Buffalo Bill" film was actually a version of the Colonel's 1913 Indian Wars film but with a different title, obviously attempting to capitalize on the Buffalo Bill name. (One interesting sidelight to Essanay's promotion for their "Adventures of Buffalo Bill" film was the need to call attention to the fact that their 1917 film was *not* the same as the similarly-titled 1912 film, "The Life of Buffalo Bill," produced by the Buffalo Bill and Pawnee Bill Film Co.) Cody's 1913 documentary/historical film was never a commercial success. (Cf. above, p. 395.) Essanay's editing and re-titling of some of the Colonel's original

material must have been an attempt to redeem its earlier failure. Why did Cody's "The Indian Wars" film not make it? It presumably did not even make it into the U.S. government departments which helped "sponsor" the production to begin with. For instance, in December 1913 the Colonel offered a copy of his film to the Department of the Interior, but there is no record of its receipt. (*Biographical and Historical Index of American Indians and Persons Involved in Indian Affairs,* vol. 2, 305, U.S. Dept. of Interior) The department had for years been criticized for its neglect in caring for its Indian wards. As Bob Lee points out, Cody, in negotiating with the Secretary of the Interior in 1913 for permission to use Indians in his film, promised to demonstrate how far the Sioux had progressed under government wardship; he would include in his film shots of the Indians at work on their farms and learning the white man's ways in their schools. Cody then promised to provide copies of the film for the government to use in silencing its social critics. In addition to Interior's not getting the film, there is no record that any government department or agency ever got the film. Lee stops far short of a conspiracy theory, but he does suggest the possibility that Cody was *too* successful in picturing historical accuracy: the War Department may well have been less than enthusiastic about the Colonel's re-creation of the army's role in, for instance, the Wounded Knee affair. As Lee says of Cody's film, one rumor had it that "the government suppressed it because it depicted the Indian wars too realistically, and not to the credit of the frontier Army." For a more detailed account of the making of Cody's films and their subsequent history (and loss), see Don Russell, "Buffalo Bill—In Action," Chicago Westerners *Brand Book,* July 1962, 33-35, 40; series of articles by Bob Lee in Rapid City *Daily Journal,* Sunday editions, June 15-August 10, 1969; [Al Horne,] "On Location at Wounded Knee," Washington *Post,* March 18, 1973, Outlook section, which reproduces from glass negatives thirteen posed stills shot during the making of the 1913 Cody film; Kevin Brownlow, *The War, the West and the Wilderness,* chapter entitled "The Die Is Cast," which picks up (from Lee, through William S. E. Coleman) the government-suppression theme.

32 Judge William L. Walls was one of Colonel Cody's attorneys, as well as a close friend. In 1919 he became attorney general of Wyoming.

33 My interview with Johnny Baker, Jr., October 1972; later printed in North Platte *Telegraph,* September 17, 1973, North Platte Centennial edition.

Chapter 38   Bunk and Fact

1 North Platte *Telegraph,* Ocotber 9, 1967.
2 The Red Room was Tammen's private office at the Denver Post.
3 *Reader's Digest,* November 1946, condensed from *American Mercury.*
4 *Time,* March 4, 1946.
5 *Rocky Mountain News* (Denver), December 18, 1950.
6 E. S. Sutton, "Hero, Showman or Heel?" *Frontier Times,* Summer 1961.
7 Unidentified newspaper clipping.
8 *Rocky Mountain News,* undated clipping.
9 Janice Holt Giles, *Six Horse Hitch,* 194-95.
10 Luther North, *Man of the Plains,* 118
11 Los Angeles *Times,* February 20, 1949, book review by Martin Conville.
12 The original blueprints, now in the ranch archives, show that no fireplace was built into the house, and certainly none has been added since.
13 I frequently visited with Cody Boal when he operated a small museum and souvenir shop in North Platte in the 1950s.

14 Cody *Enterprise,* November 28, 1934, reprinted from Billings *Gazette.*

15 From the W. F. Carver files at Nebraska State Historical Society, Lincoln.

16 *Blake's Western Stories* booklet and letter from Blake to Margaret M. McCann. Cody file at Nebraska State Historical Society.

17 John Burke, *Buffalo Bill: The Noblest Whiteskin,* 292.

18 For a text-and-photo story of the making of this Cody statue, see Sally Gray, "Buffalo Bill Comes to Persimmon Hill," *Persimmon Hill,* Summer 1977.

19 North Platte *Telegraph,* June 23, 1910.

20 Unidentified newspaper clipping.

21 The writer, Hugo Frohm, wanted to know if Buffalo Bill was a real person, as some of his friends maintained there never was a Buffalo Bill.

Chapter 39   Epilogue

1 Ruby Wilson and Jessie Morant interviews, W.P.A. project.

2 Letter to me from Edward Keliher, Omaha, January 22, 1970.

3 Jessie Morant interview with Mrs. Elmer Crawford, November 13, 1940.

4 North Platte *Telegraph,* May 19, 1971.

5 My interview with Mrs. Hettie Mesmer, North Platte, 1972.

6 North Platte *Telegraph,* September 17, 1973, North Platte Centennial edition.

7 Henry Blackman Sell and Victor Weybright, *Buffalo Bill and the Wild West,* 43.

8 Chauncey Thomas letter to Margaret M. McCann, March 19, 1929. Nebraska State Historical Society, Lincoln.

9 Louisa Frederici Cody and Courtney Ryley Cooper, *Memories of Buffalo Bill,* 326.

10 Richard J. Walsh, *The Making of Buffalo Bill,* 360.

11 Copy of Mrs. W. F. Cody's will in archives at Scout's Rest Ranch.

12 Brooklyn *Eagle,* May 10, 1932.

13 Ruby Wilson interview with Julia Siebold, April 14, 1940.

14 Wilson interview with John Pell, March 7, 1940.

15 Wilson interview with Harry Pell, November 7, 1940.

16 Wilson interview with John Little, February 26, 1940.

17 Square Top was a house of ill repute located near the depot in North Platte in the early days.

18 Wilson interviews at D'Ton Writers Guild, December 7, 1939.

19 North Platte *Telegraph,* February 1927.

20 *Masonic Tribune,* August 26, 1968.

21 Told me by John Bergstrom, Charles' son, at Chappell, Nebraska, 1968.

22 Fred Elliott, Jr., manuscript; see above, Chap. 12, note 6.

23 Custer County *Chief,* undated clipping. The party included E. R. Purcell, publisher of the *Chief,* and George Palmer, recipient of the coat.

24 My interview with Chief Red Fox, North Platte.

25 Letter to me from Keliher, January 22, 1970.

26 Unidentified North Platte newspaper, December 21, 1914.

27 Stella Adelyne Foote, *Letters from Buffalo Bill,* 47-48.

28 Ibid., 75.

29 North Platte *Telegraph,* May 29, 1913.

30 Unidentified newspaper clipping.

Bibliography

Adami, Giuseppe (ed.). *Letters of Giacomo Puccini.* Philadelphia: Lippincott, 1931.

Adamson, Archibald R. *North Platte and Its Associations.* North Platte: North Platte *Evening Telegraph,* 1910.

"Autobiography of Hester Ann Rogers Brown, 1835-1924." *Bits and Pieces,* October 1969.

Avery, Delos, "Buffalo Bill: The Story of a Reputation That Ran Away with a Man." Chicago *Tribune,* March 26, 1944, Graphic section.

Bare, Ira L. and Will H. McDonald (eds). *An Illustrated History of Lincoln County, Nebraska and Her People.* Chicago and N.Y.: American Historical Society, 1920.

Beecher, George Allen. *A Bishop of the Great Plains.* Philadelphia: Church Historical Society, 1950.

Biographical and Historical Index of American Indians and Persons Involved in Indian Affairs. Vol. 2. Boston: G. K. Hall & Co., 1966.

Boal, William Cody. *My Grandfather, Buffalo Bill.* North Platte: privately published, 1956.

Bratt, John. *Trails of Yesterday.* Chicago: Univ. Publ. Co., 1921.

Brownlow, Kevin. *The War, the West and the Wilderness.* N.Y.: Knopf, 1979.

Burke, John. *Buffalo Bill: The Noblest Whiteskin.* N.Y.: Putnam's Sons, 1973.

Burroughs, John R. *Guardian of the Grasslands.* Cheyenne: Pioneer Printing & Stationary Co., 1971.

Chrisman, Harry E. *The Ladder of Rivers: The Story of I.P. (Print) Olive.* Denver: Sage Books, 1965.

Clark, Charles M. *A Trip to Pike's Peak.* Chicago: S. P. Rounds' Steam Book and Job Printing House, 1861.

Cody, Bill. *Buffalo Bill: The Boy Who Made the Man.* Cody, Wyo.: privately published, 1969.

Cody, Louisa Frederici and Courtney Ryley Cooper. *Memories of Buffalo Bill.* N.Y.: Appleton, 1919.

Cody, W. F. *An Autobiography of Buffalo Bill (Colonel W. F. Cody.).* N.Y.: Farrar and Rinehart, 1920.

————. "Famous Hunting Parties of the Plains." *Cosmopolitan,* June 1894.

————. *Story of the Wild West and Camp-Fire Chats.* Philadelphia: Historical Publ. Co., 1888.

————. *The Life of Hon. William F. Cody.* Hartford: Bliss, 1879.

483

Cooper, Courtney Ryley. *Annie Oakley*. N.Y.: Duffield and Co., 1927.

[Davies, Henry E.] *Ten Days on the Plains*. N.Y.: privately published, 1872.

Deahl, William E., Jr. "Nebraska's Unique Contribution to the Entertainment World." *Nebraska History*, Autumn 1968.

————. "The Chadron-Chicago 1,000-Mile Cowboy Race." *Nebraska History*, Summer 1972.

Dunraven, Earl of. *Canadian Nights: Being Sketches and Reminiscences of Life and Sport in the Rockies, the Prairies, and the Canadian Woods*. London: Smith, Elder & Co., 1914.

————. *The Great Divide: Travels in the Upper Yellowstone in the Summer of 1874*. Lincoln: Univ. of Nebraska Press, 1967.

————. *Past Times and Pastimes*. Vol. I. London: Hodder and Stoughton, 1922.

Foote, Stella Adelyne. *Letters from Buffalo Bill*. Billings, Mont.: privately published, 1954.

Fort McPherson Centennial Booklet. North Platte: North Platte *Telegraph*, 1963.

Fulton, Frances I. Sims. *To and Through Nebraska*. Lincoln: Journal Co., 1884.

Giles, Janice Holt. *Six Horse Hitch*. Boston: Houghton Mifflin, 1969.

Gilman, Musetta. *Pump on the Prairie*. Detroit: Harlo Press, 1975.

Gray, John S. "Will Comstock, Scout." *Montana the Magazine of Western History*, July 1970.

Gray, Sally. "Buffalo Bill Comes to Persimmon Hill." *Persimmon Hill*, Summer 1977.

Griffin, Charles Eldridge. *Four Years in Europe with Buffalo Bill*. Albia, Iowa: Stage Publ. Co., 1908.

Haglund, Kristine. "Buffalo Bill Cody Country." Chicago Westerners *Brand Book*, October 1975.

Hardwick, Emery E. "Which 'Buffalo Bill' First Got the Famous Name?" Wichita *Eagle*, August 20, 1911.

Hebberd, Mary H. "Notes on Dr. David Franklin Powell, Known as 'White Beaver.'" *Wisconsin Magazine of History*. Summer 1952.

Holmes, Louis A. *Fort McPherson, Nebraska*. Lincoln: Johnsen Publ. Co. 1963.

————. "William F. Cody and the Nebraska Legislature." Chicago Westerners *Brand Book*, February 1958.

[Horne, Al.] "On Location at Wounded Knee." Washington *Post*, March 18, 1973, Outlook section.

Hutton, Harold. *Doc Middleton: Life and Legends of the Notorious Plains Outlaw*. Chicago: Swallow Press, 1974.

King, James T. *War Eagle: A Life of General Eugene A. Carr*. Lincoln: Univ. of Nebraska Press, 1963.

Kingsley, George Henry. *Notes on Sport and Travel*. London: Macmillan, 1900.

Knight, Oliver. *Following the Indian Wars: The Story of the Newspaper Correspondents Among the Indian Campaigners*. Norman: Univ. of Oklahoma Press, 1960.

Lemmon, Ed. *Boss Cowman: The Recollections of Ed Lemon, 1857-1946*. Nellie Snyder Yost (ed.). Lincoln: Univ. of Nebraska Press, 1969.

Leonard, Elizabeth Jane and Julia Cody Goodman. *Buffalo Bill: King of the Old West*. N.Y.: Library Publishers, 1955.

Leonard, L. O. "Buffalo Bill's First Wild West Rehearsal." *Union Pacific Magazine*, August 1922.

Logan, Herschel C. *Buckskin and Satin: The Life of Texas Jack*. Harrisburg: Stackpole Co., 1954.

McCann, Margaret M. "The Life of William F. Cody with a Criticism of the Sources." Unpublished M. A. thesis, Univ. of Nebraska, 1929.

McCoy, Tim and Ronald McCoy. *Tim McCoy Remembers the West: An Autobiography.* Garden City: Doubleday, 1977.

Medal of Honor Recipients 1863-1973. Washington: G. P. O., 1973.

Medary, Edgar F. "Reminiscenses of the Ghost Dance War of 1890-91." Chicago Westerners *Brand Book*, September 1946. (See his p. 45 caption for more specific identifications of men in photo identical to Russell, *Lives*, 406c.)

Miles, W. H. *Early History and Reminiscence of Frontier County.* Maywood, Neb.: Maywood *Eagle*, 1894.

Mills, Anson. *My Story.* Washington: privately published, 1918.

Motion Pictures, 1912-1939: Catalog of Copyright Entries. Washington: Library of Congress, 1951.

Muller, Dan. *My Life with Buffalo Bill.* Chicago: Reilly & Lee, 1948.

Nordin, Charles R. "Dr. W. F. Carver." *Nebraska History Magazine*, October-December 1927.

North, Luther. *Man of the Plains: Recollections of Luther North, 1856-1882.* Donald F. Danker (ed.). Lincoln: Univ. of Nebraska Press, 1961.

Paine, Bayard H. *Pioneers, Indians and Buffalo.* Curtis, Neb.: Curtis *Enterprise*, 1935.

[Percy, Townsend.] *Red Shirt, Chief of the Sioux Nation.* London: National Press Agency, Ltd., 1887.

Peterson, Nancy M. "Buffalo Bill, the Movie Maker." Denver *Post, Empire Magazine*, February 27, 1977.

Phillips, David R. (ed). *The West: An American Experience.* Chicago: Henry Regnery, 1973.

Phipps, Robert. "Nebraska Scene." Omaha *World-Herald Sunday Magazine*, March 19, 1950.

Price, Capt. George F. *Across the Continent with the Fifth Cavalry.* N. Y.: Van Nostrand, 1883.

Rennert, Jack (ed.). *100 Posters of Buffalo Bill's Wild West.* N.Y.: Darien House, 1976.

Rosa, Joseph G. *They Called Him Wild Bill: The Life and Adventures of James Butler Hickok.* Norman: Univ. of Okla. Press, 1974.

Russell, Don. "Buffalo Bill: A Man of Many Lives, But No Home Life". *Inland* magazine, no. 4, 1970.

———. "Buffalo Bill—In Action." Chicago Westerners *Brand Book*, July 1962.

———. *The Lives and Legends of Buffalo Bill.* Norman: Univ. of Oklahoma Press, 1960.

Scher, Zeke. "Riches of the North Rim." Denver *Post, Empire Magazine*, March 3, 1978. (Scher touches on a fall 1892 visit by Cody to the North Rim of the Grand Canyon. The Colonel, prompted by Brigham Young's son in England, escorted a group of British potential investors to the Kaibab Plateau area. Scher [p. 13] uses an interesting photo of Cody in an informal pose.)

Schuchert, Charles and Clara Mae LeVene. *O. C. Marsh.* New Haven: Yale Univ. Press, 1940.

Sell, Henry Blackman and Victor Weybright. *Buffalo Bill and the Wild West.* N. Y.: Oxford Univ. Press, 1955.

[Seymour, Silas.] *Incidents of a Trip through the Great Platte Valley.* N. Y.: Van Nostrand, 1867.

Snyder, A. B. and Nellie Snyder Yost. *Pinnacle Jake.* Caldwell, Idaho: Caxton, 1951.

Sprague, Marshall. *A Gallery of Dudes.* Boston: Little, Brown & Co., 1967.

Spring, Agnes Wright. *Buffalo Bill and His Horses.* Denver: privately published, 1968.

Sutton, E. S. "Hero, Showman or Heel?" *Frontier Times*, Summer 1961.

Thorp, Raymond W. (ed). "The Letters of Doc Carver." *Outdoor Life-Outdoor Recreation*, April 1930.

[Tucker, William W.] *His Imperial Highness the Grand Duke Alexis in the United States of America during the Winter of 1871-72.* N. Y.: Interland Publ., 1972 (reprint of 1872 ed.).

Tuttle, D. S. "Tales from Old Timers—No. 4. *"Union Pacific Magazine,* July 1923.

Utley, Robert M. *The Last Days of the Sioux Nation.* New Haven: Yale Univ. Press, 1963.

Waddill, O. B. *Saddle Strings.* Pierre, S. D.: State Publ. Co., 1975.

Walsh, Richard J. *The Making of Buffalo Bill.* Indianapolis: Bobbs-Merrill, 1928.

Ware, Capt. Eugene F. *The Indian Wars of 1864.* Lincoln: Univ. of Nebraska Press, 1960 (reprint of 1911 ed.).

Webb, Harry E. "Buffalo Bill: Saint or Devil?" *The Roundup,* January February, March 1974.

The West of Buffalo Bill: Frontier Art, Indian Crafts, Memorabilia from the Buffalo Bill Historical Center. N.Y.: Abrahms, 1974.

Wetmore, Helen Cody. *Last of the Great Scouts: The Life Story of Col. William F. Cody "Buffalo Bill"* Chicago and Duluth: Duluth Press Publ. Co., 1899.

Winch, Frank. "Buffalo Bill—Frontiersman." *Ace-High,* First April 1929.

————. *Thrilling Lives of Buffalo Bill and Pawnee Bill.* N. Y.: S. L. Parsons & Co., 1911.

Wolfenstine, Manfred R. *The Manual of Brands and Marks.* Ramon F. Adams (ed.) Norman: Univ. of Oklahoma Press, 1970.

Yost, Nellie Snyder. *The Call of the Range: The Story of the Nebraska Stock Growers Association.* Denver: Sage Books, 1966.

Acknowledgments

Without the help of the following I could never have written this book. My sincere thanks to The Nebraska State Historical Society; The Wyoming State Historical Society; the Sheridan, Wyoming, library and Mrs. Elsa Spear Byron of that city; my good friend Ruby Wilson, whose interviews of forty years back with North Platte residents were invaluable; George LeRoy, superintendent of Scout's Rest Ranch, and his good secretary, Bobbie Switzer, who have cheerfully opened Cody collections to me; Alice Arzt and Johnny Baker, Jr., the only people now living in North Platte who knew the Codys intimately (they supplied information nowhere else available); Joe Rosa of Middlesex, England, who furnished most helpful data; my friend Don Russell of Chicago, who generously let himself be asked many questions, and whose in-depth research into the lives and legends of Buffalo Bill (for his book by that title) saved me a great deal of duplicate work; Stella Adelyne Foote of Montana, whose collection of Buffalo Bill letters was of incalculable help; the North Platte *Telegraph* and its microfilms of early North Platte newspapers; and to my fine editor Durrett Wagner, of Swallow Press, whose insistence on careful documentation and whose knowledge and insight into things Western have steered me around many a pitfall in the compilation of a book as complex as this one; and all the many others who supplied bits and pieces that helped to round out the story of the W. F. Cody family.

The bulk of the illustrations used throughout the book were obtained from Scout's Rest Ranch, Buffalo Bill State Park, Nebraska Game and Parks Commission. Therefore, this acknowledgment here will serve as their credit line; other pictures are credited at the end of their captions.

Index

Italic numeral indicates illustration on that page.